THE FOOD AND CULTURE AROUND THE WORLD HANDBOOK

Helen C. Brittin

Professor Emeritus
Texas Tech University, Lubbock

Prentice Hall

Boston   Columbus   Indianapolis   New York   San Francisco   Upper Saddle River
Amsterdam   Cape Town   Dubai   London   Madrid   Milan   Munich   Paris   Montreal   Toronto
Delhi   Mexico City   Sao Paulo   Sydney   Hong Kong   Seoul   Singapore   Taipei   Tokyo

Editor in Chief: Vernon Anthony
Acquisitions Editor: William Lawrensen
Editorial Assistant: Lara Dimmick
Director of Marketing: David Gesell
Senior Marketing Coordinator: Alicia Wozniak
Campaign Marketing Manager: Leigh Ann Sims
Curriculum Marketing Manager: Thomas Hayward
Marketing Assistant: Les Roberts
Senior Managing Editor: Alexandrina Benedicto Wolf
Project Manager: Wanda Rockwell
Senior Operations Supervisor: Pat Tonneman
Creative Director: Jayne Conte
Cover Art: iStockphoto
Full-Service Project Management: Integra Software Services, Ltd.
Composition: Integra Software Services, Ltd.
Cover Printer/Binder: Courier Companies,Inc.
Text Font: 9.5/11 Garamond

Credits and acknowledgments borrowed from other sources and reproduced, with permission, in this textbook appear on appropriate page within text.

Many of the designations by manufacturers and seller to distinguish their products are claimed as trademarks. Where those designations appear in this book, and the publisher was aware of a trademark claim, the designations have been printed in initial caps or all caps.

Library of Congress Cataloging-in-Publication Data
Brittin, Helen C.
  The Food and culture around the world handbook/Helen C. Brittin.
     p. cm.
Includes bibliographical references and index.
ISBN-13: 978-0-13-507481-7 (alk. paper)
ISBN-10: 0-13-507481-9 (alk. paper)
   1. Diet—Handbooks, manuals, etc.   2. Food habits—Handbooks, manuals, etc.
3. Cookery—Handbooks, manuals, etc.   I. Title.
TX353.B6985 2011
394.1—dc22

10 9 8 7 6 5 4 3 2 1

Prentice Hall
is an imprint of

www.pearsonhighered.com

ISBN 10:   0-13-507481-9
ISBN 13: 978-0-13-507481-7

PREFACE

Culture, a pattern or design for living, allows individuals in social groups to live together in relative harmony through shared values, beliefs, and practices. The variety of social groups in the world and diversity of the environmental contexts in which they live lead to great intergroup variation in values, beliefs, and practices that arise in an attempt to meet the basic needs of existence, including food and nutrition. Similarly, individuals have many different life experiences that contribute to intragroup variation in the degree of adherence to norms in their culture. Members of a society often have different interpretations of the same situation because of factors such as age, income, education level, and religion.

Food and nutrition professionals, as well as persons from all walks of life, need quick access to information to interact effectively with individuals from different cultural groups. This is especially important now in the United States because recent population changes have resulted in an increasingly culturally diverse society. This pocket guide is a resource containing basic cultural and geographic information about cultural groups throughout the world. It is intended to provide a snapshot of the cultural diversity that exists and that we must understand to fulfill our dual roles as citizens and providers of competent education and care, including food service. The author encourages the reader to use the book as an introduction to the diversity of factors that affect values, beliefs, and practices related to food and nutrition. The reader can use the book as an initial stepping stone to multicultural competence in providing food and nutrition education and care to a culturally diverse population and to gain a better understanding of ones self.

The purpose of this guide is to help focus attention on the potential variations a culturally diverse client or student may, or may not, exhibit. One needs to be aware of the cultural factors such as availability of food, income, and religion which might influence a person's food practices and preferences in order to address them in nutrition assessment, education, and care. The facts must not be converted into stereotypes by the user. Use this guide to start increasing your awareness and understanding of potential similarities and differences. Then build on this information with an individualized cultural assessment.

This book is also about food of countries throughout the world. Included is information on influences on food, usual foods listed in food groups, seasonings, typical dishes, national dish if there is one, special occasion foods, beverages, meals and service, and street food and snacks. This information is included for each country if it is available. The information on food is designed to be used with the information on culture in this book.

The book is designed to be a convenient, brief reader and reference on food and culture of all the countries of the world. As of mid-2009, there are 195 nations in the world. The book profiles the culture and food of the 195 countries, in alphabetical order. Certain regions and territories that are not independent nations can be found in the entry for the governing nation. The book will be useful to people who are already interested in food and it may spark an interest in food of people throughout the world to others who read it.

THE AUTHOR

Helen C. Brittin, PhD, RD, LD, FADA, CFCS, Professor Emeritus of Food and Nutrition at Texas Tech University, created the course on cultural aspects of food at Texas Tech University and taught thousands of students in the course. She is a Registered Dietitian, Licensed Dietitian, Fellow of the American Dietetic Association, and is Certified in Family and Consumer Sciences. An active researcher, she has more than 100 presentations and publications, including a classic textbook. Her research is on meat, sensory evaluation, wine, iron in food, and cultural aspects of food. Active in teaching, research, and service, she has served as President of the Texas Dietetic Association and received university, state, and national awards including the Texas Dietetic Association 2000 Distinguished Dietitian Award. She was recognized by Florida State University with a Centennial Award in 2005. In addition to degrees from Florida State University and Texas Tech University, she has taken graduate courses in cultural aspects of food at New York University and Washington State University. She also did a Mini Development Leave at the University of California, Davis. Dr. Brittin has served as a Professor at the University of Tennessee, Knoxville, and Middle East Technical University in Ankara, Turkey. She has served as the International Federation for Home Economics Research Committee chairperson and was instrumental in increasing research presentations at IFHE World Congresses. She has traveled to numerous countries throughout the world in her research, teaching, and service. Dr. Brittin's avid and longtime interest in people and their food has culminated in this book.

ACKNOWLEDGMENT

The following sources were especially helpful in the preparation of this manuscript and deserve special recognition for their contributions. These sources are cited for demographic, economic, and geographical data.

Time Almanac 2009. Chicago, IL: Encyclopedia Britannica, Inc., 2009.

The World Almanac and Book of Facts 2009. Pleasantville, NY: World Almanac Books, 2009.

CONTENTS

Countries

A

B

C

DEFINITIONS

Literacy rates and population figures are supplied by the International Data Base, U.S. Census Bureau. **National population and health** figures are mid-2008 estimates. Percentage of urban population is for mid-2005. **Literacy** rates given generally measure the percent of population of adults ages 15 or over able to read and write simple statements on everyday life, not the (smaller) percent able to read and write to carry out effectively activities in the community. **Life expectancy** is at birth for persons born in 2008. **GDP**, gross domestic product, figures are 2007 estimates; figures are based on purchasing power parity calculations, which involve use of international dollar price weights applied to quantities of goods and services produced. **HIV rate** is the estimated number of adults, aged 15-49, living with HIV in 2007, divided by the total population aged 15-49. **Agriculture** livestock is listed in order of decreasing numbers of animals in 2007.

AFGHANISTAN
Islamic Republic of Afghanistan

Geography   Afghanistan is in southern Asia, bordering Pakistan, Iran, Turkmenistan, Uzbekistan, and Tajikistan. Approximately the size of Texas, it is mostly mountainous or desert, with a dry climate and extreme temperatures.

Major Languages	Ethnic Groups		Major Religions	
Dari (Afghan Persian)	Pashtun	42%	Islam (official)	
Pashto (all are official)	Tajik	27%	Sunni Muslim	80%
Six additional local languages	Hazara	9%	Shi'a Muslim	19%
	Uzbek	9%	Other	1%
	Other	13%		

Population density per sq. mi. 131
Literacy rate 28.1%
Life expectancy 44 male; 44.4 female
Per capita GDP $1,000
Labor force in agriculture 80%

Urban 22.9%
Infant mortality rate per 1,000 live births 154.7
HIV rate NA
Unemployment rate 8.5%
Arable land 12%

Agriculture   wheat, rice, grapes, opium poppy, fruits, nuts, sheep, chickens, goats, camels, cattle

Natural resources   natural gas, oil, coal, copper, salt, gemstones (especially lapis lazuli), fish

Industries   textiles, soap, furniture, shoes

History   Afghanistan occupied a favored invasion route from antiquity until the 18th century when a unified kingdom was established. In 1973 it became a republic. Soviet troops were in Afghanistan from 1978 until 1988, when an UN-mediated agreement provided for Soviet withdrawal and a neutral Afghan state. Afghan rebels achieved power in 1992; the Taliban, an insurgent Islamic radical faction, gained control in 1996. The United States and the UN demanded the Taliban hand over for trial Osama bin Laden, a wealthy Islamic radical believed to be involved in the bombing of the U.S. embassies in Kenya and Tanzania on Aug. 7, 1998. On Aug. 20, 1998, U.S. cruise missiles struck a terrorist training complex in Afghanistan, believed to be financed by bin Laden, sheltered by the Taliban. Bin Laden was also the primary suspect for the Sept. 11, 2001, terrorist attack on New York's World Trade Center towers and the Pentagon. In late 2001 a U.S.-led coalition invaded Afghanistan and overthrew the Taliban government. In 2004 a new constitution was ratified, and a U.S.-led coalition and NATO peacekeeping force were in Afghanistan to combat remnants of the Taliban and Al-Qaeda. Since 2004 violence has increased. Islamic suicide bombers and Taliban insurgents, operating from across the border in Pakistan, increased their activities such as bombing and kidnapping in 2007–2008, and U.S. air strikes intensified. In 2007 a record poppy crop accounted for almost a third of the country's GDP and 93% of the world's opium. In 2008 international donors pledged increased aid for reconstruction and to combat drugs, poverty, and violence.

Influences on food   Afghanistan was a crossroads on the ancient Silk Road that linked East and West and played an important role in the exchange of foods and knowledge. The invading armies of Alexander the Great, Genghis Khan, the Moghul Babur, the Persian Nader Shah, and the British with their Indian troops in the 19th century brought other influences. The cuisine reflects Afghanistan's diverse ethnic groups and its neighbors. Most of the people are Muslims, who do not consume pork or alcohol. Afghanistan grows wheat, rice, fruit, and nuts, and raises livestock; rivers provide some fish. Main foods are bread, rice, dairy products, lamb, and tea.

Bread and cereals   Wheat, rice, corn; bread, pastry, noodles, rice dishes. Breads, usually from wheat flour, are nan (leavened and baked in a tandoor, or clay oven) and chapati (unleavened flat circles cooked on a griddle).

Meat, poultry, fish   Lamb and mutton, goat, chicken, beef, water buffalo, camel, eggs, game, fish (e.g., trout).

Dairy products   Yogurt (mast), cheese (panir) such as white cheese, qymaq (clotted cream traditionally made from water buffalo milk). Yogurt is used extensively in cooking and is strained to make creamy chaka, which is sometimes dried and made into balls which harden (quroot).

Fats and oils   Oil, fat from fat-tailed sheep (dumba).

Legumes   Split peas.

Vegetables   Potatoes, leeks, spinach.

Fruit   Grapes, melons, raisins. Afghan melons and grapes are famous.

Nuts and seeds   Pistachios, almonds, walnuts, pine nuts, fenugreek seeds, sesame seeds, basil seeds.

Seasonings   Cardamom, fenugreek seeds, saffron, rosewater-flavored syrup.

Dishes   Pastry and noodle dishes. Pilaf, long-grain rice cooked first in oil and then with water so that grains remain separate and usually with lamb or vegetables. Chalau, the basic boiled white long-grain rice, usually accompanied by meat or vegetable stews (korma) or burani (vegetables with yogurt). Boiled or steamed short-grain sticky rice (bata) served with stew or vegetables. Lamb kebabs, usually chunks of meat on a skewer roasted or grilled; fat from fat-tailed sheep is grilled with kebabs to provide more juiciness and flavor. Chappli kebab (sandal kebab), named after its sandal-like shape, the hot specialty of Jalalabad. Shami, or lola, kebabs, made with ground meat, potatoes, split peas, and fried in oil. Jalebi, deep-fried batter soaked in syrup, served with fish during winter. Dopyasa, lamb boiled with fat from fat-tailed sheep.

Sweets   Sugar, syrup. Fruit. Milk-based puddings (e.g., firni, made with rice or corn flour). Sweet rice dishes such as shola (short-grain sticky rice cooked with other ingredients until soft and thick). Halva (confection of grain or vegetables, fruit, and sesame seeds). Baklava (pastry of layers of thin filo dough, nuts, and soaked in syrup). Elephant ear–shaped pastry (goash-e-feel). The unusual abrayshum (silk) kebab, egg prepared to form threads that are rolled up to look like kebabs and sprinkled with syrup and ground pistachios. Sweets are luxuries.

Special occasion sweets   Dried fruit and nut compote (haft mewa), traditional for the New Year festival on the first day of spring. Shola-e-zard (saffron- and rosewater-flavored sweet rice dish), for mourning and thanksgiving; it is given to the poor, neighbors, and relatives, and is served with sharbat-e-rihan (sherbet with basil seeds).

Beverages   Tea (chai), black and green, often flavored with cardamom and served with sugared almonds (noql).

Special occasion tea   Afghan tea (qymaq chai), made with green tea, adding bicarbonate of soda so that the tea becomes red, adding milk resulting in a purple pink tea, and topping with qymaq (clotted cream).

Tea houses   (chaikhana) These provide tea from a samovar and often meals and accommodation for travelers.

Meals and service   Nan (bread) with qymaq (clotted cream) is often eaten for breakfast. Bread is eaten with tea and at all meals and is used to scoop food.

Street food and snacks   Available from street vendors (tahang wala) for snacks or lunch: fried pastries such as boulanee (stuffed with leek) and sambosa (stuffed with egg, cheese, meat, vegetable, or mashed potato); and pakora (batter-fried vegetables, fish, or cheese). Nuts. White cheese with raisins (kismish panir), a spring snack.

ALBANIA
Republic of Albania

Geography   Albania is in southeastern Europe, bordering the Adriatic Sea, Montenegro, Kosovo, Macedonia, and Greece. It is mostly (70%) mountainous, with a western coastal plain where most people live.

Major Languages	Ethnic Groups		Major Religions	
Albanian (official)	Albanian	95%	Muslim (Sunni 51%)	70%
Greek	Greek	3%	Albanian Orthodox	20%
	Other	2%	Roman Catholic	10%

Population density per sq. mi. 342.2
Literacy rate 99%
Life expectancy 75.1 male; 80.7 female
Per capita GDP $6,300
Labor force in agriculture 58%

Urban 44.8%
Infant mortality rate per 1,000 live births 19.3
HIV rate NA
Unemployment rate 14.0%
Arable land 20%

Agriculture   alfalfa, wheat, corn, potatoes, vegetables, fruits, sugar beets, chickens, sheep, goats, cattle, pigs

Natural resources   oil, natural gas, coal, bauxite, chromite, copper, iron ore, nickel, timber, hydropower, fish

Industries   food processing, textiles and clothing, lumber

History   Ancient Illyria was conquered by Romans, then by Slavs, and by Turks in the 15th century. Independent Albania was proclaimed in 1912; a republic was formed in 1920. Albania was invaded by Italy in 1939. It was allied with the USSR from 1944 to 1960 and then with China until 1978. Some liberalization began, including measures in 1990 providing for freedom to travel abroad. In 1992 the first noncommunist president since World War II was elected. The collapse of fraudulent investment schemes in 1997 led to armed rebellion and anarchy; the UN authorized a force to restore order. In 1999 Albania was an outpost for NATO troops in Kosovo and took in Kosovo refugees, its fellow ethnic Albanians. In 2008 Albania signed protocols for NATO membership. Neighboring Kosovo, a province of Serbia with more than 90% Albanian population, declared independence.

Influences on food   Albania is one of the smaller Balkan countries. Influences include its conquerors, the Romans, Slavs, and Turks, religion, neighboring countries, and other foreign rule. Until the Turkish occupation in the 15th century, Albanians were Christians, Eastern Orthodox in the south and Roman Catholic in the north. By the 19th century Islam became the predominant religion. Unlike Christians, Muslims do not eat pork. Albanian cookery evolved as a result of Islamization and the influence of Turkish food practices, except in the traditionally Orthodox south, where food remained Greco-Mediterranean, and the coastal zone, where Italian influence is strong. Food traditions are strong in the older generation and in the villages populated by Albanians in the former Yugoslavia (in Kosovo, Montenegro, and in Tetovo, Macedonia), whose isolation from Albania has strengthened tradition. Traditional food habits are weakening due to women's emancipation and the breakdown of the extended family. Turkish influence is reflected in mezze, rice, pilaf, and Turkish coffee and sweets; Greek in feta cheese; and Italian in tomato sauce. Albania's land produces grain, vegetables, fruit, sugar beets, and livestock; its seacoast provides fish. Staple foods are bread (served at most meals), pasta, cheese, and yogurt.

Bread and cereals   Wheat, corn, rice; wheat bread including the standard dark, heavy, and slightly sour loaf, leavened bread, and flat breads such as pita (thin circle with hollow center, a pocket) and lavash (a large crisp bread), cornmeal bread, rice dishes, wheat flour pastry, turnovers, pasta, and dumplings, wheat kernels (bulgur).

Meat, poultry, fish   Lamb and mutton, chicken, goat, beef, pork, fish, eggs.

Dairy products   Milk (cow, sheep, goat), cream, yogurt (kos), cheese (usually from goat or sheep milk, e.g., white cheese similar to feta and a hard, tangy ewe's milk cheese similar to cheddar called kashkaval).

Fats and oils   Olive oil, butter, sesame oil, vegetable oils, rendered lamb fat.

Legumes   Chickpeas, fava beans.

Vegetables   Potatoes, olives, cabbage, eggplant, onions, tomatoes, cucumbers, peppers, mushrooms; pickles.

Fruit   Grapes, lemons, apricots, cherries, figs, dates, melons, pomegranates, pears, plums; preserves.

Nuts and seeds   Walnuts, almonds, hazelnuts, peanuts, pine nuts, pistachios, poppy seeds, sunflower seeds, sesame seeds. Nuts, especially walnuts, are used in many savory and sweet dishes.

Seasonings   Onions, mint, parsley, dill, garlic, pepper, anise, cardamom, cinnamon, oregano, lemon juice.

National appetizers   Kanelloni alla toskana (pancakes stuffed with minced veal and with a gratin finish), a regular restaurant antipasto (appetizer). Byrne me djathë, a small triangular pastry filled with white cheese and eggs.

Dishes   Rice pilaf (rice sautéed in butter or oil in which onions have been browned, then steamed or simmered with water or broth). Kofta (meatballs, fried or skewered and grilled). Shish kebabs (lamb pieces skewered and grilled). Dumplings filled with meat. Baked pasta, lamb or goat, and tomatoes. Baked macaroni, ground meat, cheese, tomato, and sauce. Pastitsio (béchamel sauce). Grape or cabbage leaves stuffed with rice or meat (dolma). Moussaka (baked minced lamb, eggplant, onions, and tomato sauce), a Balkan specialty. Tabouli, salad of onions, parsley, mint, bulgur, and fresh vegetables.

Sweets   Honey, sugar, syrup. Fresh fruit. Fruit compote. Baklava (filo dough layered with nut filling, baked, soaked in flavored syrup, often cut in diamond shape). Halvah (sweet paste made with grain and crushed sesame seeds).

Beverages   Coffee, tea, fruit juice, yogurt drinks, beer, wine, brandy, anise-flavored aperitifs including ouzo and the Turkish specialty raki (alcoholic beverages are prohibited for Muslims but are consumed in the Balkans), orme (beverage made from fermented cabbage), Turkish-style coffee (strong, thick, sweet, often with cardamom).

Meals   The poorest people eat cornmeal bread, cheese, and yogurt, with lamb or mutton when affordable. For wealthier people, three meals a day with a midafternoon snack are typical. Breakfast: bread with cheese, olives, or jam and coffee or tea. Main meal (usually at midday): mezze with ouzo or raki, perhaps soup and/or pilaf, meat dish with salad of raw vegetables, yogurt or cheese, and fruit.

Mezze   (appetizers) Salads such as liptao (feta cheese with bell pepper, deli meats, sardines, and hard-boiled egg) and tarator (soupy salad of yogurt, cucumbers, garlic, and olive oil), pickles, fish and seafood, omelets, spit-roasted lamb or entrails, and baked variety meats; usually with raki, ouzo, or orme.

Midafternoon snack   Turkish-style coffee or tea and pastries, nuts, or fresh fruit.

ALGERIA
People's Democratic Republic of Algeria

Geography   Algeria is in northern Africa, bordering the Mediterranean Sea and extending into the Sahara Desert. More than three times the size of Texas, Algeria is mostly desert. The Sahara region comprises 85% of the land, with major mineral resources, and almost completely uninhabited. Fertile plains 50 to 100 miles wide, with a moderate climate and adequate rain, are along the coast. Mountains run east to west and enclose a dry plateau.

Major Languages	Ethnic Groups		Major Religions	
Arabic (official)	Algerian Arab	59%	Islam (official)	
French	Berber	26%	Sunni Muslim	99%
Berber	Bedouin Arab	15%	Other	1%
Tamazight (national)				

Population density per sq. mi. 36.7
Literacy rate 75.4%
Life expectancy 72.1 male; 75.5 female
Per capita GDP $6,500
Labor force in agriculture 14%

Urban 63.3%
Infant mortality rate per 1,000 live births 28.8
HIV rate 0.1%
Unemployement rate 12.3%
Arable land 3%

Agriculture   wheat, potatoes, barley, oats, grapes, olives, citrus, fruits, chickens, sheep, goats, cattle, pigs

Natural resources   oil, natural gas, iron ore, phosphates, uranium, lead, zinc, fish

Industries   oil, gas, light industries, mining, petrochemical, electrical, food processing

History   Earliest known inhabitants were ancestors of Berbers, followed by Phoenicians, Romans, Vandals, and Arabs. Turkey ruled the land from 1518 to 1830. France ruled here from 1830 to 1962 when independence came and 1 million Europeans left. Algeria was socialist from 1963 to 1965 and then a military coup overthrew the government. The country entered a major recession after world oil prices plummeted in the 1980s. Fundamentalist Islamic forces gained power in 1991, and a bloody civil war ensued to 1999. Algeria remains in essence a military dictatorship. Bombings by radical Islamists and Al-Qaeda in the Islamic Maghreb occurred from 2006 to 2008.

Influences on food   Influences are from the Romans, Arabs, Turks, Spain, Italy, and especially France. France controlled Algeria for more than 130 years, leaving influences including French bread (the baguette, a long, thin, crusty loaf) and desserts such as éclairs, both now common in cities, and vineyards and winemaking. Algeria, Morocco, and Tunisia occupy the northwest corner of Africa known in Arabic as Maghreb (the west). They have similar cuisine and have influenced France by exporting foods such as couscous, merguez sausage (made from beef to comply with Islamic dietary law and spiced with red hot chili peppers), and Arab-style pastries. Also, some restaurants in Paris and other cities serve Algerian food. North African cuisine has much in common with Arabic food of the Middle East, but it has distinctions due in part to Berber, Bedouin, and French influences. In Algeria, Arab cuisine predominates although nomads consume Bedouin food: mainly dairy products (milk, clarified butter, and yogurt) from camels, sheep, and goats, thin unleavened wheat bread, boiled mutton on rice, small game, locusts, dates, and coffee. Much of Algeria is desert, which limits its cuisine compared to that of its neighbors on either side, Tunisia and Morocco. Algeria has small numbers of nomads and settlements at some oases, but most inhabitants live on the fertile coastal strip, the Tell, between the Mediterranean on the north and the plateau at the beginning of the Atlas Mountains on the south. Pork or alcohol consumption is prohibited for Muslims.

Bread and cereals   Wheat, barley, oats; kesra (round Arab bread baked in clay ovens in the countryside), French bread in the cities, couscous (made from crushed grain, usually semolina wheat, mixed with water to make a dough that is pressed into tiny pellets and dried).

Meat, poultry, fish   Lamb and mutton, beef, chicken, eggs, goat, pork, fish; merguez sausage.

Dairy products   Yogurt, cheese, cream.

Fats and oils   Olive oil, butter, vegetable oil, sheep's tail fat, rendered lamb fat.

Legumes   Chick peas (garbanzos), fava (broad) beans, black beans, navy beans, red beans, lentils, peanuts.

Vegetables   Potatoes, olives, eggplant, tomatoes, cucumbers, okra, green beans, greens, green peppers, carrots.

Fruit   Grapes, citrus fruits especially lemons, dates, figs, apricots, melon, pomegranate, plums, prunes, raisins.

Nuts and seeds   Almonds, cashews, hazelnuts, pine nuts, pistachios, walnuts, poppy seeds, sesame seeds.

Seasonings   Salt, black pepper, lemon juice, vinegar, onions, garlic, herbs (mint, parsley, basil, coriander, marjoram), cinnamon, chilie pepper, cumin, cloves, ginger, saffron, nutmeg, allspice, harisa (chili pepper and garlic paste), orange blossom water, rosewater. Food is highly seasoned.

Dishes   Steamed couscous topped with stewed meat or chicken, vegetables, and spicy hot sauce, the usual main dish. Lamb, usually grilled or stewed. Tagine (meat, poultry, fish, vegetable, or fruit stew). Sferia (simmered chicken, chickpeas, onions, and cinnamon, topped with egg yolk-lemon juice sauce and parsley), served with cheese croquettes flavored with orange blossom water and cinnamon. Lahm lhalou (braised lamb with cinnamon, almonds, sugar, orange blossom water, and prunes), often served before or after chicken couscous.

Main festive dish   Mechoui, a whole spit-roasted lamb basted with butter and spices. City dwellers often cut a lamb into halves or quarters and roast them over charcoal-filled braziers.

Sweets   Honey, sugar. Fresh fruit and nuts. Couscous with dates and cinnamon. Pastries: baklava, éclairs. Makroud el louse (cookie made of ground almonds, grated lemon peel, sugar, eggs, and orange blossom water).

Beverages   Tea with sugar and mint, coffee, fruit juice, yogurt drinks, wine.

Mezze   Small bits (e.g., olives, vegetables, cheese, small kebabs) eaten as snacks while drinking and talking.

ANDORRA
Principality of Andorra

Geography   Andorra is in southwestern Europe in the Pyrenees Mountains on the French-Spanish border. Most of the land is high mountains with narrow valleys.

Major Languages	Ethnic Groups		Major Religions	
Catalan (official)	Spanish	43%	Roman Catholic	89%
French	Andorran	33%	Other Christian	4%
Castilian	Portuguese	11%	None	5%
Portuguese	French	7%	Other	2%
	Other	6%		

Population density per sq. mi. 457.3
Literacy rate 100%
Life expectancy 80.3 male; 86.1 female
Per capita GDP $38,800,
Labor force in agriculture 0.3%

Urban 90.3
Infant mortality rate per 1,000 live births 3.7
HIV rate NA
Unemployment rate NA
Arable land 2%

Agriculture   tobacco, hay, potatoes, grapes, rye, wheat, barley, oats, vegetables, sheep, cattle, goats

Natural resources   hydropower, mineral water, timber, iron ore, lead

Industries   tourism, cattle, timber, banking, tobacco, furniture

History   Charlemagne recovered the region from the Muslims in 803. Andorra was a co-principality, with joint sovereignty by France and the bishop of Urgel, from 1278 to 1993. Ending a feudal system in place for 715 years, Andorrans adopted a parliamentary government in 1993. The traditional economy was based on sheep-raising. Tourism has been important since the 1950s and is the economic mainstay, especially skiing. In 2007 no snow until mid-March reduced the number of visitors. Andorra is a free port and an active trade center.

Influences on food   Spain, France, and Portugal are the main influences on food practices in Andorra.

Bread and cereals   Rye, wheat, barley, oats, corn; breads, pastas, porridge, rice dishes.

Meat, poultry, fish   Lamb, beef and veal, goat, pork, chicken, fish, eggs; dried salt cod.

Dairy products   Milk, cream, cheese (cow, sheep, goat).

Fats and oils   Butter, olive oil, lard, vegetable oil.

Legumes   Chickpeas, fava beans, kidney beans, lentils, white beans.

Vegetables   Potatoes, tomatoes, cabbage, cucumber, green beans, lettuce, mushrooms, olives, peas, peppers.

Fruit   Grapes, apples, bananas, grapefruit, lemons, pears, oranges, raisins.

Nuts and seeds   Almonds, hazelnuts, walnuts.

Seasonings   Onion, garlic, black pepper, parsley, pimento, lemon juice, capers, cinnamon, cloves, nutmeg, oregano, rosemary, saffron, sage, vanilla, chocolate.

Sweets   Honey, sugar.

Beverages   Coffee, wine.

ANGOLA
Republic of Angola

Geography   Angola is in southern Africa, bordering the Atlantic Ocean for more than 1,000 miles (1,609 km). Most of the land is a plateau, elevation 3,000 to 5,000 feet, rising from a narrow coastal strip. The land is mostly desert or savanna. There is a temperate highland area and a tropical rainforest.

Major Languages	Ethnic Groups		Major Religions	
Portuguese (official)	Ovimbundu	37%	Indigenous beliefs	47%
Bantu	Kimbundu	25%	Roman Catholic	38%
Other African languages	Bakongo	13%	Protestant	15%
	Other	25%		

Population density per sq. mi. 26
Literacy rate 67.4%
Life expectancy 37 male; 38.9 female
Per capita GDP $5,600
Labor force in agriculture 85%

Urban 54%
Infant mortality rate per 1,000 live births 182.3
HIV rate 2.1%
Unemployment rate 70%
Arable land 3%

Agriculture   cassava, corn, sweet potatoes, bananas, sugarcane, coffee, chickens, cattle, goats, pigs, sheep

Natural resources   oil, diamonds, iron ore, fish, phosphates, copper, feldspar, gold, bauxite, uranium

Industries   oil, mining, cement, metal products, fish and food processing

History   Bantu-speaking tribes penetrated the region during the first millennium CE and dominated it by 1500. Portuguese came in 1583 and, with the Bakongo kingdom in the north, developed the slave trade. Major colonization began in the 20th century when 400,000 Portuguese immigrated. A guerrilla war from 1961 to 1975 ended when Portugal granted independence. A 30-year civil war between rebel groups and the government lasted until 2002. Angola changed from a socialist state to a democracy in 1992. The second largest producer of crude oil in Africa south of the Sahara, Angola in 2007 became the 12th full member of OPEC and, already China's chief supplier of crude oil, began negotiations with Russia.

Influences on food   Bantu herders and the Portuguese influenced Angola's food. Angola was settled about 1,500 years ago by Bantu herders from the north who lived mainly on dairy products, grain pastes, and wild green vegetables. The Portuguese came in the early 16th century and established foods stops on routes to the Spice Islands. Portuguese trade and colonization influenced Angola's cuisine. The Portuguese brought pigs, chickens, salt cod, olives, coffee, tea, and wine. From America they introduced corn, tomatoes, potatoes, sweet potatoes, chilies, sweet peppers, and cassava; Brazilian influence is strong. From the east via Mozambique, another Portuguese colony, they brought oranges, lemons, spices, rice, beans, and probably bananas, sugar, and tropical fruits. Portuguese influence remains; examples include the use of fish and salt cod, Portuguese bread, goat, and sweet dishes containing eggs. Goober, peanut's nickname, comes from the Angolan word for the legume, nguba.

Bread and cereals   Corn, wheat, rice, grain pastes; Portuguese-style bread, rolls, cassava-flour porridge (funge).

Meat, poultry, fish   Chicken, eggs, beef, goat, pork, lamb, mutton, fish, salt cod, prawns, shrimp, clams. Blood of a slaughtered animal is used as an ingredient or in a sauce or dressing.

Dairy products   Milk (cow, goat), cream, cheese.

Fats and oils   Palm oil, olive oil, sesame oil, butter, pork fat, lard.

Legumes   Peanuts, beans, cowpeas.

Vegetables   Cassava, sweet potatoes, green leafy vegetables, tomatoes, potatoes, okra, pumpkin, onions, chilies, sweet peppers, olives.

Fruit   Bananas, coconut, oranges, lemons, limes, pineapple, papaya, strawberries.

Nuts and seeds   Sesame seeds, caraway seeds.

Seasonings   Salt, garlic, chilies, cloves, cinnamon, coriander, saffron.

Dishes   Esparrega dos de bacalao (salt cod, cassava leaves, sweet peppers, guinea pepper, and palm or sesame oil). A soup of cuttlefish with limes, ground sesame, olive oil, and tabil (a spice mixture usually of coriander, caraway seeds, garlic, and red peppers). Rice simmered with clams. Shrimp fritters. Prawns browned with onions in butter and olive oil, simmered in coconut milk, tomatoes, chopped red chilies, black pepper, and ginger; wine added; poured over pounded coconut meat, parsley, and lettuce; and served with rice. Goat meat stewed with garlic, chilies, and cloves. Assola de mais (cooked dried beans mixed with fresh corn fried in pork fat). Hot pot (simmered meat and chicken pieces, sweet and white potatoes, carrots, cabbage, beans). Fried or grilled pork served with yellow rice (rice browned in olive oil and cooked with saffron in stock made of pig blood).

Possible national dish   Muamba chicken (cut-up chicken cooked with palm oil, garlic, onion, hot red peppers, okra, pumpkin, and sweet potato leaves).

Sweets   Sugarcane, brown sugar, sugar, puddings, candies, sweet dishes containing eggs such as yellow coconut pudding (made with sugar, water, grated coconut, egg yolks, cloves, cinnamon).

Beverages   Coffee, tea, wine (port, Madeira).

ANTIGUA AND BARBUDA

Geography   These two islands lie in the eastern Caribbean Sea. Antigua, the larger island, is hilly and well wooded. Barbuda is flat, with a large lagoon in the west. The pleasant climate fosters tourism.

Major Languages	Ethnic Groups		Major Religions	
English (official)	Black	91%	Anglican	26%
Local dialects	Mixed	4%	Seventh-Day Adventist	12%
	White	2%	Pentecostal	11%
	Other	3%	Moravian	11%
			Roman Catholic	10%
			Other	30%

Population density per sq. mi. 494.6
Literacy rate 85.8%
Life expectancy 72.3 male; 76.3 female
Per capita GDP $18,300
Labor force in agriculture 7%

Urban 30.7%
Infant mortality rate per 1,000 live births 17.5
HIV rate NA
Unemployment rate 8.4%
Arable land 18%

Agriculture   cotton, tropical fruits, vegetables, chickens, goats, sheep, cattle, pigs

Natural resource   fish

Industries   tourism, construction, light manufacturing

History   Columbus landed on Antigua in 1493. The British colonized Antigua in 1632 and Barbuda in 1678. They imported African slaves to grow tobacco and sugarcane; the slaves were emancipated in 1834. Antigua and Barbuda gained independence in 1981. The land was hit hard by a hurricane in 1995. Since 1995 about 3,000 refugees fleeing volcanic eruptions on Montserrat have settled in Antigua. Crime in 2007–2008 impacted tourism.

Influences on food   The indigenous peoples, Carib and Arawak Indians, mostly disappeared following the Spanish conquest. The traces of information about their food practices indicate they ate fish, seafood, and one-pot soups or stews. Spain and Britain influenced the food customs. For example, the Spanish brought cattle, pigs, and rice, and British influence reflects in salt fish gundy (spread), biscuits, and tea. Slaves from Africa and indentured laborers, especially from India, also influenced food on these islands. As examples, African influence includes the use of okra, and Asian Indian influence includes the use of spices in dishes such as pepper pot.

Bread and cereals   Corn, rice, wheat; fried cornmeal breads, rice dishes, wheat flour breads, cassava bread (grated, squeezed, and dried cassava, fried on a griddle), biscuits or bread made with cassava and wheat flour.

Meat, poultry, fish Chicken, goat, lamb, beef, pork, fish and seafood (salt cod, snapper, lobster, crabs), eggs.

Dairy products Cow's milk (fresh, condensed, evaporated), cream, aged cheese.

Fats and oils Butter, lard, coconut oil, olive oil, vegetable oil.

Legumes Kidney beans, red beans, black-eyed peas, chickpeas (garbanzo beans), pigeon peas.

Vegetables Cassava, cucumbers, yams, malanga (taro-like plant with corms and green leaves), sweet potatoes, plantains, avocados, green leaves (cassava, malanga), squash, pumpkin, bread-fruit, tomatoes, okra, chili peppers, sweet peppers, onions. Cassava contains hydrocyanic acid, toxic in large amounts; the acid must be leached out and the tuber cooked before it can be eaten safely.

Fruit Papaya, guavas, soursops (have a cotton-like consistency), oranges, mangoes, melons, pineapple, bananas, coconut, limes, cashew apples, akee (looks similar to a peach but has segmented sections with shiny black seeds partly surrounded by a fleshy seed coat, the only edible part; other parts contain toxins, hypoglycins).

Nuts and seeds Almonds, cashew nuts, annatto seeds.

Seasonings Salt, black pepper, chilies, onion, garlic, annatto, allspice (pimento), cinnamon, coconut, cocoa, rum.

Dishes Callaloo (soup of green leaves cooked with okra, seasonings, and sometimes coconut milk and bits of salt meat or cod). Pepper pot (a meat stew containing boiled juice of cassava and highly seasoned with pepper). Ceviche (raw fish marinated in lime juice with olive oil and spices). Stuffed crab. Codfish cakes. Boiled or fried akee or plantains. Fried cassava or plantain chips. Cornmeal and okra cake. Boiled rice. Rice cooked with peas or beans. Cucumber salad. Papaya and mango jam (made with papaya, mango, sugar, and lime juice).

Sweets Sugarcane, molasses, sugar, fresh fruit, cornmeal pudding, baked bananas flambéed with rum.

Beverages Coffee often with milk, tea, iced tea with lime, fruit juices, soft drinks, milk, cocoa, beer, rum.

Meals Breakfast: coffee with milk and bread. Lunch: rice and beans or starchy vegetable and salt cod. Dinner: like lunch plus meat, vegetables, milk, and dessert when available.

Snacks Fresh fruit, sweetened fruit juice poured over crushed ice, coffee with milk.

ARGENTINA
Argentine Republic

Geography Argentina occupies most of southern South America and is its second largest country in area and in population. The land is a plain rising from the Atlantic Ocean to the Andes peaks. Aconcagua (22,834 ft) is the highest peak in the Western Hemisphere. The north is swampy. The central region, the Pampas, is fertile land used for agriculture and grazing; it supports most of the population. Patagonia, in the south, is cool, arid steppes.

Major Languages	Ethnic Groups		Major Religions	
Spanish (official)	White (mostly Spanish and Italian descent)	97%	Roman Catholicism (official)	
Italian				
English	Other (mostly Mestizo, and Amerindian)	3%	Roman Catholic	92%
German			Protestant	2%
			Jewish	2%
French			Other	4%

Population density per sq. mi. 38.3
Literacy rate 97.6%
Life expectancy 73.1 male; 79.8 female
Per capita GDP $13,300
Labor force in agriculture 1%

Urban 91.4%
Infant mortality rate per 1,000 live births 11.8
HIV rate 0.5%
Unemployment rate 12.1%
Arable land 10%

Agriculture   alfalfa, soybeans, corn, sugarcane, wheat, sunflower seeds, lemons, grapes, chickens, cattle, sheep, horses, goats, pigs

Natural resources   lead, zinc, tin, copper, iron ore, manganese, oil, uranium, fish

Industries   food processing, vehicles, consumer durables, textiles, chemicals

History   Nomadic Indians roamed the Pampas when Spaniards arrived in 1515. Most Indians were killed by the late 19th century. Argentina won independence in 1816. After 1880 Italian, German, and Spanish immigration spurred modernization. General Juan Perón was president from 1946 to 1955, exiled from 1955 to 1973, reelected president, and died 10 months later. He was succeeded by his wife Isabel, the first woman head of state in the Western Hemisphere. Military control and fighting occurred from 1976 to 1983 when democratic rule returned. Political problems and a recession followed, with an economic crisis in 2001. The economy has been rebounding. After strong economic growth in 2004–2005, Argentina repaid its debt to the International Monetary Fund in 2006. In 2007 the first woman was directly elected president. The economy grew, but inflation increased at a faster rate.

Influences on food   The rolling grassland on each side of the River Plata in central Argentina and Uruguay is the world's richest agricultural terrain. It was the home of nomadic Indians and was untilled and unexploited before the Spanish conquest. Argentina, Latin America's second largest country, includes the Pampas with agriculture and cattle- and sheep-grazing, the Andes Mountains whose foothills support vineyards, and the rugged Patagonia with many sheep. Mutton, the meat of Patagonia, was once supplemented by the guanaco (llama). Cattle were important for hides, and jerky was eaten. Now Argentina leads the world in beef consumption per capita. The Atlantic shore provides abundant fish and seafood. Argentina's food reflects influences of the Indians, Spanish, Germans, and Italians. The Spanish brought cattle, and their influence is also reflected in sweet milk confections. Italians brought pasta. German influence is evident in the charcuterie industry of Buenos Aires.

Bread and cereals   Corn, wheat; cornmeal bread, grits, hominy, wheat bread, pastries, pasta (spaghetti), pizza.

Meat, poultry, fish   Beef, lamb and mutton, chicken, eggs, goat, pork, fish and seafood, turkey; sausage. Beef is the foundation of the diet. Chicken and turkeys are esteemed.

Dairy products   Milk, cream, cheese.

Fats and oils   Butter, olive oil, corn oil.

Legumes   Soybeans, peanuts, beans.

Vegetables   Pumpkin, squash, spinach, carrots, tomatoes, olives, onions, red chili peppers, pimentos, parsley, cabbage; squash cut into strips and dried (Chichocade zapallo), a winter staple.

Fruit   Lemons, grapes, strawberries, peaches, raisins, quince.

Nuts and seeds   Almonds, sunflower seeds, pumpkin seeds.

Seasonings   Chili, onions, cinnamon, salt, black pepper, garlic, oregano.

Condiment   Chimichurri (corn oil, vinegar, onions, garlic, parsley, oregano, salt, black pepper, and chili or pimentos), a traditional sauce for grilled and roasted meats.

Dishes   Boiled corn grits porridge. Boiled corn hominy served with cabbage and sausage. Fried corncakes (humitas) made from a coarse purée of unripe corn kernels, milk, eggs, and cheese; the mixture wrapped in corn husks and steamed like tamales is humitas en chala. Beef usually grilled or roasted (asado) on the open fire; cooked con cuero (with the hide on) it is juicier. Grilled steaks. Offal dishes: tongue cooked with almond sauce, tripe, and sausages; grilled sweetbreads; and, most famous, puchero (boiled dinner of calf's head, chicken, sausage, and beef with green corn). Meat trimmings cooked and served as cold cuts (fiambres). Empanada, a crescent-shaped pastry turnover filled with spiced chopped meat and vegetables. Stews made from tougher cuts of meat and vegetables such as pumpkin and corn or fruit. Carbonada criolla (stew of beef chunks, corn, pumpkin, squash, and peaches cooked in a pumpkin shell). Locro (soup/stew of meat with wheat or corn and squash). Boiled or baked pasta (spaghetti, lasagna, ravioli) and sauce, a Sunday favorite in many homes.

National dish   Matambre ("hunger killer"), flank or rib steak rolled around spinach, whole hard-boiled eggs, carrots, and onions, tied with a string, and poached in broth or baked; served hot or cold as an appetizer.

Sweets   Sugarcane, sugar, soft fudge or a sauce on bread or pudding (dulce de leche), cream cakes, quince pie.

Beverages   Coffee, tea, milk, yerba maté (tea made from leaves of holly family plant), soft drinks, beer, wine.

Restaurant/grill   Parrilla, a restaurant specializing in grilled beef or a grill to hold meat over a bed of coals.

Street food and snacks   Empanada (spicy meat/vegetable turnover), a common street food. Maté with small snacks, often served in the afternoon.

ARMENIA
Republic of Armenia

Geography   Armenia is in southwestern Asia, in the southern Caucasus, bordering Turkey, Georgia, and Azerbaijan. The smallest of the former Soviet republics, it is a land of rugged mountains and extinct volcanoes.

Major Languages	Ethnic Groups		Major Religions	
Armenian (official)	Armenian	98%	Armenian Orthodox	95%
Yezidi	Russian	2%	Other Christian	4%
Russian	Yezidi (Kurd)	1%	Other	1%

Population density per sq. mi. 270.7
Literacy rate 99.5%
Life expectancy 68.8 male; 76.5 female
Per capita GDP $4,900
Labor force in agriculture 45.2%

Urban 64.1%
Infant mortality rate per 1,000 live births 20.9
HIV rate 0.1%
Unemployment rate 7.4%
Arable land 17%

Agriculture   potatoes, grapes, wheat, tomatoes, vegetables, chickens, sheep, cattle, pigs, goats

Natural resources   gold, copper, molybdenum, zinc, bauxite, fish

Industries   diamond processing, machine tools and machines, electric motors, tires, knitwear

History   Tradition holds that Armenia was settled by a descendant of Noah in the Lake Van region, where Noah's ark landed after the flood. Ancient Armenia extended into parts of the present Turkey and Iran. Armenia lost its independence to Rome in the 2nd century BCE and was later conquered successively by Persia, Byzantium, Islam, Mongols, Turks, Persians again, and Russia. Armenia became a Soviet republic in 1921. In 1988 an earthquake killed approximately 55,000 people and ruined several cities and towns. Armenia declared its independence in 1990 and became an -

independent state when the USSR disbanded in 1991. About a fifth of the population left the country beginning in 1993 because of an energy crisis. Economic growth has increased in recent years. In 2007 the first section of pipeline that provides Iranian natural gas to Armenia was inaugurated. Conflict over Nagorno-Karabakh, an Azerbaijan enclave with a majority population of ethnic Armenians, continues between mostly Christian Armenia and mostly Muslim neighboring Azerbaijan.

Influences on food   Armenians became Christians at the beginning of the 4th century and since then have maintained their church and related food customs, such as Lenten foods. Over the centuries Armenians have kept their culture intact and influenced others, although Armenian cuisine has been influenced by neighboring Greeks, Turks, Persians, Syrians, and other Arabs. Armenians traveled around the Caucasus more than the other nationalities and were the main commercial traders. Many Armenians emigrated to the United States and have been successful in the food industry, with specialty shops, delicatessens, restaurants, and bakeries.

Main foods   Bread, lamb, yogurt, cheese, eggplant.

Bread and cereals   Wheat, corn, rice; bread of different flours (wheat, potato, corn) combined for different flavors, flatbread (round, some topped with sesame seeds), lavash (thin crisp bread), pastries, rice dishes.

Meat, poultry, fish   Chicken, lamb, beef, pork, goat, fish (Lake Sevan is famous for trout), eggs; sausage.

Dairy products   (Cow, sheep, goat) Yogurt (mahdzoon), cheese (blue cheese, feta cheese, kashkaval). Yogurt and cheese are served at most meals and are used in cooking. Cheese is often flavored with herbs or spices.

Fats and oils   Olive oil, lamb fat (kyurdyuk from fat-tailed sheep, used in cooking), butter including from sheep.

Legumes   Lentils, beans, chickpeas.

Vegetables   Potatoes, tomatoes, eggplant, cucumbers, red peppers, cabbage, okra, squash, onions, garlic, olives; pickles.

Fruit   Grapes, raisins, apricots, prunes, damsons (small oval plums), lemons, apples, quinces, pomegranates. Armenia is noted for apricots. Fruits are common and are eaten fresh and used in soups and stews.

Nuts and seeds   Pine nuts, pistachios, walnuts, sesame seeds, pumpkin seeds.

Seasonings   Onions, garlic, peppers, lemon juice, allspice, basil, cumin, fenugreek, rosemary, mint, rosewater. Herbs are used in salads and cheeses. Spice use is moderate. There is a general liking for sweet and sour.

Dishes   Salads of cucumbers, tomatoes, and lemons. Usual soups: tomato, egg, and lemon; yogurt with onion or garlic and herbs; yogurt and cucumber. The favorite soup, bozbash (made from fatty breast of lamb plus fruit and vegetables). An unusual soup, shoushin bozbash (meat, quince, apple, and mint). Bulgur (cracked wheat) steamed and served like rice. Rice plov (pilaf). Kofta (meatballs made from a smooth paste of a meat and spicy ingredients, cooked by various methods). Trout poached; marinated with red peppers; or stuffed with fruits such as prunes, damsons, or apricots and baked. Shashlyk (grilled lamb kebabs). Luhjuman (pizza made with lamb, vegetables, and feta cheese). Keshkeg (lamb or chicken stew containing whole-wheat kernels).

Sweets   Honey, sugar. Fruit. Honey- or rosewater-flavored desserts and pastries such as paklava, or baklava (thin layers of dough with nuts and syrup). Armenian khalva (toasted walnut halves with boiled milk and sugar coating).

Beverages   Coffee, tea, tahn (diluted yogurt with mint), wine, brandy, anise-flavored aperitif raki. Armenians are world-acclaimed vintners and frequently consume wine and brandy made from various fruits.

Dinner   Mezze (appetizers) with raki, followed by soup, salad often with main course, bread, dessert, beverage.

Mezze   Cheese, eggplant, chickpea dip, toasted pumpkin seeds or pistachios, boeregs (pastries of thin layers of dough with savory filling of meat or cheese), dolma (stuffed grape leaves), basturma/pastourma (a pungent spiced meat with fenugreek), sausages, lavash. The mezze tradition (snacks with drinking) is important.

AUSTRALIA
Commonwealth of Australia

Geography   Australia, the island continent, is between the South Pacific Ocean and the Indian Ocean. Australia with the island state Tasmania off the southeastern coast is approximately the size of the United States excluding Alaska and Hawaii. The western half of Australia is a desert plateau. Mountain ranges run along the east coast. The Great Barrier Reef lies along the northeast coast. The northeast has heavy rainfall. Most of the cities and population are along the coast. Australia has many plant and animal species not found elsewhere, including kangaroos, koalas, platypuses, dingoes, Tasmanian devils, wombats, and barking and frilled lizards.

Major Languages	Ethnic Groups		Major Religions	
English (official)	White	92%	Roman Catholic	26%
Chinese	Asian	7%	Anglican	21%
Italian	Aboriginal and other	1%	Other Christian	21%
Other			Other	17%
			None	15%

Population density per sq. mi. 7.1
Literacy rate 93.4%
Life expectancy 79.2 male; 84 female
Per capita GDP $36,300
Labor force in agriculture 3.6%

Urban 88.2%
Infant mortality rate per 1,000 live births 4.8
HIV rate 0.2%
Unemployment rate 4.3%
Arable land 6%

Agriculture   wheat, grapes, barley, sugarcane, cotton, fruit, vegetables, sheep, chickens, cattle, pigs, goats
Natural resources   bauxite, coal, iron ore, copper, gold, other minerals, diamonds, natural gas, oil, fish

Industries   mining, wool, beef, industrial and transportation equipment, food processing, chemicals, steel

History   The first inhabitants, the aborigines, migrated here at least 40,000 years ago from Southeast Asia. In 1770 Captain James Cook explored the east coast when a variety of tribes inhabited the continent. In 1788 settlers (mostly convicts, soldiers, and government officials) began to arrive. Britain claimed the entire continent by 1830. In 1901 the Commonwealth was proclaimed. The 50,000 aborigines and 150,000 part aborigines are mostly detribalized, but there are several preserves in the Northern Territory; they remain economically disadvantaged. Australia's agriculture, mining, and industrialization are developed. Australia is the leading producer of wool and a leading exporter of meat, wool, and wheat. Sydney hosted the 2000 Summer Olympics. Australian troops fought in U.S.-led military operations in Afghanistan (2001) and Iraq (2003). In 2007 a decade of conservative government ended. In 2008 withdrawal of combat troops in Iraq began and the economy remained strong.

Australian External Territories   Norfolk Island, Coral Sea Islands, Territory of Ashmore and Cartier Islands, Heard Island and McDonald Islands, Cocos Islands, Christmas Island, Australian Antarctic Territory.

Influences on food   The aborigines were hunter-gatherers and subsisted on foods called bush tucker, including kangaroo, wombat, emu, duck, fish, shrimp, snakes, lizards, witchetty grubs, and wild plants such as yams, onions, wattle seeds, and quandong (a peach-like fruit). Foods were cooked over a fire, in the ashes, or boiled. The first white settlers (mostly convicts) arrived in 1788 from Britain and lived on imported food. After Britain gained control of the entire continent in 1830, many people immigrated voluntarily and accepted indigenous food such as kangaroo. During the 19th century meat was cooked on sticks over an open fire and damper (bread made with baking soda and tartaric acid because yeast was difficult to obtain) was cooked in ashes. The diet of meat, damper, and tea resulted from the abundance of meat and reflected convict rations: flour, meat, tea, and sugar. Australian meat production and consumption were among the highest in the world; meat was eaten three times a day. Vegetables including tomatoes were grown in home gardens. Thrift and economy were important, and physical labor demanded substantial meals of meat stews. Early in the 20th century women excelled at baking, and cookbooks usually contained more pages on pies, puddings, cakes, scones, and biscuits than on meat and vegetable dishes. During the first half of the 20th century the population became more urban with less reliance on native game and fruits, tastes shifted from mutton to lamb, and technological change such as refrigerators resulted in more ice cream and chilled dishes. After World War II great change occurred, including more restaurants and eating out, increased travel bringing more contact with Asian and European cultures, and more immigrants from Asia and Europe. The traditional British Sunday dinner (roast beef) and diet (meat and potatoes) gave way to the casual barbecue and a more distinctly Australian diet with Asian influence.

Bread and cereals   Wheat, barley, oats, rice; bread, pastry on meat pies and sweet pies, porridge.

Meat, poultry, fish   Beef, lamb and mutton, chicken, pork, goat, fish, seafood (oysters, crayfish, rock lobster, crabs, prawns), game (emu, wombat, kangaroo), eggs; sausage. Meat is the mainstay of the diet; beef is favored.

Dairy products   Milk, cream, cheese.

Fats and oils   Butter, lard, salt pork, bacon, vegetable oil, canola oil.

Legumes   Beans, peas, soybeans.

Vegetables   Potatoes, carrots, tomatoes, beets, peas, cabbage, corn, plantains, cucumbers, olives.

Fruit   Grapes, apples, bananas, oranges, pears, coconut, strawberries, mangoes, guavas, blackberries, currants.

Nuts and seeds   Macadamia nuts (native to Australia), pistachios, wattle seed.

Seasonings   Salt, pepper, onions, tomato sauce, ketchup, mint, rosemary, sage, ginger, soy sauce, garlic.

Dishes   Crab soup. Grilled prawns. Fried barramundi (a tropical perch) fillets with egg-oatmeal-macadamia nut batter. Roast beef. Roast lamb with rosemary and mint. Meat stew. Boiled lamb and cabbage. Colonial goose (boned leg of mutton with sage-and-onion stuffing). Carpetbagger steak (grilled or sautéed oyster-stuffed steak). Shepherd's pie (ground lamb topped with mashed potatoes). Meatloaf. Hamburgers topped with fried eggs and beet slices. Fried steak and eggs. Vegetables usually boiled, sometimes stir-fried. Salads of mixed vegetables and fruits. Stewed fruit.

Specialties   Roasted witchetty grubs. Kangaroo tail soup. Damper (soda bread).

Sweets   Sugarcane, sugar, jams, scones, biscuits (cookies), ANZAC biscuits (oatmeal cookies for Australian and New Zealand Army Corps during the world wars), pies, puddings, custards, cream puffs, cakes (fruit, sponge).

Sweet specialties   Butterfly cake (cupcake with center cut out, filled with whipped cream, and the halves of the cutout placed on the cream to resemble butterfly wings). Lamingtons (cookies with chocolate icing and coconut).

National dessert   Pavlova (meringue cake filled with strawberries and topped with whipped cream), claimed by Australia and New Zealand, and named after Anna Pavlova, the Russian ballerina who visited both in 1926.

Beverages   Tea, beer, wine. Australia is known for its beers and wines.

Meals   Three meals a day plus an afternoon break for tea or beer is typical. Outdoor barbecues are popular.

Fast-food snacks   Individual steak or sausage pies (eaten with tomato sauce or ketchup), fish and chips.

AUSTRIA
Republic of Austria

Geography   Austria is in south central Europe. It is mostly mountainous, with the Alps in the west and south. The eastern provinces and Vienna lie in the Danube River basin. Forests and woodlands cover about 40% of the land.

Major Languages	Ethnic Groups		Major Religions	
German (official)	Austrian	91%	Roman Catholic	74%
Turkish	Former Yugoslav (including		Protestant	5%
Serbian	Serbian, Croatian)	4%	Muslim	4%
Croatian (official in	Turk	2%	Other	5%
Burgenland)	Other	3%	None	12%

Population density per sq. mi. 257.8
Literacy rate 98%
Life expectancy 76.5 male; 82.4 female
Per capita GDP $38,400
Labor force in agriculture and forestry 3%

Urban 66.5%
Infant mortality rate per 1,000 live births 4.5
HIV rate 0.2%
Unemployment rate 7.2%
Arable land 17%

Agriculture   sugar beets, corn, wheat, potatoes, grapes, wine, chickens, pigs, cattle, sheep, goats

Natural resources   oil, coal, lignite, timber, iron ore, copper, zinc, antimony, magnesite, hydropower, fish

Industries   construction, machinery, vehicles and parts, food, metals, chemicals, lumber and paper, tourism

History   Around 15 BCE Rome conquered Celtic tribes in Austrian land. In 788 CE Charlemagne incorporated the land into his empire. By 1300 the House of Hapsburg gained control of the land and many other parts of Europe. The Congress of Vienna, in 1815, confirmed Austrian control of a large empire in southeastern Europe. The dual Austro-Hungarian monarchy was established in 1867, giving autonomy to Hungary. World War I started in 1914 with the assassination of the Hapsburg heir and destroyed the empire. By 1918 Austria was a small country, with present-day borders. Nazi Germany invaded Austria in 1938. Independence was restored in 1955. Austria joined the European Union in 1995. In the late 1990s and to 2006, far-right parties gained against the Social Democratic Party. In 2007 important reforms including the first national monthly minimum wage was introduced. The economy grew at the fastest rate in eight years.

Influences on food   Austria's neighbor to the south, Italy, influenced cuisine of Tyrol, the southern part of Austria, with foods such as speckknödel (dumplings with bauernspeck, cured and smoked bacon), a prominent Tyrol specialty, and nockerln, the Austrian version of Italian gnocchi (small dumplings) that accompany many dishes. Turkish influence is apparent in the pastry for strudel, layered thin dough similar to filo.

Regional foods   Some differences in foods among Austria's nine provinces are notable. Carinthia in the south has the highest mountains and lakes to provide freshwater fish. It also has nudeln, a small folded noodle square with many different fillings, of which kasnudeln (with cheese) is the best known. Styria, bordering on former Yugoslavia, has hearty food and interesting soups, such as stoss-suppe (sour cream, milk, potato, and caraway).

Bread and cereals   Corn, wheat, rye; white and dark breads, rolls, buns, croissants, pastry, dumplings, pancakes, cakes.

Meat, poultry, fish   Pork, veal and beef, chicken, eggs, lamb, goat, fish especially trout; bacon, ham, sausage.

Dairy products   Milk, cream, sour cream, cheese.

Fats and oils   Butter, lard, vegetable oil, olive oil. Lard is used for frying veal cutlets.

Legumes   Beans, lentils, split peas.

Vegetables   Potatoes, cabbage, beets, carrots, lettuce, cucumbers, tomatoes, onions, parsley, mushrooms, radishes, green peppers; sauerkraut (brined, fermented cabbage), pickles. Potatoes are prominent.

Fruit   Grapes, apples, apricots, lemons, raisins, raspberries; jam.

Nuts and seeds   Almonds, caraway seeds, poppy seeds.

Seasonings   Salt, pepper, mustard, cinnamon, cloves, horseradish, vinegar, chocolate, vanilla.

Dishes   Soups: beef broth with vegetables, potato, or mushrooms; split pea. Prominent are foods made with flour (melhspeisen): savory or sweet dishes of dumplings, noodles, pancakes, yeast pies and cakes, and strudel. Substantial main dishes: wiener schnitzel (thin slices of veal, beef, or pork, floured, dipped in egg, dipped in bread crumbs, and fried), boiled beef (especially sliced boiled beef with pan-browned whole potatoes and parsley), Viennese steaks (tender beef steak pan fried in butter in which onion slices were browned), and fried chicken (prepared like wiener schnitzel). Usual accompaniments to boiled beef: pickles, grated horseradish in vinegar, or apple-sauce. Vegetable dishes: potato salad (boiled potatoes mixed with vinegar, oil, sugar, salt, pepper, mustard, and finely chopped onion), winter vegetables simmered in water or baked and prepared with butter or cream, and sauerkraut with bacon. Green salad.

A specialty dish   Blue trout (brook trout taken out of the water and killed by a blow on the head, cleaned quickly, and boiled briefly; it turns blue and curls) with melted butter and new potatoes.

Sweets   Sugar. Kugelhopf (delicate yeast cake with raisins, in a tall ring shape, and dusted with powdered sugar). Linzertorte, from Linz (torte of nut pastry, raspberry jam filling, and lattice top).

Specialty sweets   Strudel, especially apple strudel (paper-thin sheets of dough rolled around cinnamon-spiced apple pieces and baked). Layer cakes, especially Sachertorte (a rich chocolate sponge layer cake filled with apricot jam and iced with bittersweet chocolate), served with whipped cream (as is strudel and many sweets). Sachertorte was first produced in 1832 by Franz Sacher, chef to Prince von Metternich; Sacher's descendants for many years operated the Sacher Hotel in Vienna, where the cake is still served.

Beverages   Coffee, wine, milk, hot chocolate, beer, tea.

Meals   Austrians tend to have three meals a day plus a second breakfast (gabelfrühstük) and a tea meal (jause). A typical main meal: soup, main dish with vegetable, green salad, and dessert.

Snacks   Coffee and cakes are enjoyed in establishments called konditorei, especially in Vienna.

AZERBAIJAN
Republic of Azerbaijan

Geography Azerbaijan is in southwestern Asia, bordering the western shore of the Caspian Sea. At the southeastern extremity of the Caucasus Mountains, it is mountainous. The climate is arid except in the southeast.

Major Languages	Ethnic Groups		Major Religions	
Azerbaijani (official)	Azeri	91%	Shi'a Muslim	53%
Lezgi	Dagestani (Lezgian)	2%	Sunni Muslim	34%
Russian	Russian	2%	Russian Orthodox	3%
	Armenian	2%	Armenian Orthodox	2%
	Other	3%	Other	8%

Population density per sq. mi. 246
Literacy rate 99.4%
Life expectancy 62.2 male; 71 female
Per capita GDP $7,700
Labor force in agriculture 41%

Urban 51.5%
Infant mortality rate per 1,000 live births 56.4
HIV rate 0.2%
Unemployment rate 1.4%
Arable land 21%

Agriculture wheat, vegetables, potatoes, cotton, rice, grapes, chickens, sheep, cattle, goats, pigs

Natural resources oil, natural gas, iron ore, nonferrous metals, bauxite, fish

Industries oil, natural gas, oil-field equipment, steel, iron ore, cement

History Azerbaijan was home to Scythian tribes and was part of the Roman Empire. It was overrun by Turks in the 11th century and conquered by Russia in 1806 and 1813. After the Russian revolution in 1917 it declared its independence. Taken by the Soviet army in 1920, it joined the USSR in 1922. Azerbaijan became independent when the USSR disbanded in 1991. In December 2001 the alphabet was officially changed from Latin to Cyrillic. Since 1988 Azerbaijan and Armenia have been fighting over the Azerbaijan enclave of Nagorno-Karabakh, the majority of whose inhabitants are Armenian Christians who want to secede and join Armenia. Azerbaijan has undergone rapid privatization, with Western investment in its oil resources. Construction of a 1,100-mile pipeline through Turkey and Georgia began in 2002. The pipeline opened in 2005, providing an outlet for Azerbaijan's vast oil reserves from the Caspian Sea and transforming the economy. Economic growth continued in 2007.

Influences on food Azerbaijan is the largest and most populous of the three Caucasus countries, with Georgia on the northwest and Armenia on the west and south. The other southern neighbor, Iran, now includes much of the larger Azerbaijan of former times. Neighbors and invaders (Romans, Persians, Arabs, Mongols, and Turks) have influenced Azerbaijan's cuisine. Turks dominated the country from the 11th century to the early 19th century, and Russia controlled it for most of the 19th and 20th centuries. Rice and fruit have grown here since ancient times and are important foods. Azerbaijan's coast on the Caspian Sea provides fish. Azerbaijan shares a common cuisine with its Caucasus neighbors in main foods (grain, lamb, yogurt, fruit especially grapes, and vegetables including eggplant) and liking of the sweet and sour taste combination. Azerbaijan differs from these neighbors in religion and related food practices and in mezze practice. Most Azerbaijani are Muslims, for whom consumption of pork or alcohol is forbidden, not Christians as in Georgia and Armenia. Mezze (snacks with drinking) is not typical in Azerbaijan as it is in Georgia and Armenia.

Bread and cereals Wheat, rice; bread, dumplings, pasta, rice dishes (plov).

Meat, poultry, fish Chicken, lamb, beef, goat, pork, fish (sturgeon, caviar), eggs.

Dairy products   Milk, yogurt, cheese.

Fats and oils   Butter, clarified butter, olive oil, lamb fat.

Legume   Chickpeas, beans, lentils.

Vegetables   Potatoes, eggplant, cucumbers, radishes, spring onions, tomatoes, watercress.

Fruit   Grapes, apricots, lemons, oranges, peaches, plums, damsons, pomegranate, prunes, raisins, barberries, quinces. Fruits is consumed fresh, dried, and as juice.

Nuts and seeds   Almonds, chestnuts (a specialty: roasted, shelled, and cooked in milk), walnuts, sesame seeds.

Seasonings   Juice of unripe grapes, lemon juice, herbs (coriander, tarragon, sumac, dill, mint), saffron (the national spice).

Dishes   Fresh vegetables and herbs. Fresh fruit such as peaches lightly fried. Soups: dumpling (dyushbara), pasta, rice, or yogurt with chickpeas, prunes, or chestnuts, and often with saffron and dill or mint. Kebabs (shashlik), lamb chunks, perhaps flavored with sumac, grilled on a skewer. Meat balls, sometimes stuffed with sour plums, chestnuts, quince, or prunes. Bozbash (the famous soup/stew made with fatty breast of lamb, fruits, and vegetables, and sometimes meat balls). Kavourma, or korma (braised or stewed meat slices with juice of unripe grapes or lemon juice). Fish prepared with coriander, tarragon, walnuts, and fruit such as prunes. Accompaniments: pomegranate seeds or syrup and walnuts for fish, poultry, and game; pomegranate syrup or plum sauce for kebabs. Plov, or pilaf (rice cooked first in oil so the grains remain separate and then simmered with liquid), the prize of Azerbaijan cuisine and the centerpiece of the meal. A plov may contain fish or eggs and toppings including orange peel, nuts, and dried fruit. Kazmag (a special plov with a golden brown crisp crust made by lining the bottom of a casserole with a thin layer of egg dough, adding rice and liquid, and baking).

Sweets   Honey, sugar. Pre-dessert, a thick sauce of grape juice, raisins, dried apricots, and almonds. Desserts: jams, halvah (varied sweet confections, often sweetmeats of fruit and nuts), sherbets, cakes.

Beverage   Strong black tea.

Meal   A main meal traditionally includes foods served in the following order: fresh vegetables and herbs, perhaps fresh fruit lightly fried, soup, meat dish, plov, pre-dessert, and dessert with tea.

B

BAHAMAS, THE
The Commonwealth of The Bahamas

Geography   The Bahamas is in the Atlantic Ocean, east of Florida. It is a chain of about 700 islands (29 inhabited) and over 2,000 islets.

Major Languages	Ethnic Groups		Major Religions	
English (official)	Black	85%	Baptist	35%
Creole (among Haitian immigrants)	White	12%	Anglican	15%
	Asian and Hispanic	3%	Roman Catholic	14%
			Other Christian	15%
			Other	21%

Population density per sq. mi. 79.1
Literacy rate 95.6%
Life expectancy 62.5 male; 69.0 female
Per capita GDP $25,000
Labor force in agriculture 5%; **in tourism** 50%

Urban 83.1%
Infant mortality rate per 1,000 live births 23.7
HIV rate 3%
Unemployment rate 10.2%
Arable land 1%

Agriculture   sugarcane, citrus fruits, vegetables, chickens, goats, sheep, pigs, cattle

Natural resources   salt, aragonite, timber, fish

Industries   tourism, banking, cement, oil trans shipment, salt, rum

History   Arawak Indians, the first inhabitants, lived here in 1492 when Columbus first arrived in the New World. British settlement began in 1647. The islands became a British colony in 1783 and independent in 1973. There is a big income gap between the urban middle class and poor farmers. Hurricanes regularly cause serious damage. Along with tourism, international banking and investment management have become major industries. In 2007 the newly elected president announced privatization of Bahamasair, the money-losing government-owned airline.

Influences on food   The indigenous Arawak Indians mostly disappeared after the Spanish conquest. Traces remaining about their food practices indicate they ate a wide range of fish and seafood and one-pot soups or stews. The Spanish explored and colonized the area and influenced food customs; for example, they brought cattle, pigs, and rice. British rule of The Bahamas for 200 years influenced food customs, such as the use of salt fish. Slaves from Africa brought their use of foods such as okra and black-eyed peas. Other influences include the Atlantic Ocean, which provides fish and seafood; the neighboring United States; and tourism.

Bread and cereals   Corn, wheat, rice; fried cornmeal breads, wheat flour breads, biscuits, and pasta, rice dishes, cassava bread.

Meat, poultry, fish   Chicken, eggs, goat, lamb, pork, beef, fish and seafood (dried salt cod, sea turtle, crabs).

Dairy products   Cow's milk (fresh, condensed, evaporated), cream, cheese.

Fats and oils   Lard, butter, coconut oil or cream, olive oil, vegetable oil, salt pork.

Legumes   Red beans, kidney beans, chickpeas (garbanzo beans), black-eyed peas, pinto beans, soybeans.

Vegetables   Cassava, yams, malanga, sweet potatoes, plantains, breadfruit, avocados, green leaves (taro, malanga, callaloo), squash, tomatoes, okra, cucumbers, chili peppers, sweet peppers, onions.

Fruit   Citrus fruits, bananas, coconut, mangoes, pineapple, akee (a mild apple-sized fruit), cashew apples, papaya, soursop (has a cotton-like consistency).

Nuts and seeds   Almonds, cashew nuts, annatto seeds.

Seasonings   Chilies, lime juice, salt, black pepper, garlic, onions, annatto, cilantro, cinnamon, allspice (pimento), coconut, rum, cocoa.

Dishes   Cassava bread (made by pressing, drying, grating, and frying cassava in flat loaves). Callaloo (soup of green leaves cooked with okra). Pepper pot (stew of meat and boiled juice of cassava, called cassarep, highly seasoned with pepper). Ceviche (raw fish marinated in lime juice with olive oil and spices). Escabeche (fried, marinated fish, seafood, or poultry). Dried salt cod fritters. Black-eyed pea fritters. Simmered or fried akee, cassava, or plantains. Boiled rice. Rice cooked with peas or beans. Rice cooked with meat, poultry, or fish in a pilaf. Savory pies. Salt cod gundy (spread). Hot chili sauces. Curried meat, poultry, or fish.

Sweets   Sugarcane, sugar, molasses, fresh fruit, cornmeal pudding, pies, cakes, ice cream.

Beverages   Coffee often with milk, tea, iced tea, soft drinks, milk, beer, rum.

Meals   Breakfast: coffee with milk and bread. Lunch: rice and beans or starchy vegetable and salt cod. Dinner: like lunch plus meat, vegetables, and milk when available.

Snacks   Fresh fruit, sweetened fruit juice poured over crushed ice, coffee with milk.

BAHRAIN
Kingdom of Bahrain

Geography   Bahrain is in the Middle East. It is an archipelago of sand and rock islands in the Persian Gulf off the eastern coast of Saudi Arabia. A causeway connects it to Saudi Arabia. It has a hot, humid climate with little rain.

Major Languages	Ethnic Groups		Major Religions	
Arabic (official)	Bahraini Arab	62%	Islam (official)	
English	Indo-Pakistani	15%	Shi'a Muslim	58%
Farsi	Iranian	13%	Sunni Muslim	24%
Urdu	Other	10%	Christian	9%
			Hindu, other	9%

Population density per sq. mi. 2,797.6
Literacy rate 88.8%
Life expectancy 72.4 male; 77.5 female
Per capita GDP $32,100
Labor force in agriculture 1%

Urban 88.4%
Infant mortality rate per 1,000 live births 15.6
HIV rate NA
Unemployment rate 16–18%
Arable land 3%

Agriculture   dates, vegetables (including tomatoes, onions), fruit, chickens, sheep, goats, cattle

Natural resources   oil, natural gas, fish, pearls

Industries   oil processing and refining, aluminum smelting, iron pelletization, fertilizers, Islamic and offshore banking

History   Bahrain was an important trade center by the third millennium BCE. It was ruled by Persia in the 4th century CE and then by Arabs until 1541. It was a British protectorate from 1861 to 1971, when it gained independence. Pearls, shrimp, fruits, and vegetables were economic mainstays until oil was discovered in 1932. By the 1970s oil reserves were depleted and international banking thrived. The government bought control of the oil industry in 1975. Bahrain was a Western airbase during the Persian Gulf War in 1991 and Iraq War in 2003. Since 1996 Shiites have clashed with the Sunni-led government. Democratization began in 1999 when Sheik Hamad ibnal-Khalifah succeeded his father after a four-decade rule. In 2002 women were first allowed to vote and seek office. The first female judge was appointed in 2006. In 2007 the first woman delivered a speech at the Arab League summit conference, held in conservative Saudi Arabia.

Influences on food   Bahrain's food has been influenced by Persia, many centuries of Arab rule, Britain, and surrounding cultures: Ottoman to the north, the Horn of Africa to the west, and Iran and India to the east. Religion also influences cuisine in this mostly Muslim country; for example, Muslims do not eat pork. The food in Bahrain is basically Arabian food, as it is for neighboring Saudi Arabia. Food presentation and meal format in Bahrain are similar to those in Lebanon and Syria. Bahrain's extensive coastline provides fish and shrimp. Expatriates comprise a substantial proportion of the population (38%), resulting in the availability of a wide variety of foods.

Bread and cereals   Wheat, rice; flatbread, couscous, cracked wheat, rolls, pancakes, filo pastry, rice dishes.

Meat, poultry, fish   Lamb, chicken, goat, beef, shrimp, fish (grouper, silver pomfret), eggs.

Dairy products   Yogurt (laban), labneh (fresh cheese made from draining yogurt), milk, cream, feta cheese. Yogurt and labneh are the main ones and used in various dishes.

Fats and oils   Sesame seed oil and paste (tahini), ghee (clarified butter), butter, olive oil, vegetable oils.

Legumes   Chickpeas (garbanzo beans), fava (broad) beans, lentils, red beans, peanuts.

Vegetables   Tomatoes, onions, eggplant, cucumbers, olives, parsley, spinach, mint, coriander, green onions.

Fruit   Dates, mangoes, melons, watermelon, oranges, bananas, lemons, limes, figs. Dates are consumed in large quantities, especially during the fresh date season and Ramadan, the month of fasting.

Nuts and seeds   Almonds, hazelnuts, pine nuts, pistachios, sesame seeds.

Seasonings   Baharat (a spice mix of black pepper, coriander, cassia, cloves, cumin, cardamom, nutmeg, and paprika), loomi (dried Omani limes), salt, cardamom, saffron, mint, lemon juice, onion, garlic, rosewater, orange flower water. Loomi is used in meat dishes and sweet tea.

Dishes   Boiled rice. Lamb cooked on skewers as pieces or ground (kebab mashwi). Machbous (shrimp cooked with rice, fresh herbs, and vegetables). Tharid (casserole of layered flatbread with meat stew). Hummus (simmered puréed chickpeas). Ground chickpeas or fava beans formed into small balls and fried. Foul (simmered fava beans) topped with tomato, garlic, lemon juice, olive oil, and fresh coriander. Vegetables cooked with tomatoes, sautéed onions, and a little water. Fresh salt pickles, accompaniments for meat dishes and snacks.

Possible national dish   Khouzi (baked whole lamb stuffed with chicken, eggs, and rice spiced with baharat, saffron, and onions), served on rice and garnished with almonds and ghee.

Sweets   Date molasses (dibis), honey, sugar. Baklava (pastry made of filo dough layers with nuts and soaked in honey or flavored syrup). Small stuffed pancakes (ataif), a Ramadan specialty. Many sweet dishes contain dates and date molasses. Honey is consumed in large quantities.

Beverages   Coffee, tea, fruit drinks, yogurt drinks, beer, wine, brandy. Coffee, the main drink, is strongly associated with the renowned Arabian hospitality and is prepared from well-roasted, finely ground beans and usually flavored with cardamom. Tea, the second drink, is usually consumed black and very sweet.

Street food and snacks   Freshly roasted chicken and doner kebab (vertical spit-roasted lamb pieces) sliced and served in flatbread or roll with tomato, parsley, and tahini, available from shawarma stalls.

BANGLADESH
People's Republic of Bangladesh

Geography   Bangladesh (formerly East Pakistan) is in South Asia, bordering the Bay of Bengal, and almost surrounded by India. It is mostly a low plain with a tropical monsoon climate and frequent floods and monsoons.

Major Languages	Ethnic Groups		Major Religions	
Bangla, or Bengali (official)	Bengali	98%	Islam (official)	
English	Other	2%	Muslim (mostly Sunni)	83%
			Hindu	16%
			Other	1%

Population density per sq. mi. 2,969.8
Literacy rate 53.5%
Life expectancy 63.1 male; 63.3 female
Per capita GDP $1,300
Labor force in agriculture 63%

Urban 25.7%
Infant mortality rate per 1,000 live births 57.5
HIV rate NA
Unemployment rate 4.3%
Arable land 55%

Agriculture   rice, sugarcane, potatoes, jute, tea, wheat, tobacco, chickens, goats, cattle, sheep

Natural resources   fish, natural gas, timber, coal

Industries   cotton textiles, jute, garments, tea, newsprint, cement, chemical fertilizer, light engineering, sugar

History   The historic region Bengal was a kingdom about 1000 BCE. Buddhists ruled it for centuries, but by the 10th century CE Hindus predominated. In the 12th century Muslim invaders conquered it. In 1576 it became part of the Mogul Empire, and most east Bengalis converted to Islam. British India ruled here from 1757 to 1947, when Britain withdrew and East Bengal became part of Pakistan. In 1971 Bangladesh proclaimed its independence; in the ensuing civil war 1 million died and 10 million fled to India. In 1974 Pakistan recognized Bangladesh's independence. Associated with India during the 1970s, Bangladesh became an Islamic Republic in 1988 and adopted a parliamentary system of government in 1991. In 1996 it signed a treaty with India on the use of water from the Ganges River. Jute's decline as a world commodity worsened the destitution here. Recent storms and floods have killed thousands. Militant Islamist bombing in 2005 caused deaths and injuries. Escalating political violence led to a state of emergency for most of 2007–2008. In 2008, Bangladesh also suffered from increased inflation and high food prices, floods, and a cyclone.

Influences on food   Before 1947 a part of the Bengal province of India, which was controlled by Britain from the 18th century to 1947, Bangladesh has been influenced by India and Britain. The area has been largely Muslim for nine centuries, which also influences food practices. A substantial proportion of the population is Hindu, also influencing food practices. For example, Muslims do not eat pork and Hindus do not eat beef. Geography is dominated by great rivers that flow into the Bay of Bengal and by the alluvial delta they created. The rivers sometimes flood during the monsoon season. Bangladesh has a subtropical climate with much rainfall, which supports rice, the main crop. The rivers and seacoast provide fish and seafood. Rice and fish are the staple foods. Sometimes famines occur in this densely populated country with many poor people.

Bread and cereals   Rice, wheat, corn, barley, sorghum, millet; chapati (flat, circular, whole wheat flour bread cooked on an ungreased griddle), luchi (fried bread like northern India pooris), caching (luchi stuffed as with green peas), dosa (lentil and rice pancakes), rice dishes. Rice is higher status than bread, so bread is not served with it.

Meat, poultry, fish   Fish and seafood (shrimp, crabs), chicken, eggs, goat, beef, lamb, and mutton. Fish include hilsa, a shad and full of small bones, and bekti, giant sea perch and one of the best fish in the Indo-Pacific.

Dairy products   Milk (cow, water buffalo), yogurt, cream, cheese.

Fats and oils   Ghee (clarified butter), mustard oil.

Legumes   Beans, peas, lentils. Dal is split pulse, lentils, or a combination of legumes (beans, peas, or lentils).

Vegetables   Potatoes, green leafy vegetables, onions, chili peppers, eggplant, carrots, cucumbers, green peas, jackfruit pulp (resembles breadfruit).

Fruit   Coconut, mangoes, dates, tamarind (sour pulp of bean pod). Dried dates are popular.

Nuts and seeds   Almonds, walnuts, pine nuts, pistachios, cardamom seeds, cumin seeds, mustard seeds.

Seasonings   Onion, garlic, chili pepper, mint, masala (spice mixture often of chilies, coriander, cumin, black pepper, ginger, turmeric, saffron, cardamom, cinnamon, and cloves; used in curries), rosewater.

Condiment   Chutney (spicy fruit or vegetable preserves).

Dishes   Boiled or steamed rice. Boiled potatoes. A special potato and rice dish (potato pieces browned in ghee with saffron, layered with rice and mint, water added, covered, and simmered, and unmolded to serve). Curry (meat, poultry, fish, or vegetable pieces cooked in spicy sauce), often served over rice and with chutney. Fish and seafood coated with masala (either red one with hot chilies or yellow one with turmeric) and fried in mustard oil.

Sweets   Sugarcane, sugar. Carrot or coconut pudding. Barfi (shredded coconut, and perhaps ground almonds, cooked with milk and sugar). Roshgulla (fresh cheese formed into a walnut-sized round ball, dipped in sugar syrup, and flavored with rosewater), a sweet contrast to highly seasoned seafood dishes and curries. Ladikanee (made from dough of flour and sugar mixed with other ingredients and shaped into balls, each containing a sugared cardamom seed or other candy, deep fried in ghee, then soaked in rose-flavored syrup), a popular and British-inspired confection created for Lady Canning's birthday shortly after 1858 when Lord Canning became the first viceroy of India. World-famous confections are produced. A professional sweet-maker (moira) is esteemed.

Beverages   Tea, lassi (diluted yogurt).

Daily diet   Many poor peasants eat rice, one or two onions, some chilies, and a handful of leafy greens (shak) or boiled potato. Urban workers living in slums often eat rice and dal. Persons who are better off also eat more complex dishes and sweets.

BARBADOS

Geography   Barbados is an island between the Caribbean Sea and the Atlantic Ocean. Farthest east of the West Indies, it is 21 miles long (34 km) and 14 miles wide (23 km), circled by fine beaches and narrow coastal plains.

Major Language	Ethnic Groups		Major Religions	
English (official)	Black	90%	Anglican	28%
	White	4%	Other Protestant	43%
	Mixed and Asian	6%	Other	12%
			None	17%

Population density per sq. mi. 1,694.4
Literacy rate 99.7%
Life expectancy 71.2 male; 75.2 female
Per capita GDP $19,300
Labor force in agriculture 10%

Urban 38.4%
Infant mortality rate per 1,000 live births 11.1
HIV rate 1.2%
Unemployment rate 8.1%
Arable land 37%

Agriculture   sugarcane, sweet potatoes, coconuts, vegetables, cotton, chickens, pigs, sheep, cattle, goats

Natural resources   oil, fish, natural gas

Industries   tourism, sugar, light manufacturing, component assembly

History   Barbados was probably named by Portuguese sailors in reference to bearded fig trees. It is thought to have been inhabited by Arawak Indians but was uninhabited when English ships came in 1605. In 1627 it became a British colony and British settlers came. They grew tobacco and cotton, and by the 1640s they switched to sugarcane. African slaves were brought to work on the plantations until slavery was abolished in 1834. Barbados became independent in 1966. It is one of the better developed Caribbean nations. British traditions remain. In 2007 officials announced that Barbados would import natural gas by pipeline from Trinidad and Tobago, and they launched an open-bid round for offshore exploration.

Influences on food   Arawak Indians, thought to be the original inhabitants, ate fish, seafood, and stews such as callaloo, using foods available from the sea and local greens. The same foods are used today on this tropical island. British control for more than three centuries influenced food customs; examples include salt cod, chowders, biscuits, and tea. Black African slaves also influenced foodways such as in using okra.

Bread and cereals   Corn, rice, wheat; fried cornmeal cakes, cassava bread (made from grated cassava fried in a flat loaf), cassava coconut biscuits or bread (made using wheat flour, cassava, and grated coconut).

Meat, poultry, fish   Chicken, eggs, pork, lamb, beef, goat, fish and seafood (flying fish, green sea turtles, green sea turtle eggs also called sea urchins, lobster, crabs, frogs, salt cod, snapper).

Dairy products   Cow's milk (fresh, condensed, evaporated), cream, aged cheese.

Fats and oils   Butter, lard, coconut oil, vegetable oil.

Legumes   Kidney beans, red beans, black-eyed peas, chickpeas, pigeon peas.

Vegetables   Sweet potatoes, cassava, yams, malanga, green leaves (cassava, malanga), squash, plantains, breadfruit, avocados, tomatoes, onions, chilies, sweet peppers, okra.

Fruit   Coconut, bananas, cashew apples, akee, papaya, pineapple (George Washington's favorite fruit when he visited Barbados in 1751), soursop, limes, mangoes, oranges, passion fruit, raisins.

Nuts and seeds   Almonds, cashew nuts, annatto seeds.

Seasonings   Salt, black pepper, chilies, allspice, annatto, cinnamon, garlic, cocoa, rum, hot pepper sauce.

Dishes   Callaloo (malanga leaves cooked with okra). Pepper pot (a meat stew containing boiled juice of cassava and peppercorns). Crab and greens soup made with coconut milk. Cornmeal coo-coo (flat cake made by stirring cornmeal into simmered okra slices). Codfish fritters. Lobster salad. Baked whole red snapper. Roast pig.

Specialty dishes   Fried flying fish. Green turtle and sea urchin dishes.

Special occasion dish   Conkies (cornmeal, chopped meat, raisins, and coconut in banana-leaf envelopes).

Sweets   Sugarcane, unrefined sugar, molasses, sugar, rum fruitcake, coconut custard pie, coconut-milk sherbet, mango mousse, chocolate mousse, cornmeal cake (made with cornmeal, wheat flour, raisins, cherries, and rum).

Beverages   Coffee with milk, tea, iced tea usually with lime, fruit juices, soft drinks, milk, cocoa, beer, rum (was first made in Barbados), planter's punch (lime juice, sugar or syrup, rum, and water or ice).

Meals   Breakfast: bread and coffee with milk. Lunch: rice and beans with meat, if affordable. Dinner: like lunch but with more meat, vegetables, and milk added when available.

Snacks   Sugarcane, fruit, sweetened fruit juice poured over shaved ice, tea with coconut biscuits or bread, planter's punch with plantain chips. Snacking is frequent, especially with children.

BELARUS
Republic of Belarus

Geography   Belarus is in Eastern Europe between Poland and Russia. It is a large landlocked country consisting mostly of hilly lowland with forests, swamps, peat marshes, rivers, and lakes.

Major Languages		Ethnic Groups		Major Religions	
Belarusian	(both	Belarusian	81%	Eastern Orthodox	80%
Russian	official)	Russian	11%	Roman Catholic	13%
		Polish, Ukrainian, other	8%	Other	7%

Population density per sq. mi. 120.8
Literacy rate 99.7%
Life expectancy 64.6 male; 76.4 female
Per capita GDP $10,900
Labor force in agriculture 14%

Urban 72.2%
Infant mortality rate per 1,000 live births 6.5
HIV rate 0.2%
Unemployment rate 1.2%
Arable land 27%

Agriculture   corn, other grain, potatoes, sugar beets, vegetables, flax, chickens, cattle, pigs, goats, sheep

Natural resources   forests, peat, oil, natural gas, granite, limestone, marl, chalk, sand, gravel, clay, fish

Industries   machine tools, tractors, trucks, earth movers, motorcycles

History   In the 5th century east Slavic tribes colonized Belarus. Kiev dominated it from the 9th to the 12th century. In medieval times it was subject to Lithuanians and Poles. Beginning in 1503 it was a war prize between Russia and Poland. Following the partition of Poland, 1772 to 1795, Belarus became part of the Russian empire. It proclaimed independence in 1918 but was occupied by the Red Army. The Polish-Soviet War of 1918 to 1921 was fought to decide Belarus's fate: west Belarus went to Poland and the larger eastern part became Belarussian SSR and was joined to the USSR in 1922. In 1939 the Soviet Union took west Belarus and incorporated it into Belarussian SSR. Overrun by German troops in 1941 and regained by Soviet troops in 1944, Belarus became independent in 1991 when the Soviet Union disbanded. Much of the area was contaminated from the Chernobyl accident in 1986, forcing many to evacuate. After increasing political turmoil in the 1990s, in 1996 Belarus signed a pact with Russia linking their political and economic systems. Also in 1996 a constitution was enacted that gave the president vast new powers. In 2007 Belarus resolved disputes with Russia on natural gas prices and petroleum.

Influences on food   With Russia on the east and Poland on the west, Belarus has undergone continuous social and religious upheavals. The peasants belonged to the Russian Orthodox Church, the petty gentry were mostly Unitarian, and the nobility, mostly of Polish or Lithuanian origin, were Roman Catholic. The cooking of the upper class resembled that of Poland and

Germany, whereas the cuisine of the small town merchants and artisans was influenced by Jewish cooking after the 17th-century influx of Jews. The peasants maintained the Slavic tradition of their ancestors. Most people are Eastern Orthodox: the observant do not eat animal products on fast days, and they eat special foods on holidays, especially Easter, when special cakes and decorated hard-boiled eggs are made. The cold, damp climate influences what foods are grown, mainly potatoes, rye, barley, and oats. Potatoes, rye bread, and dairy products are prominent in the diet. Lakes and rivers provide fish. Foods are often preserved by drying, pickling, or fermenting (e.g., sour cream).

Bread and cereals   Rye, barley, oats, wheat, buckwheat, millet; porridge, bread usually dark rye, dumplings, pastry, pancakes, cakes.

Meat, poultry, fish   Chicken, beef, pork, goat, lamb, fish, eggs; ham, sausages, pickled herring.

Dairy products   Milk, buttermilk, cream, sour cream, cheese. Dairy foods are eaten daily.

Fats and oils   Butter, lard, bacon, flaxseed oil, vegetable oil.

Legumes   Kidney beans, lentils, navy beans, split peas.

Vegetables   Potatoes, beets, cabbage, carrots, parsnips, cauliflower, turnips, cucumbers, onions, mushrooms. Mealy potatoes are preferred.

Fruit   Apples, apricots, blackberries, cherries, oranges, peaches, plums, raisins, rhubarb, strawberries.

Nuts and seeds   Almonds, hazelnuts, walnuts, poppy seeds, caraway seeds.

Seasonings   Vinegar, garlic, dill, horseradish, mustard, cinnamon, cloves, ginger, paprika, vanilla.

Dishes   Soups from beets (borscht), cabbage (shchi), or fish (ukha). Kasha (cooked porridge from buckwheat, barley, or millet). Boiled potatoes. Fried potatoes. Cucumbers in sour cream. Dumplings (kletski) from flour or potatoes, stuffed with meat, cheese, or fruit, and boiled. Pastry stuffed with meat or cabbage and fried or baked.

Belarus dishes unusual elsewhere   Zhur (oat soup), can be savory or sweet with honey and fruit; the savory is slightly sour from soaking the oatmeal overnight and is served hot with potatoes. Mokanka (blended curd cheese, sour cream, milk, and buttermilk, usually with chopped green onions and dill added), served as appetizer, main dish, or with pancakes. Drachona, pancake made with rye flour and buckwheat, served with sour cream and jam.

Sweets   Honey, sugar, fruit, jam, cooked fruits as in berry pudding (kisel).

Beverages   Milk, buttermilk, tea, coffee, beer, vodka.

Meals   Three hearty meals a day, with lunch the largest, are usual. Usual foods are bread, soup, and kasha, with milk, tea, or beer. Snacking is rare.

BELGIUM
Kingdom of Belgium

Geography   Belgium is in Western Europe bordering the North Sea, France, Germany, the Netherlands, and Luxembourg. It is mostly flat, with hills and forests in the southeast. Major commercial rivers trisect the country.

Major Languages		Ethnic Groups		Major Religions	
Dutch (Flemish)	(all	Flemish	58%	Roman Catholic	75%
French	are	Walloon (French)	31%	Protestant, Muslim,	
German	official)	Other	11%	Other, none	25%

Population density per sq. mi. 890
Literacy rate 99%
Life expectancy 75.9 male; 82.4 female
Per capita GDP $35,300
Labor force in agriculture 2%

Urban 97.3%
Infant mortality rate per 1,000 live births 4.5
HIV rate 0.2%
Unemployment rate 6.7%
Arable land 27%

Agriculture   sugar beets, potatoes, wheat, vegetables, fruit, tobacco, chickens, pigs, cattle, sheep, goats

Natural resources   construction materials, silica, sand, carbonates, fish

Industries   engineering and metal products, motor vehicle assembly, transportation equipment, scientific instruments, processed food and beverages, chemicals, metals, textiles, glass, oil

History   First inhabited by the Belgae, probably Celts, the area was conquered by Julius Caesar in about 50 BCE and by the Franks in the 5th century CE. It was part of Charlemagne's empire in the 8th century. Burgundy controlled it in the 15th century. Spain ruled it from 1555 to 1713, followed by Austria. During wars after the French Revolution, France occupied and then annexed it. After 1815 Belgium became part of the Netherlands. In 1830 it became an independent constitutional monarchy. Germany violated Belgium neutrality in both world wars. Language difference has been a perennial source of controversy: Dutch is the language of the Flemings of northern Belgium, whereas French is the language of the Walloons in the south. In 2000 Brussels became the "capital" of the European Union, where heads of government meet. In 2003 gay marriages and euthanasia were legalized. The economy was strong in 2007.

Influences on food   In the 1830s Belgium took its present form: the Flemish (Dutch) part in the north and Walloon (French-speaking) part in the south plus bilingual capital Brussels in the center. In Brussels some streets have food names, for example, Rue au Beurre (Butter Street). The north has flat land and coastline providing fish and seafood; the south has pastures, hills, and forests providing pork and game. The division is not only for language and geography but also for pattern of employment, wealth, birth rate, and personality profile: the more numerous and richer Flemish are go-getters, whereas the Walloons generally are more pleasure loving and gastronomically inclined. Belgium waffles and chocolates are famous throughout the world. Spanish influence includes meat, fowl, or fish fried then marinated; rice saffron torte; almond macaroons; and Seville oranges at Mardi Gras.

Bread and cereals   Wheat, rye, rice; yeast breads (whole wheat, wheat, rye), waffles, biscuits, sweet breads.

Meat, poultry, fish   Chicken, eggs, pork, beef, lamb, goat, fish, seafood (eel, crayfish, shrimp, mussels, oysters), game (rabbit, wild boar, deer); ham, sausages, charcuterie.

Dairy products   Milk, cream, cheese.

Fats and oils   Butter, lard, margarine, vegetable oil.

Legumes   Split peas, kidney beans.

Vegetables   Potatoes, endive (chicory), asparagus, Brussels sprouts, cabbage, onions, hop shoots, tomatoes.

Fruit   Pears, grapes, lemons, juniper berries, prunes, oranges, apples, cherries, raisins.

Nuts   Almonds, chestnuts, hazelnuts, pecans, walnuts, sesame seeds.

Seasonings   Herbs (celery, parsley, chervil, sorrel, tarragon, bay leaf), onions, shallots, garlic, lemon, cinnamon, nutmeg, ginger, saffron, vanilla, chocolate.

Historical dishes   Charlemagne's grandmother's soup (potage liégeois), pea and bean soup. Soupe Tchantches (vegetables, vermicelli, and milk soup). Truleye (from truler, "to crumble"), cold soup with crumbled gingerbread.

National dishes   Moules et frites (mussels with chips), served in restaurants and at roadside stalls; chips are eaten with mayonnaise. Chips or pommes frites (fried potatoes). Carbonade (beef and onions braised in beer). Anguilles au vert (eels simmered with herbs in butter and white wine, thickened with egg yolk, and seasoned with lemon juice). Waterzool (fish or chicken with herbs simmered in liquid including white wine, and the broth thickened with egg yolks and cream). Crayfish (écrevisses) simmered in white wine and cream sauce. Croquettes de crevettes (deep-fried shrimp croquettes). Tomatoes crevettes (hollowed-out tomatoes filled with shrimp and topped with mayonnaise). Cream of endive soup. Creamed oysters and shrimp. Shrimp and cheese fritters. Hochepot (meats, vegetables, and herbs poached in broth).

Northern specialties   Asperges op zijn vlaams (asparagus the Flemish way), simmered asparagus served with potatoes, boiled or braised ham, hard-boiled egg, melted butter, and grated nutmeg. Simmered hop vine shoots.

Southern specialties   In this land of châteaux and fortresses: smoked raw ham, charcuterie, pâtés, game (wild boar, deer, rabbit), tarts (baked two-crust pastry with sweet or savory filling), biscuits, sweet breads, and waffles.

Sweets   Sugar, honey. Cramique (fruit bread). Craquelin (sugar loaf). Waffles (gaufres) with butter and sugar, whipped cream, fresh fruit, or caramelized sugar. Café liégeois (mocha ice cream topped with coffee-flavored syrup and whipped cream). Speculoos (Christmas spice cookies baked in decorative molds). Belgium chocolates.

A national dessert   Dame blanche (ice cream, whipped cream, and chocolate sauce).

Beverages   Beer, coffee, tea, hot chocolate, wine. Belgium is renowned for beers.

BELIZE

Geography   Belize is in Central America, bordering Mexico, the Caribbean Sea, and Guatemala. Swamps along the coast give way to hills and mountains in the interior. Much of the land is heavily forested.

Major Languages	Ethnic Groups		Major Religions	
English (official)	Mestizo	49%	Roman Catholic	50%
Spanish	Creole	25%	Protestant	27%
Creole	Maya	11%	Other	14%
Mayan dialects	Other	15%	None	9%

Population density per sq. mi. 34.2
Literacy rate 70.3%
Life expectancy 66.4 male; 70.1 female
Per capita GDP $7,900
Labor force in agriculture 22.5%

Urban 50.2%
Infant mortality rate per 1,000 live births 23.6
HIV rate 2.1%
Unemployment rate 11.0%
Arable land 3%

Agriculture   sugarcane, oranges, bananas, cacao, chickens, cattle, pigs, sheep, goats

Natural resources   timber, fish, hydropower

Industries   garment production, food processing, tourism, construction

History   The Mayan civilization spread to this area between 1500 BCE and 300 CE and flourished until about 1200. The civilization was advanced and the population was dense. Columbus sailed along the coast in 1502. Shipwrecked English seamen began a settlement in 1638; more British settlements were established during the next 150 years. Both Spain and Britain claimed the area until Britain defeated Spain in 1798 and made it a British colony, British Honduras, in 1840. In 1973 it changed its name to Belize. Britain's last colony on the American mainland, it achieved independence in 1981. It has become a center for drug trafficking between Colombia and the United States. In 2007 Hurricane Dean caused extensive damage.

Influences on food   Belize's Caribbean coastline provides fish and seafood. The tropical climate allows growing sugarcane and fruits. The Maya influence was strong when the Spanish conquest occurred and it endures in the highlands, where the staple is corn, eaten as solid food or in drinks, gruels, tortillas, and tamales. Also, now there are posole (semi-fermented corn dough, diluted to make a beverage or used in other ways) and atole (thickened corn gruel, which can have additions of chili or beans, or can be used as an ingredient). The Spanish brought cattle, pigs, and new foods such as rice. Caribbean island foodways from native Carib-speaking Indians and from Africans and Asians imported to work influence food customs on Belize's Caribbean coast. British rule for almost two centuries had some influence on food customs. Most people are Christians, who eat special fare on religious holidays (Christmas, Easter, and Lent) and Sundays.

Staple foods   Corn, beans, rice.

Bread and cereals   Corn, rice, wheat; corn tortillas and atole, wheat flour rolls and cakes, coconut breads on the Caribbean coast.

Meat, poultry, fish   Chicken, eggs, beef, pork, lamb, goat, fish, shrimp, spiny lobster, conch, turtle, sea turtle eggs.

Dairy products   Milk (evaporated), cream, cheese.

Fats and oils   Lard, butter, vegetable oils, shortening.

Legumes   Red beans, kidney beans, black beans, white beans, chickpeas.

Vegetables   Avocados, chilies, squash, plantains, breadfruit, lettuce, onions, sweet peppers, potatoes, pumpkin, tomatoes, yams, cassava, chayote (green pear-shaped gourd), cabbage, beets, carrots.

Fruit   Oranges, bananas, coconut, pineapple, mangoes, grapes, apples, guavas, roselle fruit.

Seeds   Squash seeds, pumpkin seeds.

Seasonings   Chilies, garlic, orange-red coloring achiote/annatto, cilantro, cinnamon, cloves, lime juice, coconut milk, vanilla, cocoa.

Dishes   Cornmeal and meat dishes such as tamales (spicy meat mixture with cornmeal dough, wrapped in corn husks or banana leaves, and steamed). Rice and beans (frijoles con arroz) dishes such as gallo pinto (red beans and rice fried with onions); rice is often fried with onions before boiling in water or is cooked with coconut milk. Salads such as avocado with lime juice (guacamole). Pickled vegetables such as cabbage, beets, and carrots. Fried plantains. Soups/stews of meat, poultry, or fish with plantains, beans, or cassava and coconut milk.

Specialties   Spiny lobster soup and conch soup or fritters on the Caribbean coast. Exotic meat from forests, such as gibnut (small deerlike rodent).

Sweets   Sugarcane, sugar, honey, custards, rice puddings, ices made with fruit syrups, ice creams, cakes and fritters flavored with coconut or rum, praline-like candy (nogada), sweetened baked plantains.

Beverages   Coffee, hot chocolate, cold tropical fruit drinks (refrescas), beer, rum.

Meals   Corn and beans are eaten at every meal by the poor; rice is also common. In wealthier areas dinner also includes soup; meat, poultry, or fish; garnish such as salad or fried vegetable; and perhaps dessert.

Snacks   Sugarcane, fresh fruit, ices made with fruit syrups, ice cream.

BENIN
Republic of Benin

Geography   Benin is in western Africa, bordering the Gulf of Guinea and west of Nigeria. Dense vegetation covers most of the land: a coastal strip, a swampy forested plateau, and northern highlands. The climate is tropical.

Major Languages	Ethnic Groups		Major Religions	
French (official)	Fon	39%	Christian	43%
Fon	Adja	15%	Muslim	24%
Yoruba	Yoruba	12%	Voodoo	17%
Tribal languages	Bariba	9%	Other	16%
	Other	25%		

Population density per sq. mi. 199.8
Literacy rate 40.5%
Life expectancy 57.4 male; 59.8 female
Per capita GDP $1,500
Labor force in agriculture NA

Urban 40%
Infant mortality rate per 1,000 live births 66.2
HIV rate 1.2%
Unemployment rate 6.8%
Arable land 24%

Agriculture   cassava, yams, corn, cotton, beans, chickens, cattle, goats, sheep, pigs

Natural resources   fish, oil, limestone, marble, timber

Industries   textiles, food processing, construction materials, cement

History   The Kingdom of Abomey was established in the area in 1625 by the Dahomey, or Fon, and arose to power in wars with neighboring tribes in the 17th century; a rich cultural life flourished. In the 18th century the expanded kingdom became known as Dahomey. France dominated the area by the late 19th century, annexed it in 1893, and incorporated it into French West Africa in 1904. Dahomey gained independence in 1960 and was renamed Benin in 1975. By the late 1980s its economy nearly collapsed. Privatization and austerity measures were implemented. In 2007 a Benin scientist was granted a patent for his new treatment for a strain of sickle-cell anemia, the first time an African had been given a patent for a new drug.

Influences on food   This hot, humid, and rainy country has a coastline that provides fish and land that supports raising cassava, yams, corn, and some animals. The introduction of New World foods such as cassava, corn, peanuts, tomato, chili pepper, pumpkin, and potato during the 15th and 16th centuries greatly influenced food customs. Native African foods include black-eyed peas, watermelon, and okra. French influence is strong. Daily fare is mostly starchy vegetables with legumes and greens, with fish near the coast, seasoned with palm oil, tomatoes, hot red chili peppers, and onions. Thick, sticky, spicy dishes are enjoyed.

Bread and cereals   Corn, sorghum, millet, rice; porridge, corn flour paste, dough balls, biscuits, rice dishes.

Meat, poultry, fish   Chicken, eggs, beef, goat, lamb, pork, fish (fresh, smoked, salted, or dried), guinea fowl, rabbit, game. Chicken is a favorite and prestigious food.

Insects   Termites (often called white ants), locusts.

Dairy products   Milk, sour milk, buttermilk, curds, whey, cheese.

Fats and oils   Palm oil, shea oil, coconut oil. Palm oil, the predominant cooking fat, gives dishes a red hue.

Legumes   Beans, peanuts (groundnuts), black-eyed peas, locust beans (carob).

Vegetables   Cassava, yams, plantains, taro, green leaves, okra, bitterleaf, melokhia, tomatoes, sweet potatoes, potatoes, eggplant, pumpkin, onions, red chili peppers, cucumbers, bell peppers.

Fruit   Coconut, bananas, pineapple, akee apples, baobab, watermelon, guavas, lemons, limes, mangoes, papaya.

Nuts and seeds   Cashews, kola nuts, watermelon seeds (egusi, a popular ingredient), sesame seeds, mango seeds. Nuts and seeds thicken and flavor sauces.

Seasonings   Salt, hot red chilies, tomato, onion, garlic, dried baobab leaves, thyme, turmeric, nutmeg, ginger, coconut, stock cubes.

Dishes   Most foods are boiled or fried, and chunks are dipped in sauce and eaten by hand. Sauces: peanut (ground and pounded); palaver sauce (green leaves); and fréjon (black-eyed peas, coconut milk, and sometimes carob or chocolate). Fufu, paste of boiled and pounded starchy vegetables or boiled corn flour, formed into bite-size scoops to eat stew. Stews: fish and meat; chicken and peanut; and root vegetables, okra, or peanuts with bits of fish, chicken, or beef. Adalu (mashed vegetables). Rice boiled in coconut milk, served with many dishes including the chicken and fish ones listed here. Jollof rice (boiled rice with meats, vegetables, spices, and tomato or palm oil). Chicken or fish marinated in lemon juice, grilled, fried with onions, and simmered with the marinade. Roast chicken with onion, pepper, turmeric, and garlic; basted and served with coconut sauce.

Sweets   Honey, sugar, kanya (peanut candy), bananas baked with honey, sugar, or coconut, fried dough balls.

Beverages   Coffee, beer, red zinger (herbal tea made from flower pods of roselle (*Hibiscus sabdariffa*).

Street food and snacks   Grilled spicy kebabs, fried foods (fish, bean balls, plantain chips, sweet dough), steamed rice balls, coconut biscuits, sweet porridge.

BHUTAN
Kingdom of Bhutan

Geography   Bhutan is in southern Asia in the eastern Himalayan Mountains, bordering India and Tibet. It is composed of high mountains in the north, fertile valleys in the center, and thick forests and plains in the south.

Major Languages	Ethnic Groups		Major Religions	
Dzongkha (a Tibetan dialect) (official)	Bhote	50%	Mahayana Buddhism (official)	
Tibetan and Nepalese dialects	Nepalese	35%	Buddhist	75%
	Indigenous tribes	15%	Hindu	25%

Population density per sq. mi. 37.6
Literacy rate 55.6%
Life expectancy 64.8 male; 66.3 female
Per capita GDP $5,200
Labor force in agriculture 63%

Urban 31%
Infant mortality rate per 1,000 live births 51.9
HIV rate 0.1%
Unemployment rate 3.1%.
Arable land 2%

Agriculture   corn, potatoes, rice, citrus, food grains, dairy products, cattle, chickens, pigs, horses, goats, sheep

Natural resources   timber, hydropower, gypsum, calcium carbonate

Industries   cement, wood products, processed fruits, alcoholic beverages, calcium carbide, tourism

History   Civilization in the region dates back to at least 2000 BCE. Aboriginal Bhutanese, Monpa, are believed to have migrated from Tibet. Tibet gained control in the 16th century CE. British influence grew in the 19th century. A Buddhist monarchy was established in 1907. A 1910 treaty let Britain guide external affairs while Bhutan was internally self-governing. Upon independence India assumed Britain's rule in 1949. Until the 1960s Bhutan was isolated from the rest of the world. Fearing China after it invaded Tibet, Bhutan strengthened ties with India, with new roads and other connections. Bhutan has taken steps toward modernization, including building roads and hospitals and establishing a system of secular education. It abolished slavery and the caste system, emancipated women, and enacted land reform. In 2004 Bhutan became the first nation to ban tobacco sale and public smoking. In 2008 Bhutan changed from an absolute monarchy to a multiparty democracy.

Influences on food   Bhutan's high eastern Himalaya Mountains, fertile valleys, and forests and plains influence its foods. Other influences include neighbors Tibet (home of Bhutan's original inhabitants) and India, and also nearby countries China and Nepal. Examples include noodle dishes from Tibet and China; curry, pickles, and halva from India; and split pea pancakes from India and Nepal. British control for a century and a half also exerted some influence. Religions Buddhism and Hinduism also influence food practices. Buddhists abstain from taking life of another so they eat grains and vegetables when plentiful and hardly any meat; however, for those who have to eat meat for survival it is permitted. Nomads depend on dairy and meat products. Yak and mutton are eaten, but Buddhists abstain from fish, pork, or poultry. It is considered better to take the life of one large animal than of numerous small ones. In Hinduism, the cow is sacred and not to be killed or eaten. Products of a living cow are pure and purifying: milk, ghee, dung. Little information about food practices in Bhutan is available. Food in the mountains and north resembles that in Tibet; food in the area bordering India resembles that in northern India.

Bread and cereals   Rice, corn, other grains; bread, pancakes, dumplings, noodles. Tsampa (toasted flour of any grain) is a main staple at high altitudes.

Meat, poultry, fish   Beef, chicken, eggs, pork, goat, lamb and mutton, yak. Meat, fat, and cheese dry easily in the cold dry atmosphere in the high altitudes. Shay kampo (dried meat) can be dried in thick strips and is tender to eat whether cooked or not.

Dairy products   Milk, cream, yogurt, cheese. Dairy foods are important. The dri (female yak) is used just for milk and milk products. There are also cows and crosses between a yak and a cow.

Fats and oils   Butter, ghee (clarified butter), other animal fats. In high-altitude areas people eat a lot of fat.

Legume   Split peas.

Vegetables   Potatoes, other root vegetables, onions, garlic.

Fruit   Citrus, dates, raisins.

Seasonings   Salt, curry spices (usually black pepper, cayenne, cinnamon, coriander, cumin, fenugreek, ginger, cardamom, and turmeric), cinnamon.

Dishes   Steamed or fried breads. Split pea pancakes. Steamed meat-filled dumplings (mono). Dishes using offal because all parts of the animal are used. Noodle dishes. Curry dishes. Pickled vegetables.

Sweets   Halva, varied confections, usually made from grain, ghee, spiced syrup, and fruit.

Beverage   Tea. A lot of tea is drunk. Boeja (butter) tea, made by churning brewed tea, butter, milk or cream, and salt, is drunk throughout the day.

BOLIVIA
Republic of Bolivia

Geography   Bolivia is In western central South America. It is one of two landlocked countries in South America. Bolivia has a great high central plateau (12,000 ft; 3,658 m) between high Andes Mountains in the west and semitropical forests, plains, and lowlands in the east. La Paz is the world's highest capital city (11,910 ft; 3,630 m). Lake Titicaca is the world's highest commercially navigable lake (12,506 ft; 3,812 m).

Major Languages		Ethnic Groups		Major Religions	
Spanish	(all	Quecha	30%	Roman Catholicism (official)	
Quechua	are	Mestizo	30%	Roman Catholic	95%
Aymara	official)	Aymara	25%	Protestant (Evangelical Methodist)	5%
		White	15%		

Population density per sq. mi. 22.1

Literacy rate 90.3%

Life expectancy 63.9 male; 69.3 female

Per capita GDP $4,000

Labor force in agriculture 40%

Urban 64.2%

Infant mortality rate per 1,000 live births 49.1

HIV rate 0.2%

Unemployment rate 8.0% in urban areas

Arable land 3%

Agriculture   sugarcane, soybeans, corn, coffee, coca, cotton, rice, potatoes, chickens, sheep, cattle, pigs, llamas and alpacas, goats

Natural resources   tin, natural gas, oil, zinc, tungsten, antimony, silver, iron, lead, gold, timber, hydropower

Industries   mining, smelting, oil, food and beverages, tobacco, handicrafts, clothing

History   An advanced Tiwanaku culture existed in the Bolivian highlands in the 7th to 11th centuries. Aymara Indians inhabited this land in the 13th century when conquered by the Incas. Spain ruled from the 1530s until 1825, when Spanish forces were finally defeated. Bolivia is named for Simon Bolivar, independence fighter. It lost parts of its land to neighboring countries in wars from 1879 to 1935. Government instability occurred during much of the 20th century. In the 1990s Bolivia was a big producer of coca, from which cocaine is obtained. The government tried to eradicate the crop, although many poor farmers dependent on it resisted. Bolivia has large gas reserves and considerable oil but has remained one of the poorest South American counties. Unrest concerning the use of Bolivia's gas and oil continues. In 2005 Evo Morales was elected president, South America's first Indian president. He nationalized the hydrocarbon sector in 2006 and increased government income from natural gas and mineral resources in 2007 as tension increased between the Indian-dominated western highlands and the resource-rich eastern lowlands.

Influences on food   Once part of the Inca Empire, this interior land is high in the Altiplano that stretches east from Lake Titicaca and swoops down to a moist jungle. Potato is the staple crop of the Altiplano. Coca bush is the staple in the high mountains; its leaves counteract altitude sickness. The jungle supplies tropical produce: cassava, sweet potato, and coconut. The two great lakes, Titicaca and Poopù, provide freshwater fish; Lake Titicaca also provides giant frogs. The Indian culture was over-laid by the Inca, followed by the Spanish. Bolivia's cuisine reflects the Indian culture, the barrenness of the country, and Spanish influence. For example, the Spanish brought cattle, pigs, rice, and olives. Bolivia's cooking has much in common with other Andean countries such as Peru and Ecuador: fondness of chilies, reliance on stews and substantial vegetable dishes, and frequent use of annatto (seeds of pods from a tree native to tropical America; they are red and contain carotene) to color food. Many varieties of potatoes grow here, especially the frost-resistant white and purple varieties used to make chuño, the freeze-dried potato that provides food for the whole year. At high altitudes in the Andes around Lake Titicaca, quinoa provides a cereal staple. It has green leaves similar to spinach and seeds in large sorghum-like clusters, which are processed into flour and used in breads. Quinoa flour has high quality protein due to a high concentration of essential amino acids. Bolivia has neither coast for fish and seafood nor grassland for large meat animals. Llama is used for transport but not for meat or milk.

Staple foods   Potato, quinoa, and corn; these are also used to make alcoholic beverages.

Bread and cereals   Corn, rice, quinoa; bread, hominy.

Meat, poultry, fish   Chickens, eggs, lamb and mutton, beef, pork, goat, cuz (guinea pig), rabbit, fish, frogs. Cuz and rabbit are popular. Stews are eaten frequently.

Dairy products   Milk (cow, goat), evaporated milk, fresh and aged cheeses.

Fats and oils   Butter, lard, olive oil.

Legumes   Soybeans, kidney beans, peanuts.

Vegetables   Potatoes, cassava, sweet potatoes, yams, chilies, pumpkin, squash, plantains, green peppers, carrots, yacón (white root similar to a mild carrot), onions, tomatoes, olives.

Fruit   Coconut, bananas, apples, lemons, limes, oranges, guavas, raisins.

Nuts and seeds   Cashews, pumpkin seeds, squash seeds.

Seasonings   Chilies, annatto, allspice, cinnamon, citrus juices, garlic.

Dishes   Boiled potatoes. Substantial vegetable dishes such as chine (freeze-dried potato) sauced with hot chilies or cheese or in a stew (chupe). Beef stew made with carrots, onions, hominy, and chuño. Conejo estirado, a dish in which rabbit is stretched to make it more tender. Fried fish. Humitas, ground cornmeal dough wrapped around a meat, fish, or vegetable filling. Cornmeal-coated chicken in tomato sauce.

A specialty   Fried legs from Lake Titicaca giant frogs.

Sweets   Sugarcane, sugar, honey.

Beverages   Coffee often with milk, chichi (distilled corn liquor), brandy with orange juice (a specialty cold drink).

BOSNIA AND HERZEGOVINA

Geography   This country is in southeastern Europe on the Balkan Peninsula, bordering the Adriatic Sea. It has hills, mountains, and forests in Bosnia in the north; flat farmland in Herzegovina in the south; and a narrow coast.

Major Languages	Ethnic Groups		Major Religions	
Bosnian (official)	Bosniak	48%	Muslim	40%
Croatian	Serb	37%	Orthodox	31%
Serbian	Croat	14%	Roman Catholic	15%
	Other	1%	Other	14%

Population density per sq. mi. 232.5
Literacy rate 96.7%
Life expectancy 74.7 male; 82.2 female
Per capita GDP $7,000
Labor force in agriculture NA

Urban 45.7%
Infant mortality rate per 1,000 live births 9.3
HIV rate <0.1%
Unemployment rate 31.1%
Arable land 20%

Agriculture   corn, potatoes, wheat, fruits, vegetables, chickens, sheep, pigs, cattle, goats, beehives

Natural resources   coal, iron ore, bauxite, copper, lead, zinc, chromite, cobalt, manganese, fish

Industries   steel, coal, mining, vehicle assembly, textiles, tobacco products, wood furniture, tank and aircraft assembly, domestic appliances

History   Bosnia was ruled by Croatian kings to 958 CE and by Hungary from 1000 to 1200. It organized at 1200, later took control of Herzegovina, and from 1391 it disintegrated. The Turks conquered the area in 1463. Austria-Hungary controlled it from 1878 to 1918, when it became part of Yugoslavia. In 1946 Bosnia and Herzegovina became a republic of communist Yugoslavia. Bosnia and Herzegovina became an independent nation in 1992; its Serb population objected, and conflict ensued among Serbs, Croats, and Muslims. Leaders of Bosnia, Croatia, and Serbia signed a peace agreement in 1995. In 1996 a NATO peacekeeping force was installed there. A UN tribunal began bringing charges against suspected war criminals, leading to convictions of Bosnian Serb leaders in 2001 and 2006. In 2008 the parliament started reforms of the police force.

Influences on food   Formerly part of Yugoslavia, this mostly mountainous land with woods and fertile plains supports extensive agriculture. The small outlet on the Adriatic Sea supplies fish. Modern, large-scale agriculture is practiced, with wheat and corn the chief cereals. There are numerous orchards and extensive raising of cattle, pigs, and sheep. During the four centuries of Turkish occupation most of the Slavs in this land adopted the Muslim faith. Now most people in this country are Muslims or Orthodox Christians. Religion influences food practices; for example, Muslims do not consume pork, whereas Christians may. Although Islam prohibits alcohol consumption, Bosnian Muslims never gave up drinking wine and plum brandy.

Bread and cereals   Corn, wheat, rice; wheat kernels, bread (usually leavened loaves made from wheat flour), pocket bread, pastry (especially paper-thin dough, filo), pies, dumplings, pasta.

Meat, poultry, fish   Chicken, eggs, lamb, pork, beef, goat, fish. Pork is very popular (except with Muslims).

Dairy products   Yogurt, cheese especially feta (salty white cheese) and kasheval (hard tangy ewe's milk cheese sometimes called the cheddar of the Balkans), milk, buttermilk, cream, sour cream.

Fats and oils   Butter, olive oil, vegetable oils, rendered lamb fat.

Legumes   Chickpeas, fava beans, black beans, white beans, lentils.

Vegetables   Potatoes, cabbage, cucumbers, grape leaves, onions, green peppers, tomatoes, olives, eggplant.

Fruit   Plums, pears, apricots, cherries, grapes, apples, berries, peaches, lemons. Plum is the main fruit.

Nuts and seeds   Almonds, pistachios, walnuts, sesame seeds, poppy seeds.

Seasonings   Dill, garlic, mint, cardamom, cinnamon, oregano, parsley, pepper, lemon juice. Fruit juices, especially lemon juice, and syrups flavor many foods.

Dishes   Kofta (fried meatballs). Kebabs (lamb pieces grilled or roasted on skewers). Dolma (cabbage or grape leaves stuffed with ground meat, onion, green pepper, and tomato). A Balkan specialty, moussaka (minced lamb, eggplant, onions, and tomato sauce baked in a dish lined with eggplant slices).

Sweets   Honey, sugar. Fresh fruit. Fruit compote. Sweet yeast bread rolled with a walnut, butter, cream, and egg filling. Baklava (a pastry made with filo dough layered with a walnut, almond, or pistachio filling, then soaked in a syrup flavored with honey, brandy, rosewater, or orange blossom water, and often cut into diamond shapes), available at most cafés and bakeries. A Balkan specialty, slatko (fruits simmered in thick syrup).

Beverages   Coffee (strong, often very sweet, and flavored with cardamom), tea, wine, plum brandy (šljivovica).

Mezze   Small bites of foods (e.g., cheese, olives) eaten while drinking and gossiping. The favorite pastime is the evening gathering (akšamluk) where men have friendly conversation along with native brandy and mezze dishes.

Restaurant food tradition   The tradition of good restaurant food dates back to the second half of the 15th century (about 1462) when the first inn with a cook was recorded. Nearly 200 dishes were served at the end of the 19th century in Sarajevo eating houses. By the early 20th century many of these dishes had disappeared from menus.

Restaurant meal   A tradition is to serve small amounts of six or more complementary dishes on a plate. For example, bašĉaršikski (high street platter) might contain a skewer of lamb pieces, a stuffed onion, green pepper, and tomato, a few fried tiny meatballs, and stuffed grape or cabbage leaves (sarma in Bosnia, japrak in Herzegovina); the juices from the various saucepans are mixed together and poured over the food; and a few tablespoons of yogurt garnish are added.

Meals   Three meals a day, with the main meal at midday, is typical. Breakfast: bread with honey or preserves and tea or coffee. Lunch: soup, casserole of meat and vegetables or a fish dish, bread and cheese, and fruit compote or pastry. Dinner: leftovers or soup, wine.

Snacks   Fresh fruit, pastries, ice cream. Frequent snacking is typical.

BOTSWANA
Republic of Botswana

Geography   Botswana is in southern Africa. The Kalahari Desert occupies the southwest, supporting nomads and wildlife. In the east is rolling plains, where livestock graze. In the north are salt lakes, swamps, and farmland.

Major Languages	Ethnic Groups		Major Religions	
English (official)	Tswana (Setswana)	79%	Christian	72%
Setswana (Tswana) (national)	Kalanga	11%	Badimo	6%
	Basarwa	3%	Other	1%
	Other	7%	None	21%

Population density per sq. mi. 8.2
Literacy rate 82.9%
Life expectancy 51.3 male; 49 female
Per capita GDP $16,400
Labor force in agriculture NA

Urban 57.3%
Infant mortality rate per 1,000 live births 44
HIV rate 23.9%
Unemployment rate >20%
Arable land 1%

Agriculture   roots and tubers, sorghum, pulses, corn, millet, sunflowers, chickens, cattle, goats, sheep, pigs

Natural resources   diamonds, copper, nickel, salt, soda ash, potash, coal, iron ore, silver, fish

Industries   diamonds (world's leading producer, by value), copper, nickel, salt, soda ash, potash

History   Inhabited by Bushmen, then by Bantus, the region became the British protectorate of Bechuanaland in 1886. It gained independence in 1966, as Botswana. Cattle raising and mining have contributed to the economy, which is closely tied to South Africa. In 2001 Botswana had the highest rate of HIV infection in the world. In 2002, assisted by international doctors, Botswana started a program that provided free antiviral drugs. In 2007 controversy continued over the eviction of Bushmen from the Middle Kalahari Game Reserve and the transfer of sales and distribution of Botswana's diamonds from London to Gaborone.

Influences on food   This land of desert, plains, and farmland supports nomadic Bushmen and wildlife, livestock, subsistence farming, and mining. Most of the population is indigenously African. Botswana's neighbor to the south is South Africa. Botswana's cuisine has been influenced by European settlers of the region, including the Dutch, German, French, and especially the British because Botswana was a British protectorate for 80 years. The Dutch and Germans brought an appreciation for jams and preserves (konfyt) and baked goods. French Huguenots founded the wine industry. Muslim slaves and laborers imported from Malaysia and India to South Africa have also influenced local fare. The Malays were expert fishermen with experience in preserving fish. They founded the Cape Malay cuisine that is prominent in the region. The diet of rural people was that of their East African ancestors except that corn (from the New World and planted by European settlers) was used in porridge. Cattle were wealth and seldom eaten. Dairy products, beans, melon, pumpkin, greens, and insects were and are eaten.

Bread and cereals   Sorghum, corn, millet, wheat, rice; porridge, rice dishes, bread, pastry, doughnuts, cookies.

Meat, poultry, fish   Chicken, eggs, beef, goat, lamb and mutton, pork, fish, game (antelope, venison, ostrich); boerewors (sausages from mixed meats often game), biltong (salted meat strips dried and smoked), dried fish.

Insects   Locusts, caterpillars, termites (white ants), ant larvae.

Dairy products   Milk, cream.

Fats and oils   Fat of fat-tailed sheep, butter, fish oil, vegetable oil.

Legumes   Beans, peanuts, lentils.

Vegetables   Sweet potatoes, carrots, onions, potatoes, green leaves, pumpkin, cauliflower, cucumbers, tomatoes.

Fruit   Melons, quinces, dates, apples, apricots, tangerines, grapefruit, lemons, grapes, raisins, coconut.

Nuts and seeds   Almonds, walnuts, sunflower seeds.

Seasonings   Vinegar, lemon juice, chili pepper, garlic, cinnamon, cloves, turmeric, ginger, curry powder, bay leaf.

Dishes   Bredie (spicy mutton stew including various vegetables). Sosaties (curried, marinated mutton, either skewered and barbecued or simmered in marinade). Bobotie (meatloaf with curry, topped with a custard mixture of milk and eggs, and baked). Frikkadels (braised meat patties). Grape-stuffed chicken or suckling pig, sometimes served for special occasions. Cornmeal porridge, sometimes sour (ting). Fried or roasted insects. Simmered beans or lentils, often with melon or pumpkin. Grated raw fruit or vegetables with vinegar or lemon juice and chilies. Spicy fruit or vegetable relishes (chutney). Atjar (unripe fruit or vegetables preserved in oil with spices).

Sweets   Honey, sugar. Dried fruit. Fruit leathers (planked fruit). Fruit preserves and jams. Pastries such as tarts made with raisins, sweet potatoes, coconut, or custard. Koeksister (deep-fried braided spiced doughnuts). Soetkoekies (spice cookies flavored with sweet wine).

Beverages   Tea, wine.

BRAZIL
Federative Republic of Brazil

Geography   Brazil occupies the east half of South America and is the continent's largest country. The heavily wooded Amazon basin in the north comprises half of Brazil. The northeast is semiarid scrubland. The south central region is farmland with almost half of the population. The Brazilian Highlands are in the south. A narrow coastal belt includes most of the major cities. The entire country has a tropical or semitropical climate.

Major Languages	Ethnic Groups		Major Religions	
Portuguese (official)	White	54%	Roman Catholic	74%
Spanish	Mixed white and black	39%	Protestant	15%
English	Black	6%	Other	4%
Minor Amerindian languages	Other	1%	None	7%

Population density per sq. mi. 60.1
Literacy rate 90.5%
Life expectancy 68.2 male; 75.5 female
Per capita GDP $8,100
Labor force in agriculture 20%

Urban 84.2%
Infant mortality rate per 1,000 live births 23.3
HIV rate 0.6%
Unemployment rate 8.6%
Arable land 7%

Agriculture   coffee (leading grower), sugarcane, soybeans, corn, cassava, oranges, rice, bananas, cotton, tomatoes, wheat, dry beans, coconuts, potatoes, papayas, cocoa, chickens, cattle, pigs, sheep, horses, goats

Natural resources   bauxite, gold, iron ore, manganese, nickel, phosphates, platinum, tin, uranium, oil, hydropower, timber, fish

Industries   textiles, shoes, chemicals, cement, lumber, iron ore, tin, steel, aircraft, motor vehicles and parts

History   The land was thinly settled by various Indian tribes when the first European arrived, Portuguese navigator Pedro Alvares Cabral, in 1500. During the next centuries Portuguese colonists came, bringing large numbers of African slaves. To flee Napoleon's army, the king of Portugal moved the seat of government to Brazil in 1808. After his return to Portugal, his son Pedro proclaimed Brazil's independence in 1822. Slavery was abolished in 1888. With vast natural resources and a huge labor force, Brazil became the leading industrial power of Latin America by the 1970s, and agricultural output soared. By the 1990s it had one of the world's largest economies, although income was poorly distributed. Economic crisis began in 1999, and after tough economic reform the economy improved in 2004. A new civil code guaranteeing equality for women was enacted in 2001. Brazil is among the world's energy giants. In 2007 biofuel from sugarcane passed hydroelectricity as Brazil's second largest energy source (after petroleum). Brazil reported huge new offshore oil and natural gas finds in 2007–2008.

Influences on food   Brazil is the largest and most populous Portuguese-speaking country in the world and the largest country in Latin America. Climate, geography, native foods and customs, Europeans, and slaves from Africa have influenced the diet. Brazil's cuisine is very different from that of other South American countries due to Portuguese and African influences. The Portuguese arrived in the 16th century and first settled in the northeast, Bahia province. There they established sugarcane plantations and brought slaves from West Africa, mainly Guinea, more than 3.5 million before slave trade ceased in 1853. The Portuguese contributed dried salt cod, dried shrimp, rice, olives, wine, almonds, garlic, onions, linguiça (garlic pork sausage), sweet desserts based on sugar and eggs, and basic cooking methods including refogado (soffritto), a preliminary preparation of lightly cooking chopped onion and garlic in olive oil. Africans brought the use of palm oil (dendê oil in Brazil) with its characteristic orange color, coconut, vegetables such as okra and plantains, cowpeas (black-eyed peas), peanuts, and some dishes: vatapá (a seafood stew with peanuts, palm oil, coconut milk, and spicy hot pepper); caruru (okra, onion, dried shrimp, melegueta pepper, palm oil, green vegetables, and cashew nuts); and malho de nagô (dried shrimp, lemon juice, okra, and melegueta peppers). Bahian cooking features fish and shrimp, which are plentiful, and reflects African influence. The south of Brazil was developed later than the northeast and north coast. Coffee was the cash crop, starting around São Paulo in the 1830s. European immigrants, rather than black slaves, influenced the cuisine. The cuisine became more cosmopolitan and more Portuguese, for example the dish cuzcuz paulista (molded, steamed cornmeal, chicken, and vegetables). Germans, Italians, and others came to the industrialized area around São Paulo and to the mines; they contributed cheese-making and preserved meats. Brazil's vast land and grassland support growing coffee, grains, sugarcane, cocoa, cassava, and raising livestock. Its rivers (15,814 miles of navigable rivers, including the Amazon) and Atlantic coastline (4,603 miles) provide fish and seafood. Beef cattle are raised in the south, near Uruguay. As in Argentina, the grill is called churrasco, restaurants are churrascarias, and cowboys are gauchos. Minas Gerais, the region between Rio de Janeiro, São Paulo, and Bahia, is famous for best cooks and best food. Most Brazilians are Roman Catholic and celebrate Easter and Carnival with traditional holiday fare.

Main foods   Cassava (manioc), rice, beans and other legumes, tropical fruits.

Bread and cereals   Corn, rice, wheat, cassava; porridge, rice dishes, cassava meal.

Meat, poultry, fish   Chickens, eggs, beef, pork, lamb and mutton, goat, fish, shrimp; smoked meat, dried meat, sausage. Fresh meat is important, but preserved meat is more important in the dry northeast region. Sun-dried beef is carne sêca or charque (jerky).

Dairy products   Milk, cheese.

Fats and oils   Dendê oil, lard, butter, olive oil.

Legumes   Soybeans, beans (black beans are preferred), black-eyed peas (cowpeas), peanuts.

Vegetables   Cassava, tomatoes, potatoes, onions, avocados, plantains, greens (kale, mustard, collards), pumpkin, olives.

Fruit   Oranges, bananas, coconut, papaya, cashew apples, pineapple, grapes, lemons, limes, mangoes, apples, guavas.

Nuts and seeds   Cashews, Brazil nuts. Brazil nuts grow in very tall trees in the jungle of the Amazon basin.

Seasonings   Melegueta pepper (malagueta in Brazil), garlic, coconut, ginger, cocoa. Melegueta pepper is a small, hot, red chili; its seeds, aromatic and pungent, are often used. Typically the pepper is minced and added to dendê oil, often with dried shrimp, to make a hot sauce. Coconut or coconut milk is used in many dishes.

Dishes   Rice or cornmeal porridge (pirão). Lightly toasted cassava meal (farinha), always available on the table, in a gourd or wooden bowl, to sprinkle over most dishes. Farofa (cassava meal toasted in butter), often eaten as an accompaniment or mixed with boiling water. Feijão (beans in Portuguese), boiled beans, eaten all over Brazil. Acarajé (fritters of dried ground beans or cowpeas mixed with dried shrimp and fried in dendê oil), served with a sauce of shrimp, melegueta pepper, and ginger. Fish stew with coconut milk. Whole fish or abara (cowpeas and shrimp spiced with pepper and dendê oil) wrapped in banana leaves and cooked on a brazier. Grilled fresh meat.

Dishes of the northern region   Xinxim de galinha (chicken cooked with dried shrimp, peanuts, and dendê oil). Efó (fresh and dried shrimp cooked with greens such as mustard). Fritters of dried shrimp and cod, beans or cowpeas, peanuts, and plantains.

Diet in southern Brazil   Grilled meats, rump roast (picanba), cassava, and maté.

National dish   Feijoada completa (black beans cooked with smoked meats and sausages and served with rice, sliced orange, fresh or boiled greens, and a hot sauce mixed with lemon or lime juice), originated in Rio.

Sweets   Sugarcane, sugar. Confections of fruits and Brazil nuts. Fios de ovos (egg threads). Egg custards such as Quindim, which has coconut and is the most popular. Puddings: tapioca (processed cassava), pumpkin, coconut, and sweet cuzcuz (tapioca, grated coconut, coconut milk, sugar, salt, and water mixed with boiling water, put in mold, and chilled overnight). Cookies. Cupcakes. Romeu e Julieta (guava paste with fresh cheese), popular in restaurants and reminiscent of quince paste and cheese in Portugal. Avocado cream (blended ripe avocado mixed with lime juice and confectioners sugar, and chilled).

Beverages   Coffee (often served already sweetened), yerba maté (a tea made from dried leaves of an evergreen shrub indigenous to Latin America), fruit juice, beer, rum, guaraná (soft drink made with seeds of native guaraná, which contains caffeine), cachaça (sugarcane brandy), batidas (punch of cachaça and citrus fruit).

Meals   Light breakfast, main meal at midday, light supper, and afternoon coffee or maté are typical. For the poorer people the standard meal is black beans, rice, and cassava meal sprinkled over both.

Snacks   Acarajé (bean or cowpea fritters), coffee, fruit juice.

BRUNEI
State of Brunei Darussalam

Geography   Brunei is In Southeast Asia, on the north coast of the island of Borneo, bordering the South China Sea and Malaysia. Brunei has a narrow coastal plain, swamps, eastern mountains, and western hilly lowlands. Much of the land is covered with tropical rainforest.

Major Languages	Ethnic Groups		Major Religions	
Malay (official)	Malay	66%	Islam (official)	
English	Chinese	11%	Muslim	67%
Chinese	Other indigenous	4%	Buddhist	13%
	Other	19%	Christian	10%
			Indigenous beliefs and other	10%

Population density per sq. mi. 187.4
Literacy rate 94.9%
Life expectancy 73.3 male; 77.8 female
Per capita GDP $51,000
Labor force in agriculture 2.9%

Urban 73.5%
Infant mortality rate per 1,000 live births 12.7
HIV rate NA
Unemployment rate 4.3%
Arable land 2%

Agriculture   vegetables, pineapples, bananas, cassava, rice, chickens, buffalo, sheep, goats, pigs, cattle

Natural resources   oil, natural gas, timber, fish

Industries   oil, oil refining, liquefied natural gas, construction

History   Brunei traded with China during the 6th century. During the 13th to 15th century it came under Hindu influence. In the early 15th century widespread conversion to Islam occurred and Brunei became an independent sultanate. Powerful from the 16th to the 19th century, it ruled the northern part of Borneo and adjacent islands, including the Sulu Islands and the Philippines. It fell into decay and became a British protectorate in 1888, then a British dependency in 1905. Brunei became independent in 1984. Exploitation of the rich Seria oil field made the sultanate and sultan rich. Much of the country's oil wealth has been squandered by members of the royal family. In 2007, in an attempt to diversity the economy, Brunei with two Japanese companies built a methanol plant.

Influences on food   Brunei is on the north coast of the island Borneo, a melting pot of tribes, traders, and adventurers. Brunei shares geography and foodways with Malaysia. Brunei has two main cuisines, Malay and Chinese. Two thirds of Brunei's population are Malays and are Muslim, and 11% are Chinese (Straits Chinese, with roots in South China). Chinese influence is strong due to mass movement of labor during the colonial period, as well as immigrant elites from East and South Asia. An example is nonya (Chinese Straits) cooking, associated with Chinese immigrants who settled in the area from the 15th century to World War II. It uses chilies, shrimp paste, coconut milk, and aromatic roots and leaves as in Malaysian cooking, but it has retained the use of pork, lard, and noodles from Chinese tradition. It values hotness and sourness. Islam has been dominant since the 15th century. Muslims do not eat pork or pork products such as lard, whereas Chinese (and Christians) do. European traders and British control from 1888 to 1984 left some influence.

Bread and cereals   Rice, wheat; rice dishes, glutinous rice in sweets, noodles. Rice is the staple food.

Meat, poultry, fish   Chicken, lamb, goat, pork, beef, fish and seafood, water buffalo, eggs; prawn/shrimp pastes (blacang), dried anchovy, fish sauce, gelatin (used in sweets). Seafood is the secondary staple.

Dairy products   Milk and other dairy products are uncommon.

Fats and oils   Coconut oil, palm oil, lard, vegetable oil.

Legumes   Soybeans and soybean products such as soy sauce, mung beans, winged beans, peanuts.

Vegetables   Cassava (taro), yams, breadfruit, seaweed, greens, arrowroot (bland, mealy tuber; used to thicken dishes), green beans, eggplant, sweet potatoes, ti plant, daikon (white radish), squash, water chestnuts.

Fruit   Pineapple, bananas, coconut, tamarind, oranges, limes, lemons, mangoes, papaya, melons, durian.

Nuts   Litchis, macadamia nuts.

Seasonings   Chilies, tamarind, coconut milk and cream, lime and lemon juice, shrimp paste, aromatic roots and leaves, soy sauce, fish sauce, onions, garlic, pepper, laos (of ginger root family), ginger root, lemon grass, coriander, turmeric, cumin, cinnamon, allspice.

Dishes   Coconut milk is often used as a cooking medium. Boiled rice. Fried rice. Fried noodles (kway teow). Satay (small strips of meat, chicken, or fish/seafood on thin bamboo skewers, often marinated with soy sauce and flavorings, and grilled). Rendang ("dry beef curry," formerly venison, now water buffalo meat or beef, cubed and simmered with spices and other seasonings in coconut milk). Rempah (spice mixture, often fried before use). Gulai (curry or anything cooked in coconut milk and retaining its sauce). Chinese roast pork. Lamb shoulder braised in coconut milk with onion, garlic, and spices, served with sauce of braising liquid and coconut cream and with pineapple slices simmered in the sauce. Starchy vegetables (e.g., cassava) boiled and pounded into a paste. Cooked greens. Sambal (hot, spicy side dishes or chilies and other spices fried together and used in a dish such as prawn sambal). Achar (pickle).

Sweets   Palm sugar, sugar. Immature coconut. Baked rice rolls in banana leaves. Desserts mostly based on thick brown palm sugar syrup, with coconut milk, grated coconut, gelatin, and glutinous rice, for example, kuey lapis (has many different colored layers of gelatin). Naga sari (pudding of mung beans, sugar, and coconut).

Beverages   Tea, fruit juice, coconut juice, fermented coconut sap, kava (alcoholic drink made from pepper plant).

Meals   In many homes rice is cooked for all three meals.

Street food   Fried noodles, satay (the favorite snack: goat meat for Muslims, pork for Chinese, chicken for both, and all with hot sauce of chilies, onion, garlic, laos, and peanuts). Street food is sold by street vendors and in market stalls and night stores.

BULGARIA
Republic of Bulgaria

Geography   Bulgaria is in southeastern Europe in the eastern part of the Balkan Peninsula, bordering the Black Sea. Plains in the north and south cover two thirds of the land; mountains east to west across the center cover one third. The Danube River flows along the northern border.

Major Language	Ethnic Groups		Major Religions	
Bulgarian (official)	Bulgarian	84%	Bulgarian Orthodox	83%
Turkish	Turk	9%	Sunni Muslim	12%
Roma	Roma (Gypsy)	5%	Other	5%
	Other	2%		

Population density per sq. mi. 170.2
Literacy rate 98.3%
Life expectancy 69.2 male; 76.7 female
Per capita GDP $11,300
Labor force in agriculture 8.5%

Urban 70.2%
Infant mortality rate per 1,000 live births 18.5
HIV rate NA
Unemployment rate 10.7%
Arable land 30%

Agriculture   wheat, corn, sunflower seeds, vegetables, fruit, tobacco, wine, wheat, barley, sugar beets, chickens, sheep, pigs, cattle, goats

Natural resources   bauxite, lead, copper, zinc, coal, timber, fish

Industries   utilities, food, beverages, tobacco

History   Thracians lived here in about 3500 BCE. They were incorporated into the Roman Empire. At the decline of the Empire, Goths, Huns, Bulgars, and Avars invaded. Slavs settled here in the 6th century. Turkic Bulgars arrived in the 7th century, merged with the Slavs, became Christians by the 9th century, and established empires in the 10th and 12th centuries. The Ottomans ruled from 1396 for 500 years. Bulgaria sided with the Central Powers in World War I and with Germany in World War II. Communists took power with Soviet aid in 1946. A new constitution proclaiming a republic took effect in 1991. The economy deteriorated during the 1990s. Bulgaria joined NATO in 2004 and the EU in 2007. Foreign investment in Bulgaria increased in 2007 but wages stayed low, and prices, especially for energy and food, increased.

Influences on food   Much of Bulgaria's land is arable and the remainder is high mountains. Most of the highlands are forested, with summer pastures for sheep above the forests. Mountain forests provide game. On the Danube plain, cereals and temperate fruits are grown and livestock are raised. Along the Black Sea and lowlands, nuts, figs, and peanuts are grown. In the south, rice and lentils are grown. The Black Sea, rivers, and streams provide fish, although little fish is consumed. A national feature is red-colored food and drinks. From the 4th century onward Proto-Bulgars used crushed red rock or red clay mixed with red wine as a curative. Red is considered healthy and invigorating: red apples are preferred to other colors. Since red chilies were brought in during the 16th century, Bulgarian stew is always red with chilies. Cooking is in harmony with the season, which determines ingredients: meat of older animals is cooked with pulses, winter vegetables, or winter fruit; young animal flesh is combined with spring vegetables. Summer is the time for salads, vegetables, uncooked soups, cold yogurt drinks, unsweetened compotes, and fresh fruits. Bulgaria is famous for its attar of roses (rose oil) perfume, or essence, used in jellies, rosewater, and syrup. The 500-year Turkish rule was a strong influence on Bulgarian cuisine. Muslims do not eat pork, whereas many Christians do.

Bread and cereals   Wheat, corn, barley, rice; wheat flour yeast bread (often a large round loaf; sometimes served heated and with a spice dip), rolls, rice dishes.

Meat, poultry, fish   Chicken, eggs, lamb, pork, beef, goat, fish, water buffalo, quail, partridge, pheasant, rabbit, deer, wild boar; sausages. Many people eat fish (riba) only in month names containing the letter "r" and with no milk or yogurt in the meal.

Dairy products   Milk, yogurt, cheese (sirene, creamy white goat cheese similar to feta, and kashkaval, made from ewe's milk and similar to cheddar). Two thirds of the milk output, mostly cow's, is sold as yogurt. Thick sheep's yogurt (katuk) is most preferred; made as early as the 7th century it is still made in the highlands and rural areas and stored for winter sealed with a layer of butter. A large quantity of dairy foods is produced and consumed.

Fats and oils   Sunflower oil, lard, butter, olive oil. A main characteristic of present-day cooking is widespread use of sunflower oil rather than animal fat. Lard or butter is sometimes used in stews and pastries.

Legumes   Lentils, peanuts.

Vegetables   Cabbage, green onions, green garlic, spinach, broad beans, peas, tomatoes, potatoes, eggplant, onions, cucumbers, green beans, chilies, mild red and green peppers, olives; sauerkraut (two barrels are made each summer: one of whole cabbages for leaves for stuffing or salad, the other of shredded cabbage for cooking).

Fruit   Apples, apricots, citrus, cherries, strawberries, figs, grapes, plums, pears, peaches, quinces, melons, watermelons, prunes, raisins, currants.

Nuts and seeds   Walnuts, almonds, chestnuts, sunflower seeds. Walnuts are grown and used in many dishes.

Seasonings   Salt, black pepper, red chilies, onions, garlic, dill, parsley, ciubritsa (similar to tarragon), cumin, fenugreek, chili powder, anise, vinegar, rose oil, rosewater. Ciubritsa, one of Bulgaria's most popular seasonings, is used in stews and, mixed with salt and ground red pepper, in a dip (also called ciubritsa) for bread.

Cooking method   Frying was rarely used in old Bulgaria, probably because few utensils that could withstand high heat were available. Zapruzhka, a small stew-enrichment sauce of fried onions and flour, is a recent method used only for about the last century. Most modern fried dishes are adopted from Greece, Turkey, and Central Europe.

Dishes   Bulgarian stew (yahniya), vegetables, perhaps meat, red chilies, and onions cooked slowly for a long time so that it thickens and has a distinct flavor. Meat stews often contain fruits such as quince. Ghivetch (meat and vegetable stew with ciubritsa, small green hot peppers, and a crusty topping made by adding beaten eggs and yogurt just before the dish comes out of the oven). Grilled meat (pastermá), sausage (kebabcha), or lamb kebabs (not marinated). Roasted chicken or pork.

Spit roasted whole lamb. Baked carp stuffed with walnuts. Quail browned in butter with garlic and onions, and then steamed with a mixture of rice, currants, and raisins, in the Turkish tradition. Bird of paradise bread (round yeast loaf with cheese, olives, ham, and sweet red pepper decorating the top). Banitsa (flaky cheese roll of paper-thin pastry with cheese filling). Shopska salata (tomatoes, cucumbers, and cheese), served with no dressing but with heated round bread and a dish of mixed spices (ciubritsa). Salad dressing (chopped walnuts, garlic, vinegar, and oil). Uncooked tomato or yogurt soups (e.g., tarator, cold cucumber and yogurt soup with walnuts). Ciorba (soup served Turkish style with lemon juice). Kurban (meat stock soup with peppers and tomatoes). Roasted ears of corn. Spread of eggplant, green peppers, tomatoes, olive oil, vinegar, parsley, garlic, salt, and pepper. Peppers stuffed with sirene cheese, coated with bread crumbs, and deep fried.

Sweets   Sugar, fresh fruit, unsweetened compotes, rose jelly.

Beverages   Yogurt drinks, coffee, tea, red wine, plum brandy (slivova).

BURKINA FASO

Geography   Burkina Faso (formerly Upper Volta) is In West Africa, south of the Sahara. This land-locked country consists of extensive savannas, with desert in the north. It is arid and hot.

Major Languages	Ethnic Groups		Major Religions	
French (official)	Mossi	40%	Muslim	50%
Sudanic languages	Fulani, Bobo,		Indigenous beliefs	40%
	Lobi, Mande, other	60%	Christian (mainly Roman Catholic)	10%

Population density per sq. mi. 144.4
Literacy rate 28.7%
Life expectancy 50.7 male; 54.5 female
Per capita GDP $1,300
Labor force in agriculture 90%

Urban 18.3%
Infant mortality rate per 1,000 live births 86
HIV rate 1.6%
Unemployment rate NA
Arable land 18%

Agriculture   sorghum, millet, corn, cotton, peanuts, shea nuts, sesame, chickens, goats, cattle, sheep, pigs

Natural resources   manganese, limestone, marble, gold, phosphates, pumice, salt, fish

Industries   cotton, lint, beverages, agricultural processing, soap, cigarettes, textiles, gold

History   The Bobo, Lobi, and Gurunsi peoples originally inhabited the area. In the 11th to 13th centuries, the Mossi people entered the region and ruled until defeated by the Mali and Songhai empires. French control came by 1896. Upper Volta was established as a separate territory in 1947. It gained independence in 1960 and was renamed Burkina Faso in 1984. After independence the country was ruled by the military until 1991, when a new constitution instituted a multiparty system. The country has suffered a meningitis epidemic, low cotton prices, and flooding in recent years. A large part of the male labor force migrates annually to neighboring countries for seasonal employment. Despite years of foreign aid, Burkina Faso remains one of the world's poorest countries.

Influences on food   Burkina Faso, like most countries of Sub-Saharan Africa immediately south of the Sahara, was a former French colony. Burkina Faso is arid and hot. The Niger River provides fish. Food customs are influenced by North Africa, West Africa, France, foods brought from the New World (including corn, tomatoes, chilies, and sweet potatoes), and religion. For examples: chicken and guinea fowl are popular; as in West Africa; baguette bread is common in towns, a French influence; and tomatoes and chilies appear in many dishes. Many people are Muslim and do not eat pork. In rural areas, the traditional wood-burning hearth of three stones on which a pot sits is still used; meat may be grilled on open fires, and ovens are uncommon.

Bread and cereals   Sorghum, millet, corn, rice, wild grains, wheat; porridge, baguette bread, couscous (tiny balls of millet dough steamed and served like rice), noodles, rice dishes.

Meat, poultry, fish   Chicken, eggs, guinea fowl, pigeons, goat, beef, lamb and mutton, pork, camel, fish, game (antelope, rock rabbit, cane rat). Red meat is a luxury. Meat and fish are often dried.

Dairy products   Milk, sour milk, buttermilk, curds, whey, cheese.

Fats and oils   Shea oil and butter (from the seeds of the African shea tree), palm oil, peanut oil.

Legumes   Peanuts, beans, cowpeas, lentils.

Vegetables   Okra, greens, tomatoes, yams, plantains, cassava, sweet potatoes, onions, chilies.

Fruit   Dates, raisins, coconut, mangoes, watermelon.

Nuts and seeds   Shea nuts, kola nuts, sesame seeds, mango seeds, watermelon seeds. Nuts, seeds, and peanuts are often used to thicken sauces.

Seasonings   Chilies, onions, tomatoes.

Dishes   Mush of millet grains boiled with cassava. Corn porridge. Meatball and peanut sauce served with boiled millet or rice. Sauces of combinations of meat and fish. Meat cooked with okra. Stuffed camel stomach (resembles haggis). Boiled rice served with a thin stew of beef and tomatoes. Stews of cassava leaves with dried fish and palm oil or with okra, served with couscous or rice. Chicken dishes. Atik (dried cassava porridge with smoked fish, tomatoes, and other vegetables). Maan nezim nzedo (stew of fish, okra, greens, and tomatoes).

Festive occasion dishes   Millet and cassava mush served with two sauces (minced meat, dried fish, and dried okra powder; and diced meat and tomatoes) usually combined before serving. Jollof rice (rice with tomato paste or palm oil so is always red).

Sweets   Sugar, honey, sweet pastries, peanut candy, fried sweetened dough balls.

Beverages   Ginger beer, coffee.

Street food   Kabobs, shawerma, bean fritters, sweet pastries, grilled sweet corn. Street food is important.

BURMA (SEE MYANMAR)

BURUNDI
Republic of Burundi

Geography   Burundi is in central Africa. It is a high plateau divided by deep valleys, with grassy highlands and mountains. The southernmost source of the White Nile and Lake Tanganyika are in Burundi.

Major Languages		Ethnic Groups		Major Religions	
Kirundi	(both	Hutu (Bantu)	85%	Roman Catholic	62%
French	official)	Tutsi (Hamitic)	14%	Indigenous beliefs	23%
Swahili		Other	1%	Muslim	10%
				Protestant	5%

Population density per sq. mi. 877.6
Literacy rate 59.3%
Life expectancy 50.9 male; 52.6 female
Per capita GDP $400
Labor force in agriculture 93.6%

Urban 9.5%
Infant mortality rate per 1,000 live births 60.8
HIV rate 2.0%
Unemployment rate NA
Arable land 36%

Agriculture   bananas, sweet potatoes, cassava, coffee, cotton, tea, corn, chickens, goats, cattle, sheep, pigs

Natural resources   nickel, uranium, rare earth oxides, peat, cobalt, copper, platinum, vanadium, hydropower, fish

Industries   light consumer goods, assembly of imported components, public works, construction, food processing

History   The region was first inhabited by the pygmy Twa, then by Bantu Hutus, who were conquered in the 16th century by the Tutsi (Watusi), probably from Ethiopia. German control began in 1899, followed by Belgium rule in 1916. Burundi became independent in 1962. Ethnic conflict occurred during the following decades. Most warring groups signed a draft peace treaty in 2000. In 2005 the peaceful transfer of power to a democratically elected leader took place. In 2007 a UN Integrated Office in Burundi replaced the UN Security Council peacekeeping force authorized in 2004 for Burundi. Violence occurred in 2007 and UN calls for negotiation were turned down.

Influences on food   Burundi food customs resemble those of East African countries Kenya and Tanzania. The diet contains little meat, in spite of abundant game and the tradition of breeding cattle. Cattle were regarded as wealth, not food, and the Masai and related people lived on milk products and blood of cattle. Others lived on mostly grains, bananas, and gathered greens. The lakes supply fish, and tilapia and catfish are farmed. In the mountains, although animals are protected, game is plentiful and antelope are farmed. The earliest foreign traders, Arabs, established colonies along the coast of East Africa from about 700 CE, traded slaves and ivory, and introduced spices, onions, and eggplant. Germans and Belgium controlled this land but left little influence on food customs. British encouragement of Asians to settle in East Africa affected food customs (e.g., use of curry).

Bread and cereals   Corn, sorghum, millet, rice; porridge, flatbread, pancakes.

Meat, poultry, fish   Chicken, eggs, goat, beef, lamb, pork, fish, salted and dried seafood from the coast, game.

Insects   Locusts, crickets, grasshoppers, ants, worms (madora), caterpillars (harati). Fried insects are snacks.

Dairy products   Milk, curds, cheeses (adaptations of European ones). Milk products are important in the diet.

Fats and oils   Butter, clarified butter, palm oil, peanut oil.

Legumes   Peanuts (groundnuts), cowpeas, red kidney beans, lentils. Legumes are eaten daily.

Vegetables   Sweet potatoes, cassava, plantains (green bananas), green leaves, okra, pumpkin, tomatoes, peppers, onions, potatoes, yams, eggplant. A large amount of starchy vegetables and green leaves is eaten.

Fruit   Bananas, coconut, papaya.

Nuts and seeds   Cashews, sesame seeds, pumpkin seeds.

Seasonings   Peppers, tomatoes, dried baobab leaves, onions, coconut milk, black pepper, curry powder, cloves.

Dishes   The common staple food, ugali (thick porridge of cornmeal or millet), often served with stew of leftover cooked meat, tomatoes, peppers, and green leaves or other vegetables. Green leaves cooked with peanut paste. Curried chicken served with irio (boiled beans, corn, and potatoes or cassava, mashed to a thick pulp). Green bananas boiled in banana leaves and mashed. Fish cooked with coconut milk. Boiled and mashed beans, lentils, corn, and plantains. Plantain soup, stew, and fritters.

Sweets   Honey, plantain custard.

Beverages   Coffee, tea, beer (often home brewed from corn or millet).

Street food and snacks   Mandazi (doughnut or fritter), grilled corn cobs, rice and coconut pancakes, goat kabob.

C

CAMBODIA
Kingdom of Cambodia

Geography   Cambodia is in Southeast Asia, on the Indochina Peninsula, bordering the Gulf of Thailand. It is mostly (76%) forested, with a level central plain along the Mekong River and hills and mountains in the southeast.

Major Languages	Ethnic Groups		Major Religions	
Khmer (official)	Khmer	90%	Buddhism (official)	
French	Vietnamese	5%	Buddhist	95%
English	Other	5%	Other	5%

Population density per sq. mi. 209
Literacy rate 76.3%
Life expectancy 59.6 male; 63.8 female
Per capita GDP $1,800
Labor force in agriculture 75%

Urban 19.7%
Infant mortality rate per 1,000 live births 56.6
HIV rate 0.8%
Unemployment rate 1.8%
Arable land 20%

Agriculture   rice, cassava, corn, rubber, vegetables, cashews, chickens, cattle, pigs, buffalo, crocodiles

Natural resources   oil and gas, timber, gems, iron ore, manganese, phosphates, fish

Industries   tourism, garments, rice milling, fishing, wood and wood products, rubber, cement, gem mining, textiles

History   Early kingdoms dating from the 1st century CE led to the great Khmer empire of the 9th to 13th century, encompassing present-day Thailand, Cambodia, Laos, and southern Vietnam. The area became a French protectorate in 1863. Independence came in 1953. Conflicts with Vietnam and with the communist Khmer Rouge occurred from the 1960s to the mid-1990s. The United States provided military and economic aid. A new constitution reestablishing a monarchy took effect in 1993. The party in opposition to Khmer Rouge, in power from 1993, retained power in the 2008 elections. In 2001 the first bridge over the Mekong River opened; this river flows through Cambodia for about 300 miles and is its most important river. Cambodia's offshore oil is predicted to be large and to contribute significant revenue by 2011.

Influences on food   During the first half of the 20th century the cuisine of the royal palace and of the aristocracy had great visual appeal. During the last half of the 20th century bloodshed and turmoil were prominent. Cambodian cuisine reflects northern Indian, Malaysian, and Chinese influences, as well as French influence in foods such as haricots (green beans), potatoes, French bread, pastry, and coffee. The predominant religion, Theravada Buddhism, influences food customs. It emphasizes a person's efforts to reach spiritual perfection. The support of monks and temples is critical to one's progress through reincarnation, and the faithful contribute food to support monks. Cambodia's geography and climate allow the production of rice, corn, cassava, vegetables, fruit, cashew nuts, and livestock. The Gulf of Thailand and many lakes and rivers supply fish.

Bread and cereals   Rice (both long grain and glutinous), corn, wheat; rice dishes, rice vermicelli, noodles, French bread, pastry. Rice is the main food; rice vermicelli is the base of many dishes. White corn is grown and eaten.

Meat, poultry, fish   Chicken, beef, pork, buffalo, crocodile, fish (mostly freshwater); fish sauce, fermented fish products. As throughout Southeast Asia, fish sauce (tuk trey) is eaten, adding protein to the diet. Two special fermented fish products in Cambodia start with cleaned, not whole, fish and require weeks for preparation: prahoc (a dry paste with fish chunks) and pha-âk (fish preserved in brine with rice incorporated).

Dairy products   Condensed milk (used in coffee), whipping cream (used in pastries).

Fats and oils   Coconut cream, lard, bacon, butter, margarine, peanut oil, vegetable oil.

Legumes   Soybeans and products (soy milk, soybean curd, or tempeh), peanuts, chickpeas, lentils, mung beans.

Vegetables   Cassava, tapioca (processed from cassava or taro), cabbage, collards, carrots, green beans, cucumbers, radishes, jicama, plantains, bitter melon, potatoes, tomatoes, pumpkin, eggplant, water chestnuts.

Fruit   Coconut, bananas, limes, tamarind, durian, mangoes, papaya, oranges, lemons, melon.

Nuts and seeds   Cashew nuts, almonds, lotus seeds, pumpkin seeds, sesame seeds.

Seasonings   Fish sauce, fermented fish paste and sauce, lime juice, tamarind, lemon grass, coconut milk, chilies, garlic, shallots, ginger, turmeric, fresh coriander, mint. Seasoning is delicate and aromatic, as in the paste kroeung, made fresh by grinding herbs and spices such as galangal, garlic, kaffir lime leaves, lemon grass, shallots, and turmeric. Lemon grass is a favorite herb. Sour taste is liked.

Dishes   Steamed, boiled, or fried rice. Kutiev (rice vermicelli soup), also called soupe Chinoise. Grilled and fried dishes with freshwater fish the main ingredient. Fried noodles topped with meats and vegetables. Stir-fried vegetables. Fresh salads. Shredded raw vegetables and unripe fruits topped with meat, poultry, or fish and spicy hot dressing. Rice, vegetables, and/or meats wrapped in banana or edible leaves and steamed. Kralan (glutinous rice with coconut cream, shredded coconut, and flavorings, cooked in hollow sections of bamboo in a fire for an hour, and then the bamboo peeled away). Ansam chrouk (rice cake stuffed with green beans and pork meat or fat, wrapped in a banana leaf, and steamed), a festive dish with many variations.

National favorites   Amok (steamed leaf-wrapped fish in coconut milk). Banh choc (rice noodle and fish soup).

Sweets   Sugarcane, sugar, fruit, fried coconut, fried bananas rolled in coconut, sweet glutinous black rice.

Beverages   Tea (often blended with flowers such as rose, jasmine), soy milk, hot soup (broth), fruit and bean drinks, coffee, beer, rice wine or whiskey for special occasions.

Meals and service   Two meals a day, at about 11 a.m. and dusk, are usual. A typical meal is rice accompanied by soup (samla) and when possible a dish of each: chhâ (sauté of meat, poultry, vegetables, or vermicelli), aing (grilled meat, poultry, or fish), and chion (fried meat, poultry, or fish). All foods are served at the same time, and each person takes a portion of rice and places any additional foods on it. Spoons, chopsticks, or fingers are used.

Snacks   Fruit, beverages, tapé (a fermented glutinous rice preparation, sweet and faintly alcoholic).

CAMEROON
Republic of Cameroon

Geography   Cameroon is in central Africa on the west coast. It comprises a low coastal plain with rainforests in the south and along the coast, an interior plateau, forested mountains in the west, and grasslands in the north with marshes around Lake Chad.

Major Languages	Ethnic Groups				Major Religions	
English (both	Highlanders	31%	Northwest Bantu	8%	Indigenous beliefs	40%
French official)	Equatorial Bantu	19%	Eastern Nigritic	7%	Christian	40%
24 major African	Kirdi	11%	Other African	13%	Sunni Muslim	20%
languages	Fulani	10%	Other	1%		

Population density per sq. mi. 101.9
Literacy rate 67.9%
Life expectancy 52.5 male; 54.1 female
Per capita GDP $2,100
Labor force in agriculture 70%

Urban 54.3%
Infant mortality rate per 1,000 live births 64.6
HIV rate 5.1%
Unemployment rate NA
Arable land 13%

Agriculture   cassava, sugarcane, plantains, coffee, cocoa, cotton, rubber, bananas, oilseed, grains, chickens, cattle, goats, sheep, pigs

Natural resources   oil, bauxite, iron ore, timber, hydropower, fish

Industries   oil production and refining, aluminum production, food processing, light consumer goods, textiles, lumber

History   Bantu speakers were among the first settlers, followed by Muslim Fulani in the 18th and 19th centuries. Portuguese sailors reached Cameroon in the 15th century. Slave trade by Europeans to America followed. Germany controlled the area from 1884 to 1916. France and Britain then divided the region. French Cameroon became independent in 1960. Part of British Cameroon joined Nigeria in 1961; the other part joined Cameroon. Roads, railways, agriculture, and petroleum production have been developed. In recent decades economic problems have produced unrest. In 2007 the president of China visited and signed agreements including an interest-free loan for development projects in Cameroon. Rising food and fuel costs and discontent with the government of the president, in power since 1962, led to riots in 2008.

Influences on food   This tropical country has coastline that provides fish and prawns, rainy lowland and interior plateau that grow cocoa, coffee, and bananas, and northern grassland that supports livestock. Starchy roots in the south and grains in the more arid north are staple foods. The Portuguese, Germans, French, and British have influenced food customs. The country's name comes from the Portuguese word for prawns, camarões. Some consider Cameroon's cooks the best in central Africa. The introduction of New World foods such as cassava, corn, peanuts, tomato, chili pepper, and potato during the 15th and 16th centuries had major influence. Native African foods include black-eyed peas, watermelon, and okra. Starchy food is regarded as real food and sauces and stews as accompaniments. The diet is mostly starchy vegetables, legumes, and greens. Mucilaginous texture is liked, as in okra.

Bread and cereals   Corn, rice, millet, sorghum; mashed bananas and flour "bread," grain pastes, rice dishes.

Meat, poultry, fish   Chicken, eggs, beef, goat, lamb, pork, fish (fresh, smoked, salted, or dried), prawns, rabbit, game. Chicken is a popular, prestigious food. Fish is abundant and often used with meat in stews.

Insects   Termites (often called white ants), locusts.

Dairy products   Milk, sour milk, buttermilk, curds, whey, cheese.

Fats and oils   Palm oil, peanut oil, shea oil, coconut oil. Palm oil, used liberally on most food, gives a red hue.

Legumes   Peanuts (groundnuts), black-eyed peas (cowpeas), locust beans (carob), red beans.

Vegetables   Cassava, plantains, yams, green leaves (cassava, bitter leaf), okra, tomatoes, sweet potatoes, potatoes, eggplant, pumpkin, onions, red chili peppers, cucumbers, bell peppers.

Fruit   Bananas, coconut, pineapple, akee apples, baobab, watermelon, guavas, lemons, dates, mangoes, papaya.

Nuts and seeds   Cashews, kola nuts, watermelon seeds (egusi), sesame seeds, mango seeds, baobab seeds.

Seasonings   Salt, palm oil, onions, red chili pepper. These season most foods.

Dishes   Boiled or fried foods, of which chunks are dipped in sauce and eaten by hand. Fufu (a paste of boiled and pounded starchy vegetables or corn), formed into bite-size scoops to eat stew. Stews of root vegetables, okra, or peanuts, with bits of fish, chicken, or beef. Moin moin (steamed paste of black-eyed peas, hot peppers, and onions). Rice boiled in coconut milk. Peanut stew (peanuts, chilies, tomatoes, and herbs with beef, chicken, fish, or mixtures and potatoes, beans, or eggplant). Ntomba nam (peanut sauce with peppers, onions, and herbs) with roast chicken. Aloco (plantain cooked in palm oil with onions and chili). Sauce of pounded leaves (e.g., bitter leaf).

A specialty   Cameroon prawns grilled on wooden skewers served with spicy peanut sauce.

Sweets   Sugarcane, honey, sugar, deep-fried dough balls, peanut candy, bananas baked with coconut.

Beverages   Coffee, cocoa, beer.

Street food and snacks   Spiced kabobs, fried fish, plantain chips, balls of steamed rice or black-eyed peas.

CANADA

Geography   The Western Hemisphere's largest country in land size, Canada stretches from the Atlantic Ocean to the Pacific Ocean and from the North Pole to the United States. It includes coastline, plains, mountains, forests, and rivers, in 10 provinces and 3 territories. Climate is mostly temperate, with cold winters and hot summers.

Major Languages		Ethnic Groups		Major Religions	
English	(both	British-Canadian	28%	Roman Catholic	43%
French	official)	French-Canadian	23%	Protestant	23%
		Other European	15%	Other	6%
		Asian	6%	None	16%
		Mixed and other	28%	Unspecified	12%

Population density per sq. mi. 9.5
Literacy rate 99%
Life expectancy 78.7 male; 83.8 female
Per capita GDP $38,400
Labor force in agriculture 2%

Urban 80.1
Infant mortality rate per 1,000 live births 5.1
HIV rate 0.4%
Unemployment rate 6.1%
Arable land 5%

Agriculture   wheat, barley, oilseed, corn, potatoes, oats, soybeans, dry peas, lentils, tobacco, fruits, vegetables, chickens, cattle, pigs, sheep, goats

Natural resources   iron ore, nickel, zinc, copper, gold, lead, molybdenum, potash, diamonds, silver, fish, timber, wildlife, coal, oil, natural gas, hydropower

Industries   transportation equipment, chemicals, minerals, food and fish products, wood and paper products, oil, natural gas

History   Vikings are believed to have reached Canada centuries before Englishman John Cabot saw Newfoundland in 1497. Frenchman Jacques Cartier reached the Gulf of St. Lawrence in 1534. French settlers founded Quebec City in 1608, Montreal in 1642, and the colony New France in 1663. Britain acquired Acadia (now Nova Scotia) in 1717, Quebec in 1759, and the rest of New France in 1763; the French retained their rights to their own language, religion, and civil law. During the American Revolution many loyalists moved to Canada. Fur traders and explorers led Canadians westward to the Pacific. Upper and Lower Canada (later called Ontario and Quebec) and the Maritimes had legislative assemblies in the 18th century. The War of 1812, between Great Britain and the United States, was fought mainly in Upper Canada. Upper and Lower Canada united into one Canada in 1839. The Dominion of Canada was formed in 1867 and was proclaimed a self-governing Dominion within the British Empire in 1931. In 1982 Canada severed its last formal legislative link with Britain by gaining the right to amend its constitution; it kept its Commonwealth membership. The North American Free Trade Agreement between Canada, Mexico, and the United States took effect in 1994. In 1998 the government apologized to native people for 150 years of mistreatment and pledged to set up a "healing fund." In 1999 a homeland for the Inuit, Nunavut ("Our Land"), was established from part of the Northwest Territories. In 2001 Newfoundland was renamed Newfoundland and Labrador. Canada supported U.S. counter-terrorism operations in Afghanistan in 2001 and 2006 but not in Iraq in 2003. A severe acute respiratory (SARS) outbreak in Toronto in 2003 caused considerable loss of lives and revenue. In 2005 Parliament approved same-sex marriages. In 2006, after 12 years of Liberal Party rule, Conservatives took control of the government. In 2007 the economy performed well, with the Canadian dollar reaching above the value of the U.S. dollar. The prime minister announced plans to bolster Canadian sovereignty over the Arctic. In 2008 Canada extended the mandate for its force in Afghanistan through 2011.

Influences on food   Canada, the second largest nation in the world in area, is larger than the United States but has a tenth the population. This diverse land provides a varied diet. Canada is rich in natural resources including fish and seafood, game, and farmland. Large rugged cold areas contrast with the Niagara peninsula and Okanagan Valley (in British Columbia) that are warm enough to grow fruit. Major railroads CPR and CNR and their hotels had some of the finest dining: Canadian bacon, grilled Calgary sirloins, spring lamb chops, lake fish, cheddar cheese, hot blueberry pie, and coffee served in silver tureens. Indigenous foods, Native Americans, and immigrants from Great Britain, France, northern Europe, and Asia have influenced Canadian cuisine.

East Canada, the Atlantic Provinces   In Newfoundland, Nova Scotia, New Brunswick, and Prince Edward Island, seafood dominates the diet with potatoes a mainstay. Newfoundland has traditional dishes such as fish and brewis (hard bread in water to make broth seasoned with salt pork), and home baking continues to thrive. In the Maritimes (Nova Scotia, New Brunswick, and Prince Edward Island) French and British traditions continue in French dishes such as Acadian potato dumplings and Scottish dishes such as oatmeal bread sweetened with molasses. Eastern Canada is also home of Canadian maple syrup.

Quebec   The French-speaking province has French influence as in cretons (a pork pâté), tourtière (a hot spiced pork pie), and Québécois pea soup, made of dried yellow split peas, smoked pork hock or ham bone, and seasonings. Quebec produces much of the world's supply of maple syrup. Montreal is famous for street and snack foods such as poutine (a combination of French fries, cheese, and gravy).

Ontario   Further west is Ontario, a province of lakes and fruits and berries. Cities include Ottawa (the capital), Toronto, and Ingersoll, birthplace of the Canadian cheddar cheese industry. The cuisine shows Indian influence, as in corn and bean soup and the specialty moose muzzle, and German influence, as in sausages, dried fruit and meat pie, chicken or rabbit pot pie, and shoofly pie (molasses dessert). Specialties from the plentiful fruits include Dutch apple pie and ice wine (a dessert wine similar to German eiswein (Aspler, 1995)).

The Prairie Provinces   Manitoba, Saskatchewan, and Alberta, the next western provinces, are red meat country and the breadbasket of Canada. They have fish in rivers and lakes, beef now instead of buffalo as in the early years, and wheat and other grains including wild rice. Cuisine is influenced by European immigrants including Scandinavians and especially by immigrants from the Ukraine in Manitoba, where pierogi (sweet or savory filled pie) seems to be the national dish.

West Canada, British Columbia   This province borders the Pacific Ocean and features salmon, including the Indian wind-dried salmon known as jerky. Native foods include greens, camas bulbs, and wild berries. Now grapes are grown and wines are produced. Indian, British, and Asian influences are prominent, especially in Vancouver because the immigration pattern changed greatly during the last part of the 20th century with a major influx from Asia, particularly Hong Kong, China, and Taiwan (Powers and Stewart, 1995).

Bread and cereals   Wheat, barley, corn, oatmeal, rice, wild rice; bread, French bread, porridge, biscuits, scones.

Meat, poultry, fish   Chicken, beef, pork, lamb, goat, fish (salmon, cod), seafood (lobster), rabbit, game birds, game meat (venison); bacon, Canadian bacon, salt pork, sausages, salmon jerky.

Dairy products   Milk, cream, cheese (cheddar, Oka also called Trappist monk cheese, French types).

Fats and oils   Vegetable oil, corn oil, canola oil, safflower oil, rapeseed oil, bacon, salt pork, butter.

Legumes   Soybeans, dried yellow split peas, lentils, beans.

Vegetables   Potatoes, tomatoes, mushrooms, carrots, celery, onions, lettuce, green beans, peas, asparagus.

Fruit   Apples, cranberries, blueberries, bananas, grapes, oranges, strawberries, pears, cherries, rhubarb.

Seeds   Canary seed, mustard seed, caraway seed, rapeseed, linseed.

Seasonings   Salt, black pepper, onions, cinnamon, ginger.

Dishes   Clam or fish chowder. Lobster and corn boil. Fish and chips (fried fish and French fries). Planked salmon. Split-pea soup. Corn and bean soup. Grilled beef steak, lamb chops, or salmon. Beef pot roast or stew. Meat pie.

Sweets   Sugar, maple syrup, molasses, pie (apple, blueberry, rhubarb), pudding, cinnamon buns, cake.

Beverages   Tea, coffee, cider, beer, wine, ice wine (a dessert wine).

Street food and snacks   Fish and chips, poutine (French fries, cheese, and gravy).

CAPE VERDE
Republic of Cape Verde

Geography   Cape Verde is in the Atlantic Ocean, off the west tip of Africa. It consists of 15 volcanic islands with stark landscape and with vegetation mostly in interior valleys.

Major Languages	Ethnic Groups		Major Religions	
Portuguese (official) Crioulo (Portuguese- West African blend)	Creole (mulatto) African (mostly Fulani, Balanta) Other	71% 28% 1%	Roman Catholic (infused with indigenous beliefs) Protestant and other	88% 12%

Population density per sq. mi. 274.2
Literacy rate 83.8%
Life expectancy 68 male; 74.8 female
Per capita GDP $3,200
Labor force in agriculture NA

Urban 57.4%
Infant mortality rate per 1,000 live births 42.5
HIV rate NA
Unemployment rate 21.1%
Arable land 11%

Agriculture   sugarcane, fruits, pulses, bananas, corn, beans, sweet potatoes, sugarcane, coffee, peanuts, chickens, pigs, goats, cattle, sheep

Natural resources   salt, basalt rock, limestone, kaolin, fish

Industries   food and beverages, fish processing, shoes and garments, salt mining, ship repair

History   The Portuguese discovered these uninhabited islands in 1456 or 1460. The first Portuguese colonists arrived in 1462. African slaves were soon brought. Most Cape Verdeans descend from both groups. Cape Verde became independent in 1975. Remittances from Cape Verdean emigrants, along with money from the European Development Fund and others, provide much of the income. The country enjoyed political stability and a tourism boom in 2007.

Influences on food   Cape Verde cuisine reflects Portuguese and West African influences. The Portuguese introduced the domesticated pig, chickens, olives, salt cod, coffee, tea, and European-style bread. They brought a liking for goat and for sweet dishes especially ones made with eggs. From the Americas, especially Brazil, the Portuguese brought corn, tomatoes, potatoes, sweet potatoes, chilies, sweet peppers, and cassava. From the east via Mozambique (another Portuguese colony), they brought oranges, lemons, many spices, and probably sugar and various tropical fruits. West Africans brought a tradition of dairy products, grain pastes, starchy root vegetables, green leafy vegetables, legumes, and using blood as in sauces. Using blood from a slaughtered animal in yellow rice may reflect medieval Portuguese practice.

Bread and cereals   Corn, rice, wheat; porridge, grain pastes, rice dishes, Portuguese-style bread.

Meat, poultry, fish   Chicken, eggs, pork, goat, beef, lamb and mutton, fish, seafood.

Dairy products   Milk, cream, curds, whey, cheese.

Fats and oils   Palm oil, lard, sesame oil, butter, olive oil.

Legumes   Beans, peanuts, black-eyed peas.

Vegetables   Sweet potatoes, cassava, greens, onions, tomatoes, potatoes, sweet peppers, chilies, okra, olives, pumpkin, lettuce, parsley.

Fruit   Bananas, coconut, baobab, pineapple, oranges, lemons, limes, guavas, mangoes, papaya.

Nuts and seeds   Cashews, baobab seeds, sesame seeds.

Seasonings   Salt, black pepper, onions, garlic, chili peppers, coriander, cloves, cinnamon, saffron, ginger.

Dishes   Frejon (bean purée with coconut milk). Salt cod with cassava leaves, sweet peppers, and palm oil. Goat stew with garlic, chilies, and cloves. Boiled dried beans mixed with fresh corn fried in pork fat. Fish simmered with limes, powdered sesame, olive oil, garlic, and coriander. Prawns sautéed with chopped onions in olive oil and butter; then simmered in coconut milk with tomatoes, chopped red chilies, black pepper, and ginger; wine added and the mixture poured over pounded coconut meat, parsley, and lettuce; and served with boiled rice. Chicken cut up and cooked with palm oil, garlic, onion, hot red peppers, okra, pumpkin, and sweet potato leaves. Prawns grilled on skewers and basted with a sauce of oil, lemon juice, garlic, salt, and crushed peppers. Marinated, fried pork. Yellow rice (rice browned in olive and then simmered with saffron and broth). Goat pot roast (sliced kid layered with bacon, onions, bay leaves, garlic, cloves, and red chili powder; dry wine poured on top and covered and simmered until meat is almost tender; and cut potatoes added and covered and simmered until tender).

Sweets   Sugarcane, sugar, coconut pudding, baked bananas with coconut, puréed papaya and egg custard.

Beverages   Coffee, beer, wine (palm, Madeira, port).

CENTRAL AFRICAN REPUBLIC

Geography   This landlocked central African country is mostly plateau, average elevation 2,000 feet, covered with well-watered savanna. Tropical rainforest is in the south. Desert is in the east. Rivers drain to the Congo.

Major Languages	Ethnic Groups		Major Religions	
French (official)	Baya	33%	Indigenous beliefs	35%
Sangho (national)	Banda	27%	Protestant	25%
Tribal languages	Mandjia	13%	Roman Catholic	25%
	Sara	10%	Sunni Muslim	15%
	Mboum, other	17%		

Population density per sq. mi. 18.5
Literacy rate 48.6%
Life expectancy 44.1 male; 44.3 female
Per capita GDP $700
Labor force in agriculture NA

Urban 38.1%
Infant mortality rate per 1,000 live births 82.1
HIV rate 6.3%
Unemployment rate 23% (Bangui, the capital, only)
Arable land 3%

Agriculture   timber, cassava, yams, peanuts, cotton, coffee, tobacco, millet, corn, bananas, chickens, cattle, goats, pigs, sheep

Natural resources   diamonds, uranium, timber, gold, oil, hydropower, fish

Industries   gold and diamond mining, logging, brewing, textiles, footwear, bicycle and motorcycle assembly

History   For centuries Bantu tribes migrated through this region before the French gained control in the late 19th century, when the region was named Ubangi-Shari. Independence was attained in 1960. In 2003 rebels led by a former army chief ousted the president and installed the army chief as president; he was reelected in 2006. In 2007 fighting between dissident groups and the army forced thousands of civilians to flee; some 56,000 refugees from fighting in the northern region were living in Chad in mid-2008. In 2007 violence against health care workers led all aid agencies in the north to suspend operations.

Influences on food   This tropical country has rivers that provide fish and land that grows coffee, cassava, yams, millet, corn, and bananas and produces livestock. Starchy roots and grains are staple foods. The French have influenced food customs (e.g., French bread). The introduction of New World foods such as cassava, corn, peanuts, tomato, chili pepper, and potato had major influence. Native African foods include black-eyed peas, watermelon, and okra. Starchy food is considered real food and sauces and stews accompaniments. The diet of most people is grain, starchy vegetables, legumes, and greens. Meat is a luxury. Thick, sticky, spicy food is liked.

Bread and cereals   Millet, corn, rice, sorghum, wheat; fried cornmeal/plantain cakes, rice dishes, French bread.

Meat, poultry, fish   Chicken, eggs, beef, goat, pork, lamb and mutton, fish (fresh, smoked, salted, or dried), guinea fowl, rabbit, game. Chicken is a popular, prestigious food. Fish is often used with meat in stews.

Insects   Termites (often called white ants), locusts.

Dairy products   Milk, sour milk, buttermilk, curds, whey, cheese.

Fats and oils   Palm oil, peanut oil, shea oil, coconut oil. Palm oil, used liberally on most food, gives a red hue.

Legumes   Peanuts (groundnuts), black-eyed peas (cowpeas), locust beans (carob), red beans.

Vegetables   Cassava, yams, plantains, taro, green leaves (taro, cassava, bitterleaf), okra, tomatoes, sweet potatoes, potatoes, eggplant, pumpkin, onions, red chili peppers, cucumbers, bell peppers.

Fruit   Bananas, coconut, pineapple, akee apples, baobab, watermelon, guavas, lemons, dates, mangoes, papaya.

Nuts and seeds   Cashews, kola nuts, watermelon seeds (egusi), sesame seeds, mango seeds, baobab seeds.

Seasonings   Salt, palm oil, onions, red chili peppers, dried baobab leaves, thyme.

Dishes   Boiled or fried food; chunks are dipped in sauce and eaten by hand. Peanut sauce or stew (ground and pounded peanuts, chilies, tomatoes, and chicken, beef, fish, or mixtures of them, and perhaps potatoes, beans, or eggplant). Sauce of pounded leaves. Frejon (black-eyed pea or bean purée, coconut milk, and sometimes carob or chocolate). Gari (cassava meal). Fufu (a paste of boiled and pounded starchy vegetables or corn), formed into balls or bite-size scoops to eat stew. Stews of root vegetables or okra, with bits of fish, chicken, or beef. Moin moin (steamed ground paste of black-eyed peas, hot peppers, and onions). Rice boiled in coconut milk. Roast chicken with peanut sauce. Plantain fried in palm oil with onions and chili.

Sweets   Honey, sugar, deep-fried sweet dough balls, peanut candy, bananas baked with sugar or coconut.

Beverages   Coffee, beer.

Street food and snacks   Spiced kabobs, fried fish, plantain chips, fried bean balls, black-eyed pea fritters, balls of steamed rice, fried yams, fried sweet dough. Snacks are common and available at street stalls in urban areas.

CHAD
Republic of Chad

Geography   Chad is in central North Africa. Chad, an interior country, has a northern desert that is part of the Sahara, wooded savanna with rivers in the south, and Lake Chad along the western border. The highest peak in the Sahara is Mt. Koussi, 11,204 feet, an extinct volcano in northwestern Chad.

Major Languages	Ethnic Groups		Major Religions	
Arabic (both	Sara	28%	Sunni Muslim	53%
French official)	Arab	12%	Catholic	20%
120+ languages and dialects	Mayo-Kebbi	12%	Protestant	14%
	Kanem-Bomou	9%	Animist	7%
	Other	39%	Other	6%

Population density per sq. mi. 20.8
Literacy rate 25.7%
Life expectancy 46.4 male; 48.5 female
Per capita GDP $1,700
Labor force in agriculture 80% (subsistence)

Urban 25.3%
Infant mortality rate per 1,000 live births 100.4
HIV rate 3.5%
Unemployment rate NA
Arable land 7%

Agriculture   sorghum, millet, peanuts, gum arabic, cotton, rice, potatoes, cassava, cattle, goats, chickens, sheep, camels, pigs

Natural resources   oil, uranium, natron, kaolin, fish

Industries   oil, cotton textiles, meatpacking, brewing, sodium carbonate, soap, cigarettes, construction materials

History   Paleolithic and Neolithic cultures existed here before the Sahara Desert formed. Kingdoms and Arab slave traders dominated the region until France took control in 1900. Chad gained independence in 1960. Independence was followed by decades of civil war and intervention by France and Libya. In 2003 oil began flowing through a pipeline connecting Chad oil fields with the Cameroon coast. In 2007 Chad continued to be affected by conflict across its border in the Darfur region of Sudan. In 2008 an estimated 233,000 Sudanese refugees from Darfur were in camps in eastern Chad, and an UN-European peacekeeping force was established to protect the camps. In mid-2008, UN camps in Chad also held 56,000 refugees from the Central African Republic. A peace accord to stop cross border fighting was signed in 2008.

Influences on food   Chad, like most other countries of Sub-Saharan Africa immediately south of the Sahara, is a former French colony and sparsely populated. Food practices are influenced by North Africa, West Africa, France, foods brought from the New World, and religion. For examples: meat and fish are combined in sauces, as in West Africa; baguette bread is common in towns, a French influence; and chilies and tomatoes appear in many dishes, a New World influence. Many people are Muslim and do not eat pork, although pigs are raised and pork is eaten by many other people. Herders, such as the Fula, live in the northern part of the region. Although red meat is a luxury, some is eaten as well as game. Rivers and Lake Chad provide fish. In country areas the traditional wood-burning hearth, made of three stones on which a pot sits, is still used. Meat may be grilled on open fires. The oven is uncommon.

Bread and cereals   Sorghum, millet, rice, corn, wheat, wild grain; porridge, couscous (tiny balls of millet dough steamed and served like rice), rice dishes, baguette bread.

Meat, poultry, fish   Beef, goat, chicken, eggs, lamb, camel, pork, fish (perch, tilapia), guinea-fowl, pigeons, game (antelope, rock rabbit, cane rat). Meat and fish are often dried.

Dairy products   Milk, sour milk, buttermilk, curds, whey, cheese.

Fats and oils   Shea oil and butter (from the seeds of the African shea tree), palm oil, peanut oil.

Legumes   Peanuts (groundnuts), beans, peas, lentils. Legumes are important.

Vegetables   Potatoes, cassava, yams, plantains, sweet potatoes, tomatoes, okra, greens, chilies, onions.

Fruit   Dates, raisins, coconut, bananas, mangoes.

Nuts and seeds   Kola nuts, shea nuts, watermeon seeds, sesame seeds. Nuts and seeds thicken sauces/stews.

Seasonings   Chilies, tomatoes, onions, garlic.

Dishes   Steamed or boiled rice or other grain, often with meat and peanut sauce. Rice served with a thin stew of beef and tomatoes. Boiled millet and cassava mush. Corn porridge. Red meat and okra stew. Chicken and peanut stew with sweet potatoes and tomatoes. Cassava porridge with smoked fish, tomatoes, and other vegetables. Fish, okra, greens, and tomato stew. Stuffed camel stomach (similar to haggis). Stew of cassava leaves with dried fish and palm oil or with okra, served with couscous or rice.

Festive occasion dishes   Millet grains and cassava mush served with two sauces (minced meat, dried fish, and dried okra powder; and diced meat and tomatoes) mixed before serving. Jollof rice (rice with tomato or palm oil).

Sweets   Honey, sugar, peanut candy, baked bananas, deep-fried sweet dough balls, sweet pastries.

Beverages   Beer, coffee.

Street food   Kabobs, shawerma, bean fritters, sweet pastries, grilled sweet corn. Street food is important.

CHILE
Republic of Chile

Geography   Chile is on the west coast of southern South America, bordering the Pacific Ocean. It is a narrow long strip between the Andes Mountains, which cover a third of Chile and has some of the world's highest peaks, and the Pacific Ocean. In the north is the Atacama Desert, the driest place on earth. The center is a thickly populated valley with the agricultural area. In the south are forests and grazing lands. Punta Arenas, on a mainland peninsula, is the world's southernmost city and a sheep-raising center.

Major Languages	Ethnic Groups		Major Religions	
Spanish (official)	White and		Roman Catholic	70%
Mapudungun	White-Amerindian	95%	Protestant	15%
German	Amerindian	4%	Other	7%
English	Other	1%	None	8%

Population density per sq. mi. 56.9
Literacy rate 96.5%
Life expectancy 73.9 male; 80.6 female
Per capita GDP $13,900
Labor force in agriculture 13.6%

Urban 87.6%
Infant mortality rate per 1,000 live births 7.9
HIV rate 0.3%
Unemployment rate 7.8%
Arable land 3%

Agriculture   sugar beets, grapes, wheat, apples, pears, onions, corn, oats, peaches, garlic, asparagus, beans, chickens, cattle, pigs, sheep, goats

Natural resources   copper, timber, iron ore, nitrates, precious metals, molybdenum, hydropower, fish

Industries   copper (world's largest producer and exporter), other minerals, foodstuffs, fish processing, iron, steel, wood and wood products, transportation equipment, cement, textiles

History   Incas ruled in northern Chile before the Spanish conquest, 1536 to 1540. Araucanian Indians lived in southern Chile and resisted the Spanish until the late 18th century. Independence was attained in the period 1810 to 1818. Later in the 19th century Chile defeated Peru and Bolivia, gaining mineral-rich northern land. In 1970 a Marxist was elected president, the first Marxist head of state in Latin America. Political and financial chaos and then a military junta followed. Repression continued through the 1980s. A Socialist president took office in 2000. Chile and the United States signed a free-trade accord in 2003. Another Socialist president took office in 2006, as Chile's first woman president. In 2007 the economy was strong, and copper, the largest export, reached its highest level in 40 years.

Possessions: Cape Horn, South America's southernmost point; part of **Antarctic territory**; **Easter Island**, in the South Pacific; and part of **Tierra del Fuego**, the largest island on the archipelago of the same name at the southern tip of South America. Tierra del Fuego has majestic mountains and high winds. Magellan visited it in 1520, naming it Land of Fire because of many Indian bonfires. Part of the island is in Argentina.

Influences on food   Influence of Inca and other native Indians remains in the use of corn, potatoes, beans, tomatoes, squash, and chili peppers. *Chili* is a general term for a wide range of fruits of the genus *Capsicum* (but not including the larger, mild-tasting pimiento, or sweet, pepper). Chilies are hot because they contain capsaicin, an irritant alkaloid found mainly in the interior tissue to which the seeds adhere. Spanish influence includes the use of the pig (and lard), cattle, and olives. This long, thin country has extremely varied climate and geography. As a result, foods vary throughout the country. Little food is produced in the high desert of the northern third of the country. In wide fertile valleys in temperate to subtropical zones in the middle of the country, edible crops, grapes, and stone fruits are grown. The south has forests with climate and terrain unsuitable for agriculture; sheep are raised here. Pigs are farmed, and some pork dishes are popular. The long, deeply indented coastline, especially in the south, provides abundant seafood. The strawberry's ancestor was brought from Chile to France in 1714.

Bread and cereals   Wheat, corn, rice; wheat flour bread, pastry, and turnovers, potato bread.

Meat, poultry, fish   Chicken, beef, pork, lamb and mutton, goat, fish including congrio (a cusk eel), seafood such as giant sea urchins (erizos), mussels, scallops, abalone, clams, oysters (staples of the Indian diet), and the giant goose-necked barnacle picoroco (a delicacy found only on this coast), eggs; sausage.

Dairy products   Milk, evaporated milk, cheese.

Fats and oils   Lard, olive oil, vegetable oil, butter. Lard or oil with garlic, paprika, and perhaps chili is a popular cooking medium called color.

Legumes   Cranberry beans (porotos), kidney beans, peanuts.

Vegetables   Potatoes, squash (chayote), chili peppers, tomatoes, onions, asparagus, plantains, cassava, pumpkin, sweet potatoes, olives, carrots, parsley.

Fruit   Grapes, apples, pears, peaches, strawberries, bananas, lemons, limes, oranges, raisins.

Nuts and seeds   Cashew nuts, pumpkin seeds.

Seasonings   Salt, chili peppers (ají), onions, garlic, paprika, cilantro, vinegar.

Dishes   Porotos Granados (simmered cranberry beans, squash, and fresh corn). Pastel del choclo (beef topped with ground fresh corn sprinkled with sugar). Humitas (purée of fresh corn with onions, peppers, and tomatoes, or cornmeal dough wrapped around savory or sweet meat, fish, or vegetable filling). Cancho a la chilena (casserole of pork, vegetables, and chilies). Raw giant sea urchins served with parsley sauce. Mussels, scallops, abalone, and oysters cooked in stews such as chupe de mariscos (with bread crumbs and cheese) or steamed in stone-lined pits. Fish, tomato, and potato soup. Chilean hot sauce (olive oil, vinegar, cilantro, onions, red hot chilies, garlic, salt). Escabeche de gallina (cold pickled chicken made by browning chicken pieces in olive oil and simmering with wine, vinegar, water, onions, carrots, salt, and spices). Cold seafood salad of simmered shrimp and crab with corn and rice. Pebre (a sauce of onions, vinegar, olives, garlic, chili, and cilantro), used on cold meat. Baked or fried pastry turnovers filled with chopped abalone or beef, olives, raisins, and onions. Lamb and vegetable stew. Braised ham with chili sauce.

Specialties   Picoroco cooked in a curanto (an elaborate clambake with shellfish, pig, sausages, potato patties, peas, and beans layered with seaweed), eaten with potato bread. Chupe de loco (clam or abalone chowder with beans). Congrio (cusk eel, potatoes, onions, garlic, and white wine stew).

Sweets   Honey, sugar, brown sugar, fruit, custard, pudding.

Beverages   Coffee, fruit juice, tea, beer, wine, pisco sour (wine mixed with lemon juice, sugar, and egg whites).

Meals   Breakfast: bread and coffee. Lunch: appetizer, meat or seafood stew, side dish of beans, potatoes, or greens, dessert. Tea in the late afternoon with fruit, sandwiches, or pastry. Dinner: seafood salad or stew. Poorer people often eat a single meal of soup or stew with a side dish of potatoes, plantains, corn, rice, or beans.

CHINA
People's Republic of China

Geography   China occupies most of the habitable mainland of East Asia and borders the East China Sea and the South China Sea. It is slightly larger in area than the United States. Most of the land is mountains or desert; only a tenth is cultivated. Mountains are in the west, north, and southwest, including the Himalayas in the southwest. The Gobi Desert is in the north. Tibet is in the southwest. Eastern China is one of the world's best-watered and fertile agricultural lands, with three great river systems providing water for vast farmlands. Hong Kong and Macao are in the south.

Major Languages	Ethnic Groups		Major Religions	
Standard Chinese (Mandarin) (official)	Han Chinese	92%	Atheist (official)	8%
Yue (Cantonese)	Other	8%	None	39%
Wu (Shanghainese)			Chinese folk-religionist	29%
Other languages and dialects			Christian (mostly Protestant)	10%
			Buddhist	8%
			Traditional beliefs	4%
			Muslim	2%

(Statistical data do not include Hong Kong or macao.)

Population density per sq. mi. 369.4
Literacy rate 93.3%
Life expectancy 71.4 male; 75.2 female
Per capita GDP $5,300
Labor force in agriculture 43%

Urban 40.4%
Infant mortality rate per 1,000 live births 21.2
HIV rate 0.1%
Unemployment rate 4.2% in urban areas
Arable land 15%

Agriculture   rice, corn, wheat, barley, millet, oilseed, soybeans, peanuts, rapeseed, sunflower seeds, melons, fruits, sweet potatoes, sugarcane, potatoes, other vegetables, cotton, tobacco, tea, silkworm cocoons, ducks, chickens, pigs, goats, sheep, water buffalo, cattle
Natural resources   coal, iron ore, oil, natural gas, mercury, tin, tungsten, antimony, manganese, molybdenum, vanadium, magnetite, aluminum, lead, zinc, uranium, hydro power potential, fish

Industries   mining and ore processing, iron, steel, aluminum, coal, machine building, armaments, textiles and apparel, oil, cement, chemicals, fertilizers

History   Remains of humanlike creatures who lived several hundred thousand years ago have been found in China. From about 5000 BCE Neolithic settlements were along the Huang (Yellow) River. By 1500 to 1000 BCE bronze metallurgy and pictographic writing was used in the Shang Dynasty in northern China. Dynasties ruled China for the next 3,000 years, expanding China to the south and west and developing a culturally advanced society. Foreign rule (Mongols, 1271–1368, and Manchu in the Ch'ing Dynasty, 1644–1911) did not alter the culture. China became a republic in 1912. China and Japan were in conflict from 1894 to 1945; in 1895 China ceded Korea, Taiwan, and other areas. The Sino-Japanese War (1937–1945) became part of World War II. Defeated, Japan gave up all seized land. China came under communist domination in 1949–1950. The Kuomintang government moved to Taiwan in 1949. The People's Republic of China was proclaimed in 1949, under Mao Zedong. China and the USSR signed a 30-year treaty of "friendship, alliance, and mutual assistance." In 1971 the UN General Assembly ousted the Taiwan government and recognized the People's Republic in its place. In 1978 the United States formally recognized the People's Republic of China as the sole legal government of China, with diplomatic relations between the two nations established in 1979. China enacted economic reforms in the 1980s; since then its industries, exports, and oil demand have increased rapidly. In 1989 in Beijing students and workers marched in Tiananmen Square for political reform and were crushed, with thousands left dead, injured, or arrested. In the 1990s China had one of the world's fastest growing economies. Its economy continued its recent dramatic rise in 2007 and 2008, and the Chinese currency continued to appreciate against the U.S. dollar at an annual rate of about 5%. On the downside, in 2007 a toymaker recalled Chinese-made toys containing lead-tainted paint, and in 2008 nearly 53,000 babies were sickened by contaminated milk powder. In 2008 China hosted the Summer Olympics. An earthquake in Sichuan province destroyed more than 6,900 schools, killed more than 68,000 people, and made as many as 5 million people homeless.

Manchuria   It is the northeastern region of China, home of the Manchu, who ruled China from 1644 to 1911. It became industrialized during Japanese rule (1931–1945) and took in millions of Chinese settlers in the 20th century.

AUTONOMOUS REGIONS: Guangxi Zhuang, Inner Mongolia, Ningxia Hui, Xingjian Uygur, Tibet

SPECIAL ADMINISTRATIVE REGIONS: Hong Kong, Macao

Hong Kong   became a Special Administrative Region when Great Britain returned it to China in 1997 after a 99-year lease (it had been a British dependency since 1842); China agreed that Hong Kong would keep its capitalist system for 50 years. Hong Kong is in southeast China and includes Hong Kong Island, Kowloon Peninsula, Stone Cutters Island, and the New Territories, a mainland area. Hong Kong is a major trade and banking center.

Macao   is a small enclave of a peninsula and two small islands in Southeast China near Hong Kong. It was established as a Portuguese trading center in 1557. Portugal claimed it in 1849 and China accepted this claim in an 1887 treaty. Macao became a Special Administrative Region when Portugal returned it to China in 1999; the Chinese government guaranteed Macao it would not interfere with its capitalist system for 50 years. In 2007 the world's largest casino opened in Macao.

Influences on food   Climate and geography influence the cereal eaten (the necessary food) and the secondary foods, including the regional specialties. Chinese dietary practice involves "eating to live" and "eating for pleasure." A meal usually consists of a starchy food (the necessary one) and one or more animal or vegetable items (the secondary, eating for pleasure ones). Starchy foods are cereals (preferably) and tubers. A general difference is between northern China, a wheat area, and southern China, where rice is grown; the Blue River (Yangtze) separates these parts. In Beijing rice and wheat are eaten equally. People from poor rural areas of the north and center usually eat corn or millet foods. In areas lacking natural resources cereals are supplemented or replaced with tubers: taro in the subtropics and potatoes or sweet potatoes in cold areas. Natural products from each region, especially edible foodstuffs, were sent annually to the emperor from the provinces to represent them. From early days Chinese cooking was a skilled profession. Now four great cooking styles are recognized (below). In addition are a Muslim cuisine, in which pork is excluded, and a vegetarian cuisine, for Buddhists or other persons who do not take the lives of living creatures.

Bread and cereals   Rice, corn, wheat, barley, millet; rice dishes, rice flour noodles, glutinous rice cakes, wheat flour noodles, wonton wrappers, steamed bread, and pancakes.

Meat, poultry, fish   Duck, chicken, pork, goat, lamb and mutton, beef, water buffalo, fish, shrimp, oysters, eggs.

Dairy products   Milk (cow, water buffalo). Dairy products are rarely consumed. Many Chinese are lactose intolerant. Calcium sources are soy milk, tofu, and small bones of fish.

Fats and oils   Bacon fat, lard, butter, sesame oil, soybean oil, peanut oil, corn oil.

Legumes   Soybeans, peanuts, mung beans; tofu (soybean curd), soy milk, soy sauce, bean sprouts.

Vegetables   Sweet potatoes, potatoes, cabbage, tomatoes, cucumbers, onions, eggplant, chilies and peppers, asparagus, spinach, cauliflower, green beans, carrots, lotus roots, mushrooms, water chestnuts, taro.

Fruit   Watermelon, apples, citrus, cantaloupe, pears, bananas, lychee (has grapelike pulp and flavor).

Nuts and seeds   Almonds, cashews, chestnuts, ginkgo nuts, walnuts, rapeseed, sunflower seeds, sesame seed.

Seasonings   Soy sauce, garlic, fresh ginger, green onions, vinegar, hot chili peppers, Szechwan peppers.

Food preparation   Throughout China kitchen and dining area are separate. Food is usually cut into small pieces before cooking. In the rare instances when food is cooked whole, it is then cut in the kitchen. All foods (except fruit) are cooked or prepared (such as pickled or preserved), not served raw. Rice and bread are steamed. Stir-frying (chao) is typical for vegetables, meat, eggs, and cooked rice; this involves frying small pieces of food over intense heat, usually each ingredient separately, then reassembling and seasoning before serving. This method retains color, texture, and flavor of food and uses minimum cooking time and fuel and only one knife to cut food and one utensil to cook in (a wok).

Cookware   Woks of iron or steel are used for stir-frying, steaming, stewing, and deep-fat frying; cooking in them increases the iron content of food significantly (Zhou and Brittin, 1994). Roasting/baking is not done in homes, which do not have ovens; although in professional cooking food is roasted in big drum-shaped vertical ovens.

Dishes   Steamed rice. Soups. Battered and fried meat, poultry, or fish with sweet and sour sauce. Dumplings (steamed bread). Stir-fried vegetables, meat, fish, poultry, or rice. Noodle dishes such as chao mien (boiled noodles stir-fried with meat and vegetables). Deep-fried meatballs, fish, egg rolls, chicken, beef, pork, or tofu. Stewed pork, chicken, beef, fish, tofu, or vegetables.

Sweets   Sugarcane, honey, syrup, sugar, bean pastes, glutinous (sticky) rice cakes, saqima (pea-sized balls of fried dough bound with honey into a flat loaf).

Beverages   Tea (green and black), soy milk, soup broth, rice wine, beer.

Meals and service   A place setting: porcelain small plate, rice bowl, tea cup (no handles), soup bowl, and spoon plus bamboo chopsticks. A typical main meal: steamed rice, meat and vegetable dishes (usually the same number as the number of people at the table), soup, tea, and fruit. Rice and tea are at each diner's place; meat and vegetable dishes are placed on the table (often round) and people serve themselves; soup follows.

Street food and snacks   Xioaochi ("small foods"), tidbits that can be eaten at any time, include savory or sweet dishes, thick soups, bouillons, custards, jellies, omelets, and cakes (Newman, 2000a).

Regional cooking styles and specialties   Northern style, centered in Beijing, uses garlic, vinegar, and soy sauce. Beijing specialties include mung bean milk (douzhi) and Peking duck with its crackling skin accompanied by raw green onions and thin pancakes. In the area north of Beijing mutton with garlic and vinegar is eaten. Central and western style, concentrated around Sichuan, uses hot chili and Sichuan peppers, fermented bean paste, and sesame oil and purée. Specialties include Szechwan duck (fiery hot from Szechwan peppers and deep fried after steaming), chicken with walnuts and hot peppers, and pork. Southeastern (or coastal) style, dominant in Shanghai, uses delicate flavor of ginger and wine plus sweet and sour tastes combined. Specialties include vegetarian buns, fish balls, oyster omelet, fish, rice, and vegetables. Southern style, found in Canton, uses complex, rich flavors. Specialties include rice porridge (zhou), seafood, egg roll, dim sum (dumplings of minced meat or vegetables wrapped in dough and steamed), green vegetables, whole-roasted pigs, and lacquered meats hanging in restaurant front windows. Many Cantonese eat dim sum and tea in restaurants for breakfast or lunch.

Tibet   A province in southwest China, has unique food customs due to its isolated location in the Himalayan Mountains. In this land of high altitude and cold climate, barley is the chief grain. The main food is tsampa, gruel of toasted barley flour and water, usually mixed with tea made with yak butter. Tsampa is also made from buckwheat, wheat, corn, millet, oats, or soybeans. Flour is also mixed with butter, sugar, milk or cream, and sometimes tea to make flattened balls eaten with tea or soup. Other breads and cereals are popped grain (yet), steamed or fried bread from wheat flour, buckwheat pancakes, and momo (meat-filled dumplings). Yak and mutton are commonly eaten but most Tibetans who are Buddhist do not eat pork, poultry, or fish. Nomads get much of their food (dairy products and meat) from their herds, and they provide food to some other people. Momo and offal dishes are popular. Some meat is dried. Dairy products are important: milk (yak, cow, and yak/cow cross), butter, sour milk, milk solids preserved from butter making, and film skimmed from boiled milk and then dried. Butter tea (boeja), made by churning brewed tea, butter, milk or cream, and salt, is drunk throughout the day. Vegetables include turnips, cauliflower, beets, carrots, cabbage, radishes, onions, garlic, leeks, and potatoes. Wine, made from barley or buckwheat, is served on special occasions. A traditional Tibetan kitchen is simple, and fuel is wood or animal dung (Ang, 2000; Newman, 1999).

COLOMBIA
Republic of Colombia

Geography   Colombia is at the northwestern corner of South America, bordering the Caribbean Sea and the Pacific Ocean. Three parallel Andes mountain ranges run from to north to south. The eastern range is mostly high tableland, a high plateau and valley, the most densely populated part of the country. The eastern plains, sparsely settled by isolated Indian tribes, are drained by the Orinoco River and Amazon River systems.

Major Language	Ethnic Groups		Major Religions	
Spanish (official)	Mestizo	58%	Roman Catholic	90%
	White	20%	Other	10%
	Mulatto	14%		
	Black	4%		
	Mixed black-Amerindian	3%		
	Other	1%		

Population density per sq. mi. 112.2
Literacy rate 93.6%
Life expectancy 68.7 male; 76.5 female
Per capita GDP $6,700
Labor force in agriculture 22.7%

Urban 73.6%
Infant mortality rate per 1,000 live births 19.5
HIV rate 0.6%
Unemployment rate 11.8%
Arable land 2%

Agriculture   sugarcane, plantains, rice, cut flowers, coffee, bananas, tobacco, corn, cocoa beans, chickens, cattle, goats, sheep, horses, pigs

Natural resources   oil, natural gas, coal, iron ore, nickel, gold, copper, emeralds, hydropower, fish

Industries   textiles, food processing, oil, clothing and footwear, beverages, chemicals, cement

History   By the 1530s Spain conquered native Indians in this region and then ruled it and neighboring areas as New Granada for 300 years. Independence was won by 1819. Venezuela and Ecuador withdrew in 1829–1830 and Panama in 1903. Rural and urban violence (including that related to drug trafficking) has occurred since the mid-20th century. Colombia produces an estimated 90% of the cocaine reaching the United States. Since 2000, the United States has provided more than $5 billion to Colombia, much of it to combat the drug trade. Many leftist rebels and right-wing paramilitary groups have funded their activities through narcotics trafficking and kidnappings. In 2008, after killings including 11 provincial legislators who had been held since 2002, peace was reestablished between the two groups, and an army freed a presidential candidate and 14 other hostages from captivity by a leftist group.

Influences on food   Mountain ranges separate the areas of Colombia yielding distinctive regional cuisines: coconuts, tropical fruits, and fish on the Caribbean coast; and highland dishes of the capital Bogotá, showing Indian influences. Different altitudes allow fruits along with cassava on the coasts and coffee, corn, beans, and potatoes in the highlands. The Caribbean and Pacific coasts provide seafood, and wide rivers flowing into the Caribbean provide freshwater fish. The jungle yields sources of protein including ants and wild peccary (musk hog, looks something like a small wild pig). Cattle are raised on the eastern plains. Spanish influence remains in the use of foods such as rice, beef, cheese, cream, and capers, imported from Spain by early settlers, and in some sweet dishes combining Spanish methods and local fruits.

Staples   Rice, beans, and potatoes are universal throughout Colombia. Firm, yellow-fleshed potatoes (papas criollas) are typical Andean fare. Cassava and plantains are staples of the coasts.

Bread and cereals   Rice, corn; rice dishes, corn bread, pancakes, fritters, cassava flour "bread."

Meat, poultry, fish   Chicken, beef, lamb and mutton, goat, pork, fish, seafood including shrimp, eggs, rabbits, peccary, monkey, rodents such as paca, ants.

Dairy products   Milk, cream, cheese, curd cheese.

Fats and oils   Butter, lard, olive oil, coconut oil.

Legumes   Beans (black, cranberry, kidney), black-eyed peas, peanuts.

Vegetables   Plantains, potatoes, cassava (yucca), tomatoes, avocados, onions, carrots, olives, pumpkin.

Fruit   Bananas, coconut, raisins, guavas, papaya, pineapple, limes, other tropical fruits.

Nuts and seeds   Brazil nuts, cashews, pumpkin seeds.

Seasonings   Chili peppers, cilantro, garlic, annatto (a native tropical American tree whose red seeds are used to flavor oil or fat and are ground and used for color and flavor), cinnamon. Piquant (hot) food and cilantro are liked.

Dishes   Potatoes fried, boiled, or in casseroles or dishes such as papas chorreadas ("poured-upon potatoes," boiled potatoes covered by a sauce of tomatoes or cheese). Ajiaco de pollo (chicken stew with potatoes and corn plus sometimes cream and capers). Grilled small cornmeal patties (arepas).

Fresh corn kernel deep-fried fritters. Empanadas (savory turnovers). Cassava soup and stew such as bollito misto (chicken, sweet potatoes, cassava, plantains, and cilantro). Pan de yucca (a light bread of the highlands made from cassava flour and curd cheese). Cassava or plantains sliced and fried for a picada (chip). Hallacas (spicy meat and corn dough wrapped in plantain leaves and steamed). Bogotá chicken stew (chicken, potatoes, sweet potatoes, and cream). Beef tenderized by chopping into small pieces or twice cooking (braise in beer and spices and then roast). Sancocho (boiled beef and potatoes, plantains, or cassava). Sancocho de pescado (stew of fish or seafood). Fried fish or seafood. Avocado soup, salad, stuffed, or sauce such as aji de huevo (sauce of avocado, hard-boiled egg, and chili). Coconut in soups and stews of rabbits or rodents. Arroz con coco (rice pilaf with coconut and raisins). Spicy hot chili pepper sauce, served as a side to most dishes. Hormiga culona, a dish made from big-bottomed ants.

Sweets   Sugarcane, sugar, rice pudding with raisins and cinnamon (arroz de leche), coconut pudding, fruits boiled in light syrup, cake, candy, ice cream.

Beverages   Coffee, fresh fruit juice, batidas (tropical fruit juice drink, sometimes made with alcoholic beverages), avocado batidas (made with ripe avocado, milk, sugar, and lime), cocoa, tea, beer, wine.

Snacks   Sweetened and dried fruit leathers and pastes, toasted ants.

COMOROS
Union of the Comoros

Geography   Comoros is in the Indian Ocean between Mozambique and Madagascar. It consists of three islands (Grande Comore, Anjouan, and Moheli) of volcanic origin, with an active volcano on Grande Comore.

Official Languages	Ethnic Groups		Major Religions	
Arabic	Comorian (mix of		Islam (official)	
French	Bantu, Arab, Malay, and		Sunni Muslim	98%
Comorian (Swahili-Arabic blend)	Malagasy)	97%	Other	2%
	Other	3%		

Population density per sq. mi. 873.4
Literacy rate 75.1%
Life expectancy 60.7 male; 65.5 female
Per capita GDP $1,100
Labor force in agriculture 80%

Urban 27.9%
Infant mortality rate per 1,000 live births 68.6
HIV rate <0.1%
Unemployment rate 13.3%
Arable land 36%

Agriculture   coconuts, bananas, cassava, vanilla, cloves, ylang-ylang, perfume essence, copra, chickens, goats, cattle, sheep

Natural resources   fish

Industries   fishing, tourism, perfume distillation

History   These islands were frequently visited by travelers from Africa, Madagascar, Indonesia, and Arabia before Europeans came. Muslim sultans controlled the islands until the French gained them in the period from 1841 to 1909. The islands became a French overseas territory in 1947. Comore declared independence in 1975. Instability and coup attempts followed for decades. Anjouan and Moheli seceded from the Comoros in 1997; attempts to determine a new constitutional relationship are ongoing. A referendum in 2001 renamed the country the Union of the Comoros and granted the three islands partial autonomy. Each of the islands elected its own president in 2002 and 2007. Elections for national and island assemblies were held in 2004.

Influences on food   Influences from Africa, Madagascar, Indonesia, Arabia, France, and Islam are reflected in the food customs in Comoros. Most people are Muslims, whose religious beliefs forbid consumption of pork or alcohol.

Bread and cereals   Rice, wheat; rice dishes, baguette (French) bread.

Meat, poultry, fish   Goat, beef, lamb and mutton, chicken, fish, eggs.

Fats and oils   Coconut oil and cream.

Legumes   Cowpeas, peanuts, lentils, chickpeas.

Vegetables   Cassava, tomatoes, onions.

Fruit   Coconut, bananas, lemons.

Seasonings   Vanilla, cloves, chilies, ginger, garlic, satay (paste of chili, ginger, and garlic).

Dishes   Rice boiled, steamed, or in pilaf. Cassava boiled and mashed or fried. Stew of meat, chicken, or fish, or a mixture of them, and tomatoes. Rougaille (sauce of chilies, tomato, onion, lemon, and ginger). Achards (spicy and sweet pickled vegetables), accompanies savory dishes.

Sweets   Sugar. Vanilla-flavored pudding. Coconut pudding. Baked or fried bananas.

Beverages   Fruit juice, coffee, tea.

Breakfast   Soupy rice is often eaten for breakfast.

CONGO (FORMERLY ZAIRE)
Democratic Republic of the Congo

Geography   Congo is in central Africa with a short strip of land bordering the Atlantic Ocean. One fourth the size of the United States, it includes most of the Congo River basin. The vast central region is a low-lying plateau covered by rainforest. Surrounding it are mountains in the east and west, savannas in the south, and grasslands in the north. Lake Tanganyika is along the eastern border.

Major Languages	Ethnic Groups		Major Religions	
French (official)	200+ groups, majority Bantu		Roman Catholic	50%
Lingala	Four largest tribes:	45%	Protestant	20%
Kingwana (a Swahili dialect)	Mongo, Luba,		Kimbanguist	10%
Kikongo	Kongo (all Bantu),		Muslim	10%
Tshiluba	Mangbetu-Azande (Hamitic)		Other	10%

Population density per sq. mi. 76
Literacy rate 67.2%
Life expectancy 55.2 male; 55.8 female
Per capita GDP $300
Labor force in agriculture NA

Urban 32.1%
Infant mortality rate per 1,000 live births 83.1
HIV rate NA
Unemployment rate NA
Arable land 3%

Agriculture   cassava, sugarcane, plantains, coffee, palm oil, rubber, tea, quinine, bananas, root crops, corn, fruits, chickens, goats, pigs, game, sheep, cattle

Natural resources   cobalt, copper, oil, diamonds, gold, silver, zinc, manganese, tin, uranium, coal, hydropower, timber, fish

Industries   mining, mineral processing, textiles, footwear, cigarettes, processed food and beverages, cement

History   The earliest inhabitants may have been the pygmies, followed by Bantus from the east and Nilotic tribes from the north. When Portuguese explorers came in the 15th century, the large Bantu Bakongo kingdom ruled much of this land. King Leopold II of Belgium began exploitation in 1876 and claimed the area as the Congo Free State in 1884–1885. Exploitation of native laborers on rubber plantations led to granting a colonial charter in 1908; the colony became known as the Belgian Congo. It became independent in 1960 as the Democratic Republic of the Congo. The country's name was changed to the Republic of Zaire in 1971 and was restored to the Democratic Republic of the Congo in 1997. Economic decline and government corruption occurred in the 1980s and 1990s. In 1994 refugees fleeing massive ethnic bloodshed in Rwanda inundated Congo; violence and civil war ensued. Regional instability and the attraction of Congo's mineral wealth led to interventions by various African countries. The president was assassinated in 2001. In 2003 a new government was installed. In 2005 the legislature approved a new constitution. Strife between militia groups and the new president occurred from 2006 to 2008. Violence occurred near the borders with neighbors Rwanda and Uganda. A peace deal with militia groups was signed in 2008.

Influences on food   The Congo River and Lake Tanganyika provide fish. The tropical Congo River Basin, mountains, savannas, grasslands, and plateau produce coffee, sugarcane, tea, cassava, bananas, corn, and livestock. Cassava and plantains are dietary staples; daily fare also includes bananas, rice, corn, legumes, and green leaves. The introduction of New World foods such as cassava, corn, peanuts, tomato, chili pepper, pumpkin, and potato during the 15th and 16th centuries greatly influenced food customs. Native African foods include black-eyed peas, watermelon, and okra. Belgian control from 1885 for 75 years left some influence.

Bread and cereals   Corn, rice, millet, sorghum; grain pastes, porridge, rice dishes, plantain and flour bread.

Meat, poultry, fish   Chicken, goat, pork, lamb and mutton, beef, fish (fresh, smoked, salted, or dried), guinea fowl, eggs, rabbit, game meat such as antelope, monkey, and porcupine.

Insects   Termites (often called white ants), locusts.

Dairy products   Milk, sour milk, buttermilk, curds, whey, cheese.

Fats and oils   Palm oil, peanut oil, shea oil, coconut oil. Palm oil, the predominant fat, gives food a red color.

Legumes   Peanuts (groundnuts), black-eyed peas (cowpeas), locust beans (carob), red beans.

Vegetables   Cassava, plantains, yams, taro, green leaves (taro, cassava, bitter leaf), okra, tomatoes, sweet potatoes, potatoes, eggplant, pumpkin, onions, red chili peppers, cucumbers, bell peppers.

Fruit   Bananas, coconut, pineapple, akee apples, baobab, watermelon, guavas, lemons, dates, mangoes, papaya.

Nuts and seeds   Palm kernels, shea nuts, cashews, kola nuts, watermelon seeds (egusi), sesame seeds, mango seeds. Nuts and seeds thicken and flavor sauces and stews.

Seasonings   Salt, palm oil, onions, red chili peppers. These season most foods.

Dishes   Most foods are boiled or fried, and chunks are dipped in sauce and eaten by hand. Sauces of ground peanuts or boiled and pounded green leaves. Fufu (a paste of boiled and pounded starchy vegetables or corn), formed into balls or bite-size scoops to eat stew. Stews of root vegetables, okra, or peanuts, with bits of fish, chicken, or beef. Gari (roasted and ground cassava). Gari foto (scrambled eggs, cassava meal, onions, chilies, and tomatoes). Moin moin (steamed ground paste of black-eyed peas, hot peppers, and onions). Rice boiled in coconut milk. Plantain fried in palm oil with onions and chilies. Omelet of eggs, onions, and red peppers. A notable dish, soso (rich chicken stew).

National dish   Moambé (a spicy peanut sauce with palm oil) served with meat or chicken and rice.

Sweets   Sugarcane, honey, sugar, fried dough balls, peanut candy, baked bananas with sugar, honey, or coconut.

Beverages   Coffee, tea, cocoa, beer, palm wine.

Street food and snacks   Spiced kabobs, fried fish, plantain chips, fried bean balls, balls of steamed rice, sweet porridge, doughnuts, coconut biscuits. Snacks are common and available at urban street stalls.

CONGO REPUBLIC
Republic of the Congo

Geography   This country is in west central Africa, bordering the Atlantic Ocean and straddling the equator. Much of it is covered by thick forest. It contains a coastal plain and fertile valley, a central plateau, and the Congo River Basin with its flood plains and savanna.

Major Languages	Ethnic Groups		Major Religions	
French (official)	Kongo	48%	Christian (mostly	
Lingala	Sangha	20%	Roman Catholic)	50%
Monokutuba	Teke	17%	Animist	48%
Many local languages and dialects,	M'Bochi	12%	Muslim	2%
Kikongo most widespread	Other	3%		

Population density per sq. mi. 29.6
Literacy rate 86.8%
Life expectancy 52.5. male; 55.5 female
Per capita GDP $3,700
Labor force in agriculture NA

Urban 60.2%
Infant mortality rate per 1,000 live births 81.3
HIV rate 3.5%
Unemployment rate NA
Arable land 1%

Agriculture   cassava, sugarcane, oil palm fruit, rice, corn, peanuts, vegetables, coffee, cocoa, chickens, goats, cattle, sheep, pigs

Natural resources   oil, timber, potash, lead, zinc, uranium, copper, phosphates, gold, magnesium, natural gas, hydropower, fish

Industries   oil extraction, cement, lumber, brewing, sugar, palm oil

History   In the 15th century the Loango Kingdom and the Anzico Kingdom of the Batekes flourished here. By 1885 France controlled the region, the Middle Congo. Republic of the Congo gained independence in 1960. France remained a dominant trade partner. Political instability including ethnic and regional conflicts has been a problem since gaining independence. The country was renamed People's Republic of the Congo in 1970. In 1990 Marxism was renounced and in 1991 the country's name was changed back to Republic of the Congo. During the 1990s factional fighting occurred, devastating the capital Brazzaville in 1997; a former Marxist dictator took control of the city. He claimed victory in the presidential election in 2002. The government and rebels agreed to a cease-fire in 2003. A severe cholera outbreak in 2007 was blamed on poor hygiene. Children (400,000) were vaccinated against polio, and a special train carried 300,000 insecticide-treated anti-malaria mosquito nets for delivery along the southwestern coast. Oil accounts for about 65% of the country's GDP and 90% of export revenue.

Influences on food   The Atlantic coastline and Congo River provide fish. The tropical coastal plain, fertile valley, central plateau, and Congo River Basin with its flood plains and savannah produce cassava, sugarcane, rice, corn, peanuts, vegetables, cocoa, and livestock. Cassava and plantains are the dietary staples; daily fare also includes bananas, rice, corn, legumes, and green leaves. New World foods such as cassava, corn, peanuts, tomato, chili pepper, pumpkin, and potato introduced in Africa during the 16th and later centuries has influenced food here. Also, French control from 1885 for 75 years was an influence.

Bread and cereals   Rice, corn, millet, sorghum, wheat; rice dishes, grain pastes, dough balls, bread made from mashed plantains and flour, French bread.

Meat, poultry, fish   Chicken, goat, beef, lamb or mutton, pork, fish (fresh, smoked, salted, or dried), seafood, guinea fowl, eggs, rabbit, game. Chicken is popular.

Insects   Termites (often called white ants), locusts.

Dairy products   Milk, sour milk, buttermilk, curds, whey, cheese.

Fats and oils   Palm oil, peanut oil, shea oil, coconut oil. Palm oil, the predominant fat, gives food a red color.

Legumes   Peanuts (groundnuts), black-eyed peas (cowpeas), locust beans (carob), red beans.

Vegetables   Cassava, plantains, yams, green leaves (cassava, bitter leaf), okra, tomatoes, sweet potatoes, potatoes, eggplant, pumpkin, onions, red chili peppers, cucumbers, bell peppers.

Fruit   Bananas, coconut, pineapple, akee apples, baobab, watermelon, guavas, lemons, dates, mangoes, papaya.

Nuts and seeds   Palm kernels, shea nuts, cashews, kola nuts, watermelon seeds (egusi), sesame seeds, mango seeds. Nuts and seeds thicken and flavor sauces.

Seasonings   Salt, palm oil, onions, red chili pepper. These season most foods.

Dishes   Most foods are boiled or fried, and chunks are dipped in sauce and eaten by hand. Sauces of ground peanuts or boiled and pounded green leaves. Fufu (a paste of boiled and pounded starchy vegetables or corn), formed into balls or bite-size scoops to eat stew. Stews of root vegetables, okra, or peanuts, with bits of fish, chicken, or beef. Gari (roasted and ground cassava). Gari foto (scrambled eggs, cassava meal, onions, chilies, and tomatoes). Moin moin (steamed ground paste of black-eyed peas, hot peppers, and onions). Rice boiled in coconut milk. Plantain fried in palm oil with onions and chilies. Roast chicken with peanut sauce.

Sweets   Sugarcane, honey, sugar, fried dough balls, peanut candy, bananas baked with sugar, honey, or coconut.

Beverages   Cocoa, coffee, beer.

Street food and snacks   Spiced kabobs (coupé-coupé); fried fish, plantain chips, or bean balls; balls of steamed rice, black-eyed peas, yams, or peanuts. Snacks are common and available at street stalls in urban areas.

COSTA RICA
Republic of Costa Rica

Geography   Costa Rica, in Central America between Nicaragua and Panama, contains tropical lowlands by the Caribbean Sea, a high interior plateau (4,000 ft) with temperate climate, and a narrow strip by the Pacific Ocean.

Major Languages	Ethnic Groups		Major Religions	
Spanish (official)	White and mestizo	94%	Roman Catholicism (official)	
English	Black	3%	Roman Catholic	76%
	Amerindian	1%	Protestant (mostly Evangelical)	16%
	Chinese and other	2%	Other	8%

Population density per sq. mi. 214.5
Literacy rate 95.9%
Life expectancy 74.8 male; 80.1 female
Per capita GDP $10,300
Labor force in agriculture 14%

Urban 61.7%
Infant mortality rate per 1,000 live births 9
HIV rate 0.4%
Unemployment rate 6.6%
Arable land 4%

Agriculture   sugarcane, bananas, pineapples, coffee, melons, ornamental plants, corn, rice, beans, potatoes, chickens, cattle, pigs, goats, sheep

Natural resources   hydropower, fish

Industries   microprocessors, food processing, medical equipment, textiles and clothing, construction materials, fertilizer, plastics

History   Guaymi Indians lived here when Spaniards arrived in 1502. Independence came in 1821. Costa Rica seceded from the Central American Federation in 1838. In 1890 Costa Rica held the reputedly first free and honest election in Central America, beginning a history of democracy. Since the civil war, 1948–1949, there has been little violent conflict. Costa Rica's president was awarded the Nobel Peace Prize in 1987. The country suffered severe hurricane damage in 1996. It has a relatively high standard of living, widespread land ownership, and increasing tourism. In 2007 it established diplomatic relations with China and broke formal ties with Taiwan. Economic growth remained strong. Costa Rica was elected to serve on the UN Security Council in 2008–2009.

Influences on food   Influences are from the Guaymi Indians who lived here when the Spanish arrived, the Spanish, and the Caribbean islands. The Spanish brought new foods including rice, beef, and pork. Caribbean island foodways from native Carib-speaking Indians and laborers imported from Africa and Asia influenced food customs on Costa Rica's Caribbean coast.

Staple foods   Corn, beans, rice. These are eaten at most meals.

Bread and cereals   Corn, rice, wheat; rice dishes, tortillas (thin circles of corn bread), wheat flour bread and rolls.

Meat, poultry, fish   Chicken, beef, pork, goat, lamb and mutton, fish, eggs.

Dairy products   Milk (evaporated), cream, sour cream, cheese. Milk is not usually drunk as a beverage.

Fats and oils   Lard, butter, vegetable oils, shortening.

Legumes   Beans (black, red, kidney, white), chickpeas.

Vegetables   Potatoes, plantains, cassava, tomatoes, sweet peppers, chayote squash (green pear-shaped gourd), breadfruit, pumpkin, avocados, chili peppers, onions.

Fruit   Bananas, pineapple, melons, coconut, mangoes, oranges, roselle fruit (used to make sorrel drinks and jams/jellies), grapes, papaya, passion fruit.

Nuts and seeds   Palm tree nuts, squash seeds.

Seasonings   Onions, garlic, achiote/annatto, chili, cilantro, thyme, oregano, pimento, cinnamon, vanilla.

Dishes   Tamales (corn dough stuffed with spiced chicken or pork, wrapped in leaves or corn husks, and steamed). Posole (semi-fermented corn dough, diluted to make a beverage). Atole (thickened corn gruel) that can have additions of chili, squash seeds, or beans. Boiled rice and beans combinations (frijoles con arroz). Rice pancakes. Soups and stews of beef or seafood, plantains, and cassava in coconut milk. Fried plantains or breadfruit. Avocado salad.

Sweets   Sugarcane, honey, sugar (white, brown), nogada (praline-like candy), baked bananas, fruit ices, custard, rice pudding, ice cream, coconut- or rum-flavored cakes and fritters.

Beverages   Coffee, chocolate, tropical fruit drinks (refrescas), beer, rum.

Meals   Traditional breakfast: Gallo pinto, a rice and black bean dish, sometimes with sour cream or fried eggs. Economical meal: Casado (combination of rice and beans) with meat, fried plantains, and perhaps avocado. Typical dinner in wealthier areas: soup; meat, poultry, or fish; tortillas or bread; and salad, fried plantains, and pickled vegetables plus sometimes appetizers and dessert.

CÔTE D'IVOIRE
Republic of Côte d'Ivoire

Geography   This country is on the south coast of West Africa, bordering the Atlantic Ocean. It includes a coastal strip, sparse inland plain, and low mountains in the northwest. Forests cover the western half of the country.

Major Languages	Ethnic Groups		Major Religions	
French (official)	Akan	42%	Indigenous beliefs	37%
60 native dialects	Mandes	27%	Muslim	28%
(Dioula most widely spoken)	Voltaiques (Gur)	18%	Roman Catholic	17%
	Krous	11%	Other Christian	15%
	Other	2%	Other	3%

Population density per sq. mi. 164.4
Literacy rate 48.7%
Life expectancy 54 male; 55.4 female
Per capita GDP $1,700
Labor force in agriculture 68%

Urban 46.8%
Infant mortality rate per 1,000 live births 69.8
HIV rate 3.9%
Unemployment rate NA
Arable land 10%

Agriculture   yams, oil palm fruit, cassava, coffee, cocoa beans, bananas, corn, rice, chickens, cattle, sheep, goats, pigs

Natural resources   oil, natural gas, diamonds, manganese, iron ore, cobalt, bauxite, copper, gold, fish

Industries   foodstuffs, beverages, wood products, oil refining, truck and bus assembly, textiles, fertilizer

History   In the 15th century this region had numerous settlements and attracted French and Portuguese merchants in search of ivory and slaves. A French protectorate from 1842, it gained independence in 1960, as Ivory Coast. It changed its name to Côte d'Ivoire in 1985. In the 1990s fighting began between rebels and the government. In 2002 the country began to divide politically into north and south; civil war began, lasting nearly five years. In 2007 measures were taken to unify the country. A UN peacekeeping force was here from 2004.

Influences on food   The introduction of New World foods such as cassava, corn, tomato, peanuts, chili pepper, and potato greatly influenced food customs. Native African foods include watermelon, black-eyed peas, and okra. A French protectorate for over a century, this country retains a French influence. The Atlantic Ocean and rivers provide fish. The land in this tropical country produces food crops and grass for animal herds and game. Daily fare is mostly grains and starchy vegetables with legumes, greens, and fish. Thick, sticky, spicy food is liked.

Bread and cereals   Corn, rice, millet, sorghum, wheat; porridge, rice dishes, dough balls, French bread.

Meat, poultry, fish   Chicken, beef, lamb and mutton, goat, pork, fish (fresh, smoked, salted, or dried), guinea fowl, rabbit, game, eggs. Chicken is a popular, prestigious food.

Insects   Termites (often called white ants), locusts.

Dairy products   Milk, sour milk, buttermilk, curds, whey, cheese.

Fats and oils   Palm oil, peanut oil, shea oil, coconut oil. Palm oil, the predominant cooking fat, is red.

Legumes   Beans, peanuts (groundnuts), black-eyed peas (a variety of cowpeas), locust beans (carob).

Vegetables   Yams, cassava, plantains, taro, green leaves, okra, bitter leaf, melokhia (crain crain), tomatoes, sweet potatoes, potatoes, eggplant, pumpkin, onions, red chili peppers, cucumbers, bell peppers.

Fruit   Bananas, coconut, pineapple, akee apples, baobab, watermelon, guavas, lemons, limes, mangoes, papaya.

Nuts and seeds   Palm kernels, cashews, kola nuts, watermelon seeds (egusi), sesame seeds, mango seeds. Nuts and seeds thicken and flavor sauces.

Seasonings   Salt, hot red chili peppers, tomatoes, onions, dried baobab leaves, thyme, "African nutmeg," cocoa.

Dishes   Most foods are boiled or fried and chunks are dipped in sauce and eaten by hand. Sauces: peanut (ground and pounded peanuts); palaver sauce (green leaves); and fréjon (bean or black-eyed pea purée, coconut milk, and sometimes carob or cocoa). Fufu (a paste of boiled and pounded starchy vegetables or boiled corn flour), formed into bite-size scoops or balls to eat stew. Stews: fish and meat; chicken and peanut; and root vegetables, okra, or peanuts with bits of fish, chicken, or beef. Gari (roasted cassava meal). Adalu (mashed vegetables). Jollof rice (boiled rice with palm oil or tomato, various meats, and spices). Chicken or fish marinated in lemon or lime juice, grilled, fried with onions, simmered with the marinade, and served with boiled rice. Baked chicken with tomato, onion, okra, and peanut sauce. Egg topped with ground chilies and baked on mashed yam.

Sweets   Honey, sugar, kanya (peanut candy), baked bananas with honey, sugar, or coconut, fried dough balls.

Beverages   Coffee, cocoa, beer, red zinger (herbal tea made from flower pods of roselle, *Hibiscus sabdariffa*).

Meals and service   Two meals a day served family style is typical. Snacking is common.

Street food and snacks   Spiced kabobs, fried fish, plantain chips, fried bean balls, sweet porridge.

CROATIA
Republic of Croatia

Geography   Croatia is in southeastern Europe on the Balkan Peninsula, bordering the Adriatic Sea. It is a former Yugoslav republic. Croatia has fertile agricultural plains in the east and low mountains along the Adriatic coast.

Major Languages	Ethnic Groups		Major Religions	
Croatian (official)	Croat	90%	Roman Catholic	88%
Serbian	Serb	5%	Orthodox	4%
	Other	5%	None	5%
			Other	3%

Population density per sq. mi. 206.2
Literacy rate 98.7%
Life expectancy 71.5 male; 79.3 female
Per capita GDP $15,500
Labor force in agriculture 2.7%

Urban 56.5%
Infant mortality rate per 1,000 live births 6.5
HIV rate <0.1%
Unemployment rate 9.5%
Arable land 26%

Agriculture   corn, sugar beets, wheat, sunflower seed, barley, chickens, pigs, sheep, cattle, goats

Natural resources   oil, coal, bauxite, iron ore, calcium, gypsum, natural asphalt, silica, mica, clays, salt, hydropower, fish

Industries   chemicals, plastics, machine tools, fabricated metal, electronics

History   Once the Roman province Pannonia, Croatia was settled in the 7th century by the Croats, south Slavic people. They converted to Christianity between the 7th and 9th centuries. In 925 they established a kingdom, which flourished in the 11th century, and joined Hungary in 1102. The Croats separated from the Slavs and retained autonomy under Hungary. In 1848–1849 the area became the Austrian crown land of Croatia and Slavonia. It joined other Yugoslav areas to form the Kingdom of Serbs, Croats, and Slovenes in 1918. When Yugoslavia was reorganized in 1929, Croatia and Slavonia became Savska County, which in 1939 united with Primorje country to form Croatia County. A state from 1941 to 1945 and a republic from 1946, Croatia declared independence from Yugoslavia In 1991. Fighting between ethnic Serbs and Croats occurred; a peace accord was signed in 1995; and the last Serb-held enclave, East Slavonia, returned to Croatian control in 1998. In 2007 Croatia began trials of several suspected war criminals from its wars in the 1990s. The economy and tourism continue to grow.

Influences on food   Croatia's fertile plains support agriculture, producing grains, sugar beets, and livestock. The Adriatic Sea coastline provides fish. Influences include Latin and Roman Catholic, Slavic, and Austrian, as well as that of northern neighbors Slovenia and Hungary. Central Europe influenced the cuisine of Croatia and other north Balkan countries. Most Croatians are Roman Catholic and frequently consume pork and fish, as well as special fare at Christmas and Easter. Popular foods include pork, lamb, and veal; cool weather fruits and vegetables such as apples and cabbage; dairy foods; and bread.

Bread and cereals   Wheat, corn, barley, rice; porridge, rice dishes, bread (usually leavened wheat loaves), wheat flour in pies, turnovers, filo dough (paper-thin pastry), dumplings, and pasta.

Meat, poultry, fish   Chicken, eggs, pork, lamb, beef and veal, goat, fish; ham, bacon.

Dairy products   Milk (cow, sheep, goat), buttermilk, cream, sour cream, whipped cream, cheese. Kashkaval (hard tangy ewe's milk cheese) is called the cheddar of the Balkans.

Fats and oils   Butter, margarine, vegetable oils, olive oil.

Legumes   Chickpeas, fava beans, black beans, white beans, lentils. Legumes are important.

Vegetables   Potatoes, cabbage, cucumbers, mushrooms, tomatoes, eggplant, onions, olives; sauerkraut.

Fruit   Apples, berries, cherries, peaches, pears, plums, apricots, grapes, lemons. Fruit juice is popular.

Nuts and seeds   Almonds, walnuts, pistachios, sunflower seeds, poppy seeds.

Seasonings   Garlic, dill, mint, cardamom, cinnamon, oregano, parsley, pepper, paprika, lemon juice.

Dishes   Soups such as lentil soup. Meat and vegetable casseroles. Pork or veal stew with paprika. Fish dishes. Dumplings filled with meat or fruit. Boiled or baked stuffed vegetables such as cabbage stuffed with seasoned meat or rice. Pies and turnovers filled with meat, cheese, eggs, vegetables, nuts, or dried fruit. A Balkan specialty, moussaka (baked minced lamb, eggplant, onions, and tomato sauce).

Special occasion foods   The Easter meal often includes lamb or ham and pogaca (bread topped with painted hard-boiled eggs). The Christmas Eve meal features cod. A Christmas dish is stuffed cabbage and sauerkraut.

Sweets   Honey, sugar, fruit preserves, fruit compote, cheese- or fruit-filled dumplings and strudels, baklava (filo dough layered with nut filling that is then soaked in flavored syrup). A Balkan specialty, slatko (fruits simmered in thick syrup). A northern Balkan treat, potica (sweet yeast bread rolled in a walnut, butter, cream, and egg filling).

Beverages   Coffee (strong, sweet), tea, buttermilk, fruit juice, wine, plum brandy (sljivovica).

Meals   Three meals a day, with the main meal at midday, and frequent snacking is typical.

Street foods and snacks   Pastries and ice cream are sold by vendors in urban areas throughout the day. Small meat balls (kofta), pickles, salads, coffee, wine, and plum brandy are evening snacks in cafes and coffeehouses.

CUBA
Republic of Cuba

Geography   Cuba is 90 miles (145 km) south of Florida in the Caribbean Sea. It is the largest and westernmost island of the West Indies. The coastline is approximately 2,500 miles. Low hills and fertile valleys cover more than half of the country. The north coast is steep and rocky; the south coast is low and marshy.

Major Language	Ethnic Groups		Major Religions	
Spanish (official)	White	65%	Roman Catholic	47%
	Mulatto and mestizo	25%	Protestant	5%
	Black	10%	None	22%
			Other including Santeria	26%

Population density per sq. mi. 266.9
Literacy rate 99.8%
Life expectancy 75 male; 79.6 female
Per capita GDP $4,500
Labor force in agriculture 20%

Urban 75.8%
Infant mortality rate per 1,000 live births 5.9
HIV rate 0.1%
Unemployment rate 1.9%
Arable land 28%

Agriculture   sugarcane/raw sugar, tomatoes, plantains, tobacco, citrus, coffee, rice, potatoes, beans, chickens, cattle, sheep, pigs, goats

Natural resources   cobalt, nickel, iron ore, chromium, copper, salt, timber, silica, oil, fish

Industries   sugar, oil, tobacco, chemicals, construction, nickel

History   Arawak Indians lived here when Columbus came in 1492. They died from diseases brought by sailors and settlers. Cuba's name is derived from the Indian Cubanacan. Spain established settlements here by 1511 and frequented Havana's excellent harbor. From the 18th century a sugar plantation economy developed. African slaves were brought until slavery was abolished in 1886 to work the sugarcane plantations. Sugar remains the chief product and export. Except for British occupation of Havana (1762–1763), Spain controlled Cuba until 1898, when, after the sinking of the *USS Maine* in Havana harbor, the United States declared war on

Spain and defeated it in the Spanish-American War. After three years of U.S. occupation, Cuba gained independence in 1902. U.S. and other foreign investments began to dominate the economy. In 1952 Batista established a dictatorship. Fidel Castro led guerrilla fighting and took power in 1959. Sweeping economic and social changes began; lands, banks, and companies were nationalized. Some 700,000 Cubans emigrated, mostly to the United States. In 1962 the USSR brought nuclear missiles to Cuba; after a warning from U.S. president John F. Kennedy they were removed. The collapse of the communist bloc in the late 1980s shook Cuba's economy, dependent on aid from other communist countries. The economy, aided by tourism, gradually improved during the 1990s. In 2002 the United States began using its naval base on a leased site at Guantánamo Bay to detain prisoners captured in Afghanistan. In 2004 new U.S. sanctions limited Cuban exiles' visits and remittances. In 2006 Fidel Castro yielded power to his brother Raul. In 2007 presidents of Cuba and Venezuela signed agreements for development projects (e.g., ethanol plants), and Venezuela's state oil company announced that it would explore for offshore oil in Cuban waters. Hurricanes in 2008 devastated the sugar crop.

Influences on food   West Indies, the chain of islands between Florida and Trinidad, and the Caribbean islands are not synonymous, but the two terms are often used interchangeably. In the largest island, Cuba, the indigenous Arawak almost disappeared following the Spanish conquest, leaving only traces of their foodways. They ate a wide variety of fish and seafood. Spanish control for almost four centuries left strong influence on food customs. The Spanish brought new foods such as rice, beef, pork, lard, and olives. Slaves from Africa and indentured laborers brought other influences. This tropical island has abundant fish, seafood, fruits, and vegetables.

Bread and cereals   Rice, corn, wheat; Cuban bread (crisp roll made from wheat flour), cassava bread (a fried flat loaf made of grated cassava), fried cornmeal cakes, rice dishes.

Meat, poultry, fish   Chicken, beef, lamb, pork, goat, fish and seafood (snapper, salt cod, lobster, sea turtle, land crabs), eggs, iguana, large frogs; ham, sausage.

Dairy products   Cow's milk (fresh, condensed, evaporated), aged cheeses.

Fats and oils   Lard, salt pork, olive oil, butter, vegetable oil, coconut oil and cream.

Legumes   Black beans (the specialty), chickpeas (garbanzo beans), kidney beans, red beans.

Vegetables   Tomatoes, plantains, potatoes, cassava, yams, malanga (a mild tuber), sweet potatoes, greens (taro, callaloo, poke weed, nightshade), avocados, squash, sweet peppers, okra, onions, olives.

Fruit   Citrus, bananas, coconut, mangoes, papaya, pineapple, akee (fruit of a West Indian tree; the edible part is the fleshy seed coat surrounding three black poisonous seeds), guavas, cashew apples, passion fruit, raisins.

Nuts and seeds   Almonds, cashew nuts, annatto (achiote) seeds.

Seasonings   Salt, black pepper, chilies, onion, garlic, annatto (achiote) seeds, coconut cream, cocoa, allspice (pimento), coriander, saffron, cinnamon, cumin, capers, rum. Annatto oil, made by simmering annatto seeds in vegetable oil, is used to give a red-orange color and mild flavor to meat, poultry, and seafood.

Dishes   Simmered black beans. Simmered rice. Moros y Cristianos (Moors and Christians: black beans and rice cooked together). One-pot dishes: callaloo (green leaves of several plants plus garlic, herbs, usually some other vegetables and coconut milk, and perhaps salt pork, salt beef, salt cod, or crab); pepper pot (stew of various vegetables and bits of pork or beef, highly seasoned with crushed peppercorns); and chowders (hearty soups often containing seafood). Spicy soups. Chili sauces. Escabeche (a fish fried then sauced or marinated to be sweet and sour). Ceviche (raw fish marinated in lemon or lime juice with olive oil and spices; the citrus juice denatures the protein, an effect similar to cooking). Dried salt cod fritters. Akee simmered, baked, or fried. Foo-foo (balls of mashed cassava or plantains). Roast pork. Grilled beefsteak.

Ropa vieja (spicy beef strips). Brazo gitano (cassava pastry filled with corned beef). Fried meat, poultry, or fish. Langosta criolla (lobster Creole: lobster tail briefly fried and then cooked a few minutes in white wine, tomatoes, onions, sweet green peppers, and chili). Baked red snapper with capers, olives, garlic, and onions or with lime juice, herbs, spices, mustard, and ketchup.

Specialty Black bean soup (simmered dried black beans blended with chicken stock to a coarse purée, mixed with chopped onion and garlic cooked in annatto oil, chopped ham or sausage, chopped tomato, vinegar, cumin, and black pepper, and simmered to heat throughout), served with side dishes of rice and chopped raw onion.

Practically a national dish Picadillo (spiced boiled beef seasoned with sauce of tomato and chili pepper), garnished with olives and raisins and served with boiled rice or fried plantains, or topped with fried eggs.

Sweets Sugarcane, raw and unrefined sugar, molasses, sugar, fresh fruit, flan (custard), coquimol (coconut cream sauce), mango or papaya ambrosia, rice pudding, ice cream, pastries.

Beverages Coffee often mixed with milk (café con leche), milk, soft drinks, beer, rum, daiquiri (lime juice, sugar, rum, and ice, shaken and strained; named after the Cuban town where it was invented in 1896), Cuba libre (rum and cola with lemon slice).

Meals Breakfast: coffee with milk, bread, and perhaps egg, cereal, and fruit. Lunch: rice and beans with meat if affordable. Dinner: soup, rice and beans with meat, bread, vegetables, milk when available, and perhaps dessert.

Snacks Fresh fruit, sweetened fruit juice over shaved ice, coffee with milk. Snacking is common among children.

CYPRUS
Republic of Cyprus

Geography The third largest island in the Mediterranean Sea, Cyprus lies off the southern coast of Turkey. It has a wide fertile central plain between two mountain ranges running east and west.

Major Languages	Ethnic Groups		Major Religions	
Greek (both	Greek	77%	Greek Orthodox	78%
Turkish official)	Turkish	18%	Muslim	18%
English	Other	5%	Other	4%

Population density per sq. mi. 222.2
Literacy rate 97.7%
Life expectancy 75.8 male; 80.7 female
Per capita GDP $23,735
Labor force in agriculture 8.5%

Urban 69.3%
Infant mortality rate per 1,000 live births 6.8
HIV rate NA
Unemployment NA
Arable land 11%

Agriculture potatoes, grapes, olives, citrus, vegetables, barley, chickens, pigs, goats, sheep, cattle
Natural resources copper, pyrites, asbestos, gypsum, timber, salt, marble, clay, earth pigment, fish
Industries tourism, food and beverage processing, cement and gypsum, textiles, light chemicals, metal products
History Cyprus, the site of early Phoenician and Greek colonies, was ruled by the Ottoman Empire from 1571 to 1878, when a large Turkish colony settled on it. Britain took control in 1878, annexed it in World War I, and made it a British colony in 1925. The Greek population sought union

with Greece, the Turkish minority opposed, and violence broke out in 1955–1956. Cyprus became Independent in 1960. The National Guard, led by Greek army officers, seized the government in 1974; Turkey invaded. In 1975 Turkish Cypriots voted to form a separate Turkish Cypriot state; Greeks had been expelled from the Turkish-controlled area and were replaced by Turks, some from Turkey. In 1983 Turkish-Cypriot leaders declared independence for Turkish Republic of Northern Cyprus; the state is not recognized internationally. Conflict has continued and the UN peacekeeping mission has remained in place to the present. In 2003 Turkish Cyprus opened its border with Greek Cyprus for the first time since partition. In 2004 Turkish Cypriots approved a reunification plan but Greek Cypriots rejected it. Cyprus became a full member of the European Union (EU) in 2004. In 2007 Cypriots from both sides routinely crossed the border to shop and work, and some obstacles to pedestrian crossing were removed by both the Turkish Cypriots and the Cypriot government. EU membership stimulated the economy on both sides, and tourism revenues increased. Cyprus's first communist president was elected in 2008.

Influences on food   Influences on Cyprus's cuisine include Greece, Turkey, Byzantine cookery, the surrounding Mediterranean Sea, nearby Arab countries, and the Greek Orthodox and Islam religions. Cyprus's cuisine resembles that of Greece, Turkey, Lebanon, and Syria. Vegetables, pulses, and wheat bread are eaten frequently, and spices are used generously. Greek Cypriot cuisine resembles Greek cuisine. Turkish Cypriot cuisine resembles Turkish cuisine. Greek Orthodox faithful often eat plain boiled pulses during Lent and special dishes for Easter. Islam forbids consumption of pork or alcohol.

Bread and cereals   Barley, wheat, rice; leavened and flat breads such as pita (thin, round, with hollow center) and lavash (a larger crisp bread), pies, filo dough (paper-thin sheets of pastry), wheat kernels, rice dishes.

Meat, poultry, fish   Chicken, pork, goat, lamb, beef, fish and seafood, eggs.

Dairy products   Milk (goat, sheep, cow), buttermilk, yogurt, cream, cheese (especially feta, a white cheese).

Fats and oils   Olive oil, nut oil, corn oil, vegetable oil, butter, clarified butter (ghee), sesame oil.

Legumes   Chickpeas, lentils, yellow split peas, black-eyed peas.

Vegetables   Potatoes, olives, eggplant, greens (grape leaves, taro leaves, mallow shoots, Swiss chard, rage), cucumbers, tomatoes, onions, green peppers, parsley, celery.

Fruit   Grapes, citrus especially lemons, dates, figs, apricots, cherries, currants, melons, pomegranates, raisins.

Nuts and seeds   Almonds, pistachios, walnuts, hazelnuts, pine nuts, sesame seeds, fenugreek seeds.

Seasonings   Garlic, verjuice (juice of unripe lemons), mint, cardamom, coriander, cumin, pepper, cinnamon, anise, nutmeg, allspice, oregano, saffron, other spices, rosewater, orange blossom water.

Dishes   Boiled chickpeas or lentils with coriander and cumin; also used in dips and soups. Boiled greens. Salad of greens, tomato, cucumber, olives, and lemon juice and olive oil dressing. Rice pilav. Tavas (cubed beef or lamb, potatoes, tomatoes, and cinnamon; covered and roasted slowly). Afelia (casserole of pork, red wine, crushed coriander seeds, and cinnamon). Grilled meats, especially sheftalia (a spicy sausage made of pork or lamb wrapped in caul, the fat membrane around the intestines). Kabobs. Fried meats. Fried meat- or cheese-filled pastry. Filo dough layered with spinach and feta filling and baked. Omelet containing sautéed greens. Greek Cypriot dishes: egg-and-lemon sauces added to chicken and fish soups and casseroles; grilled and fried fish; pies; and breads such as elioti (made with olives and olive oil). Dishes reminiscent of ancient Greece: louvana (yellow split-pea purée); and trachanas (or tarhana: cracked wheat boiled with milk, rolled in thick bread crumbs, sun dried, stored until winter, and then made into a porridge-like soup). Labor-intensive and intricate dishes: koubes (koupepia, or dolmas: vegetables stuffed with a meat mixture or rice, often including greens); sweet-and-savory Easter cheese pies (flaounes). Arab dishes: hummus (chickpea dip); kibbeh (cracked wheat around a stuffing of a fried mixture of spicy minced meat, onions, and parsley), called koupes (cups).

Sweets   Honey, sugar, syrup, fruit, fig and apricot compote, gliko (fruit preserve in syrup), loukoumades (or jalebi: deep-fried batter soaked in syrup), baklava (crisp syrup- or honey-soaked pastry made with filo dough layered with a nut filling), candy (lokum, or Turkish delight: candy made from syrup and corn flour with citrus, mint, or rosewater, cut into cubes and rolled in powdered sugar).

Beverages   Tea often sweetened and with mint, coffee often sweetened and with cardamom, anise-flavored aperitifs (ouzo, raki), beer, wine, brandy.

Meals   Breakfast: bread with cheese, olives, or jam and coffee or tea. Main meal (usually at midday): mezze (appetizers such as cheese, olives, fish roe dip, hummus with pita bread, stuffed grape leaves, lamb kebabs) with ouzo, raki, or wine, meat dish, yogurt or cheese, and fruit. Late afternoon/early evening (when friends drop by): sweets and ouzo, raki, or coffee. Light supper (in late evening): similar to breakfast, soup, or leftovers.

Snacks   Fruits, kourabiedes (butter cookies), coffee or tea.

CZECH REPUBLIC

Geography   This country is in east central Europe. It is a plateau ringed by mountains, with two main rivers. Bohemia is in the west, Moravia in the east.

Major Languages	Ethnic Groups		Major Religions	
Czech (official)	Czech	90%	Roman Catholic	27%
Slovak	Moravian	4%	Protestant	2%
	Slovak	2%	Unaffiliated	59%
	Other	4%	Other	12%

Population density per sq. mi. 342.6
Literacy rate 99%
Life expectancy 73.3 male; 80.1 female
Per capita GDP $24,200
Labor force in agriculture 4.1%

Urban 73.5%
Infant mortality rate per 1,000 live births 3.8
HIV rate NA
Unemployment rate 7.1%
Arable land 39%

Agriculture   wheat, sugar beets, barley, potatoes, hops, fruit, chickens, pigs, cattle, sheep, goats, fish
Natural resources   coal, kaolin, clay, graphite, timber, fish
Industries   metallurgy, machinery and equipment, motor vehicles, glass, armaments
History   Slavic tribes settled in this region probably about the 5th century. In the 9th century Bohemia and Moravia were part of the Great Moravian Empire. Later they became part of the Holy Roman Empire. Prague was the cultural center of central Europe in the 14th century. Bohemia and Hungary became part of Austria-Hungary. The Republic of Czechoslovakia was born in 1918 through the union of Bohemia and Moravia with Slovakia. In 1939 Hitler dissolved Czechoslovakia, made protectorates of Bohemia and Moravia, and supported Slovakia's independence. In 1948 Czechoslovakia became the Czechoslovak Socialist Republic. In 1968 Soviet troops invaded Czechoslovakia. In 1989 large-scale protests resulted in Communist Party leadership resignation. Havel was elected president; the country was renamed the Czech and Slovak Federal Republic; in 1993 it split into the Czech Republic and Slovakia, with Moravia remaining in the former. Floods in 1997 and 2002 caused extensive damage. Havel left office in 2003 after 13 years as president of the Czech Republic. The country became a member of NATO in 1999 and of the EU in 2004. In 2008 Czech and U.S. leaders signed an agreement allowing construction of a radar station southeast of Prague as part of a U.S. missile-defense system in Eastern Europe.

Influences on food   The Czech and Slovak Republics were one country, Czechoslovakia, for most of the 20th century and share a culinary history. They became separate countries in 1993. The western part of Czechoslovakia was formerly Bohemia and became the Czech Republic. Neighboring countries Poland, Germany, Austria, and Slovakia have influenced Czech cuisine and have been influenced by it. Bohemia was famous for cookery skills and provided cooks for Vienna, capital of the Austro-Hungarian Empire, to which Bohemia belonged. Czech cuisine was also influenced by Hungary (e.g., goulash). Religion influences the food customs, for example, special foods for the Christian holidays Christmas and Easter. The Czech Republic has rich agricultural land, also influencing its food. Czech cuisine is robust, emphasizing bread, dumplings, root vegetables, cabbage, meat especially sausage, soups, and dairy products.

Bread and cereals   Wheat, barley, rye; bread (usually dark and usually served at all meals), dumplings (knedliky), yeast buns, strudel. Dumplings range from huge loaf-sized ones, served in slices with stews, to tiny liver dumplings, traditionally served in soup by the bride to her new husband; they include ham, cheese, and fruit ones.

Meat, poultry, fish   Chicken, pork, beef and veal, lamb, kid, fish (trout, eel, carp), eggs; ham, bacon, sausage (klobása) such as.jaternice (pork) and jelita (a blood sausage). Meats are often extended by grinding and stewing.

Dairy products   Milk (cow, sheep), cream, sour cream, cottage cheese, cheese.

Fats and oils   Butter, bacon, lard, olive oil, vegetable oil.

Legumes   Kidney beans, lentils, navy beans, split peas.

Vegetables   Potatoes, other root vegetables, cabbage, onions, mushrooms, cucumbers; sauerkraut, pickles.

Fruit   Apples, cherries, grapes, plums, apricots, raisins, prunes, sultanas (large grapes).

Nuts and seeds   Almonds, caraway seeds, poppy seeds. Poppy seeds are often used in cakes and pastries.

Seasonings   Onions, salt, black pepper, paprika, cinnamon, sour cream, vinegar, mustard, horseradish.

Dishes   Párky (steamed or boiled sausage). Simmered dumplings. Potato dumplings. Falsche (false) soups, made with vegetable stock instead of meat stock. Potato and mushroom soup. Stewed red or white cabbage with caraway seeds. Mashed potatoes. Cabbage leaves stuffed with seasoned ground meat. Hearty stews: goulash (cubed meat, onion, and paprika and other spices covered and simmered with a small amount of liquid); dušené telecí na kmíně (veal, caraway seeds, and mushrooms) served with noodles. Lungenbraten (roast fillet of beef). Svíčková na sonetane (beef roast with sour cream sauce). Mehlspeisen (foods made with flour): some savory and many sweet items (dumplings, yeast pies, noodles, pancakes, and doughs and pastes combined with vegetables, fruit, or soft cheese and cream, butter, bacon, jam, poppy seeds, and honey). Topfenknödel (cottage cheese dumplings). Liptauer cheese (made with cottage cheese, butter, sour cream, paprika, black pepper, salt, caraway seeds, mustard, capers, and onions).

Special occasion foods   Roast goose stuffed with sauerkraut and served with bread dumplings. Christmas foods: carp four ways (breaded and fried, baked with prunes, cold in aspic, and in soup) and kolaches (round yeast buns filled with poppy seeds, dried fruit, or cottage cheese). Easter foods: baked ham or roasted kid and mazanec (round loaf of sweet yeast dough with raisins and almonds).

Sweets   Sugar, honey, jam, strudel (pastry of thin sheets of dough around a soft filling), yeast buns, dumplings filed with cherries, plum jam, or apricots. Topfenpalatshcinken (thick pancakes with curdled sweet cream). škubánky (potato dumplings baked in butter and served with cinnamon sugar). Makovy kolac (poppy seed cake with sultanas). Bulblanina (bubble cake, a sponge with fruit baked in it). Streuselkuchen (crumb-topped cake).

Beverages   Coffee, tea, milk, hot chocolate, beer, wine. The Czechs are known for pilsner beer, which tastes bitter and is light in color and body. Coffeehouses and sweet treats are a Bohemian tradition.

Meals   Three meals a day with snacks is typical.

D

DENMARK
Kingdom of Denmark

Geography   Denmark is in northern Europe between the North and Baltic seas. The smallest of the Scandinavian countries, it occupies the Jutland Peninsula and about 500 neighboring islands, 100 inhabited. It is flat lowland.

Major Languages	Ethnic Groups		Major Religions	
Danish (official)	Danish	92%	Evangelical Lutheran (official)	95%
Faroese	Other	8%	Other Christian	3%
Greenlandic (Inuit dialect)			Muslim	2%
English (predominant second language)				

Population density per sq. mi. 335.1
Literacy rate 99%
Life expectancy 75.8 male; 80.6 female
Per capita GDP $37,400
Labor force in agriculture 3%

Urban 85.9%
Infant mortality rate per 1,000 live births 4.4
HIV rate 0.2%
Unemployment rate 5.0%
Arable land 53%

Agriculture   wheat, barley, sugar beets, potatoes, chickens, pigs, cattle, sheep

Natural resources   oil, natural gas, fish, salt, limestone, chalk, stone, gravel, sand

Industries   iron, steel, nonferrous metals, chemicals, food processing, machinery and transportation equipment, textiles and clothing, electronics, construction, furniture

History   From 10,000 to 1500 BCE the people evolved from a hunting/fishing society into a farming one. In ancient times Copenhagen was a fishing and trading place named Havn (port). By the end of the 8th century CE the area was called Jutland. Its mariners were among Vikings, who raided Western Europe and the British Isles from the 9th to the 11th century. Denmark was Christianized in the 10th century. The Danish kingdom was a major power until the 17th century, when it lost its land in southern Sweden. In 1815, for supporting Napoleon, it lost Norway to Sweden. Neutral in World War I, Denmark was occupied by the Nazis from 1940 to 1945 in World War II. Denmark was a founding member of NATO (1949). In 1993 voters ratified the European Union document. In 2000 they voted not to join the euro currency zone. In 1997 the island of Zealand, on which Copenhagen stands, was connected to the central island, Fenen, by a rail tunnel and bridge. In 2007 Denmark removed its troops from Iraq, but it increased its troops in Afghanistan in 2008. It has a strong economy, no foreign debt, and a budget surplus. **The Faroe Islands**, in the North Atlantic, are an administrative division of Denmark. Fish is the primary export. **Greenland** (Kalaallit Nunaat), a huge island between the North Atlantic and the Polar Sea, was a colony of Denmark that was approved for home rule in 1979. Most (84%) of its land is ice capped. Fish is the principal export.

Influences on food   Denmark's cuisine has been influenced by its southern neighbor Germany. Denmark shares with nearby Netherlands traditions of dairy farming and simplicity of food. France influenced the food of the wealthier classes. Denmark, a green and rolling land, has foods of the field and pasture, especially from pigs and dairy cattle. The North Sea and Baltic Sea provide fish and seafood. The Danes had important trade with the Orient in past centuries, which also influenced their food.

Bread and cereals   Wheat, barley, rye, oats, rice; bread (dark rye and white wheat), porridge, cereal soup, pastry.

Meat, poultry, fish   Chicken, pork, beef and veal, lamb, fish and seafood (herring, salmon, eels, shrimp, oysters, green-salted haddock, plaice, anchovies), eggs; bacon, ham, sausage.

Dairy products   Milk, sour milk, buttermilk, cream, sour cream, cheese (many types including Tybo, mellow and sometimes with caraway seeds; Danbo, firm and bland; Havarti, semi-soft and slightly acidic; Crèma Danin, soft and rich; Danish Swiss; Danish Blue; Danish Brie; and Danish Camembert).

Fats and oils   Butter, lard, margarine, salt pork, rapeseed oil.

Legumes   Yellow split peas, green split peas, lima beans.

Vegetables   Potatoes, cabbage (red and green), rape (of the cabbage family), kale, beets, carrots, cucumbers, celery, radishes, mushrooms, onions, leeks, chives, parsley; pickled beets or cucumbers.

Fruit   Apples, cherries, apricots, plums, prunes, raisins, currants, raspberries, strawberries, oranges, lemons.

Nuts and seeds   Almonds, caraway seeds, rape seeds, mustard seeds.

Seasonings   Dill, mustard, vinegar, horseradish, cardamom, ginger, cloves, curry.

Condiment   Fish mustard (fiskesennep), coarsely ground yellow and brown mustard seeds with vinegar and salt.

Dishes   Smoked Baltic herring with radish slices and chives on buttered rye bread. Postej (liver paste of pork or calf's liver with anchovy). Porridges: rice with butter; barley simmered in buttermilk. Soups: yellow split pea; beer and rye crusts. Boiled potatoes, sometimes served with salt pork gravy. Kale boiled, chopped, and served with a cream sauce. Braised cabbage with caraway seeds. Stuffed cabbage (cabbage head hollowed out, filled with minced pork and veal, and simmered). Frikadeller (meat patties of ground pork and veal, bread crumbs, onions, and eggs fried in butter). Plaice fried in butter and served with sour cream and lemon sauce. Roast pork loin stuffed with apples and prunes, served with braised red cabbage with sliced sour apple. Sautéed mushrooms. Simmered chicken stuffed with parsley and butter, served with sauce of heavy cream stirred into the drippings.

Specialties   Exported bacon and canned hams. Smørrebrød (bread and butter), open sandwiches of rye bread, butter, and various toppings (herring, cheese, liver paste, hard-cooked eggs, or sausage) or of white bread and shrimp. Danish pastries (wienerbrød, brought by bakers from Vienna), flaky pastry (made from yeast dough containing milk and egg into which butter has been folded) filled with butter creamed with sugar and almonds, apricots, or other ingredients. Danish pastries are eaten at any time, often with coffee or tea.

Sweets   Sugar, honey, molasses, cold fruit soups, butter cookies, Danish pastries. Rødgrød med fløde (red fruit pudding with cream), thickened raspberries or strawberries with sweet cream poured in. Oatmeal cakes and cold buttermilk soup. Danish apple cake made from applesauce layered with buttered bread crumbs and often topped with whipped cream. Danish Christmas fruit loaf made from rich yeast dough and candied fruits.

Beverages   Coffee, tea, milk, beer, aquavit (water of life, distilled liquor sometimes flavored with caraway).

Meals   Breakfast: oatmeal porridge with milk and sugar or herring and soup. Lunch: kole board (cold table) of bread, butter, and various items for making smørrebrød (open-faced sandwiches). Dinner: herring, soup, meat or fish dish, potatoes, fruit dessert, beer. Midmorning and late afternoon: coffee with pastry.

DJIBOUTI
Republic of Djibouti

Geography   This small country is on the east coast of Africa, bordering the Red Sea and Gulf of Aden. It is mainly a sandy desert with a low coastal plain, scattered mountains, and an interior plateau. The climate is hot and dry.

Major Languages	Ethnic Groups		Major Religions	
Arabic (both	Somali	60%	Muslim (nearly all Sunni)	94%
French official)	Afar	35%	Christian (mostly Orthodox)	6%
Somali	Other	5%		
Afar				

Population density per sq. mi. 57.1
Literacy rate 67.9%
Life expectancy 41.9 male; 44.8 female
Per capita GDP $2,300
Labor force in agriculture NA

Urban 86.1%
Infant mortality rate per 1,000 live births 99.1
HIV rate 3.1%
Unemployment rate 60%
Arable land 0.04%

Agriculture   lemons, limes, dry beans, tomatoes, goats, sheep, cattle, camels

Natural resources   geothermal areas, gold, clay, granite, fish

Industries   construction, agriculture processing

History   Able from Arabia migrated here in about the third century BCE; their descendants are Afars today. Somali Issas arrived later. Islam was brought in 825 CE. Arabs controlled trade in the region until the 16th century. Between 1862 and 1900 France gained control of the area through treaties with Somali sultans; it became the French protectorate of French Somaliland in 1888 and a French overseas territory in 1945. In 1967 it was named the French Territory of the Afars and the Issas. In 1976 Afars (ethnically related to Ethiopians) and Issas (related to Somalis) clashed. Ethiopians and Somalis immigrated here up to 1977, when the country gained independence and took the name of its capital city. In the late 20th century Djibouti received refugees from the Ethiopia-Somali war. In 2002 it became a U.S. military base to combat terrorism; French and U.S. troops are based here. Camp Lemonier is the only official U.S. military presence in Africa. The economic mainstay is French aid, with assistance from Arab countries.

Influences on food   French control for about a century until 1977 left some influence on Djibouti food. Other influences include Ethiopian, Somali, Arab, and religion. Djibouti food is similar to that of neighboring Ethiopia, Somalia, and Eritrea. For example, usual bread is flatbread as in Ethiopia, and red chili pepper is used as in all the neighboring countries. Traditional Somali foods are rice (brees) with meat (hibbib) and chili. Afars eat a typical nomadic diet of grain and dairy products. Neither Muslims nor Christians here eat pork, and Somalis avoid chicken and eggs. Lentils are popular during fasting periods required by the Christian Orthodox church.

Bread and cereals   Rice, millet (including teff), sorghum, barley, wheat, corn, oats; rice dishes, flatbread (usually like injera from Ethiopia, cooked like a huge pancake on a griddle, covered, resulting in a large circular loaf).

Meat, poultry, fish   Beef, goat, lamb and mutton, camel, fish and seafood.

Dairy products   Milk (cow, goat, sheep, camel), cheese.

Fat   Butter (usually clarified and flavored with onions, garlic, ginger, and other spices).

Legumes   Beans especially fava beans, lentils, chickpeas, split peas, peanuts.

Vegetables   Tomatoes, potatoes, plantains, kale, red chili peppers, onions, garlic.

Fruit   Lemons, limes, dates, various other fruits.

Nuts and seeds   Almonds, fenugreek seeds, sesame seeds.

Seasonings   Red hot chili peppers, onions, garlic, cayenne, cardamom (in almost all stews), ginger; hot red pepper spice mixture (allspice, cardamom, cayenne, cinnamon, cloves, coriander, cumin, fenugreek, ginger, nutmeg, and black pepper), spiced butter.

Dishes   Boiled rice. Anan geil (millet gruel with camel milk and honey). Lentil salad. Garlic- and ginger-flavored vegetable casserole. Ful (bean stew). Wat (stew). Vegetarian stew of ground legumes. Thick spicy stews of lentils, chickpeas, peanuts, vegetables, and meat or fish. Meat-stuffed vegetable. Dried raw beef mixed with spiced butter. Flatbread crumbled with butter or wat.

Sweet   Honey, sugar.

Beverages   Coffee (sometimes with butter), beer (home-brewed from millet or corn), wine (made from honey).

Meals and service   Usual is one meal in the early evening, with snacking throughout the day. A typical meal includes a spicy stew, often containing beef or lamb, and flatbread or rice. Food is often served on or picked up with swatches of flatbread.

DOMINICA
Commonwealth of Dominica

Geography   Dominica is in the eastern Caribbean Sea. It is mountainous, with a ridge running north to south. It has rich deep topsoil on the leeward side, red clay on the windward coast, and numerous thermal springs.

Major Languages	Ethnic Groups		Major Religions	
English (official)	Black	87%	Roman Catholic	61%
French patois	Carib Amerindian	3%	Protestant	28%
	Mixed	9%	Other	5%
	Other	1%	None	6%

Population density per sq. mi. 249.1
Literacy rate 94%
Life expectancy 72.4 male; 78.4 female
Per capita GDP $9,000
Labor force in agriculture 40%

Urban 72.9%
Infant mortality rate per 1,000 live births 14.1
HIV Rate NA
Unemployment rate 25%
Arable land 7%

Agriculture   bananas, citrus, root crops, mangoes, coconuts, cocoa, chickens, cattle, goats, sheep, pigs

Natural resources   timber, hydropower, fish

Industries   soap, coconut oil, tourism, copra, furniture, cement blocks, shoes

History   Caribs inhabited Dominica when Columbus explored it in 1493. Britain and France claimed it until 1763, when it was ceded to Britain. It became an English colony in 1805, was granted self-government in 1967, and gained independence in 1978. In 1979 Hurricane David devastated the island and destroyed the banana plantations, the economic mainstay. In 1983 Dominica participated in the U.S.-led invasion of nearby Granada. Dominica does not have the extremes of wealth and poverty evident in other Caribbean islands. In 2002 economic austerity measures were introduced and massive protests followed. In 2007 Dominica and Venezuela began talks about Venezuela building an oil refinery in Dominica.

Influences on food   Arawak Indians, thought to be the original inhabitants, ate fish, seafood, fruits, plants, stews, cassava bread, and hot pepper sauce using foods available from the sea and this tropical island. The same foods are used here today, plus ones brought to the region by the Spanish and to Dominica by the French, the British, and African slaves. Carib Indians from further south overcame the Arawaks, and some of the remaining Caribs live on a reservation in Dominica; they are excellent fishers. British and French claims and British control for more than two centuries influenced food customs; examples include dried salt cod, biscuits, and tea. Slaves brought from Africa also influenced floodways such as the use of okra.

Bread and cereals   Corn, rice, wheat; fried cornmeal cakes, cassava bread (made from grated, squeezed, and dried cassava, fried on a griddle pancake-style, and sun dried), cassava coconut biscuits or bread (contain wheat flour, cassava, and grated coconut).

Meat, poultry, fish   Chicken, eggs, beef, goat, lamb, pork, fish and seafood (salt cod, snapper, flying fish, mangrove-tree oysters, sea turtles, sea eggs or sea urchins, lobster, crabs), large frogs.

Dairy products   Cow's milk (fresh, condensed, evaporated), cream, aged cheese.

Fats and oils   Butter, lard, coconut oil, vegetable oil.

Legumes   Kidney beans, red beans, black-eyed peas, chickpeas, pigeon peas.

Vegetables   Cassava, yams, malanga (taro-like plant with corms and green leaves), sweet potatoes, squash, plantains, breadfruit, green leaves (cassava, malanga), avocados, tomatoes, okra, onions, chilies, sweet peppers.

Fruit   Bananas, grapefruit, pomelos, mangoes, coconut, cashew apples, akee, papaya, pineapple, soursop, guavas, passion fruit, raisins.

Nuts and seeds   Almonds, cashew nuts, annatto seeds.

Seasonings   Salt, black pepper, chilies, allspice, annatto, cinnamon, garlic, coconut, cocoa, rum; pepper sauce.

Dishes   Callaloo (green leaves cooked with okra). Pepper pot (a meat stew containing boiled juice of cassava and pepper). Salt cod gundy (spread). Fried cassava or plantain chips. Fried cornmeal and okra cake. Boiled rice. Rice cooked with peas or beans.

Specialty   Fried mountain chicken (frog legs).

Sweets   Sugarcane, unrefined sugar, molasses, sugar, rum fruitcake, coconut custard pie.

Beverages   Coffee with milk, tea, iced tea usually with lime, fruit juices, soft drinks, milk, cocoa, beer, rum, passion fruit juice punch.

Carib meal   Boiled green bananas topped with egg, fried or grilled fish, and green coconut (liquid and flesh).

Snacks   Fruit, sweetened fruit juices poured over crushed ice, tea with coconut biscuits (cookies) or bread.

DOMINICAN REPUBLIC

Geography   Bordering the Caribbean Sea and the Atlantic Ocean, this country occupies the eastern two-thirds of the island of Hispaniola, sharing it with Haiti. Mountains are in center of the country, with Duarte Peak, 10,417 feet (3,175 m), the highest point in the West Indies. Cibao Valley in the north is the major agricultural area.

Major Language	Ethnic Groups		Major Religions	
Spanish (official)	White	16%	Roman Catholic	95%
	Black	11%	Other	5%
	Mixed	73%		

Population density per sq. mi. 509
Literacy rate 89.1%
Life expectancy 71.6 male; 75.2 female
Per capita GDP $7,000
Labor force in agriculture 17%

Urban 66.8%
Infant mortality rate per 1,000 live births 26.9
HIV rate 1.1%
Unemployment rate 16.2%
Arable land 22%

Agriculture   sugarcane, rice, bananas, coffee, cotton, cocoa, tobacco, beans, potatoes, corn, chickens, cattle, pigs, goats, sheep

Natural resources   nickel, bauxite, gold, silver, fish

Industries   tourism, sugar processing, mining, textiles, cement, tobacco

History   Carib and Arawak Indians inhabited the island of Hispaniola when Columbus landed on it in 1492. The city Santo Domingo, founded in 1496, is the oldest European settlement in the Western Hemisphere; the supposed ashes of Columbus lie in its cathedral. The western third of the island was ceded to France in 1697; the rest of the island was ceded to France in 1795. The eastern two thirds was returned to Spain in 1908 and declared independent in 1821. Haitian troops occupied it soon after and until 1844. A series of dictatorships followed until 1921. U.S. Marines occupied the country from 1916 to 1924, when a constitutionally elected government was installed. In 1979 and 1998 hurricanes caused extensive damage. Floods and mudslides in 2004, fire resulting from a fight between rival prison gangs in 2005, and torrential rains in 2007 killed hundreds of people. The economy grew from 2004 to 2007, but the quality of public education and public health remained poor. The government invested less in those sectors than in the new subway system for the capital.

Influences on food   The indigenous Arawak and the Carib Indians almost disappeared following the Spanish conquest. Only traces of information about their foodways remain. They ate a wide variety of fish and seafood. Spanish control for three centuries left strong influence on food customs. The Spanish brought new foods such as rice, beef, pork, lard, olives, and citrus. Columbus brought the first citrus plants to the New World, oranges that he planted on Hispaniola in 1493. The oldest kitchen in the Americas, recreated in Santo Domingo, capital of the Dominican Republic, is in the Alcazar, the palace of Columbus's son Diego; the palace was restored in 1957. Other influences were from French control for more than a century, slaves brought from Africa, and indentured laborers. This tropical island has abundant fish and seafood, fruits, and vegetables.

Bread and cereals   Rice, corn, wheat; cornbread, fried corncakes, rice dishes, cassava bread (fried flat loaf made of grated cassava), wheat flour bread, rolls, and pastry.

Meat, poultry, fish   Chicken, beef, pork, goat, lamb, fish and seafood (snapper, shrimp, salt cod, sea turtle, land crabs), eggs, iguana, large frogs; ham, sausage.

Dairy products   Cow's milk (fresh, condensed, evaporated), aged cheeses.

Fats and oils   Lard, butter, salt pork, olive oil, vegetable oil, coconut oil and cream.

Legumes   Beans (kidney, red, black), chickpeas (garbanzo beans).

Vegetables   Potatoes, cassava, yams, malanga (a mild tuber), plantains, sweet potatoes, greens (taro, callaloo, poke weed, nightshade), avocados, squash, okra, tomatoes, sweet peppers, okra, onions, olives.

Fruit   Bananas, coconut, oranges, lemons, limes, mangoes, papaya, pineapple, guavas, cashew apples, passion fruit, sour sop, tamarind, akee, raisins.

Nuts and seeds   Almonds, cashew nuts, annatto (achiote) seeds.

Seasonings   Salt, black pepper, chilies, garlic, annatto (achiote) seeds (red-orange color and mild flavor), coconut cream, cocoa, allspice (pimento), coriander, saffron, cinnamon, rum.

Dishes   Callaloo (green leaves of several plants boiled with okra). Pepper pot (stew of boiled juice of cassava, called casserep, various vegetables, and bits of pork or beef, highly seasoned with crushed peppercorns). Hearty, spicy seafood soups. Chili sauces. Escabeche (a fish fried then sauced or marinated to be sweet and sour). Ceviche (raw fish marinated in lemon or lime juice with olive oil and spices; the citrus juice denatures the protein, a similar effect to cooking). Akee simmered, baked, or fried. Mofongo (simmered or fried plantain balls). Roast pork. Fried meat, poultry, or fish such as chicharrones de pollo (chicken pieces marinated in lime juice, sprinkled with salt and black pepper, coated with flour, and deep fried). Deep-fried shrimp and potato cakes (made with mashed potatoes and chopped shrimp mixed with grated cheese and onions, and coated with egg and bread crumbs). Pastelitos (meat-filled turnovers). Simmered beans or chickpeas with lard and salt and sometimes with onions, sweet peppers, and tomatoes. Simmered rice. Fried yam cakes (grated yams mixed with butter, grated onion, chopped parsley, salt, black pepper, and eggs; dropped by tablespoons into a thin layer of hot oil and turned to cook on both sides).

A specialty   Sancocho (a pork intestine stew).

Sweets   Sugarcane, raw and unrefined sugar, molasses, sugar, fresh fruit, custard, coconut or rice pudding, sautéed or baked banana, ice cream, pastry.

Beverages   Coffee often mixed with milk (café con leche), milk, soft drinks, tea, beer, rum.

Meals   Breakfast: coffee with milk, bread, and perhaps egg, cereal, and fruit. Lunch: rice and beans with meat if affordable. Dinner: rice and beans with meat, bread, vegetables, milk when available, and perhaps dessert.

Snacks   Fresh fruit, frio-frio (fruit syrup over crushed ice), coffee with milk. Snacking is frequent among children.

E

EAST TIMOR (See TIMOR-LESTE)

ECUADOR
Republic of Ecuador

Geography   Ecuador is in northern South America, bordering the Pacific Ocean and on the Equator. Two parallel Andes Mountain ranges cross Ecuador north to south, dividing it into three zones: hot, humid coastal lowlands; temperate highlands between the ranges; and rainy, tropical eastern lowlands. Also, Ecuador includes the Galapagos Islands. Ecuador's highest peak is 20,577 feet (6,272 m).

Major Languages	Ethnic Groups		Major Religions	
Spanish (official)	Mestizo (mixed Indian & white)	65%	Roman Catholic	95%
Amerindian languages,	Amerindian	25%	Other	5%
especially Quechua	Spanish & others	7%		
	Black	3%		

Population density per sq. mi. 130.3
Literacy rate 92.6%
Life expectancy 73.9 male; 79.8 female
Per capita GDP $7,200
Labor force in agriculture 8%

Urban 63.6%
Infant mortality rate per 1,000 live births 21.4
HIV rate 0.3%
Unemployment 10.1%
Arable land 6%

Agriculture   bananas, sugarcane, oil palm fruit, coffee, cocoa, rice, potatoes, cassava, plantains, chickens, cattle, pigs, sheep, goats

Natural resources   oil, fish, timber, hydropower

Industries   oil, food processing, textiles, wood products, chemicals

History   Tribes in the northern highlands of Ecuador formed the Kingdom of Quito around 1000. It was absorbed into the Inca Empire. The region was the northern Inca Empire, conquered by Spain in 1533. Spain was defeated in 1822. Ecuador gained independence in 1830; revolts and dictatorships followed into the mid-20th century. Border disputes with Peru occurred from 1941 to 1998, when agreement was reached. Since 1972 the economy has revolved around petroleum exports. In 1987 an earthquake destroyed much of the main oil pipeline and left 20,000 people homeless. In the 1990s Indians staged protests to demand greater rights. The president imposed austerity measures in 1996, 1998, 1999, 2002, and 2004 to cope with the continuing economic crisis. In 2008 a new constitution was approved. **The Galapagos Islands**, about 600 miles to the west, is the home of huge tortoises and other unusual animals.

Influences on food   The tropical seacoast is where bananas, a chief export, are grown, supplanting cocoa when that crop was ravaged by disease. Although the equator is in Ecuador, a temperate climate occurs in the mountains where the capital Quito is located. The primitive jungle country east of the Andes has specialties including stewed monkey and alligator steak. In the Galapagos tortoises and iguana were eaten. Coastal cuisine depends heavily on green plantains and bananas, is more varied than that of the sierra, and uses unusual combinations such as pork stuffed with shrimps. Ecuador has a heritage of the Incas, who depended on corn, beans, chili peppers, and potatoes, and of the Spanish, who brought rice, olives, cattle, pig, and cheese. Ecuador shares a common heritage and cuisine with Peru, its southern neighbor. With its northern neighbor Colombia it shares the practice of using annatto (red seeds of a native tropical American tree) for color and as a spice.

Bread and cereals   Rice, corn, wheat; rice dishes, corn atole (gruel), tortillas, and dishes, bread and cake made from banana flour and mixtures of banana flour and wheat.

Meat, poultry, fish   Beef, chicken, pork, lamb, goat, fish, shrimp, eggs, guinea pig (cuy).

Dairy products   Milk, evaporated milk, cheese.

Fats and oils   Lard, butter, olive oil, palm oil.

Legumes   Beans, peanuts (ground to make sauce and used to give texture and flavor in stew).

Vegetables   Potatoes, cassava (yucca), plantains, sweet potatoes, avocados, pumpkins, chili peppers, sweet peppers, onions.

Fruit   Bananas, oranges, other tropical fruits. Banana leaves are used for wrapping as in tamales.

Nuts and seeds   Almonds, cashews, annatto seeds, pumpkin seeds.

Seasonings   Cocoa, aji (chili pepper), annatto, coriander.

Dishes   Ceviche (raw fish or shellfish marinated in orange juice with olive oil and spices), often served as an appetizer or with corn and sweet potato. Boiled potatoes. Causas (made with mashed potatoes). Ocupas (made with boiled potatoes). Llapingachos (fried potato and cheese patties), served with fried eggs in the sierra or with fried bananas on the coast, or with a sauce of ground peanuts and tomatoes. Beef flank baked with potatoes, served with peanut-tomato sauce. Lorco (potato cheese soup) served with avocado slices. Banana chips (green bananas or plantains, sliced on a slant to make oval slices, and deep fried). Egg and shrimp with almond sauce (used on many foods). Bollos (tamale-like steamed packets of plantain dough-wrapped filling of cooked chicken meat). Humitas (fresh kernel corn or cornmeal dough wrapped around meat, fish, or vegetable filling and steamed). Pork stew with sweet peppers and coriander. Salsa de aji (fresh chopped chili, onion, and salt), served at most meals.

Sweets   Sugarcane, honey, sugar, brown sugar. Bananas cut crosswise and lengthwise, fried slowly, brown sugar added and banana pieces browned on both sides, dribbled with brandy or local rum, and dusted with powdered sugar. Bananas puréed, mixed with beaten egg, and baked as a soufflè.

Beverages   Coffee, cocoa, costa (alcoholic drink traditionally made from yucca plant by women who chew and spit out the pulp to facilitate fermentation).

EGYPT
Arab Republic of Egypt

Geography   Egypt occupies the northeast corner of Africa, bordering the Mediterranean Sea and the Red Sea. It is nearly 1.5 times the size of Texas and mostly desert. The Nile River divides Egypt into two regions: hills and mountains in the east and desert in the west. Most people live in the 550-mile-long Nile Valley.

Major Languages	Ethnic Groups		Major Religions	
Arabic (official)	Egyptian (Arab,		Islam (official)	83%
English	Berber, Bedouin)	99%	Muslim (nearly all Sunni)	90%
French	Other	1%	Coptic Christian	9%
			Other	1%

Population density per sq. mi. 212.6

Literacy rate 72%

Life expectancy 69.3 male; 74.5 female

Per capita GDP $5,500

Labor force in agriculture 32%

Urban 42.6%

Infant mortality rate per 1,000 live births 28.4

HIV rate NA

Unemployment 9.3%

Arable land 3%

Agriculture   sugarcane, wheat, corn, cotton, rice, beans, fruits, vegetables, chickens, sheep, cattle, goats, pigs, camels

Natural resources   oil, natural gas, iron ore, fish, phosphates, manganese, limestone, gypsum, talc, asbestos, lead, zinc

Industries   textiles, food processing, tourism, chemicals, pharmaceuticals, hydrocarbons, construction, cement, metals

History   Egyptian history dates back to about 4000 BCE. A unified kingdom developed about 3200 BCE. It extended south into Nubia and as far north as Syria. A high culture was built on an economic base of serfdom, fertile soil, and annual flooding of the Nile. The last native dynasty fell in 341 BCE to the Persians. Later, successive rulers were Greeks, Romans, Byzantines, and Arabs. Arabs introduced Islam and the Arabic language. The ancient Egyptian language survives only in Coptic Christian liturgy. The Mamluks, a military caste of Caucasian origin, ruled from 1250 to 1517, when defeated by Ottoman Turks. Egypt was part of the Ottoman Empire from 1517 to 1914, although Britain administered it from 1882, and it was a British protectorate from 1914 to 1922. A 1952 uprising forced King Farouk to abdicate; the republic was proclaimed in 1953. The Suez Canal, linking the Mediterranean and Red seas, was built by a French company (1859–1869) and was controlled by Britain from 1875 to 1956. The Aswan High Dam, completed in 1971, provides irrigation for more than a million acres of land. When the state of Israel was proclaimed in 1948, Egypt, along with other Arab nations, invaded Israel and was defeated. Egypt and Israel engaged in 30 years of war, ending with a treaty in 1979. Conflict between Muslim fundamentalists and Christians occurred in the 1980s. Egypt supported the Allied forces in the Persian Gulf War, 1991. Islamic fundamentalist violence increased in the 1990s. Terrorist activity against the economically important tourism industry increased in the late 1990s. Bombings occurred in 2004, 2006, and 2007. The government took measures to control dissent led by the banned Muslim brotherhood in 2007. The cost of living increased 10.5%.

Influences on food   Egyptian foodways have retained continuity since ancient times and are connected with those of the Middle East. In the 7th century Islamic influence became dominant in the Middle East, bringing with it some changes in the cuisine such as no consumption of pork or alcohol. When the Turks conquered Egypt early in the 16th century they introduced more new dishes, including those using filo pastry (dough of many paper-thin layers separated by thin films of butter) and many sweet items. These introductions mainly affected the upper and middle classes. Most people continued the diet from ancient Egypt, mainly bread along with onions, beans, fish, poultry, eggs, and olive oil. A British influence on the total population is frequent consumption of tea. Most of the people live in the Nile Valley, where the Nile River supplies fish.

Bread and cereals   Wheat, corn, rice, barley; rice dishes, wheat kernels, couscous (wheat meal moistened to form small pellets), semolina (hard wheat pasta-like product), bread, filo dough pastry, pasta. The everyday bread (eish baladi) is a round flatbread with a pocket in the center, often sprinkled with the spice mixture duqqa.

Meat, poultry, fish   Chicken, lamb and mutton, beef, goat, pork, water buffalo, fish, prawns, eggs, camel, pigeons, rabbit. Fish is generally not eaten with dairy products.

Dairy products   Milk, cream, yogurt, cheese (white and a gray salty cheese called mish).

Fats and oils   Olive oil, butter, clarified butter, corn oil, nut oil.

Legumes   Broad beans (fava beans), lentils, chickpeas (garbanzo beans), peanuts.

Vegetables   Onions, eggplant, tomatoes, green leaves (e.g., melokhia; mucilaginous when cooked), green peppers, cucumbers, turnips, zucchini, okra, sweet potatoes, spinach, beets, carrots, parsley, olives.

Fruit   Grapes, dates, lemons, currants, raisins, figs, apples, cherries, pomegranates.

Nuts and seeds   Almonds, pine nuts, pistachio nuts, sesame seeds.

Seasonings   Onions, lemons, garlic, salt, black pepper, cumin, mint, coriander, cinnamon, dill, saffron, cayenne, vanilla, rosewater; duqqa (spice mixture, usually sesame and coriander seeds, cumin, salt, and pepper).

Dishes   Falafel (small fried broad bean purée patties). Pickled turnips and beets. Beid hamine (hard-boiled eggs). Baid mutajjan (fried hard-boiled eggs). Broiled prawns. Lentil soup with garlic and cumin. Feta (a bowl layered with bread in the bottom, rice, and meat, all moistened with broth and seasoned with garlic). Roasted lamb sometimes stuffed with rice, pine nuts, almonds, and currants. Shish kabob (lamb pieces cooked on a skewer). Stew of lamb, okra, and carrots. Baked fish fillets served with rice. Rice cooked by first heating in oil in which chopped onions have been browned, then adding water, covering, and simmering. Steamed couscous served with main dish such as lamb and chicken simmered in gravy with onions. Hamam mahshi (braised or roasted pigeon with crushed wheat-mint stuffing). Biram ruzz (baked chicken and rice casserole). Bamai (baked okra and ground beef). Okra or zucchini stewed in butter. Baked or simmered vegetables such as eggplant with rice-dill or rice-lamb stuffing. Sanbusak (fried meat- or cheese-filled pastry).

National dishes   Ful medames (boiled beans, usually fava beans, seasoned with olive oil, lemon juice, and garlic, often sprinkled with parsley and served with hard-boiled eggs), eaten for breakfast, main meal, or snack. Melokhia soup (chopped melokhia leaves simmered with rabbit or poultry stock, garlic, and cumin).

Special occasion food   Kahj, a sweet bread with ample butter and nuts.

Sweets   Sugarcane, honey, sugar, syrups. Date-filled filo dough pastry. Rice pudding with rosewater. Steamed couscous with sugar and peanuts. Mihallabiyya (rice flour pudding with currants and pistachios). Bread soaked in sugar syrup, baked, and topped with thick cream. Basboosa (semolina cake topped with lemon syrup and almonds). Pastries made with filo dough, couscous, and nuts.

Beverages   Tea, coffee (both heavily sweetened), diluted yogurt drinks, beer, wine.

Mezze   Falafel, thin soft bread with mish cheese, olives. The mezze tradition of snacks with drinking is practiced.

Meals and service   Breakfast: Tea or coffee, cheese or yogurt, beans, eggs, olives. Main meal (early afternoon): bread, rice or couscous, vegetable or legume, a meat, poultry, or fish dish, salad or olives, dessert, coffee or tea. Evening meal: like breakfast, leftovers, or soup. Food is not served in courses. Bread is used to scoop up foods.

Street food and snacks   Fool (boiled, seasoned beans), tamiya (deep-fried patties of fava beans, garlic, onions, herbs, cayenne), kushari (spaghetti, rice, and lentils with fried onions and hot tomato sauce), baked sweet potato.

EL SALVADOR
Republic of El Salvador

Geography   El Salvador is the smallest Central American country and the only one without an Atlantic coastline; it borders the Pacific Ocean. Most of the land is a fertile volcanic plateau about 2,000 feet (607 m) high. Mountains with volcanoes are in the north; the south is a hot coastal plain.

Major Languages	Ethnic Groups		Major Religions	
Spanish (official)	Mestizo	88%	Roman Catholic	83%
Nahua	Amerindian	9%	Protestant, other	17%
	White and other	3%		

Population density per sq. mi. 883
Literacy rate 85.5%
Life expectancy 68.5 male; 75.8 female
Per capita GDP $5,800
Labor force in agriculture 19%

Urban 59.8%
Infant mortality rate per 1,000 live births 22.2
HIV rate 0.8%
Unemployment 7.2%
Arable land 31%

Agriculture   sugarcane, corn, sorghum, coffee, rice, beans, oilseed, cotton, chickens, cattle, pigs, goats, sheep

Natural resources   hydropower, geothermal power, oil, fish

Industries   food processing, beverages, oil, chemicals, fertilizer, textiles, furniture, light metals

History   The Pilpil Indians, descendants of the Aztecs, probably migrated to the area in the 11th century. The Spanish arrived in the area in 1524–1525 and conquered the Pipil Indians by 1539. El Salvador became independent of Spain in 1821, of the Mexican empire in 1823, and of the Central American Federation in 1839. Since its founding it has experienced political turmoil. A 12-year civil war ended in 1992. A hurricane in 1998 and earthquakes in 2001 left more than a thousand people dead and many homeless. In 2001 a severe drought destroyed 80% of the crops. In 2007 nearly a third of native Salvadorans lived in the United States, and remittances from Salvadorans working in the United States were a major source of income in El Salvador.

Influences on food   The Pacific Ocean provides fish and shrimp, and fertile land, mostly on a plateau, supports crops and livestock. The Indian influence continues, for example, corn and beans. The Spanish brought new foods including rice, beef, pork and lard, coconut, and breadfruit. Caribbean island foodways from native Carib-speaking Indians and laborers from Africa and Asia have also influenced the food customs of El Salvador.

Staple foods   Corn, rice, beans.

Bread and cereals   Corn, rice, sorghum, wheat; corn tortillas, gruel, dishes, and drinks, rice dishes, wheat bread and rolls.

Meat, poultry, fish   Chicken, beef, pork, goat, lamb and mutton, fish, shrimp, eggs, turkey; sausage.

Dairy products   Milk (evaporated), cream, sour cream, cheese. Milk is not usually drunk as a beverage.

Fats and oils   Lard, butter, vegetable oils, shortening.

Legumes   Beans (black, red, kidney, white), chickpeas.

Vegetables   Plantains, cassava, tomatoes, sweet peppers, chayote squash (green pear-shaped gourd), avocados, pumpkin, breadfruit, chili peppers, onions, potatoes, cabbage, carrots, green beans, lettuce, beets.

Fruit   Pineapple, coconut, bananas, mangoes, oranges, other citrus, roselle fruit (used to make sorrel drinks and jams/jellies), grapes, papaya, passion fruit.

Nuts and seeds   Palm tree nuts, squash seeds, sesame seeds.

Seasonings   Onions, garlic, chili, achiote/annatto (orange-red coloring), cilantro, pimento, cinnamon, vanilla, rum.

Dishes   Foods are often fried and feature indigenous ingredients such as corn, beans, tomatoes, chilies, and turkey. Atole (corn gruel). Posole (semifermented corn dough, diluted to make a beverage or used in other ways). Tamales (spicy meat-stuffed corn dough, wrapped in corn husks or leaves, and steamed). Beans simmered with spices (frijoles sancochadas), puréed, or fried; often paired with rice (frijoles con arroz). Rice often fried before boiling or cooked with coconut milk. Soups and stews of meat, chicken, or seafood and plantains or cassava in coconut milk. Roasted meat, chicken, and fish. Salads such as avocado. Fried potatoes, plantains, or breadfruit. Pickled vegetables (cabbage, carrots). Sandwiches of French bread, turkey, and pickled vegetables.

Specialties   Pineapple used in unexpected ways such as in stews. Pupusas (thick tortilla filled with cheese, black beans, or chicarrones, which are pork cracklings, topped with another tortilla, the edges sealed, and fried).

Special occasion dish   Quesadilla (cheese-flavored batter bread), served on Sundays.

National dish   La semita, a pineapple tart.

Sweets   Sugarcane, honey, sugar (white, brown), nogada (praline-like candy), baked bananas, fruit ices, ice cream, custard, rice pudding, coconut- or rum-flavored cakes and fritters.

Beverages   Coffee, chocolate, tropical fruit drinks (refrescas), beer, rum.

Meals   Corn and beans are eaten at every meal by the poor. Rice is consumed frequently, with cheese or meat added if resources permit. Dinner in wealthier areas typically includes soup; meat, poultry, or fish; tortillas or bread; and salad, fried plantains, and pickled vegetables plus sometimes appetizers and dessert.

Street food   Pupusas (small thick tortillas filled with beans, sausage, or cheese), sold by pupuserias.

Snacks   Candy, fruit ices, ice cream, custard, rice pudding, cakes, fritters.

EQUATORIAL GUINEA
Republic of Equatorial Guinea

Geography   Formerly Spanish Guinea, this country is on the west coast of Africa. It consists of Rio Muni, the mainland coastal plain, and nearby Bioko Island in the Gulf of Guinea, two volcanic mountains and a valley.

Major Languages		Ethnic Groups		Major Religions	
Spanish (both		Fang	86%	Roman Catholic	80%
French official)		Bubi	7%	Other Christian	7%
Fang		Mdowe	4%	Muslim	4%
Bubi		Other	3%	Other and none	9%

Population density per sq. mi. 56.9
Literacy rate 87%
Life expectancy 60,4 male; 62.1 female
Per capita GDP $12,900
Labor force in agriculture NA

Urban 38.9%
Infant mortality rate per 1,000 live births 83.8
HIV rate 3.4%
Unemployment 30%
Arable land 5%

Agriculture   cassava, sweet potatoes, oil palm fruit, coffee, cocoa, rice, yams, bananas, chickens, sheep, goats, pigs, cattle

Natural resources   oil, natural gas, timber, gold, fish

Industries   oil, fishing, sawmilling, natural gas

History   Pygmies originally inhabited the mainland. The Fang and Bubi migrated to the area in the 17th century. The Portuguese reached the islands in the late 15th century and ceded them to Spain in 1778. Independence came in 1968. Disputes between peoples on the islands and mainland erupted; mainlander Masie became president in 1972. His brutal reign bankrupted the nation. Most of its 7,000 Europeans emigrated. Masie was ousted by a military coup led by Obiang, who became president and has headed the government since (as of 2008). An offshore oil boom began in 1997; oil sales, especially to the United States, have greatly increased. In 2007 the country continued to have one of the highest GDP growth rates in the world, estimated at more than 20%.

Influences on food   The Gulf of Guinea provides fish and seafood. The land and tropical climate allow raising coffee, cocoa, rice, yams, cassava, bananas, and some livestock. Starchy roots and rice are staple foods. Portuguese control for nearly three centuries and Spanish control for nearly two centuries left some influence. Also, there is French influence from French control of some countries in the region, including neighboring Cameroon and Gabon. The introduction of New World foods such as cassava, corn, peanuts, tomato, chili pepper, and potato was a major influence. Native African foods include black-eyed peas, watermelon, and okra.

Bread and cereals   Rice, corn, millet, sorghum, wheat; rice dishes, bread of mashed banana or plantain and flour.

Meat, poultry, fish   Chicken, lamb and mutton, goat, pork, beef, fish and seafood (fresh, smoked, salted, or dried), guinea fowl, eggs, rabbit, game. Chicken is popular.

Insects   Termites (often called white ants), locusts.

Dairy products   Milk, sour milk, buttermilk, curds, whey, cheese.

Fats and oils   Palm oil, peanut oil, shea oil, coconut oil. Palm oil, the predominant cooking fat, is red.

Legumes   Peanuts (groundnuts), black-eyed peas (cowpeas), locust beans (carob), red beans, black beans.

Vegetables   Cassava, sweet potatoes, yams, plantains, green leaves (e.g., cassava), okra, tomatoes, potatoes, eggplant, pumpkin, onions, red chili peppers, cucumbers, bell peppers.

Fruit   Bananas, coconut, pineapple, akee apples, baobab, watermelon, guavas, lemons, dates, mangoes, papaya.

Nuts and seeds   Palm kernels, shea nuts, cashews, kola nuts, watermelon seeds (egusi), sesame seeds, mango seeds. Nuts and seeds thicken and flavor sauces.

Seasonings   Salt, palm oil, onions, red chili peppers, tomatoes, cocoa.

Dishes   Most foods are boiled or fried, and chunks are dipped in sauce and eaten by hand. Sauce of boiled, pounded green leaves. Fried yams. Fufu (boiled and pounded starchy vegetables or corn), formed into balls or scoops to eat stew. Peanut sauce or stew (ground and pounded peanuts, chilies, tomatoes, and meat, chicken, fish, or mixtures of them, and sometimes starchy vegetables). Stews of root vegetables or okra with bits of fish, chicken, or beef. Moin moin (steamed ground paste of black-eyed peas, hot pepper, and onions). Rice boiled in coconut milk. Plantain fried in palm oil. Egg, onion, and red pepper omelet. Roast chicken with peanut sauce.

Sweets   Honey, sugar, deep-fried sweet dough balls, peanut candy (kanya), baked bananas with coconut.

Beverages   Coffee, cocoa, beer.

Street food and snacks   Spiced kabobs (coupé-coupé); fried fish, plantain chips, balls of steamed rice, black-eyed peas, beans, yams, or peanuts. Snacks are common and available at street stalls in urban areas.

ERITREA
State of Eritrea

Geography   Eritrea is In East Africa, on the southwest coast of the Red Sea. It includes many islands of the Dahlak Archipelago, extremely hot and dry low coastal plains in the south, cooler central highlands with fertile valleys, and a mountain range with peaks to 9,000 feet in the north.

Major Languages	Ethnic Groups		Major Religions	
Afar	Tigrinya	50%	Muslim (nearly all Sunni)	50%
Arabic	Tigre and Kunama	40%	Coptic Christian (Orthodox)	40%
Tigre and Kunama	Afar	4%	Roman Catholic	5%
Tigrinya,	Saho	3%	Protestant	2%
Other Cushitic languages	Other	3%	Other	3%

Population density per sq. mi. 117.5
Literacy rate 58.6%
Life expectancy 59.4 male; 63.5 female
Per capita GDP $800
Labor force in agriculture 80%

Urban 19.4%
Infant mortality rate per 1,000 live births 44.3
HIV rate 1.3%
Unemployment NA
Arable land 5%

Agriculture   sorghum, roots and tubers, pulses, vegetables, corn, cotton, tobacco, sisal, sheep, cattle, goats, chickens, camels

Natural resources   gold, other minerals, potash, salt, fish

Industries   food processing, beverages, clothing and textiles

History   Part of the Ethiopian kingdom of Aksum until its decline in the 8th century, Eritrea came under control of the Ottoman Empire in the 16th century and of Egypt later. It was an Italian colony from 1890 to 1941, when it came under British control. After a period of British and UN supervision, it was awarded to Ethiopia in 1952 as part of a federation. Annexation as a province in 1962 led to a 31-year struggle for independence, declared in 1993. A border war with Ethiopia (1998–2000) ended with a peace treaty in December 2000. In 2007 Ethiopia and China signed agreements granting mineral exploration rights to China and canceling part of Eritrea's foreign debt.

Influences on food   Formerly a part of Ethiopia, later an Italian colony, and most recently the northernmost province of Ethiopia, Eritrea has been independent since 1993. Ethiopians, Italians, Arabs, and Islam and Orthodox Christianity have influenced Eritrean food customs. As in Ethiopia, foods include the flatbread injera and the spicy red pepper sauce berbere. Italian influence is reflected in pasta, pizza, frittata, ices, and ice cream. Islam forbids consumption of pork or alcohol. Bean and lentil dishes are popular during the fasting periods of the Christian Orthodox Church. The Red Sea provides fish. Eritrea's highlands and fertile valleys produce coffee, grains, lentils, vegetables, and livestock. Farmers have learned to grow foreign vegetables such as tomatoes.

Bread and cereals   Sorghum, corn, rice, millet, barley, wheat; cooked rice, flatbread injera made from millet and cooked on a griddle, covered, in a large circular loaf, pasta (e.g., spaghetti), pizza.

Meat, poultry, fish   Lamb and mutton, beef, goat, chicken, fish, eggs.

Dairy products   Milk (cow, goat, sheep, camel), cheese.

Fats and oils   Butter, clarified butter, vegetable oils, olive oil.

Legumes   Lentils, chickpeas, peas, fava beans, peanuts.

Vegetables   Potatoes, plantains, beans, peas, tomatoes, red chili peppers, sweet peppers, onions, garlic.

Fruit   Dates.

Nuts and seeds   Almonds, fenugreek seeds, sesame seeds.

Seasonings   Red hot chili peppers, onions, garlic, cayenne, ginger; berbere (hot red pepper spice mixture: allspice, cardamom, cayenne, cinnamon, cloves, coriander, cumin, fenugreek, ginger, nutmeg, and black pepper), spiced butter (clarified butter with onions, garlic, ginger, and other spices).

Dishes   Stew (wat): vegetables with ground legumes; ful (bean stew); tum 'tumo (lentil stew); and thick spicy stew of whole hard-boiled eggs, lentils, chickpeas, peanuts, vegetables, and lamb, beef, chicken, or fish. All stews are eaten with berbere. Bean-and pea-purées with vegetable oils and wat-like sauces beaten into them to make airy, soufflé-like consistencies. Garlic- and ginger-flavored vegetable casserole. Lentil salad. Flatbread crumbled with spiced butter or wat. Spaghetti and pizza (both with berbere sauce). Frittata (egg omelet with sweet peppers).

Sweets   Honey, sugar, ices, ice cream.

Beverages   Coffee, beer (home-brewed from millet or corn), wine (fermented from honey).

Meals   A typical meal: a spicy vegetable stew often with lamb or beef, or a bean-or pea-purée with vegetable oils, berbere, rice or injera, and beverage.

ESTONIA
Republic of Estonia

Geography   Estonia is in Eastern Europe, bordering the Baltic Sea and Gulf of Finland. It is mainly marshy lowland with numerous lakes, swamps, and rivers. About 40% of the land is forest. It includes some 800 islands.

Major Languages	Ethnic Groups		Major Religions	
Estonian (official)	Estonian	69%	Unaffiliated	34%
Russian	Russian	26%	Evangelical Lutheran	14%
	Other	5%	Russian Orthodox	13%
			Unaffiliated Christian	26%
			Other	13%

Population density per sq. mi. 78.4
Literacy rate 99.8%
Life expectancy 67.2 male; 78.3 female
Per capita GDP $21,000
Labor force in agriculture 11%

Urban 69.4%
Infant mortality rate per 1,000 live births 7.5
HIV rate 1.3%
Unemployment 5.9%
Arable land 12%

Agriculture   barley, wheat, potatoes, vegetables, chickens, pigs, cattle, sheep, goats

Natural resources   fish, oil, shale, peat, phosphorite, clay, limestone, sand, dolomite, sea mud

Industries   engineering, electronics, wood products, textiles

History   Estonia resisted assaults of Vikings, Danes, Swedes, and Russians from the 9th century to 1219, when the Danes gained control. In 1346 the Danes sold northern Estonia to the Teutonic

Order, German Knights, who reduced the Estonians to serfdom. Sweden gained control in 1526, followed by Russia in 1721. The next year serfdom was abolished. Estonia gained independence from Russia in 1918 and was independent until Russia occupied it in 1940 and later incorporated it as the Estonian SSR. It regained independence in 1991. Free-market reforms and foreign investments advanced the economy. In 1998 Estonia relaxed citizenship requirements that kept Russian speakers from gaining citizenship. It joined the EU and NATO in 2004. In 2007 the government accused Russia of a cyber attack against Estonia's computer network.

Influences on food   Northernmost of the three Baltic countries, Estonia has culinary traditions closest to those of the Scandinavian countries. Influences include neighbors Finland, Denmark, and Sweden, that dominated Estonia until early in the 18th century, and Russia, who dominated it most of the time since. The Estonian language, along with Finnish and Hungarian, is one of the few surviving languages in the Finno-Ugric group. Coasts on the Baltic Sea and Gulf of Finland plus numerous lakes and rivers allow important fishing and shipping industries.

Bread and cereals   Barley, wheat, rye, oats, millet, rice; porridge, bread, pancakes, pastry, dumplings.

Meat, poultry, fish   Chicken, pork, beef and veal, lamb, goat, fish and seafood, eggs, fish eggs (caviar); salted fish (Baltic herring and sprat, a small fish of the herring family), ham, sausage. Salted fish and bread are staples.

Dairy products   Milk (cow, sheep), cream, sour cream, cheese, cottage cheese.

Fats and oils   Butter, bacon, lard, vegetable oil.

Legumes   Beans, lentils, split peas.

Vegetables   Potatoes, cabbage, beets, mushrooms, cucumbers, radishes, tomatoes; sauerkraut, pickles.

Fruit   Apples, rhubarb, cherries, ligonberries, cranberries, grapes, lemons, oranges, currants, raisins.

Nuts and seeds   Almonds, chestnuts, hazelnuts, walnuts, caraway seeds, poppy seeds.

Seasonings   Sour cream, vinegar, salt, pepper, dill, mustard. Sour taste is liked.

Dishes   Skaha putra (traditional porridge of barley, sour milk, potatoes, and salt pork). Milk soups and sauces. Cabbage or beet soup. Kippers (salted smoked herring) chopped, fried in a milk-flour-egg batter with a little grated cheese, and served with tomato sauce. Kiluvõi (sprat pâté) made with salted kilu, or Baltic sprat (the most typical Estonian fish), butter, and salty fish juices; served with hot boiled potatoes. Boiled dumplings, flour or potato, sometimes stuffed with meat, cottage cheese, potatoes, or fruit. Baked or fried pastry stuffed with meat, cabbage, or rice and mushrooms. Pork cutlet lightly breaded and fried. Meatballs (fried large patties of ground pork, veal, and beef). Cabbage stuffed with ground pork, veal, and beef. Herring salad (rossolye): herring, ham or other meat, hard-cooked eggs, beets, potatoes, dill pickles, and apples, dressed with sour cream and mustard. Roasted veal stuffed with ground meat and hard-cooked eggs. Potato patties fried in butter.

Sweets   Honey, sugar, molasses. Rye bread soup with apples. Rhubarb pudding. Pancakes with ligonberries. Apple cake. Small cake with topping of cottage cheese, sugar, and raisins, Cookies. Pastries with poppy seeds.

Beverages   Milk, tea, coffee sometimes topped with whipped cream, hot chocolate, beer, kvass (sour beer from rye or beets), vodka flavored with caraway, wine.

ETHIOPIA
Federal Democratic Republic of Ethiopia

Geography   Ethiopia is in East Africa in the horn of Africa. A high central plateau, 6,000 to 10,000 feet, rises to mountains near the Great Rift Valley and descends to plains on both west and southeast. The Blue Nile, and other rivers, crosses the plateau; its chief reservoir is Lake Tana.

Major Languages	Ethnic Groups		Major Religions	
Amarigna	Oromo	32%	Ethiopian Orthodox	51%
Tigrigna	Amara	30%	Muslim	33%
Oromigna	Tigraway	6%	Protestant	10%
Guaragigna	Somali	6%	Traditional beliefs	5%
Somaligna	Gurage	5%	Other	1%
English (major foreign language taught in schools)	Sidamo	4%		
	Other	17%		

Population density per sq. mi. 190.9
Literacy rate 35.9%
Life expectancy 52.5 male; 57.5 female
Per capita GDP $800
Labor force in agriculture 80%

Urban 16.1%
Infant mortality rate per 1,000 live births 82.6
HIV rate 2.1%
Unemployment 5.0%
Arable land 10%

Agriculture   cereals, pulses, coffee, oilseed, cotton, sugarcane, potatoes, beeswax, honey, cut flowers, kat (qat), cattle, chickens, sheep, goats, camels, pigs, civets

Natural resources   gold, platinum, copper, potash, natural gas, hydropower, fish

Industries   food processing, beverages, textiles, leather, chemicals, metals processing, cement

History   Hamitic peoples migrated here from Asia Minor in prehistoric times. Ethiopia, the biblical land of Cush, was once under ancient Egyptian rule. Egypt and Greece influenced Ethiopian culture. Roman and Byzantine Empires valued Ethiopia's Red Sea ports. Coptic Christianity was brought in 341 CE; a variant became the state religion. Ancient Ethiopia was a monarchy and at its peak in the 5th century; then, isolated by the rise of Islam and weakened by feudal wars, it declined. Ethiopia's last emperor, Haile Selassie, established a parliament and judiciary system in 1931. Ethiopia maintained independence until Italians invaded in 1936. In 1941 Britain freed Ethiopia. Selassie was dethroned in 1974; the monarchy was abolished in 1975. A Marxist government controlled the country until 1991, with curtailment of Coptic Church influence, civil wars, and famine. Border conflicts with Eritrea, which was incorporated by Ethiopia in 1952 and became independent in 1993, and neighboring Somalia continued in the 1990s. The first multiparty general elections were held in 1995. A border war with Eritrea (1998–2000) cost Ethiopia nearly $3 billion; an international tribunal adjudicated the disputed boundary in 2002. Crop prices collapsed in 2001. Drought in 2002–2003 left severe food shortages. Ethnic clashes in 2003–2004 and police firing on protestors in Addis Abba in 2005 left hundreds dead, thousands fleeing to Sudan, and thousands arrested. In 2003 Ethiopia began relocating 2 million highland farmers to western land with more fertile soil; the resettled area has malaria and farmers still cannot support themselves. Food shortages due to drought and other reasons resulted in Ethiopia's appeal for $325 million in emergency aid in 2008.

Influences on food   Much of the land is high central plateau, and more than half the country is grassland. With a great diversity of climates and elevations, a wide variety of crops are grown. Tef, the smallest of all grains and grown nowhere else, accounts for almost half the grain acreage. It is the preferred grain for injera, the sour flatbread of the highlands. The other distinctive crop, ensete, also called false banana, grows at lower elevations than tef. Ensete root is scraped and the scrapings are fermented and made into flatbread, wesa. The Ethiopian diet consists largely of grain, dairy products, pulses, and kale. Usual foods include the flatbread injera, wat (stew), and berbere, the red hot pepper spice mixture used in many dishes. Ethiopian culture was influenced by Egypt, Greece, and Africa. Ethiopia's diverse climate, peoples, and religions influence food practices. About a third of Ethiopia's people, the dominant people of the western highlands, are the Amhara and the Tigre. They live in villages, are Coptic Christians who eat many vegetarian dishes based on kale and pulses because the Ethiopian Orthodox Church restricts animal products on the many fast days, and they avoid eating fruit. Neither they nor Muslims eat pork. The Gurage and Sidamo of the southwestern highlands and adjacent lowlands live mostly in individual homesteads and cultivate ensete. The Gurage are about equally divided among Christians, Muslims, and animists. The Sidamo, who have highly developed agriculture including plowing with oxen and terracing of fields, produce the famous Ethiopian coffee and are mostly animists. The largest group in Ethiopia, the Oromo, relative newcomers from Somalia, came in the 16th century and now dominate the eastern highlands and are found throughout the south. Some grow their own corn, millet, and tef and scarcely eat vegetables. They and the Somali avoid chicken and eggs. People in the arid east eat a typical nomad diet of grain (usually millet) and dairy products, spiced with red pepper.

Bread and cereals   Tef, corn, wheat, sorghum, oats, millet, barley, rice; boiled rice, ensete porridge, flatbreads injera (made from fermented tef batter cooked like a huge pancake on a griddle) and wesa (made from ensete), round leavened loaves with spice or honey. Wesa, often tough, is eaten with a moist accompaniment such as milk, butter, cheese, or zamamojat (mixture of cheese, cabbage, and spices).

Meat, poultry, fish   Beef, chicken, lamb and mutton, goat, pork, fish, eggs.

Dairy products   Milk, buttermilk, curds, whey, yogurt, cheese.

Fats and oils   Butter (usually clarified and flavored with spices), oils (e.g., cottonseed). The Gurage believe that without butter food has no taste, and they even put butter in coffee.

Legumes   Split peas, chickpeas, lentils, broad beans, peanuts.

Vegetables   Potatoes, Ethiopian kale (also called Abyssinian cabbage or mustard), ensete root, shallots (onion-like but smaller, with multi-bulbs and more delicate flavor), carrots, green beans, green peppers, chili peppers.

Nuts and seeds   Almonds, fenugreek seeds, sunflower seeds.

Seasonings   Red pepper and cardamom (used in most stews in the highlands), garlic, ginger, mustard, dill, caraway, Bishop's weed (ajowan), basil, turmeric; berbere (red-hot spice mixture of hot red pepper, paprika, allspice, cardamom, cayenne, cinnamon, cloves, coriander, cumin, fenugreek, ginger, nutmeg, and black pepper), niter kibbeh (clarified butter with onions, garlic, ginger, and other spices).

Dishes   Golo (toasted grain paste). Ilbet (broad beans boiled with sunflower seeds, garlic, and ginger). Wat (stew/sauce made from ground seeds). Ye-shimbra asa (fried "fish" of chickpea flour). Shiro wat (vegetable stew). Yeminser salatta (lentil salad), boiled lentils with chili peppers, garlic, and oil and vinegar dressing. Chopped spiced greens with buttermilk curds. Yataklete kilkil (simmered potatoes, carrots, beans, green peppers, garlic, and ginger). Kitfo (diced raw beef mixed with spiced butter). Red meat stew (wat), which includes red pepper, and green meat stew (alich'a), which does not. Chicken stewed in red pepper sauce. T'ibs (hash, or dry-fried meat dish). Stuffed tripe. Ahish (meat-stuffed vegetable). Crumbled injera with butter or wat.

National dish   Wat (stew), a thick spicy stew of whole hard-boiled eggs, lentils, chickpeas, peanuts, root vegetables, niter kebbeh, berbere, and beef, chicken, lamb, or fish, served with injera or rice.

Sweets   Sugarcane, honey (often in the comb).

Beverages   Coffee (originated in Ethiopia), tella (home-brewed beer), tej (honey wine, or mead).

Meals and service   One or two meals a day, with snacks of dried cured meat strips and bread in between, are usual. A typical meal is a spicy stew, often with chicken, beef, or lamb, and injera or rice. Food is often served on and picked up with torn pieces of flatbread.

F

FIJI
Republic of the Fiji Islands

Geography   Fiji is in the western South Pacific Ocean north of New Zealand. It consists of 322 islands (106 inhabited); the largest, Viti Levu, has over half the land area. Fiji has mountains, forests, and large fertile areas.

Major Languages		Ethnic Groups		Major Religions	
English	(all	Fijian (predominantly		Protestant (mostly Methodist)	35%
Fijian	are	Melanesian with Polynesian)	57%	Hindu	33%
Hindustani	official)	Indian	38%	Independent Christian	11%
		Other	5%	Roman Catholic	8%
				Muslim	7%
				Other	6%

Population density per sq. mi. 132.1
Literacy rate 93.7%
Life expectancy 67.9 male; 73.1 female
Per capita GDP $5,500
Labor force in agriculture 70%

Urban 50.8%
Infant mortality rate per 1,000 live births 11.9
HIV rate 0.1%
Unemployment rate 14.1%
Arable land 11%

Agriculture   sugarcane, coconuts, cassava, rice, sweet potatoes, bananas, chickens, cattle, goats, pigs, sheep

Natural resources   timber, fish, gold, copper, offshore oil potential, hydropower

Industries   tourism, sugar, clothing, copra, gold, silver

History   Inhabited since the second millennium BCE, Fiji was visited by Dutch and British explorers in the 17th and 18th centuries. It became a British colony in 1874. In the 1880s large-scale sugarcane cultivation began and contract laborers were brought from India. Fiji became independent In 1970 and a republic in 1987. Cultural differences between indigenous Fijians and descendant Indians have resulted in continuing conflicts. Military coups were frequent in recent decades, including one in 2006. In 2007 a military commander declared himself prime minister; international aid partners withheld aid until Fiji established a plan to return to civilian government.

Influences on food   Fiji is in the Melanesia group of the Pacific Islands. About 30,000 to 40,000 years ago people from Southeast Asia began to move south to the West Pacific islands and Australia, and thereafter migrated to islands further east. Magellan was the first European to see these people, when he sailed around the southern tip of South America in 1519 and across the Pacific Ocean. Europeans brought new food plants, wheat bread, and some animals. The British started large-scale sugarcane cultivation and brought indentured laborers from India, who brought curries. Asians brought rice, soybeans, noodles, and stir-frying. The islanders have great fishing prowess. Mainstays of the traditional diet are fish and seafood and starchy vegetables including taro root, breadfruit, sweet potato, and cassava. Fruits and nuts, especially coconut, are also important. Pork is a main meat, especially for festive occasions, traditionally cooked in a stone-lined pit over coals. When coals are hot, layers of banana leaves or palm fronds are added, a pig and foods such as sweet potatoes and breadfruit are added and covered with more leaves, sometimes water is poured over, the pit is sealed with dirt, and the food cooks for hours. A feast may be held on the beach at sunset, after making daylong preparations. Mats and banana and ti leaves are laid to form a "table" surface, on which are placed wooden platters, woven baskets, and coconut shell bowls to hold the foods cooked in the pit.

Bread and cereals   Rice, wheat; rice dishes, bread, noodles.

Meat, poultry, fish   Chicken, beef, goat, pork, lamb and mutton, fish (mullet), shellfish, eggs; corned beef, spam.

Dairy products   Milk and other dairy products are uncommon.

Fats and oils   Coconut oil and cream, lard, vegetable oil, shortening, butter, sesame oil.

Legumes   Soybeans, winged beans, pigeon peas, lentils, peanuts.

Vegetables   Cassava, taro root, sweet potatoes, greens leaves (taro and sweet potato), breadfruit, plantains, yams, arrowroot, bitter melon, cabbage, daikon, eggplant, green onions, seaweed.

Fruit   Coconut, bananas, lemons, limes, guavas, mangoes, papaya, pineapple, melons, tamarind. Coconut milk is the usual cooking medium. Fresh fruit is eaten as snacks.

Nuts and seeds   Candlenuts (kukui), litchis, macadamia nuts.

Seasonings   Soy sauce (the basic condiment), coconut milk or cream, lime or lemon juice, green onions, garlic, salt, pepper, ginger, curry powder, red chili peppers.

Dishes   Starchy vegetables such as taro root boiled or baked and pounded into a paste. Boiled cassava, sweet potatoes, or taro root. Steamed green leaves. Arrowroot thickened dishes (e.g., pudding). Fish and shellfish stewed, steamed, roasted, or raw and marinated. Kokonda (chunks of white fish marinated in salted lime or lemon juice, squeezed, and soaked and served in coconut milk with chili added). Boiled or steamed rice. Curry dishes such as mild Indian beef curry (korma). Foods cooked in a pit: whole pig, taro chunks and leaves, sweet potatoes, crabs, whole fish, chicken, taro leaf wrapped around a filling of coconut cream, lemon, onions, and shredded beef and all bound in banana leaves, and other leaf-wrapped puddings of taro, sweet potato, yams, or plantains.

Sweets   Sugarcane, sugar, immature coconut. Haupia (pudding of coconut milk, sugar, and arrowroot).

Beverages   Coconut juice, fruit juice, coffee, tea, kava (mildly alcoholic drink from pepper plant).

Meals   Two or three meals daily, with the evening meal the largest, are typical. Usual meal: boiled cassava, sweet potato, or rice; a fish, chicken, or meat dish; and steamed greens or seaweed.

FINLAND
Republic of Finland

Geography   Finland is In northern Europe between Russia and Sweden, stretching from above the Arctic Circle to the Gulf of Finland. It is generally lowland with heavy forests, many lakes and rivers, and extensive marshland. Finland has mountains in the north and long, cold winters.

Major Languages	Ethnic Groups		Major Religions	
Finnish (both	Finnish	93%	Lutheran	83%
Swedish official)	Swedish	6%	Greek Orthodox	1%
Russian and other	Other	1%	Other	1%
			None	15%

Population density per sq. mi. 44.6
Literacy rate 100%
Life expectancy 75.3 male; 82.5 female
Per capita GDP $35,300
Labor force in agriculture & forestry 4.4%

Urban 62.4%
Infant mortality rate per 1,000 live births 3.5
HIV rate 0.1%
Unemployment rate 7.7%
Arable land 7%

Agriculture   barley, oats, sugar beets, wheat, potatoes, chickens, pigs, cattle, sheep, goats

Natural resources   timber, fish, iron ore, copper, lead, zinc, chromite

Industries   metals and metal products, electronics, machinery and scientific instruments, shipbuilding, pulp and paper, copper refining, foodstuffs, chemicals, textiles

History   Recent archeological discoveries indicate that humans may have lived in Finland for 100,000 years. Sami ancestors probably arrived by about 7000 BCE. At about the beginning of the Christian era, the early Finns probably migrated here from the Ural Mountain area. The area was gradually Christianized from the 11th century. From 1154 to 1809 Swedish settlers also inhabited the region, which was part of Sweden. In 1809 Finland became an autonomous grand duchy of the Russian Empire. In 1917 it declared independence and in 1919 became a republic. The Soviet Union invaded in 1939, forcing cessions of territory then and additional cessions after World War II. Finland signed a treaty of mutual assistance with the USSR in 1948 and a pact with Russia in 1992. Finland joined the EU in 1995. In 2000 it elected its first woman president, who was reelected for a second term in 2006. In 2007 agreement was reached with the nurses' unions to provide raises over four years and a year-end bonus. Nokia bought the U.S. company Navteq, a maker of digital maps for mobile systems. **Aland (Ahvenanmaa)**, an autonomous province, is a small group of islands in the Gulf of Bothnia.

Influences on food   Finland is a large country with a relatively small population (5,244,749) and two languages, both spoken by almost everyone. The Finnish language, along with Estonian and Hungarian, is one of the few surviving examples of the Finno-Ugric linguistic family. Culinary traditions are based on hunting, fishing, gathering wild fungi and berries, and customs shared with other Scandinavian countries such as rye bread. Lapland, the part of Finland, Sweden, and Norway in the Arctic, is inhabited by the Lapps, who provide Father Christmas with his home territory and reindeer. The Lapps have their own culture and foodways, with strong emphasis on reindeer. In Finland's forests elk, bear, hare, and reindeer are hunted and eaten. The many lakes provide freshwater fish. The Baltic Sea provides sea fish including Baltic herring. These and other foods are displayed at markets in Helsinki harbor, with a backdrop of delicately colored classical buildings. Neighbors Sweden and Russia influenced Finnish cuisine because Finland was part of Sweden for more than 600 years and part of Russia for another 100 years. Examples include the smörgåsbord and Karelian pasties. The latter is from Karelia, the eastern province of Finland, and resembles Russian pasties.

Bread and cereals   Barley, oats, wheat, rye, rice; whole-grain porridges, rye and/or wheat flour bread, crackers, rice-filled pasties, pancakes. Finnish bread (Suomalaisleipä), round flat yeast loaf from wheat and rye flours.

Meat, poultry, fish   Chicken, pork, beef and veal, lamb and mutton, goat, eggs, fish (freshwater fish like burbot, miukku, crayfish; sea fish like Baltic herring, salmon; roe of burbot, salmon, whitefish, and sturgeon [caviar]), meat of reindeer (a large deer), elk, bear, hare; sausage. Delicacies: burbot "caviar," smoked reindeer tongue.

Dairy products   Milk, sour milk (piimä and viili, or long curd, which is eaten), cream, sour cream, cheese.

Fats and oils   Butter, lard, margarine, salt pork, vegetable oil.

Legumes   Split peas (green and yellow), lima beans.

Vegetables   Potatoes, cabbage, carrots, lettuce, spinach, peas, cucumbers, rutabagas, mushrooms; dill pickles.

Fruit   Ligonberries (small cranberries), strawberries, raspberries, blueberries, cloudberries (golden berries found mainly within the Arctic Circle), apples, lemons, oranges, raisins. Fresh berries are popular in summer.

Nuts and seeds   Almonds, marzipan (sweetened almond paste).

Seasonings   Dill (free with fish bought in Finland), parsley, salt, mustard, vinegar, peppercorns, allspice, vanilla.

Dishes   Herring with dill. Hearty savory soups: meat and potato dumplings soup, fish cooked with potatoes and dill soup. Summer vegetable soup (kesäkeitto) made from carrots, small potatoes, peas, and spinach in cream sauce. Pita-ja-joulupuuro (whole-grain barley porridge) served with fruit purée. Potatoes, loved by Finns, in many dishes including potato porridge and the favorite, boiled tiny new potatoes served with dill. Rutabagas, cubed and simmered plain or with pork and mutton in a casserole. Pork gravy. Karelian pastie (piirakka), baked shell of rye dough with rice filling, often served with egg butter (chopped hard-boiled egg stirred into soft butter). Kalakukko (fish pastry made of rye dough baked around a fish and pork fat filling), from Savo, the province in central Finland. Savo whitefish poached, in a stew, or (as above) baked in a shell of rye bread. Patakukko (baked casserole of fish and pork filling under a rye crust). Crayfish steeped in dill solution, boiled, and served cold with toast. Baked fish stuffed with rice and cucumbers. Stew of mutton, pork, and veal with allspice. Meatballs. Omelets. Roast pork or leg of lamb. Reindeer meat stew (poronkäristys), soup, or roast served with mashed potatoes, ligonberry purée, and sour cream. Salad of greens and mushrooms or cucumbers. Fish eaten outdoors: raw, salted, smoked by wrapping in newspaper layers and setting in embers, grilled on sticks, planked (pinned on a board and baked in front of open flames), or steamed on top of potatoes in a pot.

Holiday fare   On Midsummer's Day (June 24), smoked salmon and new potatoes with dill.

Sweets   Sugar, molasses. Fresh berries plain, with sugar and cream or piimä, or with whipped cream. Kiisseli (berry pudding). Vatkattu marjapuuro (whipped ligonberry pudding). Cold fruit soups. Pies and tarts containing berries. Large lacy pancakes (muurinpohjaletut) sprinkled with sugar or with berry jam. Crullers (deep-fried yeast batter, dusted with confectioner's sugar).

Easter sweet   Mämmi (rye pudding), rye flour and malt boiled, mixed with molasses and bitter orange peel, whipped, baked (traditionally in a birchbark basket), and served with cream and sugar.

Beverages   Milk, sour milk (piimä), tea, coffee, beer, vodka, cognac, golden cloudberry liqueur, homemade beer (kalja) and mead (sima).

After-sauna food   Salty food such as herring or grilled pork-and-mutton sausage to replace body salt lost in the sauna (an extremely hot, dry air bath to relax).

FRANCE
French Republic

Geography   France is in Western Europe, bordering the Atlantic Ocean and the Mediterranean Sea. France consists of a wide plain covering more than half of the country, a mountainous plateau in the center, the Pyrenees Mountains on the southwest border with Spain, and the Alps in the east (Mt. Blanc is the tallest peak in Western Europe, 15,771 ft). Major rivers include the Seine and Loire.

Major Language	Ethnic Groups		Major Religions	
French (official)	French (Celtic and Latin)	77%	Roman Catholic	83–88%
Regional dialects and languages	North African, Italian,		Muslim	5–10%
	Portuguese, Fleming, Basque,		Protestant	2%
	German, Jewish, Vietnamese,		Other and none	1–27%
	Catalan, and other minorities	23%		

Population density per sq. mi. 259.2
Literacy rate 99%
Life expectancy 77.7 male; 84.2 female
Per capita GDP $33,200
Labor force in agriculture 4.1%

Urban 76.7%
Infant mortality rate per 1,000 live births 3.4
HIV rate 0.4%
Unemployment rate 8.2%
Arable land 33%

Agriculture   wheat, sugar beets, cereals, grapes, potatoes, vegetables, fruits, chickens, cattle, pigs, sheep, goats

Natural resources   coal, iron ore, bauxite, zinc, uranium, antimony, arsenic, potash, feldspar, fluorspar, gypsum, timber, fish

Industries   machinery, chemicals, automobiles, metallurgy, aircraft, electronics, tourism

History   Archeological excavations indicate continuous settlement in this land from Paleolithic times. Gauls came around 1200 BCE. The region, Celtic Gaul, was conquered by Caesar in 58 to 51 BCE and ruled by Rome for 500 years until the Franks invaded in the 5th century. By the 8th century Charlemagne extended Frankish rule over much of Europe. After his death, in 843, the area now roughly France, Germany, and Italy was divided among his three grandsons. In 1328 when Philip VI ascended the French throne, France was the most powerful European nation. The English also claimed the French throne. The Hundred Years War (1337–1453) settled the contest with France's victory. The high point of absolute monarchy was the reign of Louis XIV (1643–1715), whose court was the center of the Western world. The monarchy was overthrown by the French Revolution (1789–1793), and the First Republic was established. Napoleon Bonaparte defended the republic from foreign attack and ruled from 1799 to 1814. After Napoleon's defeat the Congress of Vienna, 1815, tried to restore order with Louis XVIII, but growing industrialization and the middle class pressed for change. A revolution in 1848 drove Louis Philippe, last of the Bourbons, into exile. A limited monarchy followed from 1852 to 1871, when after France's defeat in the Franco-Prussian War (1870–1871), the Third Republic was formed. Germany seized Alsace and Lorraine provinces in 1871 and invaded France in World War I. Alsace and Lorraine were returned to France after World War I. Germany invaded France again in 1940; France was liberated by the Allies in 1944. France withdrew from Indochina in 1954 after a costly war and from Morocco and Tunisia in 1956; it freed most of its remaining African territories from 1958 to 1962. In 2004 the French government passed a law banning wearing Muslim headscarves and other religious symbols in public schools. In 2006 protests and strikes led to some concessions for younger workers. In 2008 France pledged additional troops to its contingent as part of NATO forces in Afghanistan. Corsica, a Mediterranean island, is a region of France and the birthplace of Napoleon I.

Overseas Departments: French Guiana, in South America; **Guadeloupe**, in West Indies; **Martinique** (birthplace of Napoleon's Empress Josephine), in West Indies; and **Réunion**, in Indian Ocean near Madagascar.

Overseas Territorial Collectivities: Saint Pierre and Miquelon, islands near the Grand Banks, south of Newfoundland, the center of the French Atlantic cod fisheries; **Mayotte**, the most populous of the four Comoros Islands in the Indian Ocean off Mozambique in Africa, and the only one that chose to remain a French dependency after Comoran independence in 1975; **St. Barthelemy** and **St. Martin**, in the West Indies, became overseas territorial collectivities in 2007.

Overseas Territories (T) and Countries (C):   French Polynesia (C), scattered islands in the South Pacific, for example, the Marquesas and Society Islands (the principal and most populous island is Tahiti, in the Society group); **New Caledonia and Dependencies (T)**, east of Australia; **Southern and Antarctic Lands (T)**, certain islands in the southern Indian Ocean and Adélie Land on the Antarctic mainland; **Wallis and Futuna Island (T)**, two island groups in the South Pacific, between Fiji and Samoa.

French Possessions: Bassas da India,   off coast of Southeast Africa; **Clipperton Island**, in the Pacific southwest of Mexico; **Europa Island**, between East Africa and Madagascar; **Glorioso Islands,** off coast of East Africa northwest of Madagascar.

Influences on food   France is famous for its cuisine. Several factors made this possible. A large and diverse country, it produces a great variety of foods, and its coasts provide fish and seafood. It also is a large food processor and the largest food exporter in Europe. Some food refinements made in Italy during the Renaissance inspired French cooking after Catherine de Medici married Henry II of France in 1533. France developed its la grande cuisine, which flourished in the French court in the 18th century. France has historically had a gastronomic capital, Paris, where resources were concentrated; chefs who advanced the art of cookery by building on the past and exploring new tastes; people who care about their food; and writers about food. Bread is a main food. At about 1900 white bread was a luxury only city dwellers could afford; a dark loaf of rye and wheat, or cornmeal bread in the south, was consumed by country folk. After World War II the baguette, made with soft wheat, spread from Paris to the rest of France. Some regional foods spread to Paris and throughout France, such as crêpes (very thin pancakes) from Brittany in the 1920s and cassoulet (a casserole of white beans, sausage, and duck, goose, pork, or mutton) from Languedoc in the 1990s. The cooking of France has been divided into classic cuisine and provincial (regional) cooking. Classic cuisine (la grande cuisine) is elegant, formal, and mostly prepared in restaurants centered in Paris, using the best ingredients from throughout France. Provincial cooking is simple fare made at home featuring fresh local ingredients.

Provincial/regional specialties   The historic provinces can be grouped into 11 regions. **Bretagne**   (Brittany) region, in northwest France, has seafood, especially Belon oysters, and is the home of crêpes. **Normandy**, also in the northwest and east of Brittany, produces dairy products including Camembert cheese, apples, and cider. **Champagne**, in the north, produces sparkling wine named after the province. **Touraine**, in the west, produces fruits and vegetables. **Ile de France**, the land surrounding Paris, the birthplace of classic cooking, uses finest foodstuffs from all the regions in dishes such as lobster bisque (lobster cooked with seasonings, chicken stock, tomatoes, white wine, and cream) and filet de boeuf béarnaise (beef filet with sauce of egg yolks, butter, lemon juice or vinegar, and tarragon). **Alsace and Lorraine** region, in northeast France, has German-influenced foods such as goose, sausages, sauerkraut, Rhine wines, and special dishes pâté de foie gras (goose liver and usually truffles baked with a finely ground pork stuffing) and quiche lorraine (egg, cream, and bacon baked in a pie crust). **Bourgogne** (Burgundy), in east France, produces wines (and snails, raised on grape vines) especially red burgundy, an ingredient in beef bourguignon (beef stew); its principal city Dijon hosts the annual gastronomic fair and is the home of mustard made with white wine and herbs. **Bordeaux**, in central and southwest France, is the other great wine-producing region, home of the bordelaise sauce (with 13 ingredients plus red Bordeaux wine, made primarily from cabernet sauvignon grape), Cognac (the brandy capital), and Perigueux, famous for truffles. **Franche-Comté**, in the mountains of east France, is noted for Bresse chicken, a small bird usually simply roasted. In the **Languedoc, Foix, Roussillon** region in central south France, Languedoc retains its Roman influence as in cassoulet, and Foix and Roussillon show influence from neighbor Spain as in omelets with tomatoes, green peppers, and ham. **Provence**, in southeast France, has more highly flavored fare than in north France and shows Mediterranean influence in cooking with garlic, olive oil, and tomatoes (à la Provençal means that a dish contains these items), all used in the famous bouillabaisse (fish stew containing various Mediterranean fish and shellfish); another specialty, named after Nice, a city in this region, is salade Niçoise (tuna, tomato, olives, lettuce, other raw vegetables, hard-boiled egg, and capers).

Bread and cereals   Wheat, corn, barley, rye; baguette (long thin white wheat loaf with a crisp crust, the "national bread," often called French bread), croissants (buttery, flaky rolls), rye-wheat loaf, cornmeal bread, and porridge.

Meat, poultry, fish   Beef and veal, chicken, pork, lamb, turkey, duck, goat, fish (cod, sole), shellfish (oysters, mussels, lobsters), eggs, snails; sausage, ham.

Dairy products   Milk, cream, yogurt, cheese (Camembert, the "national cheese," and Brie; both semisoft, mild).

Fats and oils   Butter, lard, olive oil, goose fat, walnut oil, corn oil, safflower oil. Butter is the basic cooking fat in the northwest, lard in the northeast, and olive oil on the Mediterranean coast.

Legumes   White beans, split peas, lentils.

Vegetables   Potatoes, tomatoes, carrots, lettuce, green peas, cauliflower, green beans (haricots verts), leeks, mushrooms, spinach, cabbage, asparagus, onions, eggplant, zucchini, artichokes, cucumbers, green peppers, radishes, black truffles (fungi found underground among oak roots), turnips, parsley, olives; sauerkraut.

Fruit   Grapes, apples, peaches, nectarines, pears, strawberries, raspberries, oranges, lemons, apricots, melons.

Nuts and seeds   Chestnuts, walnuts, pistachio nuts, almonds, sunflower seeds.

Seasonings   Salt, black pepper, onions, garlic, wine, vinegar, lemon juice, bouquet garni (selected herbs such as tarragon, thyme, and bay leaf), mustard, nutmeg, chocolate, vanilla.

Dishes   Pâté (mixture of finely ground meat, poultry, or fish, seasonings, and usually wine; baked in a crust). Escargot (snails cooked in garlic butter). Sauces made with white stock (from fish, chicken, or veal) or brown stock (from beef or veal), various seasonings, and roux (flour cooked in butter or fat drippings), for example béchamel sauce (cream sauce, or basic white sauce, made from white stock, milk, and roux). Onion soup (made with broth, sliced onions, and garlic, served over slices of French bread with cheese). Potage St. Germain (pea soup) Grilled steak (bifteck), sometimes peppered (au poivre), served with French fries (pommes frites). Ratatouille (tomatoes, eggplant, and zucchini cooked in olive oil). Green salad dressed with olive oil, vinegar, and seasonings. Coq au vin (chicken cooked in wine). Cheese soufflé (baked light airy dish made from thick white sauce, grated sharp cheese, and beaten egg whites). French toast (pain perdu: leftover bread sliced, dipped into egg/milk mixture, and grilled in butter; usually served with butter and syrup). Pan bagna (French bread sandwich with olive oil and various ingredients: anchovies, tomato, green pepper, onion, olives, hard-boiled eggs).

Sweets   Sugar, fruit, jam, marmalade. Strawberries with crème Chantilly (whipped cream with confectioner's sugar and vanilla). Crêpes rolled around strawberries and whipped cream. Crêpes Suzette (crêpes flavored with orange liqueur sauce). Cream-filled cakes and pastries (cream puffs, éclairs). Strawberry or cheese tarts (small baked pie crusts filled with fresh strawberries or cheese). Orange soufflé. Petits fours (small fancy cakes). Madeleines (small cakes or cookies).

Beverages   Coffee, hot chocolate, wine, champagne, liqueur. Coffee is served strong and black, at breakfast with hot milk offered, and in small cups (demitasse) after other meals and in sidewalk cafés.

Meals and service   Three meals a day is typical. Breakfast: bread or croissant, butter, marmalade, coffee or hot chocolate. Main meal: hors d'oeuvre (appetizer) such as pâté on toast; chicken, meat, fish, or egg dish and vegetable; green salad; cheese, fruit, and sometimes a dessert or petits fours; bread and butter, and usually wine, accompany the meal. The meal is served in courses.

Street food and snacks   Roasted chestnuts, crêpes filled with strawberries and whipped cream, pastries, coffee.

G

GABON
Gabonese Republic

Geography   Gabon is in central Africa, bordering the Atlantic Ocean and straddling the Equator. Gabon consists of coastal lowlands and plateaus, with mountains in the northeast. Most of the land is covered by dense forest.

Major Languages	Ethnic Groups	Major Religions	
French (official) Fang, Myene, Nzebi, Bapounou/Eschira, Bandjabi	Bantu tribes (major groups: Fang 29%, Bapounou 10%, Nzebi 9%, Obamba) French 7% Other African and European	Roman Catholic Protestant/independent Christian Muslim Traditional beliefs None	45% 28% 12% 10% 5%

Population density per sq. mi. 14.9
Literacy rate 86.2%
Life expectancy 52.5 male; 54.6 female
Per capita GDP $14,100
Labor force in agriculture 60%

Urban 83.6%
Infant mortality rate per 1,000 live births 52.6
HIV rate 5.9%
Unemployment rate 21%
Arable land 1%

Agriculture   plantains, sugarcane, cassava, cocoa, coffee, palm oil, chickens, rabbits, pigs, sheep, goats, cattle

Natural resources   oil, natural gas, diamonds, niobium, manganese, uranium, gold, timber, iron, hydropower, fish

Industries   oil extraction and refining, manganese, gold, chemicals, ship repair, food and beverages

History   Artifacts from Paleolithic times have been found in Gabon. Gabon's earliest inhabitants probably were the Pygmies. Bantus from southern and eastern Africa followed. The Fang arrived in the late 18th century. The Portuguese explored the area in the 15th century. The Dutch came in 1593. The French came in 1630, established their first settlement in 1839, and took control of the region in the second half of the 19th century. The slave trade dominated commerce in the 18th and much of the 19th century. Gabon became independent in 1960. Due to abundant natural resources, foreign private investment, and government programs, Gabon is one of the most prosperous black African countries. In 2007 food and fuel prices increased 25%. The government promised free electricity and water to the country's poorest households and also instituted price ceilings on basic commodities.

Influences on food   The ocean provides fish and seafood. The tropical lowlands, plateaus, and mountains produce cocoa, coffee, sugarcane, palm trees, and livestock. People rely on starchy roots, plantains, bananas, grains, legumes, and green leaves for daily fare. The introduction of New World foods such as cassava, corn, peanuts, tomato, chili pepper, potato, and cocoa greatly influenced food in Gabon. Native African foods include black-eyed peas, watermelon, and okra. French control in the 19th and 20th centuries also influenced the food.

Bread and cereals   Rice, corn, millet, sorghum; bread made from mashed bananas and flour.

Meat, poultry, fish   Chicken, pork, lamb and mutton, goat, beef, fish (fresh, smoked, salted, or dried), seafood, guinea fowl, eggs, rabbit, game. Chicken is popular.

Insects   Termites (often called white ants), locusts.

Dairy products   Milk, sour milk, buttermilk, curds, whey, cheese.

Fats and oils   Palm oil, peanut oil, shea oil, coconut oil. Palm oil, the main cooking fat, gives food a red color.

Legumes   Peanuts (groundnuts), black-eyed peas (cowpeas), locust beans (carob), red beans.

Vegetables   Plantains, cassava, yams, green leaves (cassava, bitter leaf), okra, tomatoes, sweet potatoes, potatoes, eggplant, pumpkin, onions, red chili peppers, cucumbers, bell peppers.

Fruit   Bananas, coconut, pineapple, akee apples, baobab, watermelon, guavas, lemons, dates, mangoes, papaya.

Nuts and seeds   Palm kernels, shea nuts, cashews, kola nuts, watermelon seeds (egusi), sesame seeds, mango seeds. Nuts and seeds thicken and flavor sauces.

Seasonings   Salt, palm oil, onions, red chili peppers, tomatoes, cocoa.

Dishes   Most foods are boiled or fried, and chunks are dipped in sauce and eaten by hand. Sauces of ground peanuts; boiled and pounded green leaves; or black-eyed pea or bean purée, fried yams. Fufu (a paste of boiled and pounded starchy vegetables or corn), formed into balls or bite-size scoops to eat stew. Stews of root vegetables, okra, or peanuts, with bits of fish, chicken, or beef. Moin moin (steamed ground paste of black-eyed peas, hot pepper, and onions). Rice boiled in coconut milk. Plantain cooked in palm oil with onions and chili. Omelet of eggs, onions, and red pepper. Roast chicken with peanut sauce.

Sweets   Honey, sugar, fried sweet dough balls, peanut candy, bananas baked with honey, sugar, or coconut.

Beverages   Cocoa, coffee, beer.

Street food and snacks   Spiced kabobs (coupé-coupé); fried fish, plantain chips, bean balls; balls of steamed rice, black-eyed peas, yams, or peanuts. Snacks are common and available at street stalls in urban areas.

GAMBIA, THE
Republic of The Gambia

Geography   Gambia is near the west tip of Africa, bordering the Atlantic Ocean. The smallest country in Africa, only miles wide, Gambia is primarily savanna and bisected by the wide Gambia River.

Major Languages	Ethnic Groups		Major Religions	
English (official)	Mandinka	42%	Muslim	90%
Mandinka (Malinke)	Fula	18%	Christian	9%
Fula (Fulani)	Wolof	16%	Indigenous	1%
Wolof	Diola	10%		
Other native dialects	Soninke and other	14%		

Population density per sq. mi. 444.9
Literacy rate 40.1%
Life expectancy 53.1 male; 55.9 female
Per capita GDP $1,300
Labor force in agriculture 75%

Urban 53.9%
Infant mortality rate per 1,000 live births 68.7
HIV rate 0.9%
Unemployment rate extremely high
Arable land 28%

Agriculture   Millet, peanuts, oil palm, sorghum, rice, corn, sesame, cassava, chickens, cattle, goats, sheep, pigs

Natural resources   fish, titanium, tin, zircon

Industries   peanut processing, fish, hides, tourism, beverages, agricultural machinery assembly

History   Since the 13th century, the Wolof, Malinke, and Fulani have settled here. The tribes here have been associated with the West African empires of Ghana, Mali, and Songhai. Gambia became Britain's first African possession, in 1588. It became independent in 1965 and a republic within the Commonwealth in 1970. Severe famine occurred in the 1970s. From 1982 to 1989 Gambia was confederated with Senegal into Senegambia. A military coup in 1994 deposed the president, who had served since 1970. The government was in turmoil during the 1990s and to 2006. In 2000 the peanut market collapsed due to mismanagement, leaving farmers unpaid after a bumper crop. In 2007 Gambia's president resisted pressure from China to drop the country's support for Taiwan. In 2008 he announced that substantial amounts of uranium had been discovered and would be exploited.

Influences on food   The Atlantic Ocean and Gambia River provide fish. Savanna provides grass for animal herds. British rule for almost 400 years left British influence. The introduction of New World foods such as corn, peanuts, chili pepper, cassava, tomato, and potato greatly influenced food customs in Gambia. Native African foods included watermelon, black-eyed peas, and okra. Daily fare is mostly starchy foods (grains and starchy vegetables) with legumes and greens. Meat is a luxury. Most foods are boiled or fried, and chunks are dipped in sauce and eaten by hand. Thick, sticky, spicy dishes are liked. Nuts and seeds thicken and flavor sauces.

Bread and cereals   Millet, sorghum, rice, corn; porridge, rice dishes, cornmeal and plantain cakes, biscuits.

Meat, poultry, fish   Chicken, beef, goat, lamb, pork, fish and seafood (fresh, smoked, salted, or dried), guinea fowl, eggs, rabbits, "Bush meat" (game, especially antelope and wild pig). Chicken is popular and prestigious.

Insects   Termites (often called white ants), locusts.

Dairy products   Milk, sour milk, buttermilk, curds, whey, cheese.

Fats and oils   Palm oil, shea oil, coconut oil. Palm oil, the predominant cooking fat, gives dishes a red hue.

Legumes   Peanuts (groundnuts), black-eyed peas (a variety of cowpeas), locust beans (carob), red beans.

Vegetables   Cassava, yams, plantains, taro, green leaves, okra, bitter leaf, melokhia (crain crain), tomatoes, sweet potatoes, potatoes, eggplant, pumpkin, onions, chili peppers, cucumbers, bell peppers.

Fruit   Coconut, akee apples, baobab, pineapple, watermelon, bananas, guavas, lemons, limes, mangoes, papaya.

Nuts and seeds   Cashews, kola nuts (contain caffeine), sesame seeds, watermelon seeds (egusi), mango seeds.

Seasonings   Salt, hot red chili peppers, tomatoes, onions, dried baobab leaves, ginger, thyme, "African nutmeg."

Dishes   Fufu (a paste of boiled and pounded starchy vegetables or boiled corn flour), formed into bite-size scoops to eat stew. Fish and meat stew. Stew of peanuts, okra, or root vegetables with chilies, tomatoes, and herbs and perhaps bits of fish, chicken, or beef. Peanut sauce. Palaver sauce (green leaves). Fréjon (black-eyed pea or bean purée, coconut milk, and sometimes carob or cocoa). Gari (roasted cassava meal). Steamed rice balls. Adalu (boiled or baked and mashed vegetables). Yassa (chicken or fish marinated in lemon or lime juice, grilled, fried with onions, and simmered in the marinade). Jollof rice (boiled rice with various meats, vegetables, and spices). Chicken baked with tomatoes, onions, okra, and peanut sauce.

Sweets   Honey, sugar, kanya (peanut candy), deep-fried sweet dough balls, banana fritters.

Beverages   Beer, red zinger (herbal tea made from flower pods of roselle, *Hibiscus sabdariffa*), ginger beer.

Street food and snacks   Shawerma (rotisserie lamb), fried fish, bean balls, puff-puff (doughnut), coconut biscuits.

GEORGIA

Geography   Georgia is in Southwest Asia bordering the east coast of the Black Sea, with the Caucasus Mountains to the northeast.

Major Languages	Ethnic Groups		Major Religions	
Georgian (official)	Georgian	84%	Orthodox Christian	84%
Russian	Azeri	7%	Muslim	10%
(official in Abkhazia)	Armenian	6%	Armenian-Gregorian	4%
	Russian, Ossetian, other	3%	Other	2%

Population density per sq. mi 172.1
Literacy rate 100%
Life expectancy 73.2 male; 80.3 female
Per capita GDP $4,700
Labor force in agriculture 55.6%

Urban 52.5%
Infant mortality rate per 1,000 live births 16.6
HIV rate 0.1%
Unemployment rate 13.8%
Arable land 12%

Agriculture   potatoes, corn, grapes, citrus, tea, hazelnuts, vegetables, chickens, cattle, sheep, pigs, goats

Natural resources   forests, hydropower, manganese, iron ore, copper, coal and oil deposits, fish

Industries   steel, aircraft, machine tools, electric appliances, mining, chemicals

History   The region became a kingdom about 4 BCE and contained the ancient kingdoms of Colchis and Iberia. It was part of the Roman Empire by 65 BCE. Christianity was introduced here in 337 CE. In the 8th century Arabs conquered Georgia, which over the centuries came to extend from the Black Sea to the Caspian Sea and to include parts of Armenia and Persia. Mongol and Turkish invasions in the 13th and 14th centuries disintegrated the kingdom. From the 16th century on, Persia and Turkey struggled here. In 1801 Russia annexed Georgia, leading to war with Persia (1804–1813). Georgia was forcibly incorporated into the USSR in 1922, became a USSR republic in 1936, and gained independence in 1991 when the Soviet Union disbanded. Since independence, conflicts have included separatist rebel movements by ethnic Abkhazis and South Ossetias, plus attempts to assassinate the president. In 1992 the northwestern republic of Abkhazia declared its independence, which Georgia does not recognize. A temporary administration for the republic of South Ossetia was endorsed by the Georgian parliament in 2007. In 2008 Russia sent forces to South Ossetia and Abkhazia, recognized the independence of both, and assaulted key Georgian cities; the United States authorized $1 billion in reconstruction for Georgia.

Influences on food   Influences include the invaders (Arabs, Mongols, and Turks), Persia, Russia (that controlled Georgia for most of the 19th and 20th centuries), and neighbors (Russia, Turkey, Armenia, and Azerbaijan). Also, it is generally agreed that Georgia has had a favorable influence on Russian cuisine. The northernmost country of the Caucasus, Georgia has a Mediterranean-type climate and some fertile land that grows grain, fruit, and vegetables. Located at the east end of the Black Sea, Georgia has fish and seafood, as well as suitable conditions for growing tea. Also, rivers and lakes provide fish. Located on the southern slopes of the Caucasus Mountains, Georgia has forests that supply nuts and game, and high pastures for grazing livestock. In western Georgia, Turkish influence is strong, corn is the main grain, and tea and citrus are grown. In eastern Georgia, Persian influence is strong, wheat bread is preferred, and grapes and other fruits flourish. Religion also influences food practices. Orthodox Christians do not consume animal products on the many fast days. Observant Muslims do not consume pork products or alcohol and fast from sunup to sundown during the month of Ramadan.

Bread and cereals   Corn, wheat, rice; lavash (thin crisp bread), peda (pita bread), mchadi (round flat cornbread), kachapuri (bread stuffed with cheese before baking), long loaves of white bread, porridge, rice dishes. Bread is often baked in a toné (an outdoor brick-lined pit oven). Bread is eaten at every meal.

Meat, poultry, fish   Chicken, beef, pork, lamb, goat, fish, eggs, game; sausage.

Dairy products   Milk (cow, sheep, water buffalo), sour cream, cultured clabber (matsoni), yogurt, cheese.

Fats and oils   Butter, clarified butter, olive oil.

Legumes   Beans especially kidney beans, lentils, split peas.

Vegetables   Potatoes, tomatoes, greens, eggplant, green beans, asparagus, cucumbers, onions, olives; pickles.

Fruit   Grapes, citrus, plums, apricots, barberries, other berries, cherries, figs, pomegranates, melon, raisins.

Nuts   Hazelnuts, walnuts, almonds, chestnuts. Walnuts are used liberally in cooking and not just as a garnish.

Seasonings   Onions, garlic, parsley, tarragon, mint, basil, dill, coriander, oregano, thyme, fenugreek, cardamom, cinnamon, cloves, saffron, black pepper, red pepper, marigold petals. Herbs and spices are used liberally.

Dishes   Soups thickened from either egg or acidic ingredients. Chikhirtma (chicken stock with egg yolks, saffron, and lemon juice added just before serving so as not to curdle). Sauces: satsivi (contains walnuts pounded with garlic, with chopped onions browned in butter and bouillon added; often used on roasted poultry and a little is often added to fruit sauces); tkemali (tart plums stewed with coriander, red pepper, and garlic); others featuring grapes, barberries, pomegranates, tomatoes, garlic, or yogurt. Meat cooked in chunks on skewers (kebab). Mtswadi (grilled marinated game or unseasoned lamb or kid). Roast suckling pig. Fish smoked, boiled, or broiled. Mountain trout fried in butter. Chicken boiled whole and covered with pomegranate sauce. Chakhokhbili (chicken pieces rolled in finely chopped onions, fried in butter, then layered with tomatoes, covered, and simmered). Kharcho (beef, onion, and tomato soup/stew with fenugreek). Chankhi (stew of a little meat, a lot of vegetables, and often with rice). Lubio (simmered kidney beans mixed with scallions, coriander, tarragon vinegar, and olive oil). Plov (rice dishes). Ghome (cornmeal porridge). Baked casserole of green beans with beaten eggs poured over. Eggplant baked with onion, garlic, lemon juice, oil, and coriander or with fried onions and tomatoes (Adzhersandal). Deep-fried cheese eaten with cornbread.

Sweets   Honey (sometimes in the comb), sugar. Fresh fruit. Apricots, cherries, or melon rind cooked in syrup. Chuchkella (walnut halves coated with grape candy). Gozinakh (walnut, almond, or hazelnut honey brittle).

Beverages   Milk, tea, wine, brandy.

Zakuski   (small appetizers served before main meal) Cheese, greens (tarragon, cress, scallions), thin bread.

GERMANY
Federal Republic of Germany

Geography   Germany is in central Europe, bordering the North Sea and the Baltic Sea. It has flat land in the north, hills in the center and west, and mountains in the south, with rivers, including the Rhine and Danube.

Major Language	Ethnic Groups		Major Religions	
German (official)	German	92%	Lutheran/Reformed	34%
	Turkish	2%	Roman Catholic	34%
	Italian	1%	Sunni Muslim	4%
	Other	5%	Other or unaffiliated	28%

Population density per sq. mi 610.9
Literacy rate 99%
Life expectancy 76.1 male; 82.3 female
Per capita GDP $34,200
Labor force in agriculture 2.8%

Urban 73.4%
Infant mortality rate per 1,000 live births 4
HIV rate 0.1%
Unemployment rate 8.0%
Arable land 33%

Agriculture   sugar beets, wheat, potatoes, barley, rapeseed, grapes, fruit, cabbage, chickens, pigs, cattle, sheep, goats

Natural resources   coal, lignite, natural gas, iron ore, copper, nickel, uranium, potash, salt, construction materials, timber, fish

Industries   iron, steel, coal, cement, chemicals, machinery, vehicles, machine tools, electronics, food and beverages, shipbuilding

History   Celts probably were the first inhabitants. German tribes followed by the end of the 2nd century BCE; they were defeated by Julius Caesar, 56 and 53 BCE. Germanic invasions destroyed the Roman Empire in the 4th and 5th centuries. Charlemagne ruled Saxon, Bavarian, Rhenish, Frankish, and other lands, the eastern part of which became the German Empire. The Holy Roman Empire, centering on Germany and northern Italy, gained strength after the 10th century. Conflict between the Holy Roman emperors and and the Roman Catholic popes, aided by Luther's revolt in 1517, divided the empire into Protestant and Roman Catholic parts and led to the Thirty Years' War, 1618 to 1648. The war left Germany in small principalities and kingdoms. Austria lost the land to Prussia in 1866. Prussian chancellor Otto von Bismarck formed the North German Confederation in 1867, defeated France in 1870, and formed the German Empire, proclaiming King Wilhelm I of Prussia the German emperor in 1871. Numerous central European states with a common culture were united to form Germany in 1871. After World War I, in 1918, the German Empire was dissolved, and Germany lost much of its land and all its colonies; it was the Republic of Germany (1919–1933). In 1933 Adolf Hitler became chancellor of the totalitarian state, the Third Reich, controlled by the Nazi Party. Hitler invaded Poland in 1939, starting World War II. After that war, defeated Germany was split into two countries, East Germany and West Germany, and Berlin, the former capital, was divided. From 1961 to 1989, the Berlin Wall surrounded West Berlin and prevented access to it from East Berlin and adjacent areas of East Germany. West Germany, with its capital in Bonn, became a prosperous parliamentary democracy. East Germany, with Berlin as its capital, was a one-party state under Soviet control. In 1990 Germany was reunited and Berlin again became the capital. Unemployment hit a postwar high in 1998. In 2002 record floods occurred. The recession continued in 2003 and the government reduced benefits. In 2007 the economy improved. In 2008 Germany agreed to add troops to its forces, part of a NATO peacekeeping force, in Afghanistan.

Influences on food   Germany is a large and diverse country that produces a variety of foods. Coasts and rivers provide fish and seafood. Other influences include the Roman Empire,

Charlemagne's uniting most of Europe into a Christian community by around 800, the Crusades and Arab conquests, spice trade, France, and the New World. Some examples are grape cuttings first planted in the Rhineland by the Romans; banquets influenced by Roman times and Charlemagne's court; marzipan from ancient Persia; spice cookies and cakes; French cuisine and French cooks brought late in the 18th century when coffee, tea, chocolate, and pastries became popular; and the potato from the New World. Prior to unification of Germany in 1871, the region was a collection of small independent states, with the separate German-speaking kingdoms of Prussia in the north and east, Saxony in the center, and Württemburg and Bavaria in the south. These divisions reflect in the culinary regions of Germany today. The north region is influenced by proximity to Scandinavia and the North and Baltic seas; its cold climate fare includes dark rye bread, seafood, pork, potatoes, and apples. The central region, with rolling hills and forests, has a rich and hearty cuisine, as depicted in a 15th-century stained-glass window in a church in the town of Soest; shown is the Last Supper but with Westphalian ham, pumpernickel bread, and beer on the sacred table. The south has lighter food, with wheat bread, Italian influence in the mountains, Rhineland white wines, Baden game and Black Forest cake, and Bavarian strudel and meatless Fridays in this Catholic area. German fare is hearty, with meat, potatoes, bread, beer, and wholesome family-type dishes, although with fancy decorated pastries. The frankfurter (a sausage from Frankfurt) and hamburger (Deutsches beefsteak) have spread around the world.

Bread and cereals   Wheat, barley, rye, rice; bread (white, wheat, and dark rye, or pumpernickel, loaves), rolls, dumplings, salty biscuits (Salzgebäck), doughnuts, pancakes, kugelhopf (round yeast cake), rice dishes.

Meat, poultry, fish   Pork, chicken, beef and veal, lamb, goat, fish and shellfish (herring, eel, sole, salmon, pike, carp), goose, duck, game (wild boar, venison, wild birds), eggs; sausages, ham (Westphalian ham, lightly smoked, cured, and cut into paper-thin slices). Sausages (wurst): rohwurst (cured and smoked; may be eaten as is); bruhwurst (the frankfurter type, smoked and scalded; may be eaten as is or simmered); knockwurst (fully cooked and like a cold cut); and bratwurst (similar to sausage links, sold raw; must be cooked before eating).

Dairy products   Milk, buttermilk, cream, sour cream, cheeses (including Emmentel, Limburger, Münster).

Fats and oils   Butter, lard, bacon, chicken fat, goose fat, vegetable oil, olive oil.

Legumes   Kidney beans, navy beans, white beans, lentils, split peas.

Vegetables   Potatoes, cabbage (red and green), beets, asparagus, spinach, peas, carrots, cucumbers, green beans, lettuce, cauliflower, celery, onions, turnips, mushrooms, artichokes, green peppers, tomatoes; sauerkraut (salted and fermented cabbage), dill pickles (made from cucumbers).

Fruit   Grapes, apples, currants, gooseberries, pears, plums, prunes, apricots, raisins, cherries, oranges, lemons.

Nuts and seeds   Almonds, chestnuts, hazelnuts, walnuts, anise seeds, caraway seeds, poppy seeds.

Seasonings   Salt, sour cream, vinegar, dill, mustard, black pepper, lemon juice, onions, garlic, allspice, cinnamon, cloves, ginger, horseradish, parsley, nutmeg, cardamom, tarragon, thyme, sage, vanilla and almond extracts, chocolate, cocoa. Sour taste and combined sweet and sour tastes are common. Meat is often cooked with fruit.

Dishes   Pickled herring. Bismarck herring (fillets soaked in vinegar with onion rings and seasonings). Rolllmops (marinated herring fillets rolled around onions and pickle). Thick soups made from potatoes, dried peas, or lentils, with sausage or bacon and onion, and thickened with flour. Cream soups such as cream of cauliflower. Fish such as sole or salmon poached or sautéed and served with butter or lemon sauce. Pike or carp stuffed, cooked in wine, and served with sour cream sauce or sweet-and-sour sauce with raisins and spices. Duck, braised in beer or wine, or stuffed with apples or prunes and roasted. Goose (a favorite) stuffed with onions, apples, and herbs and roasted.

Schwarzsauer (a stew of goose blood and giblets with dried fruit). Venison or wild boar roasted or braised and served with mushrooms and tart berry sauce (Preiselbeeren). Pork (the most common meat) or veal schnitzel (thin slice lightly breaded and fried). Grilled pork chops. Roast pork with dried apples, pears, apricots, and prunes. Roast chicken or pheasant sometimes stuffed with green grapes. Steak Tartar (raw ground beef and sometimes pork or veal) served on toast or with egg yolk, onions, anchovies, capers, and parsley. Grilled or fried hamburger. Poached meatballs. Eintoff (one-pot dish of simmered meat and vegetables). Stewed fruit (e.g., prunes for pork). Dumplings (knödel) usually boiled, large ones served with roast meat, small ones in soups, and tiny ones (spätzle) in the south. Potatoes boiled, roasted, or mashed, also in dumplings, pancakes, and salad. Himmel and Erde (heaven and earth), simmered apples and potatoes topped with bacon and onion rings cooked in bacon drippings. Red cabbage and apples simmered with vinegar and onions. Green or cucumber salad. Beets simmered with wine, vinegar, onion, and spices. Green herb sauce. Simmered asparagus with hollandaise sauce.

National dish   Braten (roast) of pork, beef, or veal (e.g., sauerbraten: roast marinated in vinegar, wine, or buttermilk, braised with a little liquid in a tightly covered pot, and served with gingersnap crumbs and sour sauce).

Festival and holiday foods   Sausage and beer for Oktoberfest, an annual festival in late September and early October. Advent and Christmas, the most holy seasons in this mostly Christian country, feature a lighted, decorated tree (the Christmas tree custom comes from Germany), gifts, and carp for dinner on Christmas Eve; roast goose with apple, raisin, and nut stuffing on Christmas Day; and spice cakes and cookies (lebkuchen and pfeffernüsse), stollen (sweet yeast bread with almonds, raisins, currants, and candied fruit), gingerbread, and marzipan (paste of almonds and sugar with rosewater or orange, colored and shaped as fruits) for the seasons.

Sweets   Honey, sugar. Rice pudding with fruit, custard, cream, and liqueur added. Hazelnut cream pudding (egg custard with ground hazelnuts folded with whipped cream and chilled). Apple pancakes with hazelnut cream. Streuselkuchen (yeast cake with cinnamon crumb topping).Cookies: spritzgebäck (pressed hazelnut); springerle (molded anise seed). Honey and spice cakes (lebkuchen and pfesserkuchen). Apple strudel (sliced apples, sugar, cinnamon, and raisins rolled in buttered paper-thin dough and baked). Black Forest cake (Schwarzwälder Kirschtorte), chocolate layer cake with kirsch (cherry liqueur), whipped cream, cherries, and chocolate curls.

Beverages   Milk, beer, coffee, wine (usually white). The most common beer is lager, a light (helles) beer; bock, a dark (dunkle) beer, has the strongest flavor and highest alcohol content.

Meals   (five a day) Breakfast: bread with butter and jam. Second breakfast (midmorning): coffee and sandwich or fruit. Midday meal: soup; meat with vegetables; dessert usually with whipped cream. Kaffee (afternoon sociable snack): coffee and small cakes or cookies. Evening meal (abend-brot): bread, butter, and assorted fish, cold cuts, cheese, sausage, ham or salad. Later in the evening guests may come for dessert and wine or beer.

Snacks   Torte and kuchen (fruit tarts and pastries like cherry tarts, cream puffs), sold in konditorei, and coffee.

GHANA
Republic of Ghana

Geography   Ghana is In West Africa, bordering the Atlantic Ocean. It consists of low fertile plains and scrubland, a coastal strip, and the Volta River and Lake Volta.

Major Languages	Ethnic Groups		Major Religions	
English (official)	Akan	45%	Christian	69%
Asante	Mole-Dagbon	15%	Muslim	16%
Ewe	Ewe	12%	Indigenous beliefs	9%
Fante	Ga	7%	None	6%
	Other	21%		

Population density per sq. mi 262.2
Literacy rate 65%
Life expectancy 58.6 male; 60.4 female
Per capita GDP $1,400
Labor force in agriculture 56%

Urban 47.8%
Infant mortality rate per 1,000 live births 52.3
HIV rate 1.9%
Unemployment rate 20.3%
Arable land 18%

Agriculture   cassava, yams, plantains, cocoa, rice, peanuts, corn, shea nuts, bananas, chickens, goats, sheep, cattle, pigs

Natural resources   gold, timber, industrial diamonds, bauxite, manganese, fish, rubber, hydropower

Industries   mining, lumbering, light manufacturing, aluminum smelting, food processing

History   Major civilizations flourished in this region: the Ghana Empire along the Niger River (400–1240 CE); the Akan civilization, starting in the 13th century; and the Ashanti Empire, in the 18th and 19th centuries. Portuguese traders came in 1470, landing on the Gold Coast, where gold-seeking Mande traders had arrived by the 14th century. The Portuguese later established a settlement, Elmira, as headquarters for the slave trade. The English came in 1553, the Dutch in 1595, and Swedes in 1640. Britain controlled this region as the Gold Coast from 1820 until it became independent in 1957 and a republic within the Commonwealth in 1960. Hospitals, schools, and development projects (the Volta River hydroelectric and aluminum plants) were built in the 1960s; however, debt and accusations of government corruption ensued. Political conflicts occurred in the following decades. The first peaceful transfer of power from one elected president to another was in 2001. Ghanaian Kofi Annan was UN secretary general from 1997 to 2006. A major offshore oil find was reported in 2007.

Influences on food   Ghana is said to have one of West Africa's best cuisines. A main influence was the introduction of New World foods such as cassava, cocoa, corn, peanuts, tomato, chili pepper, and potato during the 16th and later centuries. Native African foods include black-eyed peas, watermelon, and okra. British control for over a century left some British influence. The Gulf of Guinea, rivers, and Lake Volta provide fish. The fertile plains produce cocoa, grains, root crops, peanuts, plantains, bananas, and some animals. Daily fare is mostly grains, starchy vegetables, legumes, and greens, with fish if nearby. Spicy, thick, sticky foods are liked.

Bread and cereals   Rice, corn, millet, sorghum; millet porridge (tazafi) in the north, fermented corn balls (kenkey) steamed in corn husks in the south, rice dishes, cornmeal and plantain cakes.

Meat, poultry, fish   Chicken, goat, lamb and mutton, beef, pork, fish and seafood (fresh, smoked, salted, or dried), guinea fowl, eggs, rabbit, game, forest snails. Chicken is a popular, prestigious food.

Insects   Termites (often called white ants), locusts.

Dairy products   Milk, sour milk, buttermilk, curds, whey, cheese.

Fats and oils   Shea oil, palm oil, peanut oil, coconut oil. Palm oil, the predominant cooking fat, is red.

Legumes   Peanuts (groundnuts), black-eyed peas, locust beans (carob), red beans.

Vegetables   Cassava, yams, plantains, green leaves, okra, tomatoes, bitter leaf, melokhia (crain crain), sweet potatoes, potatoes, eggplant, pumpkin (ponkie), onions, hot red chili peppers, cucumbers, bell peppers, parsley.

Fruit   Bananas, coconut, pineapple, akee apples, baobab, watermelon, lemons, oranges, mangoes, papaya.

Nuts and seeds   Shea nuts, palm kernels, cashews, kola nuts, watermelon seeds, sesame seeds, mango seeds.

Seasonings   Salt, chili, tomato, onion, garlic, dried baobab leaves, thyme, "African nutmeg," horseradish, cocoa.

Dishes   Most foods are boiled or fried such as boiled rice, rice boiled in coconut milk, boiled okra, hard-boiled eggs, fried plantains, and fried yams. Sauces: palaver (green leaves); and fréjon (black-eyed pea or bean purée, coconut milk, and sometimes carob or chocolate). Fufu (paste of boiled and pounded starchy vegetables or boiled corn flour) formed into balls or bite-size scoops to eat stew. Peanut stew (ground peanuts with tomatoes, onions, peppers, garlic, and sometimes chicken). Pumpkin stewed with other vegetables and minced meat. Gari foto (cassava meal cooked with tomatoes, onions, peppers, and scrambled eggs). Tatali (fried cakes of cornmeal and plantain with hot peppers). Roast chicken with peanut sauce. Red snapper marinated in lemon juice and dressed with oil, chilies, thyme, parsley, and grated coconut. Imogo (fish and prawns simmered separately; boned and shelled, respectively; combined and dressed with lemon juice and chopped red pepper, tomato, onion, and minced garlic). Akotonshi (stuffed land crabs). Chicken gizzards grilled on wood skewers. Pili-pili (sauce of chili pepper, tomato, onion, garlic, and horseradish), often on the table.

Sweets   Honey, sugar, deep-fried bright colored sweet dough balls (togbei), pineapple fritters with peanut cream.

Beverages   Cocoa, coffee, beer, red zinger (herbal tea made from flower pods of roselle (*Hibiscus sabdariffa*).

Street food and snacks   Spicy kabobs, fried fish, steamed rice balls, coconut biscuits, sweet porridge.

GREECE
Hellenic Republic

Geography   Greece is in southeast Europe on the southern end of the Balkan Peninsula, bordering the Mediterranean Sea. Greece has mountains in all areas and a heavily indented coastline.

Major Language	Ethnic Groups		Major Religions	
Greek (official)	Greek	93%	Greek Orthodox (official)	98%
	Other	7%	Muslim	1%
			Other	1%

Population density per sq. mi 212.3
Literacy rate 97.1%
Life expectancy 77 male; 82.2 female
Per capita GDP $29,200
Labor force in agriculture 12%

Urban 60.4%
Infant mortality rate per 1,000 live births 5.2
HIV rate 0.2%
Unemployment rate 8.0%
Arable land 20%

Agriculture   sugar beets, corn, olives, wheat, barley, tomatoes, grapes, wine, tobacco, potatoes, chickens, sheep, goats, pigs, cattle, beehives

Natural resources   fish, lignite, oil, iron ore, bauxite, lead, zinc, nickel, magnesite

Industries   tourism, food and tobacco processing, textiles, chemicals, metal products

History   The Minoan civilization reached its peak on Crete c. 2000 BCE. It was succeeded by the Mycenaean civilization c. 1600 BCE, after invasions by Indo-Europeans. Additional invasions destroyed the Bronze Age culture, and a dark age ensued, as told about in the epics of Homer. Classical Greece began to emerge c. 750 BCE as a group of city-states. Ancient Greece excelled in art, architecture, science, mathematics, philosophy, drama, literature, and democracy, reaching its height of power in the 5th century BCE. In 338 BCE Greece was taken over by Philip II of Macedon, and his son, Alexander the Great, who spread Greek culture throughout his empire. In the 2nd century BCE the Romans conquered the Greek states. After the fall of the Roman Empire, Greece was part of the Byzantine Empire until the 15th century. After the fall of Constantinople to the Turks in 1453, Greece was part of the Ottoman Empire. It won its independence in a war with Turkey (1821–1829) and became a kingdom. It became a republic in 1924; the monarchy was restored in 1935. During World War II Nazi forces occupied Greece. In 1944 the monarchy was restored. Political and military changes occurred during the next some 20 years, King Constantine fled to Italy in 1967, democratic government returned, and in 1975 the monarchy was abolished. Greece joined NATO in 1952 and the EU in 1981. Turmoil in the Balkans in the 1990s led to strained relations between Greece and some neighbors, notably the former Yugoslavia that took the name Republic of Macedonia. Athens suffered a damaging earthquake in 1999. It hosted the Olympic Summer Games in 2004. Devastating forest fires occurred in 2007. The economy performed well, with unemployment decreasing and tourism remaining strong. The first official visit by a Greek official to Turkey in 49 years occurred in 2008.

Influences on food   The Mediterranean and Aegean coasts provide fish and seafood to this small country. Much of the land is mountainous and rocky, another important influence. Much of the terrain is terraced and planted with trees that will withstand the heat and aridity, notably the olive. Vine cultivation is also important, for fruit and especially for wine. In general, the food is frugal and relies on fresh ingredients: vegetables, fish, seafood, olive oil, and fruit. The cuisine of ancient and modern Greece shows remarkable continuity in dishes such as cracked whole wheat boiled in milk, sun dried, and stored for winter soup making (tarhana); garlic sauce that accompanies fried fish (skordalia), and yellow split-pea purée soup dressed with raw onion, olive oil, and lemon (fava). Bread- and pie-making are a long tradition. Influences on food include the Roman, Byzantine, and Ottoman Empires, as well as Arab, Turkey, and Balkan neighbors. Greece shares a cuisine with the other Middle East countries except for differences due to religion. Greek Orthodox Christianity, predominant in Greece, does not prohibit consumption of pork or alcohol, as does Islam in the Muslim countries. Judaism, predominant in Israel, also prohibits pork consumption. Also, fasting and feasting rules differ between Orthodox Christians and Muslims. The Orthodox religion limits animal food intake on its many fast days, especially during Lent, and has special foods for religious holidays, notably Easter.

Bread and cereals   Corn, wheat, barley, rice; pita bread (flat, round, hollow center), filo dough, pasta, rice dishes.

Meat, poultry, fish   Chicken, lamb, goat, pork, beef, fish and seafood, eggs; sausage, preserved salted fish.

Dairy products   Milk, yogurt, feta cheese (moist, white, salty), kefalotiri cheese (hard, yellow, often grated).

Fats and oil   Olive oil, butter.

Legumes   Beans (including fava and white beans), lentils, chickpeas, yellow split peas.

Vegetables   Olives, tomatoes, potatoes, eggplant, grape leaves, cucumbers, green peppers, squash, scallions.

Fruit   Grapes, lemons, oranges, figs, plums, cherries, apricots, raisins, currants, quinces.

Nuts and seeds   Almonds, hazelnuts, walnuts, sesame seeds.

Seasonings   Lemons, onions, garlic, olive oil, oregano, vinegar, parsley, thyme, dill, sparing use of spices (black pepper, cumin, cinnamon, cloves, allspice, aniseed) except on Aegean coast, where Arab influence is strongest.

Dishes   Moussaka (baked sliced eggplant, ground meat, tomatoes and onions covered with beaten egg or white sauce). Winter and Lenten soups of beans, lentils, and chickpeas such as fasolatha (white bean soup with tomatoes and garlic). Vegetables and grape leaves stuffed with rice, meat, and seasonings. Olive relishes. Fried strips of yellow cheese. Greek salad (greens, cucumber, tomato, scallions, black olives, and feta cheese dressed with oil and vinegar). Deep-fried fish served with skordalia (garlic, olive oil, lemon juice, and bread pieces or mashed potato). Casserole of shrimp, tomatoes, and feta cheese. Lamb shank roasted with garlic, onion, lemon juice, tomato. Intestines or caul stuffed with rice, liver, lights (lungs), heart, kidney, parsley, black pepper, and allspice. Chicken pieces braised in tomatoes, onion, garlic, and cinnamon. Spaghetti and sauce of ground beef, onions, tomatoes, cinnamon. Boiled potatoes. Sautéed squash.

Coastal and island cuisine   Light, mainly vegetables and seafood dishes such as fish soup finished with avgolémono (egg and lemon juice) sauce and psarosoupa (soup of fish, rice, tomatoes, and other vegetables).

Inland mountains and plains fare   Robust, mostly breads, cheeses, cheese or meat pies such as spanakopita (baked filo dough layered with spinach and feta cheese), and paximathia (baked barley bread slices and aniseed).

Holiday dishes   Christmas stuffed turkey. New Year roasted suckling pig. Easter spit-roasted whole baby lamb or goat, hard-boiled eggs painted red.

Sweets   Honey, sugar. Spoon sweets (fruits boiled with sugar) offered by the spoonful as a sweet welcome to any guest on arrival at a home. Halva (boiled semolina, oil, and sugar). Baklava (baked layers of filo dough, nuts, and syrup). For Christmas and New Year, traditional cakes such as melomarkaroma (honey-dipped biscuits made with olive oil and orange juice) and kourabiethes (butter cookies studded with almonds and dusted with powdered sugar). For New Year's Eve, a large, high, rich yeast cake (vasilopitta, or St. Basil's cake). For Easter, cakes decorated with red-painted hard-boiled eggs and often individually shaped as hens or rabbits for each child in the family. Fruits are served at the end of a meal; cakes and puddings are eaten with coffee.

Beverages   Wine, beer, Turkish-style coffee, ouzo (anise-flavored alcoholic drink), retsina (resinated wine).

Service   Greeks prefer flatware to fingers for eating.

Mezze   Feta cheese cubes, olives, tomato wedges, scallions, taramosalata (dip of fish roe beaten with lemon juice, olive oil, and bread pieces), lamb chopped liver and lights wrapped with intestine on skewers and roasted.

Street food   Gyro (sandwich of thin slices of souvlaki, or rotisserie lamb, in pita bread with tomato and yogurt).

GRENADA

Geography   Grenada (Pronunciation: first A is long.) is In the Caribbean Sea about 90 miles north of Venezuela. It includes a mountainous, volcanic main island and Carriacou and Petit Martinique islands.

Major Languages	Ethnic Groups		Major Religions	
English (official)	Black	82%	Roman Catholic	53%
French patois	Mixed	13%	Anglican	14%
	Indo-Pakistan and other	5%	Other Protestant	33%

Population density per sq. mi 680.2
Literacy rate 96%
Life expectancy 63.7 male; 67.5 female
Per capita GDP $10,500
Labor force in agriculture 24%

Urban 30.6%
Infant mortality rate per 1,000 live births 13.6
HIV rate NA
Unemployment rate 12.2%
Arable land 6%

Agriculture   sugarcane, coconuts, nutmeg, bananas, cocoa, mace, citrus, avocados, chickens, sheep, goats, cattle, pigs

Natural resources   timber, tropical fruit, fish

Industries   food and beverages, textiles, light assembly operations, tourism, construction

History   The first inhabitants were Arawak Indians, who were massacred by the Carib Indians. When Columbus arrived in 1498, he encountered the Caribs, who ruled here for 150 more years. French settlers came in 1650. France controlled the island from 1672 to 1762; then Britain controlled it until it became independent in 1974. In 1983, after a military coup and execution of the prime minister, four cabinet members, and six supporters, forces from the United States and six area nations invaded Granada; democratic self-government was reestablished. Hurricanes caused severe damage in 2004 and 2005. In 2007 Grenada's High Court ordered the release of 3 of the 13 imprisoned leaders of the 1983 insurrection.

Influences on food   Arawak and Carib Indians ate fish and seafood and fruits and vegetables, using foods available from the sea and grown on this tropical island. The same foods are used today, along with foods brought to the region by the Spanish, French, British, and others. French control for almost a century and British control for over two centuries left influences on Grenada's food. For example, British influence is reflected in salt cod, biscuits, and tea. Slaves from Africa also influenced foodways such as in using okra. In 1843 an English captain sailing home from the Spice Islands in the East Indies stopped in Grenada and left some small nutmeg trees. Now Grenada, a leading producer of nutmeg and mace (which grow on the same tree) is called the Spice Island.

Bread and cereals   Corn, rice, wheat; fried cornmeal cakes, rice dishes, wheat flour breads, cassava bread (made from grated cassava fried in a flat loaf), bread and biscuits made using wheat flour and cassava.

Meat, poultry, fish   Chicken, eggs, lamb, goat, beef, pork, fish and seafood (salt cod, snapper, flying fish, sea turtles, sea eggs also called sea urchins, lobster, land crabs, frogs).

Dairy products   Cow's milk (fresh, condensed, evaporated), cream, aged cheese.

Fats and oils   Butter, lard, coconut oil, vegetable oil.

Legumes   Kidney beans, red beans, black-eyed peas, chickpeas, pigeon peas.

Vegetables   Avocados, cassava, yams, malanga (taro-like plant with corms and green leaves), sweet potatoes, plantains, breadfruit, squash, tomatoes, okra, onions, chilies, sweet peppers.

Fruit   Bananas, coconut, oranges, limes, mangoes, papaya, guavas, cashew fruit, akee, pineapple, sour sop.

Nuts and seeds   Almonds, cashew nuts, annatto seeds.

Seasonings   Nutmeg, mace, salt, black pepper, chilies, cocoa, allspice, annatto, cinnamon, garlic, rum.

Dishes   Callaloo (soup of malanga leaves cooked with okra). Pepper pot (a meat stew containing boiled juice of cassava and pepper). Cold soups such as avocado soup, breadfruit vichyssoise (breadfruit simmered with butter, onions, and garlic, blended, cream added and blended, and chilled), and jellied orange consommé (made by heating gelatin in chicken stock, adding fresh orange juice, and chilling). Turtle soup. Fried cornmeal and okra bread. Codfish fritters. Fried plantains. Boiled rice. Rice cooked with peas or beans. Hot chili sauce.

Sweets Sugarcane, molasses, sugar, guava and nutmeg jelly, coconut biscuits, chocolate mousse, cornmeal cake (cornmeal, wheat flour, fruit, and rum), sour sop fool (sour sop and whipped cream, folded and chilled).

Beverages Coffee with milk, tea, iced tea usually with lime, fruit juices, soft drinks, milk, cocoa, beer, rum.

Meals Breakfast: bread and coffee with milk. Lunch: rice and beans or peas with meat if affordable. Dinner: like lunch but with more meat, vegetables, milk, and dessert added when available.

Snacks Fruits, sweetened fruit juices poured over crushed ice, coffee with milk, tea with coconut biscuits.

GUATEMALA
Republic of Guatemala

Geography The northernmost Central American country, Guatemala consists of cool central highlands and mountains, a narrow strip along the Pacific Ocean, and lowlands and fertile river valleys along the Caribbean.

Major Languages	Ethnic Groups		Major Religions	
Spanish (official)	Mestizo (mixed	64%	Roman Catholic	57%
Amerindian languages	Amerindian & Spanish)		Protestant/other Christian	40%
	Amerindian (Mayan)	33%	Indigenous Mayan beliefs	
	Black, white	3%	and other	3%

Population density per sq. mi 310.6
Literacy rate 73.2%
Life expectancy 68.2 male; 71.9 female
Per capita GDP $4,700
Labor force in agriculture 50%

Urban 47.2%
Infant mortality rate per 1,000 live births 28.8
HIV rate 0.8%
Unemployment 7.5%
Arable land 13%

Agriculture sugarcane, bananas, corn, coffee, beans, cardamom, chickens, cattle, sheep, pigs, goats

Natural resources oil, nickel, rare woods, fish, chicle, hydropower

Industries sugar, textiles and clothing, furniture, chemicals, oil, metals, rubber, tourism

History The ancient Mayan Indian Empire flourished here over 1,000 years before the Spanish conquest. Guatemala was a Spanish colony from 1524 to 1821, a part of Mexico, a part of the United States of Central America, and finally an independent republic in 1839. A series of dictators held power for the next century. An elected liberal government took control in 1945 and instituted reforms. Various governments and periods of civil war and armed conflict have ensued. Drought and weak export prices in 2001–2002 worsened the conditions of Guatemala's poor, 80% of the population. In 2004 an extremely violent crime wave occurred. In 2005 a free-trade agreement (CAFTA) with the United States was ratified. In 2007 three Salvadorans on an official visit were murdered.

Influences on food The Maya influence has endured especially in the highlands. Corn remains as a staple, and the ancient dishes tamales and tortillas are still popular. The Spanish brought new foods including rice, beef, pork and lard, coconut, and breadfruit. Caribbean island foodways from native Carib-speaking Indians and laborers from Africa and Asia imported to work influenced food on the Caribbean coast of Guatemala.

Staple foods Corn, beans, rice.

Bread and cereals Corn, rice, wheat; corn tortillas, gruel, drinks; rice dishes; wheat bread, small rolls, turnovers.

Meat, poultry, fish Chicken, beef, pork, lamb, goat, fish, seafood, eggs; sausage.

Dairy products Milk (evaporated), cream, sour cream, cheese. Milk is not usually drunk as a beverage.

Fats and oils Lard, butter, vegetable oils, shortening.

Legumes Beans (black, red, kidney, white), chickpeas. Black beans are especially popular.

Vegetables Plantains, cassava, tomatoes, sweet peppers, chayote squash (green pear shaped gourd), avocados, pumpkin, breadfruit, chili peppers, onions, potatoes, cabbage, carrots, green beans, lettuce, beets.

Fruit Bananas, oranges, other citrus, coconut, pineapple, mangoes, roselle fruit (used to make sorrel drinks and jams/jellies), grapes, papaya, passion fruit, prunes, raisins.

Nuts and seeds Palm tree nuts, squash seeds.

Seasonings Cardamom, onions, garlic, achiote (orange-red coloring), chili, cilantro, chocolate, cinnamon, vanilla.

Dishes Atole (corn gruel). Posole (semi-fermented corn dough, diluted to make a beverage or used in other ways). Mixtas (open-faced sandwich of tortilla spread with guacamole, then topped with a sausage and pickled cabbage). Tamales (spicy meat-stuffed corn dough, wrapped in corn husks or leaves, and steamed). Empanadas (small turnovers made with wheat flour dough filled with a savory meat mixture). Beans simmered with spices, puréed, or fried and often paired with rice (frijoles con arroz). Refried black beans (frijoles volteados), called Guatemalan caviar. Rice fried before boiling or cooked with coconut milk. Coconut bread, a specialty on the Caribbean coast. Soups and stews of meat, chicken, or seafood and plantains or cassava in coconut milk. In Guatemala Mayan meat stew (pepián) thickened with toasted squash seeds. Roasted meat, chicken, and fish. Salads such as avocado, tomato, and pickled cabbage. Fried potatoes, plantains, or breadfruit. Pickled vegetables (cabbage, carrots, beets). Chirmol (tomato sauce, often with chili), used liberally.

Special occasion dishes Black tamales stuffed with a mixture of chicken, chocolate, spices, prunes, and raisins. Plantains served in chocolate sauce during the Holy Week before Easter. Fiambre (a huge salad of vegetables, chicken, beef, pork, and sausages, with garnishes such as cheese and hard-boiled eggs, and dressed with vinaigrette or a sweet-and-sour sauce), shared by many family and friends at a social event on All Saints' Day.

Sweets Sugarcane, honey, sugar (white, brown), coconut candy, baked bananas, fruit ices, ice cream, custard, rice pudding, coconut- or rum-flavored cakes and fritters.

Beverages Coffee, chocolate, fruit drinks (refrescas), teas, beer, rum, wine (chica), distilled drink (venado).

Meals Breakfast: corn tortillas, beans (sometimes with eggs), coffee or juice. Lunch: beans, corn tortillas, rice (with cheese or meat added if available). Dinner: same as lunch or in wealthier areas: soup; meat, poultry, or fish dish; tortillas or bread; and salad, beans, fried plantains, pickled vegetables; sometimes appetizers and dessert.

Snacks Candy, fruit ices, ice cream, custard, rice pudding, cakes, fritters.

Incaparina A nutritious, economical dry food mixture, based on the traditional corn gruel (atole), Incaparina was developed at the Institute of Nutrition for Central America and Panama. It contains local ingredients including corn and other plant foods, and can be mixed with water to make a gruel, a soup, or a beverage as nutritious as milk.

GUINEA
Republic of Guinea

Geography   Guinea is In West Africa, bordering the Atlantic Ocean. It consists of a narrow coastal plain, mountainous middle region (source of the Gambia, Senegal, and Niger rivers), savanna upland farther inland, and forest in the southeast.

Major Languages	Ethnic Groups		Major Religions	
French (official)	Peuhl (Fulani)	40%	Muslim (nearly all Sunni)	85%
Each ethnic group's language	Malinke	30%	Christian	8%
	Soussou (Susu)	20%	Indigenous beliefs	7%
	Other	10%		

Population density per sq. mi 103.3
Literacy rate 29.5%
Life expectancy 55.1 male; 58.1 female
Per capita GDP $1,100
Labor force in agriculture 76%

Urban 33%
Infant mortality rate per 1,000 live births 67.4
HIV rate 1.6%
Unemployment rate NA
Arable land 4%

Agriculture   cassava, rice, oil palm fruit, coffee, pineapples, cassava, bananas, sweet potatoes, chickens, cattle, goats, sheep, pigs

Natural resources   bauxite, iron ore, diamonds, gold, uranium, hydropower, fish, salt

Industries   bauxite, gold, diamonds, iron, aluminum refining, light manufacturing

History   In about 900 CE   the Susu began migrating here from the desert and pushed the original inhabitants, the Baga, to the Atlantic coast. The Susu civilization reached its peak in the 13th century. In the mid-15th century the Portuguese visited the coast and established a slave trade. The Fulani dominated part of the region from the 16th century into the 19th century. The region was part of the ancient West African empires. It came under French control in 1849. French Guinea became part of the federation of French West Africa in 1895. Guinea chose independence in 1958; France withdrew all aid. Guinea's first president (1958–1984) turned to Communist nations for support and set up a one-party state. After a military coup in 1984 Guinea began westernizing its government. During the 1990s a new constitution was adopted and the first multiparty elections were held. Guinea received 300,000 refugees from civil wars in neighboring Liberia and Sierra Leone in the 1990s and early 2000s. In 2007 strikes and demonstrations demanded that the president (since 1984) resign; he agreed to yield some power to the prime minister. The government announced the discovery of substantial uranium deposits.

Influences on food   French control in the 19th and 20th centuries left French influence such as French bread in some areas. The Atlantic Ocean, coastal plain, savannah, mountains, and forests provide fish, grass for animal herds, and game. The introduction of New World foods such as cassava, corn, chili pepper, tomato, and sweet potato influenced Guinea's food. Native African foods include okra, black-eyed peas, and watermelon. The diet is mostly rice, starchy vegetables, legumes, and greens. Thick, sticky, spicy food is liked.

Bread and cereals   Rice, millet, sorghum, corn, wheat; rice dishes, porridge, pastes, steamed or fried cornmeal patties, dough balls, French bread.

Meat, poultry, fish   Chicken, beef, goat, lamb and mutton, pork, fish and seafood, (fresh, smoked, salted, or dried), guinea fowl, eggs, rabbits, "Bush meat" (game such as antelope and wild pig). Chicken is prestigious.

Insects   Termites (often called white ants), locusts.

Dairy products   Milk, sour milk, buttermilk, curds, whey, cheese.

Fats and oils   Palm oil, peanut oil, shea oil, coconut oil. Palm oil, the main predominant cooking fat, is red.

Legumes   Peanuts (groundnuts), black-eyed peas (a variety of cowpeas), locust beans (carob), beans.

Vegetables   Cassava, sweet potatoes, yams, plantains, taro, green leaves, okra, bitter leaf, melokhia (crain crain), tomatoes, potatoes, eggplant, pumpkin, onions, chili peppers, cucumbers, bell peppers.

Fruit   Pineapple, bananas, coconut, akee apples, baobab, watermelon, guavas, lemons, limes, mangoes, papaya.

Nuts and seeds   Cashews, kola nuts, palm nuts, watermelon seeds (egusi), sesame seeds, mango seeds.

Seasonings   Salt, hot red chili peppers, tomatoes, onions, dried baobab leaves, thyme, "African nutmeg," ginger.

Dishes   Most foods are boiled or fried, and chunks or balls are dipped in sauce and eaten by hand. Fufu (a paste of boiled and pounded starchy vegetables or boiled corn flour, formed into balls or bite-size scoops to eat sauce or stew). Fish and meat stew. Stew of peanuts or okra with chilies, tomatoes, onions, and chicken, beef, or fish, served with boiled rice or fufu. Sauce of ground peanuts with crushed peppers. Sauce of green leaves (palaver sauce). Fréjon (black-eyed pea or bean purée, coconut milk, and perhaps carob or chocolate). Gari (roasted cassava meal). Adalu (boiled and mashed vegetables). Jollof rice (boiled rice with various meats, vegetables, and spices).Yassa (chicken or fish marinated in lemon or lime juice, grilled, fried with onions, and simmered in the marinade), served with boiled rice. Roasted chicken with tomato, onion, okra, and peanut sauce. Roasted whole fish. Omelet of egg, sweet green pepper, and tomato, cooked on both sides.

Sweets   Honey, sugar, pineapple fritter, sweet omelet with fruit pieces, fried dough balls, kanya (peanut candy).

Beverages   Coffee, beer, red zinger (herbal tea made from hibiscus flower pods), ginger beer.

Street food and snacks   Spiced kabobs, fried fish, plantain chips, fried sweet dough bits, steamed rice balls.

GUINEA-BISSAU
Republic of Guinea-Bissau

Geography   Formerly Portuguese Guinea, Guinea-Bissau is in West Africa, bordering the Atlantic Ocean. It is mostly a swampy coastal plain, with a low savanna area in the east, and about 25 islands off the mainland.

Major Languages	Ethnic Groups		Major Religions	
Portuguese (official)	Balanta	30%	Indigenous beliefs	50%
Crioulo	Fula	20%	Muslim	45%
African languages	Manjaca	14%	Christian	5%
	Mandinga	13%		
	Other	23%		

Population density per sq. mi 139
Literacy rate 64.6%
Life expectancy 45.7 male; 49.4 female
Per capita GDP $500
Labor force in agriculture 82%

Urban 29.6%
Infant mortality rate per 1,000 live births 101.6
HIV rate 1.8%
Unemployment rate NA
Arable land 8%

Agriculture   rice, cashews, oil palm, corn, beans, cassava, peanuts, cotton, chickens, cattle, pigs, goats, sheep

Natural resources   fish, timber, phosphates, bauxite, clay, granite, limestone, unexploited deposits of oil

Industries   agriculture products processing, beer, soft drinks

History   More than 1,000 years ago, people lived along the coast in this land, grew rice, and supplied salt to the western Sudan. The land came under influence of the Mali Empire and was known as the kingdom of Gabú. In the mid-15th century Portuguese explored the area and imported slaves from it. The slave trade flourished here in the 17th and 18th centuries. Colonization began in the 19th century. In 1974 Portuguese control was overthrown and independence was attained. Political turmoil followed, with a military coup in 1980, a destructive civil war in 1998, and military coups in 1999 and 2003. In 2005 the former president who had been deposed in 1999 returned from exile in Portugal and was elected president. The UN's 2007 World Drug Report named the country as a key post for moving cocaine from Latin America to Europe. Guinea-Bissau is one of the world's 10 poorest countries.

Influences on food   Portuguese influence is strong. The introduction of New World foods such as cassava, corn, chili pepper, peanuts, tomato, potato, and cashew nuts greatly influenced food customs, adding to native African foods including watermelon, black-eyed peas, and okra. The Atlantic Ocean, swamps, wetlands, and forests provide fish and game. Daily fare is mostly grains and starchy vegetables with legumes and greens. Most foods are boiled or fried. Thick, sticky, spicy dishes are liked. Cashew nuts are the main export,

Bread and cereals   Rice, corn, millet, sorghum; rice dishes, porridge, pastes, steamed or fried cornmeal patties.

Meat, poultry, fish   Chicken, beef, pork, goat, lamb, fish and seafood (fresh, smoked, salted, or dried), guinea fowl, eggs, ducks, rabbits, "Bush meat" (game, especially antelope and wild pig). Chicken is prestigious.

Insects   Termites (often called white ants), locusts.

Dairy products   Milk, sour milk, buttermilk, curds, whey, cheese.

Fats and oils   Palm oil, shea oil, coconut oil. Palm oil, the predominant cooking fat, gives dishes a red color.

Legumes   Beans, peanuts (groundnuts), black-eyed peas (a variety of cowpeas), locust beans (carob).

Vegetables   Cassava, yams, plantains, taro, green leaves, okra, bitter leaf, melokhia (crain crain), tomatoes, sweet potatoes, potatoes, eggplant, pumpkin, onions, chili peppers, cucumbers, bell peppers.

Fruit   Coconut, bananas, akee apples, baobab, pineapple, watermelon, guavas, lemons, limes, mangoes, papaya.

Nuts and seeds   Cashew nuts, kola nuts, watermelon seeds (egusi), sesame seeds, mango seeds.

Seasonings   Salt, hot red chili peppers, tomatoes, onions, dried baobab leaves, thyme, "African nutmeg," ginger.

Dishes   Jollof rice (boiled rice with various meats, vegetables, and spices). Fufu (a paste made of boiled and pounded starchy vegetables or boiled corn flour), formed into bite-size scoops to eat stew. Fish and meat stew. Stew of peanuts, okra, or root vegetables with chilies and tomatoes and perhaps bits of fish, chicken, or beef. Peanut sauce (ground and pounded peanuts with seasonings). Palaver sauce (green leaves). Fréjon (bean or black-eyed pea purée, coconut milk, and sometimes carob or chocolate). Gari (roasted cassava meal). Steamed rice balls. Adalu (boiled and mashed vegetables). Yassa (chicken or fish marinated in lemon or lime juice, grilled, fried with onions, and simmered in the marinade). Chicken baked with tomatoes, onions, okra, and peanut sauce.

Sweets   Honey, sugar, kanya (peanut candy), banana fritters, fried sweet dough balls.

Beverages   Beer, soft drinks, red zinger (herbal tea from flower pods of roselle, *Hibiscus sabdariffa*), ginger beer.

Street food and snacks   Spiced kabobs, shawerma (thin slices of marinated lamb packed tightly on a vertical spit and roasted; thin pieces of meat are cut off the outside), fried bean balls, fried sweet dough bits, coconut biscuits.

GUYANA
Co-operative Republic of Guyana

Geography   Formerly British Guiana, Guyana is in northern South America, bordering the Atlantic Ocean. The low coastal area, where 90% of the people live, has fertile soil for agriculture. Tropical forest in the south covers more than 80% of the land. Grassy savanna divides the areas. An extensive network of rivers runs from north to south.

Major Languages	Ethnic Groups		Major Religions	
English (official)	East Indian	44%	Hindu	28%
Amerindian dialects	Black (African)	30%	Pentecostal	17%
Creole	Mixed	17%	Roman Catholic	8%
Caribbean Hindustani	Amerindian	9%	Anglican	7%
Urdu			Muslim	7%
			Other., none	33%

Population density per sq. mi 10.1
Literacy rate 98.8%
Life expectancy 63.8 male; 69.2 female
Per capita GDP $3,800
Labor force in agriculture NA

Urban 28.2%
Infant mortality rate per 1,000 live births 30.4
HIV rate 2.5%
Unemployment rate 11.7%
Arable land 2%

Agriculture   sugarcane, rice, coconuts, shrimp, fish, vegetable oils, chickens, sheep, cattle, goats, pigs
Natural resources   bauxite, gold, diamonds, hardwood timber, shrimp, fish
Industries   bauxite, sugar, rice milling, timber, textiles, gold mining
History   Indigenous inhabitants were the Warrou. Guyana became a Dutch possession in the 17th century and a British possession in 1815. African slaves were brought to work the plantations. After slavery was abolished, from the 1840s indentured laborers from India came for plantation work. Guyana gained independence in 1966. The government nationalized most of the economy, which has remained severely depressed. In 2000 border disputes with neighbors Venezuela and Suriname occurred; those for western Guyana and Venezuela have been resolved. Recent violence included assassination of the agricultural minister and others in 2006 and massacres of two villages in 2008. In 2007 the UN International Tribunal for the Law of the Seas's decision on the maritime boundary dispute between Guyana and Suriname gave Georgetown (Guyana) the far larger share of the Guyana-Suriname Basin under dispute; Georgetown was expected to resume offshore oil exploration.
Influences on food   The Dutch and the British, as well as their trade with India and Indonesia, have influenced Guyana's food. Guyana's history and cuisine are more closely linked to the West Indies than to Spanish or Portuguese possessions in Latin America. African slaves were brought to work in sugarcane and spice plantations, and Indian and Indonesian indentured laborers succeeded them. The cooking of this region reflects strongly the preferences of the imported labor as well as local resources and colonial influences. The diet depended largely on manioc (cassava) meal,

although the coastal areas had seafood. Settlements of Bush blacks (former runaway slaves) had dishes reflecting an African past. Pepper pot stew may have originated in Guyana. Other dishes resulted from importing or adapting European ones. Indian and Indonesian dishes increased as those populations increased here. Guyana cuisine resembles that of neighbors northern Brazil, Suriname (also a former Dutch possession and then a British colony), and French Guyana (a French region).

Bread and cereals   Rice, wheat, corn; rice dishes, wheat flour bread, cornmeal mush and bread, corn flour cake, fresh ears of corn, their scrapings, and liquid "milk," cassava meal bread.

Meat, poultry, fish   Chicken, lamb and mutton, beef, goat, pork, fish, shrimp, other seafood, eggs, large bird oko.

Dairy products   Milk (cow, goat), evaporated milk, cheese.

Fats and oils   Vegetable oils, butter, lard, dendé oil, olive oil.

Legumes   Beans, peas, peanuts.

Vegetables   Cassava, plantains, sweet potatoes, tomatoes, okra, callaloo (edible leaves of root vegetables especially amaranth, malanga, taro), pumpkins, potatoes, onions, chili peppers.

Fruit   Coconut (fresh, dried, flour, milk), bananas, papaya, limes, other tropical fruits.

Nuts and seeds   Brazil nuts, cashews, sesame seeds, pumpkin seeds.

Seasonings   Cinnamon, cloves, cayenne pepper, chili pepper, curry powder, black pepper, other spices.

Dishes   Pepper pot, a substantial stew of cassareep (boiled juice from grated bitter cassava root), mixed meats, cloves, cinnamon, and pepper. Boiled or steamed rice. Boiled or fried plantain, sweet potatoes, or potatoes. Okra and cornmeal mush (coo-coo). European imports such as Dutch split-pea soup and rijsttafel. Indian curries.

Sweets   Sugarcane, sugar, honey. Madou (macerated fruit). Pudding of rice, tapioca (from cassava), or corn "milk," coconut milk, evaporated milk, sugar, and spices. Couac coco (flour from grated and dried coconut, sugar, cinnamon, and lime zest). Doconon (poached leaf-wrapped cake of corn flour, banana, coconut, and spices).

Beverages   Coffee, fruit juices, soft drinks, sugarcane juice, tea, beer, sugarcane brandy (cachaça).

Street food and snack   Wang (toasted ground sesame seeds, cinnamon, lime zest, and sugar or salt).

H

HAITI
Republic of Haiti

Geography Haiti occupies the western third of the island of Hispaniola, in the Caribbean Sea. Two thirds of Haiti is mountainous, much of the rest is semi-arid, and coastal areas are warm and moist.

Major Languages	Ethnic Groups		Major Religions	
French (both	Black	95%	Roman Catholic	80%
Creole official)	Mulatto and white	5%	Protestant	16%
			Other	4%
			Voodoo widely practiced	

Population density per sq. mi. 838.7
Literacy rate 62.1%
Life expectancy 55.8 male; 59.4 female
Per capita GDP $1,300
Labor force in agriculture 66%

Urban 42.7%
Infant mortality rate per 1,000 live births 62.3
HIV rate 2.2%
Unemployment rate 32.7%
Arable land 28%

Agriculture sugarcane, cassava, fruits, coffee, rice, corn, sorghum, chickens, goats, cattle, pigs, horses, sheep

Natural resources bauxite, copper, calcium carbonate, gold, marble, hydropower, fish

Industries sugar refining, flour milling, textiles, cement, light assembly of imported parts

History Arawak Indians inhabited the area when Columbus explored it in 1492. Haiti was a French colony from 1697. It became a leading sugarcane producer, dependent on slaves. After a 1791 insurrection by the slaves, Haiti attained independence in 1804, the world's first independent black country. Following a century of wrecked economy, dictatorships, and political violence, the U.S. occupation from 1915 to 1934 brought stability. The Duvalier family controlled a dictatorship from 1957 to 1986. Poverty, political unrest, violence, and health problems have plagued Haiti for decades. Damaging hurricanes, storms, and floods have occurred as recently as 2008. Income from Haitians living overseas continued to help with survival and growth.

Influences on food The indigenous Arawak almost disappeared following the Spanish conquest, leaving only traces of their foodways. They ate a wide variety of fish and seafood. Barbacoa, the Arawak term for grilling meats, probably is the origin of the American word barbecue. Spanish control for two centuries, French control for about a century, and slaves bought from Africa influenced food customs in Haiti.

Bread and cereals Rice, corn, wheat; fried cornbread, wheat flour bread, cassava bread (fried grated cassava).

Meat, poultry, fish Chicken, goat, beef, pork, lamb, fish and seafood (salt cod, lobster), land crabs, eggs.

Dairy products Cow's milk (fresh, condensed, evaporated), aged cheese.

Fats and oils   Butter, lard, olive oil, coconut cream, vegetable oil.

Legumes   Red kidney beans, black-eyed peas, lima beans.

Vegetables   Cassava, malanga, yams, sweet potatoes, plantains, greens (cassava, malanga), avocados, breadfruit, squash, tomatoes, okra, onions, green peppers, black mushrooms.

Fruit   Bananas, mangoes, coconut, citrus, papaya, pineapple, guavas, star apples, cashew apples, soursop.

Nuts and seeds   Almonds, cashew nuts, annatto (achiote) seeds.

Seasonings   Salt, black pepper, hot red chili peppers, onions, allspice, garlic, lime juice, annatto, coriander, saffron, cinnamon, nutmeg, rum, coconut cream; Colombo powder (allspice, garlic, coriander, saffron, cinnamon).

Dishes   Callaloo (green leaves cooked with okra, garlic, and a little salt meat or fish). Pepper pot (stew of vegetables and meat, highly seasoned with pepper). Escabeche (fish fried, then sauced or marinated). Ceviche (raw fish marinated in lemon or lime juice with olive oil and spices). Spicy soups. Crab stew. Simmered akee. Colombo (prepared with Colombo powder), for example, fish. Griots de porc (fried pork) with fried plantain. Acrats de morue (codfish fritters). Sauce Ti-malice (onions marinated in lime juice, sautéed in butter with chilies and garlic, and combined with the marinade). Red beans and rice (rice heated in melted lard, then simmered in boiled bean liquid; boiled beans stirred into melted lard, heated, and served over rice).

Specialties   Riz au djon djon (simmered rice, black mushrooms, and lima beans; the mushrooms color the cooking water black). Poulet roti à la créole (roasted banana-stuffed chicken). Barbecued goat with chili peppers.

Sweets   Sugarcane, sugar, brown sugar, molasses, fruit, gâteau de patate (sweet potato bread).

Beverages   Coffee, milk, soft drinks, beer, rum.

Meals   Breakfast: coffee with milk, bread, and perhaps egg, cereal, and fruit. Lunch: rice and beans with meat if affordable. Dinner: rice and beans with meat, bread, vegetables, milk, and dessert if available.

Service   Protein foods are served first to the father in the household and then to the mother and children.

Snacks   Fresh fruit, fruit juice poured over crushed ice, coffee with milk. Snacking is frequent among children.

HONDURAS
Republic of Honduras

Geography   This Central American country has coastlines of 500 miles on the Caribbean Sea and 40 miles on the Pacific Ocean. Honduras is mountainous, with wide fertile valleys and rich forests.

Major Languages	Ethnic Groups		Major Religions	
Spanish (official)	Mestizo	90%	Roman Catholic	97%
Amerindian dialects	Amerindian	7%	Protestant and other	3%
	Black, white, other	3%		

Population density per sq. mi. 176.8

Literacy rate 83.1%

Life expectancy 67.8 male; 71 female

Per capita GDP $4,100

Labor force in agriculture 34%

Urban 46.5%

Infant mortality rate per 1,000 live births 24.6

HIV rate 0.7%

Unemployment rate 27.9%

Arable land 10%

Agriculture   sugarcane, oil palm fruit, bananas, coffee, citrus, chickens, cattle, pigs, goats, sheep

Natural resources   timber, gold, silver, copper, lead, zinc, iron ore, antimony, coal, fish

Industries   sugar, coffee, textiles, clothing, wood products

History   In the 1st millennium CE the Mayan civilization flourished in Honduras. In 1502 Columbus arrived and settlement followed. Honduras gained independence from Spain in 1821 and formed the Federation of Central America in 1838. In the 20th century Honduras was under military rule with frequent civil war. A civilian government took office in 1982. Honduras was devastated by a hurricane in 1998 that killed at least 5,600 people and caused extensive damage. In 2005 Honduras ratified a free-trade agreement (CAFTA) with the United States. In 2007 the U.S. government extended the Temporary Protected Status program that allowed 78,000 Hondurans to work in the United States because of Honduras's environmental disasters. Remittances from these workers accounted for about 25% of Honduras's GDP.

Influences on food   Honduras's long coastline on the Caribbean Sea supplies fish and shrimp. The Maya influence endures especially in the highlands, with corn the staple and tamales and tortillas reminders of the ancient past. The Spanish brought new foods including rice, beef and cheese, pork and lard, coconut, and breadfruit. Caribbean island foodways from native Carib-speaking Indians and laborers from Africa and Asia imported to work influenced food on the Caribbean coast of Honduras.

Staple foods   Corn, beans, rice.

Bread and cereals   Corn, rice, wheat; corn tortillas and gruel, rice dishes, wheat bread and rolls.

Meat, poultry, fish   Chicken, beef, pork, goat, lamb, fish and seafood (shrimp, conch, sea turtle), eggs.

Dairy products   Milk (evaporated), cream, sour cream, cheese. Milk is not usually drunk as a beverage.

Fats and oils   Lard, butter, palm oil, vegetable oils, shortening.

Legumes   Beans (black, red, kidney, white), chickpeas.

Vegetables   Plantains, cassava, tomatoes, sweet peppers, chayote squash (green pear-shaped gourd), avocados, pumpkin, breadfruit, chili peppers, onions, potatoes, cabbage, carrots, green beans, lettuce, beets.

Fruit   Bananas, citrus, coconut, pineapple, mangoes, roselle fruit, grapes, papaya, passion fruit.

Nuts and seeds   Palm tree nuts, squash seeds.

Seasonings   Onions, garlic, chili, achiote/annatto (orange-red coloring), cilantro, pimento, cinnamon, vanilla.

Dishes   Atole (corn gruel). Posole (semi-fermented corn dough, diluted to make a beverage or used in other ways). Tamales (spicy meat-stuffed corn dough, wrapped in corn husks or leaves, and steamed). Beans simmered with spices, puréed, or fried and often paired with rice (frijoles con arroz). Rice often fried before boiling or cooked with coconut milk. Coconut bread, a specialty on the Caribbean coast. Soups and stews of meat, chicken, or seafood and plantains or cassava in coconut milk. Roasted meat, chicken, and fish. Salads such as avocado. Fried potatoes, plantains, or breadfruit. Pickled vegetables (cabbage, carrots, beets).

Specialties   Conch, sea turtle, mondongo (tripe soup).

Sweets   Sugarcane, honey, sugar (white, brown), nogada (praline-like candy), baked bananas, fruit ices, ice cream, custard, rice pudding, coconut- or rum-flavored cakes and fritters.

Beverages   Coffee, chocolate, tropical fruit drinks (refrescas), beer, rum, wine (chica).

Meals   Corn and beans are eaten at every meal by the poor. Rice is consumed frequently, with cheese or meat added if resources permit. Dinner in wealthier areas: soup; meat, poultry, or fish dish; tortillas or bread; and salad, fried plantains, and pickled vegetables plus sometimes appetizers and dessert.

Snacks   Candy, fruit ices, ice cream, custard, rice pudding, cakes, fritters.

HUNGARY
Republic of Hungary

Geography   Hungary is in east central Europe. Its eastern half is a great fertile plain. The west and north are hilly. The Danube River is the border in the northwest and swings south to bisect the country.

Major Language	Ethnic Groups		Major Religions	
Hungarian (official)	Hungarian	92%	Roman Catholic	52%
	Roma (Gypsy)	2%	Other Christian	21%
	German, other	6%	Other	12%
			Unaffiliated	15%

Population density per sq. mi. 278.5
Literacy rate 98.9%
Life expectancy 69 male; 77.6 female
Per capita GDP $19,000
Labor force in agriculture 5.5%

Urban 63.3%
Infant mortality rate per 1,000 live births 8
HIV rate 0.1%
Unemployment rate 7.5%
Arable land 50%

Agriculture   corn, wheat, sugar beets, red paprika, sunflower seed, potatoes, chickens, pigs, geese, sheep, cattle, goats

Natural resources   bauxite, coal, natural gas, fertile soil, fish

Industries   mining, metallurgy, construction materials, processed foods, textiles, pharmaceuticals, motor vehicles

History   Earliest settlers were mostly Slav. By 14 BCE western Hungary was part of the Roman Empire; eastern Hungary was inhabited by Germanic and Asiatic peoples. In 896 CE the Magyars from the east invaded Hungary and founded a kingdom. Stephen I (977–1038) Christianized the country and made it into a strong, independent nation. The Mongols invaded in 1241. The Ottoman Turks invaded repeatedly in the 15th to 17th centuries. After defeat of the Turks (1687–1697), Austria dominated Hungary until it regained independence in 1849, and in 1867 the dual monarchy of Austria-Hungary was formed. Defeated with other Central Powers in World War I, in 1918 Hungary lost land to Romania, Yugoslavia, and Czechoslovakia. Hungary joined Germany in World War II, was captured by Russia, and communists took control in 1947. Hungary gained independence in 1989. Hungary joined NATO in 1999 and the EU in 2004. In 2007 the popularity of the Socialist prime minister's government fell after an austerity program to reduce the soaring budget deficit; the most controversial part was health care.

Influences on food   Influences include the earliest settlers (mostly Slav), the Roman Empire, Germanic and Asiatic peoples, Christianity, Italy, invading Mongols and Turks, New World foods, Austria, and Russia. The Magyar tribes that roamed Central Europe long before Hungary was a state ate a hot spicy meat soup/stew, gulyás; paprika was probably added in the 18th century. The Magyars also brought cabbage leaves stuffed with meat from their ancestral home in the Caucasian Mountains. Hungary as a nation began at the end of the 9th century, when Hungarian tribes that had been moving west and southwest from Asia for centuries gained control of the land. Food and music are closely linked in Hungary, mainly because of the Gypsies. Gypsies arrived in the area probably from India and were mistaken for Egyptians, from which their name derives; they brought an eastern influence as in their mystical fortunetelling, and their food and music are intertwined. Medieval Hungary reached its peak during the reign of King Matthias I (1458–1490), with royal feasts including the feast (with Gypsy music) for the wedding of the King with Princess Beatrice of

Naples. She imported cheese, onions, and garlic from Italy; Italian influence also includes sauces made with the food's own juices. After King Matthias's death Hungary declined and was defeated by invading Turks. During Turkish rule in central Hungary in the 16th and 17th centuries the Turks introduced filo pastry (which evolved into strudel), rice pilafs, pita bread, cherries, paprika, tomatoes, and corn; the latter three and potatoes originated in the New World. Much of Hungary was part of the Hapsburg Empire from 1282 for about 600 years and showed Germanic influence. After the Hapsburgs gained control of Budapest from the Turks in 1686 and stayed on, they brought French influence from their capital, Vienna. By 1867, when the Austro-Hungarian dual monarchy was established, Budapest had its famous pastry shops and a reputation for fine hotels, and Hungarian cookbooks appeared. Cookbooks continued being published and as a result Hungarian cuisine is probably the best documented of any Central European country. The basic cooking of ordinary people adapted Italian, German, and French dishes. Hungarian cuisine continued to flourish during the first half of the 20th century, suffered under the inhibiting influence of communism after World War II, and has rebounded since. The regions of Hungary are the western area with Lake Balaton, the largest lake in Central Europe; northern Hungary, where descendants of hunting tribes established there before the Middle Ages still live, and the Tokay wine area; and the Great Hungarian Plain, containing the orchard area. The land grows grains, potatoes, and fruits, as well as supporting livestock. Lakes and rivers including the Danube provide fish. Main foods are bread, meat especially pork, and potatoes. Hungarians, with peasant traditions from the East and West, have vitality and love of life, and consider that life and art are one and that food and cooking are important.

Bread and cereals   Wheat, corn, rye, rice; wheat bread, dumplings, pasta, noodles, pancakes, rice dishes.

Meat, poultry, fish   Pork, chicken, goose, lamb and mutton, beef, goat, fish, eggs, bacon, ham, sausage.

Dairy products   Milk, cream, sour cream (the favorite ingredient), curd cheese.

Fats and oils   Lard, fresh pork fat, bacon, butter, vegetable oil, sunflower seed oil.

Legumes   Kidney beans, lentils, split peas.

Vegetables   Potatoes, onions, cabbage, green peppers, tomatoes, beets, eggplant; pickles, sauerkraut.

Fruit   Sour cherries, sweet cherries, apples, apricots, grapes, raisins, oranges, lemons.

Nuts and seeds   Almonds, hazelnuts, walnuts, sunflower seeds, caraway seeds, poppy seeds.

Seasonings   Red paprika (sweet, piquant spice made from ground, dried red pepper), onion, garlic, salt, black pepper, parsley, dill, cinnamon, marjoram, thyme, ginger, vinegar, vanilla, cocoa.

Cooking methods   For most meat or vegetable dishes onions are browned in heated lard, paprika is stirred in, meat and/or vegetable pieces are stirred in, water or stock and seasonings are added, and the food is covered and simmered. For many dishes, a roux is made by browning flour in lard and then adding seasonings.

Dishes   Hungary's most famous dish, gulyás (goulash in the United States), paprika-spiced stew of beef, pork, or chicken, lard, onions, paprika, caraway seeds, water or stock, and sometimes garlic, potatoes, tomatoes, and/or green peppers. Stews served with sour cream and boiled potatoes, dumplings, or noodles. The great delicacy, goose liver pâté. Other specialties: fish soups and other fish dishes of Lake Balaton, for example, fogas (perch-pike), turned in flour with paprika and fried, grilled, stuffed with bread crumbs and seasonings and roasted, or poached in white wine. Chicken and noodle soup. Mutton and vegetable soup thickened with a roux. Lecsó (green peppers, tomatoes, and sausage simmered with onions and garlic that have been browned in heated lard or bacon fat with paprika added). Chicken paprika (paprika csirke), chicken pieces browned in heated lard, simmered with onions and garlic that have been heated in the lard, paprika, and chicken stock, with sour cream added to the juices and the chicken heated in the sauce. Rabló-hus (robbers' meat), skewered lamb or beef cooked outdoors at country inns and served with fried potatoes and pickle slices. Roast pork. Braised pork chops. Steaks Eszterházy (beef round steaks floured and browned in heated lard, then braised with vegetables and spices and decorated with carrot and pickle strips). Töltött káposzta (rolls of cabbage leaves stuffed with ground pork, rice, eggs, and paprika, simmered with sauerkraut and tomato purée). Potato paprika (boiled potatoes, and sometimes sausage, simmered with onions that have been heated in lard, paprika, stock or water, caraway seeds, tomatoes, and green peppers). Green pepper salad (pakrikasaláta), roasted, peeled, and seeded green peppers cut into strips, mixed with vinegar and seasonings, chilled, mixed with mayonnaise, and served on lettuce.

Special occasion food   Easter, the most important religious holiday, features the Easter Eve feast of chicken soup with dumplings or noodles, roasted meat, pickles, stuffed cabbage rolls, and cakes and pastries with coffee.

Sweets   Honey, sugar. Cold cherry soup (Hideg Meggyleves), simmered sour cherries, sugar, water, and arrowroot, chilled, and heavy cream and red wine stirred in before serving. Honey breads and honey cakes. Pancakes rolled around apricot jam, sprinkled with walnuts, and dusted with confectioners sugar. Dessert strudel (vargabéles, or cobbler's delight), paper-thin pastry filled with curd cheese, butter, sour cream, sugar, eggs, vanilla, and raisins. Dobos cake (Doboschtorte), cake with seven layers, chocolate filling between layers and around sides, and caramel topping. Pastries, by common consent the greatest Hungarian food, are found in bakeries, pastry shops, expresso bars, and coffeehouses.

Beverages   Coffee, hot chocolate, beer, wine (including the most noted, Tokay). A small glass of expresso is offered to any visitor, at home or office, day or night.

Meals and service   Three meals a day with snacks is typical; a main meal includes a sweet. Gypsies usually eat two meals a day, in the morning and late afternoon, with stews, fried foods, and unleavened bread the usual fare.

Street food and snacks   Pastries and expresso or hot chocolate with whipped cream at coffeehouses.

I

ICELAND
Republic of Iceland

Geography   Iceland, in the North Atlantic Ocean, touches the Arctic Circle and is Europe's most western point. A volcanic region, three quarters of the surface is wasteland: glaciers, lakes, and a lava desert. Most people live on the 7% of land that is fertile coastline. The Gulf Stream moderates the climate. There are geysers and hot springs.

Major Languages	Ethnic Groups		Major Religions	
Icelandic (official)	Icelandic (homogeneous		Lutheran Church of	
English	mixture of Norse-Celtic)	94%	Iceland (official)	86%
Nordic languages	European	4%	Other Christian	8%
German (widely spoken)	Other	2%	Unaffiliated, other	6%

Population density per sq. mi. 7.9
Literacy rate 99%
Life expectancy 78.4 male; 82.8 female
Per capita GDP $38,800
Labor force in agriculture 5.1%

Urban 92.3%
Infant mortality rate per 1,000 live births 3.2
HIV rate 0.2%
Unemployment rate 2.5%
Arable land 0.1%

Agriculture   potatoes, cereals, tomatoes, green vegetables, chickens, sheep, horses, cattle, pigs, goats

Natural resources   fish, hydropower, geothermal power, diatomite

Industries   fish processing, aluminum smelting, ferrosilicon production, tourism

History   Iceland was settled by Norwegian seafarers and Irish who left Ireland in the late 9th century. It was Christianized by 1000. Iceland was an independent republic from 930 to 1262, when it joined Norway. Denmark ruled Iceland from 1380, recognizing it as a separate state in 1918. In 1944 Iceland's assembly, Althing, proclaimed Iceland an independent republic. In 1980 Iceland elected a woman president, the world's first elected female chief of state. After the early 1990s recession, the economy rebounded. Iceland's language has maintained its purity for 1,000 years. Althing, established in 930, is the world's oldest surviving parliament. A 55-year U.S. military presence in Iceland ended with the closing of Keflavik naval air station in 2006. Following several years of vigorous growth, Iceland's economy slowed in 2007. The worldwide financial crisis in 2008 hit Iceland hard, prompting the prime minister's warning of national bankruptcy. Despite limiting the catch of codfish, codfish stock in Icelandic waters has decreased over the years.

Influences on food   In general, Iceland shares a common cuisine with the other Scandinavian countries. Iceland, a country of lava fields, glaciers, and long dark winters, is not well suited for agriculture. However, lamb and dairy products are excellent. Two important dairy products are skyr and whey. Skyr is made by adding bacterial cultures and rennet to skimmed sheep's or cow's milk; these curdle the milk, and the curds become skyr. Whey, the liquid remaining after the curds are removed from skimmed milk (as in making skyr or cheese), is used extensively for preservation of meat, fish, and butter. As in other far north countries, preserving food for winter is important. Whey-preserved items include offal (such as lamb's heart, testicles, and feet). Smoking, drying, and fermenting are other methods used to preserve meat and fish. A unique method of cooking is to bury food in a patch of hot earth to cook by itself; the abundant hot geysers in Iceland heat the earth so that it can be used to cook the food. They also provide hot water and heating for houses in Reykjavik.

Bread and cereals   Barley, oats, rye, wheat, rice; oatmeal or rice porridge, bread from rye flour, white (called French) bread, pancakes, unleavened (flat) breads, potato bread (thin, round, cooked on a griddle), bread made from Iceland moss, a lichen (a plant consisting of a fungus and a green or blue-green alga). There is a tradition of using dried fish in place of bread.

Meat, poultry, fish   Chicken, eggs, lamb, beef, pork, goat, fish (cod, halibut, salmon, trout, shark), sea birds (puffin, guillemot, cormorant); sausages, smoked items (lamb, sausages, tongues, and fish), dried fish. Greenland shark flesh, inedible when raw and untreated, is buried and allowed to ferment, making it safe to eat, although with crinkled black skin; it is sold in small pieces (hákarl). Sea birds (made less fishy tasting by steeping them in milk overnight), eaten traditionally but are eaten less often now; the large cormorant is considered the best.

Dairy products   Milk (sheep, cow), skyr (milk curds), whey, milk, cream, buttermilk, sour cream, cheese.

Fats and oils   Butter, lard, margarine, salt pork.

Legumes   Split peas (yellow and green).

Vegetables   Potatoes, tomatoes, turnips, cabbage, mustard, onions, mushrooms, carrots, lichen; sauerkraut.

Fruit   Apples, berries, currants, plums, prunes, raisins.

Nuts and seeds   Almonds, caraway seeds, almond paste (marzipan).

Seasonings   Salt, black pepper, dill, cardamom, cinnamon, ginger, cloves, mustard, horseradish, vinegar.

Dishes   Dried fish such as halibut served raw, with butter. Fjallagrasamjólk (a distinctive Icelandic soup made with milk and lichen). Pea soup, often served with pancakes. Boiled potatoes. Skate boiled in cooking liquid from smoked lamb. Roast ham or pork. Braised red cabbage.

A national dish   Sheep's head stored in whey.

Christmas food   Smoked lamb.

Sweets   Sugar. Skyr with cream, sugar, and sometimes fruit. Rice porridge with sugar and cream. Butter cookies. Cakes made with butter, cheese or cream, and cardamom. Pancakes served with fruit preserves or berry jam.

Beverages   Milk, buttermilk, mysa (whey, a traditional beverage), coffee, tea, beer, aquavit.

Meals   Three meals a day plus a coffee break midmorning, late afternoon, or after the evening meal are usual.

INDIA
Republic of India

Geography   India occupies most of the Indian subcontinent in southern Asia, bordering the Indian Ocean. It includes the Himalayan Mountains, the world's highest, in the north; the fertile, densely populated Ganges Plain in the center; plateau in the south; and great rivers with extensive deltas. Almost a fourth of the area is forested. The climate ranges from near-Arctic cold to tropical heat.

Major Languages		Ethnic Groups		Major Religions	
Hindi	(both	Indo-Aryan	72%	Hindu	81%
English	official)	Dravidian	25%	Muslim	13%
21 other official languages		Other	3%	Christian	2%
				Other	4%

Population density per sq. mi. 1,000
Literacy rate 66%
Life expectancy 66.9 male; 71.9 female
Per capita GDP $2,700
Labor force in agriculture 60%

Urban 28.7%
Infant mortality rate per 1,000 live births 32.3
HIV rate 0.3%
Unemployment rate 9.9%
Arable land 49%

Agriculture rice, wheat, corn, millet, sorghum, sugarcane, fruits, potatoes, oilseeds, pulses, coconut, cotton, vegetables, jute, tea, chickens, cattle, goats, water buffalo, sheep, pigs, camels

Natural resources coal, iron ore, manganese, mica, bauxite, titanium, chromite, natural gas, diamonds, oil, limestone, fish

Industries textiles, chemicals, food processing, steel, transportation equipment, cement, mining, oil, machinery, software

History Agriculture in India dates back at least to the 7th millennium BCE. One of the world's oldest civilizations dates back to at least 3000 BCE in the Indus Valley. Hinduism originated here about 2000 BCE. Around 1500 BCE Aryans from the northwest invaded and merged with early inhabitants to create Indian civilization. Buddhism was established in the 3rd century BCE. During the 4th to 6th centuries CE a golden age existed. Arabs invaded the west in the 8th century. Turkish Muslims gained control in the north by 1200. Mogul emperors ruled from 1526 to 1857. Vasco da Gama established trading posts (1498–1503). The Dutch followed. The British East India Company came in 1609, and the British gained control of most of the country. Nationalism grew after World War I, led by Mahatma Gandhi, who advocated self-rule and nonviolence. India was partitioned into India, predominantly Hindu, and Pakistan, predominantly Muslim. India became independent in 1947 and a democratic republic in 1950. In the 1980s and 1990s religious, ethnic, and political conflicts claimed many lives. Mother Teresa of Calcutta, famous for her work among the poor, died in 1997. A 1999 cyclone, 2001 earthquake, and 2004 tsunami caused great devastation. India is the world's most populous democracy. India's first woman president took office in 2007. The economy has grown since the 1990s, especially in high-technology industries. Bombings in recent years including 2008 have killed hundreds of people. The economy has continued to perform well.

Kashmir A northwest region bordering Pakistan, Kashmir is predominantly Muslim. In 1949 the UN gave the northwest part of Kashmir to Pakistan and the east two thirds to India, which India incorporated as its only Muslim-majority state.

Sikkim Bordering northern India, Sikkim became a protectorate of India in 1950 and an associate state in 1974.

Influences on food India, large in area and the second most populous country in the world, has a great diversity of climates, cultures, and cuisines. The climates vary from snowy Himalayas in the north to the tropical south, and the foods in the regions vary accordingly. Wheat is common in the north; rice and coconut are common in the south. The coast and rivers provide fish. India is the land of spices; pepper, the most important spice, is from a berry that grows on a vine in southwest India. India now refers to the country, whereas it used to refer to the whole subcontinent. The earliest important centers of agriculture and civilization (about 3200 BCE) were in the Indus Valley, now Pakistan; wheat and barley were staples. The next phase occurred when Aryans, agricultural and pastoral people from

Central Asia, arrived around 1500 BCE and formed the Vedic culture. Muslim invasions beginning in the 8th century CE introduced new eating patterns emphasizing meat. More recently, important culinary immigration was in the north by Moghuls, the Indian version of Mongol. The Mongol Empire at its height in the Middle Ages covered most of the known world. Through the Moghul court, beginning in the 16th century and lasting more than two centuries, introductions included the highly refined cuisine of Persia such as pilaf and sweet dishes, the tandoor (cylindrical clay oven), and fruits and nuts from other parts of the empire. The Portuguese opened the sea route to India in 1498, established Goa as a colony in 1510, and brought Portuguese and Christian Catholic influence, for example pork and spiced pork sausage. Syrian Christians, who also settled along the west coast, eat beef and prepare fine beef dishes. British control for more than three centuries resulted in Anglo-Indian cookery. These important influences increased the diversity of Indian cuisine. Throughout India cereals, lentils, vegetables, dairy products, and spices are widely consumed. Cereal is the main component of the meal, and accompanying savory dishes add flavor. An important feature of Indian cuisine is vegetarianism; Jains and a large proportion of Hindus are vegetarians. Most Indian vegetarians abstain from meat and poultry, although they consume dairy items and some eat eggs (notably the Parsi). Ahimsa, reverence for life, is basic in Indian ideology and was reinforced by Buddhism and Jains doctrine. Most Indians are Hindus; they eat no beef, and those of the higher castes are vegetarians. The principle of regarding cattle as sacred dates from the Vedas about 1800 BCE. Another important Hindu principle is division of human society into castes; traditionally a Hindu could consume only foods cooked and served by a member of an equal or superior caste, and only members of the same caste will eat together. Also, some foods are considered pure, such as milk and ghee, and others impure and to be avoided, such as meat and alcohol. In other religions, dietary laws prohibit consumption of pork and alcohol by Muslims and of onions (or any root) by Jains, who depend on lentils, leafy green vegetables, and rice (Jain is an extremist vegetarian sect).

Bread and cereals Rice, wheat; rice dishes, bread (roti), chapati (crisp flat round whole wheat bread cooked on a griddle without oil), puri (puffed circles of deep-fried unleavened whole wheat bread), paratha (unleavened whole wheat flour pancake), dosa (seasoned pancake made with ground rice and lentils), idli (steamed small pancake of ground lentils and rice), naan (individual bread loaf made of white flour and cooked on tandoor inner wall).

Meat, poultry, fish Chicken, beef, goat, lamb and mutton, pork, fish (Bombay duck, mullet, pomfret, sardines), shellfish (shrimp), eggs, water buffalo. Bombay duck, a sun-dried fish from Bombay coast, is fried or used in curry.

Dairy products Milk (cow, buffalo), buttermilk, yogurt, lassi (diluted yogurt), fresh curds, cheese (pannir).

Fats and oils Ghee (clarified butter), coconut oil, mustard oil, peanut oil, sesame seed oil, vegetable oils.

Legumes (dal) Chickpeas, kidney beans, mung beans, pigeon peas, lentils, black-eyed peas, peanuts, soybeans.

Vegetables Potatoes, eggplant, cauliflower, okra, tomatoes, green beans, carrots, spinach, cucumbers, green peas, plantains, peppers, radishes.

Fruit Bananas, mangoes, coconut, oranges, lemons, limes, apples, pineapple, grapes, melons, pomegranates, peaches, quinces, guavas, tamarind, jackfruit, papaya, rokum (a sour deep red fruit), raisins.

Nuts and seeds Almonds, betel nuts, cashew nuts, pistachios, walnuts, poppy seeds, sesame seeds, sunflower seeds, mustard seeds.

Seasonings Onion, coconut, allspice, pimento, garlic, ginger, saffron, mint, tamarind, fenugreek, rosewater. Masala, spices and herbs (such as coriander seed, red chilies, turmeric, black pepper, cumin seed, cinnamon, and others), ground together, kept dry, and used as the base for curry sauces; when yogurt, coconut milk, or other liquid is added it is a wet masala. Garam masala (a blend of spices such as coriander, cumin, fenugreek, turmeric, black pepper, cardamom, nutmeg, cloves, red pepper, and ginger), the prototype of curry powder in the West. Spice blends are usually dry and aromatic in northern India and spicy-hot wet masalas in southern India.

Cookware   The metal karhai (resembles a wok) and iron tava (griddle) are usual cookware. Cooking some usual Indian foods in iron karhais or tavas significantly increases their iron content (Kollipara and Brittin, 1996).

Cooking methods   Boiling, steaming (prevalent only in the south), simmering, stir-frying, deep frying, broiling, grilling, baking, dam (cooking food in a tightly covered or sealed pot; widespread only in the north).

Dishes   Boiled or steamed rice, sometimes with saffron. Curry (made by stirring a spicy mixture, masala, into onions heated in ghee or oil and then adding the main ingredient and simmering), for example, chicken curry (murgi kari), vegetable curry (aviyal), shrimp curry. Chutney (a spicy dish made from raw, cooked, or pickled fruits or vegetables, e.g., mango or tomato chutney) usually accompanies curry. Achar (brine pickles). Korma (lamb with curry sauce thickened with yogurt and nuts or poppy seeds). Pomfret fish stuffed with green chutney, wrapped in a banana leaf, and steamed or baked. Pakora (deep-fried vegetable such as eggplant, potato, or onion rings). Samosa (triangle-shaped deep-fried pastry filled with spicy mixture of meat or vegetable, e.g., potato). Pilaf (rice cooked first in melted fat or oil so that grains remain separate, then simmered in water covered and often with added ingredients). Biryani (layered simmered spicy lamb and boiled saffron rice, with raisins and cashews). Kababs (small pieces of lamb or other meat, poultry, seafood, fruits, or vegetables, skewered and broiled or grilled). Kofta (fried and then simmered meatballs of ground meat with spices). Rayta (cold mixture of raw or cooked vegetables, yogurt, and herbs and spices), for example, boiled potato rayta. Cachumbar (cucumber, tomato, and onion salad with green herbs). Pachadi (yogurt with ingredients such as ground coconut and red chilies). Dal (lentil purée), often stir-fried. Sambar (lentil purée cooked with vegetables and spices). Dishes decorated with gold and silver leaf. An acclaimed vegetarian dish, mutter paneer (simmered cheese cubes, green peas, and spices). A Parsi dish, ekuri (scrambled eggs with fresh herbs and peppers). Tandoori cooking, mostly done in Punjab, in northwest India, features the bread naan, lamb, and tandoori chicken (chicken marinated with lime juice, curds, and spices, speared on long spikes that are then placed in the tandoor and cooked).

Sweets   Sugarcane, jaggery (unrefined palm sugar), molasses, sugar. Khir (milk and rice pudding). Rice cooked with jaggery, spices, nuts, raisins, and coconut. Barfi (candy made by cooking milk slowly with sugar to fudge-like consistency and adding coconut, rosewater, and perhaps ground almonds or pistachios). Sweet samosas (small fried and flaky pastries stuffed with sweet filling). Halva (pudding made from milk and fruit or vegetable such as carrot). Gulab jamun (deep-fried balls of milk, flour, and ghee, soaked in rose-flavored syrup). Jalebi (pretzel-shaped deep-fried batter whorls soaked in syrup with saffron and rosewater).

Beverages   Tea in northern India, coffee in southern India, fruit drinks (sharbat), water flavored with fruit syrups, spices, or herbs, palm wine. Coffeehouses are popular meeting places.

Meals and service   Two meals a day, mid-morning and evening (the main one), plus afternoon tea or coffee with snacks is typical. A main meal, on an individual metal serving tray (thali), is a central pile of rice or bread surrounded by savory accompaniments in small containers. Persons use fingers of right hand and mix the accompaniments with rice or fold them in a piece of flatbread. Paan, a betel leaf wrapped around a betel nut with spices and lime paste, is chewed after meals as a digestive and breath freshener (and it turns the mouth red).

Tiffin,   a snack, eaten anytime but often in the afternoon, may consist of anything except the staple rice or bread.

Street food and snacks   Salty snacks (chat), for example, bhelpuri (cereals, fried lentils, herbs, and chutney), barfi, jalebi.

Kashmir   In northern India and adjoining northern Pakistan, Kashmir has rice as an important crop and milk and honey, saffron, shallots, mustard, and mustard oil, the standard cooking medium. Salt tea, served frequently, is prepared by boiling a special leaf with water, milk, salt, and soda until an almost pink color permeates the brew. Kashmir is famous for its lakes, often covered with pink water lilies from the Asian lotus and prominent in the cuisine. Also on the lakes are houseboats and floating vegetable gardens, formed with reeds and mud to provide fertile beds for vegetables. Hindus, Muslims, and Buddhists comprise the population. Many Hindus are Brahmins, of the high priestly class (men go by the title of pandit). Unlike Brahmins of the rest of India, Kashmir pandits eat meat as in the Kashmiri specialty rogan josh (curried lamb), yogurt-marinated lamb simmered with spices.

INDONESIA
Republic of Indonesia

Geography   Indonesia is in Southeast Asia, bordering the Pacific Ocean, Indian Ocean, and Malaysia, and along the equator. An archipelago off the Southeast Asia mainland, it comprises over 13,500 islands (6,000 inhabited), including Java (one of the most densely populated areas in the world), Sumatra, most of Borneo, the west half of New Guinea, Bali, and Timor. The mountains and plateaus on the major islands have a cooler climate than the tropical lowlands. With the largest number of active volcanoes in the world, earthquakes are frequent. Wallace's Line, a zoological demarcation between Asian and Australian flora and fauna, divides Indonesia.

Major Languages	Ethnic Groups		Major Religions	
Bahasa Indonesian (official,	Javanese	41%	Monotheism (official)	
modified form of Malay)	Sudanese	15%	Muslim	86%
English	Malay	9%	Protestant	6%
Dutch	Madurese	3%	Roman Catholic	3%
Local dialects (Javaanese	Minangkabau	3%	Hindu	2%
most widely spoken)	Han Chinese, other	29%	Other	3%

Population density per sq. mi. 336.8
Literacy rate 91.4%
Life expectancy 68 male; 73.1 female
Per capita GDP $3,700
Labor force in agriculture 43.3%

Urban 48.1%
Infant mortality rate per 1,000 live births 31
HIV rate 0.2%
Unemployment rate 10.3%
Arable land 11%

Agriculture   rice, sugarcane, cassava, peanuts, rubber, cocoa, coffee, palm oil, copra, chickens, goats, cattle, sheep, pigs

Natural resources   oil, fish, tin, natural gas, nickel, timber, bauxite, copper, coal, gold, silver

Industries   oil and natural gas, textiles, apparel, footwear, mining, cement, chemical fertilizers, plywood, rubber

History   People migrated to Indonesia from mainland Asia before 1000 BCE. Nearly 2,000 years ago Hindu and Buddhist influence from India reached Indonesia. Trade with China started in the 5th century CE. Arab traders brought Islam along the trade routes in the 13th century, and Islam took hold in the islands except Bali, which held its Hindu religion and culture. Portuguese traders arrived in the 16th century. The Dutch replaced the Portuguese as the most important European trader in the 17th century and ruled Indonesia until 1942. In the 20th century Indonesia was united under one rule for the first time. Following Japanese occupation from 1943 to 1945, nationalists declared independence. The Netherlands ceded sovereignty in 1949, and a republic was declared in 1950. Muslim and Christian clashes from 1999 to 2002 and terrorist bombings in 2002 and 2004 killed thousands. A massive earthquake triggered devastating tsunamis in 2004. Earthquakes in 2005 and 2006 and floods in 2007 killed thousands and caused extensive damage. A peace agreement in 2005 ended decades of conflict between pro-independence insurgents and the military. The economy continued to perform well in 2007. With oil production failing, the government said it planned to leave OPEC in 2008.

Influences on food   Indonesia, the fourth most populous country of the world, covers a vast area and consists of more than 13,500 islands. Kalimantan (Indonesian Borneo) is roughly the size of France, Sumatra of Spain, and Java of England, yet Java has nearly half of Indonesia's population. For centuries a few small islands in East Indonesia supplied the Old World with its most treasured spices. West Sumatra, Southeast Bali, and Java have very fertile volcanic soils, abundant rainfall, and a social system conducive to efficient production of staple crops, especially rice. Rice, probably brought from the Southeast Asian mainland at least 2,000 years ago, has become the main food except in East Indonesia and West Java where taro, cassava, and sago are still favored. The Indian Ocean, South China Sea, lakes, rivers, and flooded rice fields provide fish and seafood. The basic diet is rice, fish, vegetables (lalab), and hot chilies. Chili peppers were introduced from the New World after discovery voyages in the 16th century. Portuguese traders frequented these islands, known as the East Indies, during the 16th century. Dutch trade became dominant in the 17th century, and the Dutch controlled the islands to 1949. Dutch influences include baked wheat flour products (biscuits, sweet pastries, and cakes), a fried egg on fried rice, and serving dishes all at once in a rijsttafel. The spread of Islam in the 15th century broke up the last great Hindu-Javanese empire, and Islam became dominant here. Most of the Hindus fled to Bali and have maintained their culture. Muslims do not consume pork or alcohol. In Indonesia, the world's most populous Islamic nation, they observe the end of Ramadan (the fasting month) by at least two days of social visiting when junior family members or employees visit senior ones to ask forgiveness of the past year's trespasses, drink tea, and eat cakes.

Bread and cereals   Rice, wheat, corn; rice dishes, cakes, noodles, bread, fried thin rice, and wheat flour bread.

Meat, poultry, fish   Fish (fresh, salted, dried), chicken, goat, beef, lamb, pork, water buffalo (carabao), eggs.

Dairy products   Water buffalo milk, yogurt, sweetened condensed milk (used in coffee), cream (used whipped in pastries). Milk and other dairy products are uncommon, although now milk bars are popular in big towns.

Fats and oils   Palm oil, coconut oil, butter, lard, margarine, vegetable oil and shortening, peanut oil, sesame oil.

Legumes   Peanuts, soybeans and bean curd, mung beans.

Vegetables   Cassava, taro, sago, cucumbers, cabbage, green beans, long green bitter bean (peté), bean sprouts, eggplant, peppers, bitter cucumber (gourd).

Fruit   Coconut, bananas, tamarind, oranges, limes, mangoes, jackfruit, papaya, melons, durian, pomelo.

Nuts and seeds   Candlenuts, litchis, kenari nuts (similar to almonds), sesame seeds.

Seasonings   Chili peppers, tamarind, lime juice, lemon grass, turmeric, salt, soy sauce, fermented shrimp paste (trassi) and fish sauce, coconut milk, onion, garlic, ginger root, laos, cocoa. Food is hot, sour, sweet, and salty.

Food preparation   Food is cut into small pieces before cooking or is carved in the kitchen. In the past, food was sometimes wrapped in leaves and baked in a trench lined with hot stones.

Dishes   Boiled rice. Nasi goreng (fried rice: meat and vegetables fried, rice fried in the same oil, and all combined), often topped with a fried egg. Rice wrapped in banana leaves and steamed or baked. Satay, or saté (bits of skewered meat, chicken, or fish/seafood, basted with soy sauce and oil, and grilled over charcoal), dipped in a hot spicy peanut sauce. Soto ajam (ginger chicken soup), often poured over rice. Opor ajam (chicken and coconut milk curry). Rendang (dry beef curry), a dish of village origin, made by simmering cubed water buffalo or beef, frying, and then simmering with onion, garlic, chili peppers, turmeric leaf, and coconut milk until coconut milk becomes oil, brown, and very thick. Java rempah (fried patties of ground beef, spices, and coconut milk). Sambar (hot spicy relish or chili, other spices, onion, and garlic fried in a little oil and added to a main ingredient to flavor it while it cooks). Sumatra lado (a fiery sambar of chili, salt, tamarind, and onions, stir-fried); with seafood or beef added it becomes a more substantial sambar goreng. Java lalab (raw or lightly boiled vegetables such as cabbage and cucumbers served with hot sambar made with trassi). Java gado-gado (vegetables such as cabbage, cucumbers, and bean sprouts with hot spicy coconut milk and peanut sauce). Sumatra gulai (an everyday curry: anything cooked with chili, onion, salt, and turmeric—and ginger for fish—in coconut milk and retaining its sauce), such as fish, beef, or chicken gulai. Sumatra water buffalo stew.

Special occasion dishes   Bali tumpeng (rice cone), a food offering symbolizing the sacred mountain where the deities lived. Nasi kuning (yellow rice made by boiling rice with turmeric in coconut milk), eaten at weddings.

A Bali specialty   Chopped turtle meat mixed with coconut milk and spices.

Sweets   Raw sugar, palm sugar, sugar. Immature coconut. Steamed cakes of glutinous rice flour, cassava, sugar, and coconut. Sweet rice cakes sprinkled with sesame seeds. Onde-onde (simmered balls of rice flour, coconut milk, and sugar, coated with grated coconut). Moluccan candy (crisp balls of ground kenari and sugar).

Beverages   Coffee, sweet black tea, coconut juice, bean drinks, fruit drinks, iced tea, tjintjau (iced drink of brewed tjintjau leaves, fruit, and sweet bean paste bits), rice wine (brom). Many people do not drink with meals.

Meals and service   Usual meal: rice, a meat, chicken, or fish dish, vegetables, and soup. Most Indonesians mix rice with other cooked foods just before eating and eat with fingers of their right hand.

IRAN
Islamic Republic of Iran

Geography   Iran is in the Middle East, bordering the Caspian Sea and Persian Gulf. It has interior highlands and plains surrounded by mountains rising to 18,603 feet (5,670 m) in the north, a large salt desert 800 miles (1,287 km) long, and many oases and forests.

Major Languages	Ethnic Groups		Major Religions	
Persian (Farsi) (official)	Persian	51%	Islam (official)	
and Persian dialects	Azeri	24%	Shi'a Muslim	89%
Turkic and Turkic dialects	Gilaki and Mazandarani	8%	Sunni Muslim	9%
Kurdish	Kurd	7%	Other (including	
Arabic	Arab	3%	Christian)	2%
	Other	7%		

Population density per sq. mi. 104.3
Literacy rate 84.7%
Life expectancy 69.4 male; 72.4 female
Per capita GDP $10,600
Labor force in agriculture 25%

Urban 66.9%
Infant mortality rate per 1,000 live births 36.9
HIV rate 0.2%
Unemployment rate 11.5%
Arable land 10%

Agriculture   grains, tomatoes, potatoes, sugarcane, sugar beets, fruit, nuts, cotton, chickens, sheep, goats, cattle
Natural resources   oil, natural gas, coal, chromium, copper, iron ore, lead, manganese, zinc, sulfur, fish

Industries   oil, petrochemicals, fertilizers, caustic soda, textiles, cement and other construction materials, food processing, metal fabricating, armaments

History   The Iranians, an Indo-European group related to the Aryans in India, came from the east during the second millennium BCE and supplanted an earlier agricultural community. Medes occupied this land from c. 728 BCE and were overthrown in 549 BCE by the Persian king Cyrus the Great. The Persian Empire, from the Indus to the Nile, was at its zenith in 525 BCE. In 333 BCE Alexander the Great conquered Persia, which regained independence in the next century. Arabs brought Islam in the 7th century, replacing the indigenous Zoroastrian faith. Persia reasserted it autonomy in the 9th century, and arts and sciences flourished. Turks and Mongols ruled here from the 11th century to 1502. From 1502 to 1722 the Iranian Safavid dynasty ruled, with Shiite Islam the official religion. In the 19th century Britain and Russia controlled the country. Britain severed Afghanistan from Persia in 1857. Reza Khan took power in a coup in 1921, became shah in 1925, and began modernization and changed the country's name to Iran in 1935. In 1941 he abdicated and was succeeded by his son, Mohammed Reza Pahlavi, who brought economic and social change and was overthrown in 1979. Shiite leader Ayatollah Khomeini, exiled by the shah in 1963, returned and established a fundamentalist Islamic republic. In the 1980s Iran and Iraq had a long, costly war over a waterway between them. Earthquakes in 1990 and 2003 caused thousands of deaths and great damage. Militants and Islamic conservatives have clashed with the government. To halt Iran's uranium enrichment program, the UN Security Council imposed sanctions in 2006 and 2007; after talks ended in deadlock in 2008, the United States added sanctions.

Influences on food   Iran, ancient Persia, is a land bridge connecting cold northern plains with hot southern deserts and the Middle East with the Far East. The ancient silk route from China to Syria went through northern Iran, and Afro-Arab-Indian trade was through southern Iran. Centrally located in the ancient world, the Persian Empire, more than 2,500 years ago, extended from Russia to Egypt and from Greece to India. Persians carried their produce such as spinach, pomegranates, and saffron to the corners of the known world. Trade carried other products such as rice, citrus, eggplant, and tea from China and India through Persia to Greece and Rome, and later to North Africa and southern Europe. Iran's climate, from the warm Persian Gulf to cold high mountains, results in a diversity of growing seasons and grains and fruit. Mountains circle Iran, forming a high arid central plateau, cold in winter and hot in summer. The soil is fertile and water is carried in underground channels from mountains to the fields and orchards. Viticulture has flourished for thousands of years. Date and orange trees grow in oases in the south. The Caspian Sea and Persian Gulf provide fish. Iranian (Persian) cuisine resembles that of the Muslim Middle East: wheat, lamb, poultry, yogurt, eggplant, stuffed vegetables, and sweet pastries, with consumption of pork or alcohol forbidden for Muslims. Distinctive for rice dishes and use of fruit, Persian cuisine has influenced that of the Ottoman Empire, Arabs, and many countries.

Bread and cereals   Wheat, rice (long grain, white), other grains; wheat leavened flatbreads including lavash (flexible, thin bread cooked on tandoor wall; it keeps well and is used to eat food by hand), filo dough pastry, rice dishes. Bread and rice are eaten at most meals.

Meat, poultry, fish   Chicken, lamb and mutton, goat, beef, fish (herring, beluga sturgeon, swordfish, tuna), shrimp, eggs, camel, game. Meat is scarce, expensive, and eaten sparingly.

Dairy products   Yogurt, diluted yogurt drink (ayran), feta cheese.

Fats and oils   Butter, clarified butter (roghan), rendered fat of fat-tailed sheep (donbeh), vegetable oil (sunflower).

Legumes   Chickpeas, split peas, broad (fava) beans, white beans.

Vegetables   Tomatoes, potatoes, eggplant, spinach, cucumbers, onions, olives, carrots, radishes, beets.

Fruit   Melons, grapes, dates, lemons, oranges, limes, pomegranates, cherries, mulberries, barberries, peaches, apricots, nectarines, plums, persimmons, medlars (resemble apples), rhubarb, raisins, currants, quince, sumac.

Nuts and seeds   Almonds, pine nuts, pistachios, walnuts, sunflower seeds, sesame seeds; rashi (sesame paste).

Seasonings   Onion, garlic, chives, lemon juice, vinegar, herbs (parsley, tarragon, marjoram, basil, mint, dill) served fresh at every meal and used in many dishes, spices (saffron, cinnamon, nutmeg, cloves, cardamom, coriander, turmeric), rosewater. Many savory dishes taste sweet and sour or sour; meat is often cooked with fruit.

Dishes   Rice, either chelo (plain) or polo (mixed with vegetables, fruit, nuts, meat, or poultry); in either, rice is boiled, mixed with butter and saffron, and heated in a pan to produce a brown crust on the bottom. Shireen polo, "king of Persian dishes" (saffron rice, carrot shreds, orange peel, almonds, pistachios, and dried fruit, all encased in caramelized sugar, garnished with barberries and almonds, and served with saffron chicken). Meat or poultry sauces or stews (khoresht) accompany plain rice (chelo). Stew of mutton or lamb, chickpeas, broad beans, tomato, onion, and turmeric (dizzi). Chicken stew with pomegranate (fesenjan). Kabobs (meat pieces marinated in onion and lemon juice and grilled on a skewer), served with rice or eaten rolled in bread with herbs and pickles. Thick soups of pulses and herbs with fruit such as the popular ab-goosht (made with lamb bone, chickpeas, onions, and limes); the solid ingredients are beaten into a paste and served separately while the broth is served with bread. Summer soup of yogurt, cucumber, onion, mint, and raisins. Herbed omelet. Stuffed meat, especially chicken and lamb roasted in a tandoor or grilled over charcoal. Vegetables stuffed with rice and baked in sauces.

Festive occasion food   Large pieces of meat roasted (e.g., whole lamb stuffed with rice, nuts, and fruit) or grilled.

National dish   Chelo kabob (marinated lamb pieces grilled on skewers and saffron rice with egg yolk and sumac).

Sweets   Sugar, syrup. Stuffed sweet pastry (qotab, sambusak, or samosa). Desserts made with sugar, rice or rice flour, dates, wheat or chickpea flour, rosewater, saffron, cardamom, and nuts. Sweet sprouted wheat kernel pudding (samanu). Sorbets. The most popular dessert: fresh fruit followed by tea and sweetmeats, such as almonds rolled in sugar syrup (noql) or baklava (baked layers of filo pastry, nuts, and syrup).

Beverages   Sharbat (iced fruit drink, especially lime), coffee (popular for centuries), tea (grown in the Caspian region and in the 20th century superseded coffee) served hot, sweet, in small glasses throughout the day to all.

Meal   Lunch (main meal): saffron rice with lamb, salad of cucumber and tomato, olives, lavash, yogurt, melon, tea.

Mezze   The mezze perhaps originated in ancient Persia, where food and music accompanied drinking wine. The Persian word *maza* means "taste," or "relish." Mezze were first bits of tart fruit and later nuts and roasted meat bits. Alcohol prohibition for Muslims has prevented the mezze tradition from continuing in Iran.

IRAQ
Republic of Iraq

Geography   Iraq is In the Middle East. It is mostly a plain and includes the valley between the Tigris and Euphrates rivers, mountains in the north, desert in the southwest, and marshland along the Persian Gulf.

Major Languages	Ethnic Groups		Major Religions	
Arabic (official)	Arab	75–80%	Islam (official)	
Kurdish (official in Kurdish regions)	Kurdish	15–20%	Shi'a Muslim	62–65%
Turkoman (Turkish dialect)	Turkoman, Assyrian, other	5%	Sunni Muslim	32–37%
Assyrian			Christian, other	3%
Armenian				

Population density per sq. mi. 169.1
Literacy rate 74.1%
Life expectancy 68.3 male; 71 female
Per capita GDP $3,600
Labor force in agriculture NA

Urban 66.9%
Infant mortality rate per 1,000 live births 45.4
HIV rate NA
Unemployment rate 28%
Arable land 13%

Agriculture   wheat, tomatoes, potatoes, barley, rice, dates, cotton, chickens, sheep, goats, cattle

Natural resources   oil, natural gas, phosphates, sulfur, fish

Industries   oil, chemicals, textiles, leather, construction materials, food processing

History   One of the world's earliest civilizations was in Mesopotamia, in the Tigris-Euphrates valley. In 3000 BCE the Sumerians originated the culture of the Babylonians and Assyrians. Persian and Greek conquests followed. Arab Muslims held the land from the 7th century CE until the Mongols took it in 1258. The Ottomans ruled it from the 16th century to 1917. After World War I Iraq became a League of Nations mandate administered by Britain (the British occupied it in both World Wars). It became independent under a king in 1932 and a republic in 1958. Saddam Hussein became president in 1979 and ruled as a dictator until 2003, repressing Iraqi Kurds and Shiites and launching wars against Iran in 1980 and Kuwait in 1990. Iraqi resistance to UN inspection of suspected weapons of mass destruction sites led to a U.S.-led coalition invasion in 2003 and Iraqi government collapse. Saddam Hussein was captured in 2003 and charged with crimes against humanity, tried beginning in 2005, and convicted and executed in 2006. An Iraqi cabinet was named in 2003. In 2004 U.S. authorities transferred sovereignty to a transitional Iraqi government. In 2005 Iraq elected a transitional assembly and president. Insurgents continued attacks against police, civilians, and coalition forces. In 2007 a "surge" increased U.S. troop numbers in Iraq. A decrease in civilian casualties and violence followed in 2008.

Influences on food   Iraq has the same natural division as ancient Mesopotamia, which was composed of Assyria in the arid north upland and Babylonia in the marshy south. Al-Jazirah (Assyria) grows wheat, apples, and stone fruits; Al Iraq (Babylonia) grows rice and dates. Northern cuisine resembles that of neighbor Syria; southern cuisine relies on rice, fish, and dates. Ancient Mesopotamia civilizations subsisted on wheat and barley, and grain still dominates the diet. Often meat is combined with grain in a dish. Beef, from cattle or water buffalo, is more common than in most of the Arab world and often more common than mutton. Rivers and the Persian Gulf provide fish. Persian influences include meat cooked with fruit, some pastries and candies, stews served over rice, and the Persian name rashi for sesame paste instead of the Arabic name tahini. Turkish influences include strudel pastries, stuffed vegetables (Turkish dolma), Turkish-style clotted cream, pickled vegetables made pink by beets, and the sour flavoring citric acid crystals (Turkish name limon duzi). Two main minority groups in the northeast are Kurds, who speak a Persian-related language, and Assyrians, a Christian group speaking a modern dialect of Aramaic. Both cook usual northern dishes such as stews. Most Iraqis are Muslims, who do not consume pork or alcohol and fast from sunup to sundown during the month of Ramadan.

Bread and cereals   Wheat, barley, rice; cracked wheat (burghul), porridge, Arab bread (round wheat flour yeast loaves), pita bread (flatbread, round with hollow center), filo dough pastry, rice dishes.

Meat, poultry, fish   Chicken, mutton and lamb, beef, goat, water buffalo, fish (catfish, shabbut), eggs.

Dairy products   Yogurt, feta cheese, cream.

Fats and oils   Olive oil, clarified butter (ghee), vegetable oil.

Legumes   Chickpeas (garbanzo beans), broad beans (fava beans), lentils.

Vegetables   Tomatoes, potatoes, onions, eggplant, green peppers, olives, celery, green onions, parsley; pickles.

Fruit   Dates, figs, melons, grapes, lemons, limes, pomegranates, apricots, raisins, apples, quinces, tamarind.

Nuts and seeds   Almonds, pine nuts, pistachio nuts, walnuts, sesame seeds; sesame paste (rashi).

Seasonings   Onions, garlic, dill, tarragon, peppergrass, mint, lemon juice, vinegar, rosewater, salt, black pepper, paprika, cumin, turmeric, saffron, cardamom, cinnamon, oregano. More spices are used than in Syria or Turkey.

Dishes   Harissa (meat stewed with whole wheat), the universal Muslim dish. Kashki (meat and cracked-wheat porridge with dried limes, cumin, and turmeric or tomato juice), a favorite for picnics. Tharid (a casserole of flatbread layered with meat stew), reputedly Mohammed's favorite dish. Mosul kubba (kibbeh), a fried or poached flat wheat loaf stuffed with meat, almonds, raisins, and spices; in the south, boiled rice replaces wheat and tail fat of fat-tailed sheep replaces meat. A unique Iraqi dish, uruq (meat cut small, often fried, mixed with leavened dough, green onions, and celery leaves, and baked like bread). Pacha (boiled heads, stomachs, and trotters of sheep), served with bread and vegetable pickles. Lamb boiled and then glazed in clarified butter. Assyrian soup (rice and vegetable soup with dill and yogurt). Boiled rice. Onion dolma (hollowed onion stuffed with rice and meat). Grilled ground meat on skewers, called kabab in Iraq except among non-Arab Kurds and called caftan elsewhere. Fisinjan (fowl stewed with walnuts and pomegranate). Tarkhina (yogurt and cracked wheat mixed, fermented, and dried). Mutabbag (fish or meat smothered in rice).

National dish   Masquf, or masgoof (split large fish, preferably shabbut, cooked on stakes over a fire), cooked and eaten outdoors by a river, served with slices of tomato and onion and Arab bread.

Sweets   Honey, sugar. Syrups flavored with fruit or flowers such as roses. Manna (sweet substance that appears on plants), gathered in the Kurdish territory. Pastries such as baqlawa (baklava) and mutabaqa (flaky bun of puff paste), made by Assyrian women of villages around Mosul.

Beverages   Coffee, tea, both sweet and often flavored with cardamom and mint, respectively, water flavored with rose syrup, beer, arak (grape distillate).

IRELAND

Geography   Ireland is in Western Europe bordering the Atlantic Ocean. It occupies most of the island west of Great Britain and separated from it by the Irish Sea. Ireland consists of a central plateau rimmed with hills and mountains. The principal river is Shannon. The Atlantic coastline is heavily indented.

Major Languages		Ethnic Groups		Major Religions	
Irish (Gaelic),	(both	Irish	87%	Roman Catholic	87%
spoken mainly in the west	official)	Other white	8%	Church of Ireland (Anglican)	3%
English		Other	5%	Other	6%
				None	4%

Population density per sq. mi. 156.3

Literacy rate 99%

Life expectancy 75.4 male; 80.9 female

Per capita GDP $43,100

Labor force in agriculture 6%

Urban 60.5%

Infant mortality rate per 1,000 live births 5.1

HIV rate 0.2%

Unemployment rate 4.4%

Arable land 17%

Agriculture   sugar beets, barley, wheat, turnips, potatoes, chickens, cattle, sheep, pigs, goats

Natural resources   fish, natural gas, peat, copper, lead, zinc, silver, barite, gypsum, limestone, dolomite

Industries   food, brewing, textiles, clothing, chemicals, pharmaceuticals, machinery, rail transportation equipment

History   Humans settled Ireland c. 6000 BCE. The Picts and Erainn inhabited the islands during the Stone and Bronze ages. In about 300 BCE Celtic tribes migrated to the islands, assimilated the inhabitants, and established a Gaelic civilization. The Gaelic culture spread to Scotland in the 5th century CE, the same century that St. Patrick converted the Irish to Christianity. Norsemen invasions began in the 8th century and ended in 1014 with defeat by the Irish. English invasions started in the 12th century, and the Anglo-Irish struggle continued for over 700 years. The Great Famine of the 1840s resulted in death or emigration of 2 million people. The result of the civil war (1919–1921) between the Catholics in southern Ireland, who favored independence, and the Protestant majority in the north, who preferred continued union with Britain, was that Southern Ireland became the Irish Free State in 1922 and Northern Ireland remained part of the United Kingdom. Ireland became a sovereign democratic state in 1937 and a republic in 1948. Britain in 1949 recognized Ireland's independence but declared that the northern six counties' cession required the consent of Northern Ireland. Irish governments have favored peaceful reunification of all Ireland. Ireland's first woman president was Mary Robinson (1990–1997). In 2007 a power-sharing agreement was reached with a new government for Northern Ireland, ending nearly 40 years of conflict in the six northern counties of Ireland under British jurisdiction. In recent years, with expanded educational opportunities and foreign investment in high-tech industries, Ireland's economy has improved dramatically.

Influences on food   Celtic influence, established in the 4th-century BCE, has endured. The early Irish diet centered on cereals and dairy products. Cereals were made into porridge and cakes of oats and barley, baked over an open fire, and eaten with honey, onions, fish, curds, or a salted joint. Cows grazed in lush pastures and supplied abundant milk; some was made into salted butter. Wealth was calculated on the size of the dairy herd, so not much beef was eaten. Pork, usually smoked, salted bacon, and mutton were the usual meats. Medieval Ireland's vast forests, inland waterways, and coasts contributed venison, wild boar, crabapples, berries, watercress, and fish. Anglo-Normans arrived in the 11th and 12th centuries and increased the cultivation of wheat, peas, and beans, so wheat and rye breads and pea and bean soups increased in the diet. Overall, oats, dairy products, and salted meat dominated the diet until the potato arrived from the New World in the 17th century. The potato rapidly became the basic foodstuff and has remained so. The potato thrived in Ireland's cool, moist climate; everyone planted them and soon came to depend on them. In the 18th century butter exportation soared accompanied by increased cultivation and consumption of potatoes. By the end of the 18th century potato had displaced cereal and dairy products as the dominant food. The Irish added the potato to lamb or kid to become Irish stew, recognized as a national dish by 1800. By the time of the Great Famine, the 1840s, over a third of the Irish relied almost exclusively on the potato for food. Usually potatoes were boiled in a pot of water, and everyone peeled their potatoes and ate them with milk or buttermilk, plus boiled herring or salted bacon if available. A potato blight arrived in the mid-1840s; it was caused by a fungus that almost completely destroyed the potato crops. By 1851 about a million Irish had died and about a million had emigrated, reducing Ireland's population by over a fifth. In the late 19th century there were increases in grazing and dairy farming, agricultural prosperity, and meat and dairy products consumption. By the early 20th century, tea, sugar, and white bought bread replaced homemade breads and milk drinks. Ireland's cuisine is often described as simple and hearty. Irish people eat a lot of fish and potatoes, partly because Ireland produces a lot of them and partly because most Irish people are Roman Catholics. Until well into the 20th century the Irish Catholics ate fish (usually boiled salted fish with a basic white sauce) on the fast days of Wednesday and Friday and during Lent. The diet for many people is potatoes, turnips, soda bread, tea, and stout, occasionally with fish, bacon, or egg. Upper society has more diversified, refined food customs from outside.

Bread and cereals   Barley, wheat, oats, rye, rice, hops; oatmeal porridge, oatcakes, soda bread (crisp bread made with wheat flour, bicarbonate of soda, and buttermilk), wheat flour and oatmeal bread.

Meat, poultry, fish   Fish and shellfish, beef, chicken, lamb and mutton, pork, goat, eggs; pork sausage, bacon.

Dairy products   Milk (cow, sheep, goat), buttermilk, cream, curds, cheese (cheddar, Blarney—resembles Swiss).

Fats and oils   Butter, lard, margarine, vegetable oil, salt pork.

Legumes   Kidney beans, lentils, lima beans, split peas.

Vegetables   Potatoes, turnips, cabbage, greens, cauliflower, carrots, parsnips, onions, beans, peas, leeks.

Fruit   Apples, cherries, gooseberries, plums, raisins, currants, strawberries.

Nuts and seeds   Almonds, chestnuts, hazelnuts, pecans, walnuts, sesame seeds. Nuts are popular in sweets.

Seasonings   Salt, black pepper, onion, garlic, herbs (parsley for sauces, sage for poultry stuffing, rosemary for lamb, thyme in poultry stuffing, beef stews, and hearty soups, mint for lamb or peas), allspice, vanilla. Food is mildly seasoned and served with flavorful sauces and strong flavored condiments used to taste.

Condiments   Worcestershire sauce (anchovies, vinegar, soy, garlic, and spices), mint jelly (used with lamb).

Dishes   Potatoes, usually boiled, also baked. Mashed potatoes, called mash. Boxty (pancakes made with grated raw potatoes, flour, salt, and milk). Champ (mashed potatoes with milk, butter, and chopped onions). Colcannon (boiled potatoes and cabbage mashed together with milk, leeks, and butter). Bubble and squeak (leftover potatoes and cabbage chopped and fried together). Shepherd's pie (meat and onion pie topped with mashed potatoes). Bean, pea, and mustard soups. Fish and chips (deep-fried, battered fish and fried potatoes). Boiled lobster. Soused mackerel (mackerel with onions, herbs, spices, vinegar, and lemon juice, baked, and marinated). Roast beef or lamb. Roast pork with apples. Pie (meat, game, fish, vegetables, or fruit, covered with or in a crust and baked). Pudding (steamed, boiled, or baked meat and vegetables, custard, or fruit). Pickled cabbage, onions.

National dish   Irish stew (simmered mutton or kid, potatoes, onions, and water plus perhaps other vegetables).

St. Patrick's Day dish   On March 17, commemorating Ireland's patron saint, corned beef and cabbage is popular.

Sweets   Honey, sugar. Berry pudding. Gur cake (stale bread and cake, raisins, and water spread over pastry and baked, and iced with sugar and cut into squares). Irish Christmas cake (white fruitcake with nuts and allspice).

Beverages   Milk, tea (black, served with milk and sugar), beer (stout preferred; dark, rich, heavy), Irish whiskey.

Meals   Breakfast: oatmeal porridge. Dinner: meat, fish, or poultry, potatoes, and other vegetables, with white bread, butter, and tea or milk. Tea: hot tea and a light snack, taken by most people in late afternoon.

ISRAEL
State of Israel

Geography   Israel is in the Middle East, at the east end of the Mediterranean Sea. It has a fertile coastal plain, the Judean Plateau in the center, and desert in the south. The Jordan is the only principal river.

Major Languages	Ethnic Groups		Major Religions	
Hebrew (both Arabic official) English	Jewish Arab (mostly) and other	76% 24%	Judaism Muslim Christian Other	76% 16% 2% 6%

Population density per sq. mi. 906.1
Literacy rate 91.8%
Life expectancy 78.5 male; 82.8 female
Per capita GDP $25,800
Labor force in agriculture 18.5%

Urban 91.6%
Infant mortality rate per 1,000 live births 4.3
HIV rate 0.1%
Unemployment rate 8.2%
Arable land 15%

Agriculture   potatoes, tomatoes, citrus, cotton, chickens, sheep, cattle, pigs, goats

Natural resources   fish, timber, potash, copper, natural gas, phosphate rock, magnesium bromide, clay, sand

Industries   high-tech projects, wood and paper products, potash and phosphates, food, beverages, tobacco

History   Israel occupies the southwest corner of the ancient Fertile Crescent. Judaism developed in this land, called Canaan by the Hebrews, during the 2nd and 1st millennium BCE. After Babylonian, Persian, and Greek conquests, the area was controlled by Rome, renaming it Palestine, after earlier inhabitants, the Philistines. Arabs invaded in 636 CE and by a few centuries later Arabic language and Islam prevailed, although a Jewish minority remained. After four centuries of Ottoman rule, in 1917 Britain took control of the land. Jews migrated there during Nazi persecution, leading to deteriorating relations with Arabs. In 1947 the UN General Assembly partitioned Palestine into an Arab and a Jewish state. Immigration of Jews and Arabs increased. Israel became independent in 1948. Conflict with Arabs continued through the 20th century and as of late 2008. In 2008 relations between Israel and Syria were strained when Israeli planes bombed a military building in Syria.

Palestinian Territories   Gaza Strip and the West Bank are the Palestinian Territories. Since 1996 the Palestinian Authority has been responsible for civilian government. A victory by Hamas militants in legislative elections in 2006 led to a power struggle with the president of the Palestinian Authority (of the Fatah, moderate, more secular faction), who favored a negotiated settlement with Israel. In 2007 in bitter fighting in Gaza, Hamas ousted Fatah from Gaza but the president retained power in the West Bank.

Gaza Strip,   between Israel and the Mediterranean Sea, is inhabited mostly by Palestinian Arabs, more than 35% of whom live in refugee camps. Israel captured Gaza from Egypt in 1967. In 1993–1994 agreement between Israel and the Palestinian Authority provided for interim self-rule in Gaza, with Israel retaining control over security. In 2005 Israel evacuated Jewish settlers from Gaza and made a fortified barrier on its border to block infiltrators. After Hamas took over in 2007, Israel intensified military and economic pressures; in 2008 Hamas blew up part of the border wall between Gaza and Egypt.

West Bank   is bordered by Israel and Jordan. Israel captured it from Jordan in 1967. Israel controls much of the land; the Palestinians now have full or shared control of 40% of the area. In 2002 Israel began building a security barrier in the West Bank. In 2004 the World Court in a nonbinding ruling said the barrier violated international law.

Influences on food   Israel's varied cuisine is a blend of indigenous Middle Eastern cooking and that of many Jewish immigrants who settled there since nationhood. Also, many of the people adhere to the dietary laws of the Jewish religion. For many centuries inhabitants of the region have eaten wheat products, lentils, broad beans, fruit and nuts, raw vegetables, flatbreads, lamb and kid, and dairy products. Once the country was established, settlers came from colder climates with different food customs. The kibbutz (collective agricultural settlement) tradition has simple fare of local foods such as homemade bread and applesauce. Dishes from Central and East Europe include schnitzel, goulash, gefilte fish, chopped liver, and chicken soup. Jewish food includes börek, pirog, bagel, blini, kibbeh, kreplach, samosa, tzimmes, kneidlach, latkas, and lax. In Israel, although the proportion of the population that adheres strictly to Jewish dietary laws (the observant Orthodox Jews) is small, the Jewish influence on the availability and marketing of foods is disproportionally greater. Jewish food is influenced by Jewish dietary laws and two main branches: Sephardi and Ashkenazi. Sephardi refers to Jews of the Iberian Peninsula and their descendants, the majority of whom lived in countries that at one time were under the influence of Islam. Both Islam and Judaism came from a Middle Eastern nomadic pastoral culture and have much in common. Sephardic cooking developed in a geographic and cultural climate compatible with the Bible. Ashkenazi Jews are from the Rhine Valley and further east, from Germanic and Slavic areas with cuisines far removed from the biblical landscape and climate. Jewish dietary laws are based on the Torah (the first five books of the Bible, the commands of God to Moses) and the Talmud (rabbinical interpretations). In summary, these are the commands: what may be eaten (Leviticus 11 and Deuteronomy 14) is animals that both chew the cud and have cloven hooves, birds that are not prohibited, and fish that have both scales and fins; forbidden is eating swine, blood, or sciatic nerve (runs through hindquarters of quadrupeds); how to slaughter; how to cook; and food for special occasions (especially no leavened bread during Passover). Under Jewish dietary laws no work including cooking may be done on the Sabbath (sundown Friday until Saturday evening) so food must be prepared ahead of time. Separate cooking of, consumption of, and utensils for dairy and meat are required. Thus Jewish dietary laws forbid consumption of pork, blood, and shellfish, and of dairy products and meat at the same meal. Yemenites of Israel, Jews who came in the late 1940s after many centuries of exile in the southwest corner of the Arabian Peninsula, brought a hotly spiced diet and specialties such as qat, or kat (a narcotic shrub whose leaves are chewed or brewed into tea), fenugreek seeds, hilbeh, and locusts (baked and sun dried).

Bread and cereals   Wheat, rice, barley, corn; cracked wheat, bagel (dense round yeast bun with a hole in the middle), matzoh (crisp, flat, unleavened bread), white yeast loaf braid bread, yeast buns, pita bread (thin, round, with hollow center), filo dough, pasta, rice dishes.

Meat, poultry, fish   Chicken, beef, lamb, pork, goat, fish, lox (salmon), turkey, ducks, eggs.

Dairy products   Milk, cream, yogurt, cheese (usually feta); nondairy imitation dairy products.

Fats and oils   Olive oil, vegetable oil, nondairy margarine, butter.

Legumes   Broad beans (fava beans), lentils, chickpeas (garbanzo beans).

Vegetables   Potatoes, tomatoes, eggplant, onions, avocados, carrots, cucumbers, lettuce, peppers, squash, parsley, radishes, prickly pear cactus (sabra), olives.

Fruit   Grapefruit, pomelos, oranges, lemons, bananas, dates, figs, pomegranates, grapes, raisins, apples.

Nuts and seeds   Almonds, pine nuts, pistachios, walnuts, fenugreek seeds, sesame seeds, caraway seeds.

Seasonings   Onions, garlic, dill, curry powder, cardamom, ginger, black pepper, hot red pepper, cumin, coriander.

Condiment   Hilbeh (sauce of tomatoes, ground fenugreek seeds, hot red chilies, and spices), used to dip bread.

Dishes   Ful medames (boiled, seasoned fava beans). Shawerma (rotisserie lamb or beef). Tabbouleh (salad of parsley, tomato, and cracked wheat). Hummus (boiled, seasoned, pureed beans or chickpeas). Schnitzel (cutlet, or slice, of meat, usually veal or pork, breaded and fried). Goulash (meat stew seasoned with paprika and onions). Gefilte fish (fish skinned and boned and stuffed back into the skin or made into balls and poached). Börek (pastry filled with meat or cheese). Pirog (pie with savory or sweet filling, baked or fried). Blini (small pancakes). Kibbeh (paste of grain, onions, and meat). Kreplach (small filled pasta). Samosa (small crisp, flaky pastry). Tzimmes (sweet vegetable or meat dish). Kneidlach (dumpling). Latkas (potato fritters). Avocado half stuffed with nuts and fruit. Lettuce, tomato, and cucumber salad. Fried whole tilapia fish from the Sea of Galilee, a freshwater lake. French fried potatoes. Baked casserole of matzoh, chicken, chicken broth, beaten eggs, and dill. Roasted or stewed poultry or fried fish with fruits, perhaps olives, and seasonings. Stew of beef liver and lungs with lemon, parsley, and seasonings. Boiled squash with garlic and dill.

National dish   Falafel (small fried patties/balls of puréed beans or chickpeas), "Israeli hotdog," often with hilbeh.

Sabbath dish   Cholent (rice, beans, potatoes, meat, and eggs in the shell) assembled on Friday and slow cooked.

Sweets   Honey, sugar. Fresh fruit. Crepes with bananas, raisins, and figs, served with orange sauce. Honey cake with spices, raisins, citrus peel, and almonds. Figs simmered in syrup, stuffed with ice cream, frozen, and dipped in hot oil. Sesame seed candy.

Beverages   Tea, coffee, wine, brandy.

Street food and snacks   Ful medames, shawerma in pita bread, tabbouleh, falafel, ears of corn, goulash, coffee.

ITALY
Italian Republic

Geography   In southern Europe, this boot-shaped peninsula extends from the Alps Mountains into the Mediterranean Sea. Italy includes the fertile plains of the Po River Valley, northern lakes, mountains including the Apennine Mountains forming the peninsula's backbone, coastal plains, and islands including Sicily and Sardinia.

Major Languages	Ethnic Groups		Major Religions	
Italian (official)	Italian	96%	Roman Catholic	90%
German	Other	4%	Muslim	2%
French			Other, none	8%
Slovene				

Population density per sq. mi. 512.2
Literacy rate 98.9%
Life expectancy 77.1 male; 83.2 female
Per capita GDP $30,400
Labor force in agriculture 5%

Urban 67.6%
Infant mortality rate per 1,000 live births 5.6
HIV rate 0.4%
Unemployment rate 6.8%
Arable land 26%

Agriculture   sugar beets, corn, grapes, wheat, tomatoes, olives, fruits, vegetables, potatoes, soybeans, chickens, pigs, sheep, cattle, goats

Natural resources   coal, mercury, zinc, potash, marble, sulfur, natural gas, crude oil deposits, fish

Industries   tourism, machinery, iron and steel, chemicals, food processing, textiles, motor vehicles

History   Indo-Europeans migrated into the area probably from 2000 to 1000 BCE. The Etruscan civilization dominated here from the 9th to the 3rd century BCE. Rome became the major power in Italy after 500 BCE. The Roman Empire included Western Europe, the Balkans, the Middle East, and North Africa; it lasted until the 5th century CE. Germanics invaded for several centuries. From the 15th to the 18th century Italian lands were controlled by France, the Holy Roman Empire, Spain, and Austria. An advanced civilization developed in the northern city-states, resulting in the Renaissance.

Italy was reunified during the 1850s and 1860s. Italy joined the Allies during World War I. Fascism led by Benito Mussolini controlled Italy from 1919 to 1943. Italy was allied with Nazi Germany in World War II. It was a charter member of NATO (1949) and of the European Community, and it worked with other counties to establish the EU. Since World War II, Italy has improved indusrial output and living standards. Turin hosted the 2006 Winter Olympics. In 2008 the premier reaffirmed Italy's commitment to the Afghan mission.

Influences on food   The Phoenicians and Greeks probably brought the olive tree and chickpeas to the region in ancient times. The cooking of the Italian peninsula was the first fully developed cuisine in Europe. In Sicily, the cuisine was renowned during the time of classical Greece. During the time of the Roman Empire, banquets were held in Rome and spices from India were used, notably black pepper in desserts, as Apicius (1958) noted in one of the world's first cookbooks, in the first century CE. Polenta (cereal porridge) and cheese pie are two of the oldest Roman dishes. From the 9th to the 11th centuries, Arabs occupied Sicily and brought oranges, sugarcane, rice, varied spices, marzipan (almond paste), and rice flavored with saffron. They left a strong influence in sweet and savory dishes using almonds and dried fruit. Pasta was common in Italy by the 13th century. Naples was an important port in medieval times and a gateway for the entry of Catalan cookery. Catalan is a strip along the western Mediterranean. Characteristics of Catalan cuisine are the condiment olive oil with garlic; lightly frying onion with garlic and herbs as the starting point for many dishes; adding a pounded mixture of garlic, olive oil, fried bread, and herbs to a completed dish to thicken and to increase flavor; eggplant dishes; and the use of pork and lard. New World foods brought from the Americas such as corn, potatoes, pimento peppers, chocolate, vanilla, and especially tomatoes also influenced Italian cuisine. Italy led the Renaissance in the arts, including the culinary ones. Called the mother cuisine, Italian cuisine was introduced to France in 1533 when Catherine de Medici of Florence moved to France to marry King Henri II, taking expert chefs with her. Coffee and spices were brought in through the great trade center Venice in the 16th century, and coffee drinking was widespread by the late 17th century. Italy developed and spread over the world a cuisine that is tasty, varied, enjoyable, and popular. Italian foods famous worldwide include pasta, pizza, Parma ham, Parmesan cheese, and ice cream. Main foods are pasta and fish. Most Italians are Roman Catholics, who eat meatless dishes (e.g., pasta with fish) during Lent.

Regional variations   Italian cuisine differs mainly for north and south, with Bologna the capital of northern Italian cuisine and Naples the southern capital. Main differences are in fats and pasta, usually butter and flat pasta made with eggs (e.g., lasagna) in the north and olive oil and tubular pasta made without eggs (e.g., spaghetti) in the south. Also, in the north, pasta is commonly stuffed with cheese or meat and topped with a cream sauce, whereas in the south, it is usually served unfilled and with a tomato sauce. In addition, northern fare uses more dairy products and meat than the south, which uses more beans, vegetables, and seasonings. Northern foods include butter, beef, cheese, wine, and aperitifs such as vermouth. Southern cuisine features olive oil, pizza, spaghetti, macaroni, tomatoes, garlic, eggplant, and mixed-fish stews/soups. Lombardy region in the north including Milan produces rice, butter, and gorgonzola and Bel Paese cheeses. Piedmont region in the northwest including Turin invented grissini (slender breadsticks), grows rice, and produces wine and vermouth. The northwest coast, Liguria region with Genoa, features seafood and herbs. Northeastern Italy with Venice on the east coast features seafood and coffee. The northern center including Bologna has pork sausage similar to American bologna, proscuitto (a raw smoked ham served thinly sliced, often with melon or figs as an appetizer), Parma ham, and Parmesan cheese. Tuscany region is famous for olive groves, vineyards, wine (especially Chianti), and beef; its capital, Florence, is known for green spinach noodles. The regions around Rome, Italy's capital, have pecorino Romano, a hard sheep's milk cheese similar to Parmesan but with sharper flavor. Naples, home of pizza, has pasta as the staple food and the characteristic combination of tomato and pasta; cheeses of surrounding regions include mozzarella, provolone, and ricotta (a sheep's milk cottage cheese, often used in desserts). Sicily, an island in southernmost Italy, with an active volcano its highest peak, features seafood, kid, and lamb; grows grapes, vegetables, wheat, and citrus; and is best known for sweets and Marsala (sweet dessert wine). In Sardinia, also a mountainous island and west of the mainland, are mining, sheep-raising, and distinctive bread in thin sheets.

Bread and cereals   Wheat, corn, rice; pasta (spaghetti, noodles), bread, rice dishes, cornmeal porridge.

Meat, poultry, fish   Pork, lamb, beef and veal, goat, fish and shellfish (shrimp, small fish such as sardines eaten whole), chicken, eggs; ham, sausages.

Dairy products   Milk (cow, sheep, goat), cream, cheese (Parmesan, Bel Paese, mozzarella, ricotta, gorgonzola).

Fats and oils   Olive oil, butter, lard, vegetable oil, salt pork.

Legumes   Chickpeas, fava beans, kidney beans, lentils, soybeans, white beans.

Vegetables   Tomatoes, olives, potatoes, spinach, pimento peppers, broccoli, romaine lettuce, cabbage, eggplant, peas, squash, asparagus, artichoke, onions, celery, shallots, scallions, mushrooms.

Fruit   Grapes, pears, peaches, lemons, oranges, melons, raisins, currants, apricots, cherries, figs, citron.

Nuts and seeds   Almonds, chestnuts, hazelnuts, pine nuts, pistachios, walnuts, lupine seeds, poppy seeds.

Seasonings   Salt, olive oil, tomato, garlic, basil, oregano, parsley, black pepper, marjoram, thyme, sage, bay leaves, rosemary, tarragon, mint, cloves, saffron, lemon juice, vinegar, vanilla, chocolate.

Dishes   Minestrone (vegetable soup). Boiled spaghetti with seasoned tomato sauce and cheese. Veal parmigana (veal cutlet, breaded and fried, then simmered in tomato sauce with onion, garlic, and oregano, and sprinkled with Parmesan cheese), often served on pasta. Canneloni (pasta rolled around filling of seasoned meat and spinach and baked in tomato and cream sauces with Parmesan cheese). Ravioli (boiled small pasta packets filled with meat or cheese). Deep-fried seafood (shrimp, squid, smelts). Sautéed veal scallops (scaloppine). Pollo alla cacciatora (chicken braised in wine with vinegar, garlic, and rosemary). Fried cheese balls. Pesto (paste of basil, garlic, nuts, and cheese). Fried artichokes. Vegetable such as broccoli simmered in wine and olive oil with garlic.

A national dish   Polenta (cornmeal porridge) often served with cheese or sauce and especially popular in Milan.

Regional special dishes   North and Milan: panettone (coffee cake with raisins and candied fruit), often eaten for breakfast; risotto (rice cooked in butter and chicken stock, with Parmesan cheese and saffron). Alla Milanese often indicates rice in a dish. Northwest and Turin: bagna cauda (hot bath: a dip of anchovies, garlic, and olive oil or butter); baked trout with mushrooms and scallions. Northwest coast and Genoa: burrida (fish stew containing octopus and squid); pesto. Venice: scampi (broiled shrimp with garlic butter and lemon juice); risi e bisi (rice and green peas simmered in chicken stock). Bologna: lasagna Verdi al forno (spinach-flavored lasagna baked in meat and white sauces with Parmesan cheese); tortellini (boiled egg pasta rings stuffed with meat, cheese, and eggs), served in soup or with meat or cream sauce. Florence: boiled green spinach noodles served with butter and Parmesan cheese; outside of Italy alla fiorentina (Florentine) refers to a dish containing spinach. The regions around Rome: fettucine Alfredo (boiled long, flat egg noodles mixed with butter, cream, and cheese); gnocchi (semolina dumplings baked with butter and cheese). Naples and southern regions: pizza (baked yeast dough crust topped with tomato sauce and cheese); boiled pasta served with olive oil, garlic, and tomato sauce or in pasta e fagiole (pasta and bean soup); calzone (pizza dough folded over cheese, ham, or salami and baked or fried); eggplant Parmesan (baked eggplant, tomato sauce, and mozzarella and Parmesan cheeses).

Sweets   Honey, sugar. Flavored ices or sherbets (granita). Galatia (ice creams). Zabaione (custard with Marsala). Cheese pie, or cheesecake (crostata di ricotta). Amaretti (almond macaroons). Sicily:

cannoli (deep-fried pasty shells filled with sweetened ricotta cheese, chocolate, and citron), cassata (layer cake with ricotta filling and chocolate frosting), spumoni (chocolate and vanilla ice cream with a layer of whipped cream with fruit and nuts).

Beverages   Wine (Chianti, Marsala), coffee, espresso, cappuccino (coffee and hot, beaten milk), tea, chocolate drink, aperitifs (Campari, vermouth), Sambucca (anise-flavored liqueur).

Meals   Breakfast: coffee, bread, and jam. Main meal (usually lunch): antipasti (appetizers), soup or pasta, a fish, meat, or poultry dish and vegetable, green salad, bread and red wine, fresh fruit and cheese or occasionally cake or ice cream. Dinner: like lunch but lighter. Coffee, espresso, Marsala, or Sambucca may be drunk after dinner.

IVORY COAST (*SEE* CÔTE D'I.VOIRE)

J

JAMAICA

Geography Jamaica is an island in the Caribbean Sea, south of Cuba and west of Haiti. Mountains, including the Blue Mountains in the east, cover 80% of the land. Jamaica also has coastal lowlands and a limestone plateau.

Major Languages	Ethnic Groups		Major Religions	
English (official)	Black	91%	Protestant	63%
English Patois	Mixed	6%	Roman Catholic	3%
	East Indian and other	3%	None and other	34%

Population density per sq. mi. 670.6
Literacy rate 86%
Life expectancy 71.9 male; 75.4 female
Per capita GDP $7,700
Labor force in agriculture 17%

Urban 52.7%
Infant mortality rate per 1,000 live births 15.6
HIV rate 1.6%
Unemployment rate 8.9%
Arable land 16%

Agriculture sugarcane, coconuts, oranges, bananas, coffee, potatoes, chickens, goats, cattle, pigs, sheep

Natural resources bauxite, gypsum, limestone, fish

Industries tourism, bauxite/alumna, agriculture processing, light manufactures, rum, cement, metal, paper

History Arawak Indians inhabited this land c. 600 and when Columbus visited in 1494. They later died of disease under Spanish rule. Spain colonized the area in the early 16th century. Britain ruled it from 1655. Black African slaves were imported to work on the sugar plantations. Slavery was abolished in the late 1830s and the plantation system collapsed. Jamaica gained independence in 1962. It suffered during the 1981–1982 depression. Violence between government forces and West Kingston slum residents claimed some lives in 2001. Hurricane Ivan killed at least 17 people and destroyed thousands of homes in 2004. Jamaica's first woman prime minister took office in 2006. In 2007 Jamaica hosted a leg of the Cricket World Cup Tournament, the biggest sporting event ever held in the Caribbean. Jamaica's musical innovations include ska and reggae.

Influences on food The indigenous Arawak almost disappeared following the Spanish conquest. Only traces of their foodways remain. They ate a wide variety of fish and seafood. Jamaica belonged to Spain and then to Britain, and its food customs were influenced by these powers. Other influences were from slaves bought from Africa and by indentured labor from India. This tropical island has abundant fish, seafood, fruit, and vegetables.

Bread and cereals Rice, corn, wheat; rice dishes, fried cornbread, porridge, wheat bread, fried cassava bread.

Meat, poultry, fish Chicken, goat, beef, pork, lamb, fish and seafood (salt cod, lobster), eggs; blood sausage.

Dairy products Cow's milk (fresh, condensed, evaporated), cream, aged cheese.

Fats and oils Butter, salt pork, lard, olive oil, coconut cream, vegetable oil, shortening.

Legumes Pigeon peas, kidney beans, black-eyed peas.

Vegetables Potatoes, cassava, malanga, yams, sweet potatoes, plantains, greens (cassava, malanga), avocados, breadfruit, squash, tomatoes, okra, onions, green peppers.

Fruit Coconut, oranges, bananas, lemons, limes, grapefruit, ugli (orange and grapefruit cross, developed in Jamaica), coconut, mangoes, tamarind, akee, papaya, pineapple, guavas, star apples, cashew apples, soursop.

Nuts and seeds Almonds, cashew nuts, annatto (achiote) seeds.

Seasonings Salt, black pepper, hot chili peppers, Jamaica pepper (allspice), onions, garlic, annatto, coriander, saffron, curry powder, ginger, lime juice, cinnamon, thyme, coconut, rum; hot pepper sauce (chilies in vinegar).

Dishes Callaloo (green leaves of cassava or malanga cooked with okra). Pepper pot (stew of vegetables and meat, highly seasoned with crushed peppercorns). Escovitch (marinated fish). Souse (marinated pork). Spicy soups. Deep-fried green plantain chips. Akkra (bean or pea fritters). Salt fish gundy (spread). Rice cooked with peas or beans. Roast pork loin coated with a glaze of brown sugar, rum, garlic, and ginger; served with lime juice and rum sauce. Jamaican breakfast fruit bowl (fruits such as papaya, pineapple, grapefruit, and mango slices on ice). Mango chutney (mango preserves made with spices and hot chilies).

Specialty dishes Curried goat meat (meat cubes browned and simmered in a curry sauce) served with saffron rice and mango chutney. Stamp and Go (deep-fried codfish cakes made from soaked salt cod, a flour batter, onions, and annatto). Pickapeppa sauce (made from tomatoes, mangoes, raisins, vinegar, and chilies).

Specialty cuisines Jerk is a technique attributed to escaped African slaves, who spiced and smoked wild pig. Today jerk refers to barbecue seasoning (allspice, black pepper, cinnamon, ginger, nutmeg, thyme, scallions, hot chili pepper, garlic, onions, coriander, bay leaves, and brown sugar); meat is rubbed with the jerk mix, marinated for several hours, and grilled. I-tal (meaning vital) is the way of life for followers of the Rastafari religion (an Afro-Caribbean faith). Simple, unprocessed food is emphasized. Typical I-tal dishes include rice and pigeon peas or kidney beans, cassava bread, baked yams, vegetable stews, cornmeal porridge, sautéed plantains, and fresh juices. Usual seasonings are thyme, cinnamon, allspice, coconut, and perhaps marijuana.

National dish Salt fish and akee (simmered cod and simmered akee, combined and mixed with onions and hot chilies sautéed in fat rendered from salt pork, and the mixture heated).

Sweets Sugarcane, sugar, brown sugar, molasses, banana bread, coconut custard topped with whipped cream flavored with rum, pineapple fool (chopped pineapple folded into whipped cream and chilled), wedding cake (dark fruitcake made with candied citrus and soaked in rum).

Beverages Coffee, milk, soft drinks, iced tea usually with lime, beer, rum, Blue Mountain cocktail (rum, vodka, coffee liqueur, orange juice, lime juice, and ice, combined and shook). Jamaica's prized Blue Mountain coffee is sometimes flavored with orange rind, cinnamon stick, allspice, or ginger, or is topped with whipped cream or rum.

Typical meal Jerk (barbecue) chicken or pork, rice and peas or beans, cassava bread or cornbread.

Street food and snacks Jerk (barbecue) chicken or pork, fruit, fruit juice poured over crushed ice, coffee.

JAPAN

Geography Japan is an archipelago in the Pacific Ocean off the east coast of mainland Asia. The four main islands consist largely of mountains separated by narrow valleys. The coast is deeply indented. Volcanoes include Mt. Fuji, near Tokyo.

Major Language	Ethnic Groups		Major Religions	
Japanese (official)	Japanese	99%	Shinto and Buddhist	
	Other	1%	observed together	84%
			Christian and other	16%

Population density per sq. mi. 879.7
Literacy rate 99%
Life expectancy 78.7 male; 85.6 female
Per capita GDP $33,600
Labor force in agriculture 4.6%

Urban 66%
Infant mortality rate per 1,000 live births 2.8
HIV rate NA
Unemployment rate 4.1%
Arable land 12%

Agriculture   rice, sugar beets, vegetables, sugarcane, fruits, chickens, pigs, cattle, goats, sheep

Natural resources   fish

Industries   motor vehicles, electronic equipment, machine tools, steel and nonferrous metals, ships, chemicals, textiles, processed foods

History   Legend has it that the empire was founded 660 BCE. A unified Japan dates from the 4th to 5th century CE. During this time Buddhism was introduced by way of Korea. China strongly influenced Japanese civilization through the 700s. Warring clans were rising, and a feudal system dominated from 1192. Shoguns (military dictators) held power from 1192 to 1867, followed by emperors. Unification was achieved in the late 1500s. The Portuguese and Dutch traded with Japan and brought missionaries in the 16th and 17th centuries. During the period from 1603 to 1867, shoguns prohibited trade with foreign countries except for a Dutch trading post. In 1868 the shogun system was abolished, a constitution was adopted (1889), and a program of modernization and industrialization began. Also in the late 19th century, U.S. trade began, and Japan and China were at war. Japan was at war with Russia, 1904–1905. Japan annexed Korea in 1910. It attacked Pearl Harbor on Dec. 7, 1941, launching war against the United States. The United States dropped atomic bombs on Hiroshima and Nagasaki, and Japan surrendered in 1945. After World War II Japan adopted a democratic constitution in 1947, rebuilt, and became a world leader in economics and technology. A damaging earthquake in 1995 caused thousands of deaths. In 1998 Nagano hosted the Winter Olympics. In the late 1990s and into the 21st century Japan suffered a lengthy recession.

Influences on food   Japan consists of mountainous islands so that little land is available for agriculture. Much of the food supply is imported. The coastal waters supply fish and seafood. Historically isolated, Japan developed a cuisine relying on indigenous ingredients: fish, seaweed, vegetables, and fruits, with meat and game when available. Japan's earliest inhabitants were probably from Siberia, via the peninsula that later became Korea. They developed a deep appreciation for nature. China has had a strong influence on Japan. Migrations from South China merged ancestor worship with nature worship (animism) to produce Shintoism, long the principal religion of Japan. Between the 6th and 9th centuries, Chinese influences included Buddhism, soybeans, and tea. Tea, first imported from China around 800 CE, became a widespread beverage, partly through the Japanese courts' adoption of the Buddhist tea ceremony in the 15th century. The tea ceremony started in the 13th century and evolved as Zen Buddhist monks drank tea ceremoniously during their devotions, partly to stay alert. The ceremony is still important in Zen temples and also now as a social activity. Today the tea ceremony reflects harmony with nature and with one's self. A full-scale tea ceremony (chaji) includes a meal (cha kaiseki) of small courses that balance colors and tastes and reflect the season. A simpler tea party (chakai) has only a sweetmeat served before the tea. Tea is made by adding hot water to green tea powder and whisking, resulting in a frothy green drink. In the mid-16th century the Portuguese began trading with the Japanese and introduced tempura (deep frying batter-coated food). In the 1850s Japan ended a millennium as a tightly closed nation and began to industrialize and to borrow from the Western diet. Buddhist vegetarianism was gradually abandoned and beef, pork, and poultry began to appear in dishes. Fish/seafood and rice (gohan) are the main foods and eaten at most meals.

Soybean products, seaweed, vegetables, and fruit are important foods. Japanese cuisine is renowned for its careful preparation and presentation, with appreciation for the properties of each food item.

Regional variations and specialties Of Japan's four main islands, Honshu, the largest and with the largest proportion of arable land, grows most of Japan's rice; here Kyoto has vegetarian specialties, and Tokyo and Osaka feature seafood. Hokkaido, the far north island, is important for dairy products. Southern islands Shikoku and Kyushu are subtropical and produce citrus fruit. In far south Kyushu, Nagasaki has Chinese influence.

Bread and cereals Rice (short grain and glutinous), wheat, buckwheat; rice porridge, rice flour cakes, crackers, and noodles, wheat noodles (udon), buckwheat noodles (soba).

Meat, poultry, fish Fish and shellfish, chicken, pork, beef, goat, lamb, eggs. Meat is expensive and little is used.

Dairy products Milk, ice cream. Japanese do not use appreciable amounts of dairy products.

Fats and oils Sesame seed oil, peanut oil, cottonseed oil, olive oil, vegetable oil, butter.

Legumes Soybeans, adzuki beans, black beans, lima beans, peanuts; miso (fermented soybean paste), tofu (soybean curd), shoyu (soy sauce: soybean extract, wheat or barley, salt, malt, and water), azuki bean paste.

Seaweed Nori (laver), konbu (kelp); soups, crackers, food wrapper, garnish.

Vegetables Potatoes, cabbage, onions, sweet potatoes, carrots, tomatoes, cucumbers, green beans, green onions, lettuce, eggplant, spinach, daikon (giant white radish), pumpkin, mushrooms, taro root, squash, chrysanthemum greens, bamboo shoots, peas, lotus root, turnips, asparagus, yams.

Fruit Tangerines, mandarin oranges, plums, apples, pears, persimmons, cantaloupe, strawberries, peaches.

Pickles (Tsukemono: soaked things) Plums, daikon, cabbage, cucumber, eggplant, ginger (beni shoga).

Nuts and seeds Chestnuts, gingko nuts, walnuts, cashew nuts, poppy seeds, sesame seeds.

Seasonings Soy sauce (shoyu), sugar, rice vinegar, sake (rice wine), mirin (sweet rice wine), ginger, onions, scallions, dried mushrooms, hot mustard, wasabi (green horseradish paste), teriyaki (glaze of soy sauce and mirin, applied to meat near end of grilling). Seasonings provide sweet, sour, salty, bitter, and umami tastes.

Food preparation Usually food is cut into small pieces that are cooked on the range top. Cooking at the table is popular; most households and many restaurants have a portable gas or electric ring heating unit.

Dishes Boiled and steamed short-grain rice. Oyakodon (boiled chicken mixed with scrambled eggs on a bed of rice). Chameshi (rice cooked with other ingredients, e.g., adzuki beans or mushrooms). Menrui (noodles) boiled. Zensai (appetizers) such as miso-marinated asparagus. Suimono (clear soups), usually based on dashi (soup stock containing dried bonito fish and kelp). Shirumono (thick soups) such as misoshiru (soybean paste and dashi soup). Raw fish dishes: sushi (vinegared rice topped with raw fish, seafood, or vegetables, often wrapped in nori and served with soy sauce for dipping); sashimi (thinly sliced raw fish/seafood), usually dipped in soy sauce and wasabi. Salads: aemono (mixed things) with a thick dressing; and sunomono (vinegared things) with a thin dressing, for example, spinach with sesame seeds and miso. Salad dressing: rice vinegar, soy sauce, and sesame seeds. Mushimono (steamed food): horakuyaki (steamed shrimp, chicken, ginkgo nuts, and mushrooms); chawan-mushi (steamed custard of egg and dashi with small pieces of meat in the bottom), popular with children. Simmered dishes such as taro root. Nimono (long-simmered dishes) such as octopus. Agemono (fried foods): tempura (shrimp, fish, chicken or vegetables lightly battered and deep fried); tonkatsu (pork cutlet) breaded and fried. Yakimono (broiled, grilled, or cooked in a shallow pan), often on skewers: eel, fish, beef, chicken. Nabemono (one-pot dishes), including many cooked at the table: sukiyaki (beef slices and vegetables simmered in soy sauce and sake in a shallow pan); shabu-shabu (beef and vegetables simmered in broth and then dipped in a sauce); mitzutaki (chicken and vegetables cooked in broth). Teppanyaki (grilling): beef, chicken, shrimp, and vegetables cooked on a hot metal plate (teppan) in the center of the table in some restaurants, served with ponzu (soy sauce mixed with citrus juice). Fugu, a blowfish with a lethal poison in its liver and ovaries, served (e.g., as sashimi) in restaurants whose chefs must be specially licensed; it causes slight numbness of lips and tongue.

New Year's dish   Mochi (round rice cake made by pounding hot steamed glutinous rice into sticky dough).

Sweets   Honey, sugar. Steamed glutinous rice confections. Mochi gashi (rice cakes with sweet bean paste). Manju (dumplings). Yokan (sweet bean jelly). Okashi (small confections, usually adzuki bean paste), served with tea to visitors or after a formal meal.

Beverages   Green tea (nihon-cha), sake (rice wine, served warm), beer, coffee or black tea with Western foods.

Meals and service   Three meals a day plus a snack (oyatsu) are usual. Breakfast: pickled plums, rice, nori, soup. Lunch: rice with leftovers or dashi; or noodles with bits of meat or vegetable. Dinner: raw or vinegared fish, simmered dish, grilled or fried dish, soup, rice, pickles. All foods are served at once, in small individual portions, and each food in its individual dish (usually of porcelain). Tea accompanies meals. Fruit ends dinner. Japanese sip soup from a bowl and eat with wood chopsticks with slender, tapered ends; only steamed custard (chawan-mushi) is eaten with a spoon. The bento box holds a lunch or picnic (of at least 10 items).

Snacks   Crisp crackers of rice and seaweed, tsukudani (tiny fish and kelp simmered in soy sauce), fruit, sweets.

JORDAN
Hashemite Kingdom of Jordan

Geography   Jordan is in the Middle East. It shares the Dead Sea with Israel. Arid hills and mountains cover about 88% of the land, with fertile areas in the west. The Jordan River flows through the country.

Major Languages	Ethnic Groups		Major Religions	
Arabic (official)	Arab	98%	Islam (official)	
English widely understood among	Armenian	1%	Sunni Muslim	92%
upper and middle classes	Circassian	1%	Christian (majority Greek Orthodox)	6%
			Other	2%

Population density per sq. mi. 174.6
Literacy rate 93.1%
Life expectancy 76.2 male; 81.4 female
Per capita GDP $4,900
Labor force in agriculture 5%

Urban 78.3%
Infant mortality rate per 1,000 live births 15.6
HIV rate NA
Unemployment rate 14.5%
Arable land 3%

Agriculture   tomatoes, potatoes, cucumbers, citrus, olives, chickens, sheep, goats, cattle

Natural resources   phosphates, potash, shale, oil, fish

Industries   clothing, phosphate mining, fertilizers, pharmaceuticals, oil refining, cement, potash, light manufacture

History   Present-day Jordan comprises Edom, Moab, Ammon, and Bashan in biblical times. Much of eastern Jordan was incorporated into Israel under Kings David and Solomon c. 1000 BCE. The land along the Jordan River was united from ancient times to 1922. It passed to the Assyrians, Babylonians, Persians, Seleucids, and Roman Empire. Arabs conquered it in the 7th century. The Ottomans gained control in the 16th century. Britain took control of it, then known as Transjordan, in 1920. In 1921 Britain installed an Arabian, Abdullah, as emir of Transjordan, covering two thirds of Palestine. In 1946 an independent kingdom was proclaimed. During the 1948 Arab-Israeli war, the kingdom gained the West Bank and East Jerusalem, and changed its name to Jordan; it lost these lands to Israel in the 1967 war. In 1970–1971 fighting between the government and Palestine Liberation Organization resulted in expulsion of the PLO from Jordan. Hussein, king from 1952 until his death in 1999, reigned carefully between powerful neighbor Israel and rising Arab nationalism; his son Abdullah became king. Jordan and Israel agreed to end their state of war in 1994. Jordan's economy grew in 2007. About 500,000 refugees from the Iraq War were living in Jordan in mid-2008.

Influences on food   Influences include Persia, Arab, Ottoman, Britain, and the religion Islam. Traditionally food reflected the climates of Jordan's three regions: citrus, bananas, and vegetables from the Jordan Valley; cereals, pulses, olives and olive oil, and other fruits from the plateau; and dairy products from the sheep and goat herds of the desert. Until recently the food was that of the villages and the desert. The growth of large urban centers such as Amman and Irbid added new food customs from Palestine, Lebanon, and Syria. The staple diet of Jordanian villages remains cereals, pulses, wild herbs, and sheep and goat dairy products, with lentils, chickpeas, yogurt, and cracked wheat basic foods. The traditional village food freeki (corn picked green and roasted on wood) is now a specialty in urban areas. The village and desert populations were poor; a whole sheep was a luxury for a special occasion such as a marriage. Recently there has been the rise of the middle-class population and greater availability of meat. Islamic dietary law forbids consumption of pork or alcohol and requires fasting from sunup to sundown during the month of Ramadan.

Bread and cereals   Wheat, barley, rice, corn; cracked wheat (burghul, or bulgur), wheat flour flatbreads (mostly pita, round with hollow center), filo dough pastry, rice dishes, roasted corn.

Meat, poultry, fish   Chicken, lamb and mutton, goat, beef, fish, eggs, camel.

Dairy products   Milk (sheep, goat, cow), yogurt, drained yogurt (labaneh), white cheese (feta).

Fats and oils   Olive oil, butter, clarified butter (ghee), vegetable oils, tahini (ground sesame), lamb fat, margarine.

Legumes   Chickpeas, broad beans (fava beans), lentils, peanuts.

Vegetables   Tomatoes, potatoes, cucumbers, olives, eggplant, onions, carrots, green peppers, squash.

Fruit   Lemons, oranges, melons, dates, apples, bananas, grapes, figs, pomegranate, sumac, peaches, cherries.

Nuts and seeds   Almonds, pine nuts, pistachios, walnuts, sesame seed (often ground, tahini), fenugreek seed.

Seasonings   Onions, garlic, mint, parsley, lemon juice, cilantro, black pepper, cinnamon, cardamom, coriander, cumin, saffron, turmeric, oregano, basil.

Dishes   Green salad. Falafel (fried patties of bean or pea purée). Hummus (puréed seasoned boiled chickpeas). Shawerma (rotisserie lamb or beef). Tabbouleh (salad of chopped tomato, onions, parsley, and cracked wheat). Stuffed grape leaves (rice, ground lamb or beef, and herbs and spices, wrapped in leaves and simmered). Kabobs (usually small chunks of meat, sometimes ground meat balls, roasted or grilled on a skewer). Lentil soup. Foul (simmered fava beans topped with raw vegetables and herbs). Meat stews, sometimes with fruit, lemon juice, or yogurt. Pilaf (rice first heated in oil in which chopped onions have been browned, and then water or broth added and covered and simmered). Vegetables simmered and served cold, dressed with oil. Vegetable and meat stew. Vegetables stuffed with rice, ground lamb or beef, and herbs and spices, and simmered. Baked eggplant, tomato, and chickpea casserole. Fruit stewed with meat and served cold. Moussaka (minced lamb, eggplant, onions, and tomato sauce baked in a dish lined with eggplant slices). Boiled lamb shanks with tomato sauce. Roast chicken stuffed with rice and pine nuts.

National dishes   Mansaf (cracked wheat or rice with jameed, a dried form of yogurt). Flatbreads layered with yogurt, placed on a communal platter, and topped with rice and boiled lamb or chicken, with a sauce of seasoned butter or broth of whey or yogurt poured over the top).

Sweets   Honey, sugar, flavored syrups, dates. Baklava (baked pastry of thin layers of filo dough with butter and nuts, soaked in honey or syrup and often cut into diamond shapes). Halveh (sweet paste of ground sesame seeds). Chocolate candy. Jordan almonds (candy-coated almonds).

Beverages   Tea (sweet, often with mint), Arabic coffee (sweet, often with cardamom), soft drinks, beer, wine.

Meals and service   Breakfast: tea or coffee; labaneh, cheese or yogurt; foul or other bean dish; eggs; olives. Main meal (early afternoon): bread, rice or cracked-wheat dish, vegetable or legume dish, a meat, poultry, or fish dish, salad or olives, dessert, coffee or tea. Evening meal: like breakfast, leftovers, or soup. Men eat first or are served first, then women and children. One eats with the right hand if no utensils are provided.

Street food and snacks   Shawerma slices in pita bread, roasted ears of corn (Brittin, Sukalakamala, and Obeidat, 2008; Obeidat and Brittin, 2004).

K

KAZAKHSTAN
Republic of Kazakhstan

Geography   Kazakhstan is in Central Asia, bordering Russia on the north and with a 1,177-mile Caspian Sea coastline on the west. Four times the size of Texas, it is mostly steppe land with hilly plains and plateaus, with mountains on the east.

Major Languages	Ethnic Groups		Major Religions	
Kazakh (both	Kazakh	53%	Muslim	47%
Russian official)	Russian	30%	Russian Orthodox	44%
Russian used in	Ukrainian	4%	Other	9%
everyday business	Other	13%		

Population density per sq. mi. 14.9
Literacy rate 99.6%
Life expectancy 62.2 male; 73.2 female
Per capita GDP $11,100
Labor force in agriculture 32.2%

Urban 57.1%
Infant mortality rate per 1,000 live births 26.6
HIV rate 0.1%
Unemployment rate 7.8%
Arable land 8%

Agriculture   wheat, potatoes, barley, cotton, chickens, sheep, cattle, goats, pigs

Natural resources   oil, natural gas, coal, iron ore, manganese, chrome ore, nickel, cobalt, copper, molybdenum, lead, zinc, bauxite, gold, uranium, fish

Industries   oil, coal, titanium, phosphates, sulfur, tractors and other agricultural machinery, electric motors, construction materials

History   The indigenous Kazakhs were nomadic Turks belonging to Kajakh hordes. Mongols ruled here from the 13th century to the period from 1730 to 1853, when Russia gradually gained control. The Kazakhs consolidated a nomadic empire in the 15th to 16th centuries. A republic of the USSR from 1936, Kazakhstan became independent in 1991. In 1994 it agreed to dismantle nuclear missiles. In 1995 private land ownership was legalized. Oil discovered in the Caspian Sea in 2000 added to Kazakhstan's huge oil and mineral resources. President Nazarbayev encouraged Western investment in the oil industry, boosting the economy. Nazarbayev, reelected in 1999 and 2005, was authorized in 2007 to run for an unlimited number of terms. In 2007 the economy continued strong, mainly due to oil revenues. It became the first Central Asian country to donate to economic development of its neighbors. It warned foreign oil firms of suspension for failure to observe environmental regulations.

Influences on food   Kazakhstan is a vast area of steppe in Central Asia and the largest of the former Soviet republics except for Russia. Central Asia is mostly arid with extremes of climate and terrain, little rain, and frequent wind and earthquakes. Thousands of years ago inhabitants of Turkic and Iranian stock mixed with Mongolian and Chinese invaders forming major tribal groups that survive today. Later Indians, Arabs, Tatars, Russians, and Ukrainians arrived. Until the 20th century most Kazakhs were nomadic herdsmen who raised horses, goats, camels, sheep, yaks, and cattle. They dwelt in domed tents (yurts) and lived on milk and milk products, supplemented by meat, usually from fat-tailed sheep. They drank large amounts of hot green tea, with milk and salt in the morning. There were also oases dwellers, who raised grain, fruit, and vegetables, as is done today using irrigation. Influences on food in Kazakhstan include Mongols, who ruled it for centuries, Russia, who controlled it for centuries and is its neighbor to the north, and China, its neighbor to the east and the origin of noodles. Kazakhstan and the other Central Asian countries (Turkmenistan, Uzbekistan, Tajikistan, and Kyrgyzstan) share a common cuisine: lamb, thick soups, semi-liquid main courses, flatbread, dairy products, fruits, and vegetables. Kazakhstan and Kyrgyzstan share the most similar cuisine, with few eggs. Unlike Kyrgyz and some other Central Asians, Kazakhs eat fish, especially near Kazakhstan's long coast on the Caspian Sea.

Bread and cereals   Wheat, barley, millet, rice; flatbread (usually round), noodles, dumplings, pastries, rice dishes.

Meat, poultry, fish   Chicken, lamb and mutton, beef, goat, pork, camel, fish; smoked horsemeat sausage (kazy).

Dairy products   Milk (sheep, cow, goat, camel, mare, yak), cream, sour milk, clabber, yogurt, cheeses (kurt, a hard cheese, sun dried and reconstituted by soaking crumbled bits in water; airan, milk from camels, sheep, and goats simmered until it clabbers and grows sharp), kumys (fermented mare's milk), shubat (fermented camel's milk, thick and has high fat content).

Fats and oils   Butter, vegetable oil, fat from fat-tailed sheep (does not liquefy completely when rendered but retains tiny cracklings).

Vegetables   Potatoes, onions, carrots, pumpkins, greens, peppers, cucumbers, turnips, tomatoes, radishes.

Fruit   Apples, grapes, peaches, melons, figs, rhubarb, apricots, plums, pears, white mulberries, barberries, jujubes (a type of date), cherries, quinces, pomegranate.

Nuts and seeds   Walnuts, hazelnuts, pistachios, caraway seeds.

Seasonings   Onions, garlic, vinegar, salt, black pepper, dill, mint, coriander, dried red peppers.

Dishes   Kazakhstan besh barmak (thinly sliced lamb, beef, or horsemeat and diamond-cut noodles served with a bowl of meat broth). Manty (steamed dumplings filled with peppery ground lamb). Fried pastries filled with seasoned ground beef (beliashi). Shashlyk (lamb shish kebabs), lamb pieces seasoned, marinated, and roasted on skewers over charcoal embers. Palov (rice pilaf), rice heated in rendered fat from fat-tailed sheep or oil before adding water, covering, and simmering, often made with mutton pieces and onion (browned in the fat/oil before adding rice). Most dishes are eaten cold. Many include offal.

Sweets   Honey, sugar. Fruit, dried fruit, fruit preserves. Samsa (fritters filled with ground walnuts, butter, and sugar). Candy: khalva (made from flour, honey, and walnuts or hot syrup poured over nuts), bukman (made with concentrated, sweetened cream and browned flour).

Beverages   Tea, sour milk, shinni (fruit syrup drink), wine. Hot green tea is drunk throughout the day, at home and in tea houses, served in a samovar and drunk in porcelain bowls; it is served with small pastries, fruit, and candy.

Meals and service   Breakfast: clabber or cheese, flatbread, and tea. Lunch: thick hearty soup or cheese, greens, and fruit, flatbread, and tea. Evening meal: meat dish or palov, flatbread, fruit or a sweet, and tea. To dine, people sit on rugs or chairs and use hands to scoop food, flatbread as edible scoops and plates, or flatware and plates.

KENYA
Republic of Kenya

Geography   Kenya is in East Africa, on the equator and bordering the Indian Ocean. The northern 60% of the land is arid. The fertile Lake Victoria Basin is in the southwest. The Great Rift Valley, flanked by high mountains, separates the western highlands from the lowland coastal strip. Also a plateau 3,000 to 10,000 feet elevation is in the south. Mt. Kenya is Africa's second highest mountain. Large game reserves have been developed.

Major Languages		Ethnic Groups		Major Religions	
Kiswahili	(both	Kikuyu	22%	Protestant	45%
English	official)	Luhya	14%	Roman Catholic	33%
Many indigenous languages		Luo	13%	Muslim	10%
		Kalenjin	12%	Indigenous beliefs	10%
		Kamba	11%	Other	2%
		Other African	27%		
		Other	1%		

Population density per sq. mi. 172.7
Literacy rate 73.6%
Life expectancy 56.4 male; 56.9 female
Per capita GDP $1,700
Labor force in agriculture 75%

Urban 20.7%
Infant mortality rate per 1,000 live births 56
HIV rate NA
Unemployment rate 14.6%
Arable land 8%

Agriculture   sugarcane, corn, potatoes, cut flowers, tea, coffee, wheat, fruit, chickens, cattle, goats, sheep, pigs

Natural resources   limestone, soda ash, salt, fluorspar, wildlife, hydropower, fish

Industries   small-scale consumer goods (textiles, clothing, soap, cigarettes), agricultural processing, oil refining, cement, tourism

History   People may have lived here about 2 million years ago. By the 8th century CE Arab colonies exported spices and slaves from the Kenya coast. The Portuguese took control of the area in the early 1500s. The Kikuyu migrated to the area from the south and the Masai came from the north to the area in the 18th century. Britain gained control in the 19th century. Kenya gained independence in 1963. In the first two decades after independence, Kenya's rate of economic growth was among the highest in Africa, largely because Jomo Kenyatta, prime minister 1963–1964 and president from 1964 to 1978, encouraged foreign investment from other countries. Under a modified private enterprise system, industry and agriculture grew. In 1992 Kenya's first multiparty elections in three decades were held. During the early 1990s political turmoil, widespread unemployment, high inflation, and tribal conflicts occurred. In the 1990s corruption and poor economic practices led to suspension of aid and World Bank funding. In 1998 a truck bomb explosion at the U.S. embassy in Nairobi killed more than 200 people and injured about 5,000; the United States blamed this attack on Islamic terrorists associated with Osama bin Laden. Terrorist acts and violence continued as of 2008. To end the violence, the two presidential candidates in the 2007 election made a power-sharing agreement in 2008.

Influences on food   Apart from the coastal plains, much of the terrain is highland plateau, with some of the best climate in Africa. The diet of the highlands contains almost no meat, in spite of abundant game and the cattle-breeding tradition. Most indigenous peoples have long been pastoral. Cattle were regarded as wealth, not food, and the Masai and related people lived on milk products and blood of cattle. Others lived on mostly millet, sorghum, and bananas, along with gathered greens. The earliest foreign traders, Arabs, established colonies along the coast from about 700 CE; they traded in slaves and ivory and introduced spices, onions, and eggplant. The British trained many African men, never women, in European cooking. There were complex traditions of women cooking only in their homes while men cooked outdoors, grilling and barbecuing. The British encouragement of Asians to settle in East Africa affected local cooking as in using curry (mchuzi) and cooking many fish dishes with coconut milk, an ingredient more commonly used in East Africa than in other parts of Africa. Developing agriculture exists on farms and plantations established by Europeans. The Indian Ocean and Lake Victoria supply fish and seafood. Much of the seafood is salted and dried and sent inland. European hunters found game in the mountains; now although animals are protected, game is plentiful and antelope are farmed. As elsewhere in Africa, starchy food is regarded as "real food" and relishes as accompaniments.

Bread and cereals   Corn, wheat, millet, sorghum, rice; porridge, pancakes, fritters, rice dishes.

Meat, poultry, fish   Chicken, eggs, beef, goat, lamb and mutton, pork, game meat (gazelle, kudu), fish, seafood.

Insects   Locusts, crickets, grasshoppers, flying ants, worms (madora), caterpillars (harati).

Dairy products   Milk, cheese (including adaptations of European ones).

Fats and oils   Butter, lard, peanut oil.

Legumes   Peanuts (groundnuts), cowpeas, beans, lentils. Legumes, important protein sources, are eaten daily.

Vegetables   Potatoes, green bananas, green leaves (amaranth, baobab, okra), cassava, yams, sweet potatoes, tomatoes, onions, okra, eggplant. Kenyans eat a large amount of starchy vegetables and green leaves.

Fruit   Bananas, coconut, pineapple, papaya, mangoes, strawberries.

Nuts and seeds   Cashew nuts, sesame seeds.

Seasonings   Chilies, coconut milk, dried baobab leaves, curry powder, cloves.

Dishes   Sukuma wiki (Swahili for "stretch the week"), a stew of leftover meats and vegetables. Irio, a Kikuyu dish (mashed beans, corn, and potatoes or cassava) often served with curried chicken. Mashed beans, lentils, corn, plantains (green bananas), or potatoes. Green bananas boiled in banana leaves and mashed. Peanut soup, stew, and paste. Green leaves cooked with peanut paste. Fish cooked with coconut milk. Rice steamed with butter, served with beef, mutton, fowl, or fish. Game meat skewered and roasted. Gazelle, kudu, or antelope steaks marinated and braised. N'yama choma (goat kebabs), served with mashed green bananas and local beer.

National dish   Ugali, very thick cornmeal (or millet) porridge, the most common staple food.

Sweets   Sugarcane, honey, coconut pudding, plantain custard, mandazi (doughnut or fritter). Honey is important.

Beverages   Tea, coffee, beer, red wine.

Street food and snacks   Fried pastries, grilled corn on cob, rice and coconut pancakes, fried insects.

KIRIBATI
Republic of Kiribati

Geography   Kiribati (pronounced Kiribass) consists of 33 Micronesia islands in the mid-Pacific Ocean, south of the Hawaiian Islands. Formerly the Gilbert Islands, Kiribati comprises three widely separated main groups of islands: the Gilberts, the Phoenix Islands, and the Line Islands. Most of the islands are low-lying coral atolls, with erratic rainfall. In 1999 the International Date Line was moved to follow Kiribati's east border.

Major Languages	Ethnic Groups		Major Religions	
English (official)	Micronesian	99%	Roman Catholic	52%
l-Kiribati	Other	1%	Protestant (Congregational)	40%
			Other	8%

Population density per sq. mi. 352.4
Literacy rate NA
Life expectancy 59.8 male; 66.1 female
Per capita GDP $3,600
Labor force in agriculture 2.7

Urban 43.6%
Infant mortality rate per 1,000 live births 44.7
HIV rate NA
Unemployment rate 6.1%
Arable land 3%

Agriculture   coconuts, bananas, taro, copra, breadfruit, sweet potatoes, chickens, pigs

Natural resources   fish, phosphate

Industries   fishing, handicrafts

History   Austronesian-speaking people settled Kiribati before the 1st century CE. Fijians and Tongans came about the 14th century, and later merged with older groups to form the traditional culture. The Gilbert and Ellice Island colony was a British protectorate from 1892. The Phoenix Islands were included in 1937. Self-rule was granted in 1971. The Ellis Islands separated from the colony in 1975, becoming Tuvalu in 1978. In 1979 the remaining islands became the independent nation Kiribati. Kiribati gained UN membership in 1999. President Anote Tong was reelected in 2007.

Influences on food   Influences on food include the Austronesian original settlers, Fijians and Polynesians who came about the 14th century, British control for part of the area from 1892 to 1979, and U.S. control for part of the area during the 20th century. Europeans brought new food plants, wheat bread, and certain animals to the Pacific Islands. Asians brought rice, soybeans, and teas. Main foods in the traditional diet are fish and seafood, roots and tubers, breadfruit, and coconut. Pork is the main meat, especially for feasts, traditionally cooked in a stone-lined pit over coals along with other foods.

Bread and cereals   Rice, wheat; bread, noodles, rice dishes.

Meat, poultry, fish   Pork, chicken, beef, fish (mullet), shellfish (crabs, many others), eggs; corned beef, spam.

Dairy products   Milk and other dairy products are uncommon.

Fats and oils   Coconut oil and cream, lard, vegetable oil and shortening, sesame oil.

Legumes   Soybeans, winged beans, peas, lentils, peanuts.

Vegetables   Taro root and leaves, breadfruit, sweet potatoes, plantains, yams, cassava, seaweed, green leaves, arrowroot, bitter melon, cabbage, daikon, eggplant, onions, green onions.

Fruit   Coconut, bananas, lemons, limes, guavas, mangoes, papaya, pineapple, melons, tamarind.

Nuts and seeds   Candlenuts (kukui), litchis, macadamia nuts.

Seasonings   Coconut cream or milk, lime or lemon juice, salt, soy sauce, ginger, garlic, onions, red chili peppers.

Dishes   Boiled taro root, breadfruit, sweet potatoes. Boiled or steamed rice. Boiled or steamed greens. Arrowroot-thickened puddings and other dishes. Chunks of white fish marinated in lime juice, onions, and coconut cream. Dishes cooked in a pit: whole pig, taro, sweet potatoes, crabs, whole fish, chicken pieces, taro leaves wrapped around a filling of coconut cream, lemon, onions, and shredded beef and all bound in banana leaves, and other leaf-wrapped mixtures of taro, breadfruit, or sweet potatoes with coconut cream and seasonings

Sweets   Sugar, immature coconut, fresh fruit, pudding made from coconut milk with sugar.

Beverages   Coconut juice, tea, coffee, toddy (wine made from coconut palm blossoms).

Meals   Two or three meals daily are typical, with the same foods at all, and the evening meal the largest. A traditional meal is boiled taro root, breadfruit, or sweet potatoes, fish or pork, and cooked greens or seaweed.

KOREA, NORTH
Democratic People's Republic of Korea

Geography   In East Asia, Korea is a 600-mile peninsula jutting out into the Sea of Japan and the Yellow Sea. North Korea occupies the area north of the 38th parallel and is mostly mountains, with narrow valleys and plains.

Major Language	Ethnic Groups		Major Religions
Korean (official)	Korean (homogeneous) Chinese Japanese	(small numbers)	Traditionally Buddhist and Confucianist Christian (some)

Population density per sq. mi. 505
Literacy rate 99%
Life expectancy 69.5 male; 75.1 female
Per capita GDP $1,900
Labor force in agriculture 37%

Urban 61.6%
Infant mortality rate per 1,000 live births 21.9
HIV rate NA
Unemployment rate 24.1%
Arable land 14%

Agriculture   rice, potatoes, corn, soybeans, chickens, pigs, goats, cattle, sheep

Natural resources   fish, coal, lead, tungsten, zinc, graphite, magnisite, iron ore, copper, gold, salt, hydropower

Industries   military products, machine building, electric power, chemicals, mining, metallurgy, textiles

History   Korean history dates back to the Neolithic Age, when Turkic-Manchurian-Mongol peoples migrated here from China. Agricultural settlements appeared by 6000 BCE. According to legend, Korea's earliest civilization, Choson, was founded in the northern part of the Korean Peninsula in 2333 BCE. In the 17th century CE Korea became a vassal state of China. Following Japan's victory in the Sino-Japanese War, 1894–1895, Korea was granted independence. Japan annexed Korea in 1910. After Japan's surrender at the end of World War II, the Korean peninsula was partitioned at the 38th parallel into two occupied zones: the north by the USSR, the south by the United States. North Korea was founded in 1948 as a communist state in the zone occupied by Russian troops after World War II. It invaded South Korea in 1950, starting the Korean War, which ended in 1953 when a cease-fire was proclaimed. A communist regime was in power for the next four decades. The nation used its mineral and hydroelectric resources to develop its military and industry. North Korea suffered from a deteriorating economy and famine in the late 1990s. In 1994 it agreed with the United States to stop its nuclear development program in order to receive U.S. aid. In 2002 it admitted producing nuclear weapons and, in a draft accord, agreed to stop in exchange for aid. In 2007 North Korea agreed to begin closing its nuclear facilities in exchange for U.S. heavy fuel oil. In 2008 it gave an accounting of its nuclear program to China; the United States eased sanctions on it.

Influences on food   Neighbors China and Japan have influenced Korean cuisine. Koreans descended primarily from the Mongolians. Around the time of Christ there were three kingdoms in Korea. They were culturally advanced and had royal courts and centralized governments. At this time Buddhism was introduced to the area and became accepted by royalty while Confucianism flourished among the minor aristocracy. The kingdoms were unified to form Korea. Korea was a vassal state of China from the 17th century to 1895 and was controlled by Japan from 1910 until the end of World War II. In 1948 it divided into North Korea and South Korea. The colder mountainous North Korea produces less food than the fertile warm plains of South Korea. Korean cuisine is based on grains (mainly rice) flavored with spicy vegetable, meat, poultry, or fish side dishes. It is highly seasoned and recognizable by its five tastes (salty, sweet, sour, bitter, and hot) and colors (red, green, yellow, white, and black). It has been divided into everyday cooking of common people and cuisine for the royalty, the latter using more varied seasonings, complex cooking methods, and elegant presentation. Today the latter cuisine is used in meals for special occasions or guests; such meals include more dishes and both wine and dessert.

Bread and cereals   Rice (usually short grain glutinous), corn, wheat, millet, barley, buckwheat; rice dishes, dumplings, and cakes, rice with bean cakes, noodles (wheat, buckwheat, or mung bean), wheat flour pancakes.

Meat, poultry, fish   Chicken, pork, goat, beef, lamb, mutton, fish and shellfish, eggs; spam (canned pork product).

Dairy products   Milk and milk products are generally not consumed or used in cooking.

Fats and oils   Sesame oil, vegetable oils.

Legumes   Soybeans, adzuki beans, mung beans, peanuts, red beans; soybean curd (tobu), soy sauce, soy paste.

Vegetables   Potatoes, cabbage, white radish, seaweed, cucumbers, perilla (shiso), green onions, chrysanthemum leaves, bean sprouts, mushrooms, bamboo shoots, eggplant, sweet potatoes, winter melon, carrots, onions.

Fruit   Asian pears, apples, cherries, jujubes (red dates), grapes, pears, lemons, tangerines, melons, persimmons.

Nuts and seeds   Pine nuts, chestnuts, gingko nuts, hazelnuts, pistachios, walnuts, sesame seeds.

Seasonings   Soy sauce, garlic, ginger root, black pepper, green onions, chili peppers, sesame seeds or oil, salt, fermented fish sauce (saewujeot), cinnamon, hot mustard, sugar, rice vinegar.

Cooking methods   Meat is often marinated (in oil, vinegar, and soy sauce with chopped green onions and sesame seeds) before cooking. Marinated beef is often barbecued or grilled at the table over a small charcoal brazier or gas grill. Firepots, bronze or brass utensils with a bowl surrounding a central chimney that holds charcoal to cook the food, are used for special dishes. The Mongolian barbecue, stir-frying ingredients on a convex iron griddle, is uncommon although featured in some Korean restaurants outside Korea.

Dishes   Steamed rice. Kimchi (fermented vegetables, usually cabbage, with hot red chili peppers). Pickled seafood. Meatballs. Seaweed soup (miyak gook). Boiled noodles. Steamed dumplings. Bulgogi (barbecue beef), beef strips marinated in soy sauce, sesame oil, onions, and garlic and then grilled. Fire pot (sinsullo), beef or liver, cooked egg strips, vegetables, and nuts cooked in seasoned broth heated over charcoal. Dipping sauce: soy sauce, rice vinegar, lemon juice, garlic, and red pepper. Seasoned tobu (bean curd). Chrysanthemum leaf salad. Seasoned eggplant. Deep-fried, battered vegetables. Garnish: eggs cooked into a thin omelet, rolled, and sliced into strips. Seaweed laver (kim) brushed with sesame oil, salted, and toasted.

Sweets   Honey, sugar. Rice cookies. Steamed rice cakes perhaps filled with nuts, dates, or red beans. Dried fruit especially persimmons. Dates rolled in sesame seeds. Sweets are made for special occasions and snacks.

Beverages   Hot barley water, rice tea, herbal tea (ginseng), green tea, rice wine, beer, soju (sweet potato vodka).

Meals and service   Three small meals with snacks are typical. Breakfast: soup, rice gruel, and kimchi. Lunch: noodles or rice with broth and garnishes. Dinner: rice (the main dish) with accompaniments (panch'an) such as a meat or fish dish if affordable, two or three vegetables, kimchi, and soup. Wine and appetizers may be served before dinner. Fresh fruit sometimes concludes the meal. Beverages, for example, barley water or tea, are served after the meal. Each diner is served individual bowls of rice, soup, and kimchi; metal chopsticks and a metal soup spoon are provided. Bowls of accompaniment dishes are served on a tray in the center of the table for communal eating.

Street food and snacks   Grilled and steamed tidbits, sweets, rice wine (mukhuli) with scallion-flavored pancakes.

KOREA, SOUTH
Republic of Korea

Geography   South Korea, in East Asia, occupies the land below the 38th parallel on the Korean peninsula, bordering the Sea of Japan and the Yellow Sea. It is mountainous, with a rugged east coast and many harbors and islands.

Major Language	Ethnic Group	Major Religions	
Korean (official)	Korean (homogeneous)	None	49%
English widely taught in school	Chinese (some)	Christian (Protestant,	
		Roman Catholic)	26%
		Buddhist	23%
		Other	2%

Population density per sq. mi. 1,276.1
Literacy rate 97.9%
Life expectancy 75.3 male; 80.2 female
Per capita GDP $24,800
Labor force in agriculture 7.5%

Urban 80.8%
Infant mortality rate per 1,000 live births 4.3
HIV rate <0.1%
Unemployment rate 3.2%
Arable land 17%

Agriculture   rice, cabbages, citrus, fruits, root crops, barley, vegetables, chickens, pigs, cattle, goats, sheep

Natural resources   fish, coal, tungsten, graphite, molybdenum, lead, hydropower potential

Industries   electronics, telecommunications, auto production, chemicals, shipbuilding, steel

History   Civilization in the Korean Peninsula dates back to the third millennium BCE. Once called the Hermit Kingdom, Korea has a recorded history since the 1st century BCE. It was united in a kingdom in 668 CE. A vassal state of China from the 17th century, Korea gained independence at the end of the Sino-Japanese war of 1894–1895. Japan forcibly annexed Korea as Chosun in 1910. In 1945 the 38th parallel was made the line dividing the Soviet and U.S. occupations. The South Koreans formed the Republic of Korea in 1948; a communist nation was formed in North Korea. The North Korean army attacked South Korea in 1950, starting the Korean War; a 1953 armistice left Korea divided along the 38th parallel. In 2000, the presidents of South Korea and North Korea agreed to work for reunification of their two countries, and South Korea President Kim Dae Jung won the Nobel Peace Prize. Import of U.S. beef was banned from 2003 to 2006 because of concern over "mad cow disease." Ban Ki-Moon, South Korea's foreign minister from 2004 to 2006, became UN secretary-general in 2007. In 2007 South Koreans, concerned with economic issues, elected their first CEO president, a former Hyundai executive and mayor of Seoul. The North-South railway line was reconnected for the first time since the peninsula was divided in 1945.

Influences on food   Neighbors China and Japan have influenced Korean cuisine. Koreans descended primarily from the Mongolians. At around the time of Christ there were three kingdoms in Korea, one in the north and two in the south. These kingdoms were culturally advanced and had royal courts and centralized governments. Buddhism was introduced to the area and became accepted by royalty while Confucianism flourished among the minor aristocracy. Silla, one of the southern kingdoms, with Chinese aid, conquered the other two kingdoms and unified Korea in 668. Korea was associated with China until it gained independence in 1895. Japan controlled Korea from 1910 until the end of World War II. In 1948 Korea divided into North and South Korea. South Korea has fertile warm plains that produce grains, vegetables, and fruit, and support livestock; its coasts supply fish and shellfish. The diet is based on rice and includes spicy vegetables, meat, poultry, or fish side dishes and dipping sauces. Korean cuisine is highly seasoned and includes five tastes (salty, sweet, sour, bitter, and hot) and colors (red, green, yellow, white, and black) in meals. It includes everyday cooking of common people and refined cuisine for royalty, with more varied seasonings, complex cooking methods, and elegant presentation. Now the latter cuisine appears in meals for special occasions or guests and includes more dishes, wine, and dessert.

Bread and cereals Rice (usually short grain and glutinous), barley, wheat, millet, buckwheat; rice dishes, dumplings, and cakes, cakes of rice with beans, noodles (wheat, buckwheat, or mung bean), wheat flour pancakes.

Meat, poultry, fish Chicken, pork, beef including variety cuts, goat, lamb and mutton, fish and shellfish, eggs; spam (canned pork product). Beef is especially popular.

Dairy products Milk and milk products are generally not consumed or used in cooking.

Fats and oils Sesame oil, vegetable oils.

Legumes Soybeans, adzuki beans, mung beans, red beans, peanuts; soybean curd (tobu), soy sauce, soy paste.

Vegetables Cabbage, green onions, potatoes, sweet potatoes, beets, white radish, seaweed, eggplant, carrots, cucumbers, perilla (shiso), chrysanthemum leaves, bean sprouts, mushrooms, bamboo shoots, winter melon.

Fruit Asian pears, tangerines, mangoes, satsumas, apples, cherries, jujubes (red dates), grapes, lemons, oranges, melons, persimmons, plums. Fruits are usually eaten raw.

Nuts and seeds Pine nuts, chestnuts, gingko nuts, hazelnuts, pistachios, walnuts, sesame seeds.

Seasonings Soy sauce, garlic, ginger root, black pepper, green onions, red chili peppers, sesame seeds or oil, sea salt, fermented fish sauce (saewujeot), cinnamon, hot mustard, sugar, rice vinegar; marinades.

Cooking methods Meats are often marinated and grilled or broiled, often at the table over a small charcoal brazier or gas grill. Special dishes may be cooked in firepots, metal utensils with a bowl around a chimney holding charcoal. Mongolian barbecue, stir-frying on a convex iron griddle, is uncommon but used in some Korean restaurants outside Korea.

Dishes Steamed rice. Kimchi (fermented vegetables, usually cabbage, with hot red chili peppers). Pickled seafood. Meatballs. Seaweed soup (micas gook). Boiled noodles. Steamed dumplings. Bulgogi (barbecue beef), beef strips marinated in soy sauce, sesame oil, onions, and garlic and then grilled. Fire pot (sinsullo), beef or liver, cooked egg strips, and vegetables, cooked in seasoned broth heated over charcoal. Dipping sauce: soy sauce, rice vinegar, lemon juice, garlic, and red pepper; accompanies meat or vegetable dishes. Seasoned tobu (bean curd). Chrysanthemum leaf salad. Deep-fried, battered eggplant. Garnishes: egg omelet rolled and sliced into strips; seaweed laver (kim) brushed with sesame oil, salted, and toasted.

Sweets Honey, sugar. Rice cookies. Steamed rice cakes with nuts, dates, or red beans. Dried fruit especially persimmons. Dates rolled in sesame seeds, for weddings. Sweets are made for special occasions and snacks.

Beverages Soup, hot barley water, rice tea, herbal tea (ginseng), rice wine, beer, sweet potato vodka (soju).

Meals and service Three small meals with snacks are typical. Breakfast: soup, rice gruel, and kimchi. Lunch: noodles or rice with broth and garnishes. Dinner: rice (the main dish) with accompaniments (panch'an) such as a meat or fish dish if affordable, two or three vegetables, kimchi, and soup. Wine and appetizers may be served before dinner. Fresh fruit sometimes concludes the meal. Beverages (e.g., barley water or tea) are served after the meal. Each diner is served individual bowls of rice, soup, and kimchi; metal chopsticks and a metal soup spoon are provided. Bowls of accompaniment dishes are on a tray in the center of the table for communal eating.

Street food and snacks Grilled and steamed tidbits, sweets, rice wine (mukhuli) with scallion-flavored pancakes.

KOSOVO
Republic of Kosovo

Geography   Kosovo is in southeastern Europe bordering Serbia, Macedonia, Albania, and Montenegro. Kosovo is one of the smaller Balkan countries. Low flood basins are surrounded by high mountain ranges.

Major Languages		Ethnic Groups		Major Religions	
Albanian	(both	Albanian	92%	Muslim	91%
Serbian	official)	Serb	5%	Serbian Orthodox	6%
Bosnian		Other	3%	Roman Catholic	3%
Turkish					
Roma					

Population density per sq. mi. 505.9
Literacy rate NA
Life expectancy NA
Per capita GDP $1,800
Labor force in agriculture 21.4%

Urban NA
Infant mortality rate per 1,000 live births NA
HIV rate NA
Unemployment rate 44.1%
Arable land NA

Agriculture   wheat, hay, corn, potatoes, fruits (berries), wine, chickens, cattle, sheep

Natural resources   nickel, lead, zinc, magnesium, lignite, kaolin, chrome, bauxite

Industries   mineral mining, construction materials, base materials, leather, machinery, appliances

History   The area was part of the Roman and Byzantine empires. Serbs, a Slavic people, took control here in the Middle Ages. Ottoman Turks took control in 1389. The population then became predominantly Muslim and Kosovar (ethnic Albanian). Serbs regained control in the First Balkan War, 1912–1913. The Kingdom of Serbs, Croats, and Slovenes was created after Austria-Hungary's collapse at the end of World War I and was joined by Kosovo. In 1929 the country's name was changed to Yugoslavia. Axis powers invaded it in 1941 and occupied it for the rest of World War II. In 1991–1992 independence was declared by parts of Yugoslavia; Serbia and Montenegro became the new Federal Republic of Yugoslavia. Ethnic fighting continued in the 1990s, and in 1998–1999 Serbia repressed and expulsed ethnic populations in the province of Kosovo. In 2003 Yugoslavia changed its name to Serbia and Montenegro. Serbia declared its independence in 2006. From 1999 Kosovo was an autonomous region of Serbia administered by the UN. In 2008 Kosovo, a province of Serbia with more than 90% Albanian population, declared its independence from Serbia.

Influences on food   Influences include the Romans, Slavs, and Turks, neighboring countries, and religion. Until the Turkish occupation of this area in the 15th century, Albanians were Christians, Eastern Orthodox in the south and Roman Catholic in the north. By the 19th century Islam became the predominant religion. Unlike Christians, Muslims do not eat pork. Albanian cookery evolved as a result of Islamization and the influence of Turkish food practices, except in the traditionally Orthodox south, where food remained Graeco-Mediterranian. Food traditions are strong in the older generation and in the villages populated by Albanians in the former Yugoslavia, including Kosovo, whose isolation from Albania has strengthened tradition. Kosovo has cuisine of Albanian and Turkish influences. Most people are of Albanian origin. Many people live in patriarchial communities of between 50 and 90 members, where food is cooked and bread is baked collectively and people eat communally. Meals are served out of a huge cooking pot or baking pan on low round tables. Turkish influence are reflected in mezze, rice, pilaf, and Turkish coffee and sweets; Greek in feta cheese; and Italian in tomato sauce. Kosovo's land produces grain, fruits and vegetables, grapes for wine, and livestock. Main foods are bread, pasta, cheese, and yogurt.

Bread and cereals Wheat, corn, rice; wheat bread including the standard dark, heavy, and slightly sour loaf, leavened bread, and flatbreads such as pita (thin circle with hollow center, a pocket) and lavash (a large crisp bread), cornmeal bread, rice dishes, wheat flour pastry, turnovers, pasta, and dumplings, wheat kernels (bulgur).

Meat, poultry, fish Lamb and mutton, chicken, beef, goat, pork, fish, eggs.

Dairy products Milk (cow, sheep, goat), cream, yogurt (kos), cheese (usually from goat or sheep milk, e.g., white cheese similar to feta and a hard, tangy ewe's milk cheese similar to cheddar called kashkaval).

Fats and oils Olive oil, butter, sesame oil, vegetable oils, rendered lamb fat.

Legumes Chickpeas, fava beans.

Vegetables Potatoes, olives, cabbage, eggplant, onions, tomatoes, cucumbers, peppers, mushrooms; pickles.

Fruit Grapes, berries, lemons, apricots, cherries, figs, dates, melons, pomegranates, pears, plums; preserves.

Nuts and seeds Walnuts, almonds, hazelnuts, peanuts, pine nuts, pistachios, poppy seeds, sunflower seeds, sesame seeds. Nuts, especially walnuts, are used in many savory and sweet dishes.

Seasonings Onions, mint, parsley, dill, garlic, pepper, anise, cardamom, cinnamon, oregano, lemon juice.

National appetizers Kanelloni alla toskana (pancakes stuffed with minced veal and with a gratin finish), a regular restaurant antipaste (appetizer). Byrne me djathë, a small triangular pastry filled with white cheese and eggs.

Dishes Rice pilaf (rice sautéed in butter or oil in which onions have been browned, then steamed or simmered with water or broth). Kofta (meatballs, fried or skewered and grilled). Shish kebabs (lamb pieces skewered and grilled). Dumplings filled with meat. Baked pasta, lamb or goat, and tomatoes. Baked macaroni, ground meat, cheese, tomato, and sauce. Pastitsio (béchamel sauce). Grape or cabbage leaves stuffed with rice or meat (dolma). Moussaka (baked minced lamb, eggplant, onions, and tomato sauce), a Balkan specialty. Tabouli, salad of onions, parsley, mint, bulgur, and fresh vegetables.

Sweets Honey, sugar, syrup. Fresh fruit. Fruit compote. Baklava (filo dough layered with nut filling, baked, soaked in flavored syrup, often cut in diamond shape). Halvah (sweet paste made with grain and crushed sesame seeds).

Beverages Coffee, tea, fruit juice, yogurt drinks, beer, wine, brandy, anise-flavored aperitifs including ouzo and the Turkish specialty raki (alcoholic beverages are prohibited for Muslims but are consumed in the Balkans), orme (beverage made from fermented cabbage), Turkish-style coffee (strong, thick, sweet, often with cardamom).

Meals The poorest people eat cornmeal bread, cheese, and yogurt, with lamb or mutton when affordable. For wealthier people, three meals a day with a midafternoon snack are typical. Breakfast: bread with cheese, olives, or jam and coffee or tea. Main meal (usually at midday): mezze with ouzo or raki, perhaps soup and/or pilaf, meat dish with salad of raw vegetables, yogurt or cheese, and fruit.

Mezze (appetizers) Salads such as liptao (feta cheese with bell pepper, deli meats, sardines, and hard-boiled egg) and tarator (soupy salad of yogurt, cucumbers, garlic, and olive oil), pickles, fish and seafood, omelets, spit-roasted lamb or entrails, and baked variety meats; usually with raki, ouzo, or orme.

Midafternoon snack Turkish-style coffee or tea and pastries, nuts, or fresh fruit.

KUWAIT
State of Kuwait

Geography   Kuwait, in the Middle East at the north end of the Persian Gulf, is low-lying desert and extremely hot.

Major Languages	Ethnic Group		Major Religions	
Arabic (official)	Kuwaiti	45%	Islam (official)	
English widely spoken	Other Arab	35%	Sunni Muslim	60%
	South Asian	9%	Shi'a Muslim	25%
	Iranian	4%	Christian, Hindu,	
	Other	7%	Parsi, other	15%

Population density per sq. mi. 377.4
Literacy rate 93.9%
Life expectancy 76.4 male; 78.7 female
Per capita GDP $39,300
Labor force in agriculture NA

Urban 98.3%
Infant mortality rate per 1,000 live births 9.2
HIV rate NA
Unemployment rate 2.2%
Arable land 1%

Agriculture   tomatoes, cucumbers, potatoes, chickens, sheep, goats, cattle

Natural resources   oil, fish, shrimp, natural gas

Industries   oil, petrochemicals, cement, shipbuilding, water desalination, food processing, construction materials

History   Kuwait probably was part of an early civilization in the 3rd millennium BCE and traded with Mesopotamian cities. Early in the 18th century CE, the Anizah tribe of central Arabia founded Kuwait City, which became an autonomous sheikdom by 1756. The Sabah dynasty, founded in 1759, still rules Kuwait. Britain controlled foreign relations and defense from 1899 until Kuwait's independence in 1961. Most of the population is non-Kuwaiti and cannot vote; many are Palestinians. Oil provides most of Kuwait's income, paying for free medical care, education, and social security, with no taxes. Iraqi forces invaded Kuwait in 1990 and a U.S.-led coalition liberated it in 1991. In 2005 women gained political rights. In 2008 foreigners were 97% of the private sector work force.

Influences on food   Influences include Arab, neighbors Saudi Arabia and Iraq, surrounding cultures of Ottoman, Horn of Africa, and Iran and India, and Britain and Islam. Islam forbids consumption of pork or alcohol and requires fasting from sunup to sundown during the month of Ramadan. Kuwait is mostly desert so it raises practically no crops. It has an extensive coastline that provides fish and seafood. A substantial proportion of the population is expatriates, resulting in the availability of a wide variety of foods.

Bread and cereals   Wheat, rice, flatbread (e.g. pita), couscous, cracked wheat, pancakes, filo pastry, rice dishes.

Meat, poultry, fish   Chicken, eggs, lamb, goat, beef, fish, shrimp. Lamb is the most popular meat and chicken the second favorite. Shrimp and fish such as hammour (grouper) and zubaidi (silver pomfret) are also popular.

Dairy products   Yogurt (laban), labneh (strained yogurt), milk, cream, feta cheese.

Fats and oils   Sesame seed oil and paste, ghee (clarified butter), butter, olive oil.

Legumes   Chickpeas (garbanzo beans), lentils.

Vegetables   Tomatoes, cucumbers, potatoes, eggplant, onions, olives, garlic, fresh herbs (especially parsley, spinach, mint, and coriander). Fresh herbs are sold in markets.

Fruit   Dates, mangoes, melons, watermelon, oranges, bananas, lemons, limes, figs. Dates, the most important fruit, are consumed in large quantities, especially during Ramadan.

Nuts and seeds   Almonds,   sesame seeds, sesame seed paste (tahini).

Seasonings   Salt, cardamom, saffron, mint, baharat (a spice mix of black pepper, coriander, cassia, cloves, cumin, cardamom, nutmeg, and paprika), loomi (dried Omani limes), lemon juice, onion, garlic.

Dishes   Simmered or steamed rice or couscous. Lamb, pieces or ground, grilled on skewers (kebab mashwi). Shrimp simmered with rice, fresh herbs, and vegetables (machbous). Boiled chickpeas or lentils, sometimes puréed and fried. Eggplant, tomato, and onion casserole. Tomato and cucumber salad. Fresh salt pickles.

Possible national dish   Khouzi (baked whole lamb stuffed with chicken, eggs, and rice spiced with baharat, saffron, and onions), served on a bed of rice garnished with almonds and ghee.

Sweets   Dibis (date molasses), honey, sugar, baklava (pastry of thin filo dough layered with nuts and soaked in honey or flavored syrup), ataif (small stuffed pancakes, a Ramadan specialty adopted from northern neighbors).

Beverages   Coffee, tea, fruit drinks, yogurt drinks, beer, wine, brandy. Coffee, the main drink and strongly associated with the renowned Arabian hospitality, is prepared from well-roasted, finely ground beans and is usually flavored with cardamom. Tea is usually consumed black and very sweet.

Street food and snacks   Roasted chicken, lamb kebabs, shawarma (vertical spit-roasted lamb pieces) sliced thin and served sandwich style in flatbread with tomato, parsley, and tahini; available from shawarma stalls.

KYRGYZSTAN
Kyrgyz Republic

Geography   Kyrgyzstan is in Central Asia. In this rugged country, the Tien Shan and Pamir Mountains, with snow and glaciers, cover 95% of the land. Average elevation is above 9,000 feet. A large lake is 1 mile above sea level.

Major Languages		Ethnic Groups		Major Religions	
Kyrgyz	(both	Kyrgyz	65%	Muslim (mostly Sunni)	75%
Russian	official)	Uzbek	14%	Russian Orthodox	20%
Uzbek		Russian	13%	Other	5%
		Other	8%		

Population density per sq. mi. 72.5
Literacy rate 99.3%
Life expectancy 65.1 male; 73.3 female
Per capita GDP $2,000
Labor force in agriculture 65%

Urban 35.8%
Infant mortality rate per 1,000 live births 32.3
HIV rate 0.1%
Unemployment rate 8.1%
Arable land 7%

Agriculture   potatoes, wheat, corn, tobacco, cotton, vegetables, grapes, fruits, berries, chickens, sheep, cattle, goats, horses, pigs

Natural resources   hydropower, gold, rare earth metals, coal, oil, natural gas, other metals, fish

Industries   small machinery, textiles, food processing, cement, shoes, logs, refrigerators, furniture, electric motors

History   The native Kyrgyzk are a nomadic Turkic people of Central Asia who in ancient times settled in the Tien Shan Mountains. They were conquered by Genghis Khan's son Jochi in 1207. The area became part of the Qing Empire of China in the mid-18th century. In 1864 Russia annexed it. After 1917 it was an autonomous area. It came under USSR control in 1924 and was made the Kirghiz Soviet Socialist Republic in 1936. It became independent in 1991. Private land ownership was ratified in 1998. After protests about election fraud in 2005, a new constitution limiting presidential power was enacted in 2006. In 2007 political conditions continued to worsen and the continuing economic stagnation forced increased numbers to work abroad.

Influences on food   Kyrgyzstan, along with Turkmenistan, Uzbekistan, and Tajikistan, is the land of the old Silk Road, the ancient caravan route between China and the Caspian Sea. Influences on food include neighbors China and Kazakhstan, and Russia and Islam. For example, noodles came from China. Kyrgyzstan shares a similar cuisine with Kazakhstan, its huge neighbor on the north: lamb, thick soups, semi-liquid main dishes, flatbread, tea, and few eggs, although Kyrgyz have distinctive tea. Unlike Kazaks but like some other Central Asians, Kyrgyz eat little fish. Until the 20th century most people were nomadic herders who lived in domed tents (yurts), raised animals, and lived mostly on dairy products.

Bread and cereals   Wheat, rice, corn; flatbread, cereals in porridge-like soups, noodles, rice dishes (palov). Flatbread (nan) is usually round loaves often cooked in a tandyra (tandoor), large clay jar or oven.

Meat, poultry, fish   Chicken, lamb and mutton, beef, goat, pork, fish; smoked horsemeat sausage (kazy).

Dairy products   Milk (sheep, cow, goat, camel, mare, yak), cream, sour milk, clabber, yogurt, cheeses (kurt, a hard cheese, sun dried, and reconstituted by soaking crumbled bits in water; airan, from milk from camels, sheep, and goats simmered until it clabbers and becomes sharp), kumys (fermented mare's milk).

Fats and oils   Butter, vegetable oil, fat from fat-tailed sheep (when rendered retains tiny cracklings).

Legumes   Chickpeas, lentils, beans.

Vegetables   Potatoes, onions, greens, carrots, pumpkin, peppers, tomatoes.

Fruit   Grapes, apples, barberries, mulberries, melons, rhubarb, apricots, pomegranate, figs, cherries, plums.

Nuts and seeds   Walnuts, hazelnuts, pistachios, caraway seeds.

Seasonings   Onions, garlic, vinegar, salt, black pepper, dried red peppers, dill, mint.

Dishes   Porridge-like cereal soups, often sour. Boiled or roasted meat. Besh barmak (in Kyrgyzstan, thinly sliced lamb or mutton and square-cut noodles served with a bowl of meat broth). Manpar (sliced noodle), slices of dough in soup or stew. Manty (steamed dumplings filled with ground lamb, onions, and red peppers). Kaurma lagman (fried noodles and meat). Samsas (pies filled with ground meat or chopped onion and greens). Shashlyk (lamb kebabs), seasoned and usually marinated meat cubes skewered and grilled; also a popular street food. Palov (pilaf), rice heated in oil before adding water and boiling, often with mutton and onions. Lake Issyk-Kul grilled fish.

Sweets   Honey, sugar. Dried fruit. Rose-petal jam. Rhubarb compote. Samsa (fritter with walnut, butter, and sugar filling). Candies: khalva (grain, sugar or honey, and nuts), bukman (sweetened cream and browned flour).

Beverages   Tea (made with twice as much milk as water, salt, pepper, and a fried flour mixture), sour milk, wine. Hot tea is drunk at meals and between meals, at home and in tea houses.

Meals and service   Breakfast: clabber or cheese, flatbread, and tea. Lunch: thick hearty soup or cheese, greens, and fruit, flatbread, and tea. Evening meal: meat or palov, flatbread, fruit or a sweet, and tea. To dine, people sit on rugs or chairs and use hands to scoop food, flatbread as edible scoops and plates, or flatware and plates.

L

LAOS
Lao People's Democratic Republic

Geography   Laos is in Southeast Asia in the north central part of the Indochina Peninsula. Jungles dominate this landlocked country, with high mountains along the east border and the Mekong River flowing through it for 932 miles, mostly along the western border.

Major Languages	Ethnic Groups		Major Religions	
Lao (official)	Lao	55%	Buddhist	67%
French	Khmou	11%	Traditional beliefs,	
English	Hmong	8%	other, and unspecified	33%
Ethnic languages	Other	26%		

Population density per sq. mi. 74.9
Literacy rate 73.2%
Life expectancy 54.2 male; 58.5 female
Per capita GDP $2,100
Labor force in agriculture 80%

Urban 27.4%
Infant mortality rate per 1,000 live births 79.6
HIV rate 0.2%
Unemployment rate 7.0%
Arable land 4%

Agriculture   rice, sweet potatoes, sugarcane, ramie, vegetables, corn, coffee, chickens, pigs, cattle, water buffalo, goats

Natural resources   fish, timber, hydropower, gypsum, tin, gold, gemstones

Industries   mining, timber, electric power, agricultural processing, construction, garments, tourism, cement

History   People migrated here from southern China from the 8th century CE on. A kingdom was founded in the 14th century and lasted until 1713, except for rule by Burma from 1574 to 1637. Laos came under Siamese (Thai) rule in the 18th century, became a French protectorate in 1893, and regained independence in 1949. Communist forces took control in 1975 and established the Lao People's Democratic Republic. It relied on Vietnamese aid through the 1980s. Its economy was adversely affected by the Asian financial crisis in the mid-1990s. In this poor county, subsistence farmers, 80% of the population, have suffered floods and drought since 1993. In 2004 the U.S. Congress approved normalization of trade with Laos. In 2005 some international banks agreed to fund a hydroelectric dam expected to bring Laos $2 billion revenue annually. In 2007 Laos's economy continued to grow, mainly due to foreign investment, notably the construction of large hydropower dams and to mining development.

Influences on food   Chinese, Thai, French, Indian, Malaysian, and Vietnamese influenced Laos's cuisine. The Chinese introduced soy products, the French popularized French bread and coffee, and Indians and Malaysians contributed curries and coconut milk-flavored dishes. In Laos, a beautiful large country with a small number of inhabitants, the Lao gather much of their food from the countryside and cultivate rice and corn. The diet is rice, fish (abundantly supplied in landlocked Laos by the rivers and irrigated fields), fish sauces, vegetables, and fruits, with eggs, poultry, and meat as affordable. Meat, poultry, and sweets are luxuries. The Lao are not bread eaters and do not usually use dairy products. They enjoy feasts. Hmong, tribal Lao forced from the mountains to the lowlands during Southeast Asian conflicts, have food traditionally different from Laotian and resembling Vietnamese, such as a preference for long-grain rice, although seasonings are Laotian.

Bread and cereals   Rice (usually sticky, or glutinous, also long grain), corn, wheat; rice dishes, wheat flour French bread, noodles, and pastries.

Meat, poultry, fish   Chicken, eggs, pork, beef, goat, water buffalo, game such as venison, fish (fresh, salted, dried), duck; nam pla (fish sauce), padek (fermented fish sauce or paste containing fish chunks), and nam padek (the liquid from padek). Fish sauces are important sources of protein and used in many dishes.

Dairy products   Sweetened condensed milk, whipping cream.

Fats and oils   Bacon, butter, lard, coconut cream, margarine, peanut oil, vegetable oil.

Legumes   Soy products, for example, tempeh (a chewier version of tofu, or bean curd) and soy milk, peanuts.

Vegetables   Sweet potatoes, potatoes, bamboo shoots, banana leaves, bitter melon, breadfruit, plantains, cabbage, cassava, squash, celery, carrots, radishes, chrysanthemum, corn, cucumbers, eggplant, lotus root, jicama, bean sprouts, mushrooms, mustard, pumpkin, taro, water chestnuts, peas, onions.

Fruit   Bananas, coconut, pineapple, papaya, limes, mangoes, mangosteens, star fruit, soursop, guavas, custard apple, durian, jackfruit, tamarind, oranges, watermelon, lemons. Fruit is popular for dessert or snacks.

Nuts and seeds   Cashew nuts, almonds, lotus seeds, sesame seeds.

Seasonings   Coconut cream and milk, fish sauces and pastes, soy sauce, lime juice and leaves, hot chilies, fresh coriander, garlic, lemon grass, mint, basil, ginger, curry powder.

Dishes   Steamed rice. Laap (spicy ground meat, usually pork, traditionally uncooked). Stewed or grilled meat. Stir-fried vegetables. Steamed banana leaf–wrapped rice, vegetables, or meat. Dried noodles topped with meats and vegetables. Salad of raw vegetables or unripe papaya or mango with lime juice, palm sugar, and chili dressing.

Specialties   Furr (soup of pork, noodles, garlic, and hemp, or marijuana, leaves). Salty beef jerky with fish sauce.

Sweets   Sugarcane, palm sugar, fruit, candy.

Beverages   Broth (often the only available beverage), tea (often blended with blossoms such as jasmine), soy milk, coffee (with sweetened condensed milk), bean or fruit drinks, rice wine or whiskey (for special occasions).

Meals and service   One to three meals a day is typical. Most meals are rice; a fish, poultry, or meat dish; soup; cooked vegetable or fresh salad; and tea or coffee. Foods are set out at one time and people help themselves. Laotians often eat with their fingers, using balls of sticky rice to scoop up foods; they eat soup with a porcelain or wood spoon. At dinner, a time for socializing, food is served on a low rattan tray; women gather on one side, men on the other; persons of highest rank take the first mouthfuls, followed by others in descending order of age; then diners eat freely except no one serves himself or herself at the same time as another or before one of higher rank.

LATVIA
Republic of Latvia

Geography   Located in Eastern Europe on the Baltic Sea, Latvia is fertile lowland with lakes, marshes, and peat bogs; hills are in the east.

Major Languages	Ethnic Groups		Major Religions	
Latvian (official)	Latvian	58%	Orthodox	29%
Russian	Russian	30%	Lutheran	20%
Lithuanian	Belarusian	4%	Roman Catholic	19%
	Other	8%	Other	6%
			None	26%

Population density per sq. mi. 91.5
Literacy rate 99.8%
Life expectancy 66.7 male; 77.3 female
Per capita GDP $11,300
Labor force in agriculture 13%

Urban 68%
Infant mortality rate per 1,000 live births 9
HIV rate 0.8%
Unemployment 6.7%
Arable land 28%

Agriculture   wheat, potatoes, sugar beets, vegetables, chickens, pigs, cattle, sheep, goats

Natural resources   fish, peat, limestone, dolomite, amber, hydropower, wood

Industries   motor vehicles and railroad cars, synthetic fibers, agricultural machinery, fertilizers, washing machines, radios, electronics, pharmaceuticals

History   Baltic tribes settled here along the Baltic Sea in ancient times. Latvia was conquered by the Vikings in the 9th century CE and by a German order of knights in the 13th century. Latvia was part of the German-speaking state Livonia until 1561. It was ruled by Poland (1562–1629), Sweden (1629–1721), and Russia (1721–1918). After the Russian Revolution of 1917, Latvia declared its independence and was an independent republic from 1918 to 1939 until Soviet troops invaded in 1940. Germany controlled it from 1941 to 1945, when the USSR retook it. Latvia regained independence in 1991 when the Soviet Union dissolved. In 1998 Latvia eased citizenship laws that had discriminated against ethnic Russians. It elected its first woman president in 1999. Latvia joined the EU and NATO in 2004. The first NATO summit conference to be held in a former Soviet republic was held in Riga, Latvia's capital, in 2006. In 2007 the GDP grew by an estimated 25%. An agreement about the border was reached with Russia, although it accepted the seizure of Latvian border counties by the USSR.

Influences on food   Latvia is central of the three Baltic countries, between Estonia to the north and Lithuania to the south. Latvian and Lithuanian languages are rarities, sole survivors of a group closely related to Sanskrit within the Indo-European family of languages. Influences on food include Baltic tribes, Germany, Poland, Sweden, and Russia. Fertile soil allows crops (grain, sugar beets, potatoes, and vegetables), animal production, and dairying. The Baltic Sea and lakes provide fish and seafood. Bread, fish, and dairy products are main foods.

Bread and cereals   Rye, wheat, barley, millet, oats, corn, rice; barley cereal and porridge (putra), rye bread (eaten at most meals), wheat light-colored bread, dumplings, pancakes, and pastries, rice dishes.

Meat, poultry, fish   Chicken, pork, beef and veal, lamb, goat, fish and seafood (eel, sprat, herring), eggs, venison; bacon, ham, sausage, smoked sprats, pickled herring, fish eggs (caviar).

Dairy products   Milk (cow, sheep), buttermilk, sour cream, cream, cottage cheese, cheese.

Fats and oils   Butter, bacon, lard, salt pork, vegetable oil.

Legumes   Beans, lentils, split peas

Vegetables   Potatoes, cabbage, beets, cauliflower, carrots, onions, cucumbers, green peas, mushrooms, radishes, tomatoes, turnips; sauerkraut, pickles.

Fruit   Apples, apricots, cherries, currants, plums, raisins, cranberries, ligonberries, raspberries, rhubarb, lemons.

Nuts and seeds   Almonds, chestnuts, hazelnuts, walnuts, caraway seeds (often used with cabbage), poppy seeds, sesame seeds (often used in pastries), sunflower seeds.

Seasonings   Onions, lemon, vinegar, parsley, dill, salt, pepper, cinnamon, bay leaf, vanilla. Sour and salty tastes are prominent, with more spicing than in Estonia.

Dishes   Pickled herring. Smoked salmon. Cucumbers in sour cream with dill. Fish soup (zivju supa), pieces of cooked fish and potato with the broth plus fried onion rings and grated carrot. Solianka (soup of cooked, cubed fish, onions, cucumbers, and tomatoes). Fried Baltic salmon with plum compote (cepts lasis ar plumju kompotu). Cabbage and beet soups. Boiled dumplings of flour or potato sometimes filled with meat, cheese, potatoes, rice, or fruit. Baked or fried pastry filled with seasoned meat or cabbage. Kurzemes pork (floured ham slice simmered with browned onions in bouillon and cooked with sour cream and mushrooms). Chicken stewed or breaded and fried. Large fried ground meat patties (e.g., ligzdinas: mostly beef with pork and bread, and a peeled whole hard-boiled egg in the center of each patty). Boiled or fried potatoes. Cabbage stuffed with seasoned ground meat.

Possible national dish   Skaba putra (porridge of barley, sour milk, potatoes, and salt pork, fermented, and served cold with sour cream), eaten with herring or bread and butter.

Sweets   Sugar, honey, molasses. Kisels (currant or and berry juices thickened with potato flour). Pancake served with berries or jam. Alexander torte (pastry with raspberry preserve filling and powdered sugar and lemon juice icing).

Beverages   Milk, coffee sometimes topped with whipped cream, tea, hot chocolate, beer, kvass, vodka, wine.

LEBANON
Lebanese Republic

Geography   Lebanon is in the Middle East, at the eastern end of the Mediterranean Sea. It has a narrow coastal strip. Most of the land is two mountain ranges running north to south, with the fertile Bekaa Valley in between.

Major Languages	Ethnic Groups		Major Religions	
Arabic (official)	Arab	95%	Muslim (mostly Shi'a)	60%
French	Armenian	4%	Christian (mostly Catholic)	39%
English	Other	1%	Other	1%
Armenian				

Population density per sq. mi. 1,005.6
Literacy rate 87.4%
Life expectancy 70.9 male; 76 female
Per capita GDP $11,300
Labor force in agriculture NA

Urban 86.6%
Infant mortality rate per 1,000 live births 22.6
HIV rate 0.1%
Unemployment rate 8.2%
Arable land 16%

Agriculture   potatoes, tomatoes, oranges, grapes, apples, olives, tobacco, chickens, goats, sheep, cattle, pigs

Natural resources   limestone, iron ore, salt, water (surplus in a water-deficient region), fish

Industries   banking, tourism, food processing, wine, jewelry, cement, textiles, minerals and chemical products

History   Present-day Lebanon is the area of ancient Phoenicia, settled about 3000 BCE. In the 6th century CE, Christians fleeing persecution in Syria settled in the area now northern Lebanon and founded the Maronite church. Arab tradesmen settled in southern Lebanon by the 11th century and founded the Druze faith. Later the Mamluks ruled Lebanon. In 1516 the Ottoman Turks took control in Lebanon. After the Druze massacred the Maronites in 1860, France forced the Ottomans to establish an autonomous province for the Christian area, Mont Lebanon. Lebanon, formed from five former Turkish Empire districts, became independent in 1920 and was administered under French mandate from 1920 to 1941. Lebanon gained full independence in 1946. After the Arab-Israeli War, 1948–1949, Palestinian refugees settled in southern Lebanon. In 1970 the Palestinian Liberation Organization (PLO) moved its headquarters there. In 1943 public positions were divided among religious communities, with Christians the majority. By the 1970s Muslims became the majority. In a civil war, 1975–1976, several Arab countries aided Muslim factions while Israel aided Christian forces. Conflict continued in the 1980s and through the 1990s. In 1991 Lebanon and Syria signed a treaty recognizing Lebanon as a separate state for the first time since the countries gained independence (1943–1946). Israel withdrew almost all its troops in 2000, leaving Hezbollah, a Muslim extremist group, in control of much of the area. In 2005, after 29 years of occupation, Syria withdrew all of its troops. Violence increased in 2006 but eased after a power-sharing agreement by the government and Hezbollah in 2008. About 12,300 UN military personnel remained in Lebanon in mid-2008.

Influences on food   Lebanon, one of the world's smallest countries, is mountainous with a long coastline on the Mediterranean, which provides fish and seafood. The Phoenicians reached this land around 3000 BCE.   They established city-states and became the first great commercial mariners, trading spices, grains, foodstuffs, and wine at the ancient crossroads of Europe, Asia, and Africa. Egyptians, Persians, Greeks, Romans, Crusaders, and Ottomans invaded the land and the French administered it; each left influence, especially the Ottomans. The Romans merged the states between the Taurus Mountains and the Sinai desert into a province named Syria; in 1946 Lebanon became independent. Lebanon shares a similar cuisine with neighbor Syria, although it has more vegetarian dishes due to Lenten restrictions of its larger Christian community. Muslims, the majority, are forbidden consumption of pork or alcohol and are obliged to fast from sunup to sundown during the month of Ramadan.

Bread and cereals   Wheat, rice; burghul (cracked wheat), wheat bread, usually leavened flatbread including pita (thin round bread with a hollow center), filo dough, rice dishes. Bread is consumed at most meals.

Meat, poultry, fish   Chicken, goat, lamb and mutton, beef, pork, fish and shellfish, eggs.

Dairy products   Milk (goat, sheep, camel, cow), yogurt, feta cheese (white, moist, and salty).

Fats and oils   Olive oil, clarified butter, sesame oil, vegetable oil, sheep's tail fat. Lebanese use fat sparingly.

Legumes   Chickpeas (garbanzo beans), fava (broad) beans, lentils, and black, navy, and red beans.

Vegetables   Potatoes, tomatoes, olives, eggplant, cucumbers, onions, green peppers, lettuce, chicory.

Fruit   Oranges, grapes, apples, dates, figs, melons, pomegranates, apricots, cherries, quince, raisins, sumac.

Nuts and seeds   Almonds, pine nuts, hazelnuts, walnuts, pistachios, sesame seeds.

Seasonings   Tahini (sesame seed paste), onions, garlic, fresh herbs (parsley, mint, basil), spices (allspice, cinnamon, cardamom, pepper, oregano), lemon juice, rosewater, orange blossom water.

Preserved foods   Vegetables dried or pickled. Fruits dried, candied, or made into jam. Lamb or mutton cut into small pieces, cooked and covered in its own fat, and preserved in a pot. Cracked wheat fermented in yogurt, dried, and ground to produce kishk (used in soups, pastry fillings, and bread toppings).

Dishes   Stuffed pastries. Stuffed vegetables. Meat (including variety cuts) and vegetable stews. Grilled or fried meat and fish. Roasted chicken. Sanbusak (crescent-shaped fried meat- or cheese-filled pie). Grape leaves stuffed with rice. Shish kabob (grilled lamb pieces on skewers). Pilaf (rice heated in oil in which onions have been browned and then steamed with water or broth). Lahm bi-ajine (flatbread topped with minced meat, chopped onion, tomatoes, and lemon juice). Specialties: Burghul bi d'feeneh (cracked wheat, chickpeas, and meat); Hindbeh bil-zeyt (boiled wild chicory sautéed in olive oil and garnished with caramelized onion).

A favorite dish   Fattoush (salad of parsley, mint, tomatoes, cucumbers, onions, and pieces of pita bread).

National dish   Kibbeh (finely minced lamb paste with cracked wheat, onion, and basil or mint; raw or cooked).

Sweets   Honey, sugar, honey- or flower-flavored syrup. Baklava (filo dough layers filled with nuts, sugar, and rosewater or orange blossom water, baked, soaked in syrup). Baraziq (small round biscuits dipped in pistachios and sesame seeds). Square honey cakes. Candied dates. Candy made of boiled sugar, water, and lemon juice.

Beverages   Coffee, tea, yogurt drinks, fruit juices, wine, arak (anise-flavored aperitif often served with mezze).

Mezze (tasty snacks) Hummus (chickpea dip), tabbouleh (salad of chopped tomato, parsley, and cracked wheat with onions, mint, oil, and lemon juice), olives, pickles, broiled eggplant with tahini sauce, fried kibbeh. Diners tear pieces from a disk of flatbread to scoop and eat mezze. Lebanese mezze are generally considered the best.

LESOTHO
Kingdom of Lesotho

Geography Lesotho is a small country in southern Africa, surrounded by the Republic of South Africa. The country is mountainous, elevation 5,000 to 11,000 feet, with rocky tableland.

Major Languages		Ethnic Groups		Major Religions	
English	(both	Sotho	99%	Christianity (official)	
Sesotho (southern Sotho)	official)	Other	1%	Christian	80%
Zulu				Indigenous beliefs	20%
Xhosa					

Population density per sq. mi. 181.6
Literacy rate 82.2%
Life expectancy 41 male; 39.3 female
Per capita GDP $1,300
Labor force in agriculture 86% (subsistence)

Urban 23.3%
Infant mortality rate per 1,000 live births 78.6
HIV rate 23.2%
Unemployment rate 50%
Arable land 11%

Agriculture potatoes, corn, sorghum, wheat, barley, pulses, chickens, sheep, goats, cattle, pigs

Natural resources water, diamonds, sand, clay, building stone

Industries food, beverages, textiles, apparel assembly, handicrafts

History Bantu-speaking farmers settled here in the 16th century. Chiefdoms formed, and the most powerful organized the Basotho in 1824 and sought British protection from the South African Boers. Called Basutoland, the area became a British protectorate in 1868, was annexed to Cape Colony 1871 to 1884, and was restored to direct control by Britain. It gained independence as Lesotho in 1966. Conflicts with South Africa and internally have occurred since 1986, with violence and changes in kings several times in the 1990s. Most of Lesotho's GNP is from citizens working in South Africa. The chief industry is raising livestock; the chief export is diamonds. An estimated 20% of the people faced food shortages in 2007, mainly due to drought, Lesotho's worst in 30 years.

Influences on food Lesotho, mountainous and rocky, mainly raises grain and livestock. Most of the population is indigenous. The cuisine has been influenced by European settlers of the region, including the Dutch, German, French, and especially the British because Lesotho was a British protectorate for nearly a century. The Dutch and Germans brought an appreciation for baked goods and jam and preserves (konfyt). French Huguenots founded the wine industry. Muslim slaves and laborers imported from Malaysia and India to South Africa have also influenced local fare. The Malays, expert fishers experienced in preserving fish, founded the Cape Malay cuisine prominent in southern Africa. The diet of rural people was that of their East African forefathers except that corn (which the European settlers planted and the Africans soon cultivated) replaced millet in porridge. Cattle were wealth and seldom eaten. Dairy products, porridge, beans, melon, greens, and insects were and are eaten.

Bread and cereals Corn, sorghum, wheat, barley, rice; porridge, rice dishes, breads, doughnuts, tarts, cookies.

Meat, poultry, fish Chicken, lamb and mutton, goat, beef, pork, fish, seafood, game (venison, ostrich), eggs.

Insects Locusts, caterpillars, termites (white ants), ant larvae. Insects are fried or roasted.

Dairy products   Milk, cream.

Fats and oils   Fat of fat-tailed sheep, butter, fish oil, vegetable oil.

Legumes   Beans, peas, lentils, peanuts.

Vegetables   Potatoes, green leaves, pumpkin, onions, sweet potatoes, cauliflower, cucumbers, carrots, tomatoes.

Fruit   Melon, quinces, dates, apples, apricots, tangerines, grapefruit, lemons, grapes, raisins, coconut.

Nuts and seeds   Almonds, walnuts.

Seasonings   Vinegar, chili peppers, garlic, cinnamon, cloves, turmeric, ginger, curry powder, bay leaf.

Dishes   Corn porridge (putu). Boiled rice. Sosaties (lamb or mutton marinated, skewered, and barbecued or simmered in marinade, served with curry sauce). Bredie (stew of spiced mutton cooked with vegetables such as onions, chilies, tomatoes, potatoes, or pumpkin), always eaten with rice. Frikkadels (braised meat patties). Bobotie (meatloaf with spices topped with a custard mixture and baked). Biltong (salted meat strips dried and preserved over smoke). Potjie (stew such as of venison simmered in a pot). Grape-stuffed chicken or suckling pig, sometimes served for special occasions. Beans simmered (sometimes with melon or pumpkin). Grated raw fruit or vegetable salads with lemon juice or vinegar and chilies. Spicy fruit or vegetable relishes (chutney). Atjar (unripe fruit or vegetables preserved in oil with spices).

Sweets   Honey, sugar. Dried fruits. Fruit leathers (called planked fruit). Fruit preserves and jams. Tarts made with sweet potatoes or egg custard. Koeksister (deep-fried braided doughnuts). Soetkoekies (spice cookies with wine).

Beverages   Tea, wine.

LIBERIA
Republic of Liberia

Geography   Liberia is on the southwest coast of West Africa, bordering the Atlantic Ocean, It is mostly a plateau and low mountains covered with dense tropical forests, with a marshy coastline and six major rivers.

Major Languages	Ethnic Groups		Major Religions	
English (official)	African (Kpelle, Bassa, Gio)	95%	Indigenous beliefs	40%
About 20 ethnic languages	Americo-Liberian (descendants		Christian	40%
	of slaves from U.S.)	3%	Muslim	20%
	Caribbean (descendants			
	of slaves from Caribbean)	2%		

Population density per sq. mi. 89.7
Literacy rate 55.5%
Life expectancy 39.9 male; 42.5 female
Per capita GDP $400
Labor force in agriculture 70%

Urban 58.1%
Infant mortality rate per 1,000 live births 143.9
HIV rate 1.7%
Unemployment rate 85%
Arable land 3%

Agriculture   cassava, sugarcane, oil palm fruit, rubber, coffee, cocoa, rice, chickens, goats, sheep, pigs, cattle

Natural resources   iron ore, timber, diamonds, gold, hydropower, fish

Industries   rubber and palm oil processing, timber, diamonds

History   Africa's first republic, Liberia was founded in 1822 as a home for freed American slaves. It became a republic in 1847. A coup in 1980 ended Americo-Liberian political dominance over indigenous African descendants. A civil war began in 1989, and a peace agreement was reached in 1996. In 1996 modern Africa's first woman head of state was installed to lead the transitional government. In 1997 former rebel leader Charles Taylor was elected president; in 2003 he went into exile in Nigeria and the UN indicted him for war crimes; his trial began in 2007 and continued in 2008. In 2001 the UN imposed sanctions on Liberia for aiding insurgency in Sierra Leone. The UN authorized a peacekeeping force to help stabilize Liberia in 2003 and extended the mandate to 2008. In 2007 the UN Security Council lifted its ban on Liberian diamond exports, imposed in 2001 to reduce the export of illegal "blood diamonds" that had helped finance the civil war.

Influences on food   The Atlantic Ocean and rivers provide fish. The tropical climate and heavy rainfall grow crops such as cassava and sugarcane. New World foods such as cocoa, cassava, corn, chili pepper, peanuts, and tomato greatly influenced food customs. In turn, native African foods such as watermelon, black-eyed peas, and okra influenced food customs in the New World. Freed American slaves brought influence from the United States. Daily fare is mostly grains and starchy vegetables, legumes, greens, and fish. Thick, sticky, spicy food is liked.

Bread and cereals   Rice, millet, sorghum, corn; porridge, pancakes, fritters, biscuits.

Meat, poultry, fish   Chicken, goat, lamb and mutton, pork, beef, fish and seafood (fresh, smoked, salted, or dried), eggs, guinea fowl, rabbit, game. Chicken is well-liked and served to special guests.

Insects   Termites (often called white ants), locusts. Insects are roasted or fried.

Dairy products   Milk, sour milk, buttermilk, curds, whey, cheese.

Fats and oils   Palm oil, peanut oil, shea oil, coconut oil. Palm oil, the predominant cooking fat, is red.

Legumes   Peanuts (groundnuts), black-eyed peas (a variety of cowpeas), locust beans (carob), beans.

Vegetables   Cassava, yams, plantains, taro, green leaves, okra, bitter leaf, melokhia (crain crain), tomatoes, sweet potatoes, potatoes, eggplant, pumpkin, onions, chili peppers, cucumbers, bell peppers.

Fruit   Bananas, coconut, pineapple, akee apples, baobab, watermelon, guavas, lemons, limes, mangoes, papaya.

Nuts and seeds   Cashews, kola nuts, watermelon seeds (egusi), sesame seeds, mango seeds.

Seasonings   Salt, hot red chili peppers, tomatoes, onions, dried baobab leaves, thyme, "African nutmeg," cocoa.

Dishes   Most foods are boiled or fried, and chunks or balls are dipped in sauce or stew and eaten by hand. Fufu (pounded boiled starchy vegetables or boiled corn flour). Boiled rice. Stews: fish and meat; chicken and peanuts; okra, root vegetables, or peanuts with bits of fish or meat. Peanut sauce (ground peanuts, chilies, tomatoes, and onions). Palaver sauce (pounded green leaves and seasonings). Fréjon (pea or bean purée, coconut milk, and carob or chocolate). Gari (roasted cassava meal). Adalu (mashed boiled vegetables). Chicken or fish marinated in lemon juice, grilled, fried with onions, and simmered in the marinade. Chicken baked with tomatoes, onions, okra, and peanut sauce. Jollof rice (rice simmered with meats, vegetables, and spices). Hard-boiled eggs.

Sweets   Sugarcane, sugar, honey, kanya (peanut candy), banana fritters, fried sweet dough balls.

Beverages   Coffee, cocoa, beer, red zinger (herbal tea made from flower pods of roselle, *Hibiscus sabdariffa*).

Street food and snacks   Spiced kabobs; fried fish, plantain chips, bean balls, sweet dough; coconut biscuits.

LIBYA
Socialist People's Libyan Arab Jamahiriya

Geography   Libya is in North Africa, bordering the Mediterranean Sea. Most of the land (92%) is desert and semi-desert. Mountains are in the north and south. Arable land lies in a narrow coastal zone along the Mediterranean.

Major Languages	Ethnic Groups		Major Religions	
Arabic (official)	Arab and Berber	97%	Islam (official)	
Italian	Other	3%	Sunni Muslim	97%
English			Other	3%

Population density per sq. mi. 9.1
Literacy rate 86.8%
Life expectancy 74.8 male; 79.4 female
Per capita GDP $12,300
Labor force in agriculture 17%

Urban 77%
Infant mortality rate per 1,000 live births 21.9
HIV rate NA
Unemployment rate 30.0%
Arable land 1%

Agriculture   tomatoes, olives, potatoes, wheat, barley, dates, citrus, vegetables, peanuts, soybeans, chickens, sheep, goats, cattle, camels

Natural resources   oil, natural gas, gypsum, fish

Industries   oil, iron and steel, food processing, textiles, handicrafts, cement

History   Libya was first settled by Berbers. In the 7th century BCE, Phoenicians settled in the eastern part and Greeks in the western part. Libya was conquered by the Romans in the 1st century BCE   and by Arabs in 642 CE. In the 16th century it became part of the Ottoman Empire. It was ruled by Italy from 1912 and by Britain and France after World War II. Libya became independent in 1951. Oil was discovered here in 1959 and it brought wealth. A decade later Qaddafi led army officers to depose the king and made Libya an Islamic republic. Libya fought with Egypt and with Chad during the 1970s. The UN imposed sanctions in 1992 for Libya's failure to cooperate in cases about plane bombings in 1988 of an American plane over Lockerbie, Scotland, and in 1989. In 2003 Libya renounced terrorism and settled the plane bombing cases, and the UN lifted sanctions. After UN inspections, in 2004 the United States and Libya restored diplomatic relations after 24 years. In 2007 Libya was elected a nonpermanent member of the UN Security Council for a two-year term. Libya signed a contract with British Petroleum to drill for oil and gas. In 2008 the Italian prime minister visited and pledged aid as reparations for Italy's years of colonial rule.

Influences on food   Influences in ancient times included the Berbers, Phoenicians, Greeks, and Romans. Arabs were a strong influence. Rule by Spain in the 16th century followed by the Ottomans starting in the same century and Italy from 1912 to the end of World War II also influenced Libyan food. Brief rule by Britain and France also had some influence. Increased prosperity from oil and increased food imports in the last decades of the 20th century also influenced the cuisine. Most Libyans are Muslims, who do not consume pork or alcohol. Libya's mostly desert land and hot climate limit agriculture. Onions have been grown here for a long time. Now cucumbers and other vegetables are grown using new technology. Some legumes and most fruits except dates and some citrus are imported. The Mediterranean provides fish and seafood. Libyan cuisine is hot and spicy.

Bread and cereals   Wheat, barley; cracked wheat, flatbreads, baguette (French bread), couscous, pasta, pastry.

Meat, poultry, fish   Chicken, eggs, lamb and mutton, goat, beef, fish and shellfish; gargush (meat cut into long strips, salted, sun dried, chopped, fried in olive oil, cooled, and stored in its own fat; commonly used in cooking).

Dairy products   Buttermilk, yogurt, cheese.

Fats and oils   Olive oil, ghee (clarified butter), sesame oil, vegetable oil, rendered lamb fat.

Legumes   Peanuts, soybeans, chickpeas, fava beans, lentils.

Vegetables   Tomatoes, olives, potatoes, cucumbers, eggplant, pumpkin, okra, greens, carrots, peppers, parsley.

Fruit   Dates, citrus, wild crabapples, figs, peaches, apricots.

Nuts and seeds   Almonds, pine nuts, pistachios, poppy seeds, pumpkin seeds, sesame seeds, caraway seeds.

Seasonings   Hot red pepper, onion, garlic, lemon juice, black pepper, cinnamon, cumin, rosewater, orange water.

Dishes   Couscous (tiny balls of grain dough steamed and served like rice) mixed with stew or sauce. Stewed chicken. Hot red pepper sauce. Macaroni with meat and vegetables in tomato sauce. Ground lamb turnover. Deep-fried anchovy-filled pastry. Potato salad (boiled potatoes heated in oil, lemon juice, caraway seeds, and red pepper sauce). Bazin, a distinctly Libyan dish (barley flour boiled in water, beaten into a hard dough, shaped into a pyramid around which is poured a thick meat and potato stew, and decorated with whole hard-boiled eggs).

Sweets   Honey, sugar. Dates, sometimes stuffed with pistachio paste flavored with rosewater. Pastry filled with sweet almond or sesame seed paste. Fried doughnuts dipped in lemony honey syrup. Almond cookies. Baklava.

Beverage   Tea (sweetened, poured repeatedly to form foam, and served in small glasses with foam on top).

Meals   Lunch, the main meal, includes some of the above dishes; the other two meals are light.

Mezze   (snacks, appetizers) Olives. Cheese cubes. Dips such as taramosalata (fish roe spread), cucumber and yogurt, eggplant purée, and hummus (chickpea purée). Tabbouleh (salad of parsley, tomato, and cracked wheat). Falafel (small fried bean purée cakes). Dolma (stuffed vegetable). Kabob (grilled skewered small chunks of meat).

LIECHTENSTEIN
Principality of Liechtenstein

Geography   This tiny country (area 62 square miles, population 34,498) is in Central Europe, between Austria and Switzerland. The Rhine valley occupies a third of the country and the Alps Mountains cover the rest.

Major Languages	Ethnic Groups		Major Religions	
German (official)	Liechtensteiner	66%	Roman Catholic	76%
Alemannic dialect	Swiss	10%	Protestant	7%
	Austrian, Italian, German,		Muslim	4%
	Turkish, other	24%	Other, none, unknown	13%

Population density per sq. mi. 58.4

Literacy rate 100%

Life expectancy 76.4 male; 83.5 female

Per capita GDP $25,000

Labor force in agriculture 2%

Urban 14.5%

Infant mortality rate per 1,000 live births 4.5

HIV rate NA

Unemployment rate 2.4%

Arable land 25%

Agriculture   grapes, market gardening, wheat, barley, corn, apples, potatoes, cattle, pigs, sheep, goats

Natural resources   hydroelectric potential

Industries   electronics, metal manufacturing, dental products, ceramics, pharmaceuticals, food products, precision instruments, tourism

History   The people are descended from the Alamanni tribe that came to this area in 500 CE. Liechtenstein was founded in 1719 from two independent lordships of the Holy Roman Empire. It was a member of the German Confederation from 1815 to 1866, when it became an independent principality. Austria administered Liechtenstein's ports to 1920. Switzerland has administered its postal services since 1921 and is united with it by a customs and monetary union. In 2004 Prince

Hans-Adam II turned daily operations of the country over to his son, Crown Prince Alois. Taxes are low. Many international companies have headquarters here. In 2007 Liechtenstein began to modernize its justice system; it is on the Organization for Economic Cooperation and Development's blacklist of uncooperative tax havens. Nearly half of workers commute daily from nearby countries.

Influences on food   In this tiny, mountainous central European country, influences on food include neighbors Switzerland, Austria, and Germany, as well as geography and climate. The cold, often damp climate allows growing grain and potatoes, raising livestock, and producing dairy products. Lakes and rivers supply fish. Foods are often dried, pickled, or fermented. Bread, meat, dairy products, and sweets are eaten daily.

Bread and cereals   Wheat, barley, corn, rye; bread (often made with rye and other grains and thus darker than bread made from wheat flour), dumplings made with flour or potatoes, pastry.

Meat, poultry, fish   Beef and veal, pork, lamb and mutton, goat, chicken, eggs, fish; sausage, bacon, ham.

Dairy products   Milk (cow, sheep), cream, sour cream, cheese.

Fats and oils   Butter, lard, salt pork, vegetable oil.

Legumes   Kidney beans, navy beans, lentils, split peas.

Vegetables   Potatoes, cabbage, beans, carrots, beets, cucumbers, onions; sauerkraut, cucumber pickles.

Fruit   Apples, apricots, cherries, blackberries, grapes, lemons, raisins. Fruit is usually cooked.

Nuts and seeds   Almonds, chestnuts, hazelnuts, walnuts, poppy seeds, caraway seeds.

Seasonings   Sour cream, vinegar, cinnamon, dill, mustard, lemon, vanilla. Sour-tasting food is liked.

Dishes   Potatoes, boiled, mashed, fried, or baked. Pea soup. Dumplings stuffed with ground meat, potatoes, cabbage, or fruit and fried or baked. Pork or veal schnitzel (cutlet, often breaded and fried). Ground meat seasoned, mixed with bread crumbs, milk, or eggs, formed into patties, and fried. Ground meat–stuffed vegetables (e.g., cabbage) or pastry, baked or fried. Braised or fried meatballs. Cut meat cooked in stews, soups, or one-pot dishes. Meat cooked with fruit. Stewed fruit.

Sweets   Honey, sugar. Fruit/berry pudding, cakes, cookies, pastries (sometimes fruit-filled) with whipped cream.

Beverages   Coffee, beer, hot chocolate, wine.

Meals   Three meals with snacks daily is usual. Breakfast: bread, butter, and jam, perhaps with soft-boiled egg, cheese, or ham. Mid-morning snack: coffee and pastry. Lunch (the main meal): soup, fish dish, one or two meat dishes with vegetables and perhaps stewed fruit, and dessert, usually with whipped cream. A lighter lunch: stew or one-pot meal. Mid-afternoon coffee break: coffee and cake or cookies. Evening meal: breads, cold fish, cheese, ham, and sausage. Guests are usually invited not for dinner but for dessert and wine later in the evening.

LITHUANIA
Republic of Lithuania

Geography   Lithuania is in Eastern Europe on the eastern shore of the Baltic Sea. It is a lowland country, with hills in the west and south, fertile soil, and many forests, small rivers, lakes, and marshes in the north and west.

Major Languages	Ethnic Groups		Major Religions	
Lithuanian (official)	Lithuanian	83%	Roman Catholic	79%
Russian	Polish	7%	Russian Orthodox	4%
Polish	Russian	6%	Other	7%
	Belarusian, other	4%	None	10%

Population density per sq. mi. 141.6
Literacy rate 99.7%
Life expectancy 69.7 male; 79.9 female
Per capita GDP $17,700
Labor force in agriculture 15.8%

Urban 66.6%
Infant mortality rate per 1,000 live births 6.6
HIV rate 0.1%
Unemployment rate 5.6%
Arable land 45%

Agriculture   wheat, barley, potatoes, sugar beets, flax, vegetables, chickens, pigs, cattle, sheep, goats

Natural resources   fish, peat, amber

Industries   metal-cutting, machine tools, electric motors, TVs. Refrigerators and freezers, oil refining, textiles

History   Lithuanian tribes united in the 13th century. In 1386 the Lithuanian grand duke became king of Poland, and Lithuania and Poland united to oppose the Teutonic knights. They made one of Europe's largest empires, stretching to the Black Sea and almost to Moscow. Russia brought Lithuania under its rule in 1795 with its partition of Poland. Following World War I and the collapse of Russia, in 1918 Lithuania declared independence. Germany occupied Lithuania during both World Wars. Lithuania was annexed by the USSR in 1940, the USSR regained control of it in 1944, and Lithuania regained independence in 1991. UN admittance followed in 1991. The last Soviet troops left in 1993. Lithuania joined the EU and NATO in 2004. Lithuanian-American Valdas Adamkus was president from 1998 to 2003 and again in 2004. In 2007 the Baltic nations and Poland agreed to build a new nuclear power station in Lithuania. The economy grew substantially, largely due to foreign direct investment, more than US $73 billion at the beginning of 2008.

Influences on food   Lithuania is the southernmost Baltic country. It was a large territory in the Middle Ages, and in a union with neighbor Poland for four centuries extended at one time to the Black Sea. It had close trading lines with the Mongol-Tatars and the Ottoman Empire. This history influenced Lithuanian food. Lithuanian cuisine has been influenced most by Poland, Russia, and Germany. For example, dishes with Russian influence include beet soup, fruit soup, and kasha. Lithuania has kept its language and many indigenous food traditions, reflecting the agrarian country and Baltic coast. Main foods are Baltic herring, pork, rye bread, dairy products, and potatoes.

Bread and cereals   Wheat, barley, rye, buckwheat, millet, corn, oats; bread (usually rye and served at most meals), porridge, dumplings, pastry, pancakes.

Meat, poultry, fish   Chicken, pork, beef and veal, goat, lamb, fish and seafood (especially Baltic herring), eggs, goose; pickled herring, caviar, smoked ham, sausage such as sviezia desira (ground beef and pork with garlic, black pepper, parsley, and nutmeg). Meat, second in importance to bread, is often ground.

Dairy products   Milk, buttermilk, sour cream, fresh cream, cheese (fresh sweet cheese such as Lithuanian farmer's cheese, cottage cheese, hard cheeses often with caraway seeds).

Fats and oils   Butter, flaxseed oil, bacon, lard, salt pork, vegetable oil.

Legumes   Beans, split peas, lentils.

Vegetables   Potatoes, cabbage, beets, carrots, cucumbers, green beans, lettuce, onions, mushrooms, hemp (marijuana, used in traditional Lithuanian fare); sauerkraut, vegetable pickles.

Fruit   Apples, apricots, cherries, currants, plums, raisins, cranberries, ligonberries, raspberries, rhubarb.

Nuts and seeds   Almonds, chestnuts, hazelnuts, walnuts, caraway seeds, poppy seeds, sunflower seeds.

Seasonings   Sour cream, vinegar, lemon, onion, garlic, pepper, parsley, dill, cinnamon, cloves, nutmeg, ginger.

Dishes   Salad of cucumbers and sour cream with dill. Soup made from beets (eaten cold in summer), cabbage, or fish. Kasha (barley, buckwheat, or millet porridge). Boiled potatoes. Potato pancakes. Boiled dumplings, made from flour or potatoes, sometimes stuffed with potatoes, meat, or fruit. Cepelinai (dumplings made of grated potato and stuffed with meat, mushrooms, or cheese).

Baked or fried pastry dough filled with meat or cabbage. Kulduny (lamb-stuffed pastry) served with sour cream. Cutlet (slice) of pork, chicken, or veal, lightly breaded and fried. Fried patties of ground meat, moistened bread crumbs, chopped onion, and milk. A favorite dish, pig's stomach stuffed with potatoes and herring, and baked. Fried black bread with garlic.

Traditional Christmas Eve dish Avizine kose (fermented oatmeal porridge, boiled, and served with boiled syrup of pounded poppy seeds, chopped almonds, milk, and sugar).

Sweets Honey, sugar, molasses. Kiselius (thickened fruit soup). Cookies with apples and ginger. Honey cake (lekakh). A specialty, apple cheese (baked apples sieved, combined with honey and spices, pressed, and dried).

Beverages Milk, tea, coffee, beer, kvass (fizzy sour beer fermented from rye bread or beets), vodka.

National drink Krupnikas (mildly fermented beverage with cloves, cinnamon, and other spices).

Meals Three hearty meals a day are typical, the largest at lunch. Usual meal: bread, salad or soup, kasha or boiled potatoes, and milk, tea, or beer. Snacking is rare.

LUXEMBOURG
Grand Duchy of Luxembourg

Geography Luxembourg is in Western Europe, bordering France, Belgium, and Germany. It has mountains with heavy forests in the north and a low fertile plateau in the south.

Major Languages		Ethnic Groups		Major Religions	
Luxembourgish	(national)	Luxembourger	63%	Roman Catholic	90%
French	(both	Portuguese	13%	Protestant	3%
German	official)	French	5%	Muslim	2%
		Italian	4%	Orthodox	1%
		German, other	15%	Other	4%

Population density per sq. mi. 486.8
Literacy rate 100%
Life expectancy 75.9 male; 82.7 female
Per capita GDP $82,500
Labor force in agriculture 1%

Urban 82.8%
Infant mortality rate per 1,000 live births 4.6
HIV rate 0.2%
Unemployment rate 4.4%
Arable land 27%

Agriculture wine, wheat, barley, potatoes, grapes, oats, fruits, chickens, cattle, pigs, sheep, goats

Natural resources iron ore (no longer exploited)

Industries banking and financial services, iron and steel, information technology, telecommunications, cargo transport, food processing, chemicals, metal products, glass, aluminum

History Luxembourg was inhabited by Belgic tribes at the time of the Roman conquest, 57 to 50 BCE. German tribes invaded the area after 400 CE. Once part of Charlemagne's empire, Luxembourg became independent in 963. It was made a duchy in 1354 and ceded to the house of Burgundy in 1443 and to the Hapsburgs in 1477. It became part of the Spanish Netherlands in the mid-16th century. It was made a grand duchy in 1815. In 1839 the western part was given to Belgium and the eastern part continued with the Netherlands and became autonomous in 1848. In 1866 it left the Germanic Confederation. In the late 19th century it exploited its extensive iron ore deposits. Luxembourg was overrun by Germany in both world wars. In 1948 it ended its neutrality by joining a customs union with Belgium and the Netherlands. It joined NATO in 1949. It was one the founding members (1951) of the organization that became the European Union; it approved the EU constitution in 2005. In 2000 the grand duke, after 36 years on the throne, abdicated power in favor of his son. In 2007 Luxembourg's economy was ranked the fourth most competitive in the world. In 2008 the country opened a new airport terminal.

Influences on food   Luxembourg is a tiny country (area 998 square miles) between Belgium, France, and Germany. Its cuisine has been influenced by these neighbors, notably Belgium and France. Spain, who ruled the region from 1556 to 1713, and the Netherlands, who later owned this land, also influenced the food here. Other influences include Luxembourg's history of poverty and its present prosperity as an international banking center. The fertile plateau in the south sustains production of grains, potatoes, fruit, and livestock. Rivers provide fish.

Bread and cereals   Wheat, barley, oats, rye, rice; bread (whole wheat, wheat, and rye), waffles, cookies, pastry.

Meat, poultry, fish   Chicken, beef, pork, lamb, goat, fish, eggs; smoked ham, sausage, charcuterie.

Dairy products   Milk, cream, sour cream, cheese.

Fats and oils   Butter, lard, margarine, vegetable oil, salt pork.

Legumes   Split peas, kidney beans, broad beans.

Vegetables   Potatoes, cabbage, Brussels sprouts, asparagus, tomatoes, carrots, onions; sauerkraut, pickles.

Fruit   Grapes, raisins, plums, prunes, apples, cherries, pears, lemons, oranges, strawberries, melon.

Nuts and seeds   Almonds, chestnuts, hazelnuts, pecans, walnuts, sesame seeds.

Seasonings   Vinegar, pepper, shallots, capers, sage, cinnamon, cloves, nutmeg, mustard, vanilla, chocolate.

Dishes   Split pea or bean soup. Soup of entrails (gebeck). Pickled pig's trotters. Fried or grilled trout. Boiled, mashed, or fried potatoes. The suffix à la luxembourgeoise refers to a variety of dishes: fried meat served with a sauce containing any combination of gherkins, shallots, or capers; addition of a Luxembourg wine to a stew or fish dish; or mashed potatoes with red wine replacing milk or cream (mashed potatoes à la Luxembourgeoise).

National dish   Judd mat Gaardebounen (boiled smoked pork with boiled potatoes and broad beans with sage).

Special occasion fare   For Christmas (Kermesse): Soup made with pork offal (Gehäck). Yeast-raised cake with raisins (Kiirmeskuch) eaten spread with butter and a thin slice of smoked ham. Prunes soaked in local wine.

Sweets   Honey, sugar. Waffles with butter and sugar or with whipped cream and strawberries. Seasonal tarts (tartes des quetsches) made with plums. Sweet bread. Cookies.

Beverages   Coffee, tea, hot chocolate, beer, wine (white, red).

M

MACEDONIA
The Former Yugoslav Republic of Macedonia

Geography   Macedonia is in southeastern Europe, north of Greece. It is mostly mountainous, with deep river valleys and small areas of agricultural land. It has three large lakes. The Vardar is the main river.

Major Languages	Ethnic Groups		Major Religions	
Macedonian (both Albanian official) Turkish	Macedonian	64%	Macedonian Orthodox	65%
	Albanian	25%	Sunni Muslim	33%
	Turkish	4%	Other or unspecified	2%
	Roma	3%		
	Other	4%		

Population density per sq. mi. 214.8
Literacy rate 97%
Life expectancy 72 male; 77.1 female
Per capita GDP $8,500
Labor force in agriculture 19.6

Urban 65.4%
Infant mortality rate per 1,000 live births 9.3
HIV rate <0.1%
Unemployment rate 36.0%
Arable land 22%

Agriculture   wheat, grapes, potatoes, wine, tobacco, vegetables, chickens, sheep, pigs, cattle, goats

Natural resources   iron ore, copper, lead, zinc, manganese, nickel, tungsten, gold, silver, asbestos, fish

Industries   food processing, textiles, chemicals, cement, pharmaceuticals, mining

History   Macedonia has been inhabited since before 7000 BCE. Present-day Macedonia is the western half of the ancient Kingdom of Macedonia, which was defeated by Rome and became a Roman province in 148 BCE. After the Roman Empire division in 395 CE, the Byzantine Empire ruled Macedonia. Slavic tribes settled it by the mid-6th century. Bulgaria seized it in 1185. The Ottoman Empire ruled it from 1389 to 1912, when native Greeks, Bulgarians, and Slavs gained independence. In 1913 most of the land (the north and center of the area) was incorporated into Serbia; the rest went to Greece and Bulgaria. In 1918 Serbia became part of the Kingdom of Serbs, Croats, and Slovenes, which became Yugoslavia. In 1991 Macedonia declared independence. It joined the UN in 1993, under the name The Former Yugoslav Republic of Macedonia because Greece objected to its using the name of an ancient Greek province. In 2001 violence between Macedonia's ethnic Albanians, who sought greater autonomy in the heavily Albanian western part of Macedonia, and the government led to Parliament's granting broader rights to its Albanian minority and making Albanian an official language in 2002. Greece has blocked Macedonia's bid to join NATO because of its use of a Hellenic name and symbols.

Influences on food   Macedonia is a Balkan country and northern neighbor of Greece. In antiquity Macedonia was the heart of Alexander the Great's empire. It survived in various sizes and under various rulers including the Roman Empire, the Byzantine Empire, and the Ottoman

Empire in the 14th to 20th century. It was part of Yugoslavia for much of the 20th century. This history has influenced Macedonia's food. Macedonia has early springs with early fruits and vegetables followed by long hot summers. It raises grains, grapes, and livestock. Sheep is important and its yogurt is prized. Rivers provide fish. The food is typically Balkan: bread and other flour-based products with dairy products, fruits, and vegetables. Balkan people can be called grain eaters, in contrast to predominantly meat eaters. Favorite foods in Macedonia include lamb, yogurt, cheese, eggplant, and wine. Old Slavic dishes and adaptations of Greek and Turkish dishes are found, all often supplemented with hot red chilies or chili powder that gives Macedonian country food its characteristic fiery flavor. Food consumption during feasting and fasting differs for Orthodox Christians and Muslims, and, unlike Christianity, Islam forbids consumption of pork. Islam also prohibits consumption of alcohol, but wine and ouzo are popular in the Balkans.

Bread and cereals   Wheat, corn, millet, rice; rice dishes, porridge, wheat bread such as leavened loaves and pita, couscous, cracked wheat, filo dough, noodles, cheese-or meat-pies, pasta.

Meat, poultry, fish   Chicken, eggs, lamb and mutton, beef, pork, fish.

Dairy products   Milk (cow, sheep), yogurt, cheese (e.g., feta and kashkaval, a hard tangy ewe's milk cheese called the cheddar of the Balkans). Sheep yogurt (ovcho kiselo mleko), very thick, rich, and delicately flavored under a golden cream crust, is made by shepherds in alpine dairies.

Legumes   Chickpeas (garbanzo beans), fava beans, black beans, white beans, lentils.

Fats and oils   Butter (cow, sheep), olive oil, sunflower oil, corn oil.

Vegetables   Potatoes, eggplant, olives, pumpkin, tomatoes, cabbage, grape leaves, cucumbers, onions.

Fruit   Grapes, dates, figs, lemons, pears, plums, cherries, oranges, melons.

Nuts and seeds   Almonds, pistachio, walnuts, sesame seeds, sunflower seeds.

Seasonings   Anise, mint, hot red chili, cardamom, many other herbs and spices, garlic, lemon juice.

Dishes   Cornmeal porridge (bakrdan). Moussaka (eggplant, lamb, tomato, onion, and egg casserole). Dolma (stuffed vegetable, e.g., grape leaves or cabbage). Kofta (pounded meat, mixed with other ingredients, made into small meat balls, and grilled or fried). Kabob (meat chunks marinated and grilled on a skewer).

Sweets   Honey, sugar. Baklava (pastry made of layers of thin filo dough, buttered, layered with sweetened filling of mixed nuts, soaked in honey or flavored syrup, and often cut into diamond shapes).

Beverages   Coffee, tea (both sweet, with cardamom and mint, respectively), wine, ouzo (anise-flavored aperitif).

Meals   Breakfast: bread with cheese, olives, or jam and coffee or tea. Main meal (in early afternoon): appetizers such as hummus (chickpea dip), dolma; meat or bean dish with a salad of raw vegetables; yogurt or cheese; fruit. Supper: a light meal in late evening. Guests come in late afternoon for sweets and coffee, wine, or ouzo.

Street food and snacks   Mezze (tasty bits), such as hummus, dolma, olives, cheese, are widely available from street vendors and cafes for snacking, which is prevalent.

MADAGASCAR
Republic of Madagascar

Geography   The fourth largest island in the world, Madagascar lies in the Indian Ocean off the southeast coast of Africa. It has fertile valleys in the central mountainous plateau and low coastal areas.

Major Languages	Ethnic Groups		Major Religions	
Malagasy (all French are English official)	Malagasy (mixed Malayo-Indonesian, African, and Arab) French, Indian, Comoran, other	96% 4%	Indigenous beliefs Christian Muslim and other	52% 41% 7%

Population density per sq. mi. 89.3
Literacy rate 70.7%
Life expectancy 60.6 male; 64.5 female
Per capita GDP $1,100
Labor force in agriculture NA

Urban 28.5%
Infant mortality rate per 1,000 live births 55.6
HIV rate 0.1%
Unemployment rate 2.8%
Arable land 5%

Agriculture   rice, sugarcane, cassava, coffee, vanilla, cloves, cocoa, beans, bananas, peanuts, chickens, cattle, pigs, geese, goats, sheep

Natural resources   fish, graphite, chromite, coal, bauxite, salt, quartz, tar sands, semi-precious stones, mica, hydropower

Industries   meat processing, seafood, soap, brewing, hides, sugar, textiles, glassware, cement, auto assembly

History   This island was settled 2,000 years ago by Malayan-Indonesians, whose descendants, the Malagasy, still predominate. The first European to visit was Portuguese navigator Diogo Dias, in 1500. Trade in slaves and arms led to development of the Malagsy kingdom in the early 17th century. In the 18th and 19th centuries the merina kingdom dominated, unifying much of the island. The island became a French protectorate in 1885, a French colony in 1896, and independent in 1960, as the Malagasy Republic. It took its new name in 1975. After a coup in the 1970s the new regime nationalized French interests and expelled foreigners. A ban on multiparty politics in place since 1975 ended in 1990. A new constitution was adopted in 1992; political and economic instability has followed. A cholera epidemic and cyclones in 2000 claimed 1,600 lives. In 2002 a 6-month civil war occurred. In 2004 the World Bank and International Monetary Fund agreed to write off at least half of Madagascar's debt. In 2007 amendments to the constitution substantially reduced the size of the national assembly and increased the president's powers. A cyclone in 2008 killed at last 83 people and left 145,000 homeless.

Influences on food   Madagascar is almost a continent because it occupies its own tectonic plate so that indigenous species of plants and animals evolved separately than those of neighboring continent Africa. The inhabitants, the Malagasy, descended from Malay/Indonesian seafarers. Descendants of African Bantus live on the west coast. In addition to Malay/Indonesian, East African, Arab, and Indian influences, French influence is evident, reflecting the island's French rule from 1896 to 1960. Rice and cassava are main foods. Vanilla and cloves are important.

Bread and cereals   Rice, wheat; rice dishes, bread (called mofo) usually baguette (French bread).

Meat, poultry, fish   Chicken, beef, pork, goose, goat, lamb and mutton, fish and seafood, eggs.

Dairy products   Yogurt.

Fats and oils   Butter, lard, coconut cream and oil, vegetable oil.

Legumes   Beans, peanuts, lentils.

Vegetables   Cassava, green leaves, tomatoes, plantains, onions.

Fruit   Bananas, lemons, coconut.

Seasonings   Vanilla beans, cloves, chili peppers, ginger, garlic, curry, cocoa. Savory dishes are not highly spiced, although a paste of chili, ginger, and garlic (sakay) is used in some.

Dishes   Apangoro (simmered rice). Rice is frequently cooked in an earthenware pot, the center part eaten, and the rest caramelized and mixed with boiling water to make ranon' apango (rice water). Sosoa (soupy cooked rice), eaten for breakfast. Brèdes (soup made with leaves). Simmered cassava. Cassava cakes. Simmered and often mashed beans or lentils. Spicy peanut stew or sauce. Fried plantains. Malagasy pil-pil dishes, made hot and spicy with small hot chili peppers. Rougaille (a sauce of chili, tomato, onion, lemon, and ginger). Spicy pickled vegetables (achards), served with savory dishes.

National dish   Romazava (stew of beef, pork, chicken, tomatoes, and brèdes).

Sweets   Sugarcane, sugar. Coconut pudding. Vanilla-flavored pudding.

National dessert   Banana flambé, often the only dessert on a menu.

Beverages   Rice water (drunk with meals), coffee, tea.

MALAWI
Republic of Malawi

Geography   Malawi is a landlocked country in southeastern Africa. High plateaus and mountains line the Great Rift Valley, which runs north-south through the country. Malawi owns most of Lake Malawi, in the Rift Valley.

Major Languages	Ethnic Groups	Major Religions	
Chichewa (official)	Chewa 35%, Maravi 12%	Christian	80%
Chinyanja	Ngoni 9%, Lomwe 8%,	Muslim	13%
Chiyao	Tumbuka 8%, Yao 8%, Ngonde 4%;	Other	7%
Chitumbuka	Nyanja, Sena, Tonga, other 16%		

Population density per sq. mi. 383.5

Literacy rate 71.8%

Life expectancy 43.7 male; 43.1 female

Per capita GDP $800

Labor force in agriculture 90%

Urban 17.3%

Infant mortality rate per 1,000 live births 90.5

HIV rate 11.9%

Unemployment rate NA

Arable land 21%

Agriculture   sugarcane, cassava, potatoes, tobacco, cotton, tea, corn, chickens, goats, cattle, pigs, sheep

Natural resources   fish, limestone, hydropower, unexploited deposits of uranium, coal and bauxite

Industries   tobacco, tea, sugar, sawmill products, cement, consumer goods

History   Humans have inhabited the area since about 8000 BCE. Bantu-speaking people came between the 1st and 4th centuries CE. Major kingdoms established include Mravi, 1480; Ngonde, 1600; and Chikulamayembe, 18th century. A large slave trade occurred in the 18th and 19th centuries, bringing Islam, Christian missionaries, and Arab slavers. David Livingstone explored the area in the 1850s and 1860s. In 1884 Cecil Rhodes's British South African Company received a charter to develop the country, which came under British authority in 1891 and became the protectorate Nyasaland in 1907. Malawi gained independence in 1964. More than 7 million people suffered from severe food shortages in 2002, 2003, and 2005. In 2007 a recovery from drought occurred due to a bumper crop of corn for two consecutive years. Malawi provided substantial amounts of corn to drought-stricken Zimbabwe, Lesotho, and Swaziland. Cape Maclear Beach, on Lake Malawi, has fine beaches and restaurants.

Influences on food   The cuisine of Malawi resembles that of other East African countries such as neighbor Tanzania. Much of the terrain is high plateaus and mountains. The highland diet contains almost no meat, in spite of abundant game and the tradition of breeding cattle. Cattle were regarded as wealth, not food, and the Masai and related people lived on milk products and blood of cattle. Others lived on mostly grains and bananas, with gathered greens. The earliest foreign traders, Arabs, established colonies along the coast from about 700 CE, traded in slaves and ivory and introduced spices, onions, and eggplant. British control from the mid-19th century to 1964 left influence. For example, the British trained African men in European cooking and encouraged Asians to settle in the region. Asians brought practices such as using curry spices and cooking fish with coconut milk. Descendants of Dutch who trekked north from the Cape and later moved further north into southern Malawi left some influence. The diet is mostly porridge, starchy vegetables, and green leaves. Lake Malawi supplies fish; tilapia and catfish (chambo and mlamba, respectively) are farmed and exported. European hunters found game in the mountains; although animals are protected, game is plentiful.

Bread and cereals   Corn, sorghum, millet, rice; porridge (the common staple food), rice dishes, pancakes, fritters.

Meat, poultry, fish   Chicken, eggs, goat, beef, pork, lamb and mutton, fish, game, seafood (salted and dried).

Insects   Locusts, crickets, grasshoppers, ants, worms (madora), caterpillars (harati). These are fried or dried.

Dairy products   Milk, cheese (including some adapted from European ones). Milk products are important.

Fats and oils   Butter, lard, meat drippings, peanut oil.

Legumes   Cowpeas, beans, lentils, peanuts (groundnuts). Legumes, important protein sources, are eaten daily.

Vegetables   Potatoes, cassava, green bananas, yams, sweet potatoes, green leaves, eggplant, okra, pumpkin.

Fruit   Bananas, coconut, papaya, watermelon.

Nuts and seeds   Cashew nuts, sesame seeds, watermelon seeds.

Seasonings   Chilies, onions, coconut milk, dried baobab leaves, cloves, curry powder, cinnamon, saffron.

Dishes   Thick porridge of corn or millet. Peanut soup and paste. Green leaves cooked with peanut paste. Irio (mashed cooked beans, corn, and potatoes or cassava). Curried chicken. Boiled rice. Green bananas boiled in their leaves and mashed. Goat, beef, or mutton stew. Fried, grilled, or poached fish with coconut sauce.

Sweets   Sugarcane, honey, sugar, banana jam, doughnuts, rice and coconut pancakes, coconut pudding.

Beverages   Tea, beer.

Street food   Fried pastry, grilled corn on cob, fried pancake filled with minced meat and egg.

MALAYSIA

Geography   Malaysia is in Southeast Asia, bordering the South China Sea. It is the southern part of the Malay Peninsula and the northern third of the island of Borneo. Most of the land is a tropical jungle, with a mountain range running north to south the length of the peninsula, interior mountains in East Malaysia, and swampy coasts.

Major Languages	Ethnic Groups		Major Religions	
Malay (official)	Malay	50%	Islam (official)	
English	Other indigenous	11%	Muslim	60%
Chinese dialects	Chinese	24%	Buddhist	19%
Panjabi	Indian	7%	Christian	9%
	Other	8%	Hindu	6%
			Other	6%

Population density per sq. mi. 199.2
Literacy rate 91.9%
Life expectancy 70.3 male; 75.9 female
Per capita GDP $13,300
Labor force in agriculture 13%

Urban 67.6%
Infant mortality rate per 1,000 live births 16.4
HIV rate 0.5%
Unemployment rate 3.2%
Arable land 5%

Agriculture oil palm fruit, rice, natural rubber, cocoa, coconuts, pepper, chickens, pigs, cattle, goats, sheep

Natural resources fish, tin, oil, timber, copper, iron ore, natural gas, bauxite

Industries rubber and palm oil processing, light manufacturing, electronics, tin mining and smelting, timber, oil

History Malaysia has been inhabited for 6,000 to 8,000 years. Malaysian ancestors migrated to the area between 2500 and 1500 BCE. Traders from India came in the 2nd to 3rd century CE and brought Hinduism. Sumatran exiles founded Malacca about 1400. It was a trading and religious center until captured by the Portuguese in 1511; it passed to the Dutch in 1641. Islam took a firm hold in the 15th century. European traders came in the 16th century. Britain took control in 1867. Chinese began to migrate to Malaysia in the late 19th century. Japan invaded in 1941. Malaysia was created in 1963 from Malaya (which had become independent in 1957), British Singapore (where the British had founded a settlement in 1819), and Sabah (north Borneo) and Sarawak (northwest Borneo). In 1965 Singapore was separated from Malaysia. Abundant natural resources allowed prosperity, and foreign investments aided industrialization. The economy grew from the 1970s but suffered from the Asian currency crisis in the 1990s. In 2002 Malaysia passed stringent immigration laws. The Indian Ocean tsunami in 2004 took lives and displaced 8,000 people. Malaysia's economy remained strong in 2007. Its biotechnology initiative of 2006 had attracted substantial investments. Along with Indonesia and Brunei, Malaysia pledged to protect some rainforest on the island of Borneo, where palm oil plantations and logging had destroyed huge tracts of rainforest. The United States added Malaysia to its list of countries not doing enough to stop human trafficking.

Influences on food Malaysia consists of West Malaysia, on the Malay Peninsula and adjoining Thailand and Singapore, and East Malaysia, on the northern part of the large island Borneo and adjoining Brunei. Malaysia has three main cuisines, Malay, Chinese, and Indian. West Malaysia is influenced by its Thai neighbors. East Malaysia is a melting pot of tribes, traders, and adventurers. Chinese and Indian influence is strong due to mass movement of labor during the colonial period, as well as immigrant elites from East and South Asia. Nonya (Straits Chinese) cooking is associated with immigrants who settled in the 15th century and up to World War II. It uses chilies, tamarind, shrimp paste, coconut milk, and aromatic roots and leaves as in Malaysian cooking but retains the use of pork, lard, and noodles from Chinese tradition; it values hotness and sourness. Indian influence includes spices, curries, and achar (pickles). Islam, dominant in the peninsula and coastal towns of Borneo since before the 16th century, forbids consumption of pork or alcohol. Other influences include European traders and British control (1867–1963). Rice is the main food, cooked for all three meals daily, with seafood secondary.

Bread and cereals Rice, wheat; rice dishes, glutinous rice in sweets, noodles.

Meat, poultry, fish Chicken, pork, beef, goat, lamb, fish and seafood (pomfret the most prized), water buffalo, duck, eggs; prawn/shrimp pastes (blacang), dried anchovy, fish sauce, gelatin.

Dairy products Sweetened condensed milk, cream. Dairy products are uncommon, although condensed milk may be used in coffee and whipped cream in pastry.

Fats and oils Palm oil, coconut oil, lard, vegetable oil.

Legumes Soybeans and products such as soy sauce, mung beans, peanuts.

Vegetables Taro, cassava, breadfruit, seaweed, greens, yams, sweet potatoes, ti, zucchini, water chestnuts.

Fruit   Coconut, tamarind (tart pulp from tree pod), limes, pineapple, bananas, mangoes, papaya, melons, durian.

Nuts   Litchis, macadamia nuts.

Seasonings   Chilies, tamarind, coconut milk and cream, lime juice, shrimp paste, aromatic roots and leaves, soy sauce, fish sauce, garlic, onion, pepper, cumin, cinnamon, coriander, turmeric, lemon grass, ginger root, laos (of ginger root family), cocoa.

Dishes   Boiled rice (nasi). Nasi goreng (meat and vegetables fried, rice fried in the same oil, and all combined). Nasi samin (rice cooked in oil with garlic and onions, spices, broth, and chicken). Longlong (rolls of rice steamed in banana leaves). Fried noodles (kway teow). Satay (small strips of meat, chicken, or fish/seafood on thin bamboo skewers, often marinated with soy sauce and flavorings and grilled). Rendang ("dry beef curry," formerly venison, now water buffalo meat or beef, cubed and simmered with spices and flavorings in coconut milk). Chicken braised in coconut milk and chili sauce. Rempah (spice mixture of varied ingredients, often fried before use). Gulai (curry or anything cooked in coconut milk and retaining its sauce) such as shrimp curry. Baked puffs filled with ground beef curry. Sambal (hot, spicy relishes or Chilies and other spices fried together and used with a main ingredient, e.g., prawns) such as prawn sambal.

Sweets   Palm sugar, sugar. Nonya desserts mostly based on thick brown palm sugar syrup, with coconut milk, grated coconut, gelatin, and glutinous rice, for example, kuey lapis (has many different colored layers of gelatin). Naga sari (pudding of mung beans, sugar, and coconut).

Beverages   Tea, coffee, coconut juice, fruit juice, bean drinks, kava (alcoholic drink made from pepper plant).

Street food   Fried noodles, satay; sold by street vendors and in market stalls and night stores. Malays and Chinese Malays often take pork satay, Muslim Malays take goat meat, and all take chicken and hot sauces of ground Chilies, garlic, onion, laos, and peanuts.

MALDIVES
Republic of Maldives

Geography   Maldives is in the Indian Ocean southwest of India. It consists of 19 atolls with 1,190 islands, 198 inhabited. The atolls are less than 6 feet above sea level. Islands are flat and less than 5 square miles each.

Major Languages	Ethnic Groups		Major Religion
Divehi (Sinhala dialect) (official) English (spoken by most government officials)	Maldivian (South Indian, Arab) Sinhalese, other	99% 1%	Islam (official) Sunni Muslim (virtually 100%)

Population density per sq. mi. 3,331.8
Literacy rate 97%
Life expectancy 71.5 male; 76 female
Per capita GDP $4,600
Labor force in agriculture 22%

Urban 33.9%
Infant mortality rate per 1,000 live births 30.6
HIV rate NA
Unemployment rate 14.4%
Arable land 13%

Agriculture   coconuts, bananas, corn, sweet potatoes

Natural resources   fish

Industries   tourism, fish processing, shipping, boat building, coconut processing, garments

History   Maldives was settled in the 5th century BCE by Buddhist seafarers from India and Ceylon (now Sri Lanka). Islam was adopted in 1153 CE. Ceylon controlled the islands. The Portuguese dominated in Male, the capital, from 1558 to 1573. Dutch rulers of Ceylon controlled the Maldives islands during the 17th century. The British gained control of Ceylon in 1796 and made the Maldives islands a protectorate in 1887. The islands became independent in 1965 and, long a sultanate, became a republic in 1968. Inhabitants are primarily Islamic seafaring people. The Indian Ocean tsunami of 2004 killed at least 82 people and displaced more than 21,600 here. Rising sea levels threaten the country, mostly low-lying coral islands. In 2008 a boy scout reportedly saved President Gayonne (in power since 1978) from knifing by an assailant. Tourism has been developed. After a bomb explosion in Male targeting foreign tourists, the government took measures against religious groups advocating militancy and fundamentalism. In 2008 a new constitution providing for multiparty elections was adopted.

Influences on food   Maldives, consisting of approximately 1,200 islands, of which about 200 are inhabited, is a unique country in that more than 99% of its territory is sea, with land area only about the same as Singapore. The sea provides fish, the main food. Other influences include India, Arab, Islam, Ceylon, and Britain. Coconuts, bananas, corn, and sweet potatoes are grown.

Bread and cereals   Corn, rice.

Meat, poultry, fish   Fish and seafood (usually reef fish and tuna). Tuna is sold fresh, canned, smoked, or smoked and sun dried (hikimas). The latter, "Maldive fish," is important in cookery because when finely ground it thickens and flavors. Tuna is used in soup, as a paste (rihaakuru), and in filling of "short eats" gulha and bajiyaa.

Fats and oils   Coconut cream and oil.

Legumes   Beans, peas, lentils.

Vegetables   Sweet potatoes, onions.

Fruit   Coconut, bananas, limes, other tropical fruits.

Seasonings   Chili pepper, onion, lime juice, coconut milk.

Dishes   Boiled or steamed rice. Fried, grilled, or poached fish, usually served with rice, onion, coconut, chili pepper, and lime juice. Boiled or fried sweet potatoes.

National dish   Garudhiya (a soup containing chunks of tuna).

Sweets   Honey, palm tree sap, sugar. Fresh fruit. Confections made with coconut, honey, rice flour, palm tree sap, and banana.

Beverages   Tea, coffee, coconut juice, fruit juice.

MALI
Republic of Mali

Geography   Mali is in West Africa. It is a landlocked country, mostly in the Sahara. In the south are a grassy plain and the only fertile area, where the Senegal and Niger rivers provide irrigation.

Major Languages	Ethnic Groups		Major Religions	
French (official)	Mande (Bambara,		Sunni Muslim	90%
Bambara	Malinke, Soninke)	50%	Indigenous beliefs	5%
Numerous African languages	Peul	17%	Roman Catholic	5%
	Voltaic	12%		
	Tuareg and Moor	10%		
	Other	11%		

Population density per sq. mi. 26.2
Literacy rate 23.3%
Life expectancy 48 male; 51.9 female
Per capita GDP $1,000
Labor force in agriculture 80%

Urban 30.5%
Infant mortality rate per 1,000 live births 103.8
HIV rate 1.5%
Unemployment rate 8.8%
Arable land 4%

Agriculture   millet, rice, corn, cotton, vegetables, peanuts, chickens, goats, sheep, cattle, camels, pigs

Natural resources   gold, phosphates, kaolin, salt, limestone, uranium, gypsum, granite, hydropower, fish

Industries   food processing, construction, phosphates and gold mining

History   The region has been inhabited since prehistoric times. Mali was on caravan routes through the Sahara since 300. It was part of the great Mali Empire from the 12th century to the 15th century, when the Songhai Empire in the Timbuktu-Gao region gained control. Morocco conquered Timbuktu in 1591 and ruled over it for two centuries. Timbuktu was a center of Islamic study. The French subjugated the area in 1898 and named it French Sudan in 1920. Proclaimed the Sudanese Republic in 1958, it was briefly joined with Senegal to form the Mali Federation. Senegal withdrew, and the Sudanese Republic changed its name to the Republic of Mali and became independent in 1960. Political instability has continued, with military coups overthrowing the government in 1968 and 1991. In 1973–1974 famine killed 100,000 people. Drought occurred in the 1980s. In the 1990s foreign investment increased and Mali became Africa's second largest cotton producer. In 2005 locust infestation and drought threatened 10% of the people with starvation. In 2007 members of a dissident Taureg group attacked military targets in northern Mali.

Influences on food   Mali has much in common with the other countries immediately south of the Sahara. Food customs are influenced by North Africa, West Africa, France (Mali is a former French colony), foods brought from the New World, and religion. For example, leg of lamb stuffed with dates and raisins resembles Moroccan dishes. Meat and fish are often combined in sauces, and chicken and guinea-fowl are popular, as in West Africa. Baguette bread is common in towns, a French influence. Corn, tomatoes, and Chilies, all from the New World, are popular. Most people are Muslim, who do not consume pork. Much of Mali is sparsely populated desert. The fertile area is in the south, where the Senegal and Niger rivers supply fish and water for irrigation. Herders live in the north. Red meat is a luxury, but some is eaten as well as game. In country areas the traditional wood-burning hearth of three stones on which a pot sits is still used. Meat may be grilled on open fires. Ovens are uncommon.

Bread and cereals   Millet, rice, corn, wild grains, wheat; porridge, rice dishes, millet couscous (tiny balls of grain dough steamed and served like rice), noodles (kata), baguette bread.

Meat, poultry, fish   Chicken, eggs, goat, lamb, beef, pork, fish (perch, tilapia), camel, guinea fowl, pigeons, game (antelope, rock rabbit, cane rat). Meat and fish are often dried.

Dairy products   Milk, sour milk, buttermilk, curds, whey, cheese.

Fats and oils   Shea oil and butter (from the seeds of the African shea tree), red palm oil, peanut oil.

Legumes   Peanuts (groundnuts), cowpeas, beans, lentils. Legumes are important.

Vegetables   Yams, plantains, cassava, okra, sweet potatoes, tomatoes, greens, Chilies, onions.

Fruit   Dates, raisins, coconut, bananas, watermelon, mangoes.

Nuts and seeds   Kola nuts, shea nuts, watermelon seeds, sesame seeds. Nuts and seeds thicken sauces/stews.

Seasonings   Chilies, tomatoes, onions, garlic.

Dishes   Boiled millet grain and cassava mush. Cornmeal porridge. Boiled rice sometimes with a thin stew of beef and tomatoes. Meatball and peanut sauce. Stews: red meat and okra; cassava leaves with dried fish and palm oil; fish, okra, greens, and tomatoes. Steamed couscous. Dried cassava porridge with smoked fish, tomatoes, and other vegetables. Stuffed camel stomach (similar to haggis). A Bambara tribe invention, maafe (chicken and peanut stew with sweet potatoes and tomatoes).

Festive occasion dishes   Millet grain and cassava mush served with two sauces (minced meat, dried fish, and dried okra powder; and diced meat and tomatoes) mixed before serving. Jollof rice (rice and tomato or palm oil).

Sweets   Honey, sugar, peanut candy, tsnein achra (a Mali special celebration pastry of rice flour and honey).

Beverages   Beer, coffee.

Street food   Kabobs, shawerma (rotisserie lamb), bean fritters, sweet pastries, grilled sweet corn.

MALTA
Republic of Malta

Geography   Malta is an island group in the Mediterranean Sea, south of Sicily, Italy. Low hills cover the interior of the islands, Malta (95 sq. mi.), Gozo (26 sq. mi.), and Comino (1 sq. mi.). The coastline is heavily indented.

Major Languages		Ethnic Groups		Major Religions	
Maltese	(both	Maltese	97%	Roman Catholic (official)	98%
English	official)	British and other	3%	Other	2%

Population density per sq. mi. 3,307

Literacy rate 91.6%

Life expectancy 77.1 male; 81.6 female

Per capita GDP $53,400

Labor force in agriculture 3%

Urban 93.6%

Infant mortality rate per 1,000 live births 3.8

HIV rate 0.1%

Unemployment rate 6.8%

Arable land 31%

Agriculture   potatoes, melons, tomatoes, cauliflower, grapes, wheat, barley, citrus, cut flowers, green peppers, chickens, pigs, cattle, sheep, goats

Natural resources   fish, limestone, salt

Industries   tourism, electronics, shipbuilding and repair, food and beverages, pharmaceuticals

History   Malta was inhabited as early as 3800 BCE. The Phoenicians occupied it. The Carthaginians controlled it from the 6th century BCE. Present-day Maltese are descendants primarily of ancient Carthaginians and Phoenicians. Rome ruled Malta from 218 BCE. In 60 CE the apostle Paul converted the inhabitants to Christianity. Byzantine rule followed. Arabs controlled Malta from 870 until 1091 when defeated by the Normans. After rule by feudal lords, Malta came under rule by the Knights of Malta in 1530. It was seized by Napoleon in 1798, taken by the British in 1800, returned to the Knights in 1802, and reassociated with Britain from 1814. During World War II Malta was severely bombed by Germany and Italy. Malta gained independence in 1964 and became a republic in 1974. In 1979 British military forces withdrew after 179 years of presence. Malta became a full member of the EU in 2004 and joined the euro zone in 2008. In 2007 an agreement was signed to set up a SmartCity in Malta, the biggest foreign investment ever in Malta.

Influences on food   Malta's cuisine is influenced mainly by its location, in the Mediterranean Sea and near Italy. It is based on fish and seafood, pasta, and vegetables. A strong influence is the Roman Catholic Church. St. Paul was shipwrecked in Malta in 60 CE, and the Knights of St. John, drawn from the nobility of Catholic Europe, controlled Malta for centuries. Some people still eat fish on Fridays and a favorite cake, qwarezimal (which contains no fat or eggs), during Lent. Another influence is Britain, ruler of Malta for 150 years. The development of restaurants and tourism with a large proportion of British visitors emphasized British cuisine. Also, more than 1% of the population is British. Many Maltese dishes depend on local fish, vegetables, and fruits.

Bread and cereals   Wheat, barley, rice; pasta, bread, pastry, rice dishes.

Meat, poultry, fish   Chicken, pork, lamb, beef and veal, goat, eggs, fish and seafood (e.g., dolphin, anchovy).

Dairy products   Milk (cow, sheep, goat), cream, cheese (soft cheeses, e.g., ricotta, similar to cottage cheese).

Fats and oils   Olive oil, butter, lard.

Legumes   Chickpeas, fava beans, kidney beans, lentils, white beans.

Vegetables   Potatoes, tomatoes, cauliflower, green peppers, olives, spinach, zucchini, eggplant, cucumbers, peas, onions.

Fruit   Melons, grapes, citrus including the famous Maltese oranges, other fruits.

Nuts and seeds   Almonds, hazelnuts, pine nuts, walnuts, lupine seeds.

Seasonings   Salt, black pepper, tomato, onion, garlic, basil, oregano, parsley, marjoram, saffron.

Dishes   Boiled pasta, served with a tomato or cream sauce, or sometimes baked with tomato sauce or other ingredients. Ross fil-forn (baked rice, meat, tomato sauce, eggs, and saffron). Timpana (macaroni, tomato sauce, meat, eggs, and cheese baked in a flaky pastry). Lampuki pie (baked dolphin in pastry). Soppa tal-armla (widow's soup), made with green and white vegetables and garnished with a poached egg and soft cheese. Aljotta (a light fish soup flavored with garlic and marjoram). Vegetable soup containing pasta.

Sweets   Honey, sugar. Pastizzi (covered tartlets) filled with ricotta and sprinkled with sugar. Trifle (cake layered with jam and whipped cream or custard).

Beverages   Coffee, tea, wine.

Snacks   The ubiquitous pastizzi, usually filled with ricotta cheese and sprinkled with sugar, although filling can be peas, onions, and anchovy, and eaten hot, often with tall glasses of coffee or tea in mid-morning.

MARSHALL ISLANDS
Republic of the Marshall Islands

Geography   The islands are in the Pacific Ocean, halfway between Hawaii and Papua New Guinea. They are two 800-mile-long parallel chains of coral atolls of limestone and sand, only a few feet above sea level.

Major Languages		Ethnic Groups		Major Religions	
Marshallese	(both	Micronesian	89%	Protestant	55%
English	official)	U.S. white	6%	Assembly of God	26%
		Other Pacific Islander		Roman Catholic	8%
		and East Asian	5%	Other	11%

Population density per sq. mi. 902.5
Literacy rate 93.7%
Life expectancy 68.9 male; 73 female
Per capita GDP $2,900
Labor force in agriculture 21.4

Urban 70%
Infant mortality rate per 1,000 live births 26.4
HIV rate NA
Unemployment rate 33.6%
Arable land 11%

Agriculture   breadfruit, coconuts, bananas, tomatoes, melons, taro, fruits, chickens, pigs

Natural resources   coconut products, marine products, deep seabed minerals, fish

Industries   copra, tuna processing, tourism, craft items

History   First inhabited by Micronesians, the islands were explored by the Spanish in the 16th century and named for a British captain in 1788. Germany purchased them from Spain in 1899. Japan claimed them in 1914 and administered them between the world wars. After World War II, as part of the UN Trust Territory of the Pacific, they were administered by the United States from 1947 until they became independent in 1986. The Marshall Islands joined the UN in 1991. U.S. nuclear testing was done from 1946 to 1951 on Bikini and Enewetak islands. In 1986 the United States agreed to provide financial aid to the country to maintain its defense and to compensate victims of nuclear testing; the agreement was renewed in 2003.

Influences on food   The Marshall Islands are in the Micronesia group of the Pacific Islands. About 30,000 to 40,000 years ago people from Southeast Asia began to move south to the West Pacific islands and later migrated to islands further east. Influences on food in the Marshall Islands include the Micronesians who first inhabited the islands and the Spanish, British, Germans, Japanese, and Americans. Asians brought rice, soybeans, noodles, and tea. Europeans brought new food plants, wheat bread, and some animals. A New World food, the tomato, is now an important food. Main foods are fish, taro, breadfruit, rice, coconut, fruit, tomatoes, pork, and chicken. Pork, the main meat, especially for feasts, is traditionally cooked in a stone-lined pit over coals along with other foods.

Bread and cereals   Rice, wheat; rice dishes, bread, noodles.

Meat, poultry, fish   Pork, chicken, fish (mullet, mahimahi, salmon), shellfish (many kinds), eggs; spam.

Dairy products   Milk and other dairy products are uncommon.

Fats and oils   Coconut cream and oil, lard, vegetable oil and shortening, sesame oil.

Legumes   Soybeans, winged beans, peas, lentils, peanuts.

Vegetables   Breadfruit, tomatoes, taro root and leaves, sweet potatoes, plantains, yams, cassava, seaweed, green leaves, arrowroot, bitter melon, cabbage, daikon, eggplant, onions, green onions.

Fruit   Coconut, bananas, melons, lemons, limes, guavas, mangoes, papaya, pineapple, tamarind. Coconut milk is the usual liquid cooking medium. Fresh fruits are eaten as snacks.

Nuts and seeds   Candlenuts (kukui), litchis, macadamia nuts.

Seasonings   Coconut cream and milk, lime and lemon juice, salt, soy sauce, ginger, garlic, onions, chili peppers.

Dishes   Boiled taro root. Boiled or fried breadfruit. Boiled or steamed rice. Boiled or steamed greens and seaweed. Arrowroot-thickened puddings and other dishes. Fish stewed with vegetables, roasted, or marinated in lime juice and finished with onions, coconut cream, and perhaps chili peppers. Chicken or pork roasted or stewed with vegetables. Taro leaves wrapped around a filling (coconut cream, lemon, onions, and shredded beef; or a mixture of taro root, breadfruit, or sweet potato with coconut cream and seasonings) and steamed or cooked in a pit. Foods cooked in a pit: whole pig, taro, breadfruit, sweet potatoes, shellfish, whole fish, chicken pieces, taro leaves wrapped around various fillings and all bound in banana leaves.

Sweets   Sugar, immature coconuts, fresh fruit, coconut pudding.

Beverages   Coconut juice, tea, coffee, wine made from fermented sap of coconut palm blossoms.

Meals   Two or three meals daily are typical, with the same foods at all, and the evening meal the largest. A usual meal: boiled taro root, breadfruit, or rice, a fish, pork, or chicken dish, and cooked greens or seaweed.

MAURITANIA
Islamic Republic of Mauritania

Geography   Mauritania is in northern Africa, bordering the Atlantic Ocean. The fertile Senegal River valley is in the south. The wide central region is sandy plains and scrub trees. The north is arid and extends into the Sahara.

Major Languages	Ethnic Groups		Major Religions	
Arabic (official and national)	Mixed Moor/Black	40%	Islam (official)	
Pulaar (all	Moor (Maur)	30%	Sunni Muslim	99%
Soninke are	Black	30%	Other	1%
Wolof national)				
French				

Population density per sq. mi. 8.5
Literacy rate 55.8%
Life expectancy 51.6 male; 56.3 female
Per capita GDP $2,000
Labor force in agriculture 50%

Urban 40.4%
Infant mortality rate per 1,000 live births 66.7
HIV rate 0.8%
Unemployment rate 32.5%
Arable land 0.2%

Agriculture   sorghum, rice, dates, millet, corn, sheep, goats, camels, chickens, cattle

Natural resources   iron ore, gypsum, copper, phosphate, diamonds, gold, oil, fish including octopus

Industries   fish processing, iron ore and gypsum mining

History   Berbers inhabited this land in ancient times. Mauritania was a center for the Berber movement spreading Islam through western Africa in the 11th and 12th centuries. Arab tribes and the Portuguese arrived in the area in the 15th century. France gained control by the 19th century. Mauritania became a French protectorate in 1903 and part of French West Africa in 1904. It gained independence in 1960. Mauritania annexed the south of former Spanish Sahara (now Western Sahara) in 1976 and signed a peace treaty renouncing its claim in 1979. Conflicts have occurred, especially between blacks who dominate southern regions and the Moorish-Arabic people in the north. Although slavery has been abolished repeatedly, thousands continue to live in servitude. Legislation mandating prison terms for slaveholders was enacted in 2007. In a coup in 1984 Taya took control of the government; he was overthrown in a bloodless coup in 2005. In 2006 up to 10,000 people tried to emigrate in handmade boats to Spain's Canary Islands; more than 1,700 died. In 2007 Mauritania's first truly democratic presidential election since independence was held; however, the government was accused of being soft on terrorism and was overthrown by a military coup in 2008. Major oil discoveries have recently been developed.

Influences on food   Mauritania, like the other countries immediately south of the Sahara, is mostly desert and sparsely populated. Its land allows raising grains, dates, and livestock. The Atlantic Ocean and Senegal River provide fish. Mauritania's food customs are influenced by North Africa, West Africa, France, foods brought from the New World (e.g., corn, sweet potatoes), and religion. For example, the Mauritanian dish michoui (stuffed leg of lamb with dates and raisins) resembles Moroccan dishes. Meat and fish are often combined in dishes, as in West Africa. Baguette bread is common in towns, a French influence. Chilies and tomatoes are used in many dishes, a New World influence. Almost all the people are Muslim, forbidden to consume pork or alcohol. Herders live in the northern part of the country. Red meat is a luxury. In rural areas, the traditional wood-burning hearth of three stones is still used; meat may be grilled on open fires; and ovens are uncommon.

Bread and cereals   Millet, sorghum, rice, corn, wheat, wild grains; porridge, millet couscous (tiny balls of grain dough steamed and served like rice), rice dishes, noodles, baguette bread.

Meat, poultry, fish   Lamb and mutton, goat, chicken, eggs, beef, fish and seafood (e.g., octopus), guinea fowl, pigeons, camel, game (e.g., antelope, rock rabbit). Meat and fish are often dried.

Dairy products   Milk, sour milk, buttermilk, curds, whey, cheese.

Fats and oils   Shea oil and butter (from the seeds of the African shea tree), palm oil, peanut oil.

Legumes   Peanuts (groundnuts), cowpeas, beans, lentils. Legumes are important in the diet.

Vegetables   Cassava, yams, plantains, sweet potatoes, tomatoes, okra, greens, Chilies, onions.

Fruit   Dates, raisins, coconut, bananas, watermelon, mangoes.

Nuts and seeds   Kola nuts, shea nuts, watermelon seeds, sesame seeds. Nuts and seeds thicken sauces/stews.

Seasonings   Chilies, tomatoes, onions, garlic.

Dishes   Boiled millet grains and cassava mush. Corn porridge. Boiled rice, millet, or wild grains. Boiled or steamed couscous. Meatball and peanut sauce. Meat and fish sauce. Red meat stewed with okra. Stews: cassava leaves with dried fish and palm oil; fish, okra, greens, and tomatoes. Stuffed camel stomach (similar to haggis). A common dish, boiled rice with a thin stew of lamb or mutton and tomatoes. A popular dish, dried cassava porridge with smoked fish, tomatoes, and other vegetables.

Festive occasion dishes   Millet grain and cassava mush served with two sauces (minced meat, dried fish, and dried okra powder; and diced meat and tomatoes) mixed before serving. Jollof rice (rice with tomato or palm oil).

Sweets   Honey, sugar, peanut candy, baked bananas, sweet pastries, deep-fried sweetened dough balls.

Beverages   Beer, coffee.

Street food   Kabobs, shawerma (rotisserie lamb), bean fritters, sweet pastries, grilled sweet corn.

MAURITIUS
Republic of Mauritius

Geography   Mauritius is in the Indian Ocean 500 miles east of Madagascar. It is a volcanic island surrounded by coral reefs, with a central plateau encircled by mountain peaks.

Major Languages	Ethnic Groups		Major Religions	
English (official)	Indo-Mauritian	68%	Hindu	48%
Creole	Creole	27%	Roman Catholic	24%
Bhojpuri	Other	5%	Muslim	17%
French			Other	11%

Population density per sq. mi. 1,625.7
Literacy rate 87.4%
Life expectancy 70.3 male; 77.4 female
Per capita GDP $11,200
Labor force in agriculture and fishing 9%

Urban 42.3%
Infant mortality rate per 1,000 live births 12.6
HIV rate 1.7%
Unemployment rate 8.9%
Arable land 49%

Agriculture   sugarcane, tomatoes, potatoes, tea, corn, bananas, pulses, chickens, goats, cattle, pigs, sheep

Natural resources   fish

Industries   food processing (largely sugar milling), textiles, clothing, chemicals

History   Portuguese visited the island in the early 16th century. Mauritius was uninhabited when Dutch settlers came in 1638 and introduced sugarcane. In 1721 France took control and brought African slaves. Britain ruled from 1810 to 1968 and brought Indians to work on the sugarcane plantations. In the late 19th century competition from beet sugar and the opening of the Suez Canal caused economic decline. Mauritius became independent in 1968. It experienced political unrest during the 1990s. After a slowdown in two main industries, sugar production and textiles, in 2007 Mauritius tried to boost the economy through trade agreements with China and Pakistan.

Influences on food   Mauritius and its food have been influenced by the Dutch, French, British, Africans, Indians, and Chinese. The Dutch colonized Mauritius at the end of the 16th century and stayed for over a century. The French succeeded them and stayed almost another century. Britain controlled the island for a century and a half. Dutch and French colonists had imported black African slaves to work in the sugar plantations. Geographic factors allowed influences from Africa, Madagascar, the Arab world, Indian subcontinent, and Asia. Indians came to work in construction and in the sugar industry. Chinese came mainly in the 20th century and became prominent retailers and businessmen. Examples of Indian and Chinese influence on Mauritius's food are masala (curry powder) from India and min (noodles) from the Chinese. In addition to French, Indian, and Chinese cuisines, Creole cooking flourishes. Creole cookery here is a blend of black African, European (Dutch, French, British), and Indian cuisines. Mauritius is a melting pot of cuisine and language. Creole is the most common spoken language.

Bread and cereals   Corn, wheat, rice; bread, noodles, rice dishes.

Meat, poultry, fish   Chicken, goat, beef, pork, lamb, eggs, fish and seafood (red mullet, tuna, shrimp, octopus).

Dairy products   Yogurt.

Fats and oils   Butter, ghee, lard, coconut oil, vegetable oil.

Legumes   Beans, peas, lentils, peanuts.

Vegetables   Tomatoes (a small, flavorful variety, pomme d'amour), potatoes, leafy greens (brèdes), hearts of palm (palmiste), gourd (chayote, or chou chou).

Fruit   Bananas, coconut, lemons.

Seasonings   Garlic, tomatoes, mustard, saffron, Chilies, oil, vinegar, curry powder (a mixture of spices).

Dishes   Vindaye (sauce containing mustard, saffron, chilies, garlic, oil, and vinegar). Fried tuna or octopus, served topped with vindaye. Rougaille (garlic sauce dominated with tomato flavor), always served hot. Creole sauce (sauce containing tomatoes for color and flavor), served on barbecued steak, fried red mullet, boiled shrimp, omelet, or rice. Boiled or steamed rice. Brèdes (simmered leafy greens).

Sweets   Sugarcane, sugar, banana, banana flambé, coconut or rice pudding.

Beverages   Tea, sugarcane juice.

MEXICO
United Mexican States

Geography   Mexico is in southern North America, between the United States and Central America and bordering the Gulf of Mexico and the Pacific Ocean. It is a high, dry central plateau (5,000 to 8,000 ft elevation) between mountain ranges on the east and west, with tropical coastal lowlands. About 45% of the land is arid.

Major Languages	Ethnic Groups		Major Religions	
Spanish (official)	Mestizo (Amerindian-Spanish)	60%	Roman Catholic	87%
Mayan, Náhuatl, other	Amerindian	30%	Protestant	6%
indigenous languages	White	9%	Other Christian	3%
	Other	1%	Other, none	4%

Population density per sq. mi. 148.1
Literacy rate 92.4%
Life expectancy 73 male; 78.8 female
Per capita GDP $12,800
Labor force in agriculture 18%

Urban 76.3%
Infant mortality rate per 1,000 live births 19
HIV rate 0.3%
Unemployment rate 3.2%
Arable land 13%

Agriculture   sugarcane, corn, sorghum, oranges, wheat, tomatoes, bananas, beans, cotton, coffee, other fruits, chickens, cattle, pigs, goats, sheep

Natural resources   oil, silver, copper, gold, lead, zinc, natural gas, timber, fish

Industries   food and beverages, tobacco, chemicals, iron and steel, oil, mining, textiles, clothing, motor vehicles, consumer durables, tourism

History   Inhabited for more than 20,000 years, Mexico was the site of advanced civilizations from 100 to 1400 CE, the Maya, Toltec, and Aztec. The Mayas, an agricultural people, moved up from the Yucatan; they built pyramids and invented a calendar. The Toltecs were overcome by the Aztecs, who in 1325 founded Tenochtitlan, now Mexico City. The Spanish conquered the Aztec empire (1519–1521) and ruled Mexico until it became a republic in 1823. Mexico extended into the present southwestern United States, including California and Texas. Texas became a republic in 1836. The U.S.-Mexican War of 1846 to 1848 resulted in Mexico's loss of the land north of the Rio Grande. A French-supported Austrian archduke was on Mexico's throne as Maximilian I, 1864 to 1867. Dictatorial rule from 1877 to 1911 led to rebellion, a new constitution in 1917, and reform. The Institutional Revolutionary Party dominated politics from 1929 until 2000; some gains were made in agriculture, industry, and social services. In World War II Mexico declared war on the Axis Powers. It was a founding member of the UN (1945) and the Organization of American States (1948). In the mid-1970s, Mexico became a leading oil producer, and its economy grew until the 1986 collapse of oil prices. Mexico had severe economic problems in the 1980s to 1995. In 1995 an austerity plan and pledge of aid from the United States prevented collapse of Mexico's currency. In 1993 Mexico entered the North American Free Trade Agreement (NAFTA); it took effect in 1994. In 2005 Hurricane Wilma caused extensive damage in Cancun. As of 2007 more than 29 million people of Mexican ancestry were living in the United States. An estimated 7 million illegal immigrants from Mexico were in the United States. In 2008 remittances that immigrants sent back to Mexico from the United States fell sharply due to the U.S. economic slowdown. Drug-related violence intensified in 2008.

Influences on food   Most of the population lives in the high central plateau at 6,000 feet (1,800 m) or more elevation. For many, way of life and cuisine are Indian, whereas in Mexico City, one of the world's largest cities, are international influences. Throughout Mexico for centuries and still now, corn is the foundation of Mexican cuisine. To make tortillas, the bread of Mexico, corn is boiled with water and lime, soaked, drained and the skins rubbed off, ground into coarse flour (masa), mixed with water to make dough, shaped into flat circles, and cooked on a griddle. Beans and chilies are also important. The protein in beans supplements that of corn. Chilies provide flavor and vitamins. Fruits are plentiful except in the north. The Gulf of Mexico and Pacific Ocean, lakes, and rivers provide fish and shellfish. Turkeys and chocolate have long been eaten here, sometimes together and with chili, as in the national dish mole poblano. Spanish rule for three centuries was an important influence on food in Mexico. The Spanish arrival in the 16th century brought rice, wheat, onions, garlic, olives, sugar, raisins, cinnamon, nutmeg, almonds, sesame seed, cattle, pigs, sheep, and goats, thus adding meat and fats (especially lard from pigs, which made frying possible), milk, butter, and cheese to the Mexican diet. The Spanish also introduced the distillation of alcohol to native Mexican beverages, resulting in tequila and mescal (made from cactus). Thus Mexican cuisine is a blend of Indian and Spanish cuisines. Also, German immigrants introduced beer in the 19th century, and strong French influence in the second half of the 19th century resulted in rolls and sweet breads. Mexico's wide range of drinks reflects its geography and history: drinks are made from its produce including corn, cactus, sugarcane, coffee, and cocoa. Geographic diversity yields foods distinctive for the regions: Vera Cruz on the Gulf coast is famous for black beans, shrimp, fish, and fruit; the Yucatan peninsula for its seasonings, achiote (annatto), and sour orange; Puebla and Oaxaca for moles (sauces); and the northern states for beef, dairy products, and wheat flour tortillas. Also, food varies with diverse incomes, seasons, and festivals for national holidays. Religion also influences food. In this mostly Roman Catholic country, special foods are important to celebrate religious holidays and seasons, notably Christmas and Easter.

Bread and cereals   Corn, wheat, rice; tortillas, atole, bread, rolls, pan dulce (sweet bread), pastry, rice dishes.

Meat, poultry, fish   Chicken, beef, pork, goat, lamb, fish, seafood, eggs, turkey; chorizo (spicy sausage).

Dairy products   Milk (cow, goat), evaporated milk, cream, cheese.

Fats and oils   Butter, lard (manteca), vegetable oil, olive oil.

Legumes   Pinto beans, soybeans, kidney beans, black beans, green beans, chickpeas (garbanzo beans).

Vegetables   Tomatoes, chili peppers, potatoes, green onions, squash, pumpkin, prickly pear cactus, avocados, plantains, greens, onions, jicama (tuber with juicy crunchy flesh), sweet potatoes, peas, cassava, lettuce, olives.

Fruit   Oranges, bananas, guavas, mangoes, lemons, limes, papaya, pineapple, coconut, grapefruit, pomelo, melon, cactus fruit.

Nuts and seeds   Piñons (pine nuts), almonds, pepitas (pumpkin seeds), squash seeds, sesame seeds.

Seasonings   Chili peppers (fresh or dried and ground), garlic, vanilla, chocolate, achiote, cilantro, cinnamon.

Dishes   Atole (gruel or thick drink made from ground corn, water, and flavorings). Beans simmered with chilies added. Beans simmered, then pan-fried (frijoles refritos). Boiled rice. Simmered rice and beans. Rice with tomatoes and chili. Salsa (tomato, chili, and onion sauce), on the table at all meals. Hearty soups: vegetables, tortilla pieces, and chicken or meat bits; menudo (tripe and hominy). Stews (caldos) made by sautéing onion and garlic, adding meat, and simmering. Casseroles (sopas secas) made with stale tortillas or rice. Plantains boiled, mashed, and fried in oil with onions and tomatoes. Fried eggs (huevos rancheros). Carne asada (grilled beef strips). Cabrito (roasted young goat). Chicken grilled or steamed with fruit juice. Baked red snapper in achiote sauce. Mole (a sauce made of chilies, nuts, seeds, garlic, and spices, ground and fried in hot fat, water is added and the sauce is simmered; sometimes bitter chocolate is added; and cooked meat or poultry is added). Guacamole (mashed ripe avocado mixed with tomato, chopped onion, chili, and cilantro). Chilies relleños (mildly hot chili peppers stuffed with meat, fish, beans, or cheese, dipped in egg batter, and fried). Enchiladas (corn tortillas softened in hot oil or tomato-chili sauce, rolled around seasoned meat, chicken, or cheese mixture, covered with sauce and cheese, and baked). Tamales (spicy meat or chicken in corn dough, wrapped in corn husks or banana leaves, and steamed). Taco (tortilla filled with seasoned meat). Burrito (wheat flour tortilla folded around beans with salsa). Fried tortilla chips. Caesar salad (romaine lettuce with cheese and egg dressing).

National dish   Mole poblano (Pueblan sauce), turkey in a sauce made of chili, chocolate, nuts, seeds, and raisins.

Sweets   Sugarcane, raw brown cane sugar (panocha), sugar. Fruit. Crystallized fruit. Flan (sweetened egg custard topped with caramelized sugar). Arroz con leche (rice pudding).

Beverages   Coffee with milk (café con leche), atole, hot chocolate, liquefied fruit or vegetables (licuados), aguas frescas (sweetened fruit or vegetable drink with lime juice), soft drinks, beer, pulque, tequila, mescal, rum, wine, liqueur, whiskey, Margarita (tequila, lime juice, sugar, Cointreau or Triple Sec, ice cubes, with salt on glass rim).

Meals   Early breakfast: coffee, hot chocolate, or atole with fruit and pastry. Perhaps a late (midmorning) breakfast: fried eggs, bacon or beans, tomato and chili sauce, tortillas, and hot chocolate. Main meal (about 1 or 2 p.m.), five courses: soup; a dry soup of rice; a meat, chicken, or fish dish and tortillas; beans; and fruit or dessert with coffee. Evening meal: leftovers, atole, or a pastry, fruit, and hot chocolate.

Street food and snacks   Roasted ears of corn, fried pork rind (chicarrones), cut watermelon, aguas frescas, tacos, tamales, carnitas (pork chunks cooked in their own fat), candied sweet potatoes.

MICRONESIA
Federated States of Micronesia

Geography   Formerly the Caroline Islands, Micronesia consists of 607 islands in the Pacific Ocean, northeast of New Guinea. It includes the island states of Yap, Chuuk, Pohnpei, and Kosrae. The islands vary from high mountainous ones to low coral atolls. The climate is tropical.

Major Languages	Ethnic Groups		Major Religions	
English (official)	Chuukese	49%	Roman Catholic	50%
Chuukese	Pohnpeian	24%	Protestant	47%
Kosrean	Yapese	11%	Other	3%
Pohnpeian	Kosrean	6%		
Yapese	Other	10%		

Population density per sq. mi. 397.2
Literacy rate 89%
Life expectancy 68.8 male; 72.6 female
Per capita GDP $2,300
Labor force in agriculture 0.9%

Urban 66.9%
Infant mortality rate per 1,000 live births 27
HIV rate NA
Unemployment rate 22.0%
Arable land 6%

Agriculture   coconuts, cassava, sweet potatoes, black pepper, bananas, kava, betel nuts, chickens, pigs, cattle, goats

Natural resources   fish, forest products, marine products, deep seabed minerals

Industries   tourism, construction, fish processing, specialized aquaculture

History   About 30,000 to 40,000 years ago people from Southeast Asia began to move south to the West Pacific islands and later migrated to islands further east. Micronesians probably settled these islands some 3,500 years ago. Polynesians also inhabited the islands when Europeans came in the 16th century and Spain colonized these islands in the 17th century. Germany bought the islands in 1898. Japan occupied them in 1914 and ruled them after World War I. The United States seized them during World War II, after which the UN placed them in a trust territory administered by the United States. Micronesia became independent in 1986. It was admitted to the UN in 1991. A tropical storm in 2002 caused deaths and damage in Chuuk. A typhoon in 2004 destroyed much of Yap's infrastructure. In 2007, despite United States funds, Chuuk and Kosrae experienced serious economic problems. Another serious concern of Micronesians is the threat of rising sea levels inundating the low-lying islands.

Influences on food   The Pacific Ocean supplies of fish. The climate makes it possible to grow tropical fruits and vegetables. Other influences on the food of Micronesia include Asian, Spanish, German, Japanese, and the United States. Asians brought rice, soybeans, noodles, and tea. The Spanish brought new food plants, wheat bread, some animals such as cattle, milk, cheese, coffee, rice with meat dishes such as paella, and Mexican spicy cornmeal dishes such as tamales. Main foods are fish, cassava, sweet potatoes, greens, coconuts, and fruit. Pork is a main meat, especially for feasts, traditionally cooked with other foods in a stone-lined pit over coals.

Bread and cereals   Rice, wheat, corn; rice dishes, bread, noodles.

Meat, poultry, fish   Pork, chicken, beef, goat, fish (e.g., shipjack tuna), shellfish (many kinds), eggs; spam.

Dairy products   Evaporated milk (cow, goat, water buffalo), cheese. Traditionally dairy products are uncommon.

Fats and oils   Coconut oil and cream, lard, vegetable oil and shortening, butter, sesame oil.

Legumes   Soybeans, chickpeas, black beans, lentils, red beans, winged beans, peanuts.

Vegetables   Cassava, sweet potatoes, taro root and leaves, plantains, yams, breadfruit, seaweed, green leaves, arrowroot, bitter melon, cabbage, daikon, eggplant, onions, green onions.

Fruit   Coconut, bananas, lemons, limes, guavas, mangoes, papaya, pineapple, melons, tamarind. Coconut milk is the usual liquid cooking medium. Fresh fruit is eaten as snacks.

Nuts and seeds   Cashews, candlenuts (kukui), litchis, macadamia nuts.

Seasonings   Soy sauce (the basic condiment), salt, black pepper, coconut cream and milk, lime and lemon juice, ginger, garlic, onions, tamarind, chili pepper.

Dishes   Boiled cassava, sweet potatoes, or taro root. Boiled or steamed green leaves or seaweed. Boiled or steamed rice. Arrowroot-thickened puddings and other dishes. Fish and shellfish stewed with vegetables, roasted, or marinated in lime juice or vinegar, then seasoned with coconut cream or onions, ginger, and chili peppers. Meat and vegetable stews. Whole pig spit-roasted or cooked in pit with sweet potatoes, whole fish, chicken pieces, and leaf-wrapped fillings. Taro leaves wrapped around a filling (coconut cream, lemon, onions, and shredded beef; or sweet potatoes or cassava with coconut cream and seasonings), steamed or cooked in a pit.

Sweets   Sugar, immature coconut, sweet rice pudding, haupia (coconut pudding).

Beverages   Coconut juice, coffee with milk, tea, kava (mildly alcoholic drink make from pepper plant), toddy (wine made from fermented coconut palm blossom sap).

Meals   Typical are two or three meals daily, with the same foods at all, and the evening meal the largest. A usual meal: boiled cassava, sweet potatoes, or rice, a fish, chicken, or pork dish, and cooked greens or seaweed.

MOLDOVA
Republic of Moldova

Geography   Moldova is in Eastern Europe, between Romania and Ukraine. It is mainly hilly plains, with rich black soil covering three quarters of the area, and steppelands in the south.

Major Languages	Ethnic Groups		Major Religions	
Moldovan (official)	Moldovan/Romanian	78%	Eastern Orthodox	98%
(virtually the same as Romanian)	Ukrainian	8%	Jewish	2%
Russian	Russian	6%		
Gagauz (Turkish dialect)	Gagauz	4%		
	Other	4%		

Population density per sq. mi. 335.6
Literacy rate 99.2%
Life expectancy 66.8 male; 74.4 female
Per capita GDP $2,900
Labor force in agriculture 40.7%

Urban 42.6%
Infant mortality rate per 1,000 live births 13.5
HIV rate 0.4%
Unemployment rate 7.4%
Arable land 55%

Agriculture   grain, sugar beets, vegetables, grapes, sunflower seed, tobacco, chickens, sheep, pigs, cattle, goats

Natural resources   lignite, phosphorites, gypsum, limestone

Industries   sugar, vegetable oil, food processing, agricultural machinery, foundry equipment

History   The area was the independent principality of Moldavia, founded by the Viachs in the 14th century. It came under Ottoman Turkish rule in the 16th century. Russia acquired the area, Bessarabia, from Turkey in 1812. In 1918 Romania annexed it. In 1924 it became the Moldavian Autonomous Soviet Socialist Republic. In 1940 the USSR merged it with the Romanian-speaking districts of Bassarabia to form the Moldavian SSR. During World War II, Romania, allied with Germany, occupied the area. The USSR recaptured it in 1944. Moldova gained independence in 1991. Moldova legitimized the use of the Roman rather than the Cyrillic alphabet in 1989 and adopted the Romanian spelling of Moldova. During the 1990s Moldova struggled economically and with conflict between ethnic separatist groups and the majority. The Russian financial crisis in 1998 caused economic disaster in Moldova, whose foreign trade was mostly with Russia, resulting in an exodus of 600,000 Moldovans. In 2006 Russia, a major customer, imposed an embargo on Moldovan wine. In 2006 voters in Trans-Dniester (where much of Moldova's industry is located) supported independence from Moldova and eventual union with Russia; in 2007 the Moldovan president negotiated with Russia to try to end the secession of Trans-Dniester.

Influences on food   Moldova is situated between Ukraine and Romania and on what used to be a busy trade route between Western Europe and places further east. It reflects influence of its neighbors and of Byzantine cookery, Greece, and Turkey. Examples include moussaka as in Greece, Turkey, and Romania, mamaliga from Romania, and givech as in Turkey and the Balkan countries. Most people are Eastern Orthodox Christians; the observant consume no animal products during fast days and prepare special foods for holidays, notably Easter.

Bread and cereals   Corn, wheat, rye, buckwheat, barley, millet, oats; porridge, bread from rye or wheat flour, dumplings, pastry, pancakes, cakes.

Meat, poultry, fish   Chicken, lamb and mutton, pork, beef, goat, eggs; ham, sausage.

Dairy products   Milk (cow, sheep), buttermilk, cream, sour cream, cheese.

Fats and oils   Butter, bacon, lard, olive oil, vegetable oil, corn oil, sunflower seed oil.

Legumes   Kidney beans, lentils, split peas.

Vegetables   Potatoes, cabbage, beets, cucumbers, carrots, eggplant, onions, mushrooms, tomatoes, olives; pickles, sauerkraut.

Fruit   Grapes, apples, plums, apricots, cherries, blackberries, raisins, currants, quinces; jam.

Nuts and seeds   Almonds, chestnuts, hazelnuts, walnuts, sunflower seeds, poppy seeds.

Seasonings   Muzhdei (concentrated mixture of garlic and beef stock), onion, garlic, parsley, dill, ginger, tarragon.

Dishes   Moussaka (baked eggplant, ground meat, onions, and tomatoes). Mamaliga (cornmeal mush, cooked until solid and then cut into pieces). Givech, or gyuvech (earthenware dish with no lid or the food cooked in it, usually lamb or mutton with vegetables and herbs). Chorba (soup made by boiling meat with salt). Purée of kidney beans and onion with muzhdei. Meat or poultry with fruit such as braised chicken with apricot or plum sauce. Kasha (porridge of buckwheat, barley, or millet). Boiled or fried potatoes. Cucumbers in sour cream. Dumplings of flour or potatoes stuffed with meat, potatoes, or fruit and boiled. Pastry dough stuffed with ground meat or cabbage and baked or fried. Cabbage stuffed with ground meat. Fried patties of seasoned ground meat mixed with bread crumbs and milk or eggs. Meat cutlet lightly breaded and fried.

A traditional Christmas dish   Kutia (wheat grains, honey, poppy seeds, and stewed dried fruit).

Easter foods   Red or hand-decorated hard-boiled eggs. Pascha (a cheesecake with fruit and nuts). Kulich (cake made from rich sweet yeast dough, nuts, and fruit, and in a tall cylindrical shape).

Sweets   Honey, sugar. Fruit compote. Berry pudding (kisel). Spicy ginger cake.

Beverages   Milk, tea, kvass, beer, vodka, wine.

Meals   Usual is three meals a day, with lunch the largest, and snacking rare. Usual meal: soup, kasha, and bread.

MONACO
Principality of Monaco

Geography   Monaco is in Europe on the northwest coast of the Mediterranean Sea, 9 miles east of Nice, France. It is a tiny (0.75 square mile) hilly wedge of land, with magnificent scenery and a mild climate.

Major Languages	Ethnic Groups		Major Religions	
French (official)	French	47%	Roman Catholic (official)	89%
English	Monegasque	16%	Other Christian	4%
Italian	Italian	16%	Jewish	2%
Monegasque	Other	21%	Other, none	5%

Population density per sq. mi. 43,559.6
Literacy rate 99%
Life expectancy 76.1 male; 84 female
Per capita GDP $30,000
Labor force in agriculture NA

Urban 100%
Infant mortality rate per 1,000 live births 5.2
HIV rate NA
Unemployment rate 3.6%
Arable land none

Agriculture   some horticulture and greenhouse cultivation, fisheries production

Natural resources   fish, climate, scenery

Industries   tourism, construction, small-scale industrial and consumer products

History   Monaco was inhabited in prehistoric times and known to the Phoenicians, Greeks, Carthaginians, and Romans. It was taken by the Genoese in 1191. It has been independent and has belonged to the House of Grimaldi since 1297, except during the French Revolution. France annexed Monaco in 1793. After Napoleon's defeat Grimaldi rule returned and Monaco was placed under Sardinia's protection in 1815. In 1861 Monaco came under French guardianship but continued to be independent. The Prince of Monaco was an absolute ruler until the 1911 constitution. Monaco was admitted to the UN in 1993. In 1997 the 700-year rule of the Grimaldis was celebrated. Prince Rainier III ruled Monaco from 1949 until his death in 2005 and was succeeded by his son, Albert II. Monaco is famous as a tourist resort due to its climate, scenery, and elegant casinos. In 2007 planning continued to build on the surface of the water in order to increase Monaco's territory.

Influences on food   Monaco, a tiny hilly country on the coast of the Mediterranean Sea between France and Italy, is a tourist resort due to its climate, scenery, and casinos. Influences on Monaco's food include location on the Mediterranean Sea, which provides fish and shellfish, neighbors France and Italy, and the European and international tourist trade. Except for fish, food is imported.

Bread and cereals   Wheat, corn, rice; French bread (baguette), rolls, croissants, pasta, rice dishes.

Meat, poultry, fish   Fish and shellfish, beef, chicken, pork, lamb, eggs; prosciutto.

Dairy products   Milk, cream, yogurt, cheese (Brie, camembert, ricotta).

Fats and oils   Olive oil, butter, lard, margarine, vegetable oil.

Legumes   Split peas, lentils, chickpeas.

Vegetables Potatoes, tomatoes, lettuce, cucumbers, olives, green beans, eggplant, zucchini, green peppers, artichokes, peas, mushrooms, truffles, onions.

Fruit Grapes, pears, apples, cherries, strawberries, raspberries, oranges, lemons, melon, raisins.

Nuts and seeds Almonds, chestnuts, hazelnuts, walnuts, sesame seeds.

Seasonings Tomato, garlic, olive oil, vinegar, lemon juice, salt, pepper, parsley, basil, oregano, cinnamon, tarragon, thyme, bay leaf, mustard, capers, saffron, vanilla.

Dishes Bouillabaisse (fish stew made with tomatoes, garlic, olive oil, and several types of seafood, seasoned with saffron). Ratatouille (tomatoes, eggplant, and zucchini cooked in olive oil). Salade Niçoise (salad originating in Nice made with tuna, tomatoes, olives, lettuce, other raw vegetables, and sometimes hard-boiled eggs). Pan bagna (French bread sandwich made with olive oil and ingredients such as anchovies, tomatoes, green peppers, onions, olives, hard-boiled eggs, and capers). French fries. Dishes garnished with black truffles, an area specialty.

Sweets Sugar. Fresh fruit. Fruit tart. Pastry. Crepes, strawberries, and whipped cream. Petit fours. Cheesecake.

Beverages Coffee, soft drinks, wine (red, white, champagne), beer, tea, whiskey, port, sherry, gin, liqueurs.

MONGOLIA

Geography Mongolia is in north Central Asia bordering Russia and China. It is mostly a high plateau, elevation 3,000 to 5,000 feet, with mountains, salt lakes, rivers, vast grasslands, and much of the Gobi Desert in the south.

Major Languages	Ethnic Groups		Major Religions	
Khalkha Mongol (official)	Mongol (mostly Khalkha)	95%	Buddhist Lamaist	50%
Turkic	Turkic (mostly Kazak)	5%	Shamanist, Christian	6%
Russian			Muslim	4%
			None	40%

Population density per sq. mi. 5
Literacy rate 97.3%
Life expectancy 64.9 male; 69.8 female
Per capita GDP $3,200
Labor force in agriculture 39.9%

Urban 56.7%
Infant mortality rate per 1,000 live births 41.2
HIV rate 0.1%
Unemployment rate 3.2%
Arable land 1%

Agriculture hay, wheat, potatoes, barley, forage crops, goats, sheep, horses, camels, cattle, chickens, pigs

Natural resources fish, oil, coal, copper, molybdenum, tungsten, phosphates, tin, nickel, zinc, fluorspar, gold, silver, iron

Industries construction and construction materials, mining, oil, food and beverages, processing of animal products

History Mongolia is one of the oldest countries in the world. Small groups of nomads inhabited it in Neolithic times. Turkic-speaking people dominated it in the 4th to 10th centuries CE. Mongolia is the original home of the Mongols, nomadic tribes who reached greatest power in the 13th century under Kublai Khan. In the 13th century Genghis Khan united the Mongol tribes and conquered Central Asia. He and his successors ruled China and westward into Europe. His successors conquered the Chin dynasty of China in 1234 and established the Mongol (Yuan) dynasty in China in 1279. The empire disintegrated and after the 14th century the Ming dynasty of China confined the Mongols to homeland in the steppes. Mongolia was incorporated into China in 1644 and became a province of China. In 1911 with the Chinese revolution the Mongol princes declared independence from China. Aided by Russia, Mongolia became independent as the Mongolian People's Republic in 1924 and a communist regime began. In 1945 China agreed to give up Outer Mongolia and in 1946 recognized the Mongolian People's Republic. In 1992 a new constitution took effect and the country shortened its name to Mongolia. With the collapse of the USSR, Mongolia was deprived of Soviet aid and has had economic and political turmoil. Mongolia contributed troops to the U.S.-led operations in Afghanistan and Iraq. In 2005 President George W. Bush was the first U.S. president to visit Mongolia. In 2007 the United States agreed to a five-year aid program to Mongolia. Mongolia's GDP grew 9.9% in 2007 and was projected to grow significantly in 2008. Minerals such as copper and gold made up two thirds of exports in 2007, and evidence suggested gold smuggling.

Influences on food   Mongolia is the homeland of the Mongols and Tatar cuisine. The Mongolian empire stretched from China to Europe in the 13th century. Centuries later Mongolia became a Chinese province. It became independent in 1924 and was under Soviet control for most of the 20th century. This landlocked, sparsely populated country is arid (including part of the Gobi Desert) in the south and mountainous, with some pastures for cattle and land where wheat is grown, in the north. Most people were, and many still are, nomads who migrate from summer pastures to protected river valleys for the winter. Large herds of goats, sheep, horses, and camels are the mainstay of the economy. They furnish the main staples: meat, milk, cheese, and butter. Historically, Mongolians consumed red foods (meat) and white foods (dairy), and this tradition continues today, with the addition of some grain products and tea. Bread, noodles, potatoes, fruits, and imported rice and vegetables are now consumed. During summer, animals give ample milk. Horses are essential to daily life, providing milk, transport, and aid in tending herds and hunting. Mongols made horsemeat sausages, which were eaten raw, and sun-dried strips of meat (jerky). Today the cuisine remains traditional, reflecting the distinctive nomadic way of life.

Bread and cereals   Wheat, barley, millet, rice; porridge, millet grains, wheat flour pancakes, flatbreads steamed or baked on a hot metal plate (tava) over charcoal or dried dung fire, noodles, rice dishes.

Meat, poultry, fish   Lamb and mutton, goat, beef, chicken, pork, camel meat, horsemeat, fish, eggs; horsemeat sausage, dried horsemeat (jerky). Camel meat is banned in some areas.

Dairy products   Milk (sheep, goat, cow, camel, mare), sour milk (similar to yogurt), milk leather (made from the film skimmed off boiled milk and air-dried), fresh cheese, dried curds, clotted cream. Mare's milk (ayrag) is favored and is drunk half fermented, thus sour and sometimes slightly fizzy. After making butter the buttermilk is boiled to form curds, which are dried in the sun and stored for winter, then mixed with hot water and drunk.

Fats and oils   Butter (usually from cow or sheep milk), fat of fat-tailed sheep, lard. Fat of fat-tailed sheep is rendered for cooking and eaten as a delicacy.

Vegetables   Potatoes, cabbage; sauerkraut.

Fruit   Some fruits are eaten.

Seeds   Sesame seeds.

Dishes   Meat barbecued (broiled) on an open grill over charcoal, in a tava, or in a hot pot that sits on the table; it is also added to soups, stuffed into pancakes, and served on sesame seed buns (Newman, 2000b). This "Mongolian fire pot" is a covered metal (brass or tin) pot with a chimney in the center whose base is a brazier heated by coals. A slice of meat (usually lamb or mutton) can be cooked in it in 30 seconds, then taken out, dipped in sauce, and eaten. Broth can be heated in the basin, and in it pieces of food (meat, then vegetables, and sometimes noodles) are cooked, then eaten or ladled with the resulting broth into bowls as soup. Steamed or boiled noodles or rice. Millet porridge. Millet fried or roasted until it pops.

Sweet   Milk pie (cheese mixed with sugar and flour and then baked).

Beverages   Mongolian tea (tea made with milk and salt, and sometimes a little fried or roasted millet and/or a lump of raw sheep-tail fat added). Kumys (wine distilled from fermented milk, traditionally from a mare), a specialty.

Meals and service   Three meals a day are typical. Fingers are used to eat. Tea is drunk with meals and snacks (Cramer, 2001; Newman, 2000b).

MONTENEGRO
Republic of Montenegro

Geography   Montenegro is in southeastern Europe on the Balkan Peninsula, bordering the Adriatic Sea. It is rugged and mountainous, with fertile river valleys and a narrow, highly indented coastline.

Major Languages	Ethnic Groups		Major Religions	
Montenegrin (official)	Montenegrin	43%	Orthodox	70%
Serbian	Serbian	32%	Muslim	21%
Bosnian	Bosniak	8%	Roman Catholic	4%
Albanian	Albanian	5%	Other	5%
Croatian	Other	12%		

Population density per sq. mi. 127.2
Literacy rate NA
Life expectancy 74.2 male; 80.3 female
Per capita GDP $3,800
Labor force in agriculture 2%

Urban 61.2%
Infant mortality rate per 1,000 live births 10.3
HIV rate NA
Unemployment rate 30.3%
Arable land 14%

Agriculture   potatoes, grapes, tomatoes, grains, tobacco, citrus, olives, chickens, sheep, cattle, pigs

Natural resources   bauxite, hydroelectricity, fish

Industries   steelmaking, aluminum, agricultural processing, consumer goods, tourism

History   Montenegro was part of the Roman Empire and the Byzantine Empire. It had been independent since 1389. After World War I, in 1918, it was joined with the Kingdom of Serbs, Croats, and Slovenes. This country was named Yugoslavia in 1929. Germany invaded Yugoslavia in 1941, and Italian forces occupied part of Montenegro during World War II. Yugoslavia became the Socialist Federal Republic of Yugoslavia in 1945. It was comprised of the republics of Montenegro, Bosnia and Herzegovina, Croatia, Macedonia, Serbia, and Slovenia. Ethnic tensions increased in the 1980s. After a 10-year civil war, Yugoslavia broke up in the 1990s. Croatia and Slovenia declared independence in 1991. In 1992 Serbia and Montenegro proclaimed a new Federal Republic of Yugoslavia, which was renamed Serbia and Montenegro in 2003. Montenegro declared independence in 2006, severing some 88 years of union with Serbia. Montenegro became a member of the UN in 2006. Montenegro uses the euro as its official currency, even though it is not a member of the EU. In 2007 Montenegro adopted a constitution and took steps toward attaining EU membership. Direct foreign investment increased, the budget showed a surplus, and real wages increased.

Influences on food   Rome, Byzantium, the Ottoman Empire, Turkey, and neighboring Balkan countries have influenced Montenegro's food. Climate, geography, and religions have also influenced the food. The country has mountains and little cultivated land, so sheep are more important than cattle, and smoked mutton (pršuta) is a specialty. In summer the plentiful milk is made into clotted cream, butter, yogurt, and cheese. In the interior highlands, pockets of fertile soil yield corn and potatoes. Along the Adriatic, mountains are circled with vineyards, citrus orchards, and olive groves. The seacoast provides fish. Most people of Montenegro are Orthodox Christians; the observant adhere to the numerous feasting and fasting days of the church calendar. Many people of Montenegro (21%) are Muslims, who fast from sunup to sundown during the month of Ramadan and do not consume pork. Christians may eat pork.

Bread and cereals Wheat, corn, rice; porridge, rice dishes, leavened wheat loaves, pita bread (thin, round bread with pocket), wheat flour pasta, pies, dumplings, and filo dough (thin pastry), couscous. Meals include bread.

Meat, poultry, fish Chicken, eggs, lamb and mutton, beef and veal, pork, fish; ham, sausage.

Dairy products Milk (cow, sheep), buttermilk, cream, sour cream, yogurt, cheese (especially feta).

Fats and oils Butter, margarine, vegetable oils, olive oil.

Legumes Chickpeas, fava beans, black beans, white beans, lentils.

Vegetables Potatoes, tomatoes, olives, eggplant, cabbage, cucumbers, mushrooms, onions; sauerkraut.

Fruit Grapes, lemons, other citrus, apples, berries, cherries, peaches, pears, plums, dates, figs.

Nuts and seeds Almonds, walnuts, pistachios, poppy seeds, sesame seeds.

Seasonings Garlic, dill, mint, cardamom, cinnamon, oregano, parsley, pepper, paprika, lemon juice.

Dishes Soups often with legumes as important ingredients. Wheat or cornmeal porridge. Steamed wheat kernels. Boiled rice. Meat and vegetable casseroles such as moussaka (baked minced lamb, eggplant, onions, and tomato sauce). Veal stew with paprika. Fried fish. Dumplings and pies filled with meat, cheese, eggs, vegetables, nuts, or fruit (e.g., cheese and egg pie). Cabbage stuffed with meat or rice. Serbian cheese and egg pie (gibanjica). Vegetables (e.g., eggplant) cooked with tomatoes and sautéed onions and a small amount of water.

Sweets Honey, sugar. Milk pudding. Custard. Fruit preserves. Fruit compote. Slatko (fruit cooked in heavy syrup). Fruit-filled dumplings and strudels. Pastry filled with dried fruits or nuts. Baklava (baked pastry of filo dough layered with nut filling, soaked in flavored syrup). Potica (sweet yeast bread rolled in walnut, butter, cream, and egg filling). Kolijivo (wheat kernels cooked with sugar, dried fruit, and ground nuts).

Beverages Coffee (strong, thick, sweet, often flavored with cardamom; made in a long-handled metal briki), tea (sweet), fruit juice, wine, plum brandy (sljivovica). The Balkans are well known for their wines and distilled spirits.

Meals Three meals a day, with the main meal at midday, and frequent snacking is typical.

Snacks Pastries, ice cream, small kabobs, meat balls (kofta), vegetable salads, coffee, wine, plum brandy.

MOROCCO
Kingdom of Morocco

Geography Morocco is in North Africa, bordering the Atlantic Ocean and the Mediterranean Sea. The land is fertile plain on the Atlantic coast, mountains on the Mediterranean coast, the Atlas Mountains from northeast to south, a cultivated central plateau, and an arid area in the east and southeast.

Major Languages	Ethnic Groups		Major Religions	
Arabic (official)	Arab-Berber	99%	Islam (official)	
Berber dialects	Other	1%	Muslim (Sunni 97%)	99%
French (often used for business, government)			Other	1%

Population density per sq. mi. 199.3
Literacy rate 55.6%
Life expectancy 69.2 male; 74 female
Per capita GDP $4,100
Labor force in agriculture 40%

Urban 55%
Infant mortality rate per 1,000 live births 38.2
HIV rate 0.1%
Unemployment rate 9.7%
Arable land 19%

Agriculture   wheat, sugar beets, potatoes, barley, citrus, grapes, vegetables, olives, chickens, sheep, goats, cattle, pigs

Natural resources   phosphates, iron ore, manganese, lead, zinc, fish (mostly sardines), salt

Industries   phosphate rock mining and processing, food processing, leather goods, textiles, construction, tourism

History   Home of the Berbers since the second millennium BCE, Morocco was traded with by the Phoenicians along the Mediterranean during the 12th century BCE and had settlements by Carthage along the Atlantic in the 5th century BCE. In 42 CE Rome annexed Morocco as part of the province of Mauritania. The Arabs invaded in 685 CE and converted most of the inhabitants to Islam. In the 11th and 12th centuries a Berber empire throughout northwest Africa and Spain was ruled from Morocco. During the 17th and 18th centuries Morocco was one of the Barbary states, headquarters of pirates who pillaged Mediterranean traders. In the 19th century Spain gained control of part of Morocco. In the early 20th century France controlled the rest, a French protectorate from 1912. In 1956, Morocco gained independence from France and Spain and acquired the international seaport Tangier. Morocco annexed the disputed area of Western Sahara in the mid-1970s and in 1976 Spanish troops withdrew. Conflicts with Mauritania and Algeria over the region continued into the 1990s. King Hassan II reigned from 1961 until his death in 1999 and was succeeded by his eldest son. Terrorist attacks occurred in Casablanca in 2003. An earthquake in 2004 killed at least 629 people. In 2007 several bombings occurred in Casablanca and near the U.S. consulate and a U.S. cultural center. In 2008 the government arrested 32 alleged terrorists, including the leader of the Islamist party. Marrakech is the chief city of central Morocco and the first of Morocco's four imperial cities; its ancient section, the medinah, was designated a UNESCO World Heritage site in 1985.

Western Sahara,   bounded by Morocco on the north and Mauritania on the south, was the Spanish protectorate Spanish Sahara until 1976, when Spain withdrew. Morocco annexed most of the land and Mauritania annexed the remainder. Mauritania withdrew in 1979. Fighting between Morocco and guerilla forces for independence fought over the area until a cease-fire was implemented in 1991. Former U.S. secretary of state James A. Baker III served as UN envoy from 1997 to 2004, but the dispute was not resolved. Phosphates are the major resource.

Influences on food   Morocco s fertile plain, plateau, high mountains, and desert produce grain, fruit, vegetables, and livestock. The long coast on the Atlantic and Mediterranean provides fish and seafood. Other influences on Morocco's food include the indigenous Berbers and the Phoenicians, Carthaginians, Romans, Arabs, Spanish, and French. The Arabs brought thin bread (which evolved into thin pastry), eastern spices, and the sweet and sour combination to give the sweet, sour, spicy flavor that is typically Moroccan. Morocco, Algeria, and Tunisia occupy the northwest corner of Africa known in Arabic as Maghreb (the west), differentiated from the Middle East by substantial populations of nomadic Berbers. These countries have similar cuisine and have influenced France by exporting foods such as couscous, merguez sausage (made from beef instead of pork to comply with Islamic dietary law and spiced with red hot chili peppers), and Arab-style pastries. Moroccan restaurants have opened in Paris and elsewhere. In Morocco Arab cuisine predominates, although nomads eat Bedouin food (mainly dairy products such as milk, clarified butter, and yogurt from sheep, goats, and camels, thin unleavened bread, boiled mutton served on rice, dates, small game, locusts, and coffee). Consumption of pork or alcohol is prohibited, and fasting from sunup to sundown during the month of Ramadan is required for

Muslims. Moroccan cuisine is distinctive for its lamb dishes, bastilla (spicy pigeon or chicken pie), and sweet pastries with almonds and honey.

Bread and cereals Wheat, barley, corn, millet, rice; flatbreads, very thin pastry (warqa), couscous (dried tiny pellets made from grain, usually semolina wheat), pasta, rice dishes.

Meat, poultry, fish Lamb and mutton, chicken, goat, beef, pork, fish (sardines), eggs, pigeon; merguez sausage.

Dairy products Milk (cow, sheep, goat, camel), buttermilk, yogurt, cheese.

Fats and oils Olive oil, sour fresh butter (zebeda), preserved clarified butter (smen), butter, vegetable oil.

Legumes Chickpeas, fava beans, lentils.

Vegetables Potatoes, olives, cucumbers, eggplant, okra, tomatoes, greens, cabbage, sweet peppers, radishes.

Fruit Lemons, oranges, grapefruit, grapes, dates, cherries, peaches, strawberries, bananas, watermelon, raisins.

Nuts and seeds Almonds, hazelnuts, pine nuts, pistachios, sesame seeds.

Seasonings Salt, black pepper, onions, garlic, herbs (parsley, mint, basil, coriander, marjoram), spices (cinnamon, ginger, saffron, cumin, cardamom, cloves, chili peppers, anise, allspice, caraway, nutmeg, turmeric), lemon juice, rosewater, orange blossom water; harissa (chili pepper and garlic paste condiment), ras el hanout (a mixture of 10 to 25 herbs and spices).

Dishes Harira (soup of lamb, chickpeas and/or lentils, spices, lemon, cinnamon, and thickened with egg), usually the first dish eaten to break fast in the evening during Ramadan. Tagine (stew), any combination of meat, poultry, fish, vegetables, and fruits simmered slowly. Grilled marinated lamb kabobs. Lamb or chicken simmered with lemons and olives. Bastilla (spicy pigeon or chicken pie). Steamed chicken stuffed with couscous, honey, nuts, and raisins. Baked fish covered with almond paste. Marinated vegetable salad. Orange and radish salad. Salted, pickled olives. Msir (lemons salted and preserved in a tightly covered jar).

National dish Steamed couscous topped with lamb stew.

Sweets Honey, sugar. Fresh fruit. Mixed dates, nuts, and raisins. Briwat (almond paste, rice, and honey wrapped in a thin crust). Ghoriba (almond-topped cookies of flour, butter, and sugar). Gab el ghzal (crescent-shaped pastries of very thin dough wrapped around an almond and sugar paste with orange blossom water).

Beverages Mint tea (very sweet, offered to everyone entering a home or business), lemonade, coffee.

Meals and service Typical is one large midday meal and snacks. The meal usually has one main dish, salad, and bread; fresh fruit and nuts; followed with mint tea. The meal is served on a low table. Diners sit on cushions and eat from the communal dishes using fingers of the right hand; bread is used to scoop stews and sop sauces.

Snacks Sweet couscous, pudding, pastry.

Mezze Olives, cheese cubes, eggplant purée (ghanoush), hummus (chickpea dip), small kabobs, falafel (small fried bean patties). The mezze tradition (snacks with drinking) is practiced, although Muslims do not drink alcohol.

Moroccan feast (diffa) Six to 20 or more dishes served in a certain order, as follows. Bastilla (flaky, spicy pigeon or chicken pie), made of layers of paper-thin pastry enclosing layers of ground almonds mixed with sugar and cinnamon alternating with pigeon or chicken stewed with onions, ras el hanout, and saffron, bound with a lemony egg sauce, baked, and sprinkled with sugar and cinnamon. Steamed lamb (chou) or spit-roasted lamb or kid (mechoui). Tagines (the last one of lamb, onions, and honey), fish, or chicken. Couscous. Mint tea.

MOZAMBIQUE
Republic of Mozambique

Geography Mozambique is in southern Africa bordering the Indian Ocean. It is mostly coastal lowlands and low-lying plateaus rising to mountains in the west. It has rivers and ports, with the Zambezi the largest river.

Major Languages	Ethnic Groups		Major Religions	
Portuguese (official)	Makuana	15%	Roman Catholic	24%
Emakhuwa	Makhuwa	15%	Other Christian	18%
Xichangana	Tsonga	9%	Muslim	18%
Elomwe	Sena	8%	Indigenous beliefs	17%
Cisena	Lomwe	7%	None	23%
	Other African	46%		

Population density per sq. mi. 70.3
Literacy rate 44.4%
Life expectancy 41.6 male; 40.4 female
Per capita GDP $800
Labor force in agriculture 81%

Urban 34.5%
Infant mortality rate per 1,000 live births 107.8
HIV rate 12.5%
Unemployment rate NA
Arable land 5%

Agriculture cassava, sugarcane, corn, cotton, cashew nuts, tea, coconuts, sisal, citrus, tropical fruits, potatoes, sunflowers, chickens, cattle, goats, pigs, sheep

Natural resources fish, coal, titanium, natural gas, hydropower, tantalum, graphite

Industries food, beverages, chemicals, aluminum, oil products, textiles, cement

History Mozambique was inhabited in prehistoric times. Bantus migrated to Mozambique in about the 3rd century CE. Arab and Swahili traders occupied the coastal area from the 14th century. In 1505 the Portuguese established a port on the coast, on the trade route to the East, and colonized Mozambique. After Portuguese colonial rule for centuries and a 10-year war, Mozambique became independent in 1975. A communist system developed. Most of the whites emigrated. In the 1980s drought and civil war caused famine and many deaths. After civil wars in the 1970s and 1980s, a new constitution in 1990 provided for multiparty elections. A peace treaty was signed with the rebels in 1992. Government changes occurred and a free-market economy began. In 1999 and 2000, floods killed hundreds and displaced over a million people. Flooding and cyclones in 2007 left many people dead or homeless. Real GDP growth averaged nearly 8% annually during the period 2000 to 2008. In 2007 the country continued to increase food production, and donors for 2008 increased. Two oil refineries were planned.

Influences on food Arab merchants and slave traders brought spices from the East to this southeastern part of Africa. The Portuguese established a port here on the trade route to the East. Portuguese trade and colonization influenced Mozambique's cuisine. The Portuguese brought pigs, chickens, salt cod, olives, coffee, and tea. From the East they brought oranges, lemons, spices, new kinds of rice and beans, and probably bananas, sugar, and tropical fruits. From America via Angola, another Portuguese colony, they introduced corn, tomatoes, potatoes, sweet potatoes, chili and sweet peppers, pineapple, and cassava. Rice, spices, and fruits of the Orient are more prominent in Mozambique than in Angola. Portuguese influence remains, for example in sweet dishes containing eggs. Immigrants from the former Portuguese province of Goa, on the west coast of India, settled in Mozambique, adding an Indian influence of curries and coconut dishes. Mozambique's long coast supplies fish and its fine harbors provide an outlet for the interior of southern Africa. Its yellow sand beaches became a favorite holiday playground for Europeans of the interior.

Bread and cereals   Corn, rice, wheat; Portuguese-style bread, fritters, rice dishes.

Meat, poultry, fish   Chicken, eggs, beef, goat, pork, mutton, fish and seafood (salt cod, clams, shrimp, prawns).

Dairy products   Milk.

Fats and oils   Coconut butter, butter, olive oil, peanut oil.

Legumes   Peanuts, beans.

Vegetables   Cassava, potatoes, olives, tomatoes, sweet potatoes, chilies, sweet peppers, green leaves, pumpkin, onions, parsley, plantains.

Fruit   Coconut, oranges, lemons, limes, bananas, pineapple, papaya, watermelon.

Nuts and seeds   Cashew nuts (used in many dishes), sunflower seeds, sesame seeds, watermelon seeds.

Seasonings   Chilies, garlic, cinnamon, cloves, coriander, turmeric, other curry spices, lemon and lime juice.

Dishes   Boiled rice. Curries such as curried mutton. Dishes with coconut milk used as the cooking liquid: fish and shrimp stew; rice cooked in coconut milk with onions, tomatoes, and chili peppers (arroz de coco). Coastal seafood hotpots (filleted fish and shelled shrimp layered with sweet peppers, powdered chilies, tomato, onion, coriander, olive oil, and coconut milk; simmered; then topped with warmed peanut oil and eaten with rice). Shrimp fritters (circles of thin pastry folded around a sautéed mixture of shrimp, garlic, parsley, onions, red pepper, and cinnamon, deep-fried in peanut oil). Matata (clams, nuts, and pumpkin leaves). Zambezi River valley chicken simmered in coconut milk with cashew nuts, served with baked sweet potatoes or boiled rice. Mozambique's most famous dish, piri-piri (dish or sauce flavored with small hot chilies); the sauce is eaten over meat, fowl, fish, and shellfish, usually with rice. A favorite, prawns marinated or basted with piri-piri and grilled.

Sweets   Sugarcane, sugar. Coconut pudding and candy. Papaya and egg yolk pudding (puréed papaya, lime juice, water, sugar, cinnamon, and cloves, cooked and poured into beaten egg yolks while beating until thick).

Beverages   Tea, coffee.

MYANMAR
Union of Myanmar (formerly Burma)

Geography   Myanmar is in Southeast Asia, bordering the Bay of Bengal, in the northwest part of the Indochina Peninsula. It has mountains, dense forests, fertile delta, and rivers with valleys. Climate is tropical monsoon.

Major Languages	Ethnic Groups		Major Religions	
Burmese (official)	Burman	68%	Buddhist	89%
Many ethnic minority	Shan	9%	Protestant	4%
languages	Karen	7%	Muslim	4%
	Chinese, other	16%	Other	3%

Population density per sq. mi. 188.1
Literacy rate 89.9%
Life expectancy 60.7 male; 66.3 female
Per capita GDP $1,900
Labor force in agriculture 70%

Urban 30.6%
Infant mortality rate per 1,000 live births 49.1
HIV rate 0.7%
Unemployment rate 10.2%
Arable land 15%

Agriculture   rice, sugarcane, pulses, beans, sesame, peanuts, chickens, cattle, pigs, goats, sheep

Natural resources   fish, oil, timber, tin, antimony, zinc, coper, tungsten, lead, coal, marble, limestone, precious stones, natural gas, hydropower

Industries   agricultural processing, wood and wood products, construction materials, pharmaceuticals, garments

History   Myanmar, known as Burma until 1989, has long been inhabited. Indo-Aryans entered this area around 700 BCE. Burmese arrived from Tibet before the 9th century. By the 11th century a Buddhist monarchy was established. In 1272 the Mongol dynasty of China conquered this land, which China ruled until the 16th century. The Portugueese, Dutch, and English traded in Burma in the 16th and 17th centuries. Britain captured Burma through wars from 1824 to 1884 and ruled it as part of India until 1937, when it became self-governing. During World War II, Burma was occupied by Japan and was a battleground; the Burma Road was the Allies' supply line to China. The country gained independence in 1948. Burma was once the richest nation in Southeast Asia, but the regime from 1962 to 1988 advanced economic socialization and enforced isolation from other countries. The UN granted the country less-developed status in 1987. Although free elections were held in 1990, military opposition and ethnic conflict have continued. An opposition leader, Aung San Suu Kyi, was awarded the Nobel Peace Prize in 1991. The Indian Ocean tsunami of 2004 killed at least 61 people here. In 2007 soaring fuel costs led to public protests with security forces cracking down on monasteries and firing on protestors. In 2008 a cyclone caused great damage: at least 84,537 deaths, over 53,000 homeless, and loss of much of the livestock and rice crop.

Influences on food   China and India have influenced Burmese cooking: China contributed rice and noodle dishes, soy sauce, and mushrooms. India provided aromatic seasonings and curry dishes. Burma's fertile land produces rice and other food crops and supports livestock. Rice is the main staple food. The long coastline supplies fish and shellfish. Freshwater fish are preferred to sea fish, whose smell is masked by using turmeric and ginger. Inle Lake, one of Burma's scenic attractions, has semi-aquatic villages, floating island gardens, and renowned rowing; rowers use a leg wrapped around an oar to row to catch carp (ngapein). Burma shares a similar cuisine with neighbor Thailand, as in hot chilies and fish sauces and pastes, although Burmese prefer to cook in peanut or sesame oil (instead of coconut oil) and without many aromatic herbs; as a result their curries are less smooth and sweet although just as hot as Thailand's. In Shan states of northern Burma, bordering China, cooking reflects Chinese influence and is less varied than in the rest of Burma and in Thailand (e.g., soy sauce instead of fish sauces and pastes, and soups and fried dishes instead of curry sauces).

Breads and cereals   Rice, corn; steamed rice, rice noodles.

Meat, poultry, fish   Fish (carp, catfish, anchovies), shrimp, chicken, beef, pork, goat, lamb and mutton, eggs.

Dairy products   Sweetened condensed milk, whipping cream.

Fats and oils   Peanut oil, sesame oil, lard, bacon, ghee (clarified butter).

Legumes   Soybeans, mung beans, broad beans, peanuts; soybean milk, tofu (bean curd), tempeh (chewier curd).

Vegetables   Bean sprouts, bamboo shoots, cabbage, green onions, taro root, potatoes, sweet potatoes, water chestnuts, plantains, mushrooms, pumpkin, squash, lotus root.

Fruit   Coconut, limes, mangoes, pineapple, bananas, papaya, durian, tamarind, oranges, lemons, melons.

Nuts and seeds   Almonds, cashews, lotus seeds, pumpkin seeds, sesame seeds, watermelon seeds.

Seasonings   Garlic, green onions, shallots, chili peppers, lemon grass, ginger, turmeric, curry powder, salt.

Condiments   Prepared ngapi (fish paste), ngan-pya-ye (fermented liquid fish sauce), soy sauce; homemade balachaung (paste of finely shredded dried shrimp, garlic, ginger, turmeric, shrimp paste, onion, and sesame oil).

Dishes   Steamed rice, served hot at all meals, fluffy and just sticky enough to hold together when eaten with the fingers, the traditional method of eating; the dish htamin lethoke literally means rice mixed with the fingers). Other dishes may be served at room temperature. Fried rice, a one-dish meal. Danbauk (pilaf rice cooked with ghee). Oh-no kauk-swe (chicken and noodles with coconut milk curry). Bin lay (pork curry with pickled mango). Inle Lake carp stuffed with roe, seasonings, condiments, and marigold leaves. Fried fish. Unripe mango dipped in sugar, salt, and ground chilies. Spicy salads of unripe mango strips with shrimp or cashews.

Shan uplands dishes   Stir-fried pork and bamboo shoots. Fried fish with soybean cake. Three-layer pork (chunks of skin, fat, and meat from a bacon cut, fried in garlic, ginger, and shallots). Fried buffalo skin crisps. Fried garlicky shoots. Kneaded fish rice (cooked fish boned and kneaded and mixed with cooked rice and seasonings, sold at five-day bazaar meets and served with hot tea and chilies on the house, as in all Shan areas.

National dish   Mohinga (small rice flour noodles in a thin sauce of fish and coconut curry), accompanied by hard-boiled eggs, limes, fried garlic, green onions, and bite-size fried patties of shrimp or mung beans.

Sweets   Sugarcane, sugar. Fruit. Candy or other sweets made of beans, sweet potatoes, or sticky rice. Thayesa (food for salivary juices, nibbles eaten at any time).

Beverage   Tea (strong, sweet, and served with milk), hot water, soup, soybean milk, fruit and bean drinks, beer.

Meals and service   Two or more meals a day, depending on income, is usual, with soup and rice in all meals. The empty plate or cup indicates that the diner is still hungry or thirsty; leaving a small amount of food or beverage signals satiety. Pickled tea leaf (lepet) is served after a meal (to clear the palate), usually with tea and sometimes with fried garlic, toasted sesame seeds, fried broad beans, and salt.

Street food and snacks   Mohinga, fruit, tea. Snack stalls and tea houses are prevalent, and snacking is popular.

N

NAMIBIA
Republic of Namibia

Geography   Namibia is in southwestern Africa, bordering the Atlantic coast. It is a high plateau, elevation 3,000 to 4,000 feet, with woodland, savanna, four rivers, and the Namibia desert in the west and the Kalahari in the east.

Major Languages	Ethnic Groups		Major Religions	
English (official)	Ovambo	49%	Lutheran	50%
Afrikaans (most common)	Other black	38%	Other Christian	30%
German	White	6%	Indigenous beliefs	20%
Indigenous languages	Mixed	7%		

Population density per sq. mi. 6.6
Literacy rate 88%
Life expectancy 50.4 male; 49.4 female
Per capita GDP $5,200
Labor force in agriculture 47%

Urban 35.1%
Infant mortality rate per 1,000 live births 45.6
HIV rate 15.3%
Unemployment rate 5.3%
Arable land 1%

Agriculture   roots and tubers, corn, millet, sorghum, peanuts, grapes, chickens, sheep, cattle, goats, pigs

Natural resources   fish, diamonds, copper, uranium, gold, silver, lead, tin, lithium, cadmium, salt, hydropower

Industries   meatpacking, fish processing, dairy products, mining

History   San people may have inhabited this land more than 2,000 years ago. Bantu-speaking Herero came in the 1600s; Ovambo came in the 1800s. In the late 15th century Portuguese explorer Bartholomeu Dias was the first European to visit. In 1890 the land became a German protectorate, Southwest Africa. In 1915, during World War I, South Africa took the land. The League of Nations gave South Africa a mandate over the land in 1920. The UN General Assembly named the area Namibia in 1968. After many years of war for independence starting in 1966, Namibia gained independence in 1990. In 1994 Namibia's main deepwater port, Walvis Bay, which had remained in South Africa's control after independence, was returned to Namibia's control. In 2007 the government and De Biers diamond mining company agreed to establish the Namibia Trading Company as a joint venture to sell some of Namibia's diamonds to local companies. The Rossing uranium mine announced plans for expansion.

Influences on food   This large country in southern Africa has a long Atlantic coastline that provides fish and a high plateau that allows grain, roots, peanuts, grapes, and livestock production. Other influences include African, European, South African, and Southeast Asian. Portuguese Bartolomeu Dias was the first European to sail around the southern tip of Africa, thereb opening the sea route to India. In the 17th century the Dutch East India Company established a settlement at the Cape of Good Hope and began trading with the indigenous population and bringing goods from the East. Later European farmers came. They and their descendants, mainly Dutch and German and later known as Boers (or Afrikaners), imported slave labor from Southeast Asia. These Malaysian slaves founded the Cape Malay cuisine prominent in southern Africa. The British took control of South Africa in 1814 and sent British settlers, prompting the Great Trek of the Boers into the interior. Indians came to work in sugar plantations in the eastern part of the region. The Dutch and Germans brought an appreciation for jams, preserves (konfyt), and baked goods. They founded large self-sufficient estates. French Huguenots founded the wine industry. The Malays were expert at fishing and preserving fish. Spiced pickled fish and dried fish supplied provisions for ships visiting the Cape. Foods of the Great Trek were dried fish, sausages (boerewors) of mixed meats including game, biltong (dried strips of salted meat, often game), and potjiekos (food such as venison cooked in a potjie, a three-legged pot suspended over fire). The trekkers used old termite hills as ovens, first cooking a potjie food on top where a hole had been cut out and then baking sourdough bread inside after sealing the openings. Braai (barbecue), cooking on a wood fire, was used for some meats. The trekkers planted corn, a New World influence, soon cultivated by the Africans. Germany controlled the area now Namibia from 1890 to 1915 and South Africa controlled it to 1968, leaving their influences. Rural people eat much as their East African ancestors did: porridge, beans, melon, pumpkin, greens, insects, dairy products, and game; cattle were wealth and seldom eaten. Bushmen also eat desert berries, wild onions, and wild fruits.

Bread and cereals   Corn, millet, sorghum, wheat, rice; porridge, bread, doughnuts, tarts, cookies, rice dishes.

Meat, poultry, fish   Lamb and mutton, chicken, eggs, beef, goat, pork, fish, seafood, antelope (e.g., springbok), ostrich, ostrich eggs.

Insects   Locusts, caterpillars, termites (white ants), ant larvae. Insects are fried or roasted.

Dairy products   Milk, buttermilk, cream, yogurt, cheese.

Fats and oils   Fat of fat-tailed sheep, butter, fish oil, vegetable oil.

Legumes   Peanuts, beans, peas, lentils.

Vegetables   Green leaves, pumpkin, cabbage, potatoes, cucumbers, carrots, squash, tomatoes, onions, eggplant.

Fruit   Grapes, melon, quinces, dates, apples, apricots, peaches, tangerines, lemons, mangoes, desert berries.

Nuts and seeds   Almonds, walnuts.

Seasonings   Salt, pepper, vinegar, chili peppers, garlic, cinnamon, cloves, turmeric, ginger, curry powder.

Dishes   Simmered cornmeal (mealie) or millet porridge. Boiled rice. Scrambled ostrich egg. Simmered beans, sometimes cooked with melon or pumpkin. Fried, grilled, or stewed fish or meat. Springbok leg, rubbed with salt, pepper, ginger, and garlic, marinated in red wine and wine vinegar, browned, and braised with red wine and cloves in a tightly covered pot for two hours. Braised meat patties. Simmered or roasted stuffed chicken. Simmered or fried vegetables. Salads of raw vegetables or fruit with chilies and lemon juice or vinegar. Bredie (spicy mutton stew cooked with various vegetables), eaten with rice. Sosaties (kabobs of lamb or mutton marinated with spices, barbecued, and served with a curry sauce). Bobotie (baked spicy meatloaf with custard topping). Curries. Atjars (pickles in oil with spices). Chutney (spicy relish of pickled fruit or tomato).

Sweets   Honey, sugar. Dried fruit. Spicy fried doughnuts. Spice cookies. Sweet buns. Walnut and almond cake.

Beverages   Tea, coffee, wine.

NAURU
Republic of Nauru

Geography   Nauru (pronounced NAH-oo-roo) is a small island (8 sq. mi.) in the western Pacific Ocean, east of Papua New Guinea and just south of the equator. It is a plateau surrounded by a sandy shore and coral reefs.

Major Languages	Ethnic Groups		Major Religions	
Nauruan (official)	Nauruan	58%	Protestant	66%
English (widely used, including	Other Pacific Islander	26%	Roman Catholic	33%
in government, business)	Chinese	8%	Other	1%
	Australian white, other	8%		

Population density per sq. mi. 98.3
Literacy rate NA
Life expectancy 60.2 male; 67.6 female
Per capita GDP $5,000
Labor force in agriculture NA

Urban 100%
Infant mortality rate per 1,000 live births 9.4
HIV rate NA
Unemployment rate 22.7%
Arable land none

Agriculture   coconuts, mangoes, other tropical fruits, coffee, almonds, figs, pandanus (screw pine), chickens, pigs

Natural resources   phosphates, fish

Industries   phosphate mining, offshore banking, coconut products

History   Pacific Islanders inhabited the island when a British navigator, the first European to visit, arrived in 1798. In 1886 the German Empire annexed the island. Australia occupied it at the beginning of World World War I. In 1919 it became a League of Nations joint mandate of Britain, Australia, and New Zealand. During World War II Japanese occupied it. It was a UN trust territory of Australia from 1947 until it became independent in 1968. It was admitted to the UN in 1999. Phosphate exports provided Nauru with one of the highest per capita incomes in the developing world, although by 2006 phosphate reserves were nearly exhausted and damage from strip mining was severe. In the 1990s some countries paid compensation for damage from almost a century of phosphate strip mining by foreign companies. The economy collapsed in the late 1990s. In 2001 Nauru accepted some Asian refugees bound for Australia and was compensated by Australia. Nauru has become a haven for money laundering. In 2004 it defaulted on a loan payment for its real estate in Australia and was virtually bankrupt; financial reforms began. In 2008 the detention center to hold people seeking asylum in Australia was closed, an economic blow. Phosphate mining was revived, with new methods and new deposits.

Influences on food   Nauru is in the Micronesia group of the Pacific Islands. Influences on food include the Pacific Ocean, which provides fish, other Pacific Islanders, the Chinese, Britain, Germany, and Australia. Europeans brought new food plants, wheat bread, and certain animals. Chinese brought rice, soybeans, tea, noodles, and stir-frying. Main foods are fish, coconut, starchy roots and breadfruit, and fruit. Pork is the main meat, especially for feasts, traditionally cooked in a stone-lined pit over coals.

Bread and cereals   Rice, wheat; bread, noodles, rice dishes.

Meat, poultry, fish   Chicken, pork, fish (e.g., mullet), shellfish (e.g., crabs), eggs, beef; corned beef, spam.

Dairy products   Milk and other dairy products are uncommon.

Fats and oils   Coconut oil and cream, lard, vegetable oil and shortening, sesame oil.

Legumes   Soybeans, mung beans, winged beans, peas, lentils, peanuts.

Vegetables   Taro root and leaves, breadfruit, sweet potatoes, plantains, yams, cassava, seaweed, green leaves, arrowroot, bitter melon, cabbage, daikon, bean sprouts, eggplant, onions, green onions, mushrooms.

Fruit   Coconut, mangoes, figs, screw pine, bananas, lemons, limes, guavas, papaya, pineapple, melon, tamarind.

Nuts and seeds   Almonds, candlenuts (kukui), litchis, macadamia nuts.

Seasonings   Coconut cream and milk, lime or lemon juice, salt, soy sauce (the basic condiment), ginger, garlic, onions, red chili peppers, screw pine leaves.

Dishes   Boiled taro root, breadfruit, sweet potatoes, and other starchy vegetables. Boiled or steamed rice. Boiled, steamed, or stir-fried greens. Chunks of white fish marinated in lime juice and served with green onions and coconut cream. Foods cooked in a pit: whole pig, taro, sweet potatoes, crabs, whole fish, chicken pieces, taro leaves wrapped around a filling of coconut cream, lemon, onion, and shredded beef and all bound in banana leaves, and other leaf-wrapped mixtures of taro, breadfruit, or sweet potato with coconut cream and seasonings.

Sweets   Sugar. Immature coconut. Fresh fruit. Pudding made from coconut milk, arrowroot, and sugar.

Beverages   Coconut juice, tea, coffee, soy milk, toddy (wine made from coconut palm blossoms).

Meals   Two or three meals daily are typical, with the same foods at all, and the evening meal the largest. A usual meal is boiled taro root or rice; fish, pork, or chicken dish; and cooked greens or seaweed.

NEPAL
Federal Democratic Republic of Nepal

Geography   Nepal is in south-central Asia, bordering China and India. Astride the Himalayas, it contains many mountains over 20,000 feet, including Mt. Everest (29,035 ft; 8,850 m), the world's tallest mountain. It includes the Himalayas in the north, hills and fertile valleys in the center, and part of the Ganges Plain in the south.

Major Languages	Ethnic Groups		Major Religions	
Nepali (official)	Cchettri	16%	Hindu	81%
Maithali	Brahmin-Hill	13%	Buddhist	11%
English	Magar	7%	Muslim	4%
	Tharu	7%	Other	4%
	Other	57%		

Population density per sq. mi. 534
Literacy rate 56.5%
Life expectancy 61.1 male; 60.8 female
Per capita GDP $1,200
Labor force in agriculture 76%

Urban 15.8%
Infant mortality rate per 1,000 live births 62
HIV rate 0.5%
Unemployment rate 42%
Arable land 16%

Agriculture   rice, sugarcane, potatoes, corn, wheat, jute, chickens, goats, cattle, buffalo, pigs, sheep

Natural resources   quartz, water, timber, hydropower, fish, lignite, copper, cobalt, iron ore

Industries   tourism, carpets, textiles, small mills for rice, jute, sugar, and oilseed

History   Earliest civilization here was in the fertile Katmandu Valley around the 6th century BCE. Prince Gautama, born about 563 BCE, initiated Buddhism. Dynasties ruled from about the 4th century CE. As Indian influence increased, Hinduism mostly replaced Buddhism by around the 12th century. Nepal formed into a single kingdom in 1769 and fought border wars with China, Tibet, and British India in the 18th and 19th centuries. Nepal signed commercial treaties with Britain in 1792 and 1816. In 1923 Britain recognized Nepal's independence. In 1951 the system of rule by hereditary heads of the Ranas family (1846–1951) ended, the king introduced a constitutional monarchy, and a cabinet system of government was formed. In 1963 the caste system, polygamy, and child marriage were officially abolished. In 1990 a new constitution restricted royal authority and adopted a democratically elected parliamentary government; political parties were legalized; and elections were held. In 1996 the Maoist Communist Party of Nepal began an armed insurgency. Nepal signed trade agreements with India in 1997. Although closed to the outside world for centuries, now Nepal is connected to India and Pakistan by roads and air service and to Tibet by road. In 2001 the king, queen, and seven other members of the royal family were fatally shot by the crown prince, who also shot himself and died later. In 2006 a peace accord signed by the government and Maoist rebels ended Nepal's 11-year-long insurgency. In 2007, with a new constitution, the legislature agreed to Maoist demands and voted to end the monarchy, turning Nepal from a Hindu kingdom into a secular state. In 2008 legislative elections, the Maoists won the largest number of seats. In 2008 a constituent assembly voted to abolish the monarchy and make Nepal a republic.

Influences on food   Nepal, a mountainous country in the Himalayas between India and Tibet and almost isolated from the rest of the world until the 1950s, has peoples of Indo-European and Tibetan stock, with great diversity in cultures and religions. Cuisine reflects this diversity and traditionally relied on the ingredients available in each small locality. Main external influences on cuisine are from neighbor countries India and China. Religious wars between Muslims and the old Indian principalities caused Indian Brahmans (priests) and Kshatriyas (warriors) to escape to the Himalayas, bringing their culinary traditions. Tibetans continue to come. The Newars, whose ancestors ruled Nepal from about 700 BCE to 100 CE, live in the Katmandu Valley and are skilled in growing fruits and vegetables. The Ranas, hunters from India, during the 19th century took over the Himalayan mountain kingdom and brought pork and venison dishes. The Gurkhas were influenced by their service in the British army. The Sherpas, guides and porters in high mountains of eastern Nepal, cook many meat dishes. Butchers come from Tibet to slaughter yaks; they then dry and smoke the meat. Corn is grown almost everywhere, wheat and rice in the Katmandu Valley and in the Terai region in the south, and potatoes and other root crops further north. Citrus grows in the hills, mangoes in the Terai plain, and pineapples in the east. Rice (bhat), the main food, is usually served with legumes and vegetables. Meat is eaten when available but most people are Hindus who consider cattle to be sacred and do not eat beef. Chicken and goats are often used for sacrifice, then cooked and eaten. Rivers, lakes, and fish farming provide fish. Noodles (chau chau) and meat-stuffed dumplings (momo) show influence of Tibet and China. Hot, spicy pickles and chutneys add flavor and zest to the generally bland food. Numerous festivals and feasts feature special foods.

Bread and cereals   Rice, corn, wheat, millet, buckwheat; rice dishes, breads (roti, mari) made from grains and legumes, Indian breads (chapati, roti, parata, poori), steamed breads (some filled and called dumplings), noodles.

Meat, poultry, fish   Chicken, goat, beef, buffalo, pork, lamb, mutton, yak, venison, fish (carp, trout), eggs.

Dairy products   Yogurt, lassi (diluted yogurt), curds. Yogurt and curds are considered delicacies and healthful.

Fats and oils   Ghee (clarified butter), mustard oil, lard.

Legumes   Beans (mung, kidney), split peas, lentils (many kinds), chickpeas, soybeans.

Vegetables   Potatoes, roots (e.g., turnips), mustard greens.

Fruit   Oranges, tangerines, mangoes, pineapple, bael (bel in Nepali, a yellow aromatic fruit of citrus family).

Nuts and seeds   Almonds, betel nuts, pistachios, sesame seeds.

Seasonings   Ginger, garlic, onion, chives, cardamom.

Dishes   Steamed or boiled rice. Dal (boiled split peas or combined legumes). Boiled or fried potatoes (alu) or other vegetables. Boiled noodles. Steamed meat-stuffed dumplings. Kabafs (large pieces of meat cooked in their own juice). Fried fish. Kwati (made with many kinds of boiled beans), a special dish often eaten at festivals. Hot and spicy pickles (achars). Chutney (spicy vegetable or fruit relish).

Sweets Sugarcane, sugar, brown sugar. Rice fritters (sel). Indian khir (milk and rice pudding with cardamom) and jalebi (deep-fried batter soaked in syrup). Yomari (steamed rice-flour dumpling filled with roasted sesame seeds and brown sugar, usually made in a conch shape), made by Newari people for certain feasts and birthdays.

Beverages Tea, lassi (diluted yogurt, salted or sweet, and with flavorings), sherbats (fruit-based drinks).

NETHERLANDS
Kingdom of the Netherlands

Geography The Netherlands is in northwestern Europe, bordering the North Sea. It is mostly low, flat farmland. About half of the land is below sea level, requiring dikes for protection.

Major Languages	Ethnic Groups		Major Religions	
Dutch (official)	Dutch	80%	Roman Catholic	30%
Frisian	Other (11% non-Western origin,		Protestant, Lutheran	20%
	mainly Turks, Surinamese,		Muslim	6%
	Moroccans, Antilleans,		Other	4%
	Indonesians)	20%	Unaffiliated	40%

Population density per sq. mi. 1,272.4
Literacy rate 99%
Life expectancy 76.7 male; 82 female
Per capita GDP $38,500
Labor force in agriculture 3%

Urban 80.2%
Infant mortality rate per 1,000 live births 4.8
HIV rate 0.2%
Unemployment rate 6.3%
Arable land 22%

Agriculture potatoes, sugar beets, wheat, flowering bulbs, cut flowers, fruits, vegetables, chickens, pigs, cattle, sheep, goats

Natural resources natural gas, oil, peat, limestone, salt, sand and gravel, fish

Industries agro industries, metal and engineering products, electrical machinery and equipment, chemicals, oil, construction, microelectronics, fishing

History Celtic and Germanic tribes inhabited the area when Julius Caesar conquered it in 55 BCE. Germanic invasion in 406–407 CE ended Roman rule. The area was controlled by the Franks from the 4th to the 8th century, by Charlemagne's empire in the 8th and 9th centuries, then in turn by Burgundy in the 14th century, the Austrian Hapsburgs, and Spain in the 16th century. In 1648, following the Thirty Years' War, Spain recognized Dutch independence. In the 17th century the Dutch republic gained naval, economic, and artistic prominence, and Asian colonies. In 1795 France gained control of the land, Holland. In 1815 a kingdom of the Netherlands, including Belgium, was formed; in 1830 Belgium formed a separate kingdom. Neutral in World War I, the Netherlands was occupied by Germany from 1940 to 1945. After a four-year war, in 1949 the Netherlands granted independence to Indonesia. The Netherlands joined NATO in 1949 and was a founding member of the EU forerunner in 1958. Immigration from former Dutch colonies has been substantial. The Netherlands is heavily industrialized and has small farms. Rotterdam, at the mouth of the Rhine, is one of the world's leading cargo ports. Canals are extensive and important for transportation. Social policies include legal prostitution, same-sex marriage (2000), and euthanasia (2002). In 2005, concerned about immigration, the country rejected the EU constitution. The economy grew in 2007. The government, expecting a budget surplus in 2008, announced plans to reemploy many of the long-term unemployed and extended the mandate to 2010 for troops in Afghanistan.

Netherlands Dependencies: The Netherlands Antilles consists of two groups of islands: **Curaçao** and **Bonaire** in the Caribbean Sea near Venezuela; and **St. Eustatius**, **Saba**, and the southern third of **St. Maarten**, all southeast of Puerto Rico. Curaçao's main industry is refining oil from Venezuela; tourism is important. **Aruba** was separated from Netherlands Antilles in 1986 and now has the same status; industries are oil refining and tourism.

Influences on food The Netherlands' flat farmland produces food crops and livestock, and its long coastline, canals, rivers, and lakes provide fish and seafood. The Dutch have protected their agricultural low land from the encroaching sea and enlarged it by filling land in the Zuyder Zee. The Reformation led to the great Dutch painters turning from religious to secular themes; still life paintings of food reflect food customs of the 16th and 17th centuries. The Dutch explorers, traders, and the colonial period have influenced cuisine. During the 17th century the Dutch were eminent in the world spice trade, bringing spices back from the East. Also, Dutch exploration and colonization carried Dutch influence, such as baked flour goods and the use of spices, to various parts of the world including the United States, South Africa, East Indies, and West Indies. Indonesia, a Dutch possession for centuries until 1951, influenced food in the Netherlands. Indonesian restaurants are noticeable, mostly providing a rijsttafel (rice table). Indonesian takeaway (prepared) foods, such as sambals (foods in sauce of fried hot chili and other spices), satay (broiled bits of meat, chicken, or fish on tiny skewers dipped in hot curry sauce), and loempia (chopped food in a very thin wrapper), as well as market-prepared spiced strips of beef or chicken, are regular Dutch fare. In the first half of the 20th century cooking schools for the growing middle class became prominent, using a scientific approach and emphasizing nutrition. Until after World War II most families were large and not rich; thus subsistence cooking was emphasized. The traditional diet was potatoes, vegetables, and meat, supplemented with fish. During World War II food was scarce, rationed, and sometimes was famine food such as bulbs. After the war, with the improved economic situation and the influx of people from former colonies and of workers from various countries, new foods and customs developed. In recent years a shift to seafood occurred partly due to pollution in inland waterways. Dutch food generally is seasonal, such as new herring in early May, soups and stews in winter. France, ruler of this land at different times, has also influenced its cuisine.

Bread and cereals Wheat, rice, oats, semolina, rye, hops; gruels, yeast breads, rye bread, rolls, pancakes, turnovers, fritters, biscuits, cookies.

Meat, poultry, fish Chicken, eggs, pork, beef, lamb, goat, fish and seafood (eel, herring); sausage, bacon.

Dairy products Milk, cream, cheese (Edam, Gouda; both mild, semisoft; exported Edam has red rind).

Fats and oils Butter, lard, margarine, vegetable oil, salt pork.

Legumes Split green peas, brown beans, kidney beans, lentils, peanuts.

Vegetables Potatoes, cabbage, carrots, onions, cauliflower, Brussels sprouts, lettuce, celery, leeks, tomatoes.

Fruit Apples, coconut, currants, lemons, pears, raisins, pineapple, peaches, apricots, cherries, oranges.

Nuts and seeds Almonds, hazelnuts, pecans, walnuts, sesame seeds.

Seasonings Salt, black pepper, cinnamon, cloves, hot red chilies, curry powder, chutney, vanilla, chocolate.

Dishes Hutspot met klapstuk (beef stew with potatoes, carrots, and onions). Green pea soup (erwtensoep). Brown bean soup (bruinbonensoep). Cabbage with sausage (boerekool met worst). Fried, smoked, or stewed eels. Waterzooi (poached fish in its broth thickened with egg yolks and cream), served as a one-dish meal. Plaice (flounder) topped with bacon, bread crumbs, almonds, and Gouda cheese, and baked. Roasted Texel lamb. Boiled rice. Mashed potatoes and vegetables (stamppot). Pickled cabbage (kool sla, or coleslaw).

Sweets Honey, sugar. Usual dessert, gruel (pap) of oatmeal, semolina, tapioca, or rice with milk; Sunday gruel, thicker (a pudding), perhaps with vanilla, and served with biscuits and possibly fruit sauce. A famous Sunday dessert, watergruwel (pear tapioca cooked in red currant juice with lemon peel, cinnamon, currants, raisins, and sugar). Appelbeignets (fried battered apple slices, sprinkled with sugar). Pancakes with syrup, rolled, and sliced.

Special sweets for feast days   Hot chocolate with spicy biscuits (specculaas) on Sinterklass Day. Fried raisin yeast bread (oliebollen) and apple turnovers (appelflappen) on New Year's Eve.

Beverages   Hot chocolate, coffee, tea, heavy beer, Jenever (national aperitif, served cold often with smoked eel).

Meals   Breakfast: soft-boiled egg, cheese, roll, and hot chocolate, coffee, or tea. Lunch at a sandwich shop (broodjeswinkel): steak tartare (raw ground beef), half-om (liver and corned beef), or cheese toastie (grilled sandwich). A winter meal: soup with rye bread and bacon. Rijsttafel (rice table): rice, curry sauce with meat, chicken, or seafood, and accompaniments (tomatoes, fried onion rings, pineapple, peanuts, coconut, chutney).

Snack   Lightly brined herring with chopped onions, sold from pushcarts.

NEW ZEALAND

Geography   New Zealand is in the South Pacific Ocean about 1,250 miles southeast of Australia. It consists of two main islands, North and South. Both are hilly and mountainous, with fertile plains on the east coast. North Island has a volcanic plateau in the center, with hot springs and geysers. South Island has the Southern Alps, with glaciers and high mountain peaks. Other inhabited islands comprising New Zealand are Stewart Island, Chatham Islands, and Great Barrier Island.

Major Languages		Ethnic Groups		Major Religions	
English	(all	New Zealand European	70%	Anglican	15%
Maori	are	Other European	9%	Roman Catholic	12%
Sign language	official)	Maori	8%	Presbyterian	11%
		Pacific Islander	7%	Other, unspecified	31–36%
		Asian (Chinese 4%)	6%	None	26–31%

Population density per sq. mi. 40.3
Literacy rate 99%
Life expectancy 78.3 male; 82.2 female
Per capita GDP $26,400
Labor force in agriculture 7%

Urban 86.2%
Infant mortality rate per 1,000 live births 5
HIV rate 0.1%
Unemployment rate 3.8%
Arable land 6%

Agriculture   apples, potatoes, kiwifruit, wheat, barley, pulses, vegetables, sheep, chickens, cattle (dairy products), pigs, goats

Natural resources   fish, natural gas, iron ore, sand, coal, timber, hydropower, gold, limestone

Industries   food processing, wood and paper products, textiles, machinery, transportation equipment, banking and insurance, tourism, mining

History   The first inhabitants, the Maoris, arrived from Polynesia in about 1000 CE. Dutch navigator Abel Janszoon Tasman saw the islands in 1642. In 1769–1770 British captain James Cook explored the coasts. In 1840 the British colonized the islands and started settling them. Maori Wars ensued and ended in 1870 with Britain victorious. In 1907 the colony became the Dominion of New Zealand; it participated in both world wars. New Zealand gained independence in 1947 and is a member of the Commonwealth. Native Maoris elect 7 of the 120 members of the House of Representatives. New Zealand was the world's first country to allow women the right to vote, in

1893. It legalized prostitution in 2003 and same-sex unions in 2004. Much of the nation was deregulated in the 1990s. In 2007 the government introduced new environmental, education, and health measures including free part-time preschool education for three- and four-year-olds. A major settlement of Maori land claims was signed in 2008. With the country in recession, Prime Minister (since 1999) Helen Clark called for elections in November 2008. In 2008 government officials signed a free trade agreement with China.

Cook Islands and Overseas Territories: Cook Islands, half way between New Zealand and Hawaii, became self-governing in 1965, with New Zealand retaining responsibility for defense and foreign affairs; **Niue**,   west of New Zealand, gained the same status in 1974; **Tokelau**, north of Samoa, began New Zealand administration in 1925; **Ross Dependency**, part of Antarctic Territory, has been administered by New Zealand since 1923.

Influences on food   When the Polynesians arrived here they found plenty to eat: birds, fish and seafood, and plants such as ferns. They brought food plants including taro, sweet potato (kumara), ti, and bottle gourd; sweet potato became the main crop in the pre-European period. Their descendants, the Maori, cooked in a pit dug deep into the ground and lined with stones, stone-boiled using hot stones in large wooden containers, grilled by fastening fish or birds to sticks over a fire, or cooked food such as clams in the embers. The Polynesian influence is still seen in the haangi, a communal outdoor pit steaming/roasting method similar to imu. When Captain Cook arrived here in 1769, his crew collected wild celery and boiled it with soup and oatmeal. They also ate (as did the Maori) New Zealand spinach (tetragonia), a coastal plant spinach-like in flavor but belonging to the same family as the ice plant. European settlers brought new foods including mutton (from raising sheep for wool), potatoes, and wheat bread, which the Maori accepted. The settlers sometimes ate foods of the Maori including sea anemone soup, fuchsia berry pudding, sticky brown sugar crystals processed from the cabbage tree (ti), and, in the bush, rats. They tended to reproduce customary British fare. The climate here was similar to that of Britain although milder. British colonization in the 18th and 19th centuries greatly influenced the food practices here, resulting in an emphasis on meat and baked flour products. Other influences include Italian, Greek, and Asian immigrants; the introduction of deer and deer farming (now venison is a major export); and the discovery that plants such as tamarillo and kiwifruit (Chinese gooseberry) flourished here.

Bread and cereals   Wheat, barley, oats, corn; wheat bread, biscuits (cookies), pancakes, oatmeal porridge.

Meat, poultry, fish   Lamb and mutton, beef, chicken, pork, goat, venison, fish and shellfish such as oysters, mussels, scallops, lobster, abalone, and toheroa (bivalves similar to clams), duck, pheasant, eggs; sausage.

Dairy products   Milk, cream, cheese.

Fats and oils   Butter, lard, vegetable oil.

Legumes   Peas, beans.

Vegetables   Potatoes, sweet potatoes, pumpkin, tamarillo (resembles tomato but grows on bushes at high altitudes), New Zealand spinach, wild greens, eggplant, cabbage, celery, carrots.

Fruit   Apples, kiwifruit, apricots, berries, cherries, melons, pears, pineapple, oranges, lemons.

Seasonings   Salt, pepper, onions, mint, parsley, thyme, ginger, nutmeg, cocoa. Seasonings tend to be minimal.

Dishes   Soup of shellfish or pumpkin. Meat pies such as bacon and egg. Fried whole small fish. Fish fritters. Fish or oyster pie. Vegemite, a popular yeast spread. Some original dishes of New Zealand: toheroa soup (made with minced and puréed toheroas; has green color from chlorophyll in toheroa's liver due to feeding on plankton, which contains chlorophyll) and afghan (biscuit containing cornflakes and cocoa). Lamb, the centerpiece of New Zealand cuisine, roasted and served with mint sauce, roasted potatoes, and tamarillos. Roast leg of lamb stuffed with seasoned bread crumbs. Lamb chops grilled or baked in orange juice sauce. Mutton stew. Roast venison. Fried or grilled venison steaks, patties, or sausage.

Sweets   Sugar, scones, sweet pastries, cream buns (puffs), sponge cakes with cream, custard pies, ANZAC biscuits (oatmeal cookies provided by the New Zealand and Australian Army Corps during the world wars).

National specialty   Pavlova, a meringue cake with a soft center (due to the addition of corn flour and vinegar or lemon juice to the meringue mixture), filled with strawberries or kiwi, and topped with whipped cream; named after Anna Pavlova, the Russian ballerina who visited here in 1926.

Beverages   Tea, coffee.

Meals   Three meals a day is typical. Many people also break for morning and afternoon tea.

Snacks   Battered and fried sausages.

NICARAGUA
Republic of Nicaragua

Geography   Nicaragua is the largest yet most sparsely populated Central American country, bordering the Caribbean Sea and the Atlantic Ocean. It has mountains in the west, a volcanic and fertile Pacific coast, and a swampy Caribbean coast. Mountains with volcanic peaks run northwest to southeast through the country.

Major Languages	Ethnic Groups		Major Religions	
Spanish (official)	Mestizo (Amerindian-white)	69%	Roman Catholic	73%
English and indigenous languages	White	17%	Evangelical	15%
on Caribbean coast	Black	9%	None	9%
	Amerindian	5%	Other	3%

Population density per sq. mi. 124.6
Literacy rate 80.5%
Life expectancy 69.1 male; 73.4 female
Per capita GDP $2,600
Labor force in agriculture 29%

Urban 55.9%
Infant mortality rate per 1,000 live births 25.9
HIV rate 0.2%
Unemployment rate 5.2%
Arable land 15%

Agriculture   sugarcane, corn, rice, coffee, bananas, cotton, tobacco, sesame, soy, chickens, cattle, horses, pigs, goats, sheep

Natural resources   gold, silver, copper, tungsten, lead, zinc, timber, fish, seafood (lobster)

Industries   food processing, chemicals, machinery and metal products, textiles, clothing, oil refining and distribution, beverages, footwear, wood

History   Nicaragua has been inhabited for thousands of years, notably by the Maya. Various Indian tribes inhabited it when Columbus arrived in 1502. Spain conquered it in 1552 and ruled it until Nicaragua declared independence in 1821. Nicaragua was part of Mexico and then of the United Provinces of Central America until it became an independent republic in 1838. Political unrest and military conflicts occurred during the 1970s and 1980s. In 1998 Hurricane Mitch caused up to 2,000 deaths and extensive damage. In 2001 drought and low coffee prices brought an economic crisis. In 2004 the International Monetary Fund and World Bank forgave $4.5 billion of Nicaragua's debt. In 2007 Nicaragua's nearly $1 billion debt with the Inter-American Development Bank was cancelled. The government signed cooperative agreements with Venezuela, Brazil, and Iran.

Influences on food   Nicaragua has coasts on the Pacific and Caribbean that supply fish and seafood. Its fertile land and mountains produce sugarcane, grains, fruit, coffee, and livestock. Other influences on food are from the indigenous Indians, Spanish, and Caribbean islanders. Corn, the Maya staple, remains a staple. The Spanish brought new foods such as beef, pork and lard, and rice.

Caribbean island food customs from native Carib-speaking Indians and laborers imported from Africa and Asia influenced Nicaragua's cuisine, especially on its Caribbean coast. Most people are Roman Catholics, who eat special foods during Christmas, Lent, and Easter.

Bread and cereals   Corn, rice, wheat; rice dishes, corn bread (tortillas), gruel, and drinks, wheat breads and rolls.

Meat, poultry, fish   Chicken, beef, pork, goat, lamb and mutton, fish, seafood, eggs, iguana (an Indian favorite).

Dairy products   Milk (evaporated), cream, sour cream, cheese. Milk is not usually drunk as a beverage.

Fats and oils   Lard, butter, vegetable oils, shortening, sesame oil.

Legumes   Beans (black, red, kidney, white), chickpeas, soybeans.

Vegetables   Plantains, cassava, tomatoes, sweet peppers, chayote squash (green pear-shaped gourd), lettuce, avocados, pumpkin, breadfruit, potatoes, cabbage, carrots, chili and sweet peppers, onions, beets, olives.

Fruit   Bananas, coconut, mangoes, oranges, pineapple, roselle fruit (used to make sorrel drinks and jams/jellies), grapes, papaya, passion fruit, raisins.

Nuts and seeds   Palm tree nuts, squash seeds, sesame seeds.

Seasonings   Onions, garlic, chili, juice of sour oranges mixed with sweet peppers or mint, achiote/annatto (orange-red coloring), cilantro, pimento, capers, cinnamon, vanilla.

Dishes   Fried corn tortillas. From the ancient Indian past, Nicaragua tamales (nactamal), meat pie of corn dough flavored with sour orange juice around a filling of chicken or pork, potatoes, rice, tomatoes, onions, sweet pepper, and mint, wrapped in corn husks or leaves, and steamed. Posole (semi-fermented corn dough, diluted to make a beverage or used in other ways). Atole (thickened corn gruel) that can have additions of chili or beans. Simmered red beans and rice fried with onions (gallo pinto, "painted rooster"). Rice, boiled, often fried before boiling, or cooked with coconut milk. Coconut bread, a specialty on the Caribbean coast. Nicaraguan tripe soup. Stews of meat, chicken, or seafood and plantains or cassava in coconut milk. Roasted meat, chicken, and fish. Salads such as avocado. Fried potatoes, plantains, or breadfruit. Pickled cabbage, beets, or carrots.

Special occasion dishes   Sopa de rosquillas (soup made with ring-shaped corn dumplings), eaten on Fridays of Lent. Gallina rellena Navidena (chicken stuffed with papaya, chayote squash, capers, raisins, olives, onions, and tomatoes), a Christmas dish.

Sweets   Sugarcane, honey, sugar (white, brown), nogada (praline-like candy), baked bananas, fruit ices, ice cream, custard, rice pudding, coconut- or rum-flavored cakes and fritters.

Beverages   Coffee, chocolate, tropical fruit drinks (refrescas), beer, rum, tiste (a favorite, made with roasted corn, cocoa, sugar, cold water, and cracked ice).

Meals   Corn and beans are eaten at every meal by the poor. Rice is consumed frequently, with cheese or meat added if resources permit. Dinner in wealthier areas typically includes soup; meat, poultry, or fish; tortillas or bread; and salad, fried plantains, and pickled vegetables plus sometimes appetizers and dessert.

Snacks   Candy, fruit ices, ice cream, custard, rice pudding, cakes, fritters.

NIGER
Republic of Niger

Geography   Niger is in the interior of northern Africa. It is mostly desert and mountains except for the fertile basin along the Niger River in the southwest and a narrow savanna in the south.

Major Languages	Ethnic Groups		Major Religions	
French (official)	Hausa	55%	Sunni Muslim	85%
Hausa	Djerma Sonrai	21%	Shi'a Muslim	5%
Djerma	Peuhl (Fula)	9%	Indigenous beliefs	9%
	Tuareg	9%	Christian, other	1%
	Other	6%		

Population density per sq. mi. 27.1
Literacy rate 30.4%
Life expectancy 44.3 male; 44.3 female
Per capita GDP $700
Labor force in agriculture 90%

Urban 16.3%
Infant mortality rate per 1,000 live births 115.4
HIV rate 0.8%
Unemployment rate 1.6%
Arable land 11%

Agriculture   millet, sorghum, cowpeas, cotton, peanuts, cassava, rice, chickens, goats, sheep, cattle, camels

Natural resources   uranium, coal, iron ore, tin, phosphates, gold, molybdenum, gypsum, salt, oil, fish

Industries   uranium mining, cement, brick, textiles, food processing, chemicals, slaughterhouses

History   In the area now Niger is evidence of Neolithic culture. Niger was part of ancient and medieval African empires. The nomadic Tauregs and other groups established themselves in this area. Europeans came in the late 18th century. The French Colony of Niger was established in 1922. It became a French overseas territory in 1946. Niger gained independence in 1960. During the 1970s the economy flourished from uranium. A Taureg rebellion began in 1990 and ended with a peace accord in 1995. In 1993 Niger held its first multiparty elections. In 1999 Niger's president was assassinated. Elections and a new constitution restored civilian rule. In 2005 locusts and drought ruined the grain harvest and threatened famine in Niger, one of the world's poorest countries. In 2007 Taureg rebel deadly raids in northern Niger brought a government counteroffensive.

Influences on food   Like most other countries of Sub-Saharan Africa immediately south of the Sahara, Niger is a former French colony and sparsely populated. Niger is mostly desert, although the fertile area along the Niger River and the savanna in the south support crops and livestock. The Niger River provides fish. Food customs are influenced by North Africa, West Africa, France, foods brought from the New World, and religion. For example, meat and fish are commonly combined in sauces, as in West Africa; baguette bread is common in towns, a French influence; and chilies and tomatoes are used in many dishes, a New World influence. Most people are Muslims, who do not consume pork or alcohol. Herders such as the Fula live in northern Niger. In rural areas the traditional wood-burning hearth, made of three stones on which a pot sits, is still used; meat may be grilled on open fires; and ovens are uncommon.

Bread and cereals   Millet, sorghum, rice, corn, wheat, wild grain; porridge, couscous (tiny balls of millet dough steamed and served like rice), rice dishes, baguette bread, noodles.

Meat, poultry, fish   Chicken, eggs, goat, lamb and mutton, beef, pork, camel, fish (perch, tilapia), guinea fowl, pigeons, game (antelope, rock rabbit). Meat and fish are often smoked and dried.

Dairy products   Milk, sour milk, buttermilk, curds, whey, cheese.

Fats and oils   Shea oil and butter (from the seeds of the African shea tree), peanut oil, palm oil.

Legumes   Cowpeas, peanuts (groundnuts), beans, lentils. Legumes are important.

Vegetables   Cassava, yams, plantains, sweet potatoes, okra, tomatoes, greens, chilies, onions.

Fruit   Dates, raisins, coconut, bananas, watermelon, mangoes.

Nuts and seeds   Kola nuts, shea nuts, watermelon seeds, sesame seeds. Nuts and seeds thicken sauces/stews.

Seasonings   Tomatoes, chilies, onions, garlic.

Dishes   Millet grains boiled with cassava to a mush. Steamed or boiled millet, rice, or other grain, often eaten with meat and peanut sauce or stew. Cornmeal porridge. Rice with a thin stew of beef and tomatoes. Stews: red meat and okra; cassava leaves with dried fish and palm oil; chicken, peanuts, sweet potatoes, and tomatoes; or fish, okra, greens, and tomatoes. Dried cassava porridge with stew. Stuffed camel stomach (similar to haggis).

Festive occasion dishes Millet grain and cassava mush served with two sauces (minced meat, dried fish, and dried okra powder; and diced meat and tomatoes) mixed before serving. Jollof rice (rice with tomato or palm oil).

Sweets Sugar, honey, peanut candy, baked bananas, deep-fried sweet dough balls, sweet pastries.

Beverages Beer, coffee.

Street food Kabobs, shawerma (rotisserie lamb), bean fritters, sweet pastries, grilled sweet corn.

NIGERIA
Federal Republic of Nigeria

Geography Nigeria is in West Africa, bordering the Gulf of Guinea. It has tropical swamps and rainforests, a plateau of savanna and woodland, semi-desert in the north, and the Niger River in the west

Major Languages	Ethnic Groups		Major Religions	
English (official)	Hausa and Fulani	29%	Muslim	50%
Hausa	Yoruba	21%	Christian	40%
Yoruba	Igbo (Ibo)	18%	Indigenous beliefs	10%
Igbo (Ibo)	Ijaw	10%		
Fulani	Other (250+)	22%		

Population density per sq. mi. 415.9
Literacy rate 72%
Life expectancy 45.8 male; 47.3 female
Per capita GDP $2,000
Labor force in agriculture 70%

Urban 46.2%
Infant mortality rate per 1,000 live births 95.7
HIV rate 3.1%
Unemployment rate 11.9%
Arable land 33%

Agriculture cassava, yams, sorghum, millet, corn, cocoa, peanuts, palm oil, rice, rubber, chickens, goats, cattle, sheep, pigs

Natural resources natural gas, oil, tin, iron ore, coal, limestone, niobium, lead, zinc, fish

Industries crude oil, coal, tin, columbite, palm oil, peanuts, cotton, rubber, wood, hides and skins, textiles

History Nigeria, inhabited for thousands of years, was the center of the Nok culture, 500 BCE to 200 CE. The Kanuri, Hausa, and Fulani came later. The empire of Karrem controlled the area from late in the 11th century to the 14th century. Islam was introduced in the 13th century. In the 15th and 16th centuries Portuguese and British participated in the slave trade here. The Fulani ruled the region from the early 19th century until Britain gained control, 1851 to 1903. Nigeria gained independence in 1960 and became a republic in 1963. Civil war began in 1967 when the eastern part seceded, creating Biafra, and ended in 1970, when Biafra surrendered after widespread starvation and civilian deaths. Nigeria was a leading oil exporter in the 1970s. Military and government conflicts occurred in the 1980s and 1990s. Thousands of people have died in religious clashes since military rule ended in 1999. Kano region leaders banned polio immunizations in 2003; in 2004, 79% of the polio cases worldwide were in Nigeria; the Kano lifted its ban. The most populous country in Africa, Nigeria has rapid population increase, political instability, slow economic growth, and a high rate of crime. In 2007, for the first time in Nigeria's history, a civilian head of state succeeded another civilian. Rebel violence in recent years led to reduced oil output and increased worldwide oil prices. Attacks by militants and kidnappings of foreign oil workers and state officials and their relatives occurred in 2007 and 2008.

Influences on food   In this large, densely populated country, the Gulf of Guinea and Niger River provide fish, and the varied land supports growing root crops, grains, cocoa, peanuts, and palm trees, as well as herding animals in the north. The Portuguese, British, and Muslims (especially in the north) have influenced food customs. The introduction of New World foods such as cassava, corn, peanuts, tomatoes, and chili peppers has had great influence. Native African foods include black-eyed peas, watermelon, and okra. Daily fare is mostly starchy vegetables, legumes, and greens, with fish near the coast, all seasoned with palm oil, tomatoes, hot red chili peppers, and onions. Thick, sticky, spicy foods are liked. Women overweight by Western standards are admired.

Bread and cereals   Sorghum, millet, corn, rice; porridge, rice dishes, fried dough, biscuits.

Meat, poultry, fish   Goat, lamb, mutton, beef, pork, chicken, fish (fresh, smoked, dried), guinea fowl, eggs, game.

Insects   Termites (often called white ants), locusts.

Dairy products   Milk, sour milk, buttermilk, curds, whey, cheese.

Fats and oils   Palm oil, peanut oil, shea oil, coconut oil. Palm oil, the predominant cooking fat, is red.

Legumes   Peanuts (groundnuts), black-eyed peas (cowpeas), locust beans (carob), red beans.

Vegetables   Cassava, yams, plantains, taro, green leaves, okra, tomatoes, bitter leaf, melokhia, sweet potatoes, potatoes, eggplant, pumpkin, onions, red chili peppers, cucumbers, bell peppers.

Fruit   Coconut, pineapple, bananas, akee apples, baobab, watermelon, lemons, dates, mangoes, papaya.

Nuts and seeds   Palm nuts, cashews, kola nuts, watermelon seeds (egusi), sesame seeds, mango seeds.

Seasonings   Salt, chili peppers, tomatoes, onions, garlic, baobab leaves, "African nutmeg," curry powder, cocoa.

Dishes   Most foods are boiled or fried, and chunks are dipped in sauce and eaten by hand. Sauces: peanut (ground and pounded peanuts with seasonings); palaver sauce (green leaves); and fréjon (bean purée, coconut milk, and sometimes sugar). Fufu (a paste of boiled and pounded starchy vegetables or corn), formed into balls or bite-size scoops to eat stew. Thick soups or thin stews: egusi; okra; goat (served at important functions); root vegetables with bits of fish, chicken, or beef. Rice boiled in coconut milk. Fried plantains. Fried fish. Roast chicken with peanut sauce. Curries served with garnishes such as coconut and peanuts. Pili-pili (sauce of chili peppers, tomatoes, onion, garlic, and horseradish), usually on the table to season food. Moin moin (ground paste of black-eyed peas, hot pepper, and onion, steamed in molds or leaves), generally credited to Nigeria. Gari foto (cassava meal cooked with scrambled eggs, tomatoes, onions, and chilies), a popular Nigerian specialty often eaten for breakfast. Northern Nigeria dishes: boiled polished millet (jero) served with tausche (a stew of meat, pumpkin, greens, red pepper, and peanuts).

Sweets   Honey, sugar, fried dough balls, peanut candy (kanya), bananas baked with sugar, honey, or coconut.

Beverages   Cocoa, coffee, beer, red zinger (herbal tea made from flower pods of roselle (*Hibiscus sabdariffa*).

Street food and snacks   Spicy kabobs (tsire agashe), deep-fried fish, plantain chips, fried bean balls (akara), doughnut, fried crisp bit of sweet dough, coconut biscuits, sweet porridge.

NORWAY
Kingdom of Norway

Geography   Norway is in northern Europe in the western part of the Scandinavian Peninsula, bordering the North Sea and the Norwegian Sea. Europe's northernmost country, it extends from the North Sea to 300 miles (483 km) above the Arctic Circle. Mountains and plateaus cover most of the land, with glaciers, moors, and rivers; 25% is forest. Deep fjords indent the coastline, lined with thousands of islands.

Major Languages		Ethnic Groups		Major Religions	
Bokmal Norwegian	(both	Norwegian	94%	Evangelical Lutheran (official)	86%
Nynorsk Norwegian	official)	Other	6%	Other Christian	5%
Sami				Muslim	2%
				Other, none	7%

Population density per sq. mi. 39.1   **Urban** 77.3%
Literacy rate 100%   **Infant mortality rate per 1,000 live births** 3.6
Life expectancy 77.2 male; 82.6 female   **HIV rate** 0.1%
Per capita GDP $53,000   **Unemployment rate** 3.4%
Labor force in agriculture 4%   **Arable land** 3%

Agriculture   barley, wheat, oats, potatoes, chickens, sheep, cattle, pigs, goats

Natural resources   oil, natural gas, iron ore, copper, lead, zinc, lithium, purites, nickel, fish, timber, hydropower

Industries   oil and gas, food processing, shipbuilding, pulp, paper, metals, chemicals, timber, mining, textiles, fishing

History   Norwegians are of Teutonic origin. Norway's first ruler, Harold, came to power in 872. Between 800 and 1000, Vikings (Norsemen) from the area raided and occupied various parts of Europe. Several kingdoms were united into the kingdom of Norway in the 11th century. In 1015 the first king of Norway began converting Norwegians to Christianity. Norway was united with Denmark from 1381 to 1814 and with Sweden from 1814 to 1905, when it became independent. Neutral during World War I, it was occupied by Germany from 1940 to 1945. Norway joined NATO in 1949. In 1994 its voters rejected seeking EU membership. Norway's economy grew throughout the 1990s. Norway has one of the highest standards of living in the world, mainly due to hydroelectric resources, industrialization, and oil. It is a leading producer and exporter of crude oil, with extensive reserves in the North Sea. It has one of the world's largest merchant marines. It had rapid economic growth in the new millennium. The UN's Human Development Index rated Norway as the world's most livable country. In 2007 Norway's strong economy continued, with a trade surplus. The government promised to make Norway carbon neutral by 2050, partly by investing in new offshore technology to pump carbon gas into former reservoirs of oil and gas.

Dependencies: Svalbard,   a group of mountainous islands in the Arctic Ocean north of Norway, was incorporated into Norway in 1925; coal mining is the main economic activity. **Jan Mayen**, a volcanic island west-northwest of Norway, was annexed in 1929. **Bouvet Island**, an island nature reserve in the South Atlantic south-southwest of the Cape of Good Hope, came under Norway's administration in 1928 and is uninhabited.

Influences on food   Norway shares a cuisine with neighbors Denmark and Sweden because it was united with Denmark for centuries and with Sweden for most of the 19th century. Norway is a mountainous, northern country with only small areas of arable land and a short growing season. Transport used to be difficult most of the year, so food was preserved for later use. Fish was dried, salted, smoked, or pickled. Some meat was salted and dried. Milk was fermented, allowed to sour, or made into cheese. Grains were made into thin crisp flatbread, which kept for months. Fruit and berries were made into preserves. Norwegians still consume a large variety of preserved foods. The diet consists mostly of bread, dairy products, and fish. By the end of the 19th century leavened bread mostly replaced flatbread. Wide fertile valleys in eastern Norway are used for cattle; mountains and fjords for sheep and goats. Wildlife from forests and mountains provides game meat. Fish are in good supply from rivers, lakes, and the long coastline. A big change in diet followed the potato's introduction in the mid-18th century; now most meals include potato. Renewed interest in traditional foods such as lutefisk has occurred recently.

Bread and cereals   Barley, wheat, oats, rye, rice; oatmeal or rice porridge, thin crisp flatbread, leavened breads (often rye), French (white) bread, potato breads, for example, lefser (cooked on a griddle, thin, buttered, sugared, folded).

Meat, poultry, fish   Chicken, lamb and mutton, beef, pork, goat, eggs, fish and seafood (cod, herring, salmon, trout, Norway lobster, shrimp), game meat (elk, venison, hare, ptarmigan, grouse); pickled herring (usually served at breakfasts and buffets), salted and dried fish (klippfisk), dried stockfish (tørrfisk), ham, sausage.

Dairy products   Milk (cow, goat, sheep), sour milk, buttermilk, cream, sour cream, whey, cheeses: sour milk ones such as pultost (ripened, unpressed curd cheese with a strong flavor) and gammelost (dark brown, semi-hard, grainy, with sharp flavor and strong aroma); brown, sweet, whey cheese (mysost); and goat cheese (brown, tangy, sweet). Sour cream is the cream type used most in Norway, in contrast to sweet in Denmark.

Fats and oils   Butter, lard, margarine, salt pork.

Legumes   Split peas (yellow and green), lima beans.

Vegetables   Potatoes, cabbage, cauliflower, carrots, onions, celery, mustard, cucumbers, mushrooms, rhubarb.

Fruit   Apples, ligonberries, strawberries, raspberries, blueberries, cloudberries (like blackberries but gold color), apricots, cherries, currants, plums.

Nuts and seeds   Almonds, caraway seeds; marzipan (sweetened almond paste).

Seasonings   Dill, parsley, cardamom, cinnamon, cloves, ginger, mustard, horseradish.

Seasonal foods   September lamb; winter cod; May fried mackerel, rhubarb soup; summer strawberries, cream.

Dishes   Lutefisk (dried salted cod soaked in a lye solution before boiling). Yellow split pea soup with pancakes. Kjøttkaker (fried patties of minced beef served in a brown sauce; mors kjøttkaker, beef patties made by one's own mother, are always considered to be the best). Fårikål (mutton and cabbage stew). Cod sliced and boiled in salty water. Lobster brushed with melted butter and grilled. Poached salmon. Cucumber salad. Sautéed trout served with sauce of pan drippings and sour cream. Roast pork or ham. Roast venison with sauce of cream and melted goat cheese. Omelet. Soft-boiled or hard-cooked eggs. Open-faced sandwiches. Boiled potatoes with parsley butter. Sauerkraut with caraway seeds. Bergen fish soup (fish, root vegetables, sour cream, egg yolks).

National dish   Rommegrot (sour cream pudding sprinkled with cinnamon and sugar), served at weddings and on Midsummer's Day (June 24), a Scandinavian holiday.

Sweets   Honey, syrup, sugar, fruit with cheese, fruit or rhubarb soup topped with thick cream, rice porridge with sugar and cinnamon, Arctic cloudberries and cream, blueberry pancakes, waffles, cookies, cakes, pastries.

Beverages   Milk, coffee, tea, beer, aquavit (liquor distilled from potatoes or grain, often flavored with caraway). When toasting, Scandinavians say skoal, which probably derives from skull, as ancient Norsemen used empty craniums of their enemies for drinking vessels.

Meals   Three meals a day plus a coffee break at midmorning, late afternoon, or after evening meal are usual.

Snack, party food   Spekemat (assorted cured meat), for example, fenaldr (salted, dried, sometimes smoked leg of lamb).

OMAN
Sultanate of Oman

Geography   Oman is in the Middle East, on the southeast corner of the Arabian Peninsula, bordering the Arabian Sea. It has a 1,000-mile-long (1,700 km) coastline, a narrow coastal plain, a range of barren mountains, a stony arid plateau, and an enclave that controls access to the Persian Gulf.

Major Languages	Ethnic Groups		Major Religions	
Arabic (official)	Omani Arab	48%	Islam (official)	
English	Baluchi	15%	Ibadhi Muslim	75%
Baluchi	South Asian (Indian, Pakistani,		Other Muslim	14%
Urdu	Sri Lankan, Bangladeshi), other	34%	Christian	5%
Indian dialects	African	3%	Hindu, other	6%

Population density per sq. mi. 40.4
Literacy rate 84.4%
Life expectancy 71.6 male; 76.3 female
Per capita GDP $24,000
Labor force in agriculture NA

Urban 71.5%
Infant mortality rate per 1,000 live births 17.4
HIV rate NA
Unemployment rate 15%
Arable land 0.1%

Agriculture   dates, tomatoes, bananas, limes, alfalfa, vegetables, chickens, goats, sheep, cattle, camels

Natural resources   oil, fish, copper, asbestos, marble, limestone, chromium, gypsum, natural gas

Industries   crude oil production and refining, gas, construction, cement, copper

History   This land has been inhabited for at least 10,000 years. Arabs migrated here from the 9th century BCE and converted to Islam in the 7th century CE. Ibadi imams ruled until 1154, when a royal dynasty was established. Called Muscat and Oman, this land was ruled by Portugal from 1508 to 1648. Next, Ottoman Turks ruled the land until the mid-18th century, when forced out by Sultan Ahmad, whose descendants still rule today. By the early 19th century it was a major country in the region, controlling much of the Persian and Pakistan coasts and Zanzibar. Sultans and imams clashed during the 20th century until 1959, when the last Ibadi imam was evicted. In 1970 the sultan was deposed by his son, who began modernization and led Oman to join the Arab League and the UN in 1971. In 1970 the country's name became Sultanate of Oman. Western forces used airbases here in wars in Kuwait in 1990 and in Afghanistan in 2001. In 2003 the sultan extended voting rights to everyone over 21. Oman signed a free trade agreement with the United States in 2006. Most of the income is from oil. In 2007 the economy continued to grow due to high oil prices, increased natural gas exports, a new port and aluminum facility, and expansion of transportation and tourism services.

Influences on food   Arab is the dominant influence on the food of Oman. Other influences include Portuguese rule for over a century and surrounding cultures: Ottoman to the north, the Horn of Africa to the west, and Iran and India to the east. Religion also influences cuisine in this mostly Muslim country because Muslims do not consume pork or alcohol and fast from sunup to sundown during the month of Ramadan. Oman's long coastline provides fish and prawns. A substantial number of expatriates results in the availability of a wide variety of foods.

Bread and cereals   Wheat, rice; flatbread (e.g., pita), rice dishes, couscous, rolls, pancakes, filo dough pastry.

Meat, poultry, fish   Chicken, eggs, goat, lamb, beef, fish, prawns. Favorites are lamb, chicken, and fish.

Dairy products   Yogurt (laban), labneh (strained yogurt), ghee (clarified butter), milk, cream, feta cheese.

Fats and oils   Sesame seed oil and paste, ghee (clarified butter), olive oil.

Legumes   Chickpeas (garbanzo beans), lentils.

Vegetables   Tomatoes, eggplant, cucumbers, onions, olives, garlic, parsley, spinach, mint, coriander.

Fruit   Dates, bananas, limes, mangoes, melon, watermelon, oranges, lemons, figs. Dates are consumed in large quantities, especially during Ramadan.

Nuts and seeds   Almonds, sesame seeds, sesame seed paste (tahini).

Seasonings   Salt, cardamom, saffron, mint, baharat (a spice mix of black pepper, coriander, cassia, cloves, cumin, cardamom, nutmeg, and paprika), dried Omani limes (loomi), lemon juice, onion, garlic. Loomi is used in meat dishes and tea.

Dishes   Grilled or roasted lamb pieces, or balls of ground meat, on skewers (kabob mashwi). Machbous (prawns cooked with rice, fresh herbs, and vegetables). Boiled rice, often first cooked in oil and often with other ingredients as in pilaf. Steamed couscous. Boiled chickpeas or lentils. Eggplant fried or in casserole with tomatoes and sometimes lamb. Salad of cucumber, tomato, and greens. Fresh salt pickles.

Possible national dish   Khouzi (baked whole lamb stuffed with chicken, eggs, and rice spiced with baharat, saffron, and onions), served on a bed of rice garnished with almonds and ghee.

Sweets   Date molasses (dibis), honey, sugar. Baklava (pastry of filo dough layered with nuts and soaked in honey). Small stuffed pancakes (ataif), a Ramadan specialty. Many sweet dishes contain dates, dibis, or honey.

Beverages   Coffee, tea, fruit drinks, yogurt drinks, beer, wine, brandy. Coffee, the main drink, is strongly associated with the renowned Arabian hospitality; it is prepared from well-roasted, finely ground beans and usually flavored with cardamom. Tea is usually consumed black and very sweet.

Street food and snacks   Roasted chicken, lamb kabobs, shawerma (rotisserie lamb) served in pita bread.

P

PAKISTAN
Islamic Republic of Pakistan

Geography   Pakistan is in southern Asia, in the Indian subcontinent, bordering the Arabian Sea. Northern Pakistan's Hindu Kush and Himalaya Mountains include the world's second highest peak, K2 (28,250 ft; 8,611 m). Pakistan has a fertile valley, plateau, desert, plains, and the 1,000-mile long (1,609 km) Indus River.

Major Languages		Ethnic Groups		Major Religions	
English	(both	Punjabi	53%	Islam (official)	
Urdu	official)	Pashtun	13%	Sunni Muslim	77%
Punjabi, Sindhi,		Sindhi	12%	Shi'a Muslim	20%
Siraiki, Pashtu		Balochi, other	22%	Other	3%

Population density per sq. mi. 574.7
Literacy rate 54.9%
Life expectancy 63.1 male; 65.2 female
Per capita GDP $2,600
Labor force in agriculture 42%

Urban 34.9%
Infant mortality rate per 1,000 live births 66.9
HIV rate 0.1%
Unemployment rate 6.2%
Arable land 24%

Agriculture   sugarcane, wheat, rice, cotton, fruits, chickens, goats, cattle, buffalo, sheep

Natural resources   fish, natural gas, oil, coal, iron ore, copper, salt, limestone

Industries   textiles and apparel, food processing, pharmaceuticals, construction materials, paper products

History   One of the world's earliest civilizations flourished in the Indus River valley from 4000 to 2500 BCE. Aryan invaders from the northwest captured the region about 1500 BCE. A Hindu civilization began that dominated the India-Pakistan subcontinent for 2,000 years. Persians in the 6th century BCE and Alexander the Great ruled here. Arabs invaded in 712 CE and introduced Islam. Under the Mogul empire (1526–1857) Muslims ruled most of the area. Britain controlled the area from 1857 to 1947; the present-day Pakistan was part of India. In 1947 the Islamic majority areas of India became self-governing as Pakistan, which became a republic in 1956. West and East Pakistan were nearly 1,000 miles apart, on opposite sides of India. Civil war between East and West Pakistan ended with victory for East Pakistan; East Pakistan seceded, forming Bangladesh in 1971. Pakistan tested nuclear weapons in 1998. Al-Qaeda and Taliban activity increased here from 2002 until as of late 2008. Violence occurred in areas bordering Afghanistan in 2005 and as of late 2008. Many Afghan refugees fled to Pakistan during the Soviet-Afghan War in the 1980s; in 2008 most had been repatriated, but 1.8 million remained. During recent decades Pakistan has clashed with India over the disputed area of Kashmir. In 1988 Pakistan elected Benazir Bhutto, the first woman to head a modern Islamic state; she was ousted in 1990. In 2007 she returned from exile and was assassinated; wide-scale rioting followed. Elections in 2008 resulted in victory for the Pakistan People's Party, which had a platform of defeating extremism and bringing modernity and democracy.

Influences on food   The Indus River and Arabian Sea supply fish and seafood. Neighbors Afghanistan, Iran, and especially northern India also influence Pakistan's cuisine; Pakistan was part of India until 1947. Islam also influences food in this mostly Muslim country; Islam prohibits consumption of pork or alcohol and requires fasting from sunup to sundown during the month of Ramadan. Nearly all meats are processed according to Islam halal guidelines. Pakistanis eat mostly bread, rice, meat, dairy foods, legumes, and sweets.

Bread and cereals   Wheat, rice, corn, barley, sorghum, millet; flat leavened white bread (naan) traditionally baked in a tandoor (clay oven), unleavened whole-wheat chapati (circular flatbread cooked on a griddle), parata (a fried bread sometimes stuffed with vegetable or meat), rice dishes, porridge, cornmeal bread with mustard greens.

Meat, poultry, fish   Chicken, goat, lamb and mutton, beef, buffalo, fish and shellfish, eggs.

Dairy products   Milk (cow, buffalo), whole milk yogurt (dahi), cream, curds, panir (cheese), ice cream.

Fats and oils   Ghee (clarified butter, the preferred cooking fat), butter, vegetable oil.

Legumes   Chickpeas, lentils, beans, peas. Chickpea flour (besan) is used for breads and batters for fried foods.

Vegetables   Cabbage, carrots, cauliflower, cucumbers, tomatoes, peas, potatoes, spinach, mustard greens.

Fruit   Apples, apricots, dates, grapes, raisins, guavas, mangoes, oranges, papaya, plums, pomegranates, melon.

Nuts and seeds   Almonds, pistachios, betel nut, cashews, pine nuts, walnuts, poppy seeds, aniseed.

Seasonings   Onion, garlic, ginger (ample use of the preceding distinguishes the cuisine), salt, black pepper, mint, cinnamon, cloves, cardamom, cumin, saffron, turmeric, chili pepper, coriander, rosewater, kewra (screw pine).

Condiments   Chutney (spicy fruit or vegetable relish), pickles.

Dishes   Dalia (porridge of cracked whole wheat cooked with milk or water). Rayta (yogurt with vegetables). Klichri (simmered rice and legumes). Cholay (chickpeas or dried peas cooked with tomatoes and seasonings). Curry (sauce with a blend of spices and sometimes vegetables or meat). Minced and ground meat dishes sometimes with ground legumes. Basic meat dishes: korma (braised or stewed, e.g., beef stew), kabobs (grilled or pan-fried patties or skewered small chunks of meat), and kofta (fried meatballs); highly spiced and served with burani (mint yogurt sauce). Biriani (layered meat and rice with saffron). Pulao (pilau or pilaf: rice cooked first in oil so that grains remain separate, usually with meat or vegetables). Shami kabob (curried meatballs). Chicken tikka (grilled chicken). Shish kabob (skewered grilled lamb). Beef biryani (beef cubes cooked with rice and spices).

Regional specialties   Pakistan has varied geography and climate ranging from cold mountains to very hot desert. In the northeast, Pakistan's share of the Punjab raises fruit, sugarcane, and grain, and has rich elaborate dishes, tandoori fare (naan and spicy chicken roasted on a spit), and foods deep fried in the karhai (cast-iron, wok-shaped utensil). In the south, the Sind region's Indus River and long coastline supply plentiful fish, prepared as fritters, kabobs, steamed, or curried. To the west, pastoral Baluchistan has korma with plums and spit-roasted meat (sajji): whole lamb or chicken skewered on a pole, which is inserted into the dirt around a fire and hand-turned while the meat cooks. Rugged North-West Frontier emphasizes meat, especially lamb, and is home of chappli kabob (a hot minced meat cake shaped like a sandal). In the far northeast, Baltistan has Balti cookng of its Balti people: food is cooked in a Balti pan (a heavy cast-iron rounded bottom pan with two handles); and the food is aromatic but not hot with chilies and is scooped up with bread to eat.

Sweets   Sugarcane, gur (unrefined sugar), sugar. Kheer (milk-rice pudding). Halva (wheat flour or semolina pudding sometimes with nuts or vegetables such as carrots). Ladoos (balls of sweetened besan with nuts).

Specialty desserts   Zarda (sweet rice dish with saffron, almonds, pistachios, and raisins). Ras malai (rich cheesecake without a crust). Silver leaf may garnish special occasion desserts.

Beverages   Tea (heavily sweetened and boiled with milk, with cinnamon or cardamom), lassi (diluted yogurt), sharbat (fruit juice), sugarcane juice.

Meals   Two hearty meals a day, lunch and dinner, with dinner larger, are typical. Each contains meat, fish, or poultry (if affordable), rice, curry, cholay, raytas, salads, pickles, chutney, flatbread, and tea, followed at dinner by dessert (usually kheer or carrot halva) and often paan (betel leaf and nut with paste).

Street food and snacks   Meat fritters or patties, kabobs, pastries, flatbreads, and a favorite, pakora (fried, spicy besan batter coated fish or vegetables). Snacking is hearty and common.

PALAU
Republic of Palau

Geography   Palau is an archipelago of 26 islands (8 permanently inhabited) and 300 islets in the Pacific Ocean, southeast of the Philippines. It has a mountainous main island and low coral atolls, fringed with barrier reefs.

Major Languages		Ethnic Groups		Major Religions	
Palauan	(all	Palauan (Micronesian/		Roman Catholic	42%
English	are	Malayan/ Melanesian)	70%	Protestant	23%
Sonsorolese-Tobian	official)	Filipino	15%	Modekngei (indigenous)	9%
		Other Asian, white, other	15%	Other	26%

Population density per sq. mi. 119.3
Literacy rate 91.9%
Life expectancy 67.8 male; 74.4 female
Per capita GDP $7,600
Labor force in agriculture 20%

Urban 77.1%
Infant mortality rate per 1,000 live births 13.7
HIV rate NA
Unemployment rate 4.2%
Arable land 9%

Agriculture   eggs, cabbages, cucumbers, coconuts, copra, cassava, sweet potatoes

Natural resources   forests, gold and other minerals, fish, marine products, deep seabed minerals

Industries   tourism, craft items, construction, garment making

History   The original settlers probably arrived from Indonesia as early as 2500 BCE. Inhabitants arrived in successive waves from the Philippines and Polynesia. Explored by a Spanish navigator in 1543 CE, the islands were under Spanish control until Spain sold them to Germany in 1899. In 1914 Japan seized them. Occupied by American troops in 1944, they became part of the U.S.-administered UN Trust Territory of the Pacific Islands in 1947. Palau became an autonomous republic in 1981 and an independent country in 1994. The United States provides financial aid to Palau and maintains a military presence in Palau. In 2007 Palau agreed to join the United States and Russia in the fight against terrorism.

Influences on food   Palau is in the Melanesia group of the Pacific Islands. Spanish control from 1543 to 1899 left Spanish influence here as it did in the Philippines. Relationships with the United States from 1944 to the present left some influence. Asians brought rice, soybeans, noodles, and tea. The Spanish brought new food plants, wheat bread, some animals such as cattle, cheese, paella (saffron rice and meati dish), and adobo (meat stew). They also brought New World foods such as tomatoes, corn, and chili peppers and Mexican dishes such as tamales (steamed, corn husk–wrapped cornmeal dough, meat, and spices). American influence brought convenience and fast foods such as hamburgers and pizza. Main foods are fish, cassava, sweet potatoes, and coconuts. Pork is the main meat, especially for festive occasions, traditionally cooked in a stone-lined pit over coals along with other foods. Coconut milk is the usual liquid cooking medium. Fresh fruit is eaten as snacks.

Bread and cereals   Rice, wheat, corn; bread, noodles, rice dishes.

Meat, poultry, fish   Fish, shellfish, pork, chicken, beef, eggs; spam.

Dairy products   Evaporated milk (cow, goat, water buffalo), white cheese.

Fats and oils   Coconut oil, lard, vegetable oil.

Legumes   Soybeans, mung beans, chickpeas, black beans, lentils, red beans, winged beans, peanuts.

Vegetables   Cabbage, cucumbers, cassava, sweet potatoes, seaweed, taro, green leaves, tomatoes, onions, mushrooms.

Fruit   Coconut, bananas, lemons, limes, guavas, mangoes, papaya, pineapple, melons, tamarind.

Nuts and seeds   Cashews, candlenuts (kukui), litchis, macadamia nuts, palm kernels.

Seasonings   Soy sauce, fermented fish sauce, salt, coconut cream or milk, lime or lemon juice, vinegar, chili pepper, garlic, ginger, onions, tamarind.

Dishes   Boiled cassava, sweet potatoes, or taro root. Boiled or steamed greens (taro, sweet potato, seaweed). Boiled or steamed rice. Fish and shellfish stewed with vegetables, roasted, or marinated in lime juice or vinegar, then seasoned with coconut cream or onions, ginger, and chili peppers. Meat and vegetables stews. Whole pig cooked in a pit or spit-roasted. Taro leaves wrapped around a filling (coconut cream, lemon, onions, and shredded beef; or taro root, sweet potatoes, or cassava and seasonings) and steamed or cooked in a pit.

Sweets   Sugar, immature coconuts, sweet rice pudding, haupia (firm pudding made from coconut milk with sugar).

Beverages   Coconut juice, coffee with milk, tea, cocoa, soy milk, toddy (fermented coconut palm blossom sap), coconut brandy, kava (mildly alcoholic drink made from pepper plant).

Meals   Two or three meals daily are typical, with the same foods at all, and the evening meal the largest. A traditional meal: boiled cassava, sweet potatoes, or taro root; a fish or pork dish; and cooked greens or seaweed.

PANAMA
Republic of Panama

Geography   Panama is Central America's southernmost country. It has rainforests and fertile land in the east, interior hills, and mountains in the west. The Panama Canal connects the Caribbean Sea and Pacific Ocean.

Major Languages	Ethnic Groups		Major Religions	
Spanish (official)	Mestizo (Amerindian-white)	70%	Roman Catholic	71%
English	Amerindian-West Indian	14%	Protestant, independent	
	White	10%	Christian	14%
	Amerindian	6%	Other, none	15%

Population density per sq. mi. 112.8
Literacy rate 93.4%
Life expectancy 74.1 male; 79.8 female
Per capita GDP $10,300
Labor force in agriculture 15%

Urban 70.8%
Infant mortality rate per 1,000 live births 13.4
HIV rate 1.0%
Unemployment rate 9.1%
Arable land 7%

Agriculture   sugarcane, bananas, rice, corn, coffee, chickens, cattle, pigs, horses, goats

Natural resources   fish, copper, mahogany forests, shrimp, hydropower

Industries   construction, brewing, cement and other construction materials, sugar milling

History   Native Indians inhabited this land when Bastidas sighted it on Columbus's 1501 voyage, and Columbus visited it in 1502. Balboa founded the first successful Spanish settlement in 1510 and crossed the isthmus and discovered the Pacific Ocean in 1513. Spanish colonies were destroyed, partly by Francis Drake, from 1572 to 1595. Panama declared independence from Spain and joined Colombia in 1821. It declared independence in 1903, with backing by the United States, to which it ceded the Canal Zone. In 1989–1990 war between Panama and U.S. troops resulted from U.S. indictment of General Manuel Noriega for drug trafficking. Panama's first female president was elected in 1999.

Panama Canal   In 1524 the King of Spain ordered a survey across the isthmus for building a canal. In 1878 the Colombian government gave a construction concession to the French Canal Company. Nine years later the effort ended in bankruptcy and the United States paid the French for their rights and costs. In 1904 Panama granted the United States control of the Canal Zone for $10 million plus additional payment each year. The United States built the canal from 1904 to 1914; its jurisdiction was to revert to Panama in 1999. In 1978 a new treaty provided for Panama's gradual takeover of the canal and U.S. troop withdrawal before the end of the century. The United States returned control of the canal to Panama on Dec. 31, 1999. Construction to expand the canal began in 2007.

Influences on food   Panama has coasts on the Pacific Ocean and the Caribbean Sea, which supply fish and seafood. Mountains, tropical rainforests, and fertile land allow the production of sugarcane, bananas, rice, corn, coffee, and livestock. Corn was the staple for the Indians when the Spanish came, and it remains so, as solid food or in drinks or gruels. The Spanish brought cattle and dairy products, pigs and lard, rice, and other new foods. Some Andean food customs passed into Colombia and then into Panama. Caribbean island foodways from native Carib-speaking Indians and laborers from Africa and Asia have also influenced food customs on Panama's Caribbean coast. Panamanian fare is more international in flavor than that in most of the region, due to the U.S. influence while building the Panama Canal early in the 20th century and controlling it for the rest of the century and to international trade and tourism the Canal attracted. Staple foods are rice, corn, and beans.

Bread and cereals   Rice, corn, wheat; rice dishes, corn bread (tortillas), gruel, and drinks, wheat bread and rolls.

Meat, poultry, fish   Chicken, beef, pork, goat, fish, shrimp, eggs; ham, sausage.

Dairy products   Milk (evaporated), cream, sour cream, cheese. Milk is not usually drunk as a beverage.

Fats and oils   Lard, butter, vegetable oils, shortening.

Legumes   Beans (black, red, kidney, white), chickpeas.

Vegetables   Plantains, cassava, tomatoes, sweet peppers, chayote squash (green pear-shaped gourd), avocados, pumpkin, breadfruit, potatoes, cabbage, carrots, lettuce, spinach, beets, chili peppers, onions.

Fruit   Bananas, coconut, mangoes, oranges, pineapple, roselle fruit (sorrel), grapes, papaya, passion fruit.

Nuts and seeds   Palm tree nuts, squash seeds.

Seasonings   Onions, garlic, chili, achiote/annatto (orange-red coloring), cilantro, pimento, cinnamon, vanilla.

Dishes   Fried corn tortillas. Tamales (corn dough stuffed with spicy chicken or pork, wrapped in corn husks or banana leaves, and steamed). Posole (semi-fermented corn dough diluted to make a beverage). Atole (thickened corn gruel) perhaps with chili, squash seeds, or beans added. Boiled rice and beans (frijoles con arroz). Rice often fried before boiling or cooked with coconut milk. Coconut bread, a specialty on the Caribbean coast. Soups and stews of meat, chicken, or seafood and plantains or cassava in coconut milk. Roasted meat, chicken, and fish. Avocado salad. Fried plantains, breadfruit, or potatoes. Pickled cabbage, carrots, or beets.

A specialty Sancocho (a stew of beef, pork, ham, sausage, tomatoes, potatoes, squash, and plantains).

Sweets Sugarcane, honey, sugar (white, brown). Roselle fruit jam and jelly. Baked bananas. Nogada (praline-like candy). Fruit ices. Ice cream. Custard. Rice pudding. Coconut- or rum-flavored cakes and fritters.

Beverages Coffee, chocolate, tropical fruit drinks (refrescas), roselle fruit drinks, beer, rum.

Meals Corn and beans are eaten at every meal by the poor. Rice is consumed frequently, with cheese or meat added if resources permit. Typical dinner in wealthier areas: soup; meat, poultry, or fish dish; tortillas, rice, or bread; and salad, fried plantains, and pickled vegetables plus sometimes appetizers and dessert.

Street food and snacks Candy, fruit ices, ice cream, custard, rice pudding, cakes, fritters.

PAPUA NEW GUINEA
Independent State of Papua New Guinea

Geography This country is in the South Pacific Ocean, in the Melanesia group of the Pacific islands, and north of Australia. It occupies the eastern half of the island of New Guinea and about 600 nearby islands. It has thickly forested mountains and tropical coastal lowlands.

Major Languages	Ethnic Groups	Major Religions	
English (official)	Melanesian	Indigenous beliefs	34%
Melanesian pidgin	Papuan	Roman Catholic	27%
Motu	Negrito	Lutheran	20%
820 indigenous languages	Micronesian	Other Christian	19%
	Polynesian		

Population density per sq. mi. 33.9
Literacy rate 57.8%
Life expectancy 63.8 male; 68.3 female
Per capita GDP $2,000
Labor force in agriculture 85%

Urban 12.6%
Infant mortality rate per 1,000 live births 46.7
HIV rate 1.5%
Unemployment rate NA
Arable land 0.5%

Agriculture oil palm fruit, bananas, coconuts, coffee, cocoa, tea, sugarcane, rubber, sweet potatoes, chickens, pigs, cattle, sheep, goats

Natural resources gold, copper, silver, natural gas, timber, oil, fish

Industries copra crushing, palm oil processing, plywood production, mining

History Evidence indicates human settlements in Papua New Guinea about 50,000 years ago. Human remains dating back at least 10,000 years have been found here. Asian peoples probably entered the country via Indonesia. Polynesian, Melanesian, and Negrito tribes were early inhabitants. Portuguese explorers sighted the island in 1512 and the Spanish claimed it in 1548. The British founded the first colony here in 1793. In 1828 the Dutch took control of the western half of the island as part of the Dutch East Indies; Dutch New Guinea was annexed to Indonesia in 1969. In 1884 Britain claimed the southern half of the island, called British New Guinea, which was transferred to Australia in 1905, and Germany claimed the northern part, which Australia captured in World War I and administered until 1949. The two territories were administered jointly by Australia after 1949 and became independent in 1975. The country suffered severe drought in 1997, a killing tsunami in 1998, and army mutinies in 2001 and 2002. The country's decade-long war over the island of Bougainville with Bougainville independence fighters ended with peace negotiations in 2001. Michael Somare, the country's first prime minister (1975–1980, 1982–1985) regained the office in 2002 and was reelected in 2007.

Influences on food   Evidence indicates food gardens were here about 9,000 years ago. After migrations of people from southern Asia, by 4000 BCE   agriculture had mostly replaced hunting and fishing. Indigenous food crops include sago, sugarcane, banana, yam, and breadfruit. Immigrants brought taro, pigs, and perhaps coconut. The sweet potato, now a staple and main agricultural crop, and corn from America arrived later. Foods introduced after European contact include tapioca (made from cassava), peanuts, many vegetables and fruits, cattle, deer, and wheat bread. Asians brought rice, soybeans, noodles, and stir-frying. Britain, Germany, and Australia have controlled or administered the area and left some influence. Mainstays of the diet are fish and seafood, sago, roots, breadfruit, and fruits. Pork, the main meat especially for feasts, is traditionally cooked in a stone-lined pit over coals along with other foods. Coconut milk is the usual liquid cooking medium. Fresh fruit is eaten as snacks.

Foods of special interest   Sago, starch from pith of sago palms, is used to thicken puddings. Screw pine fruit is boiled and the red segments scraped off the woody core yielding a thin paste (marita); in the highlands it is mixed with sago. Lowland pitpit is unopened buds of a plant related to sugarcane.

Bread and cereals   Rice, sago, wheat, corn; rice dishes, sago pancakes and bread, wheat bread, noodles.

Meat, poultry, fish   Chicken, pork, beef, lamb and mutton, goat, fish, seafood, eggs, game (opossum, bush rat), birds (pigeons); corned beef, spam.

Insect   Large sago grub (beetle larvae).

Dairy products   Milk and other dairy products are uncommon.

Fats and oils   Coconut oil or cream, palm oil, lard, vegetable oil and shortening, butter, sesame oil.

Legumes   Soybeans, winged beans, peas, lentils, peanuts.

Vegetables   Sweet potatoes, sago, taro root and leaves, plantains, yams, breadfruit, cassava, green leaves, arrowroot, bitter melon, cabbage, daikon, eggplant, onions, green onions, seaweed.

Fruit   Bananas, coconuts, lemons, limes, guavas, mangoes, papaya, pineapple, melons, tamarind.

Nuts and seeds   Palm kernels, candlenuts (kukui), litchis, macadamia nuts.

Seasonings   Coconut cream or milk, lime or lemon juice, soy sauce, salt, ginger, garlic, green onions, tamarind.

Dishes   Boiled or roasted sago grub. Boiled sweet potatoes, sago, taro root, breadfruit, or yams. Sago flour moist cakes cooked on a griddle over an open fire. Moist sago flour, sometimes with greens added, baked in bamboo sections over an open fire. Sago mixed with fruit, vegetables, or diced meat and wrapped in leaves and cooked. Baked bread made with sago, coconut, banana, and breadfruit. Screw pine fruit cut into sections and boiled, served with pork, greens, or other vegetables. Lowland pitpit boiled, steamed, or baked. Boiled or steamed greens. Boiled or steamed rice. Raw fish chunks marinated in lime juice and coconut cream. Stir-fried vegetables and/or meat, chicken, or fish. Foods cooked in a pit: whole pig, sweet potatoes, yams, breadfruit, taro, crabs, whole fish, chicken pieces, taro leaf–wrapped filling of coconut cream, lemon, onions, and shredded beef all bound in banana leaves, leaf-wrapped puddings of coconut cream and sago, taro, sweet potato, yams, or plantains.

Sweets   Sugar. Immature coconut. Pudding made from sago, coconut milk, and sugar.

Beverages   Coffee, coconut juice, cocoa, tea, fruit juice, coconut toddy, kava (alcoholic drink from pepper plant).

PARAGUAY
Republic of Paraguay

Geography   Landlocked in central South America, Paraguay has grassy lands and fertile plains in the east, the Paraguay River bisecting the country, and the Gran Chaco plain with marshes and scrub trees in the west.

Major Languages		Ethnic Groups		Major Religions	
Spanish	(both	Mestizo (mixed Spanish		Roman Catholic	90%
Guarani	official)	and Amerindian)	95%	Protestant	6%
		White and Amerindian	5%	Other	4%

Population density per sq. mi. 44.5
Literacy rate 93.7%
Life expectancy 73 male; 78.3 female
Per capita GDP $4,500
Labor force in agriculture 31%

Urban 58.5%
Infant mortality rate per 1,000 live births 25.6
HIV rate 0.6%
Unemployment rate 11.1%
Arable land 7%

Agriculture   soybeans, cassava, sugarcane, maté, cotton, corn, wheat, tobacco, fruits, vegetables, chickens, cattle, pigs, sheep, goats

Natural resources   hydropower, timber, iron ore, manganese, limestone, fish

Industries   sugar, cement, textiles, beverages, wood products

History   The Guarani Indians were settled in this region, farming and speaking a common language, the most common language in Paraguay today, before Europeans arrived. In 1526 and 1529 Cabot explored the area, which was settled as a Spanish possession in 1535. Paraguay gained independence in 1811. Political instability and rule by three dictators followed for a century. Paraguay lost much of its land to neighbor countries in war with Brazil, Argentina, and Uruguay (1865–1870). Large areas were won from Bolivia in the Chaco War (1932–1935). After World War II, politics were unstable and military rule predominated until the election of a civilian president in 1993. Paraguay suffered a financial crisis in the late 1990s. Mass protests over the depressed economy resulted in a proclaimed state of emergency in 2002. Former Catholic bishop Fernando Largo was elected president in 2008, defeating the candidate of the party in power since 1947.

Influences on food   In South America straddling the Tropic of Capricorn, Paraguay has tropical jungle and temperate grassland with fertile plains. On the plains grows maté (*Ilex paraguariensis*), in the holly family native to Paraguay and the country's most distinctive product and favorite beverage. The cultivated plant is a shrub, not a tree as grows in the wild. The dried leaves are used to make tea, usually drunk without sugar. The dried powdered leaves, called yerba, are traditionally mixed with boiling water in a gourd and steeped; then a metal straw is inserted to drink the brew. Maté tea was drunk in pre-Columbian times and continues to be popular. Also on the grass plains lives the rhea (*Rhea americana*); its eggs and flesh are considered delicacies. Quinoa, a spinach-like plant with seeds used like wheat, is grown. Paraguay's food is hearty ample fare, with cassava the main food and emphasis on beef. Influences include the Guarani Indians, who have retained their culture, and immigrants. For example, the Spanish brought cattle, the Italians brought pasta, and the Germans added sausage.

Bread and cereals   Corn, wheat, rice, quinoa; bread especially cornbread, corn pudding, rice dishes, pasta.

Meat, poultry, fish   Chicken, beef, pork, lamb and mutton, goat, fish, eggs, guinea pig, rhea; sausage, cold cuts.

Dairy products   Milk (cow, goat), evaporated milk, fresh and aged cheeses. Milk is used in coffee and desserts.

Fats and oils   Butter, olive oil, dendê (palm) oil.

Legumes   Soybeans, beans (black, kidney), peanuts.

Vegetables   Cassava, potatoes, plantains, greens, tomatoes, peppers, pumpkin, squash, onions, olives.

Fruit   Bananas, coconut, cashew apples, grapes, guavas, oranges, lemons, mangoes, papaya, pineapple, melon.

Nuts and seeds   Cashews, pumpkin seeds.

Seasonings   Chili peppers, onions, cheese, salsas (tomatoes, chili, and other seasonings).

Dishes   Stews (locros) of meat and corn. Boiled or fried cassava. Chipá-guazu (cake of cassava, eggs, and cheese or meat). Bori-bori (beef soup with cornmeal and cheese dumplings). O-yosopy (beef soup with bell peppers, tomatoes, and vermicelli or rice, topped with Parmesan cheese). Grilled meat, chicken, or fish. Boiled or fried potatoes. Boiled beans. Boiled rice. Simmered greens. Peanut and chili sauce.

Special occasion dish   Sopa Paraguay (bread of cornmeal and cheese, sometimes with onions).

Sweets   Sugarcane, sugar, honey. Fresh fruit. Sweet custard. Tapioca made from cassava; pudding.

Beverages   Maté, coffee (strong and often with milk), fruit drinks.

Meals   Breakfast: bread and coffee. Lunch (usually the main meal): soup, meat or stew, rice, beans, potatoes, greens, and dessert. Dinner: cold cuts, salad, or stew. Afternoon break: maté and fruit, sandwich, or pastry.

PERU
Republic of Peru

Geography   Peru is in South America, bordering the Pacific Ocean. It has an arid coastal strip, which is irrigated and where most people live. In the center, high Andes Mountains cover 27% of the land, with peaks over 20,000 feet (6,096 m), plateaus, and valleys. Heavily forested slopes are in the east.

Major Languages		Ethnic Groups		Major Religions	
Spanish	(both	Amerindian	45%	Roman Catholicism (official)	
Quechua	official)	Mestizo (Amerindian-white)	37%	Roman Catholic	81%
Aymara		White	15%	Protestant	7%
Minor Amazonian languages		Other	3%	Other	12%

Population density per sq. mi. 59.1
Literacy rate 90.9%
Life expectancy 68.6 male; 72.4 female
Per capita GDP $7,800
Labor force in agriculture 9%

Urban 71.1%
Infant mortality rate per 1,000 live births 29.5
HIV rate 0.5%
Unemployment rate 9.6% urban
Arable land 3%

Agriculture   sugarcane, alfalfa, potatoes, asparagus, coffee, cotton, rice, corn, plantains, grapes, oranges, coca, chickens, sheep, cattle, llamas and alpacas, pigs, goats

Natural resources   copper, silver, gold, oil, timber, fish, iron, coal, phosphate, potash, hydropower, natural gas

Industries   mining minerals, oil extraction and refining, natural gas, fishing, textiles, clothing, food processing

History   The Inca Empire, with its capital in Cuzco, was established about 1230 CE and covered Peru, Bolivia, and Ecuador, as well as parts of Colombia, Chili, and Argentina. Andean civilization of 800 years provided the base on which Incas achieved a high level of skill in architecture, engineering, textiles, and social structure. Peru was conquered in 1532–1533 by Spaniard Francisco Pizarro and was ruled by Spain until 1824, when Simon Bolivar ousted Spanish forces and Peru gained independence. For a century thereafter, revolutions were frequent. Military coups in the 1960s and 1970s led to military rule for 12 years. In 1980 Peru returned to democratic rule but had economic problems. Conflict between guerrillas and government troops from 1980 to 2000 killed 69,000 people. A sagging economy, resurgent rebel activity, and scandals occurred in the period 2003 to 2005. A strong earthquake in 2007 took hundreds of lives and homes. In 2007 the economy continued strong, although extreme disparities remained between Peru's wealthy and poor. A scandal about oil and gas contracts led to the cabinet's resignation in 2008. The important mining industry experienced protests against low wages and environmental pollution. The U.S. Congress approved the Peru Trade Promotion Agreement.

Influences on food   Peru has a heritage of the Incas, who depended on corn, beans, chili peppers, and potatoes, and of the Spanish, who brought cattle and cheese, rice, the pig and fat for frying, and olives. Peru is large and has regional differences. The western coastline, populated mostly by mestizo with a small minority of Europeans in the capital Lima, has foodways from Spain meshed with Inca ingredients. The Andes Mountains in the center, home of the Incas, remains predominantly Indian, with mostly pre-Columbian foodways and Quechua spoken more often than Spanish. Beyond is the jungle, which is thinly populated. Peruvian diet staples are potatoes, corn, beans, and rice. Peru lacks large pastoral areas so large cuts of meat are uncommon. Cuy (guinea pig) is widely available in the mountains. Cuy and potatoes originated in Peru's highlands, where potatoes are eaten at most meals and corn is grown. Potatoes are frozen in the cold night air and then dried in the hot sunlight.

Bread and cereals   Rice, corn, wheat, quinoa (plant with seeds of high quality protein, used for flour); rice dishes, corn atole (gruel), tortillas, cornmeal and tortilla dishes, quinoa flour bread, banana bread.

Meat, poultry, fish   Chicken, lamb and mutton, beef, pork, goat, fish and seafood (shrimp, crayfish, sea bass, scallops, abalone), eggs, guinea pig, rabbit, llama.

Dairy products   Milk (cow, goat), cream, cheese. Milk is used in coffee, cocoa, fruit drinks, and puddings.

Fats and oils   Butter, lard, annatto oil, peanut oil, olive oil.

Legumes   Beans, peanuts, chickpeas (garbanzo beans).

Vegetables   Potatoes, plantains, sweet potatoes, pumpkin, tomatoes, cassava (yucca), apio (white, carrot like), ahipa (jicama), onions, chili peppers, olives, asparagus.

Fruit   Grapes, oranges, bananas, lemons, limes, pineapple, cherries, raisins.

Nuts and seeds   Almonds, walnuts, pumpkin seeds, annatto seeds (achiote), aniseed. Annatto seeds and a highland herb palillo provide the favored yellow-orange color. Annatto seeds flavor lard or oil and are ground.

Seasonings   Aji (chili) pepper, cocoa, onions, garlic, cilantro, coriander, vanilla. Food is picante with ample use of chili. Salsa de aji (chopped chili peppers, onion, and salt) is served at most meals.

Dishes   Boiled potatoes or sweet potatoes. Boiled or roasted corn on the cob (choclos). Ocopa (boiled potatoes topped cheese sauce, chili peppers, and peanuts). Llapingachos (fried patties of potato with cheese), served with fried eggs in the sierra or with fried bananas on the coast. Locro (potato soup or stew). Tamales (corn dough with meat or chicken, chili pepper, and boiled peanuts or olives and raisins, wrapped in banana leaves or corn husks, and steamed). Tamal en cazuela (tamale casserole), corn porridge added to meat fried with onions and chili. Crayfish chupe (soup/stew of crayfish with potatoes and cheese or cream). Arroz con mariscos (shellfish and rice cooked in shrimp stock and flavored with fresh coriander). Fried fish and shellfish with sauce of onions and aji. Shredded meat or small cuts of meat with rich sauces. Cuy fried, broiled, roasted, or stewed with potatoes, garlic, and aji. Chicken simmered, boned, and cut into cubes, heated in a spicy sauce of onions, garlic, aji, and walnuts, combined with slices of boiled potatoes and heated. Pork cubes marinated, simmered, finished in orange and lemon juice sauce, and served on slices of boiled sweet potatoes.

Coastal specialty Ceviche (raw fish or shellfish marinated in citrus juice with olive oil and spices).

Andes specialties   Charqui (dried strips of llama meat). Anticuchos (chunks of beef heart marinated in vinegar with chilies and cilantro, then skewered and grilled, and brushed with chili sauce).

Sweets   Sugarcane, brown sugar, sugar, honey. Manjar blanco (blanc mange), pudding made with milk, sugar, vanilla, and sometimes ground walnuts. Mazamorra morada (fruit compote with syrup thickened with purple corn). Picarones (sweet fritters of pumpkin and sweet potatoes with aniseed).

Beverages   Coffee, cocoa, beer, yerba maté, chica (distilled corn liquor), chicha morada (a drink of chica and fruit, e.g., cherries, lemons, pineapple, colored with purple corn), pisco (grape brandy that originated in Peru).

Meals and service   The colonial diet of Spanish Lima and the haciendas was rich and elaborate. Piqueo, a preliminary buffet, was served before either banquet or pachamanca (feast steamed in a pit oven: typically a young pig or goat, guinea pigs, chickens, tamales, potatoes, and corn in layers of hot stones, aromatic leaves, and herbs). Main (midday) meal courses: entradas (appetizers), soup, potato dish, meat dish, and sweet dish.

Street food and snacks   Anticuchos, ceviche, beer.

PHILIPPINES
Republic of the Philippines

Geography   The Philippines is an archipelago in Southeast Asia, between the Philippine Sea and the South China Sea. It consists of over 7,000 volcanic islands stretching 1,100 miles north to south. About 95% of the land and population is on the 11 largest islands, which are mountainous except for the heavily indented coastline and central plain on Luzon, the main island.

Major Languages		Ethnic Groups		Major Religions	
Filipino (Tagalog)	(both	Tagalog	28%	Roman Catholic	81%
English	official)	Cebuano	13%	Protestant	5%
8 major dialects		Ilocano	9%	Muslim	5%
		Bisaya/Binisaya	8%	Other Christian, other	9%
		Hiligay Ilonggo	8%		
		Other	34%		

Population density per sq. mi. 834.4   **Urban** 62.7%
Literacy rate 93.4%   **Infant mortality rate per 1,000 live births** 21.2
Life expectancy 67.9 male; 73.8 female   **HIV rate** NA
Per capita GDP $3,400   **Unemployment rate** 7.8%
Labor force in agriculture 35%   **Arable land** 19%

Agriculture   sugarcane, rice, coconuts, corn, bananas, cassava, pineapples, mangoes, chickens, pigs, goats, buffalo, cattle, sheep

Natural resources   timber, fish, oil, nickel, cobalt, silver, gold, salt, copper

Industries   electronics assembly, garments, footwear, pharmaceuticals, chemicals, wood products, food

History   Original inhabitants in ancient times migrated in various waves from the Southeast Asia mainland. They were mostly hunters, fishers, and unsettled cultivators. Magellan visited these islands in 1521. The Spanish founded Manila in 1571. Named for King Philip II of Spain, the islands were possessed by Spain for 350 years. Spain ceded them to the United States for $20 million in 1898, following the Spanish-American War. Japan invaded the islands during World War II and U.S. forces liberated them in 1944–1945. In 1946 independence was achieved. President Ferdinand Marcos ruled the country from 1965 to 1986, a dictatorial rule. Democratic rule followed. A rebellion of Muslim separatist guerrillas from 1972 claimed more than 120,000 lives and ended with a 1996 treaty providing for development of an autonomous Muslim region on Mindanao, southernmost of the two main islands. Flooding and mudslides from tropical storms in 2004 and typhoons in 2006 and 2008 killed thousands and did much damage; hundreds more died when a ferry capsized during the storm in 2008. Heavy fighting occurred in 2007–2008 in southern states between terrorist groups seeking a separate Muslim state and the government. In 2007 the economy grew and unemployment fell. The economy benefited substantially from remittances from some 8 million Filipinos working abroad.

Influences on food   The Philippines is a melting pot of cuisines, Malaysian, Polynesian, Chinese, Spanish, and American. Malaysians were early inhabitants. Traders brought Chinese foods (noodles, egg rolls) from about the 11th century. The Spanish, in control here for over 350 years, brought foods including wheat bread, desserts, adobo (meat stew), and Mexican corn dishes such as tamales. American control from 1898 to 1946 and influence brought convenience and fast foods such as hamburgers and pizza. Mainstays of the diet are rice with fish. Sunday dinner is important in this mostly Christian nation. Ancient rice terraces, 2,000 years old, in Banaue, in northern Luzon, and the International Rice Research Institute in Los Baños are located here. The shoreline of the islands, the many rivers, canals, and flooded rice fields, and commercial farming provide fish and seafood. Vegetables and fruits, especially coconut, are abundant. There are four regions. Luzon is the northernmost and largest group of islands, home of the capital Manila, and ethnically diverse; it has Spanish-influenced cuisine. Bicolandia, an ethnically homogeneous region that had contact with Malaysian and Polynesian cooking, has spicy food with chili peppers and coconut. Viscayan Islands make abundant use of seafood, seaweed, and sweets; the latter developed due to sugarcane plantations there. Mindanao, with Indonesian and Malaysian influences, has Muslim ethnic groups that consume no pork or alcohol, and it has spicy peanut and chili sauces and curries.

Bread and cereals   Rice, corn, wheat; rice dishes, rice ground into flour and made into cakes, noodles of rice, wheat, or mung bean, wheat bread loaf and bun/breakfast bread pan de sal.

Meat, poultry, fish   Chicken, pork, goat, beef, lamb, buffalo (carabao), fish such as grouper (lapu-lapu) and milk fish (banqus), seafood (oysters, prawns), duck, eggs; spicy sausage (embutido).

Dairy products   Evaporated milk (cow, goat), buffalo milk, white cheese (kesong puti).

Fats and oils   Coconut oil (the Philippines is the world's largest producer), lard, olive oil, vegetable oil.

Legumes   Soybeans, mung beans, chickpeas, black beans, lentils, red beans, winged beans, peanuts.

Vegetables   Cassava, seaweed, hearts of palm, kamis (cucumber-like), cucumbers, cabbage, green beans, spinach, taro, tomatoes, mushrooms, sweet potatoes, pumpkin, squash, eggplant, onions, green onions.

Fruit   Coconut, bananas, pineapple, mangoes, durian, oranges, limes, pomelo, mandarin, papaya, calamansi (lime-like), jackfruit, tamarind, bitter melon. Coconut milk, cream, and meat are used mostly in desserts.

Nuts and seeds   Cashews, palm seeds (kaong).

Seasonings   Fermented fish paste (bagoong) and sauce (patis), vinegar, chili pepper, garlic, ginger, onions, lime juice, soy sauce, coconut, curry powder, chocolate. Cool, sour, and salty tastes and spicy food are liked.

Dishes   Except for rice and some fish that are fried or grilled, a food is almost never cooked by itself; frying with garlic and onions, and fish/meat and vegetable soup/stews are typical. Steamed rice. Fried leftover rice. Garlic fried rice topped with bits of meat, sausage, and a fried egg. Lugao (thick, milky rice gruel). One of the oldest dishes, kinilaw (fish/shellfish marinated in vinegar or lime juice, then seasoned with onions, ginger, and chili peppers). Duck eggs often mixed with other ingredients or salted and colored red. Ginger chicken soup. Sinigang (sour soup/stew made of fish or meat and sour fruits, tomatoes, and other vegetables). Sinampalukan (fish stew made sour with tamarind leaves). Kari-kari (beef, oxtails, green beans, eggplant, and ground peanut stew). Adobo (stew of chicken and pork, or fish and prawns, marinated in vinegar and garlic, simmered in marinade, fried in lard and garlic, and simmered in its broth). Pancit (noodles with meat or shrimp in a sauce flavored with soy and garlic). Lumpia (deep-fried rolls stuffed with chicken, pork, and vegetable). Ukoy (deep-fried shrimp, sweet potato, and squash cakes). Garlic sauce (finely chopped garlic, salt, and vinegar), served with lumpia and ukoy. Deep-fried stuffed crabs. Morcon (flank steak stuffed with sausage and boiled eggs, rolled, braised, and sliced). Pickled pork hocks. Goat stew (caldereta). Tiola sapi (boiled beef curry). Bitter melon and cucumber salad with salt, onions, and vinegar. Stir-fried spinach. Deep-fried sweet potato chips. Spicy vegetable/fruit pickles.

Sunday dinner   Puchero (beef, chicken or pork, sweet potato, tomato, and chickpea stew), rice, eggplant sauce.

Fiesta dishes   Spit-roasted pig (lechon), the favorite. Chicken rellenong (roasted whole boned chicken stuffed with boiled eggs, pork, sausage, and onions).

Sweets   Sugarcane, palm sugar, sugar. Immature coconut. Fruit cooked in syrup. Puto (fluffy cake of glutinous rice, sugar, and coconut milk). Bibingha (moist rice flour cake sprinkled with cheese). Suman (glutinous rice, palm sugar, and coconut milk steamed in banana leaves or corn husks). Tsampurado (mush of sweet sticky rice and chocolate). Leche flan (custard). Bucayo (coconut cake). Halo-halo (coconut milk, other ingredients, shaved ice).

Beverages   Coconut juice, coffee with milk, cocoa, tea, soymilk, beer, coconut wine/brandy (tuba/lambanog).

Afternoon mini meal   Cakes, sweet fritters, ukoy, anything except rice (which is served at all meals).

Snacks   Fertilized duck egg with a partially grown chick inside (balut), fried pigskin (sitsaron), halo-halo.

POLAND
Republic of Poland

Geography   Poland is in east central Europe, bordering the Baltic Sea. It is primarily lowland plains with the Carpathian Mountains rising to 8,200 feet in the south and rivers in the west.

Major Language	Ethnic Groups		Major Religions	
Polish (official)	Polish	97%	Roman Catholic	90%
	German, Ukrainian, other	3%	Other (mostly nonreligious)	10%

Population density per sq. mi. 327.5
Literacy rate 99.3%
Life expectancy 71.4 male; 79.7 female
Per capita GDP $16,300
Labor force in agriculture 16.1%

Urban 61.5%
Infant mortality rate per 1,000 live births 6.9
HIV rate 0.1%
Unemployment rate 12.4%
Arable land 40%

Agriculture   sugar beets, potatoes, wheat, fruits, vegetables, chickens, pigs, cattle, sheep, goats

Natural resources   fish, coal, sulfur, copper, natural gas, silver, lead, salt, amber

Industries   machinery, iron and steel, coal mining, chemicals, shipbuilding, food, glass, beverages, textiles

History   Slavic tribes here converted to Christianity in the 10th century. Great (north) Poland was founded in 966, little (south) Poland in 1047. Later both Polands united. Poland merged with

Lithuania in 1386, forming a nation that was powerful to the 17th century. In 1466 it took western and eastern Prussia from the Teutonic Order, and its land eventually reached the Black Sea. In the 18th century it was divided among Prussia, Russia, and Austria. After 1815 former Polish land came under Russian control. Overrun by Austro-German troops in World War I, it was established as an independent nation by the Allies in 1919. In 1921 Russia took much of east Poland. In 1939 Germany and the USSR invaded Poland and divided it, starting World War I. After World War II, Poland was shifted west, losing eastern land to the USSR and gaining about half as much land on the west from Germany. Poland was reoccupied by Soviet forces in 1945 and was controlled by a Soviet-dominated government from 1947. The Solidarity labor movement in the 1980s achieved political reforms, and free elections were held in 1989. An austerity program began in 1990. Poland joined NATO in 1999 and the EU in 2004. It sent troops to Iraq in 2003. In 2007 the economy grew and unemployment dropped. In 2008 Poland pulled its troops out of Iraq, its troops were serving in Afghanistan, and agreement was reached to deploy U.S. antimissile interceptors in Poland.

Influences on food   Poland changed dramatically in size from the largest country in Europe, stretching from the Baltic to the Black Sea, to a small area in the 19th and early 20th century; now it is intermediate between these two extremes. In early times the Polish diet depended on Poland's soil and climate. Later it was influenced by trade routes, war, religion, and other factors. The rich dark soil and harsh northern climate yield cereal crops and vegetables. Poles like mushrooms, game, and meat. Mushrooms have been important since the 10th century when the introduction of Roman Catholic fasts gave them prominence as a meat substitute. Forests furnish abundant game. The Baltic Sea, lakes, and rivers provide fish and seafood. Because winters are severe, food is often preserved as dried, canned, pickled, or fermented (e.g., sour cream). In this predominantly Catholic country, holidays, especially Christmas and Easter, are important and include feasts and holiday foods. Large numbers of Jews came in the 14th century and led to Poland's having one of the largest Jewish communities in the world and being regarded as the chief source of the Ashkenazi branch of Jewish cookery. Italian influence came with Princess Bona Sforza of Milan who married Polish King Zygmunt the Old in 1518; she introduced salad items, still known as wloszczyzna (Italian things). French influence came when the last king of Poland, Stanislaw Agustus Poniatowski, ascended the throne in 1764 and employed a chef, Tremo, who brought French refinements. World War II and consequent scarcities and hardships returned Polish cuisine to its basics: simple and substantial dishes, and sweets. Hearty soups, dairy products, pork especially sausage, mushrooms, and honey are main foods. Other Influences include German, Hungarian, Austrian, and Russian; for example, Poland and Russia have appetizers, beet soup, and babka in common.

Bread and cereals   Wheat, rye, millet, barley, buckwheat; dark rye loaves, white bread, buckwheat cereal, noodles, dumplings, pastry.

Meat, poultry, fish   Chicken, eggs, pork, beef and veal, lamb, fish and seafood (carp, pike, herring), game; smoked ham, sausages especially kielbasa (garlic-flavored pork sausage), bacon. Pork is the favorite meat.

Dairy products   Milk, fresh cream, sour cream, smietana (mixture of sour and fresh cream), curd cheese.

Fats and oils   Butter, lard, flaxseed oil, vegetable oil, salt pork. Butter is the preferred cooking fat.

Legumes   Split peas (green and yellow).

Vegetables   Potatoes, mushrooms (fresh and dried), cabbage, beets, asparagus, cauliflower, cucumbers, green beans, carrots, turnips, onions; pickled vegetables such as sauerkraut (pickled cabbage).

Fruit   Apples, plums, berries, cherries, lemons, oranges, apricots, pears, rhubarb, raisins, prunes.

Nuts and seeds   Almonds, chestnuts, hazelnuts, walnuts, poppy seeds, caraway seeds, sunflower seeds.

Seasonings Sour cream, dill, horseradish, mustard, vinegar, lemon, cinnamon, cloves, ginger, vanilla, chocolate.

Dishes Hearty soups containing cereal and vegetables such as yellow pea soup with barley (grochowka). Barszcz Wigilijny (beet and mushroom soup). Chloderik (cold soup of beets, shrimp or crayfish, and sour cream). Steamed buckwheat, a side dish for meat and game. Pierogi (fried or baked small savory or sweet pies often filled with curd cheese). Simmered tiny dumplings filled with mushrooms (uszka). Bigos (hunter's stew), made with a variety of meats and vegetables always including cabbage. Pieczony schab (roast pork with applesauce glaze) and pickled spiced plums. Braised beef with mushrooms, served with sour cream sauce. Garnish of bread crumbs fried in butter (à la Polonaise). Boiled asparagus or cauliflower à la Polonaise.

Holiday foods Christmas Eve karp po zydowsku (chilled carp in sweet and sour aspic with raisins and almonds). Christmas cake (makowiec) shaped like a jelly roll and filled with black poppy seeds, honey, raisins, and almonds. Easter painted hard-boiled eggs and babka (rich sweet yeast cake with lemon and orange peel and raisins).

Sweets Honey, sugar. Fruit soups. Mazurka (a cake/pastry; can be small squares of meringue-like confection). Cheesecake made with curd cheese. Jelly doughnuts (paczki). Honey cake frosted with chocolate. Orzechowy (walnut torte). Honey ginger cookies.

Beverages Milk, coffee, tea, hot chocolate, beer, kvass (sour beer fermented from rye bread or beets), vodka (spirit distilled from rye or potatoes), goldwasser (vodka liqueur with flakes of pure gold).

Zakaski (like Russian zakuski, small bites, often served as a first course) Pickled herring, hard-boiled eggs.

Meals Three hearty meals a day are common, with the largest at lunch. Snacking is uncommon.

PORTUGAL
Portuguese Republic

Geography Portugal occupies the extreme southwest part of Europe, on the Iberian Peninsula, bordering Spain and the Atlantic Ocean; it includes islands in the Atlantic. Northern Portugal is mountainous, rainy, and cool. The central region is plains. The south is rolling plains, dry, and warm. Three large rivers flow across the country.

Major Languages		Ethnic Groups		Major Religions	
Portuguese	(both	Portuguese (homogeneous		Roman Catholic	85%
Mirandese	official)	Mediterranean stock)	92%	Other Christian	7%
		Other	8%	Other, none	8%

Population density per sq. mi. 300.7
Literacy rate 94.9%
Life expectancy 74.8 male; 81.5 female
Per capita GDP $21,700
Labor force in agriculture 10%

Urban 57.6%
Infant mortality rate per 1,000 live births 4.8
HIV rate 0.5%
Unemployment rate 7.7%
Arable land 17%

Agriculture grapes, tomatoes, potatoes, cork, grain, olives, chickens, sheep, pigs, cattle, goats

Natural resources fish, forests (cork), iron ore, tungsten, uranium, marble, hydropower

Industries textiles, footwear, wood and cork, paper, chemicals, auto parts manufacturing, wine, porcelain and ceramics, ship construction and refurbishment, tourism

History   Celtic peoples settled the Iberian Peninsula in the 1st millennium BCE. The Romans conquered the area about 140 BCE and ruled until the 5th century CE, when German tribes invaded. Muslims invaded in 711 and left only the northern part of Portugal in Christian control. Portugal won independence from Moorish Spain in 1143 and became the kingdom of Portugal. Portuguese navigators reached the Cape of Good Hope and the west coast of India in the 15th century. By the middle of the 16th century, the Portuguese Empire extended to East and West Africa, Brazil, Persia, Indochina, and the Malayan Peninsula. Portugal was a kingdom until 1910, when a revolution overthrew the king and proclaimed a republic. From 1932 to 1968 it had an oppressive government led by a virtual dictator. Economic and political upheavals followed. A new constitution was adopted in 1976, revised in 1982, and civilian rule returned. In 1989 Parliament approved replacing the socialist economy with a democratic one, denationalizing industries. Opposition socialists won a parliamentary majority in 2005. A conservative was elected president in 2006. Portugal returned Macao to China on Dec. 20, 1999. Portugal is a charter member of NATO and a member of the UN. In 2007 Parliament enacted a measure to ease abortion restriction and opened the world's largest photovoltaic generation plant. In 2008 Parliament approved changes in the Portuguese language to reflect the spellings of the hundreds of millions of Portuguese speakers in Brazil and elsewhere.

Azores Islands   These islands, in the Atlantic Ocean west of Portugal, received partial autonomy in 1976.

Madeira Islands   These islands, in the Atlantic Ocean northwest of Africa, received partial autonomy in 1996.

Influences on food   The Portuguese have a seafaring tradition dating back to the Phoenician sailors who first touched Iberian shores around 1100 BCE. Influences on Portuguese food include Rome because Portugal was part of the Roman Empire for seven centuries; the Arabs and being part of Moorish Spain until 1143; and Africa, Asia, and the Americas, notably Brazil. Portugal had a leading role in world exploration and colonization from the 15th century on. The Portuguese use some foods and dishes from Africa, Asia, and America. Asia contributed coconuts, bananas, mangoes, sweet oranges, and many spices. New World foods, including potatoes, corn, tomatoes, squash, pimentos, pineapple, chocolate, and vanilla, have greatly influenced Portuguese cuisine. In turn, the Portuguese influenced food in other parts of the world, such as introducing the tempura technique in Japan and influencing Chinese cooking through its colony Macao. Portugal and neighbor Spain have similar cuisines of simple fare with slow simmered foods, although the Portuguese use more herbs and spices. Portugal's long Atlantic coastline and rivers provide fish and shellfish, which dominate the diet.

Bread and cereals   Corn, rice, wheat; crusty country breads, cornmeal bread (broa), rice dishes, sweet bread.

Meat, poultry, fish   Chicken, lamb, pork, beef and veal, kid, fish and shellfish (cod, lamprey), game (partridge, quail, rabbit, hare), eggs; dried salt cod (bacalhau), pork sausages (especially garlic-flavored chouriço and linguiça), cured ham (presunto) a specialty.

Dairy products   Milk (cow, sheep, goat), cream, cheese such as creamy sharp white Serra (mountain cheese).

Fats and oils   Olive oil, lard, butter, vegetable oil.

Legumes   Chickpeas (garbanzo beans), fava and kidney beans, lentils, lupine seeds (tremocos), white beans.

Vegetables   Potatoes, tomatoes, olives, kale, cabbage, carrots, turnips, peas, lettuce, squash, peppers, pimentos.

Fruit   Grapes, apples, oranges, lemons, pears, raisins, figs, dates, pineapple, bananas, mangoes, quinces.

Nuts and seeds   Almonds, chestnuts, hazelnuts, pignolis (pine nuts), walnuts, lupine seeds.

Seasonings   Salt, black pepper, garlic, onion, lemon, vinegar, parsley, coriander (cilantro), mint, basil, cinnamon, nutmeg, cloves, saffron, cumin, chocolate, vanilla. Generous use of herbs and spices distinguishes the cuisine.

Dishes Codfish cakes (bolinhos de bacalhau), fried patties of cod with parsley, coriander, and mint, each often topped with a poached egg. Bacalhau dorado (salt cod scrambled with eggs). Bacalhau à Gomes de Sà (baked casserole of boiled salt cod, boiled potatoes, and onions heated in oil, garnished with black olives and hard-boiled egg slices). Sopa à portuguêsa (soup of pork, veal, cabbage, white beans, carrots, and macaroni). Cozida à portuguêsa (boiled meats, chicken, chickpeas, vegetables, and rice). Fried potato slices (batabas). Boiled rice, often served with fried potatoes. Sardines grilled or cooked in tomato sauce. Fish and shellfish stew (caldeirada). Tripe and bean stew, with rice served separately. Açordu (a dry soup of bread moistened with oil or vinegar and topped with meat, chicken, or shellfish, and vegetables). Bife à portuguêsa (pan-fried with seasonings ham over beef steak). Broiled split whole quail. Boiled cabbage or potatoes. Creamed turnip greens. Peas à portuguêsa (green peas simmered in stock with onions browned in butter, parsley, coriander, and sausage, then topped with eggs, covered, and simmered). Salad of green leaves, slices of tomato and red onion, black olives, and lemon juice. Broa (baked round loaf of yeast bread made with equal amounts of cornmeal and wheat flour). Sweet bread (massa sovada), yeast bread made using eggs and extra sugar. Roast suckling pig.

Some national dishes Caldo verde (kale and potato soup). Canja (chicken soup with lemon slices and mint).

Festive occasion dish Cabrito (a roasted whole kid).

Sweets Honey, sugar. Marmalata (quince preserves). Fresh fruit with cheese. Dried figs stuffed with almonds and chocolate (figos recheados). Rice pudding (arroz doca). Porto pudim flan (baked caramel custard with port). Cake made with almonds, eggs, and little or no flour. Ovos moles (egg yolk cooked with sugar). Chocolate mousse.

Beverages Coffee, chocolate, tea, wine, beer, port, Madeira, sherry, liqueurs, flavored sodas. Portugal is famous for its sweet rich wines, port and Madeira, often drunk with dessert.

Meals Four meals a day is typical: light and mid-morning breakfasts, lunch, and supper. The main meal is lunch, usually soup or salad, fish or meat, and dessert, with bread and red wine, and often followed by fruit and cheese.

Popular meal eaten out Broiled veal steak topped with two fried eggs, fried potatoes, rice, lettuce, and olives.

Snacks Tapa (bits of fish or other food on a small round thin piece of bread), served in cafés and bars with wine or sherry in late afternoon or evening. Tea and pastries in the late afternoon.

Special occasion meals After bullfight family supper of codfish cakes or grilled sardines with slices of country bread and wine. (Bullfights are family events because bullfighters remain on horseback and do not kill the bulls.) Christmas Eve: dinner of bacalhau (cod) and potato casserole and meringue cookies (suspiros); and post-midnight Mass buffet of finger foods such as fried cod puffs and sausages.

Food of Madeira Islands and Azores Islands Portugal includes the islands of Madeira and the Azores. Both have a less varied diet with milder seasoning than the mainland. Madeira, a beautiful Atlantic island with a balmy climate, has long been famous for its Madeira wine, a fortified wine. Prominent foods are tuna, cornbread, and fruits and vegetables such as mangoes, papaya, and avocados. The Azores has corn, bananas, pineapple, yams, and seafood, with tea the usual beverage, and a breakfast specialty açorda d'azedo (cornbread, vinegar, onions, garlic, saffron, and lard boiled together).

Q

QATAR
State of Qatar

Geography   Qatar (pronounced KAH-ter) is in the Middle East, occupying a small peninsula on the west coast of the Persian Gulf and bordering Saudi Arabia. It is mostly a flat desert with limestone ridges and scarce vegetation.

Major Languages	Ethnic Groups		Major Religions	
Arabic (official)	Arab	40%	Islam (official)	
English (commonly used	Indian	18%	Sunni Muslim	73%
as a second language)	Pakistani	18%	Shi'a Muslim	10%
	Iranian	10%	Christian (mostly Catholic)	10%
	Other	14%	Hindu, Buddhist, none	7%

Population density per sq. mi. 186.8
Literacy rate 90.2%
Life expectancy 73.5 male; 77 female
Per capita GDP $80,900
Labor force in agriculture NA

Urban 95.4%
Infant mortality rate per 1,000 live births 13.1
HIV rate NA
Unemployment rate 1.5%
Arable land 2%

Agriculture   dates, tomatoes, cantaloupes, other melons, vegetables, chickens, goats, sheep, camels, cattle

Natural resources   oil, natural gas, fish

Industries   crude oil production and refining, ammonia, fertilizers, petrochemicals, commercial ship repair

History   Bahrain partly ruled this land before Ottoman Turk control, 1872 to 1915. In 1916 Qatar became a British protectorate. Oil was discovered here in 1939, bringing wealth in following decades. In 1971 Qatar declared independence. In 1991 it was a base for air strikes against Iraq in the Persian Gulf War. In 1995 the king's son deposed him and instituted reforms including democratic elections and woman suffrage. In 1999 women first participated as voters and candidates in municipal elections. Oil and natural gas revenue provide one of the world's highest per capita incomes. A command center for the U.S.-led Iraq invasion is in Qatar. The Arab news network Al-Jazeera is based here. In 2007 state-owned Qatar Airways won international awards for superior service, and Qatar National Bank again received the highest possible credit rating from world rating organizations. Qatar's expansion in natural gas production and its high oil revenues continued.

Influences on food   Qatar's food resembles that of neighbors Saudi Arabia and Bahrain. It has been influenced by surrounding cultures, Ottoman to the north, the Horn of Africa to the west, and Iran and India to the east, as well as by Britain. Most people in Qatar are Muslims, who do not consume pork or alcohol and fast from sunup to sundown during the month of Ramadan. Expatriates comprise a substantial proportion of the population, resulting in the availability of a wide variety of foods. Qatar's land consists of desert with a coastline, which provides fish.

Bread and cereals   Wheat, rice; flatbread (e.g., pita), couscous, pancakes, filo dough pastry, rice dishes.

Meat, poultry, fish   Chicken, eggs, goat, lamb, camel, beef, fish, shellfish. Favorites are lamb, chicken, and fish.

Dairy products   Yogurt (laban), labneh (strained yogurt), milk, cream, feta cheese.

Fats and oils   Sesame seed oil and paste (tahini), ghee (clarified butter), olive oil.

Legumes   Chickpeas (garbanzo beans), lentils.

Vegetables   Tomatoes, eggplant, cucumbers, onions, olives, garlic, parsley, spinach, mint, coriander.

Fruit   Dates, cantaloupe, watermelon, mangoes, oranges, bananas, lemons, limes, figs.

Nuts and seeds   Almonds, sesame seeds, sesame seeds ground to make a paste (tahini).

Seasonings   Salt, cardamom, saffron, mint, baharat (a spice mix of black pepper, coriander, cassia, cloves, cumin, cardamom, nutmeg, and paprika), loomi (dried Omani limes), lemon juice, onion, garlic.

Dishes   Lamb, as pieces or ground, grilled on skewers (kebab mashwi). Machbous (prawns simmered with rice, fresh herbs, and vegetables). Boiled rice. Steamed couscous. Boiled chickpeas or lentils. Baked casserole of eggplant, tomato, onion, and olive oil, sometimes with lamb. Cucumber and yogurt salad. Fresh salt pickles.

Possible national dish   Khouzi (baked whole lamb stuffed with chicken, eggs, and rice spiced with baharat, saffron, and onions), served on a bed of rice garnished with almonds and ghee.

Sweets   Dibis (date molasses), honey, sugar, dates. Baklava (pastry of layers of thin filo dough filled with nuts and honey or flavored syrup). Ataif (small stuffed pancakes), a Ramadan specialty adopted from northern neighbors.

Beverages   Coffee, tea, fruit drinks, yogurt drinks, beer, wine, brandy. Coffee, the main drink, is strongly associated with the renowned Arabian hospitality; it is prepared from well-roasted, finely ground beans and usually flavored with cardamom. Tea is usually consumed black and very sweet.

Snacks and street food   Freshly roasted chicken and lamb kabobs are available from shawerma stalls, where vertical spit-roasted lamb pieces are sliced and served in pita bread or roll with tomato, parsley, and tahini.

R

ROMANIA

Geography   Romania is in southeastern Europe, bordering the Black Sea. It comprises the Carpathian Mountains, the Transylvanian Alps and plateau, plains in the south and east, and rivers of the Danube system.

Major Languages	Ethnic Groups		Major Religions	
Romanian (official)	Romanian	90%	Eastern Orthodox	87%
Hungarian	Hungarian	7%	Protestant	8%
Romany	Roma (Gypsy)	3%	Roman Catholic	5%

Population density per sq. mi. 250.2
Literacy rate 97.6%
Life expectancy 68.7 male; 75.9 female
Per capita GDP $11,400
Labor force in agriculture 29.7%

Urban 53.7%
Infant mortality rate per 1,000 live births 23.7
HIV rate 0.1%
Unemployment rate 4.1%
Arable land 39%

Agriculture   corn, wheat, potatoes, sunflower seeds, sugar beets, grapes, chickens, sheep, pigs, cattle, goats

Natural resources   oil (reserves declining), timber, natural gas, coal, iron ore, salt, hydropower, fish

Industries   electric equipment and machinery, textiles and footwear, light machinery, auto assembly, mining, timber

History   The earliest known inhabitants merged with invading Proto-Thracians centuries before the Dacian kingdom. Rome occupied the Dacian Kingdom, the Roman province of Dacia, from 106 to 271 CE. From the 3rd to the 12th century barbarians overran the population. The Bulgarian Empire subjected it in the 8th to 10th centuries and brought Eastern Orthodox Christianity. The principalities of Wallachia and Moldavia united in 1859 and became Romania in 1861. Romania became an independent kingdom in 1881. It joined the Allies during World War I and in 1918 added land, Transylvania, Bukovina, and Bessarabia, doubling its size. Much of the added land it ceded to the USSR, Bulgaria, and Hungary in 1940. In 1941 it supported Germany against the USSR. In 1944 it joined the Allies. Soviet troops occupied Romania, and it became a satellite country of the USSR in 1948 and a socialist republic in 1965. Industry, farms, and cooperatives were state owned. From 1967 to 1989, this moderately prosperous country turned into one near starvation. The communist regime was overthrown in 1989. A new constitution with a multiparty system took effect in 1991. Throughout the 1990s, Romania struggled with corruption, organized crime, and trying to stabilize the economy. Many state-owned companies were privatized in 1996. Romania joined NATO in 2004. A Western ally, it had troops in Iraq and Afghanistan. In 2007 it joined the EU and the economy grew and unemployment decreased. A strain on the economy was an influx of hundreds of thousands of Moldovans, who sought better financial opportunities and, taking advantage of Romanian laws, applied for joint Romanian-Moldovan citizenship; Moldova was part of Romania until World War II.

Influences on food   Influences from Roman rule, the 500-year Ottoman Turk period, Russia, Germany, Hungary, Eastern Orthodox Christianity, and geography and climate are evident in

Romanian cuisine. Caşcaval, a hard yellow full-fat cheese from sheep's milk, probably dates from Roman times, and the national bread, mamaliga, resembles Italian polenta. Turkish influence is reflected in dishes in the Wallachia (southern) region of Romania, baklava (baclava in Romania), moussaka (musaca), and pilaf. Russia influenced cuisine in northeastern Romania, which borders on Ukraine, with beet soup and grain porridge (kasha). German Saxon cookery retains much of its original character, as in knideln (dumplings) and bratwurst (beef or pork frying sausage), in the mountains in the north in Romania's largest province, Transylvania. Romanian, Hungarian, and German influences mix in Transylvania. In southeastern Transylvania, the Sekels (who had joined the Hungarians in 896) are said to have the true indigenous Hungarian cuisine such as székely gulyás (original Hungarian goulash). Romania is agricultural and grows corn and wheat. The colorful sunflower and poppy crops provide oil and seeds. Fruits, especially grapes, grow in higher areas. Raising cattle is a long tradition, and beef is the central food in the province of Moldova in northeastern Romania. Dairy cattle graze in pastures on the plains, water buffaloes live in the low regions of the Danube, and sheep live in the hills and mountains. Grains and walnut groves grow in the southern lowland region, Wallachia, where the capital, Bucharest, is located. The Danube and other rivers provide fish. Romania is famous for its attar of roses (rose oil), used in sweets. Most Romanians belong to the Eastern Orthodox Church, which has numerous fast days and special food for holidays, especially Easter.

Bread and cereals   Corn, wheat, barley, rice; cornmeal porridge and bread, wheat breads and cakes, rice dishes.

Meat, poultry, fish   Chicken, eggs, lamb and mutton, pork, beef and veal, goat, geese, duck, fish (pike, catfish); ground meat, sausages. A specialty, pastrama (lamb, beef, pork, or goose cured with seasonings and smoked).

Dairy products   Milk (cow, sheep, goat, water buffalo), cream, sour cream, yogurt, cheese (sheep and goat). The premier cheese (telemea), from sheep or goat milk, resembles feta but often contains aniseed.

Fats and oils   Butter, sunflower seed oil, poppy seed oil, olive oil. Sunflower seed oil is replacing animal fats.

Vegetables   Potatoes, cabbage, peppers, leeks, tomatoes, onions, olives, lettuce, eggplant; sauerkraut, pickles.

Fruit   Grapes, plums, berries, cherries, quinces, apples. Fruit is important in the diet.

Nuts and seeds   Walnuts, filberts, almonds, pistachios, sunflower seeds, poppy seeds (used on breads, sweets).

Seasonings   Vinegar, garlic, black pepper, dill, aniseed, allspice, nutmeg, hot peppers, rose oil.

Dishes   Mamaliga (cornmeal porridge), eaten hot or cool, sliced and served as bread. Fish spit-roasted, grilled, or cooked in soup (ciorba de pesta). Ciorba (soup of vegetables, e.g., peppers, onions, sauerkraut, and tomatoes, and meat, usually ground, or fish and then flavored with sour ingredients such as sauerkraut or vinegar). Mititei (grilled spicy ground beef sausages), accompanied by grilled or roasted bell peppers marinated in oil (ardei cu untdelemn). Ghiveciu (meat and vegetable stew). Sarmale (stuffed cabbage rolls), practically a national dish.

National dish   Musaca (moussaka), baked lamb or veal, vegetables (may be potatoes, celery, cabbage, or cauliflower instead of the traditional eggplant and tomatoes), and eggs.

Sweets   Sugar. Cakes. Custards (e.g., satou, resembles Italian zabaglione, flavored with sweet wine). Soufflés. Cozonac (yeast cake filled with poppy seeds) baked on Good Friday to celebrate the Romanian Orthodox Easter.

Beverages   Coffee, tea (both heavily sweetened), wine (red, white, sweet, dry), tuica (plum brandy).

Meals   One-dish meals, such as stews and soups, and bread are common. Bread or rice is eaten at most meals.

Snacks   Mititei, mamaliga, and wine.

RUSSIA
Russian Federation

Geography   The Russian Federation occupies most of Eastern Europe and northern Asia. Composed of 21 republics, it stretches from the Baltic Sea to the Pacific Ocean and also borders the Arctic Ocean, Caspian Sea, and Black Sea. The world's largest country in land area, Russia has varied topography, including vast plains, plateaus, low mountain ranges, forests, desert, and marshes, with all types of climate except tropical.

Major Languages	Ethnic Groups		Major Religions	
Russian (official)	Russian	80%	Russian Orthodox	53%
Many minority languages	Tatar	4%	Other Christian	5%
	Ukrainian	2%	Muslim	8%
	Other (including Bashkir, Chuvash,		Other	8%
	Chechen, Armenian; each 1%)	14%	None	6%

Population density per sq. mi. 21.4
Literacy rate 99.5%
Life expectancy 59.2 male; 73.1 female
Per capita GDP $14,700
Labor force in agriculture 10.8%

Urban 72.9%
Infant mortality rate per 1,000 live births 10.8
HIV rate 1.1%
Unemployment rate 7.2%
Arable land 7%

Agriculture   grain, potatoes, sugar beets, sunflower seed, vegetables, fruits, chickens, cattle, sheep, pigs, goats

Natural resources   oil, natural gas, coal, minerals, timber, fish

Industries   coal, oil, gas, chemicals, metals, machine building, defense (including radar, missiles), transportation equipment, communication equipment, agricultural machinery, construction equipment, electric power equipment, medical and scientific instruments, consumer durables, textiles

History   Part of the region was inhabited from ancient times by peoples including the Slavs. Nomadic peoples overran the area from the 8th century BCE to the 6th century CE. Slavic tribes from the west began migrating into the area in the 5th century. Tradition says the Viking Rurik came and founded the first Russian dynasty in Novgorod in 862. Rus, a confederaton of principalities, ruled from Kiev in the 10th century. The tribes were unified by the spread of Christianity in the 10th and 11th centuries. In the 11th and 12th centuries independent principalities dominated, including Novgorod in the north, the only principality to escape domination by the Mongols. In the 13th century the Mongols overran the country, which freed itself by 1480. In 1547 Ivan the Terrible was the first proclaimed czar. The Romanov dynasty began in 1613. Peter the Great (1682–1725) extended Russia's boundary to the west, made extensive reforms aimed at westernization, and in 1721 founded the Russian Empire. Catherine the Great (1762–1796) continued westernization and expanded Russia to include the Crimea, Ukraine, and part of Poland. Napoleon invaded in 1812 and after his defeat Russia received most of the grand duchy of Warsaw in 1815. Russia annexed Georgia, Armenia, and other Caucasus areas in the 19th century. Russia was defeated in the Crimean War. It sold Alaska to the United States. in 1867. Russia was defeated in the Russo-Japanese War. Alexander II (1855–1881) extended Russia to the Pacific and into central Asia.

Russia fought against the Central Powers in World War I. In 1917 the revolution overthrew the czarist, resulting in the formation of the Soviet Union. The USSR fought with the Allies in World War II. In 1941 Germany invaded Russia and the 900-day siege of Leningrad (now St. Petersburg) lasted to January 1944 and caused a million deaths. The city was not taken; with British and U.S. aid the Russians drove out the German troops. After the war, tension with the West led to the decades-long

Cold War. The Communist Party dominated all areas of national life in the USSR. After the dissolution of the USSR in 1991, the Russian Soviet Federated Socialist Republic was renamed Russia. Russia's land area is more than 76% of the area of the former USSR. Russia adopted a new constitution in 1993. During the 1990s Russia struggled with economic difficulties: steps toward privatization, inflation, and a severe economic crisis. The 1994 to 1996 Chechnya-Russian war was followed with fighting in 1999 and terrorism incidents. In 2000 Vladimir Putin was elected president. Russia supported the U.S.-led war in Afghanistan in 2001 but not the invasion of Iraq in 2003. Russia's economy and Putin's popularity rose in 2007 due to an oil boom; Putin was *Time* magazine's 2007 Person of the Year. Putin, president from 2000 to 2008, was barred from running for a third consecutive term; his protégé succeeded him and then made him prime minister. Russia suspended crude oil delivery to Belarus in 2007 and gas deliveries to Ukraine in 2008. In 2008 Russia sent troops to Georgia to support secessionists in two regions, South Ossetia and Abkhazia, and then recognized the independence of both. The world economic crisis and a drop in oil prices led to a Russian financial crisis and an emergency rescue plan with the government loaning banks $37 billion in October 2008.

Influences on food   Russia was under Mongol rule and then was the czarist empire for centuries. It was the core of the Soviet Union for most of the 20th century and became the Russian Federation in the early 1990s. Throughout this history most Russians were peasants with simple food. The usual diet was rye bread, kasha (buckwheat porridge), hearty soups of vegetables or fish, and kvass (a fermented drink made from rye bread); little meat was eaten until the 19th century, although now it is a central part of a main meal. Mushrooms, cheese, sour cream, onions, garlic, dill, and horseradish were often eaten. The Mongols invaded in the 13th century and ruled until 1480; they showed the Slavs how to broil meat, make yogurt, kumys (a mildly alcoholic drink), and curd cheese from soured or fermented milk, and preserve cabbage in brine resulting in sauerkraut. Also, they brought tea, the samovar for brewing tea, and spices from Asia. Most Russians are Orthodox Christians. The Russian Orthodox Church allows only Lenten foods (fish, fungi, vegetables) on the many fast days, whereas animal foods (eggs, milk, butter, and meat) can be eaten only on the other days, and there are special Easter foods. Czar Peter the Great in the late 17th and early 18th century brought French and Scandinavian influence on food of the wealthy and the zakuski table (little bites of food usually served with vodka before the meal). In the 19th century French chefs came to St. Petersburg and Moscow and refined food for the wealthy with dishes such as Bef Stroganov and Sharlotka (Charlotte) and service à la russe (servants serve dishes to seated guests). Russia, a vast land with varied climate and geography, produces a variety of crops and livestock. It is the main producer of buckwheat (seeds of a plant of the rhubarb family), which resembles cereals and is used as husked whole grains and flour. Russia produces much of the world's caviar (salted sturgeon eggs), from the Black and Caspian seas.

Bread and cereals   Wheat, barley, oats, corn, rye, buckwheat, millet; sour dough yeast breads of rye or rye and wheat with black rye bread most common, buckwheat porridge (kasha), pancakes (blini), pastry, pasta.

Meat, poultry, fish   Chicken, beef, lamb and mutton, pork, goat, fish, caviar, eggs; ham, sausage (spicy kolbase).

Dairy products   Milk (cow, sheep), cream, sour cream (smetana), cottage cheese, cheese.

Fats and oils   Sunflower seed oil, butter, lard, olive oil, vegetable oil.

Legumes   Beans, lentils, peas.

Vegetables   Potatoes, cabbage, tomatoes, carrots, turnips, onions, cucumbers, peas, beets, mushrooms, parsnips, swede (or rutabaga, a usually yellow root vegetable), radishes, green peppers; pickles, sauerkraut.

Fruit   Apples, grapes, strawberries, raspberries, cherries, plums, raisins, currants; preserves, jam.

Nuts and seeds   Almonds, chestnuts, hazelnuts, walnuts, sunflower seeds, poppy seeds, caraway seeds.

Seasonings   Sour cream, onion, garlic, parsley, dill, horseradish, cinnamon, ginger, saffron. Sour taste is liked.

Dishes Russia's most renowned dish, kasha (thick porridge of buckwheat, barley, or millet grains simmered in water, often with onions and mushrooms). Soups: shchi (cabbage), borsch (beet), and ukha (fish). Stuffed cabbage or green peppers. Blini (buckwheat pancakes), important in Russia as early as the Middle Ages, eaten especially during the week leading up to Lent. Coulibiar (a pie of filling such as fish, chopped hard-boiled eggs, dill, and kasha cooked inside yeast dough). Pirozhki (pirog), small meat or fish pie. Kotlety (fried patty of ground meat, onions, egg, and moistened bread), served with boiled potatoes or macaroni. Roast suckling pig, popular at feasts. Bef Stroganov (beef filet strips stir-fried, mixed with simmered onions and mushrooms, and with sour cream added), a world-famous dish. A Siberian stew (sheep's stomach filled with milk, sheep's blood, garlic, and green onions, tied with sheep intestines, and boiled with the meat in a pot).

Easter foods Kulich (tall cylindrical yeast cake with raisins and nuts and often iced). Paskha (sweet cheesecake with candied fruits, nuts, and letters XB for Christ is risen). Hard-boiled eggs dyed red or hand-decorated.

Sweets Honey, sugar, molasses. Fruit compote. Kisel (berry pudding or puréed fruit such as apple). Kutia (wheat grains, honey, poppy seeds, and stewed dried fruit). Baba (rich sweet yeast bread or cake baked in a tal, cylindrical mold). Sharlotka (Charlotte russe), a rich filling of gelatin, whipped cream, and raspberries or other flavoring, turned into a mold lined with sponge cake ladyfingers, and chilled.

Beverages Tea, beer, kvass, vodka (spirit distilled from potatoes). Strong tea is made and diluted with hot water from a samovar (brass urn heated by charcoal inserted in a vertical tube running through the center).

Zakuski (appetizers) Caviar, pickled herring, cucumbers in sour cream; served before dinner with vodka.

Meals Three hearty meals a day are typical, with the largest at lunch. Staples are bread, kasha, and soup.

Tatarstan and Tatar Cuisine Formerly part of the Soviet Union, Tatarstan is a semi-autonomous state within the Russian Federation. It lies in the Volga region. Kazan, its capital, is the northernmost Muslim community. Kazan Tatars prepare many Near Eastern dishes such as pilafs (rice dishes) and kabobs (meat grilled on skewers) using cold-climate ingredients, such as beef or goose. They are known for hearty meat pies: large rectangular belish, large round gubadia, and small round peremech, often topped with onion soup and yogurt. As in Russia, buckwheat, potatoes, and horseradish are eaten often, and hospitality centers on the samovar and pastries. Other dishes include Tatar samosa, made with puffy dough, as is the Russian pirozhki; Tatar baklava (pekhlewe), made of alternating layers of noodle paste and sweetened nuts; and chekchek, fried dough balls bound with honey into a flat loaf.

RWANDA
Republic of Rwanda

Geography Rwanda is in east-central Africa. It is mostly grassy uplands, hills, and deep valleys. A chain of volcanoes and Africa's highest lake, Lake Kivu (4,829 ft; 1,472 m), are in the northwest. Rwanda's highest point is Mt. Karisimbi (14,187 ft; 4,324 m).

Major Languages			Ethnic Groups		Major Religions	
Kinyarwanda (Bantu)	(all		Hutu (Bantu)	84%	Roman Catholic	57%
French	are		Tutsi (Hamitic)	15%	Protestant	26%
English	official)		Twa (Pygmy)	1%	Adventist	11%
Swahili					Muslim	5%
					Other	1%

Population density per sq. mi. 1,057.50
Literacy rate 64.9%
Life expectancy 48.6 male; 51 female
Per capita GDP $900
Labor force in agriculture 90%

Urban 17.5%
Infant mortality rate per 1,000 live births 83.4
HIV rate 2.8%
Unemployment rate 0.9%
Arable land 46%

Agriculture   plantains, potatoes, sweet potatoes, coffee, tea, bananas, beans, sorghum, pyrethrum (insecticide made from chrysanthemums), chickens, goats, cattle, sheep, pigs

Natural resources   gold, tin ore, tungsten ore, methane, hydropower, fish

Industries   cement, agricultural products, soap, plastic goods, textiles

History   Original inhabitants were the Twa, a Pygmy people. The Hutu were well established when the Tutsi came in the 14th century. The Tutsi conquered the Hutu and in the 15th century established a kingdom near Kigali. European explorers first visited the area in 1854. In 1890 it became part of German East Africa. Belgian troops occupied it during World War I. Afterward, in 1923, along with Burundi, it became a Belgian League of Nations mandate called Rwanda-Urundi. The mandate became a UN trust territory in 1946. For centuries the Tutsi (an extremely tall people) had dominated the Hutu. These groups spoke the same language. Their difference was mainly occupational: Hutus were agricultural; Tutsi owned cattle. A 1933 Belgian requirement was that each person carry an identity card indicating ethnicity, Hutu or Tutsi. In 1959 civil war ended the Tutsi rule and many Tutsi went into exile. In 1961 a referendum abolished the monarchy. In 1962 Rwanda gained independence, under Hutu rule. Since independence, violence in Rwanda and Burundi has increased ethnic differentiation between Hutu and Tutsi. In 1990 Tutsi exiles invaded Rwanda and attempted a coup; afterward a multiparty democracy was established. In 1994 a militia group and other Hutus slaughtered hundreds of thousands of Tutus, a genocidal slaughter. Afterward, a Tutu-led group took over the country and 2 million refugees, mostly Hutu, fled to neighboring countries. Rwanda's first Tutsi president, Kagama, took office in 2000. In 2003 Rwandans approved a new constitution that instituted a balance of political power between Hutu and Tutsi. In 2007 many alleged war criminals were released from prison and the government abolished the death penalty. Rwanda has had steady economic growth in recent years. In 2008 U.S. president Bush visited Rwanda and President Kagama; the United States has funded military training and control of HIV/AIDS and malaria in Rwanda.

Influences on food   Rwanda's food customs resemble those of East African countries Kenya and Tanzania, the latter a neighbor. The diet contains little meat, in spite of abundant game and the tradition of breeding cattle. Cattle were regarded as wealth, not food, and the Masai and related people lived on milk products and blood of cattle. Others lived on mostly grains, bananas, and gathered greens. The lakes supply fish, and tilapia and catfish are farmed. Although animals are protected, game is plentiful and antelope are farmed. The earliest foreign traders, Arabs, established colonies along the coast of East Africa from about 700 CE and introduced spices, onions, and eggplant. The Germans, the first European colonists here, and Belgium control, which followed, left little European influence on food here. The introduction of New World foods such as corn, potatoes, and tomatoes did influence Rwanda's food. The British encouraged Asians to settle in East Africa, leaving influence such as the use of curry. The diet is mostly starchy vegetables and legumes, the latter an important source of protein.

Bread and cereals   Sorghum, corn, millet, rice; porridge, flatbread, pancakes.

Meat, poultry, fish   Chicken, eggs, goat, beef, lamb, pork, fish, game.

Insects   Locusts, crickets, grasshoppers, ants, worms (madora), caterpillars (harati). Insects are collected, sometimes dried for later use, and often fried or roasted and eaten as snacks.

Dairy products   Milk, curds, cheeses (adaptations of European ones).

Fats and oils   Butter, clarified butter, palm oil, peanut oil.

Legumes   Beans, cowpeas, peanuts (groundnuts), lentils.

Vegetables   Plantains, potatoes, sweet potatoes, green leaves, tomatoes, peppers, cassava.

Fruit   Bananas, coconut, papaya.

Nuts and seeds   Cashews, sesame seeds, pumpkin seeds.

Seasonings   Peppers, tomatoes, dried baobab leaves, onions, coconut milk, black pepper, curry powder, cloves.

Dishes   Ugali (thick porridge of cornmeal or millet). Stew of leftover cooked meat, tomatoes, peppers, and green leaves or other vegetables. Green leaves cooked with peanut paste. Curried chicken. Irio (boiled beans, corn, and potatoes or cassava, mashed to a thick pulp). Plantains boiled in their peel and mashed. Fish fried or cooked with coconut milk. Simmered and mashed beans, lentils, corn, and plantains. Plantain soup, stew, and fritters.

Sweets   Honey, plantain custard.

Beverages   Coffee, tea, beer (often home-brewed from corn or millet).

Street food   Mandazi (doughnut or fritter), grilled corn cobs, rice and coconut pancakes, goat kabob.

S

SAINT KITTS AND NEVIS
Federation of Saint Kitts and Nevis

Geography   This country is in the eastern Caribbean Sea, southeast of Puerto Rico. A volcanic mountain chain dominates the central core of both islands. The Narrows, a 2-mile (3-km) wide channel, separates the islands. Saint Kitts's highest point is Mt. Liamuiga (3,792 ft; 1,156 m), with a lake in its forested crater. Nevis is a single mountain, ringed by coral reefs and beaches.

Major Language	Ethnic Groups		Major Religions	
English (official)	Black	90%	Anglican	24%
	Mulatto	5%	Methodist	23%
	Indo-Pakistani	3%	Other Protestant	28%
	White, other	2%	Roman Catholic	11%
			Other	14%

Population density per sq. mi. 395.1
Literacy rate 97.8%
Life expectancy 70.1 male; 76 female
Per capita GDP $13,900
Labor force in agriculture NA

Urban 32.2%
Infant mortality rate per 1,000 live births 14.3
HIV rate NA
Unemployment rate NA
Arable land 19%

Agriculture   sugarcane, tropical fruit, coconuts, rice, yams, vegetables, chickens, goats, sheep, cattle, pigs

Natural resources   fish

Industries   tourism, cotton, salt, copra, clothing, footwear, beverages

History   Carib Indians inhabited Saint Kitts (formerly Saint Christopher) and Nevis when Columbus reached and named them in 1493. The British settled on Saint Kitts in 1623, the first British colony in the West Indies, and on Nevis in 1628. The French settled on Saint Kitts in 1627. An Anglo-French rivalry lasted until 1783, when Britain gained control of both islands. The country became independent in 1983. A drop in prices in the 1980s depressed the economy, which the government tried to diversify by increasing tourism. Nevis attempted secession in 1998 but lacked the two-thirds majority vote needed. Most inhabitants are descendants of African slaves. This country is the smallest in the Western Hemisphere (area 101 sq. mi.; population 39,817). In 2007 at least four members of the National Assembly were identified as having dual citizenship, alleged to be in violation of the constitution.

Influences on food   The original inhabitants of the region, the Arawak and Carib Indians, mostly disappeared following the Spanish conquest. The traces of information that remain about their food practices indicate that they ate a wide range of fish and seafood, one-pot soups or stews, and cassava bread. The Spanish explored the region and influenced food customs, for example, they brought cattle, pigs, and rice. The French and British settled the islands and left influences such British salt cod gundy (spread), biscuits, and tea. Influences also came from African slaves, as in the use of okra, and from laborers from India, as in the use of spices in pepper pot.

Bread and cereals   Rice, corn, wheat; rice dishes, fried cornmeal cakes, wheat flour breads, cassava bread (grated, squeezed, and dried cassava, fried on a griddle), cassava and wheat flour biscuits and bread.

Meat, poultry, fish   Chicken, goat, lamb, beef, pork, fish and seafood (salt cod, snapper, lobster, crabs), eggs.

Dairy products   Cow's milk (fresh, condensed, evaporated), cream, aged cheese.

Fats and oils   Butter, lard, coconut oil, olive oil, vegetable oil.

Legumes   Kidney beans, red beans, black-eyed peas, chickpeas (garbanzo beans), pigeon peas.

Vegetables   Yams, cassava, malanga, sweet potatoes, plantains, avocados, green leaves (cassava, malanga), squash, pumpkin, breadfruit, tomatoes, okra, chili peppers, sweet peppers, onions.

Fruit   Coconut, bananas, mangoes, pineapple, oranges, limes, cashew apples, papaya, soursop, guavas, akee.

Nuts and seeds   Almonds, cashew nuts, annatto seeds.

Seasonings   Salt, black pepper, chilies, onion, garlic, annatto, allspice (pimento), cinnamon, coconut, cocoa, rum.

Dishes   Callaloo (soup of green leaves cooked with okra, seasonings, and sometimes coconut milk and bits of salt meat or cod). Pepper pot (meat stew containing boiled juice of cassava and ample pepper). Fish soup. Pumpkin soup. Stuffed crab. Fried codfish cakes. Salt cod with avocado. Boiled or fried yams, plantains, or akee. Cornmeal and okra cake. Boiled rice. Boiled peas or beans. Rice cooked with beans or peas.

Sweets   Sugarcane, molasses, sugar. Fresh fruit. Cornmeal pudding. Coconut biscuits.

Beverages   Coffee often with milk, tea, iced tea with lime, fruit juices, soft drinks, milk, cocoa, beer, rum.

Meals   Breakfast: coffee with milk and bread. Lunch: rice and beans or starchy vegetable and salt cod. Dinner: like lunch plus meat, vegetables, milk, and dessert when available.

Snacks   Fresh fruit, sweetened fruit juice poured over crushed ice, coffee with milk.

SAINT LUCIA

Geography   St. Lucia is an island in the eastern Caribbean Sea and Atlantic Ocean, south of Martinique. It is of volcanic origin, with wooded mountains running north to south, streams, fertile valleys, and a tropical climate.

Major Languages	Ethnic Groups		Major Religions	
English (official)	Black	83%	Roman Catholic	68%
French patois	Mixed	12%	Seventh-Day Adventist	9%
	East Indian	2%	Pentecostal	8%
	White, other	3%	Other	10%
			None	5%

Population density per sq. mi. 682.1
Literacy rate 90.1%
Life expectancy 73.6 male; 79 female
Per capita GDP $10,700
Labor force in agriculture 21.7%

Urban 27.6%
Infant mortality rate per 1,000 live births 13.8
HIV rate NA
Unemployment rate 17.0%
Arable land 6%

Agriculture   bananas, coconuts, citrus, tropical fruits, root crops, cocoa, chickens, pigs, sheep, cattle, goats

Natural resources   forests, pumice, sandy beaches, mineral springs, geothermal potential, fish

Industries   clothing, electronic components assembly, beverages, cardboard boxes, tourism, fruit processing

History   Arawak Indians first inhabited the island. The Carib Indians replaced them c. 800 to 1300 CE. Spain and then France explored St. Lucia. The French settled it in 1650 and France ceded it to Britain in 1814. It became independent in 1979. St. Lucians are primarily descendants of black African slaves. The 1999 European Union decision to end its preferential treatment of bananas from former colonies led to efforts to diversify the economy. A 2002 storm devastated the banana crop. In 2007 the government reestablished diplomatic relations with Taiwan, reversing the former administration's decision, which had switched recognition to China in the mid-1990s.

Influences on food   The earliest inhabitants, Arawak and Carib Indians, ate fish, seafood, stews, and cassava bread, using foods available from the sea and this tropical island. The same foods are used today, plus foods brought to the region by the Spanish, French, and British. British control for 165 years influenced food customs; examples include salt cod, biscuits, and tea. Slaves from Africa also influenced food practices such as in using okra and black-eyed peas. Laborers from India also influenced food customs, for example in using curry powder.

Bread and cereals   Corn, rice, wheat; fried cornmeal cakes, rice dishes, wheat flour bread, cassava bread (made from pressed, grated cassava fried on a griddle), biscuits made with wheat flour, cassava, and grated coconut.

Meat, poultry, fish   Chicken, eggs, pork, lamb, beef, goat, fish and seafood (33.6% tuna; also salt cod, snapper, flying fish, sea turtles, sea eggs also called sea urchins, lobster, crabs, frogs).

Dairy products   Cow's milk (fresh, condensed, evaporated), cream, aged cheese.

Fats and oils   Butter, lard, coconut oil, vegetable oil.

Legumes   Kidney beans, red beans, black-eyed peas, chickpeas, pigeon peas.

Vegetables   Cassava, yams, malanga, green leaves (cassava, malanga), sweet potatoes, squash, plantains, breadfruit, avocados, okra, tomatoes, onions, chilies, sweet peppers.

Fruit   Bananas, coconut, limes, other citrus, mangoes, cashew apples, akee, papaya, pineapple, soursop, passion fruit, raisins.

Nuts and seeds   Almonds, cashew nuts, annatto seeds.

Seasonings   Salt, black pepper, chilies, garlic, allspice, annatto, curry powder, cinnamon, coconut, cocoa, rum, pepper sauce.

Dishes   Callaloo (malanga leaves cooked with okra). Pepper pot (a meat stew containing boiled juice of cassava and highly seasoned with pepper). Soup of crab, sea urchin, or green turtle. Codfish fritters. Fried flying fish with bananas. Baked snapper. Roast pig. Curried chicken, meat, or fish. Boiled or fried cassava, yams, plantains, breadfruit, or akee. Boiled rice. Boiled black-eyed peas, other peas, or beans. Rice cooked with beans or peas. Cornmeal and okra cake.

Sweets   Sugarcane, unrefined sugar, molasses, sugar. Coconut custard pie. Lime coconut or chocolate mousse. Cornmeal cake (made with cornmeal, wheat flour, fruit, and rum). Rum fruitcake.

Beverages   Coffee often with milk, tea, iced tea with lime, fruit juices, soft drinks, milk, cocoa, beer, rum.

Meals   Breakfast: bread and coffee with milk. Lunch: rice and beans with meat if affordable. Dinner: like lunch but with more meat, vegetables, and milk added when available.

Snacks   Fruits, sweetened fruit juices poured over crushed ice, tea with coconut biscuits or bread, plantain chips.

SAINT VINCENT AND THE GRENADINES

Geography   These islands are in the eastern Caribbean Sea, north of Trinidad and Tobago. They are mountainous and thickly forested. Saint Vincent, the chief island, is dominated by volcano Mt. Soufrière (4,048 ft; 1,234 m). The Grenadines is a chain of 8 islands and about 600 islets, area 17 square miles (27 sq. km).

Major Languages	Ethnic Groups		Major Religions	
English (official)	Black	66%	Anglican	47%
French patois	Mixed	19%	Methodist	28%
	East Indian	6%	Roman Catholic	13%
	Other	9%	Other	12%

Population density per sq. mi. 788.5
Literacy rate 96%
Life expectancy 72.4 male; 76.3 female
Per capita GDP $9,800
Labor force in agriculture 26%

Urban 45.9%
Infant mortality rate per 1,000 live births 13.6
HIV rate NA
Unemployment rate 12.0%
Arable land 18%

Agriculture   bananas, sugarcane, starchy roots and tubers, coconuts, spices, chickens, sheep, pigs, goats, cattle

Natural resources   fish, hydropower

Industries   food processing, cement, furniture, clothing, starch

History   The Carib Indians inhabited St. Vincent before Columbus's arrival there on Jan. 22 (St. Vincent's Day), 1498. Britain and France alternately claimed Saint Vincent and the Grenadines in the 17th and 18th centuries until 1763, when France ceded them to Britain. The Caribs revolted in 1795, most were deported, and many who remained died in volcanic eruptions in 1812 and 1902. Sugarcane cultivation brought African slaves and, later, Portuguese and East Indian laborers. Independence was achieved in 1979; the same year Mt. Soufrière erupted, causing mass evacuation. The eruption and a 1980 hurricane seriously damaged the banana crop and the economy, which began to rebound by the 1990s. In 1999 the European Union decision to end its preferential treatment of bananas from former colonies led to efforts to diversify the economy. In 2007 the prime minister defended the increasing assistance from Cuba and Venezuela.

Influences on food   Carib Indians ate a wide variety of fish and seafood, stews, and cassava bread using foods available from the sea and grown locally. The same foods are used today on this tropical island plus foods brought to the region by the Spanish, French, British, and others. For example, breadfruit trees were brought to the Caribbean area from the South Seas by Englishman captain William Bligh in 1793. The tall tree has spread from Jamaica to virtually all the islands. Its sustaining quality is so valued that the men on Saint Vincent have a saying, "Give me a good working woman and a breadfruit tree and I never need work again." British control for more than two centuries, slaves from Africa, and laborers from India influenced food practices in this country.

Bread and cereals   Corn, rice, wheat; fried cornbread, rice dishes, wheat bread, cassava bread (pressed, grated cassava fried on a griddle), biscuits or bread made from wheat flour, cassava, and grated coconut.

Meat, poultry, fish   Chicken, eggs, lamb, pork, goat, beef, fish and seafood (salt cod, snapper, flying fish, sea eggs also called sea urchins, lobster, shrimp, crabs, frogs).

Dairy products   Cow's milk (fresh, condensed, evaporated), cream, aged cheese.

Fats and oils   Butter, lard, coconut oil, vegetable oil.

Legumes   Kidney beans, red beans, black-eyed peas, chickpeas, pigeon peas.

Vegetables   Sweet potatoes, breadfruit, cassava, yams, malanga, green leaves (cassava, malanga), plantains, avocados, okra, squash, pumpkin, tomatoes, onions, chilies, sweet peppers.

Fruit   Bananas, coconut, mangoes, limes, oranges, papaya, pineapple, cashew fruit, akee, soursop, passion fruit.

Nuts and seeds   Almonds, cashew nuts, annatto seeds.

Seasonings   Salt, black pepper, chilies, garlic, spices including allspice, cinnamon, and curry powder, annatto, coconut, cocoa, rum, hot pepper sauce, mango chutney (hot spicy preserves).

Dishes   Callaloo (malanga leaves cooked with okra). Pepper pot (a meat stew containing boiled juice of cassava and pepper). Crab soup made with coconut milk. Codfish fritters. Tree-tree cake (fritters of fresh tiny fish). Boiled or grilled lobster. Stewed shark. Roast pig. Chicken, lamb, goat, beef, or shrimp curry. Boiled rice. Boiled black-eyed peas, other peas, or beans. Rice cooked with beans or peas. Simmered cassava, yams, plantains, or akee. Fried sweet potatoes, breadfruit, akee, plantains, or chickpea balls. Cornmeal and okra cake.

Sweets   Sugarcane, unrefined sugar, molasses, sugar. Fruit. Breadfruit pudding. Coconut pie with meringue.

Beverages   Coffee with milk, tea, iced tea with lime, fruit juices, soft drinks, milk, beer, rum.
Meals   Breakfast: bread and coffee with milk. Lunch: rice and beans with meat if affordable. Dinner: like lunch but with more meat, vegetables, and milk added when available.

Snacks   Fruits, sweetened fruit juices poured over crushed ice, tea with coconut biscuits, coffee, plantain chips.

SAMOA (FORMERLY WESTERN SAMOA)
Independent State of Samoa

Geography   Samoa is in the South Pacific Ocean, near the International Date Line and about halfway between Hawaii and New Zealand. The main islands, Savaii and Upolu, are ruggedly mountainous and of volcanic origin. Most cultivation is in the small amount of level land in coastal areas. The small islands are Manono and Apolima.

Major Languages		Ethnic Groups		Major Religions	
Samoan (Polynesian)	(both	Samoan	93%	Congregationalist	35%
English	official)	Euronesian		Roman Catholic	20%
		(European-Polynesian)	7%	Methodist	15%
				Latter-Day Saints	13%
				Other	17%

Population density per sq. mi. 191.6
Literacy rate 98.7%
Life expectancy 68.8 male; 74.5 female
Per capita GDP $5,400
Labor force in agriculture NA

Urban 22.4%
Infant mortality rate per 1,000 live births 25
HIV rate NA
Unemployment rate NA
Arable land 21%

Agriculture   coconuts, bananas, taro, yams, coffee, cocoa, chickens, pigs, cattle

Natural resources   hardwood forests, fish, hydropower

Industries   food processing, building materials, auto parts

History   Polynesians, perhaps from Tonga, inhabited the islands of the Samoan archipelago for thousands of years. Dutch and French traders explored the islands in the 18th century. In the late 19th century, conflicting interests of the United States, Britain, and Germany were settled in a 1899 treaty that recognized U.S. interest for American Eastern Samoa and German interest for Western Samoa. Western Samoa was a German colony from 1899 to 1914. New Zealand received it as a League of Nations mandate in 1920 and, in 1945, it became a UN Trustee administered by New Zealand. It gained independence in 1962. In 1990 most women gained the right to vote. In 1997 the word "western" was dropped from the country's name. Cyclones regularly damage the mainly agrarian economy; Samoa is increasing its tourism. In 2007 the economy grew and the UN Economic and Social Council removed Samoa from its list of least developed countries, although the government remained dependent on remittances from some 200,000 Samoans living abroad.

Influences on food   Samoa is in the Polynesia group of the Pacific Islands. About 30,000 to 40,000 years ago people from Southeast Asia began to move south to the western Pacific islands and Australia, and they later migrated to islands further east. Influences on food in Samoa include Polynesians, perhaps from Tonga, who first settled Samoa, Dutch and French traders, the United States, Britain, Germany, and New Zealand. The Europeans brought new food plants, wheat bread, and some animals. Asians brought rice, soybeans, noodles, and teas. Many foods in some Samoa markets are from the United States, New Zealand, and Australia. Samoa's main foods are fish, taro, yams, coconuts, pork, and chicken. Pork is the main meat, especially for feasts (held nearly every Sunday), traditionally cooked in a pit (umu, or hima'a, in Samoa). A fire is built on stones lining the pit, and when coals are hot, layers of banana leaves or palm fronds are added; pig and foods such as yams and breadfruit are added and covered with more leaves; the pit is sealed with dirt; and the food cooks for hours.

Bread and cereals   Rice, wheat; bread, noodles, rice dishes.

Meat, poultry, fish   Chicken, pork, beef, fish (mullet, others), shellfish (giant crabs, palolo eggs "caviar of the South Pacific," others), eggs; corned beef, spam.

Dairy products   Milk and other dairy products are uncommon. Coconut milk has many uses, much as cow's milk.

Fats and oils   Coconut oil and cream, lard, butter, vegetable oil and shortening, sesame oil.

Legumes   Soybeans, winged beans, peas, lentils, peanuts.

Vegetables   Taro root and leaves, yams, sweet potatoes, plantains, breadfruit, cassava, green leaves, seaweed, arrowroot, bitter melon, cabbage, daikon, eggplant, squash, onions, green onions.

Fruit   Coconut, bananas, lemons, limes, guavas, mangoes, papaya, pineapple, melons, tamarind. Fresh fruit is eaten as snacks or added to dishes.

Nuts and seeds   Candlenuts (kukui), litchis, macadamia nuts.

Seasonings   Coconut cream and milk, lime and lemon juice, salt, soy sauce, ginger, garlic, onions, tamarind.

Dishes   Most dishes are cooked in coconut milk or cream. Cheese-like chunks of fermented coconut. Papaya and coconut cream soup (supo 'esi). Deep-fried dumplings filled with bananas or pineapple (pani keki). Boiled taro root or yams. Boiled or steamed rice. Boiled or steamed greens or seaweed. Arrowroot-thickened puddings and other dishes. Oka (chunks of raw white fish marinated in lemon juice and coconut cream). Stewed or roasted fish and shellfish. Ti leaf–wrapped packets of fish steamed or cooked in umu. A delicacy, fried Samoan caviar (palolo fish eggs). Steamed banana leaf–wrapped packets of fruit. Foods cooked in a pit: whole pig, taro, yams, sweet potatoes, breadfruit, shellfish, whole fish, chicken pieces, taro leaves wrapped around a filling of coconut cream, lemon, onions, and shredded beef and all bound in banana leaves, and other leaf-wrapped mixtures of taro, yams, or breadfruit with coconut cream and seasonings.

Sweets   Sugar. Immature coconut. Haupia (pudding made from coconut milk, sugar, and arrowroot). Sweet biscuit made with flour, grated coconut, and papaya.

Beverages   Coconut juice, coffee, cocoa (koko Samoa: ground cacao beans mixed with water), tea, fruit juice, kava (mildly alcoholic drink made from pepper plant). A kava ceremony often precedes a feast.

Meals   Typical are two or three meals daily, with the same foods at all, and the evening meal the largest. Coconut is eaten at every meal: in soup for breakfast, the cream with fruit, fish, or breadfruit for main meals, and grated coconut in a sweet biscuit at almost any time. It is considered rude to eat in front of someone without sharing.

SAN MARINO
Republic of San Marino

Geography   This tiny country (area 24 sq. mi., 61 sq. km; population 23,973) is in southern Europe, surrounded by Italy. It is in central north Italy, on the slopes of Mt. Titano, in the Apennines, and near the Adriatic Sea.

Major Language	Ethnic Groups	Major Religion
Italian (official)	Sammarinese Italian	Roman Catholic

Population density per sq. mi. 1,268.5
Literacy rate 96%
Life expectancy 78.4 male; 85.6 female
Per capita GDP $34,100
Labor force in agriculture 0.2%

Urban 94.1%
Infant mortality rate per 1,000 live births 5.4
HIV rate NA
Unemployment rate 3.3%
Arable land 17%

Agriculture   wheat, grapes, barley, corn, olives, cattle, sheep, pigs, horses

Natural resources   building stone

Industries   tourism, banking, textiles, electronics, ceramics, cement, wine

History   San Marino claims to have been founded about 350 CE by St. Marinus. By the 12th century it had developed into a commune. It remained independent, surviving the Renaissance as a self-governing city-state, and remained an independent republic after the unification of Italy in 1861. It has had a treaty of friendship with Italy since 1862. Persons born in San Marino remain citizens and can vote no matter where they live. San Marino joined the UN in 1992. It is very densely populated. San Marino is one of the smallest republics in the world and may be the oldest one in Europe. In 2007 the economy was reported to be strong.

Influences on food   Italy surrounds this tiny country and influences its food. San Marino is in the southern part of the Italian province Emilia-Romagna, whose capital is Bologna, the gastronomic center of northern Italy. This area has robust cuisine and the richest style of cooking in Italy. It is best known for pasta, pork (ham and sausages), and cheeses from Parma.

Bread and cereals   Wheat, barley, corn, rice; white wheat bread, rolls, pasta (tortellini, lasagna), corn dishes, rice dishes.

Meat, poultry, fish   Beef and veal, lamb, pork, chicken, eggs, fish and seafood; sausages, Parma ham (proscuitto).

Dairy products   Milk, cream, cheese (Parmesan, provolone, mozzarella, ricotta, Gorgonzola, Bel Paese).

Fats and oils   Butter, lard, olive oil, vegetable oil, margarine.

Legumes   Chickpeas, fava beans, kidney beans, white beans, lentils, peanuts.

Vegetables   Olives, tomatoes, spinach, lettuce, potatoes, onions, asparagus, carrots, celery, egg-plant, bell peppers, parsley.

Fruit   Grapes, cherries, apples, pears, peaches, lemons, figs, apricots, oranges, tangerines, raisins, melon.

Nuts and seeds   Almonds, hazelnuts, pignolis (pine nuts), walnuts, lupine seeds.

Seasonings   Salt, black pepper, onions, garlic, basil, oregano, nutmeg, sage, vinegar, lemon, vanilla, cocoa.

Dishes   Boiled pasta served with meat sauce, or stew (ragù), of pork and beef, onions, carrots, celery, and tomatoes. Boiled lasagna, then layered with meat and cream sauces, sprinkled with Parmesan cheese, and baked. Lasagne verdi al forno (like the previous dish except with spinach-flavored lasagna noodles). Tortellini (circles of dough stuffed with meat, cheese, and eggs, boiled, and served with butter, cream, and grated cheese). Polenta (cornmeal porridge). Risotto (rice sautéed in butter, then simmered with stock, and butter and grated Parmesan cheese added). Braised veal scallop rolls stuffed with chicken liver, proscuitto, and sage (involtini alla cacciatora). Baked chicken breasts topped with proscuitto and cheese slices, and sprinkled with Parmesan cheese. Pickled eels. Pickled pig's foot (zampone). Fish chowder (brodetto). Green salad. Pickled vegetables.

Sweets   Honey, sugar. Jam. Fresh fruit and cheese, for example, Gorgonzola or Bel Paese. Zabaglione (wine custard). Cheesecake. Pampeto (a sweet yeast roll with cocoa, spices, almonds, and lemon peel). Ice cream.

Beverages   Coffee, tea, chocolate, wine (Chianti, Marsala).

SÃO TOMÉ AND PRÍNCIPE
Democratic Republic of São Tomé and Príncipe

Geography   These tiny volcanic islands are about 125 miles (240 km) off the west coast of central Africa in the Gulf of Guinea. São Tomé, covered by dense mountainous jungle and large plantations, is where 95% of the population lives. Príncipe consists of jagged mountains. Other islands are Pedras Tinhosas and Rolas.

Major Language	Ethnic Groups		Major Religions	
Portuguese (official)	Black-white mixture	80%	Roman Catholic	80%
	Fang	10%	Protestant	15%
	Angolan slave descendants	8%	Muslim	3%
	Portuguese, other	2%	Other	2%

Population density per sq. mi. 533.5
Literacy rate 87.9%
Life expectancy 66.3 male; 69.7 female
Per capita GDP $1,600
Labor force in agriculture subsistence agric., fishing

Urban 58.1%
Infant mortality rate per 1,000 live births 38.4
HIV rate NA
Unemployment rate 30%
Arable land 8%

Agriculture   oil palm fruit, taro, bananas, cocoa, coconuts, cinnamon, pepper, coffee, copra, papayas, beans, chickens, goats, cattle, sheep, pigs

Natural resources   fish, hydropower

Industries   light construction, textiles, soap, beer, fish processing, timber

History   In 1471 Portuguese navigators visited these islands, believed to have been uninhabited. The Portuguese colonized São Tomé and Príncipe in the 16th century and used them in the slave trade. The islands were a major sugar producer, using slave labor, during the 17th century. Sugarcane was replaced by the slave trade as a more important economic activity. Coffee and cocoa were introduced in the 19th century and replaced sugar as major crops. Independence came in 1975. During recent decades the country's economy depended heavily on international assistance. For good governance and stable economy, the International Monetary Fund offered debt relief in 2008 under its Heavily Indebted Poor Countries initiatives. This poor country is expected to gain billions of dollars from oil in the Gulf of Guinea. Although no oil has been pumped from the country's waters, millions of dollars had been received from investors, and most of it has been invested in interest-bearing securities.

Influences on food   These islands are off the coast of Equatorial Guinea. In general, the food is West African with Portuguese influence. Portugal, a leader in world exploration and colonization from the 15th century, controlled these islands for five centuries. The Portuguese brought foods such as sugarcane, citrus, and spices from Asia and corn, tomatoes, chilies, potatoes, and chocolate from the New World, mostly from their possession Brazil.

Bread and cereals   Corn, wheat, millet, rice; porridge, cornbread, rice dishes, Portuguese bread.

Meat, poultry, fish   Chicken, goat, beef, lamb and mutton, pork, fish and shellfish, eggs, guinea fowl.

Dairy products   Milk, cream.

Fats and oils   Palm oil, coconut oil, peanut oil, butter, lard, olive oil.

Legumes   Red beans, black-eyed peas, locust beans (carob), peanuts (groundnuts).

Vegetables   Taro, greens, okra, cassava, plantains, yams, potatoes, tomatoes, eggplant, bell peppers, pumpkin.

Fruit   Bananas, coconut, papaya, lemons, baobab, mangoes, watermelon, pineapple, guavas, oranges, limes.

Nuts and seeds   Kola nuts, mango seeds, watermelon seeds (egusi), sesame seeds.

Seasonings   Cocoa, cinnamon, onion, black pepper, chili pepper, garlic, coconut milk, turmeric, ginger, vanilla.

Dishes   Porridge of corn, millet, or cassava. Boiled vegetables (e.g., okra with fermented locust beans). Fufu (starchy paste of boiled and mashed yams, plantains, cassava, or sweet potatoes, or of corn flour), formed into scoops to eat stew. Spicy peanut sauce with chili and palm oil served with chicken or meat stew and boiled rice. Stews of ground peanuts, root vegetables, or okra, with chilies, tomatoes, and herbs, plus small amounts of fish, shellfish, chicken, or beef. Accompaniments: hard-boiled eggs, raw onion, bell pepper. Sauce of pounded green leaves. Fréjon (purée of black-eyed peas, coconut milk, and sometimes carob or cocoa). Fried fish. Gari (cassava meal) cooked with eggs, tomatoes, onions, and peppers. Yassa (chicken and fish marinated in lemon or lime juice, grilled on a barbecue, and then fried with onions and simmered with the marinade). Jollof rice (rice first sautéed in oil, then boiled with water or broth, tomatoes, and meat, chicken, fish, shellfish, vegetables, legumes, and spices; palm oil and/or tomatoes are used to give a red color). Fish stew. Prawns browned with onions in oil and butter, then simmered with coconut milk, tomatoes, red chilies, and other spices, and Madeira wine added before serving. Fish and shrimp salad (simmered fish and shrimp mixed with tomatoes, onions, garlic, chilies, oil, and vinegar). Marinated and fried pork. Goat soup. Kid stew with chili potatoes. Fried cornbread. Steamed paste of black-eyed peas, onion, and hot pepper. Fried yams. Fried plantains. Black-eyed pea fritters.

Sweets   Sugarcane, honey, brown sugar, sugar. Sweet porridge. Coconut biscuits. Banana or pineapple fritters.

Beverages   Coffee, cocoa, wine (ordinary Portuguese, port, and Madeira).

SAUDI ARABIA
Kingdom of Saudi Arabia

Geography   Saudi Arabia is in the Middle East, bordering the Red Sea and the Persian Gulf. It occupies most of the Arabian Peninsula. It has mountains up to 9,000 feet in the west and the world's largest continuous sand desert, the Rub Al-Khali. Its oil region is mainly in the east along the Persian Gulf.

Major Language	Ethnic Groups		Major Religions	
Arabic (official)	Saudi Arab	74%	Islam (official)	
	Expatriates (Indian 5%,		Sunni Muslim	84%
	Bangladeshi 4%, Pakistani 4%,		Shi'a Muslim	10%
	Filipino 3%, Egyptian 3%,		Roman Catholic	3%
	other)	26%	Hindu, other	3%

Population density per sq. mi. 33.9

Literacy rate 86%

Life expectancy 74 male; 78.2 female

Per capita GDP $23,200

Labor force in agriculture 12%

Urban 81%

Infant mortality rate per 1,000 live births 11.9

HIV rate NA

Unemployment rate 6.3%

Arable land 2%

Agriculture   wheat, alfalfa, dates, barley, tomatoes, melons, citrus, chickens, sheep, goats, cattle, camels

Natural resources   oil, natural gas, iron ore, gold, copper, fish

Industries   oil production and refining, petrochemicals, cement, fertilizers, plastics, metals, construction

History   Saudi Arabia is the homeland of the Arabs, believed to have originated here, and of Islam. Numerous warring tribes and small kingdoms inhabited this land. Muhammad united the area in the early 7th century and founded Islam in 622 CE. His successors conquered the Near East and North Africa, bringing Islam and the Arabic language. During medieval times, various invaders sought to control the Arabian Peninsula and by 1517 the Ottoman Empire dominated. In the middle of the 18th century it was divided into two principalities. Central Arabia came under Turkish rule. In 1913 Ibn Saud overthrew the Turks. The British held Saudi lands as a protectorate from 1915 to 1927 and then acknowledged the sovereignty of the Kingdom of the Hejaz and Najd. The two kingdoms were united in 1932 to form the Kingdom of Saudi Arabia. Ibn Saud, founder of the Saudi dynasty, reigned until his death in 1953; succeeding kings have been his sons. Oil was discovered in 1936 and production began during World War II, transforming Arabia into a wealthy country that provided free health care and education while not collecting taxes from the people. Since World War II, Saudi Arabia has supported the Palestinian cause in the Middle East and maintained close relations with the United States Saudi Arabia is the home of Islam and contains Islam's holy cities: Mecca, Muhammad's birthplace; and Medina, location of his tomb. Each year more than 2 million Muslims make pilgrimage to Mecca. The Islamic religious code is the law of the land. Alcohol and public entertainment are restricted. Women have an inferior legal status. There is no constitution or parliament, although in 1993 the king established a Consultative Council. The Sept. 11, 2001, terrorist attacks on the United States included Saudis among the Al-Qaeda hijackers. Much of Saudi Arabia's influential religious establishment has supported anti-Americanism and Islamic militancy. Saudi Arabia is a UN charter member. In 2005, Saudi Arabia held its first election, to choose half of the new council members in Riyadh; the other half continues to be appointed, in keeping with the previous Saudi system. Women were not allowed to vote. Suicide bombers who attempted to attack a huge oil and gas facility in 2006 were arrested in 2007. Oil revenues soared from 2004 to 2008, providing investment funding for plans including diversifying the economy and redeveloping Mecca. In 2008 the Saudis disclosed a program to retrain Muslim clerics.

Influences on food   Arabian food is common to Saudi Arabia, Kuwait, Bahrain, Qatar, the United Arab Emirates, Oman, and Yemen. The large area and population, including a substantial population of expatriates, results in a wide range of foods. The indigenous Bedouin tribes (desert dwellers) have a basic Bedouin food culture. Arabian food has been influenced by Islam and by surrounding cultures: Ottoman to the north, the Horn of Africa to the west, and Iran and India to the east. Food presentation and meal format are similar in Lebanon and Syria. Saudi Arabia, the largest country of the region, has a long coast that supplies fish and prawns. It is the home of Islam.

Bedouin food   Bedouins are nomads of the Arabian, Syrian, or North African deserts. Camels, goats, and sheep provide meat and milk. The basic diet is milk, bread, and dates. A usual dish is boiled mutton on a bed of wheat or rice. Bread, the staple, is thin unleavened bread cooked on a metal sheet over the fire. Meat from a large animal is cooked in a large metal stew pot for a feast; small game are thrown on a fire to cook. Important milk products are buttermilk, yogurt, and samn (butter made from churned milk, then heated with a little flour and occasionally coriander or cumin). Samn flavors rice and wheat. Yogurt is also drained and sun-dried to make a traveler's food to gnaw or to reconstitute with water. One meal a day is usual, sometimes only camel milk and a few dates.

Muslims and food   Islam is the faith of most Arabs and of nearly 15% of the world's population. The Koran, revealed to Muhammad by the messenger of God, praises food as one of God's gifts to humanity and states that all food is permitted to the faithful with four exceptions: blood, pig meat, any animal that has not been purposefully slaughtered for food, and any food slaughtered in the name of a pagan deity. Relative to these last two prohibitions, any living creature intended as food for human beings must be slaughtered while conscious and after the slaughterer has spoken the words: 'In the name of God; God is most great.' Such meat is halal, lawful. Alcohol is forbidden, even in cooking. During the month of Ramadan, fasting is practiced from sunup to sundown.

Main foods   Lamb, rice, flatbread, yogurt, legumes, vegetables, dates.

Bread and cereals   Wheat, rice, barley; wheat flatbread (e.g., pita, thin round bread with hollow center), cracked wheat (bulgur), rice dishes.

Meat, poultry, fish   Lamb and mutton, chicken, eggs, goat, beef, fish, prawns. Favorites are lamb, chicken, fish.

Dairy products   Milk (goat, sheep, cow, camel), yogurt (labia), strained yogurt (labneh), feta cheese (white). Mostly fermented products (yogurt, cheese) are consumed.

Fats and oils   Butter, ghee (clarified butter), samn, olive oil, sesame oil.

Legumes   Fava beans, chickpeas, lentils.

Vegetables   Tomatoes, eggplant, onions, cucumbers, olives, fresh herbs (parsley, spinach, mint, and coriander).

Fruit   Dates, melons, oranges, lemons, limes, mangoes, bananas, pomegranates. Dates are consumed in large quantities, especially during Ramadan. Juice of unripe lemons (verjuice) is used to provide sour taste to dishes.

Nuts and seeds   Almonds, sesame seed, walnuts, pistachios, hazelnuts, pine nuts. Tahini (sesame seed paste) is eaten often and used as a cooking ingredient and in a sweet dessert paste halvah.

Seasonings   Onions, saffron, cardamom, turmeric, baharat (a mixture of black pepper, coriander, cassia, cloves, cumin, cardamom, nutmeg, and paprika). Loomi, dried Omani limes, is used in meat dishes and sweet tea.

Dishes   Pilaf (rice sautéed in butter or oil in which chopped onions have been browned, then broth is added, saffron or turmeric may be added, and rice is steamed). Lamb cooked on skewers, in pieces or meatballs (kabob mashwi). Roasted chicken. A whole roasted lamb or sheep, a festive food. Kish'ka (an Arab specialty of bulgur and yogurt, dried, ground, and later reconstituted with water to use in pita filling or soup). Tabouli (salad of fresh vegetables, onions, parsley, mint, and wheat kernels). Moussaka (baked eggplant, tomato, onions, and olive oil). Hummus (cooked puréed chickpeas). Falafel (fried small balls of ground chickpeas or fava beans). Machbous (prawns cooked with rice, fresh herbs, and vegetables). Tharid, reputedly Muhammad's favorite dish, a casserole of layered flatbread with meat stew. Simmered vegetables or legumes. Fresh salt pickles.

Possible national dish   Khouzi (baked whole lamb stuffed with chicken, eggs, and rice spiced with baharat, saffron, and onions), served on rice and garnished with almonds and ghee.

Sweets   Dates, dibis (date molasses), honey. Baklava (thin sheets of dough layered with nuts and soaked in flavored syrup, often cut into diamond shapes). Ataif (small stuffed pancakes), a Ramadan specialty adopted from northern neighbors. Dates and dibis are used in many sweet dishes. Honey is consumed in large quantities.

Beverages   Coffee, tea. Coffee, the main drink, is strongly associated with the renowned Arabian hospitality and is strong, thick, sweet, and often flavored with cardamom. Tea is usually consumed black and very sweet.

Snacks and fast food   Shawerma, vertical spit-roasted lamb pieces, sliced thin and served in pita bread; sold at stalls (Obeidat and Brittin, 2004).

SENEGAL
Republic of Senegal

Geography   Senegal is the westernmost country in Africa and borders the Atlantic Ocean. Low rolling plains cover most of the land, with semi-desert in the north and northeast, and forests, swamps, and jungles in the southwest.

Major Languages	Ethnic Groups		Major Religions	
French (official)	Wolof	43%	Sunni Muslim	89%
Wolof	Pular	24%	Shi'a Muslim	5%
Pular	Serer	15%	Christian (mostly	
Jola	Mandinka	10%	Roman Catholic)	5%
Mandinka	Other	8%	Indigenous beliefs	1%

Population density per sq. mi. 173.4
Literacy rate 42.6%
Life expectancy 55.7 male; 58.5 female
Per capita GDP $1,700
Labor force in agriculture 77.5%

Urban 41.6%
Infant mortality rate per 1,000 live births 58.9
HIV rate 1%
Unemployment rate 40%
Arable land 13%

Agriculture　sugarcane, peanuts, millet, corn, sorghum, rice, cotton, tomatoes, green vegetables, chickens, sheep, goats, cattle, pigs

Natural resources　fish, phosphates, iron ore

Industries　agriculture and fish processing, phosphate mining, fertilizer production, oil refining

History　The peoples of Senegal and North Africa had established links in the 10th century CE. The Toucouleur people, early inhabitants, converted to Islam in the 11th century. In the 15th century Portuguese settlers arrived. Throughout the 17th and 18th centuries Europeans exported slaves, ivory, and gold from Senegal. The first French settlement was in 1659. French control grew from the 17th century. The French gained possession of the area in 1840 and made it part of French West Africa in 1895. Dakar became the capital. Independence came in 1960. In 1982 Senegal and Gambia joined to form a confederation, Senegambia, which was dissolved in 1898. French political and economic influence has remained strong. Senegal has been a bridge between the Islamic and black African worlds. In 2001 a new constitution granted women equal property rights with men. In 2002 a state-owned ferry sank and at least 1,863 passengers died. Forty years of Socialist Party rule ended with the election of a Democratic Party leader as president in 2000; he was reelected in 2007. A peace accord was signed with separatists in southern Senegal in 2004 seeking to end a 22-year-old insurgency. In 2007 Senegal increased its number of troops in the African Union peacekeeping force in the Darfur region of the Sudan.

Influences on food　Portuguese influence came with settlers in the 15th century. French influence grew from the 17th century and remains strong. The introduction of New World foods such as cassava, corn, chili pepper, peanuts, pumpkin, tomato, and potato greatly influenced food customs. Native African foods included watermelon, black-eyed peas, and okra. Most people are Muslims and do not eat pork. The Atlantic Ocean and rivers provide fish. Animals are herded in the semi-desert area in the north and are eventually eaten. The diet of most people is starchy vegetables, legumes, and greens. Spicy, thick, sticky foods are liked.

Bread and cereals　Millet, corn, sorghum, rice, wheat; rice dishes, French bread.

Meat, poultry, fish　Chicken, lamb and mutton, goat, beef, pork, fish (fresh, smoked, salted, or dried), seafood, guinea fowl, eggs, ducks, rabbits, 'Bush meat' (such as antelope, wild pig). Chicken is popular and prestigious.

Insects　Termites (often called white ants), locusts. Insects are sometimes dried and usually roasted or fried.

Dairy products　Milk, sour milk, buttermilk, curds, whey, cheese.

Fats and oils　Palm oil, peanut oil, shea oil, coconut oil. Palm oil, the predominant cooking fat, is red.

Legumes　Peanuts (groundnuts), black-eyed peas (a variety of cowpeas), locust beans (carob), red beans.

Vegetables　Tomatoes, green leaves, okra, bitter leaf, melokhia (crain crain), yams, plantains, cassava, taro, sweet potatoes, potatoes, eggplant (green), pumpkin, onions, chili peppers, cucumbers, bell peppers.

Fruit   Coconut, akee apples, baobab, guavas, lemons, limes, mangoes, papaya, pineapple, watermelon, bananas.

Nuts and seeds   Cashews, kola nuts (contain caffeine, extract was used in original Coca-Cola recipe), egusi (watermelon seeds), sesame seeds, mango seeds, baobab seeds. These thicken and flavor sauces and stews.

Seasonings   Salt, tomatoes, hot red chili peppers, onions, mint, dried baobab leaves, thyme, "African nutmeg," ginger, cocoa, vanilla.

Dishes   Most foods are boiled or fried, and chunks are dipped in a sauce and eaten by hand. Possibly the best-known African dish outside of Africa, Jollof rice (rice and bits of meat, vegetables, and spices plus tomatoes or palm oil). Fufu (a paste of boiled and pounded starchy vegetables or corn flour); it is formed into bite-size scoops to eat stew. Fish and meat stew (e.g., futu, a stew with twice as much meat as dried fish). Peanut stew (peanuts, chilies, tomatoes, herbs, and perhaps meat, chicken, or fish, or mixtures of them, and perhaps potatoes, beans, okra, or eggplant). Stews of okra or root vegetables with bits of fish, chicken, or beef. Peanut sauce. Palaver sauce (pounded green leaves). Fréjon (pea or bean purée, coconut milk, and sometimes carob or cocoa). Gari (roasted cassava meal). Gari foto (gari cooked with scrambled eggs). Steamed rice balls. Adalu (simmered and mashed vegetables). Yassa (chicken, meat, or fish marinated in lemon juice, grilled, fried with onions and chilies, and simmered in the marinade). Boiled rice. Baked chicken, tomatoes, and peanut sauce. Grilled or roasted fish.

National dish   Thieboudienne, or chep-bu-jen (fish and rice), usually served with vegetables.

Sweets   Sugarcane, honey, sugar. Kanya (peanut candy). Baked bananas. Fried dough balls. Vanilla custard.

Beverages   Beer, bissap rouge (sweet drink made from hibiscus), ginger beer, sweet mint tea.

Meals and service   Two meals a day, one late morning and one evening, is typical. Service is family style or more formal, with the men served first, then the boys, then the girls, and the women served last.

Street food and snacks   Spiced kabobs, shawerma (rotisserie lamb), fried fish, plantain chips, sweet porridge.

SERBIA
Republic of Serbia

Geography   Serbia is in southeast Europe on the Balkan Peninsula. It is part of the rich, fertile Danube Plain drained by the Danube River in the north. It has mountains in the southeast and limestone basins in the east.

Major Languages	Ethnic Groups		Major Religions	
Serbian (official)	Serb	83%	Orthodox	85%
Hungarian	Hungarian	4%	Roman Catholic	6%
	Romany	1%	Muslim	3%
	Other	12%	Protestant, other	6%

Population density per sq. mi. 297.8
Literacy rate 96.4% (including Montenegro)
Life expectancy 72.7 male; 78.1 female
Per capita GDP $10,400
Labor force in agriculture 30%

Urban 51.5%
Infant mortality rate per 1,000 live births 11.9
HIV rate 0.1%
Unemployment rate 20.9%
Arable land NA

Agriculture   corn, sugar beets, wheat, sunflowers, tobacco, olives, chickens, pigs, sheep, cattle, goats

Natural resources   oil, gas, coal, antimony, copper, zinc, gold, pyrite, limestone, marble, fish

Industries   sugar, agricultural machinery, electrical and commercial and transportation equipment, paper and pulp

History   Serbia had been a Turkish principality from 1389 until it became an independent kingdom in 1878. It annexed Old Serbia and Macedonia in 1913 after the Balkan wars. The Kingdom of the Serbs, Croats, and Slovenes (formerly the provinces of Croatia, Dalmatia, Bosnia, Herzegovina, Slovenia, and Vojvodina) was created after Austria-Hungary collapsed at the end of World War I. Yugoslavia was formed in 1918 from Montenegro and the Kingdom of Serbs, Croats, and Slovenes. This country was named Yugoslavia in 1929 and divided into regions without regard to ethnic boundaries. Germany invaded Yugoslavia in 1941. The Socialist Federal Republic of Yugoslavia was established in 1945. It included the republics of Bosnia and Herzegovina, Croatia, Macedonia, Montenegro, Serbia, and Slovenia. After a 10-year civil war, it broke up in the 1990s. Croatia and Slovenia declared independence in 1991. Macedonia and Bosnia and Herzegovina declared independence in 1991–1992. In 1992 Serbia and Montenegro proclaimed the new Republic of Yugoslavia (containing roughly 45% of the population and 40% of the area of its predecessor), which was renamed Serbia and Montenegro in 2003. Ethnic violence continued. In 1998–1999 Serbia repressed and expulsed ethnic populations in Kosovo, a province in southern Serbia. In 2004 ethnic violence erupted again in Kosovo. Montenegro voted to separate from Serbia and Serbia declared independence in 2006. Kosovo declared independence from Serbia in 2008; its independence was recognized by the United States and most European countries but not by Serbia and Russia.

Influences on food   Serbian cuisine is based on Slavic traditions with influences during centuries of domination by Rome, Byzantium, and Turkey. Neighboring Balkan countries have also influenced food here. The many Christians frequently eat pork. Muslims do not consume pork. Usual foods are kajmak (clotted cream), sir and kačkavalj (sheep's milk cheeses), yogurts (from cow's milk and luxury kiselo mleko from sheep's milk), and slatko (syrupy fruit conserve), offered with water and Serbian (Turkish) coffee to the afternoon visitor. Vojvodina, the province north of Belgrade, shares a border with Hungary and Romania and supplies grain, sugar, beef, pork, and fresh-water fish. Settled by Serbs, other Slavs, Hungarians, Romanians, and Slovaks, it has varied cuisine with Central European influence, especially in Hungarian- or Viennese-like cakes and pastries.

Bread and cereals   Corn, wheat, rice; porridge, rice dishes, leavened wheat bread, pita bread (thin, round bread with pocket), wheat flour pasta, pies, dumplings, and filo dough (paper-thin pastry). Most meals include bread.

Meat, poultry, fish   Chicken, eggs, pork, lamb and mutton, beef and veal, goat, fish; ham, sausage.

Dairy products   Milk (cow, sheep, goat), buttermilk, cream, sour cream, yogurt, cheese.

Fats and oils   Butter, margarine, vegetable oils, olive oil.

Legumes   Chickpeas, fava beans, black beans, white beans, lentils.

Vegetables   Potatoes, olives, cabbage, cucumbers, mushrooms, tomatoes, eggplant, onions; sauerkraut.

Fruit   Apples, berries, cherries, peaches, pears, plums, grapes, lemons. Fruit juice is important.

Nuts and seeds   Almonds, walnuts, pistachios, poppy seeds, sesame seeds.

Seasonings   Garlic, dill, mint, cardamom, cinnamon, oregano, parsley, pepper, paprika, lemon juice.

Dishes   Soups often with legumes as important ingredients. Wheat or cornmeal porridge. Steamed wheat kernels. Boiled rice. Meat and vegetable casseroles such as moussaka (baked minced lamb, eggplant, onions, and tomato sauce). Veal stew with paprika. Fried fish. Dumplings and pies filled with meat, cheese, eggs, vegetables, nuts, or fruit. Cabbage stuffed with meat or rice. Serbian cheese and egg pie (gibanjica).

Special occasion food   Serbian Krsna Slava (Patron Saint's Day) Krsni kolac (ritual bread decorated with the religious Serbian emblem and other designs made in dough).

Sweets Honey, sugar. Fruit preserves. Fruit compote. Slatko (fruit cooked in heavy syrup). Fruit-filled dumplings and strudels. Baklava (baked pastry of filo dough layered with nut filling, soaked in flavored syrup). Potica (sweet yeast bread rolled in walnut, butter, cream, and egg filling). Serbian kolijivo (wheat kernels cooked with sugar, dried fruit, and ground nuts).

Beverages Coffee (strong, thick, sweet, often flavored with cardamom; made in a long-handled metal briki), tea (sweet), fruit juice, wine, plum brandy (sljivovica). The Balkans are well known for their wines and distilled spirits.

Meals Three meals a day, with the main meal at midday, and frequent snacking is typical.

Snacks Pastries, ice cream, small kabobs, meat balls (kofta), vegetable salads, coffee, wine, plum brandy.

SEYCHELLES
Republic of Seychelles

Geography Seychelles is a group of 86 islands in the Indian Ocean northeast of Madagascar. About half of the islands are of coral; the other half are of granite and are mountainous.

Major Languages	Ethnic Groups		Major Religions	
English (both Creole official) French	Seychellois Creole (mixed French, African, Indian, Chinese, Arab) British, French, other	93% 7%	Roman Catholic Anglican Other Christian Other	82% 6% 5% 7%

Population density per sq. mi. 468.2
Literacy rate 91.8%
Life expectancy 67.3 male; 78.1 female
Per capita GDP $16,600
Labor force in agriculture 3%

Urban 52.9%
Infant mortality rate per 1,000 live births 14.4
HIV rate NA
Unemployment rate 2.6%
Arable land 2%

Agriculture coconuts, bananas, tea, cinnamon, vanilla, sweet potatoes, cassava, chickens, pigs, goats, cattle

Natural resources fish, copra, cinnamon trees

Industries fishing, tourism, coconut and vanilla processing, coir (coconut fiber), rope, boat building

History The islands were uninhabited when the British first visited in 1609. They were claimed by France in 1756 and surrendered to Britain in 1810. They were ruled as part of Mauritius until 1903, when they became a separate colony. They gained independence in 1976. Seychelles, a one-party socialist state since 1979, adopted a new constitution in 1993 that provided for a multiparty state. In 1995 a new law granted amnesty from prosecution to anyone investing $10 million in the country. To gain revenue, in 1996 the government initiated a program whereby foreigners can obtain a Seychelles passport for $25,000. In 2007 Seychelles continued efforts to strengthen its economy, one of the strongest in Africa, by making foreign trade agreements, including one with China that cancelled a debt and pledged United States $12 million in aid.

Influences on food A group of islands in the Indian Ocean east of the African mainland and near the equator, Seychelles has a diet based on seafood plus rice, starchy vegetables, coconut, bread-fruit, and tropical fruits. Influences on food in Seychelles include African, French, British, Indian, Malay, and Chinese.

Bread and cereals Rice, wheat; rice dishes, bread.

Meat, poultry, fish   Chicken, pork, goat, beef, fish (many species, e.g., snapper, tuna), eggs, fruit-eating bats.

Dairy products   Milk.

Fats and oils   Coconut oil, coconut cream, lard, butter.

Legumes   Beans, peas, lentils.

Vegetables   Sweet potatoes, cassava, breadfruit, plantains (including giant red ones).

Fruit   Coconut, bananas, mangoes, papaya, jackfruit, custard apple (zat). Jackfruit, the largest of tree fruits, has green exterior covered with spikes and interior with seeds resembling chestnuts and yellow, banana-pineapple-flavored flesh; the flesh is used as a starchy vegetable. Custard apple, not related to true apple, has creamy, custard-tasting pulp.

Nuts and Seeds   Almonds, jackfruit seeds. The latter are boiled and made into flour or are candied.

Seasonings   Cinnamon, vanilla, curry, onion, chili pepper.

Dishes   Fish fried, baked, or poached and often including a sauce. Fish, meat, or chicken curries using coconut cream. Marinated, skewered, and grilled meat, chicken, and fish. Fried fruit-eating bat. Boiled rice. Boiled sweet potatoes, cassava, breadfruit, plantains, and jackfruit. Fried sweet potatoes, breadfruit, plantains, and jackfruit. Fried cassava and jackfruit flour bread. Boiled legumes, sometimes puréed and fried. Fresh fruit salads with mango a main ingredient and dusted with cinnamon.

Sweets   Sugar. Fresh fruit. Fried banana dessert with coconut cream. Candied jackfruit.

Beverages   Coffee, tea, fruit juices.

SIERRA LEONE
Republic of Sierra Leone

Geography   Sierra Leone is in West Africa, bordering the Atlantic Ocean. It has swamps along the heavily indented coastline, wooded hills and a plateau in the interior, and mountains in the east.

Major Languages	Ethnic Groups		Major Religions	
English (official)	Mende	30%	Muslim	60%
Mende (principal vernacular in south)	Temne	30%	Indigenous beliefs	30%
Temne (principal vernacular in north)	Other tribes	30%	Christian	10%
Krio (English Creole)	Creole (Krio)	10%		

Population density per sq. mi. 227.6
Literacy rate 38.1%
Life expectancy 38.6 male; 43.3 female
Per capita GDP $700
Labor force in agriculture NA

Urban 36.8%
Infant mortality rate per 1,000 live births 156.5
HIV rate 1.7%
Unemployment rate NA
Arable land 8%

Agriculture   rice, cassava, oil palm fruit, coffee, cocoa, peanuts, chickens, goats, sheep, cattle, pigs

Natural resources   diamonds, titanium, bauxite, iron ore, gold, chromite, fish

Industries   diamonds, small-scale manufacturing (beverages, textiles), oil refining

History   The Bulom people were probably the first inhabitants, followed by the Mende and Temne in the 15th century, and later the Fulani. The Portuguese explored the land and named it Sierra Leone, "lion mountains," in the 15th century and by 1495 established a fort on the site of present-day Freetown. European ships visited the coast to trade for slaves and ivory, and the British built trading posts on offshore islands in the 17th century. British abolitionists and philanthropists founded Freetown in 1780 for freed and runaway slaves. Their descendants are Creoles. The area became a British colony in 1808, a British protectorate in 1896, and independent in 1961. Mismanagement and corruption have plagued the economy. In the 1990s civil war killed thousands as rebels sought political power and control of the diamond fields. Rebellion continued in 2001 and was declared over in 2002. For the past several years, Sierra Leone has been listed by the UN as the world's least livable country, based on its poverty and poor quality of life. This poor though mineral-rich country ranked last out of 177 countries in the UN Development Program's human development index for 2007–2008. Major priorities of the president inaugurated in 2007 included restoring electricity and continuing the crackdown on the "blood diamond" trade. In 2008, under an anti-corruption law, the new president became the first president to declare all his assets.

Influences on food   The Atlantic Ocean provides fish and shellfish. The hills, plateau, and mountains support some crops and animal herds. Food habits were influenced by the introduction of New World foods such as cassava, corn, tomato, chili pepper, peanuts, potato, and cocoa. Native African foods include watermelon, black-eyed peas, and okra. British control for more than 150 years left some influence. Daily fare is mostly cereals and starchy vegetables with legumes and greens, plus fish in coastal areas. Thick, sticky, spicy dishes are liked.

Bread and cereals   Rice, millet, corn, sorghum; porridges, pastes, rice dishes, biscuits.

Meat, poultry, fish   Chicken, goat, lamb and mutton, beef, pork, fish (fresh, smoked, or dried), prawns, eggs, guinea fowl, rabbits, game. Chicken is the most popular flesh food and a special dish for guests.

Insects   Termites (often called white ants), locusts. Insects are sometimes dried and usually fried or roasted.

Dairy products   Milk, sour milk, buttermilk, curds, whey, cheese.

Fats and oils   Palm oil, peanut oil, shea oil, coconut oil. Palm oil, the main cooking fat, is red and colors food.

Legumes   Peanuts (groundnuts), black-eyed peas (a variety of cowpeas), locust beans (carob), beans.

Vegetables Cassava, yams, plantains, taro, green leaves, tomatoes, okra, bitter leaf, melokhia (crain crain), sweet potatoes, potatoes, onions, chili peppers, eggplant, pumpkin, cucumbers, bell peppers.

Fruit   Coconut, pineapple, akee apples, baobab, guavas, lemons, mangoes, papaya, watermelon, bananas.

Nuts and seeds   Cashews, kola nuts, palm kernels, watermelon seeds (egusi), sesame seeds, mango seeds.

Seasonings   Salt, hot red chili peppers, tomatoes, onions, dried baobab leaves, thyme, "African nutmeg." cocoa.

Dishes   Most foods are boiled or fried and small chunks or balls are dipped in a sauce and eaten by hand. Fufu (a paste of boiled starchy vegetables or corn flour), formed into balls or scoops to eat stew. Fried plantains. Adalu (boiled and mashed starchy vegetables). Fish and meat stew. Chicken and peanut stew. Stew of okra or root vegetables and fish, chicken, or beef. Peanut sauce or stew (ground and pounded peanuts, chilies, tomatoes, and herbs; perhaps beef, chicken, or fish, or mixtures of them; and sometimes potatoes, beans, or eggplant). Palaver sauce (pounded green leaves with seasonings). Fréjon (boiled and puréed black-eyed peas or beans with coconut milk and perhaps carob or cocoa). Gari (roasted cassava meal). Roast chicken with peanut sauce. Prawns cooked with sweet peppers, onions, and tomatoes in a small amount of palm oil, served with boiled rice.

Native dish   Jollof rice (chicken or meat or both simmered in water then browned in oil; tomatoes, onions, and crushed red peppers sautéed in the same oil; rice browned in a small amount of the oil and simmered in the stock; the other ingredients added to the rice and all covered and simmered for a few minutes).

Sweets   Honey, sugar. Kanya (peanut candy). Fried sweet dough balls. Pineapple fritters.

Beverages   Coffee, cocoa, beer, red zinger (herbal tea made from flower pods of roselle, *Hibiscus sabdariffa*).

Street food and snacks   Spiced kabobs, shawerma (rotisserie lamb), fried fish, bean balls, coconut biscuits.

SINGAPORE
Republic of Singapore

Geography   Singapore is in Southeast Asia off the tip of the Malayan Peninsula. The country consists of the main island, Singapore, and 40 nearby islets. Area is 264 square miles. Singapore is a flat, formerly swampy island.

Major Languages		Ethnic Groups		Major Religions	
Chinese	(all	Chinese	77%	Buddhist	43%
Malay	four	Malay	14%	Christian	15%
Tamil	are	Indian	8%	Muslim	15%
English	official)	Other	1%	Taoist	9%
Hokkien, Cantonese, Teochew				Hindu, other, none	18%

Population density per sq. mi. 17,482.2
Literacy rate 94.4%
Life expectancy 79.3 male; 84.7 female
Per capita GDP $49,700
Labor force in agriculture NA

Urban 100%
Infant mortality rate per 1,000 live births 2.3
HIV rate 0.2%
Unemployment rate 3.6%
Arable land 1%

Agriculture   vegetables, orchids, rubber, copra, fruit, ornamental fish, chickens, pigs, goats, cattle
Natural resources   fish
Industries   electronics, chemicals, financial services, oil drilling equipment, oil refining, rubber processing and rubber products, processed food and beverages, offshore platform construction, life sciences

History   Inhabitants first migrated to the area between 2500 and 1500 BCE. Long inhabited by fishers and pirates, Singapore was an outpost of the Sumatran Empire until the 14th century, when it passed to Java and then Siam. It was part of the Malacca Empire in the 15th century. It was controlled by the Portuguese in the 16th century and by the Dutch in the 17th century. British and Dutch interest in the area grew with the spice trade. Ceded to the British East India Company in 1819, Singapore became the center of the British colonial activity in Southeast Asia. The Japanese occupied the islands from 1942 to 1945. Singapore became a British crown colony in 1948 and gained independence in 1965. Singapore developed into one of the cleanest, safest, and most prosperous cities in Asia. Standards in health, education, and housing are generally high. It is one of the world's largest ports and a major center of manufacturing, banking, and commerce. In 2007 the property market and inflation surged, and the overall economy grew by 7.8%. In 2008 prices for food, housing, and transportation soared, as did inflation, while demand for Singapore's exports declined.

Influences on food   Singapore shares geography and cuisine with neighbor Malaysia. Singapore's three main cuisines are Malay, Chinese, and Indian. The vast majority of the people are Chinese (Straits Chinese, with roots in southern China). Chinese and Indian influence is strong due to mass movement of labor during the colonial period, as well as immigrant elites from East and South Asia. Nonya (Chinese Straits) cooking, associated with Chinese who settled in the area in the 15th century and in Singapore up to World War II, uses chilies, shrimp paste, coconut milk, and aromatic roots and leaves as in Malaysian cuisine but retains the use of pork, lard, and noodles from its Chinese tradition. It values hotness and sourness. Indian influence includes spices, curries, and achar (pickles). Islam, dominant in the Malay Peninsula and coastal towns of Borneo since the 15th century, is the religion of 15% of Singapore's population. Muslims do not consume pork or lard. Singapore is one of the world's greatest entrepôts for spices. Dutch traders influenced the area. Britain established Singapore as a trading post in 1819 and controlled it until 1965, leaving an influence. Rice is the staple food. Seafood is the secondary staple.

Bread and cereals   Rice, wheat; rice dishes, glutinous rice in sweets, noodles.

Meat, poultry, fish   Fish and seafood, chicken, pork, goat, beef, water buffalo, eggs, duck; prawn/shrimp pastes (blacang), dried anchovy, fish sauce, gelatin (used in sweets).

Dairy products   Sweetened condensed milk (used in coffee), cream (used as whipped cream in pastries).

Fats and oils   Coconut oil and cream, palm oil, lard, vegetable oil.

Legumes   Soybeans and soy products (e.g., soy sauce, soy milk, tofu), mung beans, winged beans, peanuts.

Vegetables   Taro, cassava, breadfruit, seaweed, greens, yams, green beans, eggplant, sweet potatoes, ti plant, daikon (white radish), squash, arrowroot, water chestnuts.

Fruit   Coconut, tamarind, bananas, limes, pineapple, oranges, lemons, mangoes, papaya, melons, durian.

Nuts   Litchis, macadamia nuts.

Seasonings   Chilies, shrimp paste, coconut milk and cream, tamarind, lime juice, aromatic roots and leaves, soy sauce, fish sauce, onions, garlic, laos (Malay plant of ginger root family), ginger root, lemon grass, black mushroom-like "cloud ears," cumin, cinnamon, coriander, turmeric.

Dishes   Coconut milk is often used as a cooking liquid. Boiled rice. Fried rice. Fried noodles (kway teow). Stir-fried greens. Satay (small strips of meat, chicken, or fish/seafood on thin bamboo skewers, marinated with soy sauce and flavorings, and grilled). Rendang, or "dry beef curry," (cubed beef or water buffalo meat simmered with seasonings in coconut milk). Rempah (spice mixture, often fried before use). Gulai (curry, cooked in coconut milk and retaining its sauce). Chinese roast pork. Indian peppery soup. Hot curries. Sambal (hot, spicy side dishes or chilies and spices fried together and used in a main dish). Prawn sambal (prawns fried in a hot, spicy mixture).

Singapore delicacy   River oysters fried with eggs and sweet potatoes.

Sweets   Palm sugar, sugar. Immature coconut. Baked rice rolls in banana leaves. Desserts based on thick brown palm sugar syrup with coconut milk, grated coconut, gelatin, and glutinous rice, for example, kuey lapis (has many different colored layers of gelatin). Naga sari (pudding of mung beans, sugar, and coconut).

Beverages   Tea, coffee, coconut juice, fruit juice, bean drinks, kava (alcoholic drink made from pepper plant).

Street food and snacks   Fried noodles, satay (the favorite snack: pork for Chinese, goat meat for Muslims, chicken for both and for Malays, and all with hot sauce of chilies, onion, garlic, laos, and peanuts). Street food is sold by street vendors and in market stalls and night stores. In Singapore, a parking lot by day is transformed in the evening into a ring of food stalls with a communal eating area in the middle. People love to eat outdoors.

SLOVAKIA
Slovak Republic

Geography   Slovakia is in east central Europe. The Carpathian Mountains, rich in mineral resources and with vast forests and pastures, are in the north. The fertile Danube plain is in the south.

Major Languages	Ethnic Groups		Major Religions	
Slovak (official)	Slovak	86%	Roman Catholic	69%
Hungarian	Hungarian	10%	Protestant (Lutheran 7%)	11%
	Roma (Gypsy)	2%	Other	7%
	Other	2%	None	13%

Population density per sq. mi. 289.5
Literacy rate 99.6%
Life expectancy 71.2 male; 79.3 female
Per capita GDP $20,300
Labor force in agriculture 5.8%

Urban 56.2%
Infant mortality rate per 1,000 live births 7
HIV rate <0.1%
Unemployment rate 10.0%
Arable land 29%

Agriculture   sugar beets, wheat, corn, potatoes, hops, fruit, chickens, pigs, cattle, sheep, goats

Natural resources   brown coal and lignite, iron ore, copper, manganese, salt, fish

Industries   metal and metal products, food and beverages, electricity, gas, coke, oil, nuclear fuels, chemicals and manmade fibers, machinery, paper and printing

History   Slovakia was inhabited in the first 11 centuries CE by Illyrian, Celtic, and Germanic tribes. Slovaks settled it in about the 6th century. In the 9th century Slovakia became part of the Moravia North Empire. It was under Hungarian (Magyar) control from the 10th century until 1918, except in the 15th century when overrun by Czech Hussites and then restored to Hungarian rule in 1526. After World War I it separated from Hungary and joined the Czechs of Bohemia to form Czechoslovakia in 1918. In 1939 Germany invaded Czechoslovakia and declared Slovakia independent. Slovakia rejoined Czechoslovakia in 1945. Slovakia with Czechoslovakia came under Soviet domination in 1948 and became the Slovak Socialist Republic of Czechoslovakia in 1969. Communist rule ended in 1989 when Václav Havel became president and democratic reform began. In 1993 Czechoslovakia split into two nations, the Czech Republic and Slovakia. Slovakia joined NATO and the EU in 2004 and ratified the EU constitution in 2005. One of Europe's fastest growing economies, Slovakia's economy grew at its record pace in 2007 and inflation fell, although Slovakia recorded the highest unemployment rate in the EU.

Influences on food   Slovakia and the Czech Republic, neighbor on the west, were Czechoslovakia for most of the 20th century and share a culinary history. The cuisine is robust, with emphasis on bread, dumplings, root vegetables, cabbage, meat, soups/stews, and dairy products. Slovakia was a part of Hungary for centuries and has accepted dishes from this southern neighbor, notably goulash (meat stew with paprika). German and Slavic were early influences. Most Slovakians are Christians, who observe Christmas and Easter with special foods.

Bread and cereals   Wheat, corn, rye, rice; wheat and rye bread (served at most meals), dumplings (large loaf-sized ones to tiny ones, including ones with savory or sweet fillings), yeast buns, strudel, cakes, rice dishes.

Meat, poultry, fish   Chicken, pork, beef, lamb, goat, fish (trout, eel), eggs, duck, goose; ham, sausages (klobása) such as jaternice (pork) and jelita (a blood sausage). Meat is often extended by grinding or stewing.

Dairy products   Milk (cow, sheep), cream, sour cream, cottage cheese, cheese.

Fats and oils   Butter, bacon, lard, olive oil, vegetable oil.

Legumes   Kidney beans, lentils, navy beans, split peas.

Vegetables   Potatoes, other root vegetables, cabbage, onions, mushrooms, cucumbers; sauerkraut, pickles.

Fruit   Apples, cherries, grapes, plums, apricots, raisins, prunes, sultanas (large grapes).

Nuts and seeds   Almonds, caraway seeds, poppy seeds (often used in cakes and pastries).

Seasonings   Onions, paprika, cinnamon, other spices, sour cream, vinegar, mustard, horseradish.

Dishes   Párky (steamed or boiled sausage). Simmered dumplings. Potato dumplings. Falsche (false) soups, made with vegetable stock instead of meat stock. Potato and mushroom soup. Stewed red or white cabbage with caraway seeds. Mashed potatoes. Cabbage leaves stuffed with seasoned ground meat. "Hungarian goulash" (pirkilt), meat pieces coated with paprika and seared in fat, onions, and a small amount of liquid are covered and simmered, with paprika added again just before the dish is finished. Dušené telecí na kmině (veal, caraway seeds, and mushrooms) served with noodles. Lungenbraten (roast fillet of beef). Svíčková na sonetaně (beef roast with sour cream sauce). Mehlspeisen (foods made with flour), an important food category that includes some savory and many sweet items (dumplings, yeast pies, noodles, pancakes, and doughs and pastes combined with vegetables, fruit, or soft cheese and cream, butter, bacon, jam, poppy seeds, and honey).

Special occasion foods   Roast duck or goose. Christmas foods: oplatky (small communion wafer spread with honey), eaten to break the Advent fast on Christmas Eve; and babalky (bread slices scalded, drained, and rolled in poppy seeds with sugar or honey), a Christmas dessert. Easter foods: ham; Easter cheese (syrek); imitation cheese ball made from eggs (brudka); and paska (pyramid-shaped dessert containing cheese, cream, butter, eggs, sugar, and candied fruits, and decorated with a cross).

Sweets   Honey, sugar. Jam. Yeast buns. Strudel (pastry of thin sheets of dough around a soft filling, often apple pieces). Dumplings filled with fruit or jam. Škubánky (potato dumplings baked in butter and served with cinnamon sugar). Topfenpalatshcinken (thick pancakes with curdled sweet cream). Makovy kolac (poppy seed cake with sultanas). Bulblanina (bubble cake), a sponge cake with fruit baked in it. Streuselkuchen (crumb-topped cake).

Beverages   Coffee, milk, hot chocolate, beer, wine.

Meals   Three meals a day with snacks is typical.

SLOVENIA
Republic of Slovenia

Geography   Slovenia is in southeastern Europe, bordering the Adriatic Sea and Italy. It is mostly hilly and mountainous, with forest covering 42% of the land and hilly plains in the central and eastern regions.

Major Languages	Ethnic Groups		Major Religions	
Slovenian (official)	Slovene	91%	Roman Catholic	58%
Serbo-Croatian	Croat	2%	Orthodox	2%
	Serb	2%	Muslim	2%
	Bosniac	2%	Other and unspecified	28%
	Other	3%	None	10%

Population density per sq. mi. 258.1
Literacy rate 99.7%
Life expectancy 73 male; 80.7 female
Per capita GDP $27,200
Labor force in agriculture 2.5%

Urban 49.5%
Infant mortality rate per 1,000 live births 4.3
HIV rate <0.1%
Unemployment rate 5.6%
Arable land 9%

Agriculture   corn, sugar beets, wheat, potatoes, hops, grapes, chickens, pigs, cattle, sheep, goats

Natural resources   lignite, lead, zinc, mercury, uranium, silver, hydropower, timber, fish

Industries   ferrous metallurgy and aluminum products, electronics (including military), trucks, electric power equipment, wood products, textiles, chemicals, tools

History   Slovenia, first settled by Illyrian and Celtic peoples, became part of the Roman Empire in the 1st century BCE. The Slovenes, a south Slavic group, settled here in the 6th century CE. In the 8th century the area was taken into the Frankish empire of Charlemagne. German domination, as part of the Holy Roman Empire, began in the 9th and 10th centuries. Except for the period 1809 to 1814, when Napoleon ruled the area, most of the land belonged to Austria until 1918. After 1848 the Slovenes, divided among several Austrian provinces, began struggling to unify. Slovenia and Croatia became part of the Austro-Hungarian kingdom when it was established in 1867. Following Austria-Hungary's defeat in World War I, Slovenia gained independence in 1918 and became part of the Kingdom of Serbs, Croats, and Slovenes, renamed Yugoslavia in 1929. Yugoslavia, occupied by Germany in World War II, in 1945 became communist Yugoslavia. Slovenia became a constituent republic of Yugoslavia in 1946 and received a section of the former Italian Adriatic coastline in 1947. Slovenia declared independence in 1991. It joined the UN in 1992 and the EU and NATO in 2004. It adopted the euro currency in 2007. Slovenia assumed the (rotating) presidency of the EU in 2008.

Influences on food   Formerly the northernmost province of Yugoslavia, Slovenia borders Italy, Austria, Hungary, and Croatia. Mostly mountainous, it produces grains, sugar beets, potatoes, grapes, and livestock. Early Slovenes were under Roman influence, followed by a millennium of Austrian domination. Many dishes, such as kaša (kasha, buckwheat thick porridge), from ancient Slavonic times have survived. The oldest Slavonic ritual leavened bread, kolač, can be round, ring shaped, and often elaborately decorated. Another ancient dish, juba, a meat and vegetable soup, is an essential part of meals. The Slovenes appear to be the only Europeans still using millet in traditional cooking. Like the Russians and Poles, they like buckwheat, a plant of the same family as rhubarb and grown for its seeds, which are used as husked whole grains and as flour. Many Slovenes continue to use traditional ingredients and dishes. Most Slovenes are Roman Catholic and frequently consume pork.

Bread and cereals   Corn, wheat, hops, buckwheat, oats, millet, barley, rye, rice; porridge, leavened wheat bread (consumed at most meals), pies, turnovers, filo dough (paper-thin pastry sheets), rice dishes.

Meat, poultry, fish   Chicken, eggs, pork, beef and veal, lamb, goat, fish; sausages such as ded and vratnik (chopped pork packed into pig stomach, bladder, or large intestine and poached, smoked, or air dried).

Dairy products   Milk (cow, sheep, goat), buttermilk, cream, sour cream, whipped cream, cheese, for example, kashkaval (hard tangy ewe's milk cheese, called the cheddar of the Balkans). Fresh dairy items are widely consumed.

Fats and oils   Butter, margarine, vegetable oils, olive oil.

Legumes   Chickpeas, fava beans, black beans, white beans, lentils. Legumes are important ingredients.

Vegetables   Potatoes, cabbage, cucumbers, mushrooms, tomatoes, eggplant, onions, olives; sauerkraut, pickles.

Fruit   Grapes, plums, apples, berries, cherries, pears, apricots, peaches, lemons. Fruit juice is popular.

Nuts and seeds   Almonds, walnuts, pistachios, poppy seeds, sesame seeds.

Seasonings   Dill, garlic, mint, cardamom, cinnamon, oregano, parsley, pepper, paprika, lemon juice.

Dishes   Soups. Baked or fried pies and turnovers filled with meat, cheese, eggs, vegetables, nuts, or dried fruits, for example, burek (a fried meat- or cheese-filled pastry). Dumplings filled with meat (cmoki) or fruit. Cabbage or grape leaves stuffed with meat or rice. Meat and vegetable casseroles such as moussaka (baked minced lamb, eggplant, onions, and tomato sauce), a Balkan specialty.

Specialty   Struklji, from strudel but made with stretched or rolled pastry, made from dough of wheat or buckwheat flour and mashed potatoes with fillings savory (cheese, rice, potatoes, beans, kaša, cracklings, meat or pork, eggs, and pig's blood) or sweet (apples, plums, cherries, walnuts, poppy seed, or millet).

Sweets   Honey, sugar. Fruit preserves. Fruit compote. Cheese- or fruit-filled dumplings and strudels. Baklava (filo dough layered with nut filling, baked, and soaked in flavored syrup). A Balkan specialty, slatko (fruit simmered in thick syrup). A northern Balkan treat, potica (sweet yeast bread rolled in a walnut, butter, cream, and egg filling).

Beverages   Coffee (strong, sweet), tea, buttermilk, fruit juice, wine (e.g., civek, a rosé), plum brandy (sljivovica).

Meals   Three meals a day, with the main meal at midday, and frequent snacking is typical.

Street food and snacks   In urban areas vendors sell pastries and ice cream throughout the day. Evening snacks in cafés and coffeehouses: small kabobs, meat balls, vegetable salads, pickles, coffee, wine, and plum brandy.

SOLOMON ISLANDS

Geography   The Solomon Islands is in the southwestern Pacific Ocean, east of Papua New Guinea, in Melanesia. It is an archipelago of ten large, volcanic, rugged, mountainous islands and four groups of smaller, low-lying ones.

Major Languages	Ethnic Groups		Major Religions	
English (official)	Melanesian	95%	Anglican	33%
Melanesian pidgin	Polynesian	3%	Roman Catholic	19%
120 indigenous languages	Micronesian	1%	Evangelical	17%
	Other	1%	Adventist	11%
			Other	20%

Population density per sq. mi. 54.7

Literacy rate NA

Life expectancy 70.9 male; 76.1 female

Per capita GDP $1,900

Labor force in agriculture 75%

Urban 17%

Infant mortality rate per 1,000 live births 19.7

HIV rate NA

Unemployment rate 15.2%

Arable land 1%

Agriculture   coconuts, oil palm fruit, sweet potatoes, cocoa, beans, rice, vegetables, fruit, chickens, pigs, cattle

Natural resources   fish, forests, gold, bauxite, phosphates, lead, zinc, nickel

Industries   fish (tuna), mining, timber

History   Austronesian people probably settled here c. 2000 BCE. A Spanish explorer visited the islands in 1565. The islands were explored by the Dutch, French, and British. The islands were inhabited by Melanesians in the 1890s when they became a British protectorate, the British Solomon Islands. In World War II, the Japanese invaded the islands and major battles occurred here, including the Battle of Guadalcanal. In 1945 the British regained control of the islands. Independence was attained in 1978. (Another island group named Solomon Islands, which includes Bougainville, is part of Papua New Guinea.) A coup attempt in 2000 led to three years of violence. To restore order, troops led by Australia began arriving in 2003 and in mid-2005 nearly all had left. In 2007 an earthquake and tsunami left at least 52 people dead. The economy was growing rapidly but was heavily dependent on logging, which had been growing rapidly and at unsustainable levels.

Influences on food   About 30,000 to 40,000 years ago people from Southeast Asia began to move south to the western Pacific islands and Australia, and they later migrated to islands further east. Asians brought rice, soybeans, noodles, teas, and stir-frying. Europeans brought new food plants, wheat bread, and some animals to the area. Melanesians inhabited the Solomon Islands when they became a British protectorate. British control for nearly a century left some influence. Mainstays of the diet are fish and seafood, roots and tubers, and breadfruit. Fruits and nuts, especially coconut, are also important. Fresh fruits are eaten as snacks. Pork is the main meat, especially for festive occasions, traditionally cooked in a stone-lined pit over coals along with other foods.

Bread and cereals   Rice, wheat; rice dishes, bread, noodles.

Meat, poultry, fish   Chicken, pork, beef, fish (mullet), seafood (crabs, many others), eggs; corned beef, spam.

Dairy products   Milk and milk products are uncommon.

Fats and oils   Coconut oil and cream, palm oil, lard, vegetable oil and shortening, butter, sesame oil.

Legumes   Soybeans and soybean products, winged beans, pigeon peas, lentils, peanuts.

Vegetables   Sweet potatoes, taro root and leaves, yams, breadfruit, plantains, cassava, seaweed, green leaves, arrowroot, bitter melon, cabbage, daikon, eggplant, onions, green onions.

Fruit   Coconut, bananas, lemons, limes, guavas, mangoes, papaya, pineapple, melons, tamarind.

Nuts and seeds   Candlenuts (kukui), litchis, macadamia nuts, palm kernels, sesame seeds.

Seasonings   Soy sauce, coconut milk or cream, lime or lemon juice, salt, green onions, ginger, garlic, cocoa.

Dishes   Coconut milk is the usual liquid cooking medium. Boiled taro root, breadfruit, cassava, yam, or sweet potato. Stir-fried or steamed greens (taro, yam, ti, sweet potato). Boiled or steamed rice. Arrowroot-thickened puddings and other dishes. Fish and seafood stewed, roasted, or marinated in lemon or lime juice and coconut cream. Dishes cooked in a pit: whole pig, taro, sweet potato, breadfruit, yams, crabs, whole fish, chicken pieces, taro leaves wrapped around a filling of coconut cream, lemon, onions, and shredded beef and all bound in banana leaves, and leaf-wrapped fillings of taro, sweet potato, yams, or plantains with coconut cream and seasonings.

Sweets   Sugar. Immature coconut. Haupia (firm pudding made from coconut milk, sugar, and arrowroot).

Beverages   Coconut juice, cocoa, coffee, fruit juice, tea, kava (mildly alcoholic drink made from pepper plant).

Meals   Typical are two or three meals daily, with the same foods at all, and the evening meal the largest. Traditional meal: boiled taro root, breadfruit, yam, or plantain, fish or pork dish, and cooked greens or seaweed.

SOMALIA

Geography Somalia occupies the eastern horn of Africa, bordering the Indian Ocean. It has a 1,700-mile coastline and two main rivers. The land is generally arid, barren, and flat, with hills in the north.

Major Languages		Ethnic Groups		Major Religions	
Somali	(both	Somali	85%	Islam (official)	
Arabic	official)	Bantu and other	15%	Sunni Muslim	99%
Italian				Other	1%
English					

Population density per sq. mi. 39.5

Literacy rate 37.8%

Life expectancy 47.4 male; 51.1 female

Per capita GDP $600

Labor force in agriculture 71%

Urban 35.2%

Infant mortality rate per 1,000 live births 111

HIV rate 0.5%

Unemployment rate 47.4%

Arable land 2%

Agriculture sugarcane, corn, sorghum, bananas, coconuts, rice, mangoes, sesame seeds, beans, tree/bush products (kat, frankincense, myrrh), sheep, goats, camels, cattle, chickens, pigs

Natural resources fish, uranium, iron ore, tin, gypsum, bauxite, copper, salt, natural gas, oil

Industries a few light industries including sugar refining, textiles, wireless communication

History From the 7th to 10th centuries, Arabs and Persians established trading posts along the coast. By the 10th century nomadic tribes occupied the interior, and pastoral Oromo peoples inhabited the south and west. In the 16th century Turks ruled the northern coast, and Zanzibar sultans controlled the south. In the late 19th century, Britain and Italy set up protectorates, British Somaliland in the north and Italian Somaliland in the center and south. Italy lost its African colonies in World War II. In 1960 the two parts of Somaliland united and became the independent Somalia. It claimed eastern Ethiopia, inhabited mostly by Somalis. Civil war starting in 1977 and drought produced a famine that threatened over 1.5 million people with starvation in 1992. From 1992 to 1994 a multinational force tried unsuccessfully to stabilize the region. Violence and food shortages have continued, especially in the south. The 2004 Indian Ocean tsunami killed at least 150 Somalis and displaced about 5,000. In 2006 Islamist militia took over the capital, Mogadishu, and much of the country. Violence escalated in 2007 and reached the worst level in more than a decade. In 2008 more than a million people were internally displaced and more than 400,000 were refugees in neighboring countries. Pirates in coastal waters hijacked 25 ships in 2008.

Influences on food The mostly desert land and 1,700-mile coastline influence the food of Somalia. The Indian Ocean provides fish and seafood. Other influences include Arab, Turkish, British, Italian, Ethiopian, and Islam. For example, the Italians introduced spaghetti and expresso coffee. Traditional Somali foods are rice (brees) with meat (hibbib) and chili. As in neighboring Ethiopia, flatbread and spicy stew are popular. Almost all Somalis are Muslims, who do not consume pork or alcohol and fast from sunup to sundown during the month of Ramadan.

Bread and cereals Corn, sorghum, rice, millet, barley, wheat; rice dishes, flatbread (cooked like a huge pancake on a griddle, covered, making a large circular loaf), pasta.

Meat, poultry, fish Lamb and mutton, goat, camel, beef, chicken, pork, fish and seafood, eggs.

Dairy products Milk (cow, goat, sheep, camel), cheese.

Fats and oils Butter (often clarified and flavored with onions, garlic, ginger, and other spices), vegetable oil.

Legumes   Beans, chickpeas, lentils, peanuts.

Vegetables   Plantains, potatoes, kale, eggplant, red chili peppers, onions, garlic.

Fruit   Bananas, coconut, mangoes, dates.

Nuts and seeds   Almonds, fenugreek seeds, sesame seeds.

Seasonings   Hot red chili peppers, onions, garlic, ginger; hot red spice mixture (allspice, cardamom, cayenne, cinnamon, cloves, coriander, cumin, fenugreek, ginger, nutmeg, and black pepper), clarified butter with spices.

Dishes   Anan geil (millet gruel with camel milk and honey), a traditional dish. Boiled or steamed rice with meat and chili. Stews of legumes, root vegetables, chili peppers, and lamb, goat, camel, beef, chicken, or fish. Boiled lentils in a salad. Boiled spaghetti with meat sauce.

Sweets   Sugarcane, honey, sugar.

Beverages   Beer (home-brewed from millet or corn), honey wine, coffee (especially espresso).

Meals and service   Typical is one meal in the early evening, with snacking throughout the day. A usual meal includes rice or flatbread and spicy stew. Food is often served on or picked up with pieces of flatbread.

SOUTH AFRICA
Republic of South Africa

Geography   South Africa comprises the southern tip of Africa, bordering the Atlantic Ocean and the Indian Ocean. It is mostly a large plateau with a 1,739-mile coastline. Rainfall is sparse in the west and more plentiful in the east.

Major Languages	Ethnic Groups		Major Religions	
Afrikaans, English, Ndebele,	Black African	79%	Independent Christian	37%
Pedi, Sotho, Swazi,	White	10%	Protestant	26%
Tsonga, Tswana,	Colored (mixed)	9%	Traditional beliefs	9%
Xhosa, Zulu, Venda	Asian	2%	Roman Catholic	7%
(all 11 are official			Muslim, Hindu, other	21%

Population density per sq. mi. 103.6
Literacy rate 88%
Life expectancy 49.6 male; 48.1 female
Per capita GDP $9,800
Labor force in agriculture 9%

Urban 59.3%
Infant mortality rate per 1,000 live births 45.1
HIV rate 18.1%
Unemployment rate 23.0%
Arable land 12%

Agriculture   sugarcane, corn, wheat, fruits, vegetables, chickens, sheep, cattle, goats, pigs

Natural resources   gold, fish, chromium, antimony, coal, iron ore, manganese, nickel, phosphates, tin, uranium, gem diamonds, platinum, copper, vanadium, salt, natural gas

Industries   mining (especially gold, platinum, chromium), auto assembly, metalworking, machinery, textiles, chemicals, fertilizer, foodstuffs

History   Original inhabitants were the San and Khoikhoi peoples, who roamed the area as hunters and gatherers in the Stone Age. Bantus, including Zulu, Xhosa, Swazi, and Sotho, followed. The Khoikhoi had developed a pastoral culture by the time of European contact. Dutch began settling the Cape of Good Hope area in 1652. Called Boers, or Afrikaners, they spoke a Dutch dialect, Afrikaans. Britain took control in 1806 and freed slaves in 1833. In the 1830s the Dutch settlers began the Great Trek north and founded the independent Boer republics of Orange Free State and the South African Republic (later Transvaal). In 1867 diamonds were discovered in this land, and in 1886 gold was discovered. Britain won the Anglo-Boer (Dutch) War (1899–1902) and in 1910 created the Union of South Africa, incorporating Cape and Natal with Transvaal and Orange Free State. In 1948 the policy of separate development of the races, apartheid, became official, with limited rights and opportunities to all but whites. The Union of South Africa became the independent Republic of South Africa in 1961 and left the Commonwealth. Violence ensued for almost three decades. In 1986, Nobel Peace Prize winner Bishop Desmond Tutu called for sanctions against South Africa to force an end to apartheid. In 1990 the government lifted its ban on the African National Congress and released Black Nationalist leader Nelson Mandela after 27 years in prison. In 1991 President de Klerk announced plans to end apartheid laws. In 1994 Mandela was elected the country's first black president and the country rejoined the Commonwealth. A post-apartheid constitution became law in 1996. In 2004 Mandela retired from public life. In 2006 South Africa became the first country in Africa to legalize same-sex marriage. For the 2006–2007 financial year there was an unprecedented budget surplus. In 2007 the economy grew, although strikes were a problem.

Influences on food South Africa's temperate and subtropical climate and fertile land allow the production of sugarcane, grains, fruits and vegetables, and livestock. In 1488 Portuguese Bartolomeu Dias was the first European to sail around the southern tip of Africa, opening the sea route to India. In 1652 the Dutch established a settlement at the Cape of Good Hope to produce food for Dutch ships sailing between Europe and the East. They began trading with the indigenous nomads, who herded cattle. European farmers, mainly Dutch and German, immigrated. They and their descendants, later known as Boers (Dutch word for farmers), imported slaves from Southeast Asia. These slaves spoke Malay, were Muslims, and founded the Cape Malay cuisine prominent in South Africa. The British took control of the area and sent British settlers, prompting the Boers' Great Trek into the interior. Also, Indians came to work in sugarcane plantations. British control influenced the food, for example, sugarcane plantations. The Dutch and Germans brought an appreciation for jams, preserves (konfyt), and baked goods; they founded large self-sufficient estates. French Huguenots founded the wine industry. Many dishes show Indonesian influence. The Malays were expert fishers, who preserved fish by frying them in oil and adding vinegar and spices. Spiced pickled fish, dried fish, fruits, and vegetables supplied provisions for ships visiting the Cape. Early settlers diced large fish and simmered them in onions; mullet and herring were salted and dried. Foods of the Great Trek were dried fish, boerewors (sausage made from mixed meats including game), biltong (dried strips of salted meat), and potjiekos (food such as venison cooked in a potjie, a three-legged pot over fire). The trekkers planted corn, a New World food, which was soon cultivated by the Africans. The trekkers used old termite hills to cook, first cooking a potjie food on top where a hole had been cut out and then baking sourdough bread inside after sealing the openings. Some meat was cooked on a wood fire and called braai (barbecue). The diet of rural people remains like that of their East African ancestors except that corn often replaces millet in porridge. Cattle were wealth and seldom eaten; dairy products were used.

Bread and cereals Corn, wheat, millet, oats, rice; millet, oatmeal, or cornmeal porridge (mealie pap), rice dishes, breads of wheat flour or cornmeal, cookies, pastry, ready-to-eat cereals, pasta.

Meat, poultry, fish Chicken, lamb and mutton, beef, goat, pork, fish and shellfish such as crayfish, or rock lobster (fresh, pickled, salted, dried), eggs, antelope, springbok, ostrich, ostrich eggs; sausage, bacon, biltong.

Insects Locusts, caterpillars, termites (white ants), ant larvae. These are usually fried or roasted.

Dairy products Milk, cream, buttermilk, yogurt, cheese, ice cream.

Fats and oils Fat of fat-tailed sheep, fish oil, vegetable oil, butter, coconut oil, peanut oil.

Legumes Beans, lentils, peanuts, green peas.

Vegetables Greens, pumpkin, cabbage, potatoes, sweet potatoes, carrots, tomatoes, cucumbers, turnips.

Fruit Grapes, melons, apples, citrus, apricots, peaches, dates, bananas, mangoes, papaya, pineapple, marula, gooseberries, strawberries, coconut, raisins, prunes.

Nuts and seeds Almonds, walnuts, macadamia nuts.

Seasonings Vinegar, lemon juice, onions, chili peppers, garlic, cinnamon, cloves, nutmeg, turmeric, ginger, curry powder, bay leaf, saffron.

Dishes Soups (potato, green pea). Lobster bisque. Pickled fish (Ingelegde Vis), fish fried in oil and soaked in vinegar and spices. Greens and tomato salad. Date and onion salad (dadel-slaai), blanched dates and onion slices dressed with brown sugar, salt, and vinegar or lemon juice. Steamed rice, sometimes with saffron and raisins. Bredie (spicy stew of mutton and/or vegetables). Sosaties (skewered marinated spicy lamb, barbecued, and served with curry sauce). Bobotie (baked ground lamb with curry and custard topping). Frikkadels (braised meat patties). Biriyani (spicy layered meat and saffron rice). Baked packet of thin, crisp dough enclosing antelope stew. Springbok leg marinated and braised with red wine and spices. Grilled lamb chops. Fish and chips (fried fish and potatoes). Meat, vegetable, or fruit curry (kerry), such as dried apples, raisins, and prunes curry. Grape-stuffed chicken. Ostrich egg omelet. Simmered beans, perhaps with melon or pumpkin. Sweet potatoes, stewed or baked. Cabbage layered with bacon, covered, and baked. Grated raw fruit or vegetable with chilies and vinegar or lemon juice (sambal), such as carrot sambal. Atjar (unripe fruit or vegetables preserved in oil heated with spices), such as mango atjar. Blatjang (chutney), spicy fruit or vegetable relish, such as apricot blatjang.

A national dish Gesmoorde Vis (salt cod simmered with fried onions, boiled potatoes, tomatoes, chili, and garlic).

Sweets Sugarcane, honey, sugar, brown sugar. Gooseberry jam. Malva (pudding). Custard tart (melktart). Deep-fried braided crullers dipped in cinnamon sugar (koesisters). Spiced cookies (soetkoekies). Sweet buns leavened with grape must (mosbolletjies). Tameletjie (brown sugar candy).

Beverages Tea, coffee, wine, sherry, brandy, tangerine-flavored liqueur, amarula (marula fruit liqueur).

SPAIN
Kingdom of Spain

Geography Spain is in southwestern Europe, occupying 85% of the Iberian Peninsula, and bordering the Atlantic and the Mediterranean, with Africa 10 miles (16 km) away. In northern Spain, the Pyrenees Mountains separate Spain from France. The interior is a high, arid plateau. The south is lowland with a Mediterranean climate.

Major Languages		Ethnic Groups	Major Religions	
Castilian Spanish	(official)	Mixed Mediterranean and Nordic:	Roman Catholic	94%
Catalan	(each	Spaniard 45%, Catalonian 28%,	Muslim	3%
Galician	official	Galacian 8%. Basque 6%,	Protestant	1%
Basque	regionally)	Aragonese 5%, other 8%	None, other	2%

Population density per sq. mi. 209.9
Literacy rate 97.4%
Life expectancy 76.6 male; 83.5 female
Per capita GDP $30,100
Labor force in agriculture 5.3%

Urban 76.7%
Infant mortality rate per 1,000 live births 4.3
HIV rate 0.5%
Unemployment rate 9.6%
Arable land 27%

Agriculture alfalfa, barley, grapes, vegetables, olives, sugar beets, citrus, chickens, pigs, sheep, cattle, goats

Natural resources   fish, coal, lignite, iron ore, uranium, tungsten, mercury, pyrites, fluorspar, gypsum, kaolin, potash, hydropower

Industries   textiles and apparel, food and beverages, metals, chemicals, shipbuilding, automobiles, machine tools, tourism, pharmaceuticals, medical equipment

History   Remains of Stone Age populations dating back some 35,000 years have been found in Spain. Iberians and Basques were settled here when Celtic people arrived in the 9th century BCE. Spain was successively ruled by Carthage, Rome, and the Visigoths. In 711 CE Muslims invaded from North Africa. Moorish rule ended in 1492, when Christians from the north regained control of the land. Roman Catholicism was established as the official state religion, and most Jews were expelled in 1492 and Muslims in 1502. With Columbus's discovery of America in 1492 and the conquest of Mexico by Cortes and of Peru by Pizarro, Spain gained great wealth and a vast colonial empire in the Americas. It also controlled the Netherlands and parts of Italy and Germany. The Spanish Hapsburg monarchy (1516–1700) became the world's most powerful. In 1588, the defeat of the Spanish Armada by Britain led to Spain's decline. When Hapsburg rule ended in 1700, Philip V became the first Bourbon king of Spain. Following his ascendancy, the War of Succession resulted in loss of many European possessions and triggered revolutions in most of Spain's South American colonies. Spain lost its American colonies in wars and revolutions during the 18th and 19th centuries. It lost Cuba, the Philippines, and Puerto Rico in the Spanish-American War, 1898. In 1931 Spain became a republic, separating church and state. The Spanish Civil War (1936–1939) ended in victory for the Nationalists under Gen. Francisco Franco, who ruled as dictator until his death in 1975. His successor as head of state, King Carlos I, restored the monarchy. In 1978 a new constitution provided for a parliamentary monarchy. Spain was officially neutral in World War II, although it had friendly relations with fascist countries. Catalonia and the Basque country were granted autonomy in 1980, although Basque separatist violence continued. Spain joined the UN in 1955, NATO in 1982, and the EU in 1986. In 2004, commuter train bombings in Madrid killed at least 191 people; evidence indicated the bombings were caused by Islamic extremists angered by Spain's having troops in Iraq. The opposition party led by Zapatero won elections three days later and removed Spanish troops from Iraq; Prime Minister Zapatero was reelected for a second term in 2008. Same-sex marriage became legal in 2005. In 2008 Spain agreed to add troops to its contingent in Afghanistan. As the worldwide financial crisis spread, Spain announced in October 2008 it would spend up to 50 billion euros to buy assets of its troubled banks.

Provinces of Spain: The **Balearic Islands,** in the west Mediterranean, include **Majorca, Minorca, Cabrera, Ibiza,** and **Formentera**; the **Canary Islands,** in the Atlantic west of Morocco, form two provinces and include the islands of **Tenerife, Palma, Gomera, Hierro, Grand Canary, Fuerteventura,** and **Lanzarote. Ceuta** and **Melilla** are small enclaves on Morocco's Mediterranean coast that gained limited autonomy in 1994.

Influences on food   Spanish food was influenced by the Phoenicians, who founded the city now Cadiz in 1100 BCE; the ancient Greeks and Carthaginians, who may have started wine production in Spain; and the Romans, who planted olive trees. Now Spain is a leading producer of olives and olive oil. The Arab occupation for more than seven centuries brought the use of almonds and introduced citrus fruits, sugarcane, many vegetables especially eggplant, many spices, rice cultivation in the tidal flatland now Valencia, and the use of saffron in paella, whose origin is Valencia. The Jews in Spain called their country Sepharad; thus when they were expelled in 1492 and were dispersed they were called the Sephardic Jews, who developed one of the two main branches of Jewish cookery. The same year Columbus's voyage to the New World led to the Spanish Conquest and the spread of Spanish foodways there and in the Philippines. Foods brought back from the New World, such as corn, tomatoes, potatoes, and chocolate, influenced Spain's cuisine. Spain's long coastlines provide seafood, prominent in coastal areas. From Andalusia and Extremadura, in southern and western Spain, come prize hams and sausages. The mountains and central plateau are arid and sparsely populated; there the food is seasonal, simple, and hearty. Spain includes two other major cuisines, Basque and Catalan.

Basque cuisine   The Basque people have lived since prehistoric times in the area at the southeast corner of the Bay of Biscay at the western end of the Pyrenees Mountains, mostly in Spain with a little part in France. The Basque have long depended on the sea and the mountains. Important foods include salt cod, roast lamb, dried red beans, bread, mushrooms, fruit, chestnuts, and cider. Almost unique to the Basque are many gastronomic societies for men.

Catalan cookery   The Catalan region is where Catalan is spoken: Catalonia, Valencia, the Balearic Islands, and Roussillon. Catalan cookery survives in Catalonia (northeast Spain) and the Balearic Islands. During the late medieval period Catalan was enlarged temporarily by the incorporation of Sicily in the 13th century, Sardinia in the 14th century, and Naples in the 15th century. As a result, Catalan cuisine influenced Italian cuisine. The Catalan region in Spain is unique for its Roman heritage. The Romans ruled the region from the third century BCE until 476 CE. The Arabs also influenced the region, improving the food supply with irrigation and the introduction of new plants, such as eggplant, sugar, bitter orange, and saffron, all prominent in Catalan cookery. Four basic preparations are characteristic of Catalan cuisine: allioli (an emulsion of garlic and olive oil), the main condiment; sofregit (onion and often tomato lightly fried with garlic and herbs), the start for many dishes; picada (garlic, fried bread, olive oil, and nuts, herbs, and spices pounded together with a mortar and pestle), added to a dish at the end to thicken and flavor; and samfaina (casserole of eggplant, tomatoes, squash, and sweet peppers), a basic dish. Pork is a main food, and lard is as commonly used as olive oil. Unusual combinations such as chicken and lobster, nuts in savory dishes, and bitter chocolate in meat and seafood dishes are used. The region is unique in Spain for meat and poultry dishes cooked with fruits.

Bread and cereals   Barley, wheat, corn, rice; crusty bread, rolls, cornbread, rice dishes.

Meat, poultry, fish   Chicken, pork, lamb, beef, goat, rabbit and other game, fish and shellfish (tuna, cod), eggs, snails; dried salt cod (bacalao), ham, sausages especially chorizo (made with pork, paprika, and garlic).

Dairy products   Milk (cow, sheep, goat), cheese (queso). In most of Spain there is a tradition of local cheese making. Many cheeses are made with sheep milk or goat milk or a mixture of the two.

Fats and oils   Olive oil, lard, butter. Olive oil is used in many dishes and for deep frying.

Legumes   Chickpeas, fava and kidney beans, white beans, lentils.

Vegetables   Olives, eggplant, tomatoes, potatoes, squash, sweet red and green peppers, carrots, mushrooms, cucumbers, peas, cabbage, asparagus, spinach.

Fruit   Grapes, oranges, lemons, apples, apricots, bananas, figs, dates, melons, strawberries, currants, raisins.

Nuts and seeds   Almonds and almond paste (marzipan), hazelnuts, pine nuts, chestnuts, walnuts, sesame seeds.

Seasonings   Garlic, tomatoes, onion, sweet peppers, vinegar, lemon, black pepper, cinnamon, nutmeg, saffron, coriander, aniseed, paprika, cloves, cumin, mint, chocolate.

Dishes   Cocida (meat, chickpea, and vegetable stew), served in three courses: soup, vegetables, and meat. Ollo podrida (meat and vegetable stew), served in two courses: soup and meat with vegetables. Garlic soup (sopa de ajo), garlic, bread slices, and paprika sautéed in olive oil, water and eggs added, and simmered (or the egg may be dropped in the simmered soup and poached). Escabecho (fried fish, cooled, and marinated in vinegar with other ingredients). Shellfish stew (zarzuela de mariscos). Bacalao al pil-pil (salt cod sautéed in olive oil and garlic). Grilled fish or lamb chops. Sautéed chicken with tomatoes, peppers, and olives. Braised rabbit. Roast suckling pig (cochinillo asada). Empanada (meat pie). Gazpacho (cold soup of tomato, cucumber, garlic, onion, and pepper). Tortilla, a round thin omelet (beaten eggs fried in buttered pan). Red beans simmered with chorizo. Alioli (garlic, olive oil, salt, and lemon juice), used with grilled or broiled meat or fish.

Romescu (sauce of ground almonds, garlic, paprika, and tomatoes with vinegar and olive oil), sometimes mixed with alioli to taste by each diner at the table. Migas (bread chunks fried in olive oil with garlic and perhaps bits of ham). Fried eggplant.

National dish   Paella (rice cooked with saffron, seafood, chicken, sausage, peas, tomato, and sweet peppers).

Sweets   Honey, sugar. Fresh fruit. Fruit compote. Rice pudding. Flan (sweet egg custard topped with caramel). Banana fritters. Fried cylindrical doughnuts (churros). Cake with rum cream filling. Almond honey nougat.

Easter Holy Week sweets   Tortas de aceite (cakes with olive oil, sesame seeds, and anise). Yemas de San Leandro (egg yolks poured through tiny holes into boiling syrup making "angel hair." with almond paste).

Beverages   Coffee with milk (café con leche), hot chocolate, cider, wine, sherry, sangria (red wine, fruit punch).

Meals   Four meals a day plus snacks is typical: early breakfast of bread and coffee or cocoa; mid-morning breakfast of grilled sausages, bread with tomato, or an omelet; early afternoon main meal of soup or salad, fish or meat, and dessert, often with fruit and cheese; and late supper of three courses such as soup, omelet, and fruit.

Street food and snacks   Churros and fritters (fried pastries), sold on streets. Tapas (tidbits, or finger foods), such as raw thinly sliced jamón serrano (mountain ham), served with wine or sherry in the evening in bars and cafés. The first tapas (lids) were pieces of bread used to cover wine-glasses to keep out flies.

Balearic Islands   A part of Spain, the Balearic Islands (Majorca, Minorca, Ibiza, and Formentera) are in the western Mediterranean. Along with Catalonia in northeast Spain, these islands are where Catalan cookery survives, although the island cuisine is peasant style and less sophisticated than that of Catalonia, especially Barcelona. The islands share many of the same foods with Spain, such as rice with rabbit and other game, snails, vegetables, and spices. Typical dishes include bread and garlic or cabbage soups. Typical Majorca ingredients include pork, sausages, lard, currants, pine nuts, cinnamon, peppercorns, and cloves. Majorca is famous for its apricots and almonds, often served as dessert. Minorca and Ibiza specialties include dried figs and plums. Other desserts, of Moorish (Arab) influence, are baked goods with almonds, almond ice cream, and a sweet iced almond milk drink.

Canary Islands   These islands are off the northwest coast of Africa in the Atlantic Ocean. Called "the fortunate isles" by the Romans, they have an agreeable subtropical climate. The first inhabitants arrived about 2000 BCE, probably from southwestern France. Spain has ruled here from the end of the 15th century. The Spanish introduced sugarcane, the main crop for a century. Then corn from the New World and wine production superseded sugarcane, followed by bananas, potatoes, tomatoes, and citrus fruits. Dishes include gofio (bread made from roasted and ground wheat, corn, or barley mixed with water), seafood grilled or in fish soup, and jacket potatoes (papas arrugadas) boiled in salty water and eaten with their jackets, which have a white deposit of salt. Mojo, a sauce of oil, vinegar, garlic, and herbs (parsley and coriander in the green version; red peppers and saffron in the red version), flavors many foods. Many sweets are based on corn or almonds.

SRI LANKA
Democratic Socialist Republic of Sri Lanka

Geography   Formerly Ceylon, Sri Lanka is an island in the Indian Ocean southeast of India. Most of the land is flat and rolling, with hills and mountains in the south central region.

Major Languages	Ethnic Groups		Major Religions	
Sinhala (both	Sinhalese	74%	Buddhist	69%
Tamil official)	Tamil	18%	Muslim	8%
English (used in government)	Sri Lankan Moor	7%	Hindu	7%
	Other	1%	Christian	6%
			Other	10%

Population density per sq. mi. 845.3
Literacy rate 91.5%
Life expectancy 73 male; 77.1 female
Per capita GDP $4,100
Labor force in agriculture 34.3%

Urban 15.1%
Infant mortality rate per 1,000 live births 19
HIV rate NA
Unemployment rate 6.5%
Arable land 14%

Agriculture   rice, sugarcane, coconuts, oilseed, spices, tea, rubber, chickens, cattle, buffalo, goats, pigs, sheep

Natural resources   forests, rubber, fish, limestone, graphite, mineral sands, gems, phosphates, clay, hydropower

Industries   rubber processing, tea and coconuts, insurance, banking, clothing, textiles, cement, oil refining, tobacco, telecommunications

History   Indo-Aryans from northern India overcame the indigenous aborigines about 543 BCE. Their descendants, the Sinhalese, comprise most of the present population. Buddhism was introduced during the 3rd century BCE. Immigrants from southern India, the Tamil, came between the 3rd century BCE and 1200 CE. Between 1200 and 1505, Sinhalese and Tamil rulers fought for dominance; the Sinhalese, primarily Buddhists, controlled southern Ceylon and the Tamils, primarily Hindus, claimed the north and established the Tamil kingdom in the 14th century. Invasions from India, China, and Malaya occurred in the 13th to 15th centuries. In 1505 the Portuguese arrived and by 1619 controlled most of the land. In 1658 the Dutch occupied part. Britain gained control of the island in 1796 and developed coffee, tea, and rubber plantations. Ceylon became a crown colony in 1802, gained independence in 1948, became the Republic of Sri Lanka in 1972, and was renamed its present name in 1978. Land reform and nationalization of foreign-owned plantations began in the mid-1970s. Civil war between the Sinhalese and Tamil in the 1980s and 1990s ended with a truce accord in 2002. The Indian Ocean tsunami in 2004 killed over 31,000 Sri Lankans. Fighting has continued, with Tamils seeking a separate independent state in northern Sri Lanka. In 2005 the foreign minister was assassinated and a state of emergency was declared. In 2007 violence between the government and a Tamil liberation group included fighting, suicide bombings, assassinations, and abductions. Violence increased substantially in 2008. Economic growth slowed in 2007, although the garment industry continued strong and worker remittances provided foreign exchange.

Influences on food   Sri Lanka is a very large island southeast of India. Influences on its food include India and the Portuguese, Dutch, and British. Indian-type breads and chutney are common. Burghers, descendants of intermarriages between colonists and local women, use some dishes showing European influence. Dutch influence shows in sophisticated use of spices and some Dutch terms such as frikkadel. British influence reflects in tea plantations. Influence from further east shows in the use of blachan (shrimp paste) and sambal (spicy uncooked pickles). In this tropical country, rice is the staple; breadfruit, jackfruit, and yams are secondary staples; and coconut is often used in curry-type dishes. Many spices are grown and used. In this island country fish is important. Little meat is eaten by the predominantly Buddhist population. Unlike Indian cuisine, Sri Lankan food often includes dried and grated tuna fish from Maldives; it uses a somewhat different mixture of spices in curry.

Bread and cereals   Rice, grains; rice dishes, hopper (pancake or noodle-like string made from leavened rice batter), Indian-type breads dosa (here thosai, rice and lentil pancakes) and idli (small round breakfast cakes made from ground rice and dal, fermented overnight). Dal is grains, legumes, or seeds.

Meat, poultry, fish Chicken, beef, buffalo, goat, pork, lamb, fish (tuna), shellfish (shrimp), eggs.

Dairy products Milk, yogurt.

Fats and oils Coconut oil, coconut cream, butter, ghee (clarified butter).

Legumes Chickpeas, split peas, lentils, beans, peanuts.

Vegetables Breadfruit, jackfruit, yams, plantains, tomatoes, onions.

Fruit Coconut, mangoes, bananas, limes, goraka (about the size of an orange and fluted on the outside), billing (sour fruit of a tree; has smooth, yellow-green skin, resembles a gherkin; is used as a vegetable and in pickles).

Nuts and seeds Almonds, beetle nuts, sesame seeds.

Seasonings Curry powder (cumin, black cumin, cinnamon, cardamom, cloves, coriander, fenugreek), chili.

Dishes Steamed rice. Fried rice. Curried meat, chicken, fish, shellfish, or vegetables (cooked with a mixture of spices or curry powder). Sambal (uncooked mixture of vegetables, fruits, and seasoning, usually onions, chilies, and an acid ingredient such as vinegar). Vegetables or fruit pickles. Chutney (spicy fruit or vegetable preserves). Fried fish or shrimp. Fried breadfruit, yams, or plantains. Boiled vegetables. Boiled chickpeas or lentils. Pittu (compressed steamed cake of rice or wheat flour and grated coconut), eaten with coconut milk and curries, sambals, or jaggery. Mallums (fruit or vegetable, finely shredded or grated, and cooked with coconut).

Wedding and festival food Kiri bath (rice cooked in coconut milk to form a sticky cake), served with curries, sambals, or jaggery (palm sugar made from the sap of palm trees).

Sweets Sugarcane, palm sugar (jaggery), molasses, fruit.

Beverages Tea, coffee, toddy (drink containing alcoholic liquor made from coconut or other palm tree).

SUDAN
Republic of the Sudan

Geography Sudan is in northern Africa, at the east end of the Sahara desert, with a 500-mile coast along the Red Sea. Africa's largest country and about one-fourth the size of the United States, Sudan is mostly desert. In the north are the Libya Desert in the west and the mountainous Nubian Desert, with the narrow Nile valley between. The Nile River crosses Sudan north to south. Fertile, rainy areas with fields, pastures, and forests are along the Nile and in the south, which has a tropical climate.

Major Languages	Ethnic Groups		Major Religions	
Arabic (official)	Black	52%	Sunni Muslim	70%
English (principal in southern Sudan)	Arab	39%	Indigenous beliefs	11%
Nubian	Beja	6%	Roman Catholic	10%
Ta Bedawie	Other	3%	Protestant (Anglican 5%)	9%
Dialects: Nilotic, Nilo-Hamitic, Sudanic				

Population density per sq. mi. 43.8
Literacy rate 60.9%
Life expectancy 49.4 male; 51.2 female
Per capita GDP $2,200
Labor force in agriculture 80%

Urban 40.8%
Infant mortality rate per 1,000 live births 87
HIV rate 1.4%
Unemployment rate NA
Arable land 7%

Agriculture   sugarcane, sorghum, millet, cotton, peanuts, wheat, gum Arabic, cassava, mangoes, papayas, sheep, goats, cattle, chickens

Natural resources   fish, oil, iron ore, copper, chromium ore, zinc, tungsten, mica, silver, gold, hydropower

Industries   oil, cotton ginning, textiles, cement, edible oils, sugar, pharmaceuticals, armaments

History   Northern Sudan, ancient Nubia, came under Egyptian rule periodically from the end of the 4th millennium BCE. An Egyptian and Nubian civilization, Cush, flourished from the 11th century BCE to 350 CE. In the 6th century missionaries converted the population in Sudan's three principal kingdoms to Christianity. These three black Christian kingdoms coexisted with their Muslim Arab neighbors in Egypt for centuries until the influx of Arab immigrants caused their collapse in the 13th to 15th centuries. In the 15th century Arab conquests brought Islam. In the 1500s several black African groups settled in Sudan, especially in the south. In the 1820s Egypt regained control and had conquered all of Sudan by 1874. After a revolution in the 1880s, Britain gained control in 1898 and ruled until Sudan achieved independence in 1956. Since independence, unstable governments and military regimes have ruled. In the 1980s and 1990s economic problems, civil war, influx of refugees from neighboring countries, and famine claimed over 2 million lives. A new constitution based on Islamic law took effect in 1998. The non-Muslim population of the south has engaged in rebellion against the Muslim-controlled government of the north. During the period 2003 to 2008, a rebellion in the western province of Darfur led to militia retaliation, killing up to 300,000 people and causing displacement of another 2.5 million. In 2007, mainly due to high oil prices, Sudan had one of Africa's fastest growing economies.

Influences on food   Sudan, between the deserts of North Africa and the tropical forests of West and East Africa, has cuisine that reflects both African and Middle Eastern influences. For example, okra stew and Sudanese bread might be served in a meal with fava beans and cucumber with yogurt salad. Sudan and its food customs have been influenced by Egypt, the Arabs, Britain, and religion. Sudan, the 12th largest country in the world and the largest in Africa, is arid in the north and rainy and tropical in the south. Rivers including the Nile and Blue Nile and the coastline on the Red Sea provide fish. The main staple food crop is great, or Indian, millet (dura, sorghum bicolor). Other major food crops are millet, wheat, groundnuts (peanuts), sugarcane, cassava, and fruit. The palmyra palm, an important famine food, grows in most regions. The roselle (kerkade, *Hibiscus sabdariffa,* also called red sorrel) pod provides a distinctive, delicious, deep rose red–colored drink. The main food animal is sheep; the desert sheep are well adapted to local conditions. Most people are Muslims, who do not consume pork or alcohol. A considerable part of the Sudan is called "the meatless region" because the tsetse fly prevents raising domestic animals; any wild animal caught is eaten. Traditions of hospitality and customs are that men have priority for food over women, with the result that in general women are not fed as well as men. The men eat first, except that if the meal is much delayed small children may be fed something. Guests who come before the men finish eating must be invited to partake, which may result in little food left for others in the household.

Bread and cereals   Sorghum, millet, wheat, barley, corn, rice; porridge, bread, rice dishes. The staple bread, kisra, is nearly identical to Ethiopian injera (flatbread made from fermented dough of teff, a variety of millet unique to Ethiopia, cooked on a griddle in a large circular loaf).

Meat, poultry, fish   Mutton and lamb, goat, beef, chicken, pork, fish and seafood, wild animals (snakes, bush rats, tortoises), eggs; salted and dried meat (sharmut). Mutton is preferred, except that beef is preferred in the south.

Dairy products   Milk, yogurt, curds.

Fats and oils   Sesame seed oil, cottonseed oil, peanut oil, butter, ghee (clarified butter).

Legumes   Peanuts, cowpeas, lentils, fava beans.

Vegetables   Cassava, sweet potatoes, plantains, potatoes, okra, green leafy vegetables (melokhia, rocket, amaranth), cucumbers.

Fruit   Mangoes, papaya, bananas, dates, baobab tree fruit, palmyra fruit, roselle, other tropical fruits in the south.

Nuts and seeds   Sesame seeds, baobab tree seeds.

Seasonings   Onions, salt, black pepper, hot red pepper, cinnamon, saffron.

Dishes   Boiled cassava. Boiled rice. Stewed okra or green leafy vegetables (cooked okra and melokhia have a mucilaginous texture). Boiled or fried sweet potatoes, potatoes, or plantains. Stews of meat, chicken, fish, or game with vegetables. Fried, grilled, or roasted meat, chicken, or fish. Cucumber and yogurt salad.

Sweets   Sugarcane, honey, sugar, fruit especially dates.

Beverages   Sugarcane juice, palmyra fruit juice, roselle sweet beverage, roselle herbal tea.

SURINAME
Republic of Suriname

Geography   Formerly Dutch Guiana, Suriname is in northern South America, bordering the Atlantic Ocean. It consists of a flat coastal strip where dikes permit agriculture, interior forests, and hills covering 75% of the land.

Major Languages	Ethnic Groups		Major Religions	
Dutch (official)	East Indian	37%	Hindu	27%
English widely spoken	Creole (mixed white and black)	31%	Protestant	25%
Sranang Tongo (Surinamese)	Javanese	15%	Roman Catholic	23%
Caribbean Hindustani	Maroons (descendants of		Muslim	20%
Javanese	escaped slaves)	10%	Other	5%
	Amerindian, other	7%		

Population density per sq. mi. 7.6

Literacy rate 90.4%

Life expectancy 70.8 male; 76.4 female

Per capita GDP $7,800

Labor force in agriculture 8%

Urban 73.9%

Infant mortality rate per 1,000 live births 19.4

HIV rate 2.4%

Unemployment rate 9.5%

Arable land 0.4%

Agriculture   rice, sugarcane, bananas, palm kernels, coconuts, plantains, peanuts, chickens, cattle, pigs, sheep

Natural resources   timber, hydropower, fish, kaolin, shrimp, bauxite, gold, nickel, copper, platinum, iron ore

Industries   mining, alumina production, oil, food processing, fishing

History   Suriname is named for its original inhabitants, the Surinen Indians, who were supplanted by other South American Indians by the 16th century. Spanish explorers claimed Suriname in 1593. The Dutch started settling here in 1602, followed by the English. In 1667 the Dutch acquired the area from Britain in exchange for New Netherlands (New York), and the area became the Dutch colony, Dutch Guiana. African slaves furnished labor for coffee and sugar plantations until slavery ended in 1863. African slaves who escaped into the interior were called "Bush Negroes." Their descendants are the Maroons. After 1870 indentured laborers were imported from India and the Dutch East Indies to work on the plantations. The Dutch colony Guiana was granted independence as Suriname in 1975, despite objections from its East Indians. Some 40% of the population, mostly East Indians, emigrated to the Netherlands in the months before independence. Political turmoil and military coups in the 1980s and until 1992 disrupted the economy. Suriname is known for drug trafficking; former dictator Bouterse was sentenced in

1998 in the Netherlands for transporting cocaine. In 2007 the UN International Tribunal for the Law of the Sea awarded neighboring Guyana 65% of the contested maritime area, containing oil and natural gas deposits. Improvement occurred in Suriname's economy, credit rating, tax revenues, and trade surplus.

Influences on food   Suriname, a British possession and then a Dutch colony for more than three centuries, has history and cuisine more closely linked to the West Indies than to Spanish or Portuguese possessions in South America. The Amerindian population is tiny compared to the descendants of African slaves, brought to work in sugarcane and coffee plantations, and of Indian and Indonesian laborers, who succeeded them. The cooking reflects the preferences of the imported slaves and laborers, as well as local resources and colonial influences. The diet depends largely on manioc meal (cassava), plantains, and bananas, with seafood in coastal areas. Bush blacks (former runaway slaves) had dishes reflecting an African past. Pepper pot stew originated in neighbor country Guyana. Other common dishes resulted from adapting European ones. The use of rice and Indian and Indonesian dishes increased as Indians and Indonesians here increased. Suriname cuisine resembles that of neighbors, northeast Brazil (e.g., cassava meal and fruit), Guyana (also a former British and Dutch possession), and French Guyana (a French region).

Bread and cereals   Rice, corn, wheat; rice dishes, cornmeal bread and mush, corn flour, fresh ears of corn (and scrapings and liquid "milk"), cassava meal bread, wheat flour bread and cookies.

Meat, poultry, fish   Chicken, beef, pork, lamb and mutton, goat, fish, shrimp, other seafood, eggs, large bird oko.

Dairy products   Milk (cow, goat), evaporated milk, cheese.

Fats and oils   Palm oil, coconut oil, butter, lard.

Legumes   Peanuts, beans, split peas.

Vegetables   Plantains, cassava, okra, sweet potatoes, potatoes, callaloo (edible leaves of root vegetables especially amaranth, malanga, taro), tomatoes, pumpkin, onions, chili peppers.

Fruit   Bananas, coconut (fresh, dried, flour, milk), papaya, limes, other tropical fruits.

Nuts and seeds   Brazil nuts, palm kernels, sesame seeds, pumpkin seeds.

Seasonings   Cinnamon, cloves, cayenne pepper, chili pepper, curry powder, black pepper, other spices.

Dishes   Boiled or steamed rice. Pepper pot (a substantial stew of cassareep juice from grated bitter cassava root, mixed meats, cloves, cinnamon, and peppers). Okra and cornmeal mush (coo-coo). Fried fish, shrimp, or other seafood. Dutch split-pea soup adapted by adding chilies. Indonesian dishes. Indian curries.

Sweets   Sugarcane, sugar, honey. Madou (macerated fruit). Pudding of rice, corn flour, or tapioca (made from cassava). Doconon (cake of corn flour, banana, coconut, and spices, leaf wrapped and poached). Couac coco (made by grating and drying coconut to make flour, then adding sugar, cinnamon, and lime zest). Wang (a confection of toasted ground sesame seeds, cinnamon, lime zest, and sugar or salt). A traditional dessert made with corn "milk," coconut milk, evaporated milk, sugar, and spices.

Beverages   Coffee, fruit juices, soft drinks, sugarcane juice, tea, beer, sugarcane brandy (cachaça).

Street food and snack   Wang, sold in a paper cone or formed in small balls.

SWAZILAND
Kingdom of Swaziland

Geography   Swaziland is in southern Africa near the Indian Ocean and almost surrounded by South Africa. This small country consists of arid low regions in the west and plateaus and mountains from 1,500 feet (457 m) to 6,000 feet (1,829 m) in the east. The climate is temperate.

Major Languages	Ethnic Groups		Major Religions	
Swati (both	Swazi	82%	Christian-indigenous	40%
English official)	Zulu	10%	Roman Catholic	20%
	Tsonga	2%	Protestant	18%
	Afrikaner	1%	Muslim	10%
	Mixed black-white, other	5%	Other	12%

Population density per sq. mi. 170
Literacy rate 79.6%
Life expectancy 31.7 male; 32.3 female
Per capita GDP $4,800
Labor force in agriculture NA

Urban 24.1%
Infant mortality rate per 1,000 live births 69.6
HIV rate 26.1%
Unemployment rate 31%
Arable land 10%

Agriculture   sugarcane, oranges, grapefruit and pomelo, cotton, corn, tobacco, rice, pineapples, chickens, cattle, goats, pigs, sheep

Natural resources   asbestos, coal, clay, cassiterite, hydropower, gold, diamonds, quarry stone, talc

Industries   coal mining, wood pulp, sugar, soft drinks concentrates, textiles and apparel

History   Stone tools and rock paintings indicate prehistoric habitation of the region. The royal house of Swaziland traces back 400 years and is one of Africa's last ruling dynasties. The Swazi, a Bantu people, migrated from the north to the Mozambique area in the 16th century. Some clans moved to Swaziland in the 18th century and organized as tribes in the 19th century. After the Boer War, Britain assumed control in 1903. Independence came in 1968. In 1973 the king repealed the constitution and took full powers. In 1978 the new constitution banned political parties. Since 1986, King Mswati III has ruled as sub-Saharan Africa's last absolute monarch. In 2003, after three years of drought and lavish expenditures for the king's new luxury jet, many people faced starvation. AIDS is a serious threat, and the huge gap between rich and poor has led to student and labor unrest in recent years. In 2007 the budget showed a surplus. The Prevention of Corruption Act was promulgated in response to corruption in both government and the private sector. The prevalence of HIV/AIDS dropped sharply.

Influences on food   The temperate climate allows the production of sugarcane, corn, rice, citrus, pineapples, peanuts, and livestock. Influences include South Africa (which almost surrounds this small country), Europeans, Malaysians, and East Africans. In 1488 Portuguese Bartolomeu Dias was the first European to sail around the southern tip of Africa, thereby opening the sea route to India. In the 17th century the Dutch East India Company established a settlement at the Cape of Good Hope that began trading with the indigenous population. Later some farmers from Europe settled there. They and their descendants, mainly Dutch and German, were later known as Boers. The Dutch and Germans brought baked goods and jams and preserves (konfyt). They established farms and imported slave labor from Southeast Asia. These Malaysians founded the Cape Malay cuisine that is prominent in the region. The Malays were expert fishers with experience in preserving fish; spiced pickled fish and dried fish supplied provisions for ships visiting the Cape. The British took control of South Africa in 1814 and sent thousands of British settlers there, prompting the Great Trek north by the Boers. Indians came to work in the sugar plantations. British control of Swaziland from 1903 to 1968 also influenced the food. The diet of rural people remains much like that of their East African ancestors (dairy products, beans, melon, greens, and insects) except that corn replaced millet in porridge. Cattle were wealth and seldom eaten.

Bread and cereals   Corn, rice, sorghum, millet, wheat; cornmeal porridge (putu), rice dishes, wheat breads, doughnuts, tarts, cookies.

Meat, poultry, fish   Chicken, beef, goat, pork, lamb and mutton, eggs, fish, seafood, antelope, venison, ostrich.

Insects   Locusts, caterpillars, termites (white ants), ant larvae. These are usually fried or roasted.

Dairy products   Milk, cream, cheese.

Fats and oils   Fat of fat-tailed sheep, butter, fish oil, vegetable oil.

Legumes   Peanuts, beans, lentils.

Vegetables   Green leaves, pumpkin, cauliflower, potatoes, sweet potatoes, cucumbers, carrots, onions, tomatoes.

Fruit   Oranges, grapefruit, pomelo, lemons, tangerines, pineapple, grapes, melon, quinces, dates, apples.

Nuts and seeds   Almonds, walnuts.

Seasonings   Vinegar, chili peppers, garlic, cinnamon, cloves, turmeric, ginger, curry powder, saffron, bay leaf.

Dishes   Bredie (spicy mutton stew with various vegetables), eaten with boiled rice. Sosaties (skewered, curried mutton). Bobotie (minced meat with spices, topped with custard, and baked). Frikkadels (braised meat patties). Simmered beans, sometimes with melon or pumpkin. Salads of grated raw fruit or vegetables with lemon juice or vinegar and chilies). Breyani (spicy meat layered with saffron rice and simmered). Kerry (curry) with boiled rice. Atjars (unripe fruit or vegetables preserved in oil with spices). Chutney (fruit or vegetable pickles with chilies).

Sweets   Sugarcane, honey, sugar. Cinnamon-flavored egg custard tart (melktart). Spicy doughnuts (koeksisters).

Beverages   Tea, wine.

SWEDEN
Kingdom of Sweden

Geography   Sweden is in northern Europe, on the Scandinavian Peninsula, bordering the Baltic Sea. The northern boundary extends into the Arctic Circle. Forests cover half of the land. Mountains along the northwest border comprise 25% of the land. Flat or rolling terrain with fertile valleys and plains are in the south and east.

Major Language	Ethnic Groups		Major Religions	
Swedish (official)	Swedish	84%	Lutheran	87%
	Finnish	3%	Other Protestant	5%
	Asian	4%	Muslim	4%
	Other	9%	Roman Catholic, other	4%

Population density per sq. mi. 57
Literacy rate 99%
Life expectancy 78.5 male; 83.1 female
Per capita GDP $36,500
Labor force in agriculture 2%

Urban 84.3%
Infant mortality rate per 1,000 live births 2.8
HIV rate 0.1%
Unemployment rate 6.3%
Arable land 6%

Agriculture   sugar beets, wheat, barley, chickens, pigs, cattle, sheep, reindeer

Natural resources   fish, iron ore, copper, lead, zinc, gold, silver, uranium, timber, hydropower

Industries   iron and steel, precision equipment, bearings, radio and phone parts, armaments, wood pulp and paper products, processed foods, motor vehicles

History   The first inhabitants probably were hunters who crossed the land bridge from Europe about 9000 BCE. Swedes have lived in this land for at least 5,000 years. Tribes from Sweden helped break up the Roman Empire. Other Swedes helped form the first Russian nation in the 9th century.

During the Viking era, 9th to 10th centuries, the Swedes raided western European lands. In the 11th century Swedes were Christianized and a monarchy developed. Sweden was conquered by the Finns in the 12th century. In the 14th century Sweden united with Norway and Denmark in a single monarchy. In 1435 Sweden formed Europe's first parliament, with all classes of society represented. A Danish king conquered Sweden in 1520 and ruled to 1523, when Gustavus Vasa led a revolt resulting in Swedish independence, a Swedish king (Gustavus I, 1523–1560), and the establishment of the Lutheran Church. In the 17th century Sweden was a major European power and gained most of the Baltic seacoast. In 1814, it united with Norway, which became independent in 1905. It maintained armed neutrality in both world wars. Sweden pioneered in public health, housing, and job security. It established old-age pensions in 1911. It is a constitutional monarchy and had a socialist government for most of the 20th century. Sweden was a charter member of the UN and joined the EU in 1995, although voters rejected the euro in 2003. In 1997 it began to shut down its nuclear power industry. In 2007 Sweden's economy grew and a sizable number of jobs were added. In 2008 Parliament authorized a security agency to monitor cross-border phone calls, e-mail, and other electronic communications.

Influences on food   Sweden, the largest Scandinavian country, has cuisine based on native food traditions overlaid with German and French influences. Foods often reflect preservation methods of previous centuries such as drying, salting, smoking, and pickling fish and fermenting and souring milk. The many lakes and long coastlines on the Baltic and North Seas provide fish and seafood. Göteborg, on the west coast and Sweden's greatest fishing port, has a large variety of Atlantic species, including turbot. Fertile valleys and plains in the south and east grow grains, sugar beets, and potatoes. Cattle and sheep graze in summer mountain meadows in the west and supply dairy products and meat. In the north is a Lapp region, known for reindeer meat, milk, and cheese. In the 16th century the great Gustav Vasa encouraged Swedes to grow rye and make crisp rye bread (knäckebrïd), now ubiquitous. Sweden has both homely fare (husmanskost) and sophisticated cuisine.

Bread and cereals   Wheat, barley, rye, rice; leavened and unleavened rye bread, crisp rye bread (knäckebrïd), thin crisp bread from barley flour and potatoes, French (white) bread, buns, pancakes, biscuits, rice dishes.

Meat, poultry, fish   Chicken, pork, beef and veal, lamb, reindeer meat, fish and seafood (herring, sprat, turbot, salmon, eels, crayfish), eggs; ham, pickled herring, Sürstromming (whole herring fermented with salt and natural summer heat), Sprat (small fish of the herring family; canned in oil, known as "Swedish anchovies"). Meat is often chopped or ground and extended by mixing with other ingredients.

Dairy products   Milk, cream, buttermilk, sour cream, cheese.

Fats and oils   Butter, lard, margarine, vegetable oil, salt pork.

Legumes   Split peas (yellow and green), lima beans.

Vegetables   Potatoes, onions, cabbage, cucumbers, beets, mushrooms, carrots, peas, mustard, asparagus.

Fruit   Ligonberries (small cranberries), strawberries, other berries, apples, apricots, cherries, lemons, prunes, currants, raisins. Berries are eaten fresh in summer and in preserves and soups in winter.

Nuts and seeds   Almonds, almond paste (marzipan), caraway seeds, dill seeds.

Seasonings   Salt, cardamom, ginger, cinnamon, cloves, saffron, dill, peppercorns, vinegar, mustard.

Dishes   Gravlax (cured salmon), made by marinating fresh salmon in dill, salt, sugar, and peppercorns, served uncooked with mustard-dill sauce. Boiled potatoes (often eaten twice a day). Baked potatoes. Lacy potato pancakes (grated potatoes seasoned and fried in butter and oil). Swedish meat balls (ground beef, onion, bread crumbs, and eggs, fried in butter and oil; cream may be added at end to make sauce). Jannson's temptation (casserole of anchovies and julienne potatoes with cream and onions). Baked onion or cabbage rolls (leaves stuffed with seasoned ground meat). Mushroom omelet. Poached salmon. Roast pork, ham, beef, or venison. Veal Oscar (veal topped with béarnaise sauce, white asparagus, and lobster or crab), named after Swedish King Oscar II (1872–1907), a gourmet. Homely fare dishes: yellow pea soup, often served with pancakes, and pytt i panna ("bits and pieces"), a hash of leftover cooked meat and diced potatoes fried with salty bacon and onions and topped with a fried egg.

Special event fare   On the morning of December 13, St. Lucia's Day, the eldest daughter in the home, wearing a long white dress and crown of ligonberry greens with lit candles, serves saffron yeast buns and coffee to her parents in bed. On Midsummer's Day (June 24), a holiday, fish, boiled new potatoes, and wild strawberries are eaten.

Christmas dishes   On Christmas Eve, the most special meal of the year includes lutefisk (cod or other fish dried, soaked in lye solution, rinsed, and boiled) and rice porridge (julgrot) with sugar and cinnamon.

Sweets   Sugar, honey. Fruit soups and rose hip soup, served cold with almonds and whipped cream. Fruit compote. Pancakes served with ligonberries. Deep-fried, sweet, brandy-flavored dough. Biscuits (cookies) with cardamom, ginger, cinnamon, and cloves; cut into hearts or other shapes and iced. Apple cake. Spettekaka (a yard-high cake of eggs and confectioners sugar). Ostkaka (cheesecake with almonds).

Beverages   Milk, buttermilk, tea, coffee, beer, aquavit ("water of life," liquor distilled from potatoes or grain).

Meals and service   Three meals a day plus a coffee break is typical. The smörgåsbord originated in Sweden and, although it means "bread and butter table." is a buffet meal of a large assortment of dishes served with aquavit and eaten in this order: herring, then other fish; cold meats and salads; hot dishes; and desserts.

SWITZERLAND
Swiss Confederation

Geography   Switzerland is in central Europe. The Alps Mountains, in the south, cover 60% of the land; the Jura Mountains, in the northwest, cover 10%; and the midland plateau, in between, covers 30%. The three largest lakes straddle borders with France, Germany-Austria, and Italy. The Rhine is the main inland waterway.

Major Languages		Ethnic Groups		Major Religions	
German	(all	German	65%	Roman Catholic	42%
French	are	French	18%	Protestant	35%
Italian	official	Italian	10%	None	11%
Romansch	and national)	Other	7%	Muslim	4%
				Other	8%

Population density per sq. mi. 493.7
Literacy rate 99%
Life expectancy 77.9 male; 83.7 female
Per capita GDP $41,100
Labor force in agriculture 4.6%

Urban 73.3%
Infant mortality rate per 1,000 live births 4..2
HIV rate 0.6%
Unemployment rate 2.8%
Arable land 10%

Agriculture   sugar beets, wheat, potatoes, fruits, vegetables, chickens, pigs, cattle, sheep, goats

Natural resources   hydropower potential, timber, salt, fish

Industries   machinery, chemicals, watches, textiles, precision instruments, tourism, banking, insurance

History   The original inhabitants were the Helvetians, who were conquered by Rome in the first century BCE. Switzerland was the Roman province of Helvetia. German tribes entered the region from the 3rd to the 6th century CE. Muslims and Magyars raided the region in the 10th century. It became part of the Holy Roman Empire in the 11th century. Switzerland's modern history began in 1291, when three cantons formed a defense league. Other cantons were added. The Swiss Confederation gained independence from the Holy Roman Empire in 1648. Switzerland was a center of the Reformation, which divided the country. The French organized Switzerland as the Helvetic Republic in 1798. In 1815 the Congress of Vienna recognized Swiss independence, and Switzerland has maintained armed neutrality since 1815. In 1848 a federal constitution joined the cantons and a new state was formed with Bern as the capital. Women were granted the right to vote and hold office in 1971. Many UN and other international agencies are in Geneva. Switzerland is an international banking center, the world's leading repository for international accounts. It joined the UN in 2002. Abortion was decriminalized in 2002. A 2007 highlight was the opening of the Transalpine Lötschberg Tunnel, the world's longest overland tunnel (21.5 mi; 34.6 km), which took eight years to build and halved the train journey time between Germany and Italy. In 2007 the country's economy grew, unemployment fell, and the government budget showed a surplus. Hiking is popular.

Influences on food   Switzerland is a small, mountainous, and pastoral country with 23 cantons. Grains, sugar beets, fruit, and vegetables are grown, and dairy cattle and other livestock are raised. Many dishes resemble ones in neighboring France, Germany, and Italy; however, Swiss cuisine is distinguished by emphasis on cheese and baked goods. Cheese and chocolate are important industries. An example of the cantonal cuisines is in Ticino, by the Italian border, where Italian dishes are popular. The French-speaking Swiss are influenced by French cuisine because of their proximity to France and their Burgundian ancestors. Some of Switzerland's largest lakes are in the French-speaking part, providing lake fish that are frequently served. Classical French cuisine has long been emphasized in the Alpine climate. In the Alps in the canton of Fribourg, the town Gruyères gives its name to a favorite cheese. Swiss German cuisine includes hearty soups preceding pork dishes with cabbage, sausages, and potatoes. Chefs and hotel managers are trained in Switzerland's many hotel schools.

Bread and cereals   Wheat, rye, barley, corn; porridge, bread, rolls, croissants, pastries, dumplings, Sunday bread (braid of white bread made with extra sugar and butter, often homemade and served to guests).

Meat, poultry, fish   Chicken, beef and veal, pork, lamb, goat, fish, eggs; sausages, ham, bacon, dried beef.

Dairy products   Milk (cow, sheep), cream, sour cream, cheese (e.g., Emmentaller, the cheese with the big holes called Swiss cheese throughout the world, and Gruyère, with fewer and smaller holes and more pungent flavor).

Fats and oils   Butter, lard, vegetable oil, olive oil.

Legumes   Kidney beans, lentils, navy beans, split peas.

Vegetables   Potatoes, cabbage, carrots, green beans, spinach, lettuce, tomatoes, celery, asparagus, peas, onions, cucumbers; sauerkraut, cucumber pickles, pickled onions.

Fruit   Apples, pears, oranges, currants, cherries, raspberries, strawberries, apricots, lemons, plums, raisins.

Nuts and seeds   Almonds, hazelnuts, walnuts, poppy seeds, caraway seeds.

Seasonings   Vinegar, onions, garlic, salt, black pepper, cinnamon, nutmeg, anise.

Dishes   Busecca (tripe and vegetable soup). Cream soups. Boiled whole finger potatoes. Rösti potatoes (potato pancake made of coarsely grated cold boiled potatoes, packed into a skillet of hot melted butter, fried on one side, turned, and fried on the other). Cornmeal porridge; riebeles when cooled, cubed, and fried in butter. Croque monsieur (toasted ham and cheese sandwich). Émincé de veau (veal strips sautéed in butter and simmered in white wine and cream). Fried perch fillets. Berneplatte, a platter of simmered meats (smoked pork chops, brisket, bacon, sausages) with boiled potatoes and garlic-flavored green beans. Simmered, buttered asparagus. Onion, cheese, and custard tart. Wähen (large single-crust tart filled with vegetables, fruit, or cheese), eaten communally.

National dish   Cheese fondue (melted cheese usually with white wine into which chunks of bread are dipped). Another internationally known cheese dish, raclette (made by exposing a cut edge of cheese to an open fire and then scraping the melted cheese onto a warm plate; racler means "to scrape"), served with a boiled potato.

Sweets   Honey, sugar. Fruit preserves. Fruit and cheese. Cakes. Cookies. Chocolate candy (e.g., truffles). Marzipan (almond and sugar paste) in candies and desserts. Birnbrot (pear bread with dried fruits, nuts, and spices). Luzerner kuchen (pear cake with cinnamon and anise), a small square is served topped with whipped cream and pear syrup. Linzenberry tart (shallow pie of raspberries with a lattice top). Chocolate mousse. A national favorite, apricot wähen (a large tart filled with fresh apricots and topped with whipped cream).

Beverages   Coffee, beer, milk, hot chocolate, tea, mineral water, wine, plum brandy (grappa).

Meals   Three meals a day with snacks is usual. A typical meal is salad, cold cuts, cheese, and bread; or a hot dish of veal, pork, chicken, or fish, potato, and bread.

SYRIA
Syrian Arab Republic

Geography   Syria is in the Middle East at the eastern end of the Mediterranean Sea. It has a short Mediterranean coastline, fertile lowlands and plains, the Syrian Desert in the east, and the Jebel Druze Mountains in the south.

Major Languages	Ethnic Groups		Major Religions	
Arabic (official)	Arab	90%	Sunni Muslim	74%
Kurdish	Kurd	7%	Other Muslim	16%
Armenian	Armenian	3%	Christian	10%
Aramaic				
Circassian				

Population density per sq. mi. 277.9
Literacy rate 83.1%
Life expectancy 69.5 male; 72.3 female
Per capita GDP $4,500
Labor force in agriculture 19.2%

Urban 53.2%
Infant mortality rate per 1,000 live births 26.8
HIV rate NA
Unemployment rate 8.5%
Arable land 25%

Agriculture   wheat, sugar beets, cotton, barley, lentils, chickpeas, olives, chickens, sheep, goats, cattle

Natural resources   oil, phosphates, chrome, manganese, asphalt, iron ore, rock, salt, marble, gypsum, hydropower, fish

Industries   oil, textiles, food processing, beverages, tobacco, phosphate and rock mining

History   Syria has been inhabited for several thousand years. From the 3rd millennium BCE, at various times it came under the control of the Sumerians, Akkadians, and Amorites. Syria was conquered by the Egyptians about 1500 BCE and thereafter successively by the Hebrews, Assyrians, and Babylonians. In the 6th century BCE, it became part of Persia, which in 330 BCE fell to Alexander the Great. The center of the Seleucid Empire from 301 to 164 BCE, it later was part of the Roman Empire from 64 BCE to 300 CE and part of the Byzantine Empire 300 to 634 CE. Next it was absorbed by the Arab empire. Ottoman Turks ruled it from 1516 until the end of World War I. Administered under a French League of Nations mandate from 1920 to 1941, Syria became independent in 1945. It joined the Arab invasion of Israel in 1948. During the Six-Day War (1967), it lost the Golan Heights to Israel. Since 1967 it has been in conflict with Israel and Lebanon. In 2004, the United States imposed economic sanctions on Syria for alleged continued support of terrorism and, after a 29-year occupation, Syria withdrew all its troops from Lebanon. In 2008 violence in Syria included bombings and assassination of a military aide close to the president.

Influences on food   Phoenicians reached this land at the eastern end of the Mediterranean Sea around 3000 BCE. They established city-states and became the first great commercial mariners, trading spices, grains, foodstuffs, and wine at the ancient crossroads of Europe, Asia, and Africa. Egyptians, Persians, Greeks, Romans, Crusaders, and Ottomans invaded and each left influence, especially the Ottomans, who ruled here from 1516 for four centuries. Although Syria has large desert areas, it produces grains, sugar beets, legumes, olives, and livestock. Its short Mediterranean coastline makes fish available. Most Syrians are Muslims, who do not consume pork or alcohol and fast from sunup to sundown during the month of Ramadan. Syrian food is often spicier than that of other Arab nations. Bread is eaten at most meals.

Bread and cereals   Wheat, barley, rice; cracked whole wheat (burghul), leavened flat wheat bread usually pita (thin round bread with a hollow center), round Arab loaf, thin sheets of bread, filo dough pastry, rice dishes.

Meat, poultry, fish   Chicken, lamb and mutton, goat, beef, fish, eggs.

Dairy products   Milk (goat, sheep, camel, cow), yogurt (laban), cheese usually feta (white, moist, salty).

Fats and oils   Olive oil, clarified butter, sesame oil, corn oil, sheep's tail fat.

Legumes   Lentils, chickpeas (garbanzo beans), fava (broad) beans.

Vegetables   Olives, tomatoes, cabbage, eggplant, cucumbers, potatoes, onions, green peppers, lettuce, truffles.

Fruit   Apples, apricots, cherries, dates, figs, grapes, lemons, melons, pomegranates, pears, sumac, raisins.

Nuts and seeds   Almonds, pine nuts, hazelnuts, walnuts, pistachio nuts, sesame seeds.

Seasonings   Onions, garlic, tahini (sesame seed paste), lemon, fresh herbs (parsley, mint, dill, coriander, basil), salt, spices (allspice, cinnamon, cardamom, ginger, cayenne, oregano), rosewater, orange blossom water.

Condiment   Tarator sauce (tahini, garlic, and lemon juice), often served with fish.

Preserved foods   Vegetables dried or pickled. Fruits dried, candied, or made into jam. Mutton or lamb cut into small pieces, cooked, covered in its own fat, and preserved in a pot. Cracked wheat fermented in yogurt, dried, and ground to produce kishk (used in soups, pastry fillings, and bread toppings).

Dishes   Sfeehas (small baked lamb pies seasoned with cayenne), a famous Syrian dish. Fattoosh (a salad of parsley, mint, tomatoes, cucumbers, onions, pieces of fried seasoned pita bread, and small pieces of white cheese, with oil, salt, and sumac), a favorite. Lahm bi-ajine (flatbread topped with minced meat, chopped onion, and pomegranate syrup). Stuffed vegetables, meat and vegetable stews, and grilled meat and chicken, all with herbs and other seasonings (plus hot pepper in Aleppo). Fruit in meat dishes, such as apricot sauce with chicken. Steamed cracked wheat. Pilaf (rice cooked in oil in which onions have been browned, then covered and simmered in broth or water). Fried eggs. Green salad with pomegranate seeds. Roasted leg of lamb with garlic and onion. Truffles sliced and broiled or sautéed.

National dish   Kibbeh (a paste of finely minced lamb with cracked wheat, onion, and basil or mint).

Sweets   Honey, sugar, syrups flavored with honey or flowers. Baklava (made with thin layers of filo dough) and borma ("bird's nest" pastry), both filled with nuts, sugar, and rosewater or orange blossom water, baked, and coated with syrup. Baraziq (small round thin biscuits liberally coated with pistachio nuts on one side and sesame seeds on the other). Karabeege halab (pistachio-filled semolina fingers, with matef, a sweet mousse). Candied green walnuts and fruits. Qamar al-deen (dried sheets of sweetened apricot purée). Candied pears with cinnamon, cardamom, and ginger. Dried apricots cooked in syrup, topped with almonds, and rolled in sugar. Ground and sweetened almonds with essence of rose petals.

Beverages   Coffee, tea (both heavily sweetened), fruit juices, yogurt drinks, wine.

Mezze   (tasty bits, or appetizers) Hummus (chickpea dip). Tabbouleh (salad of parsley, tomato, and cracked wheat with onion, mint, olive oil, lemon juice, and spices).

T

TAIWAN
Republic of China

Geography   Taiwan is 100 miles (161 km) southeast of mainland China, in the East and South China seas. A central mountain range divides Taiwan island, with the west a fertile, well-watered, cultivated plain and the east steep and craggy, with mountains on the east coast. Taiwan also includes two offshore islands and nearby islets.

Major Languages	Ethnic Groups		Major Religions	
Mandarin Chinese (official)	Taiwanese including Hakka	84%	Buddhist/Taoist mix	93%
Taiwanese	Mainland Chinese	14%	Christian	5%
Hakka dialects	Indigenous	2%	Other	2%

Population density per sq. mi. 1,840.2
Literacy rate 96.1%
Life expectancy 74.9 male; 80.9 female
Per capita GDP $30,100
Labor force in agriculture 5.3%

Urban NA
Infant mortality rate per 1,000 live births 5.5
HIV rate NA
Unemployment rate 3.9%
Arable land 24%

Agriculture   rice, sugarcane, citrus fruits, corn, vegetables, fruits, tea, pigs, cattle

Natural resources   fish, coal, natural gas, limestone, marble, asbestos

Industries   electronics, oil refining, armaments, chemicals, textiles, iron and steel, machinery, cement, food processing, pharmaceuticals

History   Aborigines of Malayan descent inhabited Taiwan when Chinese settlers came in the 7th century. The island was named Ilha Formosa (the beautiful) by Portuguese sailors on their way to Japan early in the 16th century. The Portuguese explored the area in 1590. After Dutch rule from 1620 to 1662, the island came under China's control and large-scale Chinese immigration began. The Manchus took Formosa in 1683, and it was not open to Europeans until 1858. After the Sino-Japanese War, Japan ruled Formosa from 1895 to 1945; it was a Japanese military center during World War II and was frequently bombed. After World War II it was returned to China. In 1949, defeated by the communists, the Nationalist government of Generalissimo Chiang Kai-shek and 2 million supporters fled from China to Formosa and established it as Taiwan, the Republic of China. Taiwan President Chiang Kai-shek and the United States signed a mutual defense agreement in 1954, and for almost three decades Taiwan received U.S. support. The UN seat went from Taiwan to China when China was admitted to the UN in 1971. In 1978 the United States recognized China and severed diplomatic ties with Taiwan but kept a long trading relationship. In 2003 China replaced the United States as Taiwan's leading trade partner. Taiwan has resisted China's efforts at reunification. Taiwan has one of the world's strongest economies. In the presidential election in 2008, both candidates proposed referenda to join the UN, and both referenda were rejected.

Influences on food   This island has been inhabited for 10,000 or more years. The several hundred thousand aboriginal Taiwanese and their food customs are less prominent than those of the Hakka. The Hakka comprise over a tenth of the population and are distinctive. They were a persecuted minority in northern China who moved south, then east across islands to Taiwan, where they were the first Chinese arrivals. Their foodways reflect their agricultural background, with emphasis on the pig. Beginning in the 17th century, foreign powers or Chinese authorities controlled the island. In 1949 the Chinese government, defeated by communists on the mainland, came to Taiwan, along with hundreds of thousands of people and their cuisines from all regions of China. Chinese and Taiwanese cuisines now dominate. Taiwanese cuisine resembles that of Fujian on the mainland, with emphasis on seafood. Japanese rule from 1895 until 1945 influenced the cuisine, for example, with many Japanese restaurants. Taiwan grows rice, sugarcane, citrus fruits, corn, vegetables, and tea (many kinds) and raises livestock especially pigs. The long coastline provides seafood. Taiwan has many peaceful, quiet teahouses and busy street food venues.

Bread and cereals   Rice, corn, wheat, buckwheat; rice dishes, buckwheat noodles, wheat flour noodles, dumplings, pancakes, steamed bread, wrappers for egg rolls, wontons, and spring rolls. Rice is the main staple.

Meat, poultry, fish   Pork, poultry (chicken, duck), beef, fish and seafood, eggs.

Dairy products   Milk (cow, buffalo). Dairy products are not routinely used. Many people are lactose intolerant.

Fats and oils   Soybean oil, peanut oil, corn oil, lard, butter, bacon fat, sesame seed oil.

Legumes   Soybeans and soybean products (tofu, soy milk, soy sauce), mung beans, red beans, peanuts.

Vegetables   Cabbage (leafy bok choy), long beans, green snow peas, mushrooms, bamboo shoots, bean sprouts, greens, seaweed, taro, water chestnuts, small eggplant, large white radish, lotus root, bitter melon, onions.

Fruit   Oranges, tangerines, kumquats, limes, apples, bananas, coconut, litchi (tough scaly exterior, whitish grapelike flesh, dark seed), longan (dragon's eye, related to litchi), mangoes, persimmon, pineapple, watermelon.

Nuts and seeds   Almonds, cashews, chestnuts, ginkgo nuts, walnuts, sesame seeds, watermelon seeds.

Seasonings   Soy sauce, rice wine, ginger root, herbs (e.g., basil, parsley), green onions, garlic, hot mustard, five-spice powder (anise, star anise, cinnamon, cloves, Szechwan pepper), monosodium glutamate.

Preparation   Most food is cooked; only fruit is often eaten raw. Food is usually cut into bite-size pieces and cooked quickly to minimize use of the limited available fuel.

Dishes   Steamed rice. Congee (rice porridge), eaten for breakfast or as soup throughout the day. Cooked rice stir-fried with vegetables and/or bits of meat. Stir-fried green vegetables. Simmered or steamed starchy vegetables (e.g., taro root). Vegetable pickles. Kumquat preserves. Stir-fried or deep-fried fish, shellfish, pork, chicken, or beef. Red foods (pork, poultry, or soup dishes cooked with red rice wine or paste). Dim sum (small bites) such as steamed or fried dumplings stuffed with meat or seafood. Roasted food (e.g., duck), usually bought from a shop or eaten in a restaurant, not prepared in the home.

Sweets   Sugarcane, honey, syrup, sugar. Fresh fruit. Sweet sticky (glutinous) rice cakes. Bean pastes.

Beverages   Tea, bubble tea, soup, beer, rice wine. Oolong tea, made from partially fermented leaves, is a Taiwanese specialty. Bubble tea (with pea-size balls of tapioca that are sucked up through large straws) was created in Taiwan.

TAJIKISTAN
Republic of Tajikistan

Geography   In Central Asia, earthquake-prone Tajikistan is 93% mountainous, with glaciers the source of rivers.

Major Languages	Ethnic Groups		Major Religions	
Tajik (official)	Tajik	80%	Sunni Muslim	85%
Russian (widely used in	Uzbek	15%	Shi'a Muslim	5%
government and business)	Russian	1%	Other (mostly Christian),	
	Tatar, other	4%	none	10%

Population density per sq. mi. 130.9
Literacy rate 99.6%
Life expectancy 62 male; 68.2 female
Per capita GDP $1,800
Labor force in agriculture 67.2%

Urban 26.4%
Infant mortality rate per 1,000 live births 42.3
HIV rate 0.3%
Unemployment rate 2.4%
Arable land 7%

Agriculture   potatoes, wheat, cotton, grain, fruits, grapes, vegetables, chickens, sheep, cattle, goats, camels, pigs

Natural resources   fish, hydropower, oil, uranium, mercury, lead, zinc, antimony, tungsten, silver, gold

Industries   aluminum, zinc, lead, chemicals and fertilizers, cement, vegetable oil, metal-cutting machine tools

History   From about 3000 BCE this region was inhabited by settled societies. The Tajiks, whose language closely resembles Persian, were part of the ancient Persian Empire that was conquered by Alexander the Great in 333 BCE. In the 7th and 8th centuries, Arabs conquered the region and brought Islam. In the 15th to 18th centuries, the Tajiks were successively ruled by Uzbeks and then Afghans until Russia took over in the 1860s. The USSR took control of the region from 1918 to 1925. In 1924 it became an autonomous republic under the administration of the Uzbek Soviet Socialist Republic. In 1929 the Tajik SSR was proclaimed. Tajikistan gained independence when the Soviet Union disbanded in 1991. Civil war between Muslim rebels and government troops occurred until a peace accord was signed in 1997. In 1997 constitutional changes included legalization of Islamic political parties. In 2007 the president appointed family and personal clique to top government posts. He dropped the Russian suffix "ov" from his surname. The country experienced power shortage due to low water levels in reservoirs behind the country's power dams and Uzbekistan's failure to meet its commitment to supply power in winter.

Influences on food   Tajikistan, a mostly mountainous country in Central Asia, was part of the old Silk Road, the ancient caravan route between China and the Caspian Sea. Influences on food include ancient Persia, Arabs, Islam, neighbors Uzbeks and Afghans, Russia, and neighbor country China (e.g., noodles from China). Until the 20th century, most people in Tajikistan were oasis dwellers who lived in settlements along rivers fed by mountain snows and glaciers. They grew grain, vegetables, and fruit, and raised animals, as they do today. Tajikistan shares a common cuisine with Uzbekistan and Turkmenistan: flatbread, lamb, thick soups, semi-liquid main dishes, and tea. Also, Tajikistan shares with Uzbekistan a very limited use of fish and eggs.

Bread and cereals   Wheat, barley, millet, rice; flatbread, noodles, rice dishes (palov). Flat disks of bread are often baked in a tandyra (tandoor), clay oven or large clay jar, in which dough is slapped on the heated inside.

Meat, poultry, fish   Lamb and mutton, chicken, beef, goat, camel, pork, fish, eggs; sausage.

Dairy products   Milk (cow, sheep, goat, mare, camel), sour milk, clabber (kumys), yogurt, cheese (kurt, a hard cheese; airan, a sharp cheese). Bowls of sour milk are offered by locals to visitors to show hospitality.

Fats and oils   Vegetable oil, fat from fat-tailed sheep, butter.

Legumes   Chickpeas, beans, lentils.

Vegetables   Potatoes, onions, carrots, pumpkin, greens, red peppers, cucumbers, turnips, tomatoes, radishes.

Fruit   Grapes, melons, pomegranates, pears, plums, apricots, cherries, apples, peaches, white mulberries, jujubes (a type of date), rhubarb, figs, barberries, quinces.

Nuts and seeds   Walnuts, hazelnuts, pistachios, caraway seeds.

Seasonings   Onions, garlic, vinegar, salt, black pepper, dried red pepper, coriander, dill, mint, aniseed.

Dishes   Lamb shish kabob (shashlyk), lamb pieces mixed with diced onion, coriander or dill, pepper, and salt; marinated in vinegar; and roasted on sticks over charcoal embers. Besh barmak (a thick lamb soup with meat slices). Noodle dishes, often with mutton cubes and onions. Kaurma lagman (fried noodles and meat). Manty (steamed dumplings filled with ground lamb, onions, and pepper). Palov (pilaf), rice heated in oil before adding water and simmering, often with mutton cubes and onions. Samsas (meat pies).

Sweets   Honey, sugar. Fruit (fresh, dried, or preserves). Samsa (fried dough filled with ground walnuts, butter, and sugar). Yanchmish (balls of roasted ground walnuts). Khalva (candy made with flour, honey, and walnuts). Bukman (candy made with cream, sugar, and flour).

Beverages   Tea, sour milk, fruit syrup drinks, wine. Tea is drunk at meals and between meals, at home and in teahouses, from porcelain bowls.

Meals and service   Breakfast: clabber or cheese, flatbread, and tea. Lunch: thick hearty soup or cheese, greens, and fruit, flatbread, and tea. Evening meal: meat dish or palov, flatbread, fruit or a sweet, and tea. To dine, people sit on rugs or chairs. Flatbread may be used as edible scoops and plates, or flatware and plates are used.

Street food   Shashlyk (sticks of grilled lamb), cooked by vendors on city streets.

TANZANIA
United Republic of Tanzania

Geography   Tanzania is in East Africa, bordering the Indian Ocean. Africa's highest point, Mt. Kilimanjaro, 19,340 feet (5,895 m), is in the north. Tanzania has a hot, arid central plateau, surrounded by the lake region in the west, temperate highlands in the north and south, and coastal plains in the east. Tanzania has three of Africa's best-known lakes, Victoria in the north, Tanganyika in the west, and Nyasa in the south. The Serengeti plains and Ngorongoro Crater have abundant wild game. Tanzania includes the islands of Zanzibar and Pemba.

Major Languages		Ethnic Groups		Major Religions	
Swahili	(both	Bantu	95%	Indigenous beliefs	35%
English	official)	Other African (130+ tribes)	4%	Muslim	35%
Local languages		Other	1%	Christian	30%
				(on Zanzibar, Muslim	99+%)

Population density per sq. mi. 117.6
Literacy rate 72.3%
Life expectancy 50.1 male; 52.9 female
Per capita GDP $1,300
Labor force in agriculture 80%

Urban 24.2%
Infant mortality rate per 1,000 live births 70.5
HIV rate 6.2%
Unemployment rate 3.7%
Arable land 4%

Agriculture   cassava, corn, sweet potatoes, coffee, sisal, tea, cotton, cashews, pyrethrum (insecticide from chrysanthemums), tobacco, cloves, chickens, cattle, goats, sheep, pigs

Natural resources   hydropower, tin, phosphates, iron ore, coal, diamonds, gemstones, gold, natural gas, fish

Industries   agricultural processing, mining (diamond, iron, and gold), oil refining, apparel

History   Some of the earliest evidences of humans were found in the Olduvai Gorge in Tanzania. The area was inhabited from the 1st millennium BCE. Arabs colonized the area in the 8th century CE and slaving began. Indian traders and Bantu-speaking peoples occupied the area by the 10th century. Portuguese explored the coast by about 1500 and held some control until the 17th century, when Arabs of Oman and Zanzibar took power. German settlers arrived in the 1880s, and in 1885 Germany established German East Africa, comprised mostly of this land. Britain administered it after World War I as a League of Nations mandate under the name of Tanganyika and after World War II as a UN trust territory. Tanganyika became independent in 1961 and united with Zanzibar to form Tanzania in 1964. Privatization of the economy began in the 1990s. A U.S. embassy bombing in the largest city, Dar-es-Salaam, in 1998 killed 11 people and injured 70. The United States blamed the attack on Islamic terrorists associated with Osama bin Laden; four were convicted in 2001. The UN International Criminal Tribunal for Rwanda was located in Arusha. AIDS care and prevention are major public health issues. In 2007 the government announced plans to attract investors, including a deep-water harbor with Kuwait, a hydroelectric plant, and an oil refinery. The president announced that, with peace restored in Burundi, the refugee camps in the northwest would close by the year's end. Coffee is a major crop and export. **Zanzibar**, separated from the Tanzania mainland by a 22-mile channel, was controlled by Portugal from 1503 until Arabs took it over in 1698. It was the center for Arab slave traders for centuries. A British protectorate from 1890, it gained independence in 1963, followed quickly by revolt and then union with Tanganyika in 1964. Zanzibar, called Isle of Cloves, and **Pemba**, 21 miles northeast of Zanzibar, produce most of the world's cloves.

Influences on food   Tanzania has temperate highlands in the north and south, with some of the best climate in Africa. The diet contains almost no meat, in spite of abundant game and the tradition of breeding cattle. Cattle were regarded as wealth, not food, and the Masai and related people lived on milk products and blood of cattle. Others lived on mostly millet, sorghum, and bananas, along with gathered greens. The earliest foreign traders, Arabs, established colonies along the coast from about 700 CE, traded in slaves and ivory, and introduced spices, onions, and eggplant. Another example of Arab influence is eating camel hump in Zanzibar. German control for about 30 years had little influence on food customs. British administration left some influence. The British trained many African men in European cooking because there were traditions of women cooking only in their homes. Also, the British encouraged Asians to settle in East Africa, which affected cooking. For example, it increased the use of curry and of coconut milk. European hunters found game here; now although animals are protected, game is plentiful and antelope are farmed. Tanzania's coast on the Indian Ocean and three important lakes provide fish and seafood. Tilapia and catfish are farmed and now exported. Much seafood is salted, dried, and sent inland. Starchy food is regarded as "real food" and relishes as accompaniments. Corn or millet porridge is a main food. Starchy vegetables, green leaves, and legumes, an important protein source, are eaten daily.

Bread and cereals   Corn, wheat, millet, sorghum, rice; porridge, pancakes, fried pastries, rice dishes.

Meat, poultry, fish   Chicken, beef, goat, lamb and mutton, pork, game meat (antelope, gazelle, waterbuck), camel hump, fish and seafood (shark, turtle, prawns, shrimp), eggs including ostrich (one egg feeds a family).

Insects   Red locusts, crickets, grasshoppers, ants, worms, caterpillars. Fried or dried insects are eaten as snacks.

Dairy products   Milk, cheese (including adaptations of European ones).

Fats and oils   Butter, lard, meat drippings, peanut oil, vegetable oil.

Legumes   Peanuts (groundnuts), cowpeas, beans, lentils.

Vegetables   Cassava, sweet potatoes, plantains (green bananas), yams, potatoes, green leaves (amaranth, baobab, sesame, okra, cowpea, pumpkin), eggplant, okra, pumpkin, onions, chilies, sweet peppers.

Fruit   Bananas, coconut, papaya, oranges, limes.

Nuts and seeds   Cashew nuts, sesame seeds.

Seasonings   Salt, coconut milk, cloves, dried baobab leaves, chilies, curry powder, nutmeg, saffron.

Dishes   Thick porridge of corn or millet (ugali). Plantain boiled in its leaves and mashed. Plantain soup (sometimes with beef), stew, fritters, and custard. Peanut soups, stews, and paste. Green leaves boiled with peanut paste. Irio (beans, corn, and potatoes or cassava, mashed), often served with curried chicken. Roasted or grilled antelope, gazelle, or waterbuck. Ostrich egg omelet. Prawn soup. Zanzibar duck (duck browned in oil, braised in stock with cloves and chili, and finished with a sauce of the cooking stock and orange and lime juice). Steamed papaya chunks mixed with butter, nutmeg, and salt, served with meat or game meat. Boiled rice. Curry. Fish poached in coconut milk.

Sweets   Honey, sugar, plantain custard, coconut pudding with meringue topping.

Beverages   Coffee, tea, beer, plantain wine, red wine.

Street foods   Grilled corn on cob, fried pancake filled with minced meat and egg, fried pastries.

THAILAND
Kingdom of Thailand

Geography   Thailand (formerly Siam) is in Southeast Asia, on the Indochinese and Malayan peninsulas, bordering the Gulf of Thailand. Thailand has a plateau in the northeast, fertile valley of the Chao Phraya River in the center, forested mountains in the north, and rainforests in the south.

Major Languages	Ethnic Groups		Major Religions	
Thai (official)	Thai	75%	Buddhist	95%
English (secondary language of elite)	Chinese	14%	Muslim (Sunni),	
Ethnic and regional dialects	Malay, Khmer, other	11%	Christian, other	5%

Population density per sq. mi. 331.5
Literacy rate 94.2%
Life expectancy 70.5 male; 75.3 female
Per capita GDP $7,900
Labor force in agriculture 49%

Urban 32.3%
Infant mortality rate per 1,000 live births 18.2
HIV rate 1.4%
Unemployment rate 1.2%
Arable land 28%

Agriculture   sugarcane, rice, cassava, rubber, corn, coconuts, soybeans, chickens, pigs, cattle, goats, sheep

Natural resources   fish, tin, rubber, natural gas, tungsten, tantalum, timber, lead, fish, gypsum, lignite, fluorite

Industries   tourism, textiles and garments, agricultural processing, beverages, tobacco, cement, light manufacturing such as automobiles and parts, electric appliances, computers and parts

History   The region has been inhabited for 20,000 years. It was part of the Mon and Khmer kingdoms in the 9th century CE. During the 10th century Thai-speaking peoples began migrating from southern China. In the 13th century two kingdoms were founded: the Sukhothai in about 1220 after a revolt against the Khmer; and Chiang Mai in 1296 after the defeat of the Mon. In 1350 a unified Thai kingdom was established. The Chakri dynasty came to power in 1782 and moved the capital from Chiang Mai to Bangkok and extended the empire along the Malay Peninsula and into Laos and Cambodia. Known as Siam from 1856 until 1939, Thailand is the only Southeast Asian country never colonized. The monarchy ruling from 1851 to1910 modernized the country and signed trade treaties with Britain and France. Siam entered World War I on the side of the Allies. In 1932, after a bloodless military coup, it became a constitutional monarchy, with the monarchy limited to titular status and representative government with universal suffrage. Japan occupied Thailand in World War II. Thailand participated as a UN forces member in the Korean War and was allied with South Vietnam in the Vietnam War. After several years of economic growth, Thailand suffered from the Asian financial crisis in 1997. After bailout by the International Monetary Fund and restructuring, the economy improved. By the end of the 1990s, UN estimates indicated more than 750,000 people here had HIV/AIDS; a nationwide prevention campaign has limited the number of new infections. The Indian Ocean tsunami of 2004 killed about 5,300 people here. During 2005 to 2008, violence in Muslim-dominated southern Thailand killed more than 3,200 people. In 2006 a military coup ousted the prime minister; in late 2007 an ally of the ousted prime minister was named the first democratically elected prime minister since the coup.

Influences on food   Thailand's distinctive cuisine has been introduced in English-speaking countries in recent decades by the increasing number of Thai restaurants. Thai cuisine is one of the world's hottest due to lavish use of very hot chili peppers. It differs from that of its neighbors because of its flavors and refinements, which grew out of court cuisine. Geography and climate allow diversity in the cuisine. The hot monsoonal climate in the central plains is ideal for rice cultivation; rice dominates the economy and diet. The long coastline and major rivers provide fish and seafood. Tropical and temperate fruits and vegetables are grown. Corn now grows in the uplands in the east and north. Thailand, unique in Southeast Asia in that it never was a European colony, has a long history as a monarchy. The royal court advanced the cuisine. Kings of Thailand have written cookbooks. The population is mostly Buddhist. Buddhists believe in abstaining from taking life. Some Buddhists do not eat beef; some eat soy products. Monks depend on voluntary contributions of food from the people. A feast is part of weddings and funerals. There are cookbooks for funeral food. Many people make small cookbooks for distribution as keepsakes to mourners at their funerals. Rice, the most frequently eaten and most liked food, is part of most meals. Noodles, soups, curries, and stir-fried dishes are eaten daily.

Bread and cereals   Rice, corn, wheat; rice dishes, noodles (rice, wheat, mung bean). Long-grain rice is usual; glutinous rice is used in sweets and in the north.

Meat, poultry, fish   Chicken, eggs, pork, beef, goat, lamb, fish (fresh, dried), seafood (especially shrimp), duck.

Dairy products   Milk (cow), ice cream.

Fats and oils   Vegetable oil, coconut cream, butter, lard.

Legumes   Soybeans, peanuts, mung beans; soy milk, tofu (soybean curd).

Vegetables   Cassava, plantains, bean sprouts, cucumbers, tomatoes, mushrooms, cabbage, bamboo shoots, taro, yams, lotus, corn, green beans, pumpkin, Thai eggplant, broccoli, carrots, onions, scallions, chili peppers.

Fruit Coconut, mangoes, oranges, bananas, watermelon, papaya, pineapple, grapes, apples, strawberries, pomelo, cantaloupe, lychees, durian.

Nuts and seeds Sesame seeds, lotus seeds.

Seasonings Fish sauce (nam pla), fish or shrimp paste (kapi), hot chili peppers, coconut milk and cream, garlic, ginger root, lemon grass, tamarind, basil, coriander, lime juice, palm sugar, galingale (spice of a ginger family plant of this name; flavor is like ginger and pepper), cumin, cardamom, turmeric. Thais like sour, salty, sweet, and umami (savory) tastes and hot chilies. Fermented fish sauce or paste (with salty and umami tastes) is added to many dishes. Nam prik (fish sauce and hot red chilies) accompanies many dishes as a sauce or dip.

Dishes Boiled or steamed long-grain rice. Kaeng chud (mild soup, clear broth). Kaeng tom (rice soup). Kaeng tom yam kung (lemony shrimp soup). Curry (meat or vegetable with curry sauce), usually very hot and yellow from turmeric, red from red chilies, or green from green chilies. Pad Thai (stir-fried noodles). Kai yang (grilled chicken). Yam (spicy fresh vegetables). Laap (spiced ground pork). Nam (highly spiced pork sausage), raw or fried.

A famous dish Mee krob (a mound of stir-fried rice noodles mixed with pork and shrimp stir-fried with seasonings and sugar, topped with fried egg lace, and garnished with bean sprouts, scallions, and chilies).

Sweets Sugarcane, sugar, palm sugar. Coconut custard. Fruit jelly. Glutinous rice or yam pudding. Khanom (small individual items made of glutinous rice or yams and prepared in banana-leaf parcels).

Beverages Tea (hot, strong, sweet) served with milk, soft drinks, coffee.

Meals and service Typically the first meal is rice soup; lunch is noodles and rice; and the evening meal is rice and a stir-fried dish. The evening meal may also include appetizers, soup, curry, fried dish, salad of raw vegetables and grilled meat, and nam prik. All dishes are served at the same time, on low tables surrounded by pillows; fingers and spoons are usual implements plus forks to push food onto spoons. Appearance is important; frequently elaborately carved fruit or sometimes dessert on a leaf-lined plate concludes the meal.

Street food and snacks Noodles, sweets (e.g., coconut custard, fruit jelly, ice cream), tea. Snacking is common (Brittin, Sukalakamala, and Obeidat, 2008; Sukalakamala and Brittin, 2006).

TIMOR-LESTE (EAST TIMOR)
Democratic Republic of Timor-Leste

Geography Timor-Leste is in Southeast Asia, south of Indonesia and bordering the Timor Sea. It consists of the eastern half of Timor Island plus an enclave on the western end. It is semiarid and mountainous, rising to 9,721 feet at Mt. Ramelau.

Major Languages		Ethnic Groups	Major Religions	
Tetum	(both	Austronesian (Malayo-Polynesian)	Roman Catholic	98%
Portuguese	official)	Papuan	Muslim	1%
Indonesian			Protestant	1%
English				
About 16 indigenous languages				

Population density per sq. mi. 196.6
Literacy rate 58.6%
Life expectancy 64.6 male; 69.4 female
Per capita GDP $2,500
Labor force in agriculture NA

Urban 26.1%
Infant mortality rate per 1,000 live births 42
HIV rate NA
Unemployment rate 50%
Arable land 8%

Agriculture   corn, rice, cassava, coffee, sweet potatoes, chickens, pigs, buffalo, beehives, cattle, goats, sheep

Natural resources   fish, gold, oil, natural gas, manganese, marble

Industries   printing, soap manufacturing, handicrafts, woven cloth

History   The Portuguese settled Timor Island in 1520. The Dutch took control of the western part in 1613. An 1860 treaty gave Portugal the eastern half plus the western enclave of Decussi (the first Portuguese settlement on Timor). In 1949, the Netherlands gave up its colonies in the East Indies, including West Timor, and Indonesia was born. East Timor remained under Portuguese control until 1975, when Portugal's sudden withdrawal led to factional fighting and an invasion by Indonesia. Indonesia annexed East Timor in 1976. During the following 20-some years, 200,000 Timorese died as a result of civil war, famine, and persecution by Indonesian authorities. In 1996 two East Timorese received the Nobel Peace Prize for their efforts to gain freedom peacefully. Under UN oversight, a referendum was held in 1999 and Timorese voted for independence. In 2002, Timor-Leste gained independence, the first new country of the millennium, and entered the UN. A dispute with Australia over the oil-rich Timor Sea was resolved in 2004. Gang violence in 2006 brought peacekeepers from Australia. In 2007 Prime Minister José Ramos-Horta, co-recipient of the 1996 Nobel Prize for Peace, was elected president. After he appointed the former president as prime minister, rioting followed. In 2008 President Ramos-Horta was seriously wounded in a failed attempt at assassination and military coup.

Influences on food   Portugal controlled this land for more than four centuries and influenced the language and religion. Portuguese trade here and Dutch trade in the area influenced the food. For example, the Portuguese used sweet wheat flour breads and the Dutch introduced baked goods such as pastries and cakes. Other influences include neighbors Indonesia and Australia, as well as Malayans, Polynesians, Papuans, and Chinese.

Bread and cereals   Rice, corn, wheat; rice dishes, bread, sweet bread, cassava and rice cakes.

Meat, poultry, fish   Fish and seafood, chicken, pork, beef, goat, lamb, eggs.

Dairy products   Milk and other dairy products are uncommon. Now there are milk bars in big towns.

Fats and oils   Coconut oil, lard, butter, vegetable oil.

Legumes   Soybeans, peanuts.

Vegetables   Cassava, sweet potatoes, cabbage, taro, sago.

Fruit   Mangoes, bananas, coconut, tamarind, limes.

Nuts and seeds   Kemiri (candlenut), kenari nut (resembles almond).

Seasonings   Chili peppers, coconut milk, tamarind, lemon grass, turmeric, soy sauce, shrimp paste, ginger, laos, onions, garlic, salt, vanilla. The cuisine is hot with chili peppers.

Dishes   Food is cut before cooking or carved in the kitchen. Boiled cassava. Boiled rice. Nasi goring (fried rice), often with a fried egg on top. Boiled or fried sweet potatoes. Cabbage and taro leaves raw or lightly steamed. Taro root boiled and pounded. Sour soup such as chicken broth with tamarind. Sambal goreng (spices, onions, garlic, and chili fried in a little oil and added to the main ingredient to flavor it while it cooks, e.g., fish sambal). Rendang (beef simmered in coconut milk). Curry (cooked with spices in coconut milk and retaining the sauce in the dish) such as chicken curry. Gulai (everyday curry with fewer spices: chili, salt, onion, and turmeric plus ginger for fish). Stuffings. Marinades. Satay, or sate (bits of chicken, meat, or fish/seafood skewered, basted or marinated in soy sauce or lime juice, and grilled over charcoal), served with a spicy chili-peanut sauce. Rice, chicken, meat, or fish wrapped in banana leaves or placed in split bamboo to retain juices and steamed or baked (in the past in a trench lined with hot stones).

Sweets   Honey, sugar, palm sugar. Fresh fruit. Immature coconut. Steamed cakes of glutinous rice flour, cassava, sugar, and coconut milk. Puddings of cassava (tapioca), glutinous rice, or sago with sugar, and coconut.

Beverages   Coffee, tea, coconut juice, fruit juice, bean drinks.

Meals and service   Usual meal: cassava or rice with other dishes (meat, chicken, or fish, vegetables, soup). Rice is mixed with other dishes to eat. Many people use their fingers to eat and do not drink with a meal.

TOGO
Togolese Republic

Geography   Togo is in West Africa, bordering the Gulf of Guinea. It is a small strip of a country east of Ghana. It consists of hills, savanna plains, and a small low sandy coastal plain. The climate is hot and humid.

Major Languages		Ethnic Groups		Major Religions	
French	(official)	37 African tribes:		Indigenous beliefs, other	51%
Ewe	(in	Ewe	22%	Christian (mostly Roman Catholic)	29%
Mina	south)	Kabre	13%	Muslim	20%
Kabye	(in	Mina	6%		
Dagomba	north)	Other	59%		

Population density per sq. mi. 279
Literacy rate 53.2%
Life expectancy 56.2 male; 60.4 female
Per capita GDP $800
Labor force in agriculture 65%

Urban 39.9%
Infant mortality rate per 1,000 live births 57.7
HIV rate 3.3%
Unemployment rate 32%
Arable land 44%

Agriculture   cassava, yams, corn, coffee, cocoa, cotton, chickens, sheep, goats, pigs, cattle

Natural resources   fish, phosphates, limestone, marble

Industries   phosphate mining, agricultural processing, cement, handicrafts

History   The earliest known inhabitants were the Voltaic peoples and the Kwa. The Ewe arrived in the 14th century and the Ane in the 18th century. The Danes claimed the land in the 18th century. In 1884 it became part of the Togoland German protectorate. After World War I, Togoland was split and administered as League of Nations trusteeships, the east part by France and the west part by Britain. In 1946 the two territories became UN trustees. The French part became independent Togo in 1960. The British part joined Ghana, independent in 1957. Togo president Etienne Eyadema, Africa's longest serving ruler (38 years), died in 2005. In 2007 the UN announced it would close refugee camps in neighboring countries for some 25,000 refugees who fled violence in Togo in 2005 following the disputed presidential election. Severe floods left 20,000 homeless in Togo; the EU pledged aid.

Influences on food   Togo's coast provides fish and its plains and hills produce coffee, cocoa, cassava, yams, corn, and livestock. New World foods such as cassava, corn, tomato, chili pepper, potato, and cocoa greatly influenced food here. Native African foods include black-eyed peas, watermelon, and okra. Various tribes and European countries especially France have influenced Togo's food. Daily fare is mostly grain and starchy vegetables, with fish near the coast. Thick, sticky, spicy food is liked.

Bread and cereals   Corn, millet, rice, sorghum; porridge, rice dishes, fried bread, French bread, biscuits.

Meat, poultry, fish   Chicken, lamb and mutton, goat, pork, fish and seafood (fresh, smoked, salted, or dried), guinea fowl, eggs, rabbit, game. Chicken is a favorite and prestigious food.

Insects   Termites, locusts. These are sometimes dried, usually fried or roasted, and often eaten as snacks.

Dairy products   Milk, sour milk, buttermilk, curds, whey, cheese.

Fats and oils   Palm oil, peanut oil, shea oil, coconut oil. Palm oil, the predominant cooking fat, is red.

Legumes   Peanuts (groundnuts), black-eyed peas, locust beans (carob), beans.

Vegetables   Cassava, yams, plantains, taro, green leaves, okra, bitter leaf, melokhia (crain crain), tomatoes, sweet potatoes, potatoes, eggplant, pumpkin, onions, red chili peppers, cucumbers, bell peppers.

Fruit   Coconut, bananas, pineapple, akee apples, baobab, watermelon, guavas, lemons, limes, mangoes, papaya.

Nuts and seeds   Palm kernels, shea nuts, cashews, kola nuts, watermelon seeds (egusi, a popular ingredient), sesame seeds, mango seeds. Nuts and seeds thicken and flavor sauces and stews.

Seasonings   Salt, hot red chili peppers, tomatoes, onions, cocoa, dried baobab leaves, thyme, nutmeg, ginger.

Dishes   Most foods are boiled or fried, and chunks are dipped in sauce and eaten by hand. Sauces: peanut (ground and pounded peanuts); palaver sauce (green leaves); and fréjon (black-eyed pea or bean purée, coconut milk, and sometimes carob or cocoa). Corn or millet porridge. Boiled rice. Fufu (a paste of boiled and pounded starchy vegetables or boiled corn flour), formed into balls or scoops to eat stew. Stews: fish and meat; chicken and peanut; and root vegetables, okra, or peanuts with bits of fish, chicken, or beef. Adalu (boiled and mashed vegetables). Jollof rice (rice cooked with meat, vegetable, spices, and tomatoes or palm oil). Chicken or fish marinated in lemon juice, grilled, fried with onions, and simmered in the marinade.

Sweets   Honey, sugar. Kanya (peanut candy). Baked bananas with sugar, honey, or coconut. Fried sweet dough.

Beverages   Coffee, cocoa, beer, red zinger (herbal tea made from pods of roselle, *Hibiscus sabdariffa*).

Street food and snacks   Spicy kabobs, fried fish, plantain chips, bean balls, sweet dough, steamed rice balls.

TONGA
Kingdom of Tonga

Geography   Tonga is in the South Pacific Ocean northeast of New Zealand. It consists of about 170 volcanic islands and coral atolls, of which 36 are inhabited.

Major Languages		Ethnic Groups		Major Religions	
Tongan	(both	Polynesian	95%	Mormon	35%
English	official)	Mixed race (Euronesian)	1%	Protestant (Methodist 25%)	30%
		Other	4%	Roman Catholic	12%
				Other Christian, other	23%

Population density per sq. mi. 429.3
Literacy rate 99.2%
Life expectancy 67.9 male; 73.1 female
Per capita GDP $5,100
Labor force in agriculture 65%

Urban 24%
Infant mortality rate per 1,000 live births 11.9
HIV rate NA
Unemployment rate 5.2%
Arable land 20%

Agriculture   coconuts, pumpkins, squash, gourds, cassava, copra, bananas, vanilla beans, cocoa, coffee, ginger, black pepper, chickens, pigs, goats, horses, cattle

Natural resources   fish

Industries   tourism, construction, fishing

History   The Polynesians have lived here for at least 3,000 years. The Tongans developed a stratified social system headed by a ruler, whose domain by the 13th century spread as far as the Hawaiian Islands. Tonga was first explored by the Dutch in 1616. British explorer James Cook visited the islands in 1773 and 1777, calling them the Friendly Islands. A series of civil wars ended in 1843 with the establishment of the Tupou dynasty. The current royal dynasty of Tonga was founded by George Tupou I. His great-grandson, George II, signed a treaty of friendship with Britain, whereby Tonga became a British protectorate in 1900. In 1970 it became independent and a member of the Commonwealth. In Tonga, a constitutional monarchy, the government is largely controlled by the king. In the 1990s, a movement to curtail the monarchy's power began. In 1999 Tonga joined the UN. In 2005, discontent with economic and social inequities increased and civil servants held a strike. In 2006 George Tupou V became king following the death of his father, Taufa ahau Tupou IV, who had reigned since 1965. In 2006 rioting caused some US$200 million damage and destroyed about 80% of the capital's central business district. Australia, New Zealand, and other international aid donors contributed to the reconstruction in the capital city.

Influences on food   Tonga is in the Polynesia group of the Pacific Islands. About 30,000 to 40,000 years ago people from Southeast Asia began to move south to the western Pacific islands and Australia, and thereafter they migrated to islands further east. Influences on food in Tonga include the Polynesians, Dutch explorers, and Britain. Captain Cook visited here and Tonga was a British protectorate from 1900 to 1970. The Europeans brought new food plants, wheat bread, and some animals to the region. Asians brought rice, soybeans, noodles, and teas. The traditional diet is mostly fish, roots and tubers (especially taro and sweet potatoes), and fruits and nuts (especially coconut). Now pumpkin, squash, cassava, bananas, chicken, pork, goat, and beef are also important. Pork, the main meat, especially for feasts, is traditionally cooked in a stone-lined pit (umu in Tonga) over hot coals. Leaves are laid on the hot coals, the pig and foods are placed on the leaves, leaves are placed on the foods, the pit is sealed with a layer of dirt, and the food cooks for hours. Fresh fruit is eaten as snacks.

Bread and cereals   Rice, wheat; bread, noodles, rice dishes.

Meat, poultry, fish   Chicken, pork, goat, beef, fish and seafood, eggs; corned beef, spam.

Dairy products   Milk (cow, goat). Milk and other dairy products are uncommon. Coconut is used much as milk.

Fats and oils   Coconut oil and cream, lard, butter, vegetable oil and shortening, sesame oil.

Legumes   Soybeans, winged beans, peas, lentils, peanuts.

Vegetables   Taro root and leaves, sweet potatoes, yams, cassava, pumpkin, squash, breadfruit, plantains, green leaves, seaweed, arrowroot, bitter melon, cabbage, daikon, eggplant, onions, green onions.

Fruit   Coconut, bananas, lemons, limes, guavas, mangoes, papaya, pineapple, melons, tamarind.

Nuts and seeds   Candlenuts (kukui), litchis, macadamia nuts.

Seasonings   Coconut cream and milk, lime and lemon juice, soy sauce, salt, black pepper, ginger, garlic, onions, tamarind, vanilla, cocoa. Many foods are cooked in coconut milk or cream.

Dishes   Boiled taro root, sweet potatoes, or yams. Boiled or steamed rice. Boiled or steamed squash, greens, or seaweed. Arrowroot-thickened puddings and other dishes. Fish and shellfish stewed, roasted, or raw and marinated in lemon juice and coconut cream. Steamed ti leaf–wrapped packets of fish. Steamed banana leaf–wrapped packets of fruit. Foods cooked in a pit: whole pig, taro, sweet potatoes, yams, breadfruit, shellfish, whole fish, chicken pieces, taro leaves wrapped around a filling of coconut cream, lemon, onions, and shredded beef and all bound in banana leaves, and other leaf-wrapped mixtures of taro, sweet potatoes, yams, or breadfruit.

Sweets   Sugar, immature coconut, haupia (firm pudding made from coconut milk, sugar, and arrowroot).

Beverages   Coconut juice, cocoa, coffee, fruit juice, tea, kava (mildly alcoholic drink made from pepper plant).

Meals   Typical are two or three meals daily, with the same foods at all, and the evening meal the largest. A usual meal is boiled taro root or sweet potatoes, a fish, chicken, or pork dish, and cooked squash, greens, or seaweed.

TRINIDAD AND TOBAGO
Republic of Trinidad and Tobago

Geography   These islands are in the Caribbean Sea and Atlantic Ocean, northeast of Venezuela. Trinidad, the larger island and where most people live, is a plain with mountains and swampy coasts. Tobago is forested.

Major Languages	Ethnic Groups		Major Religions	
English (official)	Indian (South Asian)	40%	Roman Catholic	26%
Caribbean Hindustani	Black (African)	38%	Hindu	23%
French	Mixed	21%	Protestant	15%
Spanish	Chine, white, other	1%	Muslim	6%
Chinese			Other	30%

Population density per sq. mi. 529
Literacy rate 98.7%
Life expectancy 66.1 male; 68 female
Per capita GDP $18,300
Labor force in agriculture 4%

Urban 12.2%
Infant mortality rate per 1,000 live births 23.6
HIV rate 1.5%
Unemployment rate 6.2%
Arable land 15%

Agriculture   sugarcane, fruits, coconuts, cocoa, rice, coffee, vegetables, chickens, goats, pigs, cattle, sheep

Natural resources   fish, oil, natural gas, asphalt

Industries   oil, chemicals, tourism, food processing

History   Arawaks inhabited Trinidad when Columbus sighted it in 1498; Carib Indians inhabited Tobago. The Spanish settled the islands in the 16th century. In the 17th and 18th centuries slaves were imported for plantation labor. Spain ceded Trinidad to Britain in 1802. Tobago passed back and forth between Britain and France until given to Britain in 1814. France captured Tobago in 1781 and changed it into a sugar-producing colony. After slavery ended in the islands in the period 1834 to 1838, indentured workers from India came to work on the sugarcane plantations. Trinidad and Tobago became one colony in 1889 and independent in 1962. Tension between East Indians and blacks has persisted. In 1970 conflict prompted a two-year state of emergency. In 1990 some Muslim fundamentalists attempted a coup against the government. The nation, among the Caribbean's most prosperous, has increased oil with offshore finds. It refines Middle Eastern oil, exporting it mostly to the United States The commercialization of natural gas has resulted in rapid industrialization in recent years. In 2007 it was confirmed that the country's share of natural gas in the reservoirs straddling the country and Venezuela could be 27%.

Influences on food   The indigenous peoples, Arawak and Carib Indians, almost disappeared following the Spanish conquest, leaving only traces of their foodways. They ate fish and game (covered with mud and baked in a pit or grilled over an open fire), pepper pot (a meat stew made with the boiled juice of cassava, called cassarep), fruits and vegetables, hot pepper sauce, and cassava bread. Spain, France, and Britain owned these islands and influenced their food customs (e.g., rice). Other influences were from slaves bought from Africa and indentured labor from India. These tropical islands have abundant fish and seafood and fruits and vegetables.

Bread and cereals   Rice, corn, wheat; rice dishes, fried cassava bread (made of grated cassava), fried corn bread, wheat flour bread, fried baking powder or yeast biscuits, and Asian Indian bread.

Meat, poultry, fish   Chicken, pork, goat, beef, lamb, fish and seafood (salt cod, sea turtle, large frogs, flying fish, mangrove oysters), land crabs, iguana, eggs; blood sausage.

Dairy products   Cow's milk (fresh, condensed, evaporated), cream, aged cheeses.

Fats and oils   Butter, lard, olive oil, salt pork, coconut oil and cream, vegetable oil, ghee (clarified butter).

Legumes   Red beans, chickpeas (garbanzo beans), split peas, pigeon peas, black-eyed peas, soybeans.

Vegetables   Cassava, yams, malanga, sweet potatoes, plantains, greens (taro, malanga), breadfruit, avocados, potatoes, squash, okra, tomatoes, peppers, onions, olives.

Fruit   Oranges, lemons, limes, coconut, bananas, mangoes, papaya, tamarind, akee, pineapple, guavas, cashew apples, passion fruit, soursop, star apples, raisins, pomerac (red, pear shape, with white flesh that smells like a rose).

Nuts and seeds   Almonds, cashew nuts, annatto (achiote) seeds.

Seasonings   Salt, black pepper, chilies, allspice (pimento), annatto seeds, garlic, curry powder, coriander, saffron, cinnamon, cloves, thyme, coconut, vinegar, cocoa, rum.

Dishes   Boiled or steamed rice. Callaloo (taro or malanga leaves cooked with okra and perhaps coconut milk and salt meat or salt cod). Boiled akee, potatoes, or yams. Simmered rice and peas. Black-eyed pea or soybean fritters. Sancoche (stew of beef and onions, split peas, potatoes, cassava root, yams, hot chilies, and coconut cream, topped with cornmeal dumplings, and covered and simmered). Pudding and souse (blood sausage and fresh pork hocks simmered, then marinated in lime juice, and served cold). Roast pork with simmered rice and red beans. Flying fish fried with bananas. Red snapper stuffed with pigeon peas and salt pork, brushed with lime and orange juice, and glazed with herbs, spices, mustard, and ketchup. Shrimp curry with sliced tomatoes. Poulouri (deep-fried chickpea meal balls). Mango relish (unripe mangoes, chilies, garlic, salt, olive oil). Pepper sauce.

Specialties   Trinidadian accra (salt cod fritters), served with "floats" (fried yeast biscuits). Tobago crab pilau (braised rice, crab, and coconut milk).

Possible national dish   Trinidad pepper pot (chicken and pork stew with cassarep, onion, brown sugar, hot chilies, cinnamon, cloves, thyme, and vinegar) or pilau (chicken, meat, or seafood simmered with saffron rice).

Special occasion foods   Pre-Lenten carnival is especially festive in Port of Spain, Trinidad, with parades of costumed dancers. Foods sold by Asian Indians at booths along the parade route include rotis (bread stuffed with split-pea purée and potato curry), coconut candy, and fried chickpea balls.

Sweets   Sugarcane, raw and unprocessed sugar, molasses, banana desserts, ginger mousse.

Beverages   Coffee often mixed with milk, teas, soft drinks, milk, beer, rum, sorrel drink (deep red and aromatic, made from the flower sorrel, cinnamon, orange peel, cloves, sugar, and rum).

Meals   Breakfast: coffee with milk and bread and perhaps egg, cereal, and fruit. Lunch: rice and peas or beans with meat if affordable. Dinner: rice and peas or beans with meat, bread, vegetables, milk, and dessert when available. An Asian Indian meal: curried dish with rice and garnished with coconut, fried plantains, and pineapple.

Snack   Oranges cut in half and sprinkled with salt.

TUNISIA
Tunisian Republic

Geography   Tunisia is in North Africa, bordering the Mediterranean Sea. The north is fertile and wooded, with the Atlas Mountains. The central coastal plain has grazing and orchards. The south, near the Sahara Desert, is arid.

Major Languages	Ethnic Groups		Major Religions	
Arabic (official)	Arab (Bedouin 27%)	98%	Islam (official)	
French (used in commerce)	European	1%	Sunni Muslim	97%
	Jewish and other	1%	Shi'a Muslim	2%
			Other	1%

Population density per sq. mi. 173,1
Literacy rate 77.7%
Life expectancy 73.8 male; 77.5 female
Per capita GDP $7,500
Labor force in agriculture 55%

Urban 65.3%
Infant mortality rate per 1,000 live births 23.4
HIV rate 0.1%
Unemployment rate 14.3%
Arable land 17%

Agriculture   wheat, olives, tomatoes, citrus, sugar beets, dates, almonds, chickens, sheep, goats, cattle, camels, pigs

Natural resources   fish, oil, phosphates, iron ore, lead, zinc, salt

Industries   oil, mining, tourism, textiles, footwear, agribusiness, beverages

History   The Phoenicians settled this land in the 12th century BCE. By the 6th century BCE, the great city-state Carthage dominated the area. The Punic Wars with Rome destroyed Carthage. The area was part of the Roman Empire from 146 BCE until the Arab conquest (648–669). Arabs and Berbers ruled it until the Ottoman Turks conquered it in the period 1570 to 1574 and held it until 1881. In the 16th century, it was the place of the Barbary pirates. It became a French protectorate in 1881. In World War II, after a brief occupation, U.S. and British troops captured it in 1943. France granted it independence in 1956. The first president, Habib Bourguiba, had a pro-Western foreign policy and served until 1987. Ben Ali succeeded him. In 2007 Tunisia had a record cereal harvest and GDP growth was 8.9%.

Influences on food   Phoenicians, Carthage (near the city of Tunis), Rome, Arabs, the Ottoman Empire, Italy, and France have influenced Tunisian cuisine. The Arabs brought eastern spices, thin breads, and the sweet and sour taste combination. Tunisia, Algeria, and Morocco occupy the northwest corner of Africa known in Arabic as Maghreb (the west). They differ from the Middle East by substantial populations of nomadic Berbers. They share a similar cuisine and have influenced France by exporting foods such as couscous, merguez sausage (hot with red chili peppers and made from beef instead of pork to comply with Islamic dietary law), and Arab-style pastries. Influences from the New World include tomatoes (now a main crop), corn, potatoes, and chili peppers. In Tunisia Arab cuisine predominates, although nomads eat Bedouin food (dairy products milk, clarified butter, and yogurt from camels, sheep, and goats, thin unleavened bread, boiled mutton on rice or wheat, dates, small game, locusts, and coffee). Most Tunisians are Muslims, who do not consume pork or alcohol. The Mediterranean coast provided plentiful fish until the last two decades of the 20th century; now, with increased tourism and over fishing, few Tunisians can afford it. Tunisian food is highly seasoned.

Bread and cereals   Wheat, corn, barley, rice; couscous (dried tiny pellets made from a dough of crushed grain, usually semolina wheat, and water), cracked wheat (bulgur), pita bread (thin, round, with a pocket), breadsticks (kaaki), pasta, paper-thin pastry (warqa), rice dishes.

Meat, poultry, fish   Chicken, lamb and mutton, goat, beef, camel, pork, fish, seafood, eggs; merguez sausage.

Dairy products   Buttermilk, yogurt, cheese.

Fats and oils   Olive oil, butter, clarified butter, vegetable oil.

Legumes   Chickpeas, fava beans, lentils.

Vegetables   Olives, tomatoes, eggplant, cucumbers, carrots, celery, turnips, zucchini, cauliflower, potatoes, green bell peppers, pumpkin, okra, mushrooms.

Fruit   Oranges, lemons, limes, dates, grapes, figs, peaches, apricots, wild crabapples.

Nuts and seeds   Almonds, pistachios, caraway seeds, sesame seeds.

Seasonings   Salt, black pepper, garlic, onions, chili peppers, herbs (mint, parsley), spices (allspice, cardamom, cumin, cinnamon, cloves, ginger, nutmeg, turmeric, saffron), vinegar, lemon, orange water, rosewater; harissa (ground dried hot red peppers, cumin, and salt), used on most foods except sweets.

Dishes   Steamed couscous topped with stew of lamb, beef, merguez sausage, chicken, or fish, chickpeas, and vegetables, and hot chili sauce (harissa). Tagine (lamb, chicken, or beef browned in oil; spices, tomatoes, eggplant, chickpeas, garlic, and water added; and the mixture boiled in a covered ceramic pot by the same name), often served over couscous. Couscous and tagine are often cooked simultaneously, the couscous steamed over boiling tagine. Mechoui (a lamb roasted on a spit). Grilled merguez sausage. Charcoal-grilled mullet or tuna steak served with chopped parsley and lemon. Salade meshouiwa (canned tuna; seared sweet peppers, tomatoes, garlic, and onion; hard-boiled eggs, caraway, lemon juice, and olive oil). Potato salad (boiled potatoes heated with oil, lemon juice, harissa, and caraway seeds). Salted cucumber slices with lime juice.

A favorite dish   Brik (fried turnover of very thin pastry filled with a savory mixture topped with an egg), such as brik bil lahm (with a seasoned ground lamb filling) and brik bil anchouwa (with anchovies and Parmesan cheese).

Sweets   Honey, sugar. Fresh fruit and nuts. Samsa (paper-thin pastry layers filled with ground almonds and sesame seeds, baked, and topped with syrup flavored with lemon juice and rosewater). Baklava (very thin pastry layers filled with almonds, baked, and soaked in honey). Dates stuffed with rosewater-flavored pistachio paste (tmar mihchi). Orange-flavored doughnuts dipped in lemon-flavored honey syrup (yo-yo). Almond cookies (twajin).

Beverages   Mint tea (with sugar), coffee, buttermilk, lemonade, fig brandy (boukha).

Meal service   Tunisians sit on a rug or mat around a big bowl of food such as couscous and eat with their fingers. They may use bread to scoop, dip, or sop the food. The common bowl may be set on a low table

Snacks/foods for a light meal in the evening   Steamed couscous with dates and cinnamon, pastries, puddings.

Mezze   Breadsticks, olives, cheese cubes, cucumber and yogurt, brined uncooked vegetables, eggplant purée, hummus (chickpea dip), tabbouleh (salad of parsley, tomato, and bulgur), falafel (small fried patties of bean purée), dolma (stuffed vegetables), small kabobs (meat chunks roasted on a skewer). The mezze tradition (snacks with drinking) is practiced; Muslims drink lemonade and others drink aperitifs (e.g., boukha).

TURKEY
Republic of Turkey

Geography   Turkey is in southwestern Asia and stretches into southeastern Europe, bordering the Mediterranean Sea and the Black Sea. It occupies Asia Minor. Turkey in Asia (Anatolia) is about the size of Texas. Central Turkey is a wide fertile plateau. Mountains with more than 20 peaks over 10,000 feet ring the interior, except in the west. Fertile coastal plains are in the south and west. Turkey has hot, dry summers and cold winters.

Major Languages	Ethnic Groups		Major Religions	
Turkish (official)	Turkish	80%	Muslim (mostly Sunni)	99.8%
Kurdish	Kurdish	20%	Other	0.2%
Dimli, or Zaza				

Population density per sq. mi. 241.6
Literacy rate 88.7%
Life expectancy 70.7 male; 75.7 female
Per capita GDP $12,900
Labor force in agriculture 35.9%

Urban 67.3%
Infant mortality rate per 1,000 live births 37
HIV rate NA
Unemployment rate 9.7%
Arable land 30%

Agriculture   wheat, sugar beets, tomatoes, barley, potatoes, tobacco, cotton, olives, pulse, citrus, chickens, sheep, cattle, goats, only 1,362 pigs

Natural resources   fish, coal, iron ore, copper, chromium, antimony, mercury, gold, barite, borate

Industries   textiles, food processing, autos, electronics, mining, steel, oil, construction

History   Ancient inhabitants of Turkey were among the world's first agriculturalists. The Indo-European Hittites occupied Anatolia from about 1900 to 1200 BCE, followed by Phrygians and Lydians. The area was part of the Persian Empire in the 6th century BCE. Greek civilization flourished here. Next, Turkey was part of the Roman Empire. After the fall of Rome in the 5th century CE, Constantinople (now Istanbul) was the capital of the Byzantine Empire for 1,000 years. In 1453 it fell to Ottoman Turks, who ruled a vast empire for over 400 years, until 1918. Just before World War I, Turkey (the Ottoman Empire) ruled present-day Syria, Lebanon, Iraq, Jordan, Israel, Saudi Arabia, Yemen, and islands in the Aegean Sea. Turkey joined Germany and Austria in World War I and lost much territory. Turkey became a republic in 1923, with Mustafa Kemal (later Ataturk) as president until his death in 1938. He started reforms, moved the capital from Istanbul to Ankara, modernized and secularized Turkey, and reduced Islam's dominant role in 1924. Turkey was neutral most of World War II. It joined NATO in 1952. In 1974 Turkey invaded Cyprus, off Turkey's south coast, to prevent Cyprus from uniting with Greece; since then Cyprus has been divided into Greek and Turkish zones. Since the early 1990s, strife between Kurdish separatists and the government and between fundamentalist Muslims and secularists has occurred. A major earthquake in 1999 killed over 17,000 people and injured thousands. In 2003 suicide bombings in Istanbul by Islamic extremists killed 58 people and caused extensive damage. An Islamic group won elections in 2002 and 2007. In 2007 and 2008 militants of the Kurdistan Workers Party (PKK) with its chief base in northern Iraq raided Turkish security forces, and other PKK terrorists set off bombs in metropolitan areas; in return, Turkish raids were made on PKK camps.

Influences on food   Influences include Chinese, Central Asian, Iranian, Anatolian, Mediterranean, and Islam. The earliest Turks were nomads wandering in western China. The earliest settled Turkish culture was in the mid-8th century in the present Xinjiang. Manti (stuffed pasta, or dumpling) probably entered the Turks' diet then. The Turks moved west through Central Asia. Recorded history of Turkish cuisine began in about the 10th century when Turks came into contact with Iran-Islamic culture. The Turks added yogurt, bulgur (cracked wheat), börek (meat- or cheese-filled pastry), and güveç (stew). By the late 11th century, Muslim Turks cooked bread on griddles, used the rolling pin, cooked in the tandir (clay oven), and liked yogurt, ayran (yogurt drink), and cheese, all practices unlike Chinese traditions. The Turks absorbed part of Iranian cuisine such as fruit in meat stews. The nomadic Turks were already used to cooking meat on skewers. Rice was cultivated in Iran and used in desserts and as an accompaniment. Pilaf (rice cooked with flavorings such as oil or fat and meat or vegetables) emerged from the combined Turkish and Islamic cultures. In the late 11th century, one branch of Turks began to settle in Anatolia. Eventually the Ottoman Turks were installed in Istanbul, at the junction of Europe and Asia, where for centuries they controlled the Balkans, the Arab world, and much of the Mediterranean area. Prior to the Ottoman period here, the Seljuks ruled much of the eastern Islamic world; their diet included vegetables, pulses, nuts, fruits, breads, pastries, sweets, milk products, sherbet, halva, and pickles. The Ottoman period in Turkey, rooted in the 13th century, flourished with the conquest of Istanbul in 1453. Istanbul, after the fall of the Roman Empire, was the center of Byzantine cookery and a major center of the spice trade. It became the center of Ottoman culture, exerting strong influence on the Balkans and some countries of Central Europe. Art and cuisine flourished. In Topkapi Palace a staff of over a thousand fed 10,000 people. People ate well, and there were food-related guilds. The large rural population has eaten mainly bread and yogurt for many centuries. The Mediterranean Sea and Black Sea provide fish. In Istanbul, the spice bazaar still sells spices, and street vendors sell a great variety of foods. Turkey joins two continents and their food traditions. It exports the popular sweet, Turkish delight. Most Turks are Muslim, who do not consume pork or alcohol and fast from sunup to sundown during the month of Ramadan.

Bread and cereals   Wheat, barley, corn, millet, oats, rice; bulgur (cracked wheat), wheat bread leavened and unleavened, for example yufka (lavash, crisp thin bread), pita bread (round with hollow center), filo pastry, rice pilaf.

Meat, poultry, fish   Chicken, lamb and mutton, beef, goat, fish and seafood, eggs; pastirma (spicy dried beef).

Dairy products   Milk (cow, sheep, goat, buffalo), yogurt, ayran (diluted yogurt), feta cheese (white, moist, and salty), kaymak (rich clotted cream). Yogurt is eaten at most meals.

Fats and oils   Butter, clarified butter, olive oil.

Legumes   Broad beans (fava beans), chickpeas.

Vegetables   Tomatoes, potatoes, olives, eggplant, spinach, cabbage, carrots, onions, green peppers, cucumbers.

Fruit   Lemons, oranges, grapes, figs, cherries, apples, pomegranate, currants.

Nuts and seeds   Almonds, pine nuts, pistachio nuts, walnuts, hazelnuts, sesame seeds.

Seasonings   Salt, black pepper, onions, garlic, parsley, mint, anise, allspice, cinnamon, cloves, paprika, cardamom, mastic (aromatic resin of plant), juice of unripe lemons, vinegar, rosewater, bergamot oil.

Appetizers   Pastirma, lamb meatballs, stuffed grape leaves, hummus (bean or chickpea dip), olives.

Dishes   Bean soup. Soups thickened with egg and flavored with lemon juice. Tripe soup with vinegar and garlic. Stuffed pasta. Dolma (grape or cabbage leaves stuffed with rice, currants, and pine nuts or with ground meat and spices. Eggplant hollowed out and stuffed with rice or meat mixture. Two outstanding main dishes: türlü güveç (lamb pieces and onions browned in butter; okra, zucchini, tomato, and small amount of water added; covered and baked); and döner kebab (seasoned mutton or lamb chunks alternating with fat pieces on a rotisserie, roasted, and sliced into thin strips). Köfte (broiled skewered seasoned lamb or mutton patties). Pilaf (rice heated with onions in fat, flavoring items such as meat added, water added, covered and simmered). Börek (noodle enclosing savory lamb filling, coated with butter and baked briefly). Ispanakli börek (baked filo dough layered with spinach and feta cheese filling). Raw vegetable salad with lemon juice and olive oil. Eggplant or zucchini sautéed with olive oil, tomatoes, onions, and garlic, and served cold.

Special occasion dish   "Wedding soup" (dügün çorbasi), lemony, slightly thickened lamb and vegetable soup.

Sweets   Honey, sugar, syrup. Dried fruit. Pekmez (grape juice concentrate). Fruit compote. Güllâç (dough layers boiled in milk, with sweet rosewater added and topped with kaymak). Keskul (almond and rice flours, cream, and milk pudding). Kurabiye (butter cookies with a whole clove on each and dusted with powdered sugar). Turkish delight, or lokum (candy made from syrup and corn flour with citrus, mint, or rosewater, cut into cubes and rolled in powered sugar). Noah's pudding (asure), made from foods remaining after the flood waters receded: legumes, dried fruit, and nuts. Baklava (baked layers of filo dough with nuts and syrup or honey).

Beverages   Hot tea (served in small glasses, offered on entering shops or homes). Turkish coffee (made in a long-handled metal briki, is strong, sweet, often flavored with cardamom, and served in small cylindrical cups). Raki (anise-flavored distilled alcoholic beverage, clear but becomes milky when water is added, "lion's milk").

Meals and service   Three meals with dinner the main meal. Turks use flatware and communal serving dishes.

TURKMENISTAN

Geography   Turkmenistan is in Central Asia, bordering Iran and the Caspian Sea. The Kara Kum Desert, one of the world's largest sand deserts, covers 80% of the land. Many irrigation canals and reservoirs have been built.

Major Languages	Ethnic Groups		Major Religions	
Turkmen (official)	Turkmen	85%	Muslim (mostly Sunni)	89%
Russian	Uzbek	5%	Eastern Orthodox	9%
Uzbek	Russian	4%	Other	2%
	Other	6%		

Population density per sq. mi. 27.5
Literacy rate 99.5%
Life expectancy 65.5 male; 71.8 female
Per capita GDP $5,200
Labor force in agriculture 48.2%

Urban 47.3%
Infant mortality rate per 1,000 live births 51.8
HIV rate <0.1%
Unemployment rate 60%
Arable land 5%

Agriculture   wheat, cotton, tomatoes, grain, sheep, chickens, cattle, goats, pigs

Natural resources   oil, natural gas, sulfur, salt, fish

Industries   natural gas, oil, oil products, textiles, food processing

History   The earliest traces of human settlement in Central Asia, dating back to Paleolithic times, have been found in Turkmenistan. Once part of the ancient Persian Empire, the area has been inhabited by Turkic tribes since the 10th century CE. The Turkmen were originally pastoral nomads, and some of them continued this way of life into the 20th century, living in transportable dome-shaped felt tents. Seljuk Turks ruled the area in the 11th century. The Mongols of Ghenghis Khan conquered the area in the 13th century and ruled until the Uzbeks invaded in the 15th century. The area became part of Russian Turkistan in 1881, the Turkmen Soviet Socialist Republic in 1924, and independent under the name Turkmenistan when the USSR disbanded in 1991. Once the poorest Soviet republic, Turkmenistan now has a stronger economy than other former Soviet republics due to its extensive oil and gas reserves. In the early 1990s, Turkmenistan exported gas through a Russian pipeline, which Russia closed in 1993. In 1996 a new rail line linked Turkmenistan and Iran. Gurbanguly Berdymukhammedov, elected in 2007, restored the 10th year of basic education, the 5th year of university, and pensions that his predecessor (who led the country from 1991 to 2006) had canceled. A U.S. firm announced it would construct the pipeline to carry Turkmen natural gas to Pakistan via Afghanistan.

Influences on food   Turkmenistan is mostly desert. Its western border is on the Caspian Sea, which provides fish. Other influences on food of this country include ancient Persia (of which it was a part), Turks, Mongols, Uzbeks, and Russia. Turkmenians, mostly nomadic shepherds, until the 20th century lived on milk and milk products supplemented by meat. Turkmenistan shares a common cuisine with Uzbekistan and Tajikistan: flatbread, lamb, thick soups and semi-liquid main dishes, and tea. Turkmenian cuisine has some distinctions: Turkmenians eat fish, especially near the Caspian Sea; and some tribes eat young camel and brew tea with hot camel's milk.

Bread and cereals   Wheat, rice; flatbread, noodles, rice dishes (palov). Flatbread is eaten at all meals and made in round loaves, often cooked in a tandyra, or tandoor (clay oven or large jar); dough is slapped on the insides.

Meat, poultry, fish Lamb and mutton, chicken, beef, goat, pork, young camel, horsemeat, yak, fish and seafood, eggs; sausage such as kazy (horsemeat sausage). Meat is usually boiled or roasted.

Dairy products Milk (cow, sheep, goat, mare, camel), sour milk, clabber (kumys: traditionally fermented mare's milk, "desert champagne"), yogurt, cheese (e.g., kurt, a hard cheese, sun dried and reconstituted by soaking crumbled bits in water; airan, made from still-warm milk from camels, sheep, and goats simmered until it clabbers and grows sharp). Locals offer bowls of sour milk to visitors to show hospitality.

Fats and oils Fat from fat-tailed sheep, butter, vegetable oil.

Legumes Chickpeas, beans, lentils.

Vegetables Tomatoes, onions, carrots, pumpkin, greens, cucumbers, radishes, turnips, peppers.

Fruit Melons, grapes, apricots, pomegranates, pears, apples, plums, figs, cherries, peaches, white mulberries, jujubes (a type of date), rhubarb, barberries, blackberries, quinces.

Nuts and seeds Walnuts, hazelnuts, pistachios, caraway seeds.

Seasonings Onions, garlic, vinegar, salt, black pepper, dried red peppers, coriander, dill, mint, aniseed.

Dishes Kabobs (grilled skewered seasoned with red pepper and usually marinated pieces of meat), such as shashlyk (lamb shish kabobs). Besh barmak (thick meat soup or stew of thinly sliced meat and noodles). Manty (steamed dumplings stuffed with lamb, onion, and red pepper). Kaurma lagman (fried noodles and meat). Samsas (meat pies). Fish grilled and in dishes with fruit, fruit juice, or a sweet and sour sauce. Palov (made by browning mutton pieces in rendered fat or oil, adding onion slices and rice and heating, adding water, covering, and simmering; variations include meatballs, chicken, eggs, chickpeas, raisins).

Sweets Honey, sugar. Fruit. Dried fruit. Fruit preserves (e.g., melon rind). Jam (e.g., rose petal).

Beverages Tea (drunk at meals and throughout the day, at home and in teahouses), sour milk, fruit drinks, wine.

Meals and service Breakfast: clabber or cheese, flatbread, tea. Lunch: cheese, greens or thick hearty soup, fruit, flatbread, tea. Evening meal: meat or palov, fruit, flatbread, tea. To dine, people sit on rugs or chairs and may scoop food from the pot with the hand, although plates and forks are usually used. **Street food** Shashlyk (sticks of grilled lamb), cooked by vendors on city streets.

TUVALU

Geography Tuvalu is in the Pacific Ocean east of New Guinea and near the equator. It consists of nine small islands, area 10 square miles (26 sq. km), scattered over 500,000 square miles. The islands are low-lying coral atolls, with the highest point 5 feet above sea level. The climate is tropical.

Major Languages	Ethnic Groups		Major Religions	
Tuvaluan	Polynesian	96%	Church of Tuvalu	
English	Micronesian, other	4%	(Congregationalist)	97%
Samoan			Other Christian, other	3%

Population density per sq. mi. 1,213
Literacy rate NA
Life expectancy 66.7 male; 71.4 female
Per capita GDP $1,600
Labor force in agriculture People make a living mainly from fishing and wages sent home by those working abroad (mostly workers in phosphate industry and sailors)

Urban 48.1%
Infant mortality rate per 1,000 live births 19
HIV rate NA
Unemployment rate 6.5%
Arable land none

Agriculture   coconuts, fruits, bananas, breadfruit, sweet potatoes, taro, pandanus fruit, chickens, ducks, pigs

Natural resources   fish

Industries   fishing, tourism, copra

History   The islands's first Polynesian settlers probably came from Samoa or Tonga. The Spaniards sighted the islands in the 16th century. Europeans settled them in the 19th century. In 1856 the United States claimed the four southern islands for guano mining. In 1865 missionaries from Europe came and converted the islanders to Christianity. In 1892 the islands became a British protectorate. They joined the British Gilbert Islands and became the Gilbert and Ellice Islands Colony in 1916. They separated from the Gilberts (now Kiribati, whose people are Micronesian) in 1975 and became Tuvalu. Tuvalu became independent in 1978. In 1979 the United States relinquished it claims. Tuvalu joined the UN in 2000. Tuvalu's Trust Fund, which invested in major economies and funded a substantial part of the government budget, suffered from the global economic problems in 2007. Sea levels were rising at about an inch annually, causing deterioration of coastal and underground water.

Influences on food   Tuvalu, formerly the Ellis Islands, is in the Polynesia group of the Pacific Islands. About 30,000 to 40,000 years ago people from Southeast Asia began to move south to the western Pacific islands and Australia, and they later migrated to islands further east. British control from 1892 to 1978 also influenced Tuvalu's food. Europeans brought new food plants, wheat bread, and certain animals to the Pacific Islands. Asians brought rice, soybeans, noodles, and teas. Tuvalu's main foods are fish, roots and tubers, breadfruit, coconuts, and fruit. Pork is the main meat, especially for feasts, traditionally cooked with other foods in a stone-lined pit over coals.

Bread and cereals   Rice, wheat; rice dishes, bread, noodles.

Meat, poultry, fish   Chicken, duck, pork, beef, fish (e.g., mullet), shellfish (e.g., crabs), eggs; corned beef, spam.

Dairy products   Milk and other dairy products are uncommon.

Fats and oils   Coconut oil and cream, lard, vegetable oil and shortening, sesame oil.

Legumes   Soybeans, winged beans, peas, lentils, peanuts.

Vegetables   Breadfruit, sweet potatoes, taro root and leaves, pandanus fruit, pawpaws, plantains, yams, cassava, green leaves, seaweed, arrowroot, bitter melon, cabbage, daikon, eggplant, onions, green onions.

Fruit   Coconut, bananas, lemons, limes, guavas, mangoes, papaya, pineapple, melons, tamarind. Coconut milk is the usual liquid cooking medium. Fresh fruit is eaten as snacks.

Nuts and seeds   Candlenuts (kukui), litchis, macadamia nuts.

Seasonings   Coconut cream and milk, lime and lemon juice, salt, soy sauce, ginger, garlic, onions, chili peppers.

Dishes   Boiled taro root, sweet potatoes, or breadfruit. Boiled or steamed rice. Boiled or steamed greens or seaweed. Chunks of white fish marinated in lime juice, onions, and coconut cream. Fish grilled, fried, or leaf-wrapped and steamed. Foods cooked in a pit: whole pig, taro, sweet potatoes, breadfruit, shellfish, whole fish, chicken pieces, taro leaves wrapped around a filling of coconut cream, lemon, onions, and shredded beef and all bound in banana leaves, and leaf-wrapped mixtures of taro, breadfruit, or sweet potatoes and seasonings.

Sweets   Sugar. Immature coconut. Pudding made from coconut milk, sugar, and arrowroot.

Beverages   Coconut juice, tea, coffee, toddy (coconut palm wine), kava (alcoholic drink made from pepper plant).

Meals   Two or three meals daily are typical, with the same foods at all, and the evening meal the largest. A usual meal is boiled taro root, sweet potatoes, or rice, a fish, pork, or chicken dish, and cooked greens or seaweed.

U

UGANDA
Republic of Uganda

Geography   Uganda is in east central Africa, on the equator, and bordering Lake Victoria to the south. This landlocked country is mostly a high fertile plateau (3,000 to 6,000 ft), with wooded hills, a high mountain range, swampy lowlands, and desert.

Major Languages		Ethnic Groups		Major Religions	
English	(both	Baganda	17%	Protestant	42%
Swahili	official)	Banyakole	10%	Roman Catholic	42%
Ganda, or Luganda		Basogo	8%	Muslim	12%
		Bakiga	7%	Other	4%
		Teso	7%		
		Other	51%		

Population density per sq. mi. 406.8
Literacy rate 73.6
Life expectancy 51.3 male; 53.4 female
Per capita GDP $900
Labor force in agriculture 82%

Urban 12.5%
Infant mortality rate per 1,000 live births 66
HIV rate 5.4%
Unemployment rate 3.5%
Arable land 22%

Agriculture   plantains, cassava, sweet potatoes, coffee, tea, cotton, tobacco, corn, millet, pulses, cut flowers, chickens, goats, cattle, pigs, sheep

Natural resources   fish, copper, cobalt, hydropower, limestone, salt

Industries   sugar, brewing, tobacco, cotton textiles

History   By the 19th century, the region comprised several kingdoms inhabited by various peoples, including Bantu- and Nilotic-speaking tribes. Arab traders first explored the area in 1844 and European explorers arrived in 1862. Protestant and Roman Catholic missionaries came in the 1870s. Uganda became a British protectorate in 1894 and independent in 1962. In 1967 it adopted a republican constitution and abolished the traditional kingdoms. Political unrest, guerrilla war, military coups, and human rights abuses occurred during the 1970s and until 1985. An ongoing guerrilla insurgency has killed more than 100,000 people, forced 2 million to flee their homes, and abducted 30,000 children to serve as soldiers and sex slaves over the last decade ending in 2007. A cease-fire accord was signed in 2008. An intensive public health and education campaign has reduced the rate of new AIDS infections. Coffee is a leading crop and export.

Influences on food   Uganda's food customs resemble those of East African neighbor Kenya. The diet contains little meat, in spite of abundant game and the tradition of breeding cattle. Cattle were regarded as wealth, not food, and the Masai and related people lived on milk products and blood of cattle. Others lived on mostly grains, bananas, and gathered greens. The earliest foreign traders, Arabs, established colonies along the coast of East Africa from about 700 CE and introduced spices, onions, and eggplant. Britain's control of Uganda from 1894 to 1962 influenced food customs. For example, the British trained East African men in cooking and service. Also, the British encouraged Asians to settle in East Africa, bringing influences such as the use of curry. New World foods such as cassava, sweet potatoes, and corn have become major crops and foods in Uganda. Uganda borders Lake Victoria, which supplies fish. Tilapia and catfish are farmed. In the mountains, although animals are protected, game is plentiful and antelope are farmed. Cornmeal or millet porridge is the common main food.

Bread and cereals   Corn, millet, sorghum, rice; porridge, fritters, pancakes, rice dishes.

Meat, poultry, fish   Chicken, goat, beef, pork, lamb and mutton, fish, game, eggs.

Insects   Locusts, crickets, grasshoppers, ants, worms (madora), caterpillars (harati). Insects are collected, sometimes dried for later use, and fried or roasted and often eaten as snacks.

Dairy products   Milk, buttermilk, sour milk, curds, cheese (adaptations of European ones).

Fats and oils   Butter, clarified butter, palm oil, peanut oil.

Legumes   Peanuts (groundnuts), cowpeas, beans, lentils. Legumes, an important protein source, are eaten daily.

Vegetables   Plantains, cassava, sweet potatoes, green leaves (especially amaranth, baobab, sesame, okra, cowpea, pumpkin), tomatoes, peppers, onions, yams, eggplant.

Fruit   Bananas, coconut, papaya, wild berries.

Nuts and seeds   Cashews, sesame seeds, pumpkin seeds.

Seasonings   Chilies, tomatoes, onions, coconut milk, dried baobab leaves, black pepper, curry powder, cloves.

Dishes   Thick porridge of cornmeal or millet (ugali), often served with leftover cooked meat, tomatoes, chilies, and green leaves. Boiled and mashed cassava, plantains, or sweet potatoes. Fried plantains or sweet potatoes. Green leaves simmered with peanut paste. Peanut soup. Curried chicken. Irio (simmered beans, corn, and potatoes or cassava). Beef and cassava stew. Fish and peanut curry. Boiled rice. Janjalo muchuzi (boiled red kidney beans with fish, onions, and tomato). Plantains boiled in banana leaves and mashed, a main part of the Ugandan dish Matoke n' yama (bananas and meat, flavored with tomatoes). Steamed papaya.

Sweets   Honey, sugar. Banana pudding. Coconut pudding.

Beverages   Coffee, tea, beer (often home-brewed from corn or millet), native banana gin (waragi).

Street food   Mandazi (doughnut or fritter), grilled corn cobs, rice and coconut pancakes, mkate mayai (fried pancake filled with minced meat and egg).

UKRAINE

Geography   Ukraine is in Eastern Europe, bordering the Black Sea. It is largely a plain of fertile black soil steppes, with Carpathian Mountains in the southwest, the Crimean chain in the south, and forests and lakes in the north.

Major Languages	Ethnic Groups		Major Religions	
Ukrainian (official)	Ukrainian	78%	Ukrainian Orthodox	50%
Russian	Russian	17%	Ukrainian Greek Catholic	8%
Romanian	Other	5%	Autocephalous Orthodox	7%
Polish			Protestant, Roman Catholic	4%
Hungarian			Other	31%

Population density per sq. mi. 197.3

Literacy rate 99.7%

Life expectancy 62.2 male; 74.2 female

Per capita GDP $8,900

Labor force in agriculture 25%

Urban 67.8%

Infant mortality rate per 1,000 live births 9.2

HIV rate 1.6%

Unemployment rate 2.3%

Arable land 54%

Agriculture   sugar beets, potatoes, wheat, cherries, sunflowers, vegetables, chickens, pigs, cattle, sheep, goats

Natural resources   fish, iron ore, coal, manganese, natural gas, oil, salt, sulfur, kaolin, nickel, timber, graphite, titanium, magnesium

Industries   coal, electric power, metals, machinery and transportation equipment, chemicals, food processing

History   From 6000 to 1000 BCE Trypilians lived along Ukraine's main artery, the Dnieper River. Slavic ancestors inhabited the area before the first century CE. The area was occupied in the first millennium CE by the Goths, Huns, Bulgars, Avars, Khazars, and Magyars. In the 9th century the princes of Kiev established a strong state, Kievan Rus, with Kiev the major political and cultural center in Eastern Europe. Kievan Rus, at the crossroads of European trade routes, reached its peak from 1019 to 1054 and adopted Byzantine Christianity. The Mongol conquest in 1240 ended Kiev's power. The area was ruled by Lithuania in the 14th century and by Poland in the 16th century. The Turks gained control of part of the area in 1478. The area came under Russian rule in the 18th century. After the Russian Revolution, Ukraine declared independence in 1918. It was reconquered in 1919 and became the Ukrainian Soviet Socialist Republic of the USSR in 1922. The northwestern part was held by Poland from 1919 to 1939. In 1932–1933 Soviet authorities confiscated Ukraine grain, leading to a famine that killed at least 5 million Ukrainians. Ukraine was taken by Axis troops in 1941 and retaken by the Soviets in 1944. In 1986 an accident at a Soviet-built nuclear power plant in Chernobyl killed or disabled many thousands of people. Ukraine regained independence in 1991 with the Soviet Union breakup. Ukraine's nuclear arsenal was moved to Russia for destruction in the mid-1990s. In 2007 Ukraine's GDP increased by 32.6% and industrial output increased, although agricultural output decreased and consumer prices increased substantially. Russia agreed to increase the volume of gas through Russia to Ukraine. The EU did not accept Ukraine's request for membership, but it lifted restrictions to allow free travel from Ukraine to the EU for Ukrainians under age 18 or of retirement age.

Influences on food   Occupiers (Mongols, Poles, Lithuanians, and Turks), neighbors (Belarus, Poland, Slovakia, Hungary, Romania, Moldova, and Russia), and Christianity have influenced Ukrainian cuisine. Russia dominated Ukraine for much of the last several centuries and was a strong influence. Rich black soil, abundant rain, and mild climate make this one of the world's most fertile croplands. For centuries the Ukraine was called the breadbasket of Europe; now it also grows sugar beets and potatoes. Rivers provide fish. Bread is the main food, followed by pork, potatoes, and beets. Ukraine, a large country, has some regional cuisines, such as in the Carpathian Mountains where corn is the main cereal. Most Ukrainians are Orthodox Christians, who do not eat animal products on the many fast days and eat special foods at Christmas and at Easter, the most important holiday.

Bread and cereals   Wheat, buckwheat, rye, millet, corn, barley, rice; dark rye bread, whole wheat bread, white bread (usually round loaf served with tea or coffee), pancakes (bliny), porridge, dumplings, noodles, rich sweet bread, cakes, cornbread, rice dishes. A round loaf of bread with a mound of salt in the center is offered to guests.

Meat, poultry, fish   Chicken, pork, beef and veal, lamb, goat, fish (sturgeon, herring, pike), eggs; ham, sausage.

Dairy products   Milk (cow, sheep), buttermilk, sour cream, yogurt, cream, cottage cheese, other cheeses.

Fats and oils   Butter, bacon, lard, sunflower seed oil, vegetable oil.

Legumes   Beans, peas, lentils.

Vegetables   Potatoes, beets, cabbage, eggplant, cucumbers, spinach, carrots, radishes, corn, grape leaves, tomatoes, mushrooms, green peas, celery, onions, parsley; pickled vegetables, sauerkraut.

Fruit   Cherries, apples, plums, apricots, grapes, strawberries, other berries, melons, raisins, currants.

Nuts and seeds   Almonds, chestnuts, hazelnuts, walnuts, sunflower seeds, poppy seeds, caraway seeds.

Seasonings   Sour cream, vinegar, onion, garlic, dill, parsley, cinnamon, cloves, nutmeg. Sour taste is liked.

Dishes   Soups: beet, cabbage, lamb. Kasha (porridge of buckwheat, barley, or millet). Stuffed dumplings. Pyrizhky (small yeast rolls stuffed with meat, mushrooms, cabbage, or cottage cheese). Vereshchaka (a casserole of pork and beets). Pork roast glazed with applesauce. Pork chops baked with caraway seeds. Beef steaks spread with seasoned bread crumbs, rolled up, and oven or pot roasted. Fish stuffed with bread crumbs and baked, fried in butter, or simmered in sour cream. Kotlety (fried patties of ground meat, moistened bread crumbs, egg, and milk). Cabbage leaves stuffed with cooked rice, meat, or mushrooms and simmered. Steamed cabbage soufflé (nakypliak). Apple and cabbage salad with sour cream dressing. Deep-fried potato straws. Beets shredded and baked in vinegar and butter. Egg noodles (lokshyna) boiled, drained, and fried. Halushky (boiled bits of dough), served with sour cream or onions browned in sunflower seed oil. Boiled corn on the cob. Cornmeal mush (kulesha). Soft cornbread made with milk, butter, and beaten egg; eaten with a spoon.

Best known dish   Chicken Kiev (chicken breasts wrapped around butter with herbs, breaded, and deep-fried), named for the city of its origin.

National soup   Borsch (beets, pork and beef, onions, tomatoes, garlic, and perhaps other ingredients).

National dish   Varenyky (dumpling) stuffed with cottage cheese and boiled.

Christmas Eve dish   Kutia (wheat grains with honey, poppy seeds, and stewed dried fruit).

Easter foods   Red or decorated hard-boiled eggs. Pascha (cheesecake with candied fruit and nuts baked in a pyramid-shaped mold). Kulich (yeast cake with raisins, nuts, and candied fruit baked in a tall, cylindrical mold).

Sweets   Sugar, honey. Dumpling filled with plums and boiled in honey and water. Berry pudding. Torte of rye bread crumbs and almonds with wine syrup. Spiced honey cake (medivnyk). Baba (rich sweet tall yeast cake).

Beverages   Tea, beer, kvass (beer fermented from beets or rye bread), vodka, wine.

Meals   Three hearty meals a day, with lunch the largest. Staples are bread, soup, kasha, and tea, beer, or kvass.

Snack   Roasted sunflower seeds.

UNITED ARAB EMIRATES

Geography   The United Arab Emirates is in the Middle East, onß the Arabian Peninsula, bordering the Persian Gulf and the Gulf of Oman. The land is mostly desert, with flat barren coastal plains and uninhabited sand dunes.

Major Languages	Ethnic Groups		Major Religions	
Arabic (official)	Emirati	19%	Islam (official)	
Persian	Other Arab and Iranian	23%	Sunni Muslim	80%
English	South Asian	50%	Shi'a Muslim	16%
Hindi	Other expatriates	8%	Hindu, Christian, other	4%
Urdu				

Population density per sq. mi. 143.2
Literacy rate 90.4%
Life expectancy 73.3 male; 76.6 female
Per capita GDP $37,300
Labor force in agriculture 7%

Urban 77.7%
Infant mortality rate per 1,000 live births 13.1
HIV rate NA
Unemployment rate 2.4%
Arable land 1%

Agriculture   dates, tomatoes, eggplants, watermelons, chickens, goats, sheep, camels, cattle

Natural resources   oil, natural gas, fish

Industries   oil, petrochemicals, fishing, aluminum, cement, fertilizers, construction materials

History   Important trade centers were in the Persian Gulf area as early as Sumerian times. Original inhabitants were a seafaring people who were converted to Islam in the 7th century. Later the Carmathians established a powerful sheikdom. After it disintegrated, its people became pirates and the area became known as the Pirate Coast. The Portuguese arrived in the early 16th century and the British came in the early 17th century. In the 19th century, the rulers of the seven "Trucial Sheikdoms" along the east coast of the Arabian Peninsula gave Britain control of defense and foreign relations. Britain administered the region from 1853, but the states remained sovereign and maintained internal control. In 1971 the sheikhs terminated defense treaties with Britain, merged the sheikdoms to form an independent state, and established the six-member federation, the United Arab Emirates (UAE), which Ras al-khaymah joined in 1972. The UAE aided coalition forces against Iraq in the Persian Gulf War (1991). The UAE signed a military defense agreement with the United States in 1994 and one with France in 1995. U.S. troops were stationed here during the 2003 Iraq War. Oil revenues have made the UAE one of the world's wealthiest nations. International banking, investment, and construction have boomed. In 2007 Dubai, the UAE's largest city, became the largest shareholder in the London Stock Exchange and acquired a 20% stake in the NASDAQ stock market index. Most (81%) of the population and nearly all the private work force are foreign.

Influences on food   The land is mostly desert with a coastline, which supplies fish. The country's food has been influenced by neighbor Saudi Arabia and surrounding cultures: Ottoman to the north, the Horn of Africa to the west, and Iran and India to the east. Britain, with a presence here for more than three centuries, has had some influence. Islam, the official religion and the faith of most of the people here, influences the food practices. Islam forbids consumption of pork or alcohol and requires fasting from sunup to sundown in the month of Ramadan. Expatriates comprise much of the population, resulting in the availability of a wide variety of foods.

Bread and cereals   Wheat, rice; flatbread such as pita, couscous, cracked wheat, rolls, pancakes, filo dough pastry, rice dishes. Flatbread or rice accompanies savory dishes.

Meat, poultry, fish   Chicken, goat, lamb, camel, beef, fish and shellfish, eggs. Favorites are lamb, chicken, and fish such as hammour (grouper) and zubaidi (silver pomfret).

Dairy products   Yogurt (laban), labneh (strained yogurt), milk, cream, feta cheese.

Fats and oils   Sesame seed oil and paste, ghee (clarified butter), butter, olive oil.

Legumes   Chickpeas (garbanzo beans), fava beans, lentils.

Vegetables   Tomatoes, eggplant, cucumbers, spinach, onions, green onions, olives, fresh herbs (parsley, mint, basil, dill, coriander, fenugreek). Fresh herbs are sold in markets.

Fruit   Dates, watermelon, mangoes, melons, oranges, bananas, lemons, limes, figs.

Nuts and seeds   Almonds, sesame seeds, sesame seed paste (tahini).

Seasonings   Salt, cardamom, saffron, mint, baharat (black pepper, coriander, cassia, cloves, cumin, cardamom, nutmeg, and paprika), loomi (dried Omani limes; used in meat dishes and sweet tea), lemon juice, onion, garlic.

Dishes   Steamed couscous. Rice boiled or steamed or as pilaf (cooked first with fat or oil and seasonings, then water or broth and perhaps other ingredients added and simmered). Lamb, as pieces or ground, cooked on skewers (kabob mashwi). Fried or grilled fish. Machbous (simmered prawns, rice, fresh herbs, and vegetables). Boiled and sometimes puréed chickpeas, fava beans, or lentils. Eggplant fried or baked in casserole with lamb, tomatoes, onions, and olive oil (moussaka). Salad of cracked wheat and fresh herbs. Yogurt and cucumber salad. Fresh salt pickles (accompany meat and snacks).

Possible national dish   Khouzi (baked whole lamb stuffed with chicken, eggs, and rice spiced with baharat, saffron, and onions), served on a bed of rice and garnished with almonds and ghee.

Sweets   Dibis (date molasses), honey, sugar. Dates, especially during Ramadan. Baklava (pastry of thin filo dough layered with nuts and soaked with honey or syrup). Ataif (small stuffed pancakes), a Ramadan specialty.

Beverages   Coffee, tea, fruit drinks, yogurt drinks, beer, wine, brandy. Coffee, the main drink and strongly associated with the renowned Arabian hospitality, is prepared from well-roasted, finely ground beans, and is usually flavored with cardamom. Tea is usually consumed black and very sweet.

Street food and snacks   Freshly roasted chicken and lamb are available from shawerma stalls, where lamb pieces are roasted on a vertical spit and are sliced and served in pita bread or roll with tomato, parsley, and tahini.

UNITED KINGDOM
United Kingdom of Great Britain and Northern Ireland

Geography   The United Kingdom is in Western Europe, between the North Sea and the Atlantic Ocean. It consists of Great Britain (England, Wales, and Scotland) and Northern Ireland. England, in the southeast, is mostly rolling land. Scotland, in the north, has central lowlands, granite highlands in the north, and an indented west coast. Wales, in the west, has steep hills and valleys. Northern Ireland is the northern part of the island of Ireland, westernmost of the British Isles. There are several important rivers and ample rainfall. The Gulf Stream moderates the climate.

Major Languages	Ethnic Groups		Major Religions	
English (official)	White (English 84%,		Christian (Anglican,	
Welsh	Scottish 9%, Welsh 4%		Roman Catholic	
Scottish form of Gaelic	Northern Irish 3%)	92%	Presbyterian, Methodist)	72%
	Black	2%	Muslim	3%
	Indian	2%	Other, unspecified, none	25%
	Other	4%		

Population density per sq. mi. 653.4
Literacy rate 99%
Life expectancy 76.4 male; 81.5 female
Per capita GDP $35,100
Labor force in agriculture 1.4%

Urban 89.7%
Infant mortality rate per 1,000 live births 4.9
HIV rate 0.2%
Unemployment rate 5.4%
Arable land 23%

Agriculture   cereals, sugar beets, potatoes, oilseed, vegetables, apples, chickens, sheep, cattle, pigs, goats

Natural resources   fish, coal, oil, natural gas, iron ore, lead, zinc, gold, tin, limestone, salt, clay, chalk, gypsum

Industries machine tools, electric power automation equipment, railroad equipment, shipbuilding, aircraft, motor vehicles and parts, electronics and communication equipment, metals, chemicals, coal, oil, paper and paper products

History Britain was part of the continent until about 6000 BCE. Britain's earliest inhabitants left Stonehenge and other examples of prehistoric culture. Celts followed, arriving 2,500 to 3,000 years ago. Their language survives in Welsh and Gaelic enclaves. Roman invasion brought the area into the Roman Empire in 55–54 BCE. The Roman province of Britannia lasted until the 5th century and included present-day England and Wales. In the 5th century Nordic tribes invaded. Christianity began to grow in the 6th century. Jutes, Angles, and Saxons invaded from German lands and struggled with Danes for control from the 8th through 11th centuries. In 1066 William and French-speaking Normans invaded and united Britain with their area of France. The French language of the Normans eventually merged with the Anglo-Saxon of the common people to form English. The Scots became dominant in Scotland, which was unified in the early 11th century, and from the 11th century Scotland came under the influence of the English throne. In the late 12th century Ireland was conquered by Henry II. His sons, Richard I and John, had trouble with the clergy and nobles, and John was forced to grant concessions to the nobles in the Magna Carta.

In 1215 King John signed the Magna Carta, a guarantee of rights and the rule of law. During the 13th century, statute law developed to supplement English common law, and the first parliament was convened. In 1314 Scotland won independence. France defeated England in The Hundred Years' War (1338–1453), with England losing almost all the English territory in France. Then the Black Death plague killed a third of the population. A civil war, The War of the Roses (1455–1485), ended with establishing the Tudor monarchy. Henry VIII established the Church of England (1534), separate from the authority of the pope, and took Wales into his realm. During the reign of Queen Elizabeth I (Henry VIII's daughter), England became a major world power: defeated the Spanish Armada in 1588, founded colonies in the new world, and expanded trade with Europe and the Orient. Scotland was united with England when James VI of Scotland (Elizabeth's heir) was crowned James I of England in 1603. Struggle between Parliament and the monarchy led to civil war from 1642 to 1649, the execution of Charles I, and the establishment of a republic. After Puritan rule under Oliver Cromwell and his son (1649–1660), the monarchy was restored with Charles II in 1660. Parliament's sovereignty was confirmed in 1688. A Bill of Rights was granted in 1689.

In the 18th century, England and Scotland formed the Kingdom of Great Britain (1707); the Hanoverians ascended to the English throne when George of Hanover became George I of Great Britain (1714); and technological innovations led to the Industrial Revolution. Wars with France expanded the British Empire all over the world, especially in Canada and India, although the 13 North American colonies were lost. In the 19th century, Great Britain and Ireland united to form the United Kingdom of Great Britain and Ireland (1801). Struggle with France continued with the Napoleonic Wars, ending with British victory at Waterloo in 1815. Universal public education developed, industrialization and urbanization spread, and much of Asia and Africa were added to the empire during Queen Victoria's reign from 1837 to 1901.

In the 20th century, Britain suffered high casualties in World War I. Ireland became independent in 1921, but the six counties of Ulster remained in the United Kingdom as Northern Ireland. Britain suffered major bombing damage during World War II. After the war, industrial growth continued, but Britain lost much of its empire as India gained independence in 1947 and its colonies and dependencies gained independence into the 1970s. The UK participated with UN forces in the Korean War (1950–1953). In 1956 it intervened militarily in Egypt during the Suez Crisis. In 1982 it defeated Argentina in the Falkland Islands War. The Channel Tunnel linking Britain to the continent came into use in 1994. In 1996 the European Union banned British beef because of the threat of "mad cow" disease. In 2001 an epidemic of foot-and-mouth disease had a strong impact on farming and tourism. The UK participated in the U.S.-led war against terrorism, in the bombing of Afghanistan in 2001, and sending troops to Iraq in 2003. In 2005, in the worst attack in Britain since World War II, terrorist bombings of three underground trains and a bus killed 56 people and injured more than 700. In 2007, Northern Ireland's Assembly reconvened following almost 5 years of inactivity after Sinn Féin, the Roman Catholic Nationalist Party, ended its policy of noncompliance with the police, and Ian Paisley, leader of the Protestant Democratic Unionist Party, was sworn in as first minister with Sinn Féin's Martin McGuiness as his deputy. In 2007 house prices increased every month at an annual rate of 11%, peaked in August, and fell every month thereafter. In 2008, due to the global financial crisis, the prime minister initiated a plan to nationalize three of Britain's largest banks with up to $63 billion.

Overseas Territories (OT) and Crown Dependencies (CD) of the United Kingdom: Channel Islands (CD), Jersey and Guernsey, lie off the northwest coast of France in the English Channel.

Isle of Man (CD), in the Irish Sea west of Scotland, is famous for the Manx tailless cat. Chief occupations are farming, tourism, and fishing (kippers, scallops).

Gibraltar (OT), on the southern coast of Spain, British since 1704, guards the entrance to the Mediterranean Sea.

British West Indies, an arch of islands from north of Venezuela toward Puerto Rico, includes many self-governing British possessions and ones still associated with the UK: **Montserrat** (OT); **British Virgin Islands** (OT), with tourism the main industry; **Anguilla** (OT); **Cayman Islands** (OT), three islands including Grand Cayman, a free port which in the 1970s became a tax-free refuge for foreign funds with branches of many Western banks; and the **Turks and Caicos Islands** (OT), at the southeast end of the Bahamas, where salt production gave way to tourism, offshore financial services, and fishing, and main exports are salt, shellfish, and conch shells.

Bermuda (OT) is a group of about 150 small islands in the western Atlantic Ocean, with tourism and international finance the main industries and per capita income among the world's highest. A 2003 storm caused much loss.

South Atlantic possessions are the **Falkland Islands** (OT), at the southern end of South America, whose major revenue is from licensing foreign fishing vessels, main industry is sheep-raising, and main export is wool; **British Antarctic Territory** (OT), south of 60° S latitude, formerly a dependency of Falkland Islands, became a separate colony in 1962, and includes South Shetland Islands, South Orkneys, and the Antarctic Peninsula; **South Georgia and the South Sandwich Islands** (OT), southeast of the Falklands, became a separate dependency in 1985; **St. Helena** (OT), an island off the coast of West Africa, where Napoleon after his defeat at Waterloo lived in exile from 1815 until his death in 1821, with flax, lace, and rope making the chief industries; **Tristan da Cunha**, principal island in an island group between Cape of Good Hope and South America, dependencies of St. Helena; **Ascension,** island northwest of and administered by St. Helena, has sea turtles.

British Indian Ocean Territory (OT), the Chagos Archipelago, is in the Indian Ocean south of India.

Pacific Ocean Territory: Pitcairn Island (OT), in the Pacific, halfway between South America and Australia, uninhabited until 1790 when mutineers of the *Bounty* landed there, is administered by New Zealand.

ENGLAND

Influences on food   Celts, Romans, Vikings, Saxons, Angles, Normans, Germans, Scots, Irish, West Indians, Asians (especially from Pakistan and India), refugees (Jews, Poles), Americans, Australians, Middle Easterners, and Africans have influenced England's cuisine. Influences also include continental Europe, the Protestant schism from the Roman Catholic Church, Puritan influence, the gain and loss of a global empire, and the Industrial Revolution. As examples, Romans planted apple trees; the Dutch introduced tea imported from China; and the New World furnished potatoes, fruit, and rum. English cuisine features meat, potatoes, baked goods, puddings, cheese, eggs, tea (drink and meal), and breakfast; it endures in former British possessions such as Australia.

Bread and cereals   Wheat, barley, oats, rye, hops, rice; wheat flour bread, scones (biscuits containing egg and sugar), biscuits (cookies, crackers), buns, crumpets (yeast-egg batter cooked in butter), pies, puddings, cakes.

Meat, poultry, fish   Chicken, lamb, beef, pork, fish, shellfish, eggs, turkey, game (rabbit, grouse, pheasant); bacon, ham, sausage, potted meat (smooth mixture of meat and lard or butter preserved in pots or jars).

Dairy products   Milk (cow, sheep), cream (double, with twice usual fat, and clotted, or slightly fermented), cheese (cheddar, Cheshire, Stilton, a blue cheese).

Fats and oils   Butter, lard, margarine, vegetable oil, salt pork, rapeseed oil.

Legumes   Kidney beans, lentils, lima beans, split peas.

Vegetables   Potatoes, carrots, onions, cabbage, turnips, celery, green beans, parsnips, green peas, cauliflower, Brussels sprouts, cucumbers, lettuce, tomatoes, green onions, radishes, parsley; pickles.

Fruit   Apples, strawberries, raspberries, pears, peaches, plums, oranges, apricots, raisins; jam, jelly, marmalade.

Nuts and seeds   Almonds, chestnuts, hazelnuts, pecans, walnuts, rapeseed, caraway seeds, sesame seeds.

Seasonings   Salt, black pepper, parsley, mint, mustard, horseradish, rosemary, basil, thyme, cinnamon, allspice, ginger, nutmeg, vanilla, malt vinegar, Worcestershire sauce (anchovies, vinegar, soy, garlic, spices), chutney (fruit or vegetable spicy preserve). Seasoning is mild. Flavorful sauces and gravies are added to taste.

Dishes   Roast beef with Yorkshire pudding (baked popover batter on beef drippings) and horse-radish sauce. Potatoes, boiled, mashed, fried, or roasted. Roast leg of lamb with mint jelly. Shepherd's pie (leftover meat and onions topped with mashed potatoes). Steak and kidney pie. Toad in the hole (sausage baked in a batter pudding). Cornish pasties (pie filled with meat, potato, onion, and turnip). Pork pie. Boiled lobster. Rabbit stew. Roast pheasant with chips (fried potato slices). Baked beans with bacon. Hasty pudding (flour and milk porridge). Lancaster hot pot (lamb chop, potato, and onion casserole). Boiled beef (corned brisket) with onions, carrots, and dumplings, served with pease pudding (puréed and seasoned boiled split peas). Dover sole steamed or grilled, served with herb butter. Mixed green salad. Peas simmered with a spring of mint.

Special occasion foods   Christmas: hot punch or mulled ale, roast goose or turkey, plum pudding (steamed suet and fruit pudding), mincemeat pie (made with suet, fruit, nuts, spices), Christmas cake (dark fruitcake with white frosting). Easter: hot cross buns (yeast buns with raisins and spice, and a pastry cross design on top).

Sweets   Sugar, brown sugar, honey. Steamed pudding of bread or flour and fruit. Summer pudding (molded ripe berries and sugar in a bread-lined bowl). Flummery (molded oatmeal or custard pudding). Puddings and pies served with custard, whipped cream, or rum butter (butter, sugar, and rum beaten together and chilled). Burnt cream pudding (baked cream custard topped with sugar and broiled to caramelize it). Baked apples, sugar, and spice topped with bread crumbs. Tart (pastry shell filled with fruit or jam). Fool (fruit, e.g., raspberry, purée folded with custard or whipped cream). Trifle (layered cake soaked in sherry, raspberry jam, custard, and whipped cream in a glass dish). Sally Lunn (sweet yeast cake split and topped with whipped cream, said to have been sold in Bath). Shrewsbury simnel (rich spice cake topped with 12 balls of marzipan). Chocolate cake.

Beverages   Milk, tea (black, with milk and sugar), beer (bitter ale), coffee, cider, whiskey, gin, port, sherry, wine.

Meals   Breakfast, lunch, afternoon tea, and dinner are usual. Breakfast: fried bacon and eggs, kippers (salted, smoked herring), bread, butter, marmalade, tea. Lunch: Ploughman's lunch (cheddar cheese, bread, pickled onions, and a pint of beer), served in pubs (public houses that serve alcoholic drinks and light meals). Tea: tea and small sandwiches, crumpets, scones, cakes, and jam in afternoon; high tea, a substantial late afternoon or early evening meal with tea and using fine tableware. Favorite dinner dessert: Stilton cheese, crackers, and port.

Favorite meal out   Prawn cocktail, steak garni, Black Forest cake (chocolate layers, whipped cream, cherries).

Fast food   Fish and chips (battered, deep-fried fish and fried potatoes, seasoned with salt and malt vinegar).

SCOTLAND

Influences on food   Scotland, further north than England, has different staple foods and less prosperity, with more frugal cuisine. Oats thrive in the cool, moist climate. Scotland is known for its special breeds of cattle and sheep. Fisheries have large catches of herring, cod, and whiting. Whisky is the biggest export. The Hebrides is an island group off the west coast, with industries of sheep-raising and weaving. Orkney and Shetland are islands northeast of the mainland. Orkney raises cattle, sheep, pigs, oats, barley, and turnips. Shetland, home of Shetland ponies, raises sheep and features mutton and fish.

Bread and cereals   Oats, wheat, barley; oatmeal porridge, oatcakes (bannock, griddle-cooked flatbread), scones.

Meat, poultry, fish   Lamb and mutton, beef, fish (e.g., salmon), chicken, eggs, grouse, pheasant, rabbit; sausage.

Dairy products   Milk (cow, sheep), cream, cheese (Dunlop the main one, also cottage cheese called crowdie).

Dishes   Scotch broth (boiled beef and barley with carrot, onion, and parsley). Scotch egg (hard-boiled egg enclosed in sausage and then fried). Scotch pie (small mutton pie with crust standing up above the filling, the rim above the meat often filled with hot gravy, peas or beans, and potato). Cockaleekie (chicken and leek soup). Colcannon (mashed boiled white vegetables with onions). Stovies (potatoes slow cooked in water and butter or meat drippings). Finnan haddie (smoked haddock poached in milk with onions and pepper). Grouse roast or pie.

National dish   Haggis (sheep stomach stuffed with oatmeal and sheep's innards), traditional on New Year's Eve.

Sweets   Honey, sugar, syrup. Shortbread (sweet buttery biscuit, or cookie). Dundee cake (dark fruitcake topped with almonds). Black buns (fruitcake encased in pastry). Gingerbread (made with flour, honey, and ginger).

Beverages   Tea, coffee, Scotch whisky.

Breakfast   Oatmeal porridge, kippers (salted, smoked salmon), oatcakes, bread, butter, orange marmalade, tea.

High tea   Ham, meat pie, salad, baked goods, butter, jam, and hot tea, perhaps liquor; often eaten after work.

WALES

Influences on food   The wet climate of Wales allows growing cereals and grass; sheep and cattle are raised. Rivers, lakes, and coasts provide fish. Prior to the 18th century the Celts were semi-nomadic and took flocks to high land for summer and to lower land for winter. In medieval times, chiefs and kings and their courts visited communities, and the people provided food: beer, bread, meat, honey, oats, cheese, butter, leeks, and cabbages. In good times most people ate these same foods plus sometimes fish and shellfish. Many people lived almost entirely on oats and dairy produce. Porridge, soup, and bread were the staples for centuries. Leek is the national emblem.

Special foods   Lamb, fish, cockles (bivalves, shellfish), laver (red edible seaweed), soft cheeses, leeks.

Dishes Laver bread (boiled laver seaweed mixed with oatmeal and fried in bacon or sausage fat). Welsh rabbit (melted cheese on toasted bread). Chicken and leek pie. Bara brith (fruit loaf). Small spicy Welsh cakes.

Beverage Metheglyn (strong, highly spiced mead, or honey wine).

NORTHERN IRELAND As in Ireland, foods include fish, beef, lamb, potatoes, Irish soda bread (made with flour, salt, soda, and buttermilk), Irish stew (lamb, potatoes, and onions, with seasoning), Irish Christmas cake (fruitcake), and whiskey.

UNITED STATES
United States of America

Geography The United States is in southern North America, bordering the Atlantic and Pacific oceans. It has a temperate climate and varied topography, including fertile farmland and rivers and lakes. The land includes a vast central plain, mountains and deserts in the west, and hills and low mountains in the east.

Major Languages	Ethnic Groups		Major Religions	
English	White	80%	Protestant	51%
Spanish	Black	13%	Roman Catholic	24%
Hawaiian (official in Hawaii)	Asian	4%	Mormon	2%
	American Indian and Alaska native	1%	Other Christian	2%
	Other	2%	Jewish	2%
	(Hispanic, of any race 15%)		Other or none	19%

Population density per sq. mi. 85.9
Literacy rate 99%
Life expectancy 75.3 male; 81.1 female
Per capita GDP $45,800
Labor force in farming, forestry, and fishing 0.6%

Urban 80.8%
Infant mortality rate per 1,000 live births 6.3
HIV rate 0.6%
Unemployment rate 4.6%
Arable land 18%

Agriculture corn, soybeans, alfalfa, hay, wheat, cotton, grapes, vegetables, fruits, chickens, cattle, pigs, horses, sheep, goats

Natural resources fish, coal, copper, lead, molybdenum, phosphates, uranium, bauxite, gold, iron, mercury, nickel, potash, silver, tungsten, zinc, oil, natural gas, timber

Industries oil, steel, motor vehicles, aerospace, telecommunications, chemicals, electronics, food processing, consumer goods, lumber, mining

History American Indian peoples probably migrated from Asia to North America. By 12000 BCE North American Indian cultures flourished in the territory that is now the United States In 1492 Columbus, sailing for Spain, landed in the Bahamas. In 1513 Spanish explorer Ponce de Léon explored Florida. In 1565 the Spanish settled St. Augustine, Florida, the first permanent European settlement in North America. In 1607 the British settled Jamestown, Virginia. In 1619 Dutch brought the first African black slaves to Jamestown. In 1620 Pilgrims from England arrived on the *Mayflower* and established the Plymouth, Massachusetts, colony. In 1624 and 1626 the Dutch established colonies in New York, purchased Manhattan, and named it New Amsterdam.

With the July 4, 1776, Declaration of Independence and the American Revolution: War of Independence (1775–1783), the American colonies became an independent nation. In 1803 the

United States purchased from the French the Louisiana Territory, land west of the Mississippi River to the Rocky Mountains. The Lewis and Clark Expedition (1804–1806) explored the West (now the northwestern United States) and a route to the Pacific Ocean. In 1819 Spain ceded Florida to the United States. In 1830 the Indian Removal Act authorized removal of Native Americans in the east to lands west of the Mississippi; 50,000 were relocated by the end of the decade. In 1836 Texas declared independence from Mexico, fought to gain independence, and in 1845 the United States annexed Texas. In the Mexican War (1846–1848), the United States gained land north of the Rio Grande in Texas, present-day California, and the southwest. In 1848 gold discovery in California led to the gold rush. In the period 1861 to 1865, the Civil War between the North and South, over secession and slavery, resulted in prohibition of slavery in 1865; in 1870 blacks gained the right to vote. In 1863 the Homestead Act allowed settlers to claim land (160 acres) after they had lived on it for five years. In 1867 the United States purchased Alaska from Russia and the first transcontinental railroad was completed. In 1890 Indian Wars ended and the Census Bureau announced that the West was settled and the frontier closed. In 1898 at the end of the Spanish-American War, defeated Spain ceded Puerto Rico, Guam, and the Philippines to the United States. In 1898 the United States annexed Hawaii.

Major weather disasters include the 1900 Galveston hurricane leaving 6,000 to 8,000 people dead and the 1906 San Francisco earthquake. In 1903, the United States acquired the Panama Canal Zone and the Wright brothers made the first airplane flight. During World War I (1914–1918), the United States declared war on Germany and Austria-Hungary in 1917. In 1916 the United States purchased the Virgin Islands from Denmark. In the period 1918 to 1920 the world-wide influenza epidemic struck the United States killing 500,000. In 1919 women gained the right to vote. In 1927 Charles Lindbergh made the first solo nonstop transatlantic flight. The 1929 stock market crash precipitated the Great Depression of the 1930s. In 1933 President Franklin Roosevelt's New Deal recovery measures were enacted by Congress. Social Security was enacted in 1935. The Fair Labor Standards Act, including the first minimum wage, passed in 1938. During World War II (1939–1945), after the 1941 Japan attack on Hawaii, the United States declared war on Japan and later on Germany and Italy. The Philippines became independent in 1946. In the Korean War (1950–1953), the North Korean communists invaded South Korea and the United States sent troops. During the Vietnam War (1964–1975) between North Vietnam communists, with China and USSR backing, and noncommunist South Vietnamese, the United States backed South Vietnam. In 1952 Puerto Rico became a United States Commonwealth. In 1959 Alaska became the 49th state and Hawaii the 50th. In 1969 astronauts Neil Armstrong and Edwin Aldrin, Jr., were the first men to land on the moon. In the 1991 Persian Gulf War, the United States led an international coalition to drive Iraqis from Kuwait.

On Sept. 11, 2001, two hijacked jets rammed the twin towers of the World Trade Center in New York, plus a third hijacked plane flew into the Pentagon, and a fourth crashed in rural Pennsylvania; more than 3,000 people died. The United States and Britain launched air attacks in Afghanistan after the Taliban government there failed to turn over Saudi terrorist Osama bin Laden, the suspected mastermind of the Sept. 11 attack. In 2003, a U.S.- and British-led coalition invaded Iraq for its failure to allow UN inspections of suspected nuclear weapons sites. In 2004 the United States returned sovereignty to an interim Iraqi government but maintained troops in Iraq to fight a growing insurgency. In 2005 Hurricane Katrina caused catastrophic damage in Louisiana and Mississippi, with 80% of New Orleans flooded. In 2007 President George W. Bush increased United States forces in Iraq in a "surge" of some 30,000. Islamic radicals sheltered in western Pakistan and financed partly by opium production increased armed clashes in Afghanistan, and the United States increased its troops there. A major economic concern was the real estate market that brokers had fueled by offering adjustable rate mortgages at low initial rates. By mid-2007 many homeowners could not make their payments when their interest rates were adjusted upward, leading to foreclosures. An estimated $500 billion worth of "subprime" mortgage securities were devalued, reducing the lending capacity of financial institutions. In 2008 the worst financial crisis since the Great Depression occurred in the United States, and the first African American was elected president.

U. S. TERRITORIES (T) AND OUTLYING AREAS

Puerto Rico, Commonwealth of Puerto Rico,   in the Caribbean Sea east of Cuba, consists of mountainous tropical Puerto Rico Island and three islets. Peaceful Arawak Indians lived here when Columbus came in 1493. Spain controlled the area until 1898, when it was ceded to the U.S. Puerto Ricans were granted U.S. citizenship in 1917 and since 1952 have administered their internal affairs. The population is almost entirely Hispanic and mostly Roman Catholic. Sugarcane, coffee, pineapples, plantains, bananas, cattle, pigs, and chickens are produced.

Guam, Territory of Guam (T), in the western Pacific Ocean, probably explored by Magellan for Spain in 1521, was claimed by Spain from 1565 until 1898, when ceded to the United States Japan occupied it from 1941 to 1944. Its people have been United States citizens since 1950. The religion of most people (85%) is Roman Catholic. The economy is based on tourism and U.S. military spending (U.S. bases occupy a third of the land). Main agricultural products are fruits, copra, vegetables, eggs, pork, poultry, and beef.

U.S. Virgin Islands, United States Virgin Islands   (T). The Virgin Islands consist of nine main islands and about 75 islets in the West Indies, originally inhabited by the Arawak Indians and later by the Carib Indians, and explored by Columbus in 1493. Britain has held six of the main islands since 1666. The remaining three, St. Croix, St. Thomas, and St. John, and about 50 islets, were acquired by Denmark and in 1917 were purchased by the U.S. citizenship was granted in 1927. Most people are West Indian black (76%) and Protestant (51%). The main economic activity is tourism. Main agricultural products are fruits, ornamental plants, vegetables, and cattle.

American Samoa, Territory of American Samoa   (T), a group of islands in the South Pacific, was settled by Polynesians around 1000 BCE and became a U.S. territory in 1900. Most people are Samoan (88%), speak Samoan and English, and are Christian (more than 70%). Coconuts, taro, bananas, vegetables, breadfruit, yams, copra, pineapples, dairy foods, chickens, and pigs are produced. Canned tuna is the primary export, mainly to the United States.

Northern Mariana Islands, Commonwealth of the Northern Mariana Islands,   includes seven islands east of the Philippines. They were sighted by Spanish navigator Magellan in 1521 but were not settled by Europeans until 1668, when missionaries converted the indigenous Chamorro people to Catholicism. Ruled successively by Spain, Germany, and Japan, after World War II they became a U.S.-administered UN Trusteeship and in 1986 a U.S. Commonwealth. Spanish traditions remain strong. Religion is predominantly Roman Catholic. Major industries are tourism and garments. Main agricultural products are coconuts, fruits, vegetables, and cattle.

Midway Islands   (T) is a circular atoll of two islands northwest of Hawaii, with only 2 square miles in area and no indigenous inhabitants. The area was first explored by a U.S. captain in 1859, declared a U.S. possession in 1867, and made a U.S. naval reservation in 1903. The U.S. Navy named it "Midway" because it is between California and Japan. The Battle of Midway, in 1942, was a major battle in World War II. The Midway stop for commercial air traffic was eliminated in 1950; the airbase closed in 1992.

Wake Island   (T), about halfway between Midway and Guam, is an atoll of three islets, total area about 2.5 square miles, with no inhabitants. The British discovered it in 1796. The United States annexed it in 1899 and began commercial use in 1938. The Japanese occupied it from 1941 to 1945. Economic activity consists of providing services to U.S. military personnel and contractors on the island. All food and manufactured goods are imported.

Johnston Atoll   (T), a coral atoll southwest of Hawaii, consists of four small islands. An English navigator discovered it in 1807. Hawaii claimed it in 1858. Later it became a U.S. possession. It has no indigenous inhabitants and 396 U.S. military and civilian personnel; the military is gradually departing. Used to conduct nuclear missile launching and to dispose of plutonium-contaminated waste, the atoll will become a wildlife refuge.

Baker, Howland, and Jarvis Islands   (T). The United States claimed these Pacific islands under the Guano Act of 1856. Guano is composed of phosphates and was used as fertilizer in the 19th century.

Kingman Reef   (T), about 1,000 miles south of Hawaii and a U.S. possession since 1922, is a Naval Defensive Sea Area and Airspace Reservation and closed to the public.

Navassa Island   (T) is in the Caribbean Sea, between Cuba, Haiti, and Jamaica, with an area of about 2 square miles. Claimed by the United States in 1857 under the Guano Act, the island was mined for phosphates until 1900.

Palmyra Atoll   (T), in the North Pacific Ocean, southwest of Honolulu, is privately owned. Its area is 4.6 square miles (11.9 sq. km). It was a U.S. military base in World War II.

UNITED STATES

Influences on food   A variety of climates and ethnic groups in the United States make for diverse food customs. Groups influencing the cuisine include the indigenous North American Indians, English in the east and south, Spanish and French in the south, black slaves from Africa in the south, Spanish, Mexican, and cowboys in the southwest and west, Germans in Pennsylvania and the midwest, Scandinavians in the midwest, and Italians and the Jewish community in New York City. Cuisines of some groups are described here. (Hawaii and Puerto Rico are discussed after the food groups for the United States). The United States has influenced cuisine worldwide with many uses of New World foods (e.g., turkey, corn, potato, and tomato), raising cattle on a large scale and having a pattern of meat consumption, and adapting foodways to the widespread use of automobiles by developing fast-food places with ample parking space, especially hamburger chains, such as McDonald's. At the end of the 20th century McDonald's, Coca-Cola, Pepsi-Cola, and others had spread American food around the world. Advertising (e.g., on television) influences food practices. Many Americans like novelty and try new foods.

Indian food   Main foods include corn, chili peppers, squash, beans, camas, game (e.g., buffalo, venison), wild rice, pemmican, and succotash. Camas, edible bulbs of a plant in the Pacific Northwest, were boiled or baked and the meal formed into cakes for storage food. Wild rice, grown mostly in Minnesota where it was gathered by Indians in canoes, is used like regular rice, but it is brown because the seed coat is not removed and it has a stronger flavor. Pemmican is dried strips of meat, pounded and mixed with melted fat and berries, packed in skins and dried. Succotash is a dish of simmered corn kernels and lima beans seasoned with butter or salt pork.

African, or soul, food   The term *soul food,* introduced in the 1960s, expressed the idea that the soul of African Americans would be fortified by consuming foods from their culture such as corn grits, cornbread, black-eyed peas, greens, chitterlings, and ham hocks. These foods are popular in the south.

Cowboy food   Cowboys often ate food prepared from a chuck wagon by a cook: meat stew (e.g., son-of-a-gun stew: newly killed calf heart, liver, tongue, tenderloin pieces), sourdough bread, biscuits, beans, and coffee.

Creole food   Creole food, eaten by the descendants of parents from very different culinary traditions, includes food with African, American Indian, and English influences in the south (e.g., sweet potatoes, corn, wheat); and food with American, Japanese, Chinese, and Hawaiian influences in Hawaii (meat, fish, rice, poi).

Cajun food   Acadians ("Cajuns") descended from French settlers of 17th-century Nova Scotia, named Acadia. Some went to the French colony of Louisiana. The dominant influence is African (okra, field peas, peanuts, rice), due to the close proximity of Creoles of African descent. Cajun foods include rice, Tabasco (hot red pepper sauce), crawfish (crayfish), boudin (pork sausage), and gumbo (spicy soupy stew made of flour and fat cooked to make a brown roux, okra or filé powder from dried sassafras leaves, and pieces of sausage, shrimp, chicken, game, crab claws, or shucked oysters).

Pennsylvania Dutch "Dutch" refers to a corruption of Deutsch, meaning German. The cuisine centered in Pennsylvania and spread widely. A main characteristic is combining sweet and salty tastes by cooking fruit with meat, such as schnitz un grepp (stew of ham, dumplings, and dried apples). Foods include sausages, scrapple (loaf of pork, cornmeal, and other ingredients; chilled, sliced, and fried), one-pot dishes such as chicken pot pie, pickles, and baked goods especially shoofly pie (one-crust pie with a spice crumb and molasses filling).

Bread and cereals Wheat, corn, rice, barley, oats; breads (white yeast loaf, whole wheat yeast loaf, rolls (dinner, hamburger, hot dog), prepared cereals (e.g., corn flakes), cooked cereals (e.g., oatmeal), rice dishes.

Meat, poultry, fish Beef, pork, lamb, chicken, goat, fish, seafood (mullet, shrimp), eggs; ham, bacon, sausage.

Dairy products Milk (cow, goat) (whole, reduced fat, low fat, skim), buttermilk, nonfat dry milk, cream, sour cream, cheese (American, cheddar, many kinds), cottage cheese, cream cheese, fruit-flavored yogurt.

Fats and oils Butter, margarine, vegetable oil, vegetable shortening, lard, salad dressings, olive oil.

Legumes Soybeans, beans (kidney, pinto, white navy), peanuts, black-eyed peas; soybean products.

Vegetables Potatoes, tomatoes, lettuce, onions, mushrooms, peppers, carrots, broccoli, cucumbers, cabbage, sweet potatoes, avocados, celery, peas, green beans, corn, spinach.

Fruit Bananas, apples, lemons, strawberries, cherries, peaches, watermelon, oranges, blueberries, grapefruit, pears, grapes, cantaloupe, pineapple, limes, plums, pumpkin, raisins; jelly, jam, preserves.

Nuts and seeds Almonds, pistachios, walnuts, pecans, sunflower seeds, poppy seeds.

Seasonings Salt, black pepper, cinnamon, nutmeg, cloves, chili, onions, garlic, tomatoes, vanilla, chocolate.

Condiments Salsa (tomato sauce with chili), ketchup, mustard, mayonnaise, pickle relish, steak sauce.

Cookware Iron deficiency is widespread throughout the U.S. and world (Scrimshaw, 1991) and is due mostly to inadequate intake of iron and poor availability of iron in food (Cook, 1977). Iron utensils are used to cook food by many people (Brittin and Nossaman, 1986b). Cooking food in iron utensils increases its iron content (Brittin and Nossaman, 1986a). Iron added to food by cooking in iron utensils is bioavailable (Mistry, Brittin, and Stoecker, 1988). Used iron cookware increases iron in food as much as new iron cookware does (Cheng and Brittin, 1991). Stainless steel cookware is also frequently used. Cooking food in stainless steel utensils increases its iron content (Park and Brittin, 1997). Cooking food in iron utensils does not affect sensory quality or consumer acceptance of hamburger patties but adversely affects color and flavor, and decreases consumer acceptance of applesauce (Park and Brittin, 2000).

Dishes Hamburger. Hot dog. Sandwiches. French fries. Baked potato. Green salad. Broiled steak. Roast beef. Fried chicken. Fried fish. Roasted turkey and dressing. Spaghetti with tomato ground beef sauce. Pizza.

Regional dishes New England: Indian pudding (cornmeal, molasses, spices), clam chowder (clams, milk, potatoes, corn, onions, bacon), lobster. Mid Atlantic: shoofly pie. South: hushpuppies (fried cornmeal batter), simmered black-eyed peas or greens, baked sweet potato. Midwest: potato salad, strawberry shortcake. Southwest: chili con carne (boiled pinto beans, beef, and chili). West: sourdough bread, apple torte. Alaska: king crab sauté, baked Alaska (ice cream on cake and all covered with meringue). Hawaii: pineapple chicken on rice.

Sweets Sugar, honey. Apple pie. Vanilla ice cream. Cake (chocolate, yellow, or white). Cheesecake. Cookies.

Beverages Milk, coffee, tea (iced, hot), soft drinks, orange juice, beer, wine, whiskey.

Meals Usual is three meals a day with the evening meal the largest and snacks (Weaver and Brittin, 2001).

HAWAII (U.S. STATE)

Influences on food   Hawaii, a group of islands, is in the Polynesia group of the Pacific Islands. Annexed by the United States in 1898, it was a U.S. territory from 1900 to 1959 and has been a state since 1959. Influences on food include the Polynesians, Britain, the United States, Chinese, Japanese, Koreans, Filipinos, Asian Indians, and Portuguese. About 30,000 to 40,000 years ago people from Southeast Asia began to move south to the western Pacific islands and Australia, and thereafter migrated to islands further east. The first humans arrived in the Hawaiian Islands probably from the Marquesa Islands and Tahiti in the 3rd to 5th century CE.   They brought edible plants, notably taro and sweet potato, pigs, and dogs. The main food was poi, usually made with taro, baked in an earth oven (imu) or boiled, pounded, and mixed with water to make a paste. Fish, the main protein source, were cultivated in ponds and were eaten raw or cooked. Pigs and dogs were eaten, mostly by the nobility. Salt, seaweed, and nuts of the kukui (candlenut) tree added flavor to the diet. Soon after Captain James Cook sighted the islands in 1778, they became part of world trade. Europeans and Americans, including missionaries, came and brought cows, goats, and plants. From the 1880s, sugarcane and pineapple plantations flourished and brought laborers including Chinese, Japanese, Koreans, Filipinos, and Asian Indians, who brought their food customs with them. By the early 20th century rice was a major crop. During the 20th century U.S. influence increased in Hawaii, a U.S. territory and then a state. Hawaiian fare today includes traditional native dishes, U.S. foods including beef and dairy products, and popular foods introduced by traders and immigrants. Examples include rice brought by Chinese and now the diet staple; Japanese teriyaki-grilled meat, sashimi (raw, thinly sliced fish), and noodles; Portuguese sweet bread and donuts, sausage, bean soup; Korean kimchi (hot cabbage relish) and spicy beef dishes; Filipino lumpia (egg roll); and Indian curries.

Luau   Hawaiian feast, traditionally a religious ceremony but now an informal feast, features a whole pig and other foods cooked in a pit (imu). The foods include poi, luau (taro leaf–wrapped packets of chopped taro leaves, chicken or fish, and coconut milk), laulau (ti leaf–wrapped packet of stir-fried pork, chicken, and chopped taro leaves), and perhaps fish, shellfish, chicken, and sweet potatoes. A fire is built on stones lining the pit, banana leaves or palm fronds are laid on the hot stones and coals, pig and other foods are added and covered with more leaves, the pit is sealed with dirt, and the food cooks for hours. A luau is often held on the beach at sunset. Luau means several things: taro leaf, a dish cooked in taro leaves, and the feast at which it is eaten. Although old taboos barred women from touching food for a luau, now women can eat the food but a luau remains man's work.

Bread and cereals   Rice, wheat; rice dishes, bread including Hawaiian bread (Portuguese sweet bread), fried donuts without a hole (Portuguese malasadas), noodles, hardtack (crackers).

Meat, poultry, fish   Pork, chicken, beef, fish (mullet, mahimahi, salmon), seafood (many kinds), eggs; Pipikaula (jerked beef), sausage, corned beef, spam.

Dairy products   Milk, cream, cheese. Traditionally milk and other dairy products were uncommon.

Fats and oils   Coconut oil and cream, lard, butter, margarine, vegetable oil and shortening, sesame oil.

Legumes   Soybeans, winged beans, black beans, peas, lentils, peanuts; soy milk, tofu.

Vegetables   Taro, sweet potatoes, plantains, yams, breadfruit, cassava, green leaves, seaweed, arrowroot, bitter melon, cabbage, daikon, eggplant, lotus root, onions, green onions, bok choy, water chestnuts.

Fruit   Coconut, pineapple, bananas, lemons, limes, guavas, mangoes, papaya, melons, mountain apples.

Nuts and seeds   Macadamia nuts, candlenuts (kukui), litchis.

Seasonings   Coconut cream and milk, lime or lemon juice, soy sauce, salt, ginger, onions, garlic, curry powder.

Dishes Poi (cooked, pounded taro root; is purple). Poi stews. Taro cakes. Steamed rice. Local fish dish, poke (raw fish chunks dressed with salt and seaweed). Meat, fish, or fowl, usually grilled or pan fried with teriyaki (glaze of soy sauce, sake, and mirin sweetener) used near end of cooking. Green papaya chowder. Chicken with taro leaves and coconut milk. Coconut chips (coconut sliced paper thin, salted, and baked). Steamed, boiled, or stir-fried greens. Sweet and sour pork. Mild smooth curries made with coconut cream or milk. Pineapple pickles.

Specialties Lomi-lomi (salmon, tomatoes, and onions marinated with lime juice). Steamed laulau (see earlier).

Sweets Sugarcane, sugar. Immature coconut. Haupia (coconut pudding). Macadamia chiffon pie.

Beverages Coconut juice, coffee, fruit juice, tea, fruit (pineapple, coconut, lime) and rum drinks such as mai tai.

Meals Lunch: poi and laulau; plate lunch (a scoop of rice, large serving of meat, and macaroni salad or potato salad), available at most restaurants; or saimin (ramen noodles topped with pork), a popular quick lunch or snack.

Snacks Pupu (bite-size appetizers): cherry tomatoes stuffed with marinated salmon; rumaki (water chestnuts-chicken liver-bacon skewers); Chinese chicken wings, spareribs, wontons, or dumplings; roast pork; poi; coconut chips; Portuguese sausage; Korean meatballs; curried fritters; small skewers of fish, chicken, or meat.

PUERTO RICO (U.S. AREA)

Influences on food The Arawak Indians lived here when the Spanish came. They ate a wide variety of fish and seafood. Spanish control for four centuries left a strong influence including rice, pigs, cattle, citrus, and olives. Other influences include slaves brought from Africa, and the United States after Puerto Rico was ceded to it.

Bread and cereals Rice, corn, wheat; cornbread, wheat flour bread and rolls, fried breads, cassava bread.

Meat, poultry, fish Chicken, pork, beef, goat, fish and seafood (dried salt cod, lobster, shrimp, land crabs, mangrove oysters), eggs; ham, sausage.

Dairy products Cow's milk (fresh, condensed, evaporated), aged cheeses.

Fats and oils Lard, salt pork, olive oil, butter, vegetable oil, coconut oil and cream.

Legumes Kidney beans, chickpeas (garbanzo beans), pigeon peas.

Vegetables Plantains, potatoes, cassava, breadfruit, yams, malanga, sweet potatoes, avocados, tomatoes, okra, onions, green peas, sweet green peppers.

Fruit Pineapple, bananas, coconut, mangoes, papaya, guavas, oranges, limes.

Nuts and seeds Almonds, cashew nuts, annatto seeds.

Seasonings Salt, black pepper, tomatoes, onions, hot chili peppers, garlic, pimento (allspice), annatto, rum.

Dishes Rice and kidney beans. Legumes simmered, flavored with lard and salt, and sometimes with onions, sweet peppers, and tomatoes added. chili sauce. Alcaparrado (pickle mix of capers, olives, and pimento). Recaito (cilantro, onions, garlic, and bell pepper). Sofrito (the previous two dishes combined with tomatoes and fried in lard colored with annatto seeds to form a thick paste), the foundation of many dishes. Adobo (lemon, garlic, salt, pepper, and other spices), seasons some foods. Surrulitos (deep-fried cornmeal and cheese sticks). Mofongo con chicharron (plantain with cracklings). Bacalaitos (dried salt cod fritters). Serenata (cod with potatoes). Arroz con pollo asapao (chicken and rice stew with onions, green peppers, ham, tomatoes, green peas, cheese, olives, capers, and pimento). Achichuelas guisada (marinated beans or peas). Fried plantains.

Sancocho (beef and vegetable stew). Baby goat fricassee. Meat or fish marinated in lime juice and grilled.

A Christmas specialty   Pasteles (a mixture of meat, raisins, olives, capers, and almonds placed on a plantain leaf spread with cornmeal or mashed plantains, the leaf folded to make a packet, and the packet steamed).

Sweets   Sugarcane, sugar, molasses. Fresh fruit. Flan (custard).

Beverages   Coffee with milk (café con leche), milk, soft drinks, beer, rum.

Meals   Breakfast: bread and coffee. Lunch: rice and beans or a starchy vegetable perhaps with cod. Dinner: rice, beans, starchy vegetable, a meat, chicken, or fish dish if available, or soup.

Snacks   Fresh fruit, banana or cod fritters, fried meat or cheese turnovers, fried meat-filled plantain strips.

URUGUAY
Oriental Republic of Uruguay

Geography   Uruguay is in southern South America, bordering the Atlantic Ocean, Argentina, and Brazil. It has grassy plains in the south and plateaus and hills in the north. It is well watered by rivers. The climate is temperate.

Major Languages	Ethnic Groups		Major Religions	
Spanish (official)	White	88%	Roman Catholic	66%
Portunol	Mestizo	8%	Protestant	11%
Brazilero (Portuguese-Spanish)	Black	4%	None or other	23%

Population density per sq. mi. 51.9
Literacy rate 98%
Life expectancy 72.9 male; 79.5 female
Per capita GDP $11,600
Labor force in agriculture 9%

Urban 92%
Infant mortality rate per 1,000 live births 11.7
HIV rate 0.6%
Unemployment rate 10.1%
Arable land 8%

Agriculture   rice, soybeans, wheat, corn, barley, chickens, cattle, sheep, pigs, goats

Natural resources   hydropower, minor minerals, fish

Industries   food processing, electrical machinery, transportation equipment, oil products, textiles

History   Indigenous Charrua Indians inhabited the area when the Spanish came in 1516. In 1624 Spanish settlers began to replace the Charrua Indians. Portuguese from Brazil began to settle here at about the same time. Spain owned Uruguay from 1778 until it gained independence in 1811. The Portuguese took it in 1821 and incorporated it with Brazil. Uruguay revolted in 1825 and was recognized as an independent country in 1828. Prosperous from meat and wool exports, Uruguay adopted social measures in the early 1900s. During the last half of the 20th century, political and military strife, inflation, rise in national debt, and recession occurred. The state maintains a dominant role in industries such as the power, telephone, railroad, cement, and oil refining. The 1990s brought a general economic upturn. Some privatization began in the early 2000s. In 2003 the economy began improving. The standard of living is one of the highest in South America, and political and labor conditions among the freest. In 2007 steady economic growth continued. A dispute over two pulp paper plants on the Uruguay side of the Uruguay River had not been resolved by mid-2008.

Influences on food   Influences on Uruguay's cuisine include the native Indians, Spain, Portugal, Italy, and its large neighbor Argentina, with whom it shares food customs. Before the Spanish arrived in the 16th century, the only inhabitants were a few nomadic Indians. The Spaniards introduced cattle and brought settlers. By the mid-19th century Indians had almost disappeared. Uruguay has part of the Pampas, grassland on fertile soil with almost ideal rainfall and temperate climate. Some food traditions come from the gauchos, the nomadic part-Indian herdsmen who roamed the Pampas, living on half-wild cattle. They ate meat, roasted or boiled, with some pieces of pumpkin. Meat was often cooked and eaten immediately after killing an animal. The general diet was mutton and biscuits, with potatoes, pumpkin, corn, and vegetables where there was a garden. In a ranch house kitchen meat was boiled in a large iron pot hung from rafters over the fire or roasted on a long spit. Diners carved meat from the roast with their knives. Now Uruguay has pastoral agriculture on the Pampas with sheep in the south and west and cattle everywhere else. Most people are of European ancestry, mostly Spanish and Italian. The Italians brought foods such as pasta and pizza. Many dishes show European influence, especially evident in the capital, Montevideo. Indian influences include the wide use of squash, pumpkin, and corn, all ancient Indian crops. Uruguay has hearty fare with emphasis on beef. Meat-processing factories along the River Uruguay supply much of the world's corned beef. Uruguay is located between the rivers Plate and Uruguay and on the Atlantic Ocean, which provide fish and large frogs, a favorite food.

Bread and cereals   Rice, wheat, corn, barley; rice dishes, wheat bread, biscuits, and pasta, cornbread.

Meat, poultry, fish   Beef, mutton and lamb, chicken, pork, goat, fish, shellfish, frogs, eggs.

Dairy products   Milk (cow, sheep), evaporated milk, cheese.

Fats and oils   Butter, olive oil, dendé (palm) oil.

Legumes   Beans (black, kidney), soybeans, black-eyed peas, peanuts.

Vegetables   Pumpkin, corn, squash, potatoes, sweet potatoes, tomatoes, plantains, carrots, avocados, cassava, green peppers, onions, okra, spinach.

Fruit   Apples, bananas, coconut, grapes, lemons, limes, oranges, melon, raisins, strawberries.

Nuts and seeds   Brazil nuts, cashews, pumpkin seeds.

Seasonings   Onions, green peppers, tomatoes, salt, sugar, red pepper, cinnamon.

Dishes   Grilled or broiled steaks. Roasted or boiled beef. Soups such as one made using whole body of frogs. Stews including carbonada criolla (beef stew baked in a squash). Humitas (unripe corn kernels cooked with seasonings). Matambre (a marinated flank steak spread with spinach, hard-boiled egg halves, whole carrots, and onion slices, rolled and tied with string or cheesecloth, and poached). Pasta dishes. Pizza.

Sweets   Sugar, brown sugar, honey.

Beverages   Coffee, yerba maté, fruit juices, beer, brandy, distilled corn liquor, wine. Yerba maté, made from dried leaves of a shrub from the holly family, contains caffeine and is drunk hot or cold.

UZBEKISTAN
Republic of Uzbekistan

Geography   Uzbekistan is in Central Asia. Two thirds of the land is desert or semi desert, with the rest mostly plains. The republic also includes the Karakalpakstan Autonomous Republic

Major Languages		Ethnic Groups		Major Religions	
Uzbek (official)	Uzbek	80%	Karakalpak	2%	Muslim (mostly Sunni)	88%
Russian	Russian	6%	Tatar	3%	Eastern Orthodox	9%
Tajik	Tajik	5%	Other	1%	Other	3%
	Kazakh	4%				

Population density per sq. mi. 166.5
Literacy rate 96.9%
Life expectancy 68.7 male; 74.9 female
Per capita GDP $2,300
Labor force in agriculture 44%

Urban 36.7%
Infant mortality rate per 1,000 live births 24.2
HIV rate 0.1%
Unemployment rate 0.2%
Arable land 11%

Agriculture wheat, cotton, tomatoes, vegetables, fruits, grain, chickens, sheep, cattle, goats, camels, pigs

Natural resources natural gas, oil, coal, gold, uranium, silver, copper, lead, zinc, tungsten, molybdenum, fish

Industries textiles, food processing, machine building, metallurgy, gold, natural gas, chemicals, gold

History Once part of the ancient Persian Empire, this land was conquered by Alexander the Great in the 4th century BCE. In the 8th century Arab invaders converted the nomadic Turkic tribes living here to Islam. In 1220 the Mongols under Genghis Khan overran the area. Genghis Khan's grandson Shibaqan received the Uzbekistan territory as his inheritance in the 13th century. His Mongols ruled the Turkic tribes, who eventually intermarried with the Mongols to form the Uzbeks and other Turkic peoples of Central Asia. In the 14th century Uzbekistan became the center of the native Timurid Empire. Later, Muslim feudal states comprised the area. Russia conquered the area in the mid-19th century. Uzbekistan became independent in 1924 and a Soviet Socialist Republic in 1925. It grew cotton, causing environmental damage. Uzbekistan regained independence when the Soviet Union disbanded in 1991. Since then a former communist has led the authoritarian government. During the 1990s the economy was considered the strongest in Central Asia. In 2004 Islamic militants killed 50 people and damaged the U.S. and Israeli embassies. In 2004 a Russian oil producer signed a $1 billion agreement to develop Uzbekistan's natural gas fields. In 2005 armed conflict between rebels and security forces killed more than 1,000 people. In 2005 the president of Uzbekistan and Russia signed a military cooperation agreement and the United States was ordered to vacate the airbase used to support operations in Afghanistan. In 2007 the GDP rose, agricultural and industrial output increased, and unemployment dropped. The authorities liquidated a gold-extraction venture with the United States and gave the assets to a local firm.

Influences on food Uzbekistan, in Central Asia, was part of the old Silk Road, the ancient caravan route between China and the Caspian Sea. Uzbeks were originally nomadic shepherds, who raised animals and lived on milk and milk products supplemented by meat, and oasis dwellers, who lived along rivers and grew grain, vegetables, and fruit. Influences on food include the mostly desert land, ancient Persia, Arabs, Islam, Mongols, China, and Russia. Examples include noodles from China and Russian samovars. Uzbekistan shares a common cuisine with neighbors Tajikistan and Turkmenistan: flatbread, lamb, thick soups, semi-liquid main dishes, and tea.

Bread and cereals Wheat, barley, millet, rice; flatbread, noodles, rice dishes (palov). Uzbeks are known for flatbread (non) such as onion flatbread (made by adding chopped onions browned in butter to unleavened flour dough, forming small balls of dough, flattening them, and cooking them on a heated griddle or in a heavy pan).

Meat, poultry, fish Chicken, lamb and mutton, beef, camel, goat, pork, horsemeat, game birds, eggs; smoked horsemeat sausage (kazy), smoked lamb sausage (damlama khasip). Uzbeks eat almost no fish and few eggs.

Dairy products Milk (cow, sheep, goat, mare, camel), cream, sour milk, clabber (kumys), yogurt, cheese (kurt, a hard cheese, sun dried; airan, a sharp cheese made from camel, sheep, or goat milk). Bowls of sour milk are offered to visitors to show hospitality.

Fats and oils Fat of fat-tailed sheep (when rendered it retains tiny cracklings), butter, vegetable oil.

Legumes   Chickpeas, beans, lentils.

Vegetables   Tomatoes, onions, carrots, pumpkin, greens, red peppers, cucumbers, turnips, radishes.

Fruit   Melons, grapes, pomegranates, pears, plums, apples, white mulberries, jujubes (a type of date), apricots, cherries, rhubarb, figs, barberries, quinces.

Nuts and seeds   Walnuts, hazelnuts, pistachios, caraway seeds.

Seasonings   Onions, garlic, vinegar, salt, black pepper, dried red peppers, coriander, dill, mint, aniseed.

Dishes   Thick meat soups. Noodle dishes: kaurma lagman (fried noodles and meat); manpar (slices of dough in stew or soup); shima (fine noodles) in soup. Shashlyk (lamb shish kabobs), lamb pieces seasoned, marinated, and roasted on skewers over charcoal. Kabobs of fat-tailed sheep or game birds. Samsas (meat pies). Uzbek palov (lamb cubes browned in oil, strips of carrots and onions added and heated in the oil, rice added and stirred to coat with oil and heated, water added and the pot covered, and simmered).

A national dish   Uzbek Manty (steamed dumplings filled with peppery ground lamb), often served with yogurt.

Sweets   Honey, sugar. Fruit, fresh, dried, preserves. Rhubarb jelly and compote. Rokhati dzhou (apricot syrup on shaved ice). Candies: yanchmish (balls of roasted ground walnuts), bukman (made of thick, concentrated sweetened cream and browned flour), khalva (made of grain, honey or syrup, and nuts).

Beverages   Tea (hot, green, sometimes with milk and salt), sour milk, shinni (fruit syrup drink), wine. Tea is drunk at meals and throughout the day, in teahouses (roofed pavilions) by men and at home by women. Tea is served in a samovar and drunk from porcelain bowls. Offered with tea may be little savory pastries, fruit, or candy.

Meals and service   Breakfast: clabber or cheese, flatbread, and tea. Lunch: thick hearty soup or cheese, greens, and fruit, flatbread, and tea. Evening meal: a meat dish or palov, fruit or a sweet, flatbread, and tea. To dine, people sit on rugs or chairs. Flatbread may be used as edible scoops and plates, and food may be scooped from the pot with the right hand, although forks and plates are usually used.

Street food   Shashlyk (sticks of grilled lamb) cooked on portable grills by vendors on city streets.

V

VANUATU
Republic of Vanuatu

Geography   Vanuatu is an archipelago of 83 islands in the western South Pacific Ocean, part of the Melanesia group of islands, east of Australia. It has dense forest and narrow coastal strips of cultivated land. It is in the "Ring of Fire," an area with frequent earthquakes and volcanic eruptions.

Major Languages	Ethnic Groups		Major Religions	
Bislama (pidgin) (all	Ni-Vanuatu (Melanesian)	99%	Presbyterian	31%
English are	Other	1%	Anglican	13%
French official)			Roman Catholic	13%
Local languages (100+)			Other Christian	14%
			Seventh-Day Adventist	11%
			Indigenous beliefs, other	18%

Population density per sq. mi. 45.7
Literacy rate 78.1%
Life expectancy 62 male; 65.3 female
Per capita GDP $3,900
Labor force in agriculture 65%

Urban 23.5%
Infant mortality rate per 1,000 live births 50.8
HIV rate NA
Unemployment rate 1.7%
Arable land 2%

Agriculture   coconuts, copra, bananas, cocoa, coffee, taro, yams, fruits, kava, chickens, cattle, pigs, goats

Natural resources   manganese, hardwood forests, fish

Industries   food and fish freezing, wood processing, meat canning

History   About 30,000 to 40,000 years ago people from Southeast Asia began to move south to the western Pacific islands and Australia, and they later migrated to islands further east. The first settlers in the islands of Vanuatu are believed to have arrived by canoe from New Guinea and the Solomon Islands about 3,500 years ago. Magellan was the first European to see these islands when he sailed around the southern tip of South America in 1519 and across the Pacific Ocean. French navigator Louis Antoine de Bougainville rediscovered the islands in 1768. British navigator James Cook charted the islands in 1774 and named them New Hebrides. Sandalwood merchants and European missionaries arrived in the mid-19th century. British and French cotton planters followed. Britain and France claimed the islands and in 1906 agreed to joint administration. The island plantation economy, based on imported Vietnamese labor, prospered until the 1920s. Diseases brought by traders, missionaries, and others helped reduce the population from 1 million in 1800 to 45,000 in 1935. The islands were a major Allied naval base in World War II. The New Hebrides became the independent Republic of Vanuatu in 1980. A hurricane in 1987 destroyed much of Vanuatu's housing. In 2007 political stability and a steady rate of economic growth continued. The government successfully used coconut oil-based biofuel for power generation. Tourism was growing rapidly as a result of investment in hotels and increased airline services from major markets.

Influences on food   Europeans brought new food plants, wheat bread, and some animals to the area. Asians brought rice, soybeans, noodles, and stir-frying. British and French administration and labor imported from Vietnam left influences on food. The islanders have great fishing prowess. Seafood and starchy vegetables, especially roots and tubers including taro and yams, are mainstays of the traditional diet. Fruits and nuts, especially coconut, are also important. Pork is a main meat, especially for festive occasions, traditionally cooked in a stone-lined pit. A fire is built in the pit, and when coals are hot, layers of banana leaves or palm fronds are added, a pig and various foods are added and covered with more leaves, the pit is sealed with dirt, and the food cooks for hours. A feast may be held on the beach at sunset after day-long preparations. Mats and banana and ti leaves are laid to form a table surface, on which are placed wood platters, woven baskets, and coconut shell bowls to hold the foods cooked in the pit.

Bread and cereals   Rice, wheat; rice dishes, bread, noodles.

Meat, poultry, fish   Chicken, beef, pork, goat, fish and shellfish (e.g., mullet, crabs), eggs; corned beef, spam.

Dairy products   Milk and other dairy products are uncommon.

Fats and oils   Coconut oil and cream, lard, vegetable oil, shortening, sesame oil.

Legumes   Soybeans, winged beans, pigeon peas, lentils, peanuts.

Vegetables   Taro root and leaves, yams, sweet potatoes, plantains, breadfruit, cassava, seaweed, green leaves, arrowroot, bitter melon, cabbage, daikon, eggplant, onions, green onions, scallions.

Fruit   Coconut, bananas, lemons, limes, guavas, mangoes, papaya, pineapple, melons, tamarind. Coconut liquid is the usual cooking medium. Fresh fruit is eaten as snacks.

Nuts and seeds   Candlenuts (kukui), litchis, macadamia nuts.

Seasonings   Coconut cream or milk, lime or lemon juice, salt, soy sauce, onion, ginger, garlic, chilies, cocoa.

Dishes   Starchy vegetables such as taro root cooked and pounded into a paste. Boiled taro root, yams, or sweet potatoes. Steamed green leaves. Fish and shellfish stewed, steamed, roasted, or raw and marinated in lime juice and served with coconut cream. Boiled or steamed rice. Foods cooked in a pit: whole pig, taro chunks, yams, sweet potatoes, plantains, breadfruit, crabs, whole fish, chicken pieces, taro leaf wrapped around a filling of coconut cream, lemon, onions, and shredded beef and all bound in banana leaves, and other leaf-wrapped "puddings" of taro, yams, sweet potatoes, or plantains with coconut cream and seasonings.

Sweets   Sugar. Immature coconut. Haupia (firm pudding made from coconut milk with sugar and arrowroot).

Beverages   Coconut juice, cocoa, coffee, fruit juice, tea, kava (mildly alcoholic drink from root of pepper plant).

Meals   Two or three meals daily are typical, with the same foods at all, and the evening meal the largest. A traditional meal is boiled taro root, yam, breadfruit, or plantain, fish or pork, and greens or seaweed.

VATICAN CITY
State of the Vatican City (Holy See)

Geography   The Vatican City State is in southern Europe, within Rome, Italy. It is on the right bank of the Tiber River on Vatican Hill. Area is 0.17 square miles.

Major Languages	Ethnic Groups	Major Religion
Italian	Italian	Roman Catholic
Latin	Swiss	
French	Other	
Various others		

Population 824
Population density per sq. mi. 4,850.3
Labor force essentially services; nearly all dignitaries, priests, nuns, an army of
100 Swiss guards, and approximately 3,000 lay workers who live outside the Vatican
Urban 100%

Industries banking and finance, printing, tourism, production of coins, medals, and postage stamps

History Vatican City is the smallest independent state in the world. For many centuries the popes held temporal sovereignty over mid-Italy. This territory was incorporated in the new Kingdom of Italy, 1861, with sovereignty of the pope confined to the palaces of the Vatican, the Lateran in Rome, and the villa of Castel Gandolfo. The Lateran Treaty of 1929 between the Vatican and Italy established the independent state of the Vatican City. It includes the Basilica of Saint Peter, the Vatican Palace and Museum covering over 13 acres, the Vatican gardens, and certain neighboring buildings. Frescoes by Michelangelo are in the Sistine Chapel. The Vatican Library contains a priceless collection of manuscripts. The pope has full legal, executive, and judicial powers within Vatican City. The pope appoints a commission of cardinals, who have executive power and, upon the pope's death, elect his successor for life. In 2005, after the death of Pope John Paul II, German cardinal Joseph Ratzinger was elected pope, known as Pope Benedict XVI. In 2007 Vatican City received formal visits from U.S. president George W. Bush and the British prime minister. Stronger ties were pursued with Muslims, who in 2008 outnumbered Roman Catholics for the first time.

Influences on food Italy and Rome, in which Vatican City is located, influence the food in Vatican City. Also, the Roman Catholic Church influences food because the pope has full legal, executive, and judicial power in Vatican City.

Bread and cereals Wheat, corn, rice; pasta, bread, rolls, cornmeal porridge, rice dishes.

Meat, poultry, fish Pork, lamb, beef and veal, goat, fish and shellfish, chicken, eggs; ham (prosciutto), sausage. Prosciutto is raw smoked ham, often served thinly sliced with melon as an appetizer.

Dairy products Milk (cow, sheep, goat), cream, cheese (Parmesan, Bel Paese, mozzarella, ricotta, gorgonzola, pecorino). Pecorino is an old cheese of the region made from sheep's milk.

Fats and oils Olive oil, butter, lard, vegetable oil, salt pork.

Legumes Chickpeas, fava beans, kidney beans, lentils, soybeans, white beans.

Vegetables Potatoes, olives, spinach, tomatoes, broccoli, peppers, lettuce, cabbage, celery, eggplant, peas, artichokes, onions, mushrooms, truffles.

Fruit Grapes, pears, peaches, lemons, oranges, melon, raisins, currants, apricots, cherries, figs.

Nuts and seeds Almonds, chestnuts, hazelnuts, pine nuts, pistachios, walnuts, lupine seeds, poppy seeds.

Seasonings Salt, olive oil, tomato, onion, garlic, basil, oregano, parsley, black pepper, mint, rosemary, saffron, sage, lemon, vinegar, vanilla, chocolate.

Dishes Minestrone (vegetable soup). Polenta (cornmeal porridge), often served with cheese or sauce. Risotto (rice cooked in butter and chicken stock with saffron and Parmesan cheese). Fettuccine Alfredo (boiled long, flat egg noodles mixed with butter, cream, and cheese). Gnocchi (semolina dumplings baked with butter and cheese). Saltimbocca (thin slices of ham laid on veal slices, seasoned with sage, sautéed in butter, and braised in white wine). Cannelloni (pasta rolled around filling of seasoned meat and spinach and baked in tomato and cream sauces with Parmesan cheese). Pollo alla cacciatore (chicken braised in wine with vinegar, garlic, and rosemary). Veal parmigana (veal cutlet, breaded and fried, then simmered in tomato sauce with seasonings, and sprinkled with Parmesan cheese), often served on pasta. Snails simmered with garlic, anchovy, tomato, mint, and pepper. Filetti di baccalà (thin strips of salted cod dipped in batter and fried in olive oil). Boiled spaghetti with seasoned tomato sauce and cheese. Pizza (baked yeast dough crust topped with tomato sauce and cheese). Pesto (a paste of basil, garlic, nuts, and cheese). Fried artichokes. Broccoli alla romana (broccoli simmered in white wine and olive oil, with garlic).Braised peas with prosciutto (ham). Green salad with olive oil and vinegar.

Festive favorites   Porchetta (suckling pig stuffed with herbs and roasted whole). Roasted lamb with rosemary.

Christmas Day dish   Roasted capon stuffed with bread crumbs, seasoning, giblets, sausage, and grated cheese.

Sweets   Honey, sugar. Fruit and cheese. Ices, sherbets, ice creams. Zabalone (wine custard). Bigné (small deep-fried pastry puffs). Amaretti (almond macaroons). Cheesecake. Maritozzi (buns with nuts and candied and dried fruit), for Lent. Pizza Pasquale (little Easter cake made with eggs, ricotta cheese, and honey). Chocolates.

Beverages   Wine, coffee, espresso, cappuccino, tea, Sambucca (anise-flavored liqueur).

VENEZUELA
Bolivarian Republic of Venezuela

Geography   Venezuela is in northern South America, bordering the Caribbean Sean and the Atlantic Ocean. It has coastal plains along the Caribbean Sea, Andes Mountains in the north and northwest, the Orinoco Delta plains and forests, and the Guiana Highlands and plains south of the Orinoco River, comprising nearly half of the land. The 1,600-milelong Orinoco River drains 80% of the land. The climate is tropical but cooler in the Andes.

Major Languages				Ethnic Groups		Major Religions	
Spanish	(all	Mestizo	64%	Other white	3%	Roman Catholic	96%
31 indigenous Indian	are	Local white	20%	Amerindian	1%	Protestant, other,	
languages	official)	Local black	10%	Other	2%	none	4%

Population density per sq. mi. 77.6
Literacy rate 93%
Life expectancy 70.4 male; 76.7 female
Per capita GDP $12,200
Labor force in agriculture 13%

Urban 92.3%
Infant mortality rate per 1,000 live births 22
HIV rate NA
Unemployment rate 9.4%
Arable land 3%

Agriculture   sugarcane, corn, rice, sorghum, bananas, vegetables, coffee, chickens, cattle, pigs, goats, sheep

Natural resources   oil, natural gas, iron ore, gold, bauxite, other minerals, hydropower, diamonds, fish

Industries   oil, construction materials, food processing, textiles, iron ore mining, steel, aluminum, auto assembly

History   Arawak, Carib, and Chibcha Indians lived here when Columbus sighted the area in 1498. In 1499 Spanish explorer Alonso de Ojeda arrived at Lake Maracaibo and called the land Venezuela, meaning Little Venice, because the natives had houses on stilts. A Spanish missionary established the first European settlement about 1520. Spain dominated the land until it won independence with Simón Bolivar's victory in 1821. The republic was formed in 1830. Military dictators ruled from 1830 to 1958. Since 1959, Venezuela has had democratically elected governments and has been one of the most stable democracies in Latin America. In 1935 it became a major oil exporter. A founding member of OPEC, it became relatively prosperous from oil production in the 1970s. Depressed oil revenues in the 1980s and 1990s resulted in a severe economic crisis. Floods and mudslides in 1999 killed 30,000 people. Hugo Chávez, president since 1998, brought about a new constitution in 1999. He was reelected in 2002, and great political and economic tumult followed. In 2007 President

Chávez took steps to sever ties with the International Monetary Fund and the World Bank, and he modified the contracts under which foreign oil companies exploited some oil projects. In 2008 he increased government control of the steel, cement, and sugar industries. In 2007 the GDP grew 23.6%, although inflation for 2007 to April 2008 reached 32.7%.

Influences on food   Venezuela was the first territory on mainland South America colonized by the Spanish. Along its tropical Caribbean coastline with rivers and islands are fish, palmetto tops (palm hearts), and fruit. Jungle people, usually Indian or African, plant yucca (sweet cassava), plantains, corn, and beans, and eat anything they catch. Venezuela also has highland culture in Andean valleys in the west and wide plains (llanos) where cattle graze. Recently oil has made Venezuela the richest and most urbanized Latin American country. Venezuela shares a common cuisine with neighbor Colombia. Influences on Venezuela's cuisine include Spanish (e.g., rice, beef, and olives), African, Caribbean, and Mexican (e.g., avocado). Main foods are corn, rice, bananas, cassava, and black beans. German immigrants in the 20th century brought beer.

Bread and cereals   Corn, rice, sorghum, wheat; corn bread (arepa), fritters, rice dishes, wheat bread, cake.

Meat, poultry, fish   Beef, pork, goat, lamb and mutton, chicken, fish and shellfish, eggs, turtle, venison, peccary (similar to wild pig), monkey, carassow (prized game bird); bacon, ham.

Insects   Ants. Fried ants are considered a delicacy.

Dairy products   Milk (cow, goat), evaporated milk, cream, cheese.

Fats and oils   Olive oil, coconut oil, palm oil, lard, butter.

Legumes   Black beans (caviar criollo), peanuts.

Vegetables   Cassava, plantains (sancocho), potatoes, tomatoes, hearts of palm, avocados, chili peppers (ajiaco), onions, white root (apio), sweet potatoes, okra, squash, pumpkin, green peppers, cabbage, carrots, olives.

Fruit   Bananas, coconut, pineapple, guava, grapes, raisins, lemons, limes, apples.

Nuts and seeds   Cashews, Brazil nuts, pumpkin seeds.

Seasonings   Annatto (achiote, flavors and colors red/gold), garlic, capers, chili, cilantro, allspice, cinnamon, cumin, aliño preparado (mixture of cumin, oregano, annatto, pepper, paprika; sold in supermarkets), citrus juice.

Dishes   Arepa (cornmeal, water, and salt dough formed in 1-inch thick patties and cooked on a lightly greased griddle), the main food. Pancakes made with fresh corn kernels. Boiled rice. Boiled black beans with cumin. Fried cassava. Plantains, boiled, grilled, fried, and used in soups and stews. Bananas cakes with cinnamon, served with meat. Beef and mutton are tenderized by simmering before roasting, cutting into small cubes, or cutting slits and filling with bacon or pork fat and whole carrots, onions, and garlic cloves and then roasting. Stew or soup of meat or fish with cassava and plantains (sancocho) or with corn, potatoes, avocado, and chilies (ajiaco). Stew of red snapper, pumpkin, root vegetables, lemons, and tomatoes. Arepa dough stuffed with seasoned meat, then simmered or deep fried (bolos). Corn dough, meat, and seasonings wrapped in banana leaves and steamed (hallacas). Grilled steaks. Shredded flank steak with tomato sauce, black beans, and plantains (pabellón caraqueño or criollo). Avocado sauce (guasacaca), mashed avocado with olive oil. Hot chili pepper sauce.

Christmas/New Year's dish   Pan de jamón (soft white bread with swirls of sliced ham, green olives, and raisins).

Sweets   Sugarcane, sugar, honey. Wine-soaked cake topped with coconut cream (bien me sabe de coco).

Beverages   Coffee, fruit juice, sugarcane juice, cachaça (brandy-like alcoholic beverage distilled from sugarcane), batidas (punch of fruit juice and cachaça), distilled corn liquor, beer, wine.

VIETNAM
Socialist Republic of Vietnam

Geography   Vietnam is in Southeast Asia on the east coast of the Indochinese Peninsula. Long and narrow, it has a 1,400-mile coast on the South China Sea, the densely settled Red River valley in the north, coastal plains in the center, the marshy Mekong River Delta in the south, and semiarid plateaus, mountains, and tropical rainforests.

Major Languages	Ethnic Groups		Major Religions	
Vietnamese (official)	Viet (Kinh)	86%	Buddhist	48%
English	Tay	2%	New-Religionist	11%
French	Thai	2%	Traditional beliefs	10%
Chinese	Muong	2%	Roman Catholic	7%
Khmer	Khmer and other	8%	None and other	24%

Population density per sq. mi. 685.5
Literacy rate 90.3%
Life expectancy 68.5 male; 74.3 female
Per capita GDP $2,600
Labor force in agriculture 55.6%

Urban 26.4%
Infant mortality rate per 1,000 live births 23.6
HIV rate 0.5%
Unemployment rate 4.8%
Arable land 20%

Agriculture   rice, sugarcane, cassava, coffee, rubber, cotton, tea, pepper, soybeans, cashews, peanuts, bananas, chickens, pigs, cattle, buffalo, ducks, goats

Natural resources   fish, phosphate, coal, manganese, bauxite, chromate, offshore oil and gas, forests, hydropower

Industries   food processing, garments, shoes, machine building, mining

History   Nomadic Mongols, Viets, from central China settled the land. A distinct group began to emerge about 200 BCE in the independent kingdom of Nam Viet, which China annexed in the 1st century BCE. It was held by China from 111 BCE to 939 CE and subsequently was a vassal state. The Vietnamese defeated Kublai Khan's armies in 1288. The Vietnamese also descended from migrants from Indonesia. The southern region was gradually overrun by Vietnamese from the north in the late 15th century. The Portuguese were the first Europeans to enter the area, in the 16th century. In the early 17th century, the country was divided into two parts: Tonkin in the north and Cochin-China in the south. The French took the country in the period from 1858 to 1884 and controlled it until World War II. The Japanese occupied Vietnam from 1940 to 1945. After World War II, the French and Vietnamese fought until French forces were defeated in 1954, and an agreement divided Vietnam at the 17th parallel into North Vietnam and South Vietnam. Communists in the North tried to take over South Vietnam, leading to the Vietnam War (1964–1973), which claimed lives of 1.3 million Vietnamese and 58,000 Americans who aided South Vietnam. The civil war resumed in 1975, North Vietnam invaded South Vietnam, and the South Vietnamese government collapsed. The country was officially reunited as the Socialist Republic of Vietnam in 1976. From the mid-1980s, the government made economic reforms and began to open up to Asian and Western nations. The United States lifted its 19-year-old trade embargo in 1994 and in 2005 was Vietnam's main export market. Floods in 1999 killed over 550 people and left over 600,000 families homeless. In 2007 Vietnam became a member of the World Trade Organization and was elected a nonpermanent member of the UN Security Council.

Influences on food   Vietnam's cuisine reflects indigenous ingredients (fish and seafood, tropical fruits and vegetables, and glutinous rice) and Chinese, French, and Indian/Malaysian influences. Chinese influence, resulting from more than a millennium of Chinese control, reflects in long grain rice, tea, stir-frying, hot pots, and chopsticks. European influence started in 1516 with the Portuguese arrival and continued with French control from 1883 until World War II. French influence shows in the use of potatoes, asparagus, green beans, French bread, cream-filled pastries, meat and fish pâtés, coffee, and sugarcane. The Vietnamese, especially in the north, retain Chinese cooking and eating methods; popular are soups, cooked vegetables, cooking meat pieces in a pot of boiling liquid at the table, and eating with chopsticks. Central Vietnam has more refined cuisine with spicier dishes from chili peppers (introduced by the Portuguese), fermented fish sauce, and game. The tropical south shows Indian/Malaysian influence as in curries and dishes with coconut milk. Southern food is more varied (more fresh fruits and vegetables and more sweets) and spicier than northern food. The leaf-wrapping custom (diners assemble their own packets of cooked meat mixture on a green leaf, add herbs, and wrap) existed before Chinese occupation and is still practiced, mainly in the south, the region least influenced by China. Vietnamese food is mainly rice, soups, vegetables, fruits, soybean products, fish, shrimp, and pork, flavored with salty fish sauce and lemon-grass. Vietnamese Buddhists eat soybean products on the 1st, 15th, and last day of the lunar month, when meat is prohibited. Vietnamese food spread to North America and Australia, where refugees from Vietnam settled after the Vietnam War.

Bread and cereals   Rice (long and short grain), corn, wheat; rice dishes, sticks, noodles, paper, and cakes, wheat noodles, pastry, and French bread. Rice is usually eaten at every meal.

Meat, poultry, fish   Chicken, pork, beef, buffalo, duck, goat, wild boar, deer, fish and seafood, eggs.

Dairy products   Sweetened condensed milk (used in coffee); whipping cream (used in pastries).

Fats and oils   Vegetable oil, salt pork, coconut oil. Fat is disliked; many foods are eaten raw or boiled, not fried.

Legumes   Soybeans, peanuts, mung beans; soy milk, tofu (bean curd), tempeh (chewier tofu).

Vegetables   Cassava, Chinese cabbage, green leaves, potatoes, lettuce, carrots, bean sprouts, onions, mushrooms, green beans, cucumbers, lotus root, radishes, asparagus, jicama, scallions, plantains; pickles.

Fruit   Bananas, coconut, jackfruit, mangoes, papaya, oranges, limes, melons, pineapple.

Nuts and seeds   Cashews, almonds, sesame seeds, lotus seeds, watermelon seeds.

Seasonings   Fermented fish sauce (nuoc mam), nuoc cham (nuoc mam plus chilies, vinegar, sugar, garlic, and citrus juice), lemon grass, ginger, mint, basil, pepper, coriander, basil, chilies, garlic, lime leaves, vinegar, citrus juice, coconut milk, curry powder. Nuoc mam tastes salty and umami (savory) and is put on many dishes.

Dishes   Steamed rice. Chao (rice gruel). Boiled cassava. Pho (beef and rice noodle soup) with fresh vegetable garnish. Mien ga (chicken noodle soup) with herb garnish. Beef broth, squid, shark fin, or crab and asparagus soup. Fried noodles topped with meat and vegetables. Leaf-wrapped mixtures of cooked meat and herbs. Banh cuon (steamed rice dumpling rolled around cooked minced meats, shrimp, mushrooms, and onions), dipped in nuoc cham. Rice cakes. Fish steamed, stewed, barbecued, or minced for fish cakes and fillings. Fried red snapper with sweet and sour sauce. Bo noung xa (pork or beef marinated in fish sauce with minced lemon grass and grilled). Stir-fried bean curd with vegetables. Boiled or fried potatoes. Raw salads such as goi go (shredded cabbage and unripe papaya topped with cooked chicken and cashews). Curries. Spicy peanut sauce. Garnishes: fresh herbs; fresh vegetables. Dips: nuoc mam; nuoc cham.

A specialty dish   Cha gio (small rolls of minced meat and vegetables wrapped in rice paper and deep fried).

Sweets   Sugarcane, sugar. Fruit. Sweet custard. Sweet rice cakes. Cream-filled pastries.

Beverages   Broth, tea (often with lotus blossoms), coffee, soy milk, fruit juice, soft drinks, beer, rice wine, whiskey.

Street food   Pho, sugarcane chunks on bamboo skewers, chao tom (grilled shrimp pâté–coated sugarcane).

WESTERN SAMOA (*SEE* SAMOA)

YEMEN
Republic of Yemen

Geography   Yemen is in the Middle East on the Arabian Peninsula, bordering the Red and Arabian seas. About 82% the size of France, it has a sandy coastal plain in the south and well-watered fertile mountains in the interior.

Major Language	Ethnic Groups		Major Religions	
Arabic (official)	Arab	93%	Islam (official)	
	Somali	4%	Sunni Muslim	58%
	Black, Indo-Pakistani, other	3%	Shi'a Muslim	42%

Population density per sq. mi. 112.9
Literacy rate 58.9%
Life expectancy 61 male; 64.9 female
Per capita GDP $2,300
Labor force in agriculture and herding 75%

Urban 28.9%
Infant mortality rate per 1,000 live births 56.3
HIV rate NA
Unemployment rate 16.2%
Arable land 3%

Agriculture   sorghum, potatoes, tomatoes, grains, fruits, kat, pulses, coffee, cotton, chickens, sheep, goats, cattle, camels

Natural resources   oil, fish, rock salt, marble, small deposits of coal, gold, lead, nickel, and copper

Industries   oil production and refining, small-scale production of cotton textiles and leather goods, food processing

History   Once part of the ancient Kingdom of Sheba, Yemen was a prosperous link in trade for gold, spices, and gemstones between Africa and India. It was invaded by the Romans in the 1st century CE and by the Ethiopians and Persians in the 6th century. It converted to Islam in the 7th century. After Ottoman Turkish rule from 1517, Yemen became independent in 1918. The northern part was ruled by imams until in a civil war (1962–1969), revolutionaries for a Yemen Arab Republic defeated the royalists. South Yemen came under British control in 1839; it consisted of the British colony Aden and the British protectorate South Arabia and gained independence in 1967. A boundary agreement was reached in 1934 between the northern imam-controlled territory, which became the Yemen Arab Republic (North Yemen), and the southeastern British-controlled territory, which became the People's Democratic Republic of Yemen (South Yemen). After two decades of fighting, the two Yemens united in 1990, establishing the Republic of Yemen. Its 1993 elections were the first free, multiparty general elections held in the Arabian Peninsula, and they were the first in which women participated. A 10-month civil war followed in 1994, with the north victorious, and a new constitution was approved. While on a refueling stop in Aden in 2000, the *USS Cole* was bombed, killing 17 Americans and injuring more than 36. The United States blamed the attack on Islamic extremists associated with Osama bin Laden, whose ancestral home is Yemen. Terrorist incidents and clashes between Shiite rebels and government forces occurred from 2003 to 2007. In 2007 and 2008 many thousands of people entered Yemen illegally from East Africa to escape poverty and war. Bombings of a mosque and of Spanish tourists at a temple occurred in 2007. Yemen continued efforts to fight Al-Qaeda, members of which allegedly travel in Yemen.

Influences on food   Yemen is the southwestern corner of the Arabian Peninsula. Northern Yemen includes the highest part of the Arabian plateau with areas of the highest rainfall, which comes with the summer monsoon. Grains and coffee grow here. Summer rains allow Yemen to support an unusually large population for the Arabian Peninsula. The oases of Shabwa, Ma'rib, and Nejran were prosperous towns on the Spice Road to the Mediterranean. Southern Yemen, formerly the British colony Aden, borders on the Red Sea and Indian Ocean, which provide fish. Yemen's food is similar to that of neighbor Saudi Arabia; however, isolated from other Arab population centers and with a maritime tradition, Yemen was influenced by India and Indonesia. Yemen is the only country that still regularly uses carved soapstone cookware (migla), which is durable and, Yemenis claim, produces better tasting food than that cooked in metal. Britain controlled South Yemen for more than a century and influenced food customs. Islam influences food practices in this predominantly Muslim country: it forbids consumption of pork or alcohol and requires fasting from sunup to sundown during the month of Ramadan. Jews from Yemen who emigrated to Israel have influenced Israeli cuisine, such as the use of fenugreek and kat.

Bread and cereals   Sorghum, millet, wheat, corn, rice; porridge, Arab pocket bread (pita), lahuh (a sourdough crêpe cooked on one side only and made from white sorghum), rice dishes. Sorghum and broomcorn millet are 80% of the grain produced.

Meat, poultry, fish   Chicken, lamb, goat, beef, camel, fish and shellfish (e.g., grouper, prawns), eggs.

Dairy products   Yogurt, white cheese.

Fats and oils   Samneh (ghee, or clarified butter), olive oil.

Legumes   Chickpeas, beans, lentils.

Vegetables   Potatoes, tomatoes, fenugreek (leguminous plant related to clover) greens, eggplant, onions, chili, parsley. Fenugreek greens are a main food.

Fruit   Dates, mangoes, melon, watermelon, oranges, bananas, limes, grapes, raisins.

Nuts and seeds   Almonds, fenugreek seeds, sesame seeds. Fenugreek seeds are widely used.

Seasonings   Hilbeh (fenugreek seed paste), cinnamon, cardamom, cloves, cumin, ginger, nutmeg, saffron, dried limes, rosewater, in South Yemen the spicy sauce s'hûg (which contains fenugreek), in North Yemen sahâwig (condiment of tomato, onion, and chili). Hilbeh is the symbol of Yemeni cuisine.

Dishes   Fatout (toasted bread with honey, scrambled eggs, or any other food). Boiled rice. Moraq (a soupy stew), topped with hilbeh beaten to foam. Lamb pieces cooked on skewers (kabobs). Roasted chicken, goat, or lamb.

Festive occasion dish   Bint al-sahn (flaky crêpe pastry made from egg-rich dough formed into thin layers, which are covered with samneh, stacked on top of each other, and baked), served with samneh and sometimes honey.

Peasant food   Asîd (sorghum porridge) with spiced butter or yogurt.

Sweets   Honey, dibis (date molasses), sugar. Dates. Baklava (layers of pastry with nuts and honey or syrup).

Beverages   Coffee (with cardamom and rosewater), tea (sweetened with sugar in the pot), quishr (a tea of ground coffee husks, with perhaps spices and sugar). Mocha is a fine variety of coffee that began in Yemen and is named after Yemen's Red Sea port al Makhâ; its production is restricted. Few Yemenis can afford coffee.

Eating customs   The usual Arab eating customs prevail: men eat first and women and children eat afterward or in another room. Food is eaten communally from pots, platters, and bowls on a cloth spread on the carpet. As in other Muslim countries, food is eaten with the right hand. Kat (or qat, a mildly narcotic plant whose leaves are used to make tea or to chew) leaves are often chewed (and not swallowed) after lunch or during the afternoon, especially in North Yemen.

YUGOSLAVIA (*SEE* SERBIA and MONTENEGRO)

Z

ZAIRE (*SEE* CONGO)

ZAMBIA
Republic of Zambia

Geography   Zambia (formerly Northern Rhodesia) is a landlocked country in central southern Africa. It is mostly high, thickly forested plateau drained by large rivers, including the Zambezi. The climate is subtropical.

Major Languages	Ethnic Groups		Major Religions	
English (official)	African (Bemba 22%, Tonga 11%,		Christian	82%
Bemba, Kaonda, Lozi,	Lozi 5%, Nsenga 5%, Tumbuka 4%		Indigenous beliefs	14%
Lunda, Luvale, Nyanja,	Ngoni 4%, Chewa 3%, other 45%)	99%	Muslim, other	4%
Tonga, about 70 others	Other	1%		

Population density per sq. mi. 40.8
Literacy rate 68%
Life expectancy 38.5 male; 38.7 female
Per capita GDP $1,300
Labor force in agriculture 85%

Urban 35%
Infant mortality rate per 1,000 live births 101
HIV rate 15.2%
Unemployment rate 12.7%
Arable land 7%

Agriculture   sugarcane, cassava, coffee, corn, sorghum, flowers, rice, peanuts, sunflower seeds, vegetables, tobacco, cotton, chickens, cattle, goats, pigs, sheep

Natural resources   fish, copper, cobalt, zinc, lead, coal, emeralds, gold, silver, uranium, hydropower

Industries   copper mining and processing, construction, foodstuffs

History   Early humans inhabited this land 1 to 2 million years ago. Ancestors of the Tonga tribe reached the area early in the 2nd millennium BCE. Peoples from Congo and Angola reached the area in the 17th and 18th centuries CE. Today the country is made up almost entirely of Bantu-speaking people. Portuguese trading missions were established early in the 18th century. The area was administered by the British South Africa Company from 1889, when Cecil Rhodes obtained mining concessions from the king of the Barotse and sent settlers soon thereafter, until 1924, when it became a British protectorate, Northern Rhodesia. It was united with Nyasaland (now Malawi) and Southern Rhodesia (now Zimbabwe) to form the Central African Federation of Rhodesia (1953–1963). It became independent as Zambia in 1964. In the 1980s and 1990s, lowered copper prices damaged the economy and severe drought caused famine. By the end of the 1990s, the AIDS epidemic had orphaned over 650,000 children. In 2002 food shortages affected more than 2 million Zambians; the government refused to distribute shipments of U.S. food because the grain was genetically modified. In 2005 the World Bank approved a $3.8 billion debt relief package for Zambia. The government has made some progress in treating HIV/AIDS, which affects nearly a million adults in Zambia. In 2007 China made a loan to repair flood damage; Western donors gave US$50 million to help clean up mining pollution; the United Kingdom agreed to provide about US$800 million to relieve poverty over the next decade; the United Kingdom, South Africa, and the United States contributed US$250 million to improve the railway system; and Japan agreed to help improve Zambia's infrastructure.

Influences on food   The cuisine of Zambia resembles that of East African countries and neighbor Zimbabwe. The land is high forested plateaus. The diet of the highlands contains almost no meat, in spite of abundant game and the tradition of breeding cattle. Cattle were regarded as wealth, not food, and the Masai and related people lived on milk products and blood of cattle. Others lived on mostly millet, sorghum, and bananas, along with gathered greens. The earliest foreign traders, Arabs, established colonies along the East Africa coast from about 700 CE, traded in slaves and ivory, and introduced spices, onions, and eggplant. British control of the country from late in the 19th century to 1964 influenced the food. The British trained many African men, never women, in European cooking because there were traditions of women cooking only in their homes while men cooked outdoors. Also, the British encouraged Asians to settle in East Africa, which affected local cooking, for example using curry spices. Dutch descendants, who trekked north from the Cape and later moved into southern Zambia, left some influence, such as baked goods. Some people are Muslims, who do not consume pork or alcohol. Europeans hunted game in the highlands; now, although animals are protected, game is plentiful and antelope are farmed. Large rivers including the Zambezi supply fish. As elsewhere in Africa, starchy food is regarded as "real food" and relishes as accompaniments. Porridge is the main food. Zambians eat a large amount of starchy vegetables and green leaves. Legumes are eaten daily. Milk products are important.

Bread and cereals   Corn, sorghum, rice, millet; porridge, rice dishes, pancakes, fritters.

Meat, poultry, fish   Chicken, beef, goat, pork, lamb and mutton, game meat, fish, salted and dried seafood, eggs.

Insects   Locusts, crickets, grasshoppers, ants, worms (madora), caterpillars (harati). These are collected, fried or roasted, sometimes dried for later use, and often eaten as snacks.

Dairy products   Milk, sour milk, buttermilk, curds, cheese (including some adaptations of European ones).

Fats and oils   Butter, lard, meat drippings, peanut oil, coconut oil, palm oil.

Legumes   Peanuts (groundnuts), cowpeas, beans, lentils.

Vegetables   Cassava, green bananas, yams, potatoes, sweet potatoes, green leaves (especially amaranth, baobab, sesame, okra, cowpea, and pumpkin), tomatoes, onions, eggplant.

Fruit   Bananas, coconut, papaya, lemons, watermelon.

Nuts and seeds   Sunflower seeds, cashew nuts, sesame seeds, watermelon seeds.

Seasonings   Salt, pepper, chili, onions, garlic, coconut milk, lemon juice, dried baobab leaves, cloves, curry powder, cinnamon, saffron.

Dishes   Thick porridge of corn or millet. Boiled rice. Boiled cassava. Peanut soup. Irio (mashed cooked beans, corn, and cassava or potatoes), often served with curried chicken. Green bananas boiled in their leaves and mashed. Greens cooked with coconut milk and peanut paste. Beef and cassava stew. Fish with coconut sauce. Zambezi chicken (cut-up chicken rubbed with salt, pepper, garlic, and chili powder, marinated in lemon juice, and braised in coconut milk and oil). Marinated chicken grilled and basted with coconut milk and oil. Steamed papaya.

Sweets   Sugarcane, honey, sugar. Rice and coconut pancakes. Banana jam. Doughnut. Coconut pudding.

Beverages   Coffee, tea, beer.

Street food   Fried pastries, fritters, grilled corn on cob, fried pancake filled with minced meat and egg.

ZIMBABWE
Republic of Zimbabwe

Geography   Zimbabwe, formerly Southern Rhodesia, is in southern Africa. It is a high plateau with mountains on the eastern border. The climate is subtropical.

Major Languages	Ethnic Groups		Major Religions	
English (official)	Shona	82%	Syncretic (Christian-	
Shona	Ndebele	14%	Indigenous Mix)	50%
Sindebele	Other African	2%	Christian	25%
Minor tribal dialects	Other	2%	Indigenous beliefs	24%
			Muslim and other	1%

Population density per sq. mi. 76
Literacy rate 91.2%
Life expectancy 45.1 male; 43.5 female
Per capita GDP $200
Labor force in agriculture 66%

Urban 35.9%
Infant mortality rate per 1,000 live births 33.9
HIV rate 15.3%
Unemployment rate 70%
Arable land 8%

Agriculture   sugarcane, corn, cotton, tobacco, wheat, coffee, peanuts, chickens, cattle, goats, pigs, sheep

Natural resources   fish, coal, chromium, asbestos, gold, nickel, copper, iron ore, vanadium, lithium, tin, platinum

Industries   mining, steel, wood products, cement, chemicals

History   Remains of early humans from 500,000 years ago have been found in the area. The Koisan settled here by 200 BCE. Bantu-speaking peoples arrived during the 5th to 10th centuries. They dominated for a time, then the Shona, followed by the Nguni and Zulu peoples. The Ndebele descended from the latter two groups and established a powerful kingdom by the mid-19th century. A second migration of the Bantu speakers began in 1830. Also during this time, the British and Afrikaners moved up from the south. In the 1850s, the first British explorers, colonists, and missionaries arrived, leading to the establishment of the territory Rhodesia, named after Cecil Rhodes of the British South Africa Company. In 1897 Rhodes took over the area, called Southern Rhodesia. In 1923 Britain took control of the area and granted internal self-government. The colony was united with Nyasaland (now Malawi) and Northern Rhodesia (now Zambia) to form the Central African Federation of Rhodesia and Nyasaland (1953–1963). After guerrilla warfare and black nationalist movements in the 1970s, the white minority agreed to hold multiracial elections in 1980. The country gained independence as Zimbabwe in 1980. In 1992 a national disaster was declared due to drought. In 2004 the International Monetary Fund estimated the country had grown a third poorer in the last five years. In mid-2005 Zimbabwe demolished urban slums and shantytowns, leaving 700,000 people homeless. During the period 2006 to 2008 inflation soared.

Influences on food   Zimbabwe's cuisine resembles that of East African countries such as Tanzania and neighbors Malawi and Zambia. The land is a high plateau. The diet of the highlands contains almost no meat, in spite of abundant game and the tradition of breeding cattle. Cattle were regarded as wealth, not food, and the Masai and related people lived on milk products and blood of cattle. Others lived on mostly millet, sorghum, and bananas, along with gathered greens. The earliest foreign traders, Arabs, established colonies along the coast from about 700 CE and traded in slaves and ivory; they introduced spices, onions, and eggplant. British control, starting in the mid-19th century and lasting for much of the 20th century, influenced the food. The British trained many African men in European cooking. Also, they encouraged Asians to settle in East Africa, which affected local cooking; examples are using curry and cooking fish with coconut milk. Descendants of Dutch colonists in the Cape who moved north and later into the present Zimbabwe influenced food customs (e.g., baked goods and fruit preserves). European hunters found game in the highlands; now although animals are protected, game is plentiful and antelope are farmed. Lakes and rivers supply fish. The diet is mainly porridge, starchy vegetables, green leaves, legumes, and milk products. Porridge, the staple food, was formerly of millet but now is usually corn.

Bread and cereals   Corn, wheat, millet, sorghum, rice; porridge, pancakes, fritters, rice dishes.

Meat, poultry, fish   Chicken, beef, goat, lamb and mutton, pork, game meat, fish, salted and dried seafood, eggs.

Insects   Locusts, crickets, grasshoppers, ants, worms (madora), caterpillars. These are collected, usually fried or roasted, sometimes dried for later use, and eaten as snacks.

Dairy products   Milk, sour milk, buttermilk, curds, cheeses (some adapted from European ones).

Fats and oils   Butter, lard, peanut oil, meat drippings, coconut oil, palm oil.

Legumes   Peanuts (groundnuts), cowpeas, beans, lentils.

Vegetables   Green bananas (plantains), cassava, yams, potatoes, green leaves, tomatoes, onions, eggplant.

Fruit   Bananas, coconut, papaya, watermelon.

Nuts and seeds   Cashew nuts, sesame seeds, sunflower seeds, watermelon seeds.

Seasonings   Chilies, onions, coconut milk, dried baobab leaves, curry powder, cloves, cinnamon, nutmeg.

Dishes   Thick porridge of corn or millet. Boiled rice. Peanut soup. Irio (mashed cooked beans, corn, and potatoes or cassava), often served with curried chicken. Green bananas boiled in their leaves and mashed. Cassava or potato fritters. Greens simmered with coconut milk and peanut sauce. Beef or mutton and cassava stew. Roasted or curried lamb, goat, or pork. Braised springbok (venison). Fish cooked with coconut milk or peanut curry.

Sweets   Sugarcane, honey, sugar. Banana jam. Rice and coconut pancakes. Banana custard. Spiced cookies.

Beverages   Coffee, tea, beer, plantain wine.

Street food   Fritters, grilled corn cobs, pancake filled with meat and egg.

BIBLIOGRAPHY

Abraham, N. 1995. Arab Americans. In R. J. Vecoli, J. Galens, A. Sheets, and R. V. Young, eds., *Gale Encyclopedia of Multicultural America*. New York: Gale Research.

Algert, S. J., Brzezinski, E., and Ellison, T. H. 1998. *Mexican American Food Practices, Customs, and Holidays*. Chicago: American Dietetic Association/American Diabetes Association.

American Dietetic Association. 2004. HOD Backgrounder: Meeting the challenges of a culturally and ethnically diverse US population. http://www.eatright.org (accessed October 1, 2008).

American Dietetic Association. 2007. HOD Backgrounder: Health disparities. Fall 2007. http://www.eatright.org/ HOD Backgrounders Fall 2007 (accessed October 1, 2008).

Anderson, A. W. 1956. *Plants of the Bible*. London: Crosby Lockwood & Sons.

Ang, C. 2000. Tibetan food and beverages. *Flavor & Fortune* 6(3): 21.

Apicius. *The Roman Cookery Book*. Translated by B. Flower and E. Rosenbaum. 1958. London: P. Nevill.

Archer, S. L. 2005. Acculturation and dietary intake. *Journal of the American Dietetic Association* 105: 411–12.

Arrington, L. R. 1959. Foods of the Bible. *Journal of the American Dietetic Association* 35: 816–20.

Aspler, T. 1995. Icewine. In J. M. Powers and A. Stewart, eds., *Our Northern Bounty: A Celebration of Canadian Cuisine*. Toronto: Random House.

Ayala, G. X., Baquero, B., and Klinger, S. 2008. A systematic review of the relationship between acculturation and diet among Latinos in the United States: Implications for future research. *Journal of the American Dietetic Association* 108: 1330–44.

Bachman-Carter, K., Duncan, R. M., and Pelican, S. 1998. *Navajo Food Practices, Customs, and Holidays*. Chicago: American Dietetic Association/American Diabetes Association.

Bailey, A. 1969. *The Cooking of the British Isles*. New York: Time-Life.

Balagopal, P., Ganganna, P., Karmally, W., Kulkami, K, Ran, S., Ramasubramanian, N., and Siddiqui-Mufti, M. 2000. *Indian and Pakistani Food Practices, Customs, and Holidays,* 2nd ed. Chicago: American Dietetic Association/ American Diabetes Association.

Basaran, P. 1999. Traditional foods of the Middle East. *Food Technology* 53(6): 60–66.

Bennion, M. 1976. Food preparation in colonial America. *Journal of the American Dietetic Association* 69:16–23.

Bodenheimer, R. S. 1951. *Insects as Human Food*. The Hague: Dr. W. Junk Publishers.

Brittin, H. C. 1978. Argentina Food and Culture. Personal observations.

Brittin, H. C. 1990. Australia Food and Culture. Personal observations.

Brittin, H. C. 1968, 1984, 1986. Austria Food and Culture. Personal observations.

Brittin, H. C. 1998. Barbados Food and Culture. Personal observations.

Brittin, H. C. 1984. Belgium Food and Culture. Personal observations.

Brittin, H. C. 1978. Brazil Food and Culture. Personal observations.

Brittin, H. C. 1963, 1964, 1999. Canada Food and Culture. Personal observations.

Brittin, H. C. 1980. China Food and Culture. Personal observations.

Brittin, H. C. 1968, 1984. Denmark Food and Culture. Personal observations.

Brittin, H. C. 1998. Dominica Food and Culture. Personal observations.

Brittin, H. C. 2000. Ethiopia Food and Culture. Personal observations.

Brittin, H. C. 1972, 1991, 2002. Finland Food and Culture. Personal observations.

Brittin, H. C. 1968, 1984, 1985, 1987, 1988, 1989, 1990, 1991, 1992, 1993, 1994, 1995, 1996. France Food and Culture. Personal observations.

Brittin, H. C. 1968, 1984, 1992. Germany Food and Culture. Personal observations.

Brittin, H. C. 2000. Ghana Food and Culture. Personal observations.

Brittin, H. C. 1975, 1980, 1996. Hong Kong Food and Culture. Personal observations.

Brittin, H. C. 1968. Ireland Food and Culture. Personal observations.

Brittin, H. C. 1968, 1984. Italy Food and Culture. Personal observations.

Brittin, H. C. 1975, 2004. Japan Food and Culture. Personal observations.

Brittin, H. C. 2000. Kenya Food and Culture. Personal observations.

Brittin, H. C. 1968, 1984. Liechtenstein Food and Culture. Personal observations.

Brittin, H. C. 1998. Martinique Food and Culture. Personal observations.

Brittin, H. C. 1967, 1971, 1972. Mexico Food and Culture. Personal observations.

Brittin, H. C. 1968, 1984. Monaco Food and Culture. Personal observations.

Brittin, H. C. 1968, 1984. Netherlands Food and Culture. Personal observations.

Brittin, H. C. 1990. New Zealand Food and Culture. Personal observations.

Brittin, H. C. 1968, 1972, 1984. Norway Food and Culture. Personal observations.

Brittin, H. C. 1978. Peru Food and Culture. Personal observations.

Brittin, H. C. 1980. Philippines Food and Culture. Personal observations.

Brittin, H. C. 1972. Russia Food and Culture. Personal observations.

Brittin, H. C. 1998. St. Maarten/St. Martin Food and Culture. Personal observations.

Brittin, H. C. 2006. South Africa Food and Culture. Personal observations.

Brittin, H. C. 1989. South Korea Food and Culture. Personal observations.

Brittin, H. C. 1968. Spain Food and Culture. Personal observations.

Brittin, H. C. 1968, 1972, 1984. Sweden Food and Culture. Personal observations.

Brittin, H. C. 1968, 1984, 2008. Switzerland Food and Culture. Personal observations.

Brittin, H. C. 1975. Taiwan Food and Culture. Personal observations.

Brittin, H. C. 2000. Tanzania Food and Culture. Personal observations.

Brittin, H. C. 1996. Thailand Food and Culture. Personal observations.

Brittin, H. C. 1991. Turkey Food and Culture. Personal observations.

Brittin, H. C. 1968, 1984, 1985, 1986, 1994. United Kingdom Food and Culture. Personal observations.

Brittin, H. C. 1968, 1984. Vatican City Food and Culture. Personal observations.

Brittin, H. C. 1999. U.S. Region Alaska Food and Culture. Personal observations.

Brittin, H. C. 1975, 2006. U.S. Region Hawaiian Islands Food and Culture. Personal observations.

Brittin, H. C. 1961–1963, 1964, 1970, 1973, 1977, 1990, 1993. U.S. Region Mid-Atlantic Food and Culture. Personal observations.

Brittin, H. C. 1964, 1970, 1993, 1994, 2004. U.S. Region Midwest Food and Culture. Personal observations.

Brittin, H. C. 1961, 1963, 1970, 1990. U.S. Region New England Food and Culture. Personal observations.

Brittin, H. C. 1960–1961, every year since. U.S. Region South Food and Culture. Personal observations.

Brittin, H. C. 1963–2009. U.S. Region Southwest Food and Culture. Personal observations.

Brittin, H. C. 1960, 1973, 1999, 2004, 2005, 2006, 2007, 2009. U.S. Region West Food and Culture. Personal observations.

Brittin, H. C. 1964, 1998. U.S. Puerto Rico Food and Culture. Personal observations.

Brittin, H. C. 1964, 1998. U.S. Territory Virgin Islands Food and Culture. Personal observations.

Brittin, H. C. 2001. *Food Preparation Essentials,* 4th ed. Dubuque, IA: Kendall/Hunt.

Brittin, H. C., and Nossaman, C. E. 1986a. Iron content of food cooked in iron utensils. *Journal of the American Dietetic Association* 86: 897–901.

Brittin, H. C., and Nossaman, C. E. 1986b. Use of iron cookware. *Home Economics Research Journal* 15: 43–51.

Brittin, H. C., Sukalakamala, S., and Obeidat, B. A. 2008. Food practices, changes, preferences, and acculturation of Arabs and Thais in the United States: A cross cultural comparison. Presentation at the International Federation for Home Economics XXI Congress, Lucerne, Switzerland.

Brittin, H. C., and Zinn, D. W. 1977. Meat-buying practices of Caucasians, Mexican-Americans, and Negroes. *Journal of the American Dietetic Association* 71(6): 623–28.

Brothwell, D., and Brothwell, P. 1969. *Food in Antiquity.* New York: Frederick A. Praeger.

Brown, D. 1968. *American Cooking.* New York: Time-Life.

Brown, D. 1968. *The Cooking of Scandinavia.* New York: Time-Life.

Burke, C. B., and Raia, S. P. 1995. *Soul and Traditional Southern Food Practices, Customs, and Holidays.* Chicago: American Dietetic Association/American Diabetes Association.

Chaudry, M. M. 1992. Islamic food laws: Philosophical basis and practical implications. *Food Technology* 46: 92–93, 104.

Cheng, Y. J., and Brittin, H. C. 1991. Iron in food: Effect of continued use of iron cookware. *Journal of Food Science* 56: 584–85.

Claiborne, C., and Claiborne, P. F. 1970. *Classic French Cooking.* New York: Time-Life.

Claudio, V. S. 1994. *Filipino American Food Practices, Customs, and Holidays.* Chicago: American Dietetic Association/American Diabetes Association.

Coates, R. J., and Monteilh, C. P. 1997. Assessments of food-frequency questionnaires in minority populations. *American Journal of Clinical Nutrition* 65(suppl):1108S–1115S.

Cook, J. D. 1977. Absorption of food iron. *Federation Proceedings* 36: 2028–32.

Cramer, M. 2001. Mongolian culture and cuisine in transition. *Flavor & Fortune* 8(2): 12–14, 16.

Crane, N. T., and Green, N. R. 1980. Food habits and food preferences of Vietnamese refugees living in northern Florida. *Journal of the American Dietetic Association* 76: 591–93.

Curry, K. R. 2000. Multicultural competence in dietetics and nutrition. *Journal of the American Dietetic Association* 100: 1142–43.

Davidson, A. 2002. *The Penguin Companion to Food.* New York: Penguin.

Feibleman, P. S. 1969. *The Cooking of Spain and Portugal.* New York: Time-Life.

Field, M., and Field, F. 1970. *A Quintet of Cuisines.* New York: Time-Life.

Fisher, M. F. K. 1968. *The Cooking of Provincial France.* New York: Time-Life.

Geissler, E. M. 1998. *Pocket Guide to Cultural Assessment.* St. Louis: Mosby.

Gordon, B. H. J., Kang, M. S. Y., Cho, P., and Sucher, K. P. 2000. Dietary habits and health beliefs of Korean-Americans in the San Francisco Bay Area. *Journal of the American Dietetic Association* 100: 1198–1201.

Grivetti, L. E., and Paquette, M. B. 1978. Nontraditional food choices among first generation Chinese in California. *Journal of Nutrition Education* 10: 109–12.

Hahn, E. 1968. *The Cooking of China.* New York: Time-Life.

Halderson, K. 1998. *Alaska Native Food Practices, Customs, and Holidays.* Chicago: American Dietetic Association/American Diabetes Association.

Hammoud, M. M., White, C. B., and Fetters, M. D. 2005. Opening cultural doors: Providing culturally sensitive healthcare to Arab American and American Muslim patients. *American Journal of Obstetrics & Gynecology* 193(4): 1307–11.

Harding, T. S. 1949. Native foods of the Western Hemisphere. *Journal of the American Dietetic Association* 24: 609–14.

Harris-Davis, E., and Haughton, B. 2000. Model for multicultural nutrition counseling competencies. *Journal of the American Dietetic Association* 100: 1178–85.

Hatahet, W., Khosla, P., and Fungwe, T. V. 2002. Prevalence of risk factors to coronary heart disease in an Arab-American population in Southeast Michigan. *International Journal of Food Sciences and Nutrition* 53: 325–35.

Hazelton, N. S. 1969. *The Cooking of Germany.* New York: Time-Life.

Higgins, C., Laredo, R., Stollar, C., and Wardshaw, H. S. 1998. *Jewish Food Practices, Customs, and Holidays.* Chicago: American Dietetic Association/American Diabetes Association.

Hussaini, M. M. 1993. *Islamic Dietary Concepts and Practices.* Bedford Park, IL: Islamic Food and Nutrition Council of America.

Ikeda, J. P. 1999. *Hmong American Food Practices, Customs, and Holidays.* Chicago: American Dietetic Association/American Diabetes Association.

Jaber, L. A., Brown, M. B., Hammad, A., Zhu, Q., and Herman, W. H. 2003. Lack of acculturation is a risk factor for diabetes in Arab immigrants in the U.S. *Diabetes Care* 26: 2010–14.

Kilara, A., and Iya, K. K. 1992. Food and dietary practices of the Hindu. *Food Technology* 46: 94–102, 104.

Kittler, P. G., and Sucher, K. P. 2004. *Food and Culture,* 4th ed. Belmont, CA: Wadsworth/ Thomson Learning.

Kollipara, U. K., and Brittin, H. C. 1996. Increased iron content of some Indian foods due to cookware. *Journal of the American Dietetic Association* 96: 508–10.

Lau, G., Ma, K. M., and Ng, A. 1998. *Chinese American Food Practices, Customs, and Holidays.* Chicago: American Dietetic Association/American Diabetes Association.

Lee, R. D., and Nieman, D. C. 2003. *Nutritional Assessment,* 3rd ed. New York: McGraw-Hill.

Lee, S. K., Sobal, J., and Frongillo, E. A. 1999a. Acculturation and dietary practices among Korean Americans. *Journal of the American Dietetic Association* 99: 1084–89.

Lee, S. K., Sobal, J., and Frongillo, E. A.1999b. Acculturation, food consumption, and diet-related factors among Korean Americans. *Journal of Nutrition Education* 31: 321–30.

Leistner, C. G. 1996. *Cajun and Creole Food Practices, Customs, and Holidays.* Chicago: American Dietetic Association/American Diabetes Association.

Leonard, J. N. 1968. *Latin American Cooking.* New York: Time-Life.

Liou, D., and Bauer, K. D. 2007. Exploratory investigation of obesity risk and prevention in Chinese Americans. *Journal of Nutrition Education and Behavior* 39:134–41.

Liou, D., and Contento, I. R. 2001. Usefulness of psychosocial theory variables in explaining fat-related dietary behavior in Chinese Americans: Association with degree of acculturation. *Journal of Nutrition Education* 33: 322–31.

Lowenberg, M. E., Todhunter, E. N., Wilson, E. D., Savage, J. R., and Lubawski, J. L. 1979. *Food and People,* 3rd ed. New York: Wiley.

Mead, M. 1970. The changing significance of food. *American Scientist* 258: 176–81.

Meilgaard, M., Civille, G. V., and Thomas, C. 1999. *Sensory Evaluation Techniques,* 3rd ed. Boca Raton, FL: CRC Press.

Meiselman, H. L., ed. 2000. *Dimensions of the Meal: The Science, Culture, Business, and Art of Eating.* Gaithersburg, MD: Aspen.

Mermelstein, N. H. 1992. Seeds of change: The Smithsonian Institution's Columbus quincentenary exhibition. *Food Technology* 46(10): 86–89.

Mistry, A. N., Brittin, H. C., and Stoecker, B. J. 1988. Availability of iron from food cooked in an iron utensil determined by an in vitro method. *Journal of Food Science* 53: 1546–48, 1573.

Newman, J. M. 1999. Tibet and Tibetan foods. *Flavor & Fortune* 6(4): 7–8, 12.

Newman, J. M. 2000a. Chinese meals. In H. L. Meiselman, ed., *Dimensions of the Meal: The Science, Culture, Business, and Art of Eating*. Gaithersburg, MD: Aspen.

Newman, J. M. 2000b. Mongolians and their cuisine. *Flavor & Fortune* 7(1): 9–10, 24.

Nickles, H. G. 1969. *Middle Eastern Cooking*. New York: Time-Life.

Obeidat, B. A., and Brittin, H. C. 2004. Food practices, changes, preferences, and acculturation of Arabs in the United States. *Journal of the American Dietetic Association* 104 (Suppl. 2): A-34.

Packard, D. P., and McWilliams, M. 1993. Cultural foods heritage of Middle Eastern immigrants. *Nutrition Today* (May–June): 6–12.

Painter, J., Rah, J., and Lee, Y. 2002. Comparison in international food guide pictorial representations. *Journal of the American Dietetic Association* 102: 483–89.

Pan, Y. L., Dixon, Z., Himburg, S., and Huffman, F. 1999. Asian students change their eating patterns after living in the United States. *Journal of the American Dietetic Association* 99: 54–57.

Papashvily, H., and Papashvily, G. 1969. *Russian Cooking*. New York: Time-Life.

Park, J., and Brittin. H. C. 1997. Increased iron content of food due to stainless steel cookware. *Journal of the American Dietetic Association* 97: 659–61.

Park, J., and Brittin, H.C. 2000. Iron content, sensory evaluation, and consumer acceptance of food cooked in iron utensils. *Journal of Food Quality* 23: 205–15.

Park, S. Y., Paik, H. Y., Skinner, J. D., Ok, S. W., and Spindler, A. A. 2003. Mothers' acculturation and eating behaviors of Korean American families in California. *Journal of Nutrition Education and Behavior* 35: 142–47.

Perl, L. 1965. *Red-Flannel Hash and Shoo-Fly Pie*. Cleveland, OH: World Publishing.

Powers, J. M., and Stewart, A., eds. 1995. *Northern Bounty: A Celebration of Canadian Cuisine*. Toronto: Random House.

Raj, S., Gangnna, P., and Bowering, J. 1999. Dietary habits of Asian Indians in relation to the length of residence in the United States. *Journal of the American Dietetic Association* 99: 1106–08.

Ratner, M. 1995. Thai Americans. In R. J. Vecoli, J. Galens, A. Sheets, and R. V. Young, eds., *Gale Encyclopedia of Multicultural America*. New York: Gale Research.

Rau, S. R. 1969. *The Cooking of India*. New York: Time-Life.

Root, W. 1968. *The Cooking of Italy*. New York: Time-Life.

Sakr, A. H. 1971. Dietary regulations and food habits of Muslims. *Journal of the American Dietetic Association* 53: 123–26.

Sakr, A. H. 1975. Fasting in Islam. *Journal of the American Dietetic Association* 67:17–21.

Satia, J. A., Patterson, R. E., Taylor, V. M., Cheney, C. L., Shiu-Thornton, S., Chitnarong, K., and Kristal, A. R. 2000. Use of qualitative methods to study diet, acculturation, and health in Chinese-American women. *Journal of the American Dietetic Association* 100: 934–40.

Satia-Abouta, J., Patterson, R. E., Neuhouser, M. L., and Elder, J. 2002. Dietary acculturation: Applications to research and dietetics. *Journal of the American Dietetic Association* 102: 1105–18.

Scrimshaw, N.S. 1991. Iron deficiency. *Scientific American* 265: 46–52.

Skipper, A., Young, L. O., and Mitchell, B. E. 2008. Accreditation standards for dietetics education. *Journal of the American Dietetic Association* 108: 1732–35.

Southeastern Michigan Dietetic Association. n.d. Cultural food pyramids. http://www.semda.org/info/ (accessed October 1, 2008).

Stang, J., Kong, A., Story, M., Eisenberg, M. E., and Neumark-Sztainer, D. 2007. Food and weight-related patterns and behaviors of Hmong adolescents. *Journal of the American Dietetic Association* 107: 936–41.

Stein, K. 2004. Cultural literacy in health care. *Journal of the American Dietetic Association* 104: 1657–59.

Steinberg, R. 1969. *The Cooking of Japan.* New York: Time-Life.

Steinberg, R. 1970. *Pacific and Southeast Asian Cooking.* New York: Time-Life.

Sukalakamala, S., and Brittin, H. C. 2006. Food practices, changes, preferences, and acculturation of Thais in the United States. *Journal of the American Dietetic Association* 106: 103–08.

Thompson, F. E., Subar, A. F., Brown, C. C., Smith, A. F., Sharbaugh, C. O., Jobe, J B., et al. 2002. Cognitive research enhances accuracy of food frequency questionnaire reports: Results of an experimental validation study. *Journal of the American Dietetic Association* 102: 212–24.

U.S. Department of Agriculture. 1992. Food guide pyramid: A guide to daily food choices. *Home and Garden Bulletin* no. 252. Washington, DC.

U.S. Department of Agriculture. 2005. MyPyramid.gov. http://www.mypyramid.gov/ (accessed September 11, 2008).

U.S. Department of Agriculture. 2008. Cultural and ethnic food and nutrition education materials: A resource list for educators. http://www.nal.usda.gov/fnic/pubs/bibs/gen/ethnic.html#6 (accessed October 1, 2008).

Van der Post, L. 1970. *African Cooking.* New York: Time-Life.

Vecoli, R. J., Galens, J., Sheets, A., and Young, R. V., eds. 1995. *Encyclopedia of Multicultural America.* New York: Gale Research.

Weaver, M. R., and Brittin, H. C. 2001. Food preferences of men and women by sensory evaluation versus questionnaire. *Family and Consumer Sciences Research Journal* 29(3): 288–302.

Wechsberg, J. 1968. *The Cooking of Vienna's Empire.* New York: Time-Life.

Weigley, E. S. 1964. Food in the days of the Declaration of Independence. *Journal of the American Dietetic Association* 45: 35–40.

Wenkam, N. S., and Wolff, R. J. 1970. A half century of changing food habits among Japanese in Hawaii. *Journal of the American Dietetic Association* 57: 29–32.

Wiecha, J. M., Fink, A. K., Wiecha, J., and Herbert, J. 2001. Differences in dietary patterns of Vietnamese, White, African-American, and Hispanic adolescents in Worcester, Mass. *Journal of the American Dietetic Association* 101: 248–51.

Wolfe, L. 1970. *The Cooking of the Caribbean Islands.* New York: Time-Life.

Woolf, N., Conti, K. M., Johnson, C., Martinez, V., McCloud, J., and Zephier, E. M. 1999. *Northern Plains Indian Food Practices, Customs, and Holidays.* Chicago: American Dietetic Association/American Diabetes Association.

World Health Organization. 2008. Chronic Disease Information Sheet—Obesity and Overweight. http://www.who.int/dietphysicalactivity/publications/facts/obesity/en/print.html (accessed September 29, 2008).

Yang, E. J., Chung, H. K., Kim, W. Y., Bianchi, L., and Song, W. O. 2007. Chronic diseases and dietary changes in relation to Korean Americans' length of residence in the United States. *Journal of the American Dietetic Association* 107: 942–50.

Zhou, Y. D., and Brittin, H. C. 1994. Increased iron content of some Chinese foods due to cooking in steel woks. *Journal of the American Dietetic Association* 94: 1153–56.

REGIONAL INDEX